# HOW TO GROW MORE VEGETABLES*

(and fruits, nuts, berries, grains, and other crops)

## *THAN YOU EVER THOUGHT POSSIBLE ON LESS LAND THAN YOU CAN IMAGINE

### BY JOHN JEAVONS

Ecology Action of the Midpeninsula

A primer on the life-giving GROW BIOINTENSIVE®
method of sustainable horticulture

TEN SPEED PRESS
Berkeley

Copyright © 1974, 1979, 1982, 1991, 1995, 2002, 2006 by Ecology
Action of the Midpeninsula, 5798 Ridgewood Road, Willits, CA 95490-9730
www.growbiointensive.org

Published in the United States by Ten Speed Press, an imprint of the
Crown Publishing Group, a division of Random House, Inc., New York.
www.crownpublishing.com
www.tenspeed.com

Ten Speed Press and the Ten Speed Press colophon are registered
trademarks of Random House, Inc.

The Library of Congress has cataloged the 6th edition
as follows:

Jeavons, John.
    How to grow more vegetables : and fruits, nuts, berries, grains, and
other crops than you ever thought possible on less land
than you can imagine / by John Jeavons.
        p. cm.
Includes bibliographical references and index.
    1.  Vegetable gardening. 2.  Organic gardening.  I. Title.
    SB324.3 .J424 2002
    635—dc21
                    2001006451

ISBN 9781580087964

Printed in the United States

Cover illustration by Sue Ellen Parkinson
Cover design by Katy Brown and Sue Ellen Parkinson
Interior design by Katy Brown, Linda Davis (Star Type),
and Brenton Beck (Fifth Street Design Associates)
Illustrations  by Pedro J. Gonzalez, Ann Miya, Susan Stanley,
Sue Ellen Parkinson, and Betsy Jeavons Bruneau

16 15 14 13 12 11 10 9 8

Seventh Edition

# CONTENTS

## BY ALICE WATERS

In the early days at Chez Panisse, thirty-five years ago, we had to scrounge for decent beans, pick lemons from neighbors' trees, and hunt far and wide for a variety of produce of any quality whatsoever. But farming has evolved in California. We now work with, at last count, nearly fifty local, small-scale, family-run farms that grow—organically and sustainably—the seasonal fruits and vegetables that are the foundation of our cooking. In large part, we have John Jeavons to thank for this.

I met John on the twentieth birthday of Chez Panisse just as he was preparing for the twentieth anniversary of Ecology Action. We both had a lot to celebrate. The work that John had begun in a small garden at Stanford had inspired small farms on nearly every continent; he had already worked with the Peace Corps in Togo, helped found an agricultural center in Kenya, taught in Mexico, and supported programs in Russia and the Phillipines. His work has gone right on inspiring, and at a pace that is fast enough to give us real hope that we will be able to grow sustainable communities around the world.

John's methods are nothing short of miraculous. He has shown that almost any soil can be prepared for the planting of food, and that astonishing quantities of high-quality produce can be grown on even the most devastated land. He has worked tirelessly to bring self-sufficiency to the poorest people in the poorest parts of the world. As I write, he's preparing to share his methods with the five thousand small-scale farmers from one hundred and thirty-one countries who are expected at Terra Madre, the biannual gathering of farmers in Turin, Italy, organized by the eco-gastronomes of Slow Food International. I can think of no more appropriate place for the dissemination of his ideas.

Vandana Shiva, the outspoken Indian food activist, has said that farms are zones of peace on this planet. A peaceful revolution in agriculture—what I like to call the delicious revolution—has begun, and John is one of its most brilliant leaders. *How to Grow More Vegetables* may be one of the most important how-to guides ever written.

# Ecology Action and the Common Ground Project
# by the Ecology Action Staff

**ECOLOGY ACTION GOAL:** *Act as a catalyst, teach teachers, and train students*

In September 1971, Larry White, Director of the Nature and Science Department for the City of Palo Alto, invited Stephen Kafka, Senior Apprentice at the University of California Santa Cruz Student Garden, to give a 4-hour class on the biodynamic/ French intensive method of gardening. Two years before, the city had made land available to the public for gardening, and residents appeared eager to hear more about this method. Alan Chadwick had brought the method to Santa Cruz 5 years earlier, and with love, vision, and apparent magic, the master horticulturist had converted a barren slope into a Garden of Eden. Vegetables, flowers, and herbs flourished everywhere. The method's techniques were primarily available through training in a 2-year apprentice program at Santa Cruz and through periodic classes given by Alan Chadwick or Stephen Kafka. However, neither detailed public classes nor vegetable yield research were being conducted regularly at Santa Cruz or in Palo Alto.

In January 1972, the board of directors of Ecology Action, a young nonprofit environmental research and education organization, approved a Biointensive research and education project.[1] The Ecology Action project would include a garden (called the Common Ground Garden), and its purposes were to: teach regular classes; collect data on the reportedly fourfold yields produced by the environmentally sound Biointensive method; make land available for gardening to additional Midpeninsula residents; and publish information on the method's techniques.

In May, after a 5-month search for land, the Syntex Corporation offered 3¾ acres of their grounds in the Stanford Industrial Park with all the water needed for the project at no cost. Frank Koch, Syntex Public Affairs Director, told Dr. Alejandro Zaffaroni of the Alza Corporation about the project,

---

1. For more information about Ecology Action's history, current programs, workshops, and classes, or to become a member and support our work, go to www.growbiointensive.org or write to Ecology Action, 5798 Ridgewood Road, Willits, CA 95490-9730. To order Ecology Action's other publications, go to page 261 of this book, or order online at www.bountifulgardens.org.

and Dr. Zaffaroni subsequently contributed the first money to the project, $5,000, without which we never could have begun. Commitment by Frank Koch, Don Keppy, Chuck and Dian Missar, Ruth Edwards, Ibby Bagley, numerous other individuals, several corporations, and the Point Foundation enabled the project to continue.

Alan Chadwick soon visited the garden site and gave us basic advice on how to proceed. We then attended a series of lectures given by Mr. Chadwick in Saratoga, California. Using the classes taught by Alan Chadwick and Stephen Kafka as a base, we began teaching our own classes in the spring of 1972. Further study and experience in the garden made it possible to increase the original class to a 5-week series.[2]

In starting the Common Ground Garden, we hoped to determine what agricultural techniques would make food raising by small farmers and gardeners more efficient. We call the results "mini-farming." Mini-farms can flourish in nonagricultural areas, such as mountainous regions, arid areas, and in and around urban centers. Food can be produced where people live. With knowledge and skill, the yield per hour can be high without using the expensive machinery that is the preoccupation of our current agriculture. Mini-farming is available to everyone.

We began by concentrating on the exciting possibilities presented by the Biointensive method—would this method really produce 4 times the yield, as Alan Chadwick claimed? If so, would it take more water? Would it consume vast amounts of fertilizer and organic matter? Would it exhaust the soil? Or the people working? The only way to answer these questions was to plunge in and try it. Initially, we worked mainly on the quantitative aspects, developing the tools and data to maximize yields within the framework of Biointensive's life-giving approach. This involved experimentation with and evaluation of plant spacings, fertilizer inputs, various watering methods, and other variables.

The work has always been worthwhile despite the continuing challenge of attracting strong, ongoing support. The biggest single asset to this undertaking is John Jeavons' unfailing stamina and dedication. Over and over, when we all ask, "Can it work?" he answers, "How are we going to make it work?" It is becoming increasingly clear that GROW BIOINTENSIVE[3] sustainable mini-farming will be an important part of the solution to starvation and malnutrition, dwindling energy supplies, unemployment, and exhaustion and loss of arable land, if the social and political challenges can be met.

---

2. The classes led to the development of information sheets on topics such as vegetable spacings and composting techniques. Many people asked for a book containing all the information we gathered. Those who were unable to attend our Saturday classes or who had friends living outside the area were especially insistent. The first edition of this book was the result.

3. In this book you will see the terms GROW BIOINTENSIVE and Biointensive. The latter refers to individuals, projects, and programs before Ecology Action's 1999 trademark registration of GROW BIOINTENSIVE and/or not using all of the GROW BIOINTENSIVE features.

After more than 30 years of testing, GROW BIOINTENSIVE farming has produced amazing benefits. *Yields* can average 2 to 6 times those of U.S. agriculture, and a few range up to 31 times higher. But there's still more to learn; for example, we are still working to develop an optimally healthy soil system. *Compost and calorie crops* present the most challenges because they are crucial in meeting the nutritional needs of people and the soil. Experiments include alfalfa, fava beans, wheat, oats, cardoon, and comfrey. So far our yields are from 1 to 5 times the U.S. average for these crops. *Water* use is well below that of commercial agriculture per pound of food produced, and is about 33% to 12% that of conventional techniques per unit of land area.

Energy expenditure, expressed in kilocalories of input, is 1% to 6% of that used by commercial agriculture. The human body is still more efficient than any machine we have been able to invent. Several factors contradict the popular conception that this is a labor-intensive method. Using hand tools may seem to be more work, but the yields more than compensate. Even at 50¢ a pound *wholesale,* zucchini can bring as much as $18 to $32 per hour depending on the harvest timing because it is easy to grow, maintain, and harvest. Time spent in soil preparation is more than offset later in less need for weeding, thinning, cultivation, and other chores per unit of area and per unit of yield. Hand watering and harvesting appear to take the most time. Initial soil preparation, including fertilization and planting, may take 5 to 9½ hours per 100-square-foot raised bed. Thereafter, the time spent decreases dramatically. A new digging tool, the U-bar, has reduced subsequent bed preparation time to as little as 20 minutes, when that is desirable. A new hand watering tool that waters more quickly *and* more gently is also being developed.

Nature has answered our original queries with an abundance even greater than expected, and we have narrowed our research to the most important question that can be asked of any agricul-

Lush growing beds at Common Ground make optimal use of garden space.

tural system: Is it sustainable? The GROW BIOINTENSIVE method currently uses 50% or less of the purchased *fertilizer* that commercial farmers use. Can we maintain all nutrient levels on site, once they have been built up and balanced? Or is some outside additive always necessary? We need to look more closely at all nutrients: nitrogen, phosphorus, potash, calcium, and trace minerals. Anyone can grow good crops on good soil, cashing in on nature's accumulated riches. The GROW BIOINTENSIVE method appears to allow anyone to take "the worst possible soil" (Alan Chadwick's appraisal of our original Palo Alto research site) and turn it into a bountiful garden or mini-farm. Preliminary monitoring of our soil-building process by a University of California soil scientist was probably the most important information garnered about our initial site. Continued monitoring will unlock new secrets and provide hope for people with marginal, worn-out, or desertified soils. However, a complete answer to the long-term question of sustainable soil fertility will require at least 50 years of observation as the living soil system changes and grows! We continue to work on that issue.

Nine years of growing and testing in Ecology Action's urban garden mini-farm came to an end in 1980 due to the termination of our lease and new construction on that land. Like so much other agricultural land in the United States, our lovingly tended beds succumbed to the press of urbanization. The city growing area prepared us for a rural site. The facilities of grocery store and electric lines were exchanged for open skies and room to grow more herbs, flowers, vegetables, beans, grains, and compost crops than we ever imagined. At the Common Ground mini-farm in Willits, California, we are enjoying a permanent site where we can grow trees of all kinds—for food, fuel, and beauty. Other projects include a self-fertilizing lawn composed of fragrant herbs and clovers, and a working mini-farm. In 1973, we initially estimated that a 1-person small holding (⅛ to ½ acre) could grow crops bringing in a net income of $5,000 to $20,000 a year (about $100 to $400 a week) after 4 to 5 years. However, one woman in Vancouver, British Columbia, was earning about $400 a week growing gourmet vegetables for restaurants on ¹⁄₁₆ of an acre 20 years after we began. At first she thought it could not be done, but when she tried growing crops for income it worked. She then passed her skills on to 12 other women. Crops grown may include collards, chard, beets, mangels, spinach, green onions, garlic, radishes, romaine and Bibb lettuce, zucchini, pattypan squash, cucumbers, and lavender. Rather than solely looking to Ecology Action for answers, we hope you will dig in and try GROW BIOINTENSIVE for yourself! The techniques are simple to use, as this book shows. No large capital expenses are necessary to get started. The techniques work in varied climates and soils. American farmers are feeding the world, but mini-farming can give people the knowledge to feed themselves.

Posted on the wall of our local environmental center, there once was a tongue-in-cheek guide called "50 Really Difficult Things You Can Do to Save the Earth." The second item was to "grow all your own vegetables." We had to laugh. We moved up to our new mini-farm in Willits with a plan for short-term food self-sufficiency. That was more than 20 years ago. We still take a neighborly ribbing for racing down to the farmers' markets to buy sweet corn, carrots, and other vegetables and fruits to feed an extended family of staff, apprentices, interns, and friends at our research site. Research priorities often interfere with growing all our vegetables and fruits. It is difficult to research, write, publish, teach, do outreach around the world, and farm—all at the same time!

Rachael Leler said, "My first garden was a total failure. I planned, dug, and planted, but I had not really learned how to garden yet. Now my favorite class to teach is compost. I bring a glass jar of waste—a slimy brew of potato peels, coffee grounds, and last week's rotting roses. The other jar has compost—sweet smelling, earthy, and alive and, by the way, nothing like the sifted and homogenized product sold at garden centers. These 2 jars remind me of the magical transformation of a garden: health from garbage, riches out of waste. I can 'see' that magic immediately, though it may take me years to fully comprehend it!"

Betsy Bruneau, a senior staff person, has an affinity for tiny life-forms. She taught us to appreciate the infinitely variable lichens that cling to bare rock and fallen trees, creating soil for larger life-forms to follow. People used to bring insects into our store for identification. Betsy's first response was usually a hushed "How beautiful!" She marvels at the intensely colorful tomato hornworms, the intricate markings on the shells of wise old snails, and the fact that earwigs are wonderful mothers.

We live in an age of consumption, when we are constantly exhorted to measure ourselves by our possessions. Yet no matter how rich we manage to become, something human in us says our true worth is reflected by what we ourselves create. Why not make it full of life and beauty rather than pollution? Our neighbor Ellen spent all day putting up jars of string beans and piccalilli, then worked until midnight to finish up a batch of raspberries. One of her notes reads, "There is no rest for the gardener . . . but there is always dessert!"

Gardening is not always easy, but the rewards are personal and fun. For most of us, the environment is what is around us, separate from human activity. Gardening offers the chance to become partners with nature. The reward is not just a salad from the backyard or a gleaming jar of peaches. Gardening is the process of digging the soil, starting small seeds, watching an apple tree grow. Gardening is an education in observation, harmony, honesty, and humility—in knowing and understanding our place in the world.

But the impact is also global. Alan Chadwick felt that gardening was the only way to prevent another world war—to bring a living, active peace on Earth by working with healthy, creative, positive life forces. In doing this, we become one with those life forces. The homegrown tomato requires no fuel for transportation, no packaging to be sent to the landfill, no political decisions about who will be allowed to work the fields or what level of pollutants is acceptable in our groundwater. Nature is not always a Garden of Eden. Some partnership is required to bring out the best in both nature and people. "Give to Nature, and she will repay you in glorious abundance," was one of Chadwick's favorite sayings. Gardening and mini-farming give us the opportunity to participate in the subtle transformation of desert to "dessert." All we need to do is to start with one growing bed and tend it well, and we have begun the exciting, expansive, giving process of enlivening and healing the Earth and ourselves.

## Acknowledgments

Betsy Bruneau, Rachael Leler, Tom Walker, Craig Cook, Rip King, Bill Spencer, Claudette Paige, Keven Raftery, Marion Cartwright, Paka, Phyllis Anderson, Wayne Miller, Paul Hwoschinsky, Dave Smith, Steve and Judi Rioch, Louisa Lenz, Bill Bruneau, Dean Nims, Tommy Derrick, Carol Cox, Cynthia Raiser Jeavons, Dan Whittaker, Shirley Coe, David Basile, Jed Diamond, Sensei, John Raiser, Helen Raiser, Jennifer Raiser, Phill Raiser, Sheila Hilton, John Beeby, Salvador Diaz, Bill Liebhardt, Jack and Virginia Jeavons, John Doran, Emmanuel Omondi, Joshua Machinga, Sandra Mardigian, Fernando Pia, Juan Manuel Martinez Valdez, Mercedes Torres Barrones, Carol Vesecky, Vicci Warhol, Mary Zellachild, William Wardlaw and Patricia Arnold, Maryanne Mott and Herman Warsh, Mike and Diane Griggs, Steve and Carol Moore, Clancy Drake, Jasmine Star, Langtry Williams, Mark Larratt-Smith, Gayle Fillman, Jed Diamond, Karina McAbee, Julian Gorodsky, members of Ecology Action, and friends have all made important contributions to the book's content and spirit.

We assume responsibility for any inaccuracies that may have been included; they are ours and not Alan Chadwick's or Stephen Kafka's. This book is not intended to be an exhaustive work on the subject, but rather one of simple completeness. Most of us at Ecology Action are only beginning to intermediate GROW BIOINTENSIVE gardeners. The purpose of this book is to turn on as many people as possible to a beautiful, dynamically alive method of horticulture and life.

# BUILDING SOIL,
# BUILDING THE FUTURE

There is an exciting challenge ahead of us. How can we revitalize our extraordinary planet, ensuring life and health for the environment, the life-forms of a myriad of ecosystems, humankind, and future generations? The answer is as close to each of us as the food we consume each day. We can begin to create a better world from right where we are—in home gardens and mini-farms, in virtually all climates and soils. Millions of people are already doing this in over 130 countries around the world, using GROW BIOINTENSIVE® sustainable mini-farming techniques.

We "farm" as we eat. For example, if we consume food that has been grown using methods that inadvertently deplete the soil in the growing process, then *we are responsible for depleting the soil.* If, instead, we raise or request food grown in ways that heal the Earth, then *we are healing the Earth and its soils.* Our daily food choices will make the difference. We can choose to sustain ourselves while increasing the planet's vitality. In the bargain we preserve resources, breathe cleaner air, enjoy good exercise, and eat pure food.

What are the dimensions of this challenge? Current agricultural practices reportedly destroy approximately 6 pounds of soil for each pound of food produced.[1] United States croplands are losing topsoil about 18 times faster than the soil formation rate. This is not sustainable. In fact, worldwide only about 42 to 84 years' worth of topsoil remains.[2]

Why is this happening? Conventional agricultural practices often deplete the soil 18 to 80 times more rapidly than nature builds soil. This happens when the humus (cured organic matter) in the soil is used up and not replaced, when cropping patterns

"They're making more people every day, but they ain't makin' any more dirt."
—Will Rogers

"Population will increase rapidly, more rapidly than in former times, and 'ere long the most valuable of all arts will be the art of deriving a comfortable subsistence from the smallest area of soil."
—Abraham Lincoln

1. Developed from U.S. Department of Agriculture statistics.
2. Developed from P. Buringh, "Availability of Agricultural Land for Crop and Livestock Production," in D. Pimentel and C. W. Hall (eds.), *Food and Natural Resources* (San Diego: Academic Press, 1989), pp. 69–83, as noted in "Natural Resources and an Optimum Human Population," David Pimentel et al., *Population and Environment: A Journal of Interdisciplinary Studies*, Vol. 15, No. 5, May 1994; and with statistics from the United Nations.

are used that tend to deplete the soil's structure, and when minerals are removed from the soil more rapidly than they are replaced. Even organic farming probably depletes the soil 17 to 70 times faster than nature builds it, by importing organic matter and minerals from other soils, which thereby become increasingly depleted. The planetary result is a net *reduction* in overall soil quality.

It is interesting to note that during the last 56 years, since mechanized and chemical agricultural approaches have been used in China (as opposed to traditional Biointensive practices), China has lost as much as 33% of her farmland.[3] In contrast, when properly used, the techniques included in GROW BIOINTENSIVE sustainable mini-farming's *miniaturization of agriculture* can build the soil up to 60 times faster than in nature,[4] while making possible:

**Note**
Up to 6 billion microbial life-forms can live in 5 grams of cured compost, about the size of a quarter.

- A 67% to 88% *reduction* in water consumption per unit of production
- A 50+% *reduction* in the amount of purchased fertilizer required per unit of production
- A 94% to 99% *reduction* in the amount of energy used per unit of production
- A 100+% *increase* in soil fertility, while productivity increases and resource use decreases
- A 200% to 400% *increase* in caloric production per unit of area
- A 100+% *increase* in income per unit of area

Gandhi observed that "to forget how to dig the earth and tend the soil is to forget ourselves." In *Candide,* Voltaire points the way: "The whole world is a garden and what a wonderful place this would be, if only each of us took care of our part of the Garden!" Each of us is needed. Building a truly sustainable agriculture is an essential part of building sustainable communities. As we build soils, we also build a culture made up of healthy living and effective farming, as well as enduring communities. In order to accomplish this, we need to shift our agricultural perspective. We need to *stop growing crops* and *start growing soil!* Granted, in order to grow soil, we need to grow crops. But rather than growing crops for the sole purpose of consumption, the goal changes to one of giving and creating life—producing, in the process, an abundance of food. We must begin by educating ourselves, then sharing what we have learned by teaching *people to understand the importance of growing soil.* Life makes more life, and we have the opportunity to work together with this powerful force to expand our own vitality and that of this planet.

Generally, the challenges of world hunger, soil depletion, and diminishing resources seem so overwhelming that we tend to look for big solutions, such as shipping massive amounts of grain,

3. *New York Times,* March 27, 1994.
4. "Worldwide Loss of Soil and a Possible Solution," Ecology Action, 1996.

breeding high-yield miracle crops, or establishing infrastructures—bank loans, machinery and fertilizer purchases, markets, and roads. These solutions create long-term dependency. What is so exciting about a personal approach is that it seeks to answer the question "How do we enable ourselves to take care of our own needs?" Personal solutions will have as many varied applications as there are people, soils, climates, and cultures. Our work is one way for people to begin to develop those solutions.

Our work grows out of a personal concern about worldwide starvation and malnutrition, augmented by a sober assessment of the unsustainability of the most dominant current methods of producing our food. We came to believe that if we could determine the smallest amount of land and resources needed for 1 person to supply all of his or her own needs in a sustainable way, we might arrive at a personal solution. What if a person could, in a tiny area, easily raise all the crops that would supply all food, clothes, building materials, compost materials, seeds, and income for an entire year? We asked whether others knew the smallest area required to do this, and no one did—so we began our 35-year (and counting) quest to help solve an ongoing problem and make possible a better quality of life.

How can we live better on fewer resources? It is possible! The way humankind is currently living and increasing in population, *we will not be able to provide for our own food needs soon if we do not grow soils*. The charts in the appendix on page 248 illustrate how, in as little as 7 years, there may be an average of just 9,000 square feet (or less) of farmable land per person to feed most people on Earth. But regardless of the amount of arable land available, as early as 1992, many countries had only enough water to irrigate 4,000 square feet per person. However, GROW BIOINTENSIVE sustainable mini-farming may make it possible to grow all the food for one's own nutrition, as well as food for the soil, on as little as 4,000 square feet, without a great amount of difficulty. We also believe GROW BIOINTENSIVE can produce more net income per acre than commercial agriculture. In striving for quality gardening, a person may thus be able to provide a diet and income more than sufficient for his or her needs. The effort will produce a human renaissance and a cornucopia of food for all.

The GROW BIOINTENSIVE method is very energy efficient, in large part because it relies on the work of the capable and efficient human body rather than on the work of machines. One person annually consumes in food the energy equivalent of 32.6 gallons of gasoline.[5] In contrast, the most efficient economy car will use that much gas in a month or two of ordinary driving. Imagine the fuel consumed by a tractor or industrial machine in a year!

5. Michael Perelman, "Efficiency in Agriculture: The Economics of Energy," in Richard Merrill (ed.), *Radical Agriculture* (New York: Harper & Row, 1976), p. 86.

However, GROW BIOINTENSIVE sustainable mini-farming (or any other sustainable farming practice), if used alone or improperly, is not a panacea. If *not* used properly, GROW BIOINTENSIVE practices can deplete the soil more rapidly than other farming practices because of the high yields. But above all, using only a single agricultural approach to grow food could be unhealthy. This would be another form of "monocropping" in a living world ecosystem that needs diversity. Agriculture in the future will probably be a synthesis, a *sustainable collage,* of:

- GROW BIOINTENSIVE mini-farming
- Agroforestry
- No-till Fukuoka food raising
- Traditional Asian blue-green algal wet rice farming
- Natural rainfall "arid" farming
- Indigenous farming

Also, to preserve the plant and animal genetic diversity upon which we all depend, we need to keep ½ of the world's farmable land in wild. As we begin to use sustainable, land- and resource-conserving food-raising approaches, more wilderness areas can remain untouched so more of the endangered plant and animal diversity on this Earth can be preserved. This wealth of genetic diversity is necessary if the planet on which we live is to support abundance.

## The History and Philosophy of the GROW BIOINTENSIVE Method

The GROW BIOINTENSIVE method of horticulture is a quiet, vitally alive art of organic gardening that relinks people with the whole universe—a universe in which each of us is an interwoven part of the whole. People find their place by relating and cooperating in harmony with the sun, air, rain, soil, moon, insects, plants, and animals rather than by attempting to dominate them. All of these elements will teach us their lessons and do the gardening for us if we will only watch and listen. We become gentle shepherds providing the conditions for plant growth.

*Biologically intensive farming* dates back to 4,000 years ago in China, 2,000 years ago in Greece, and 1,000 years ago in Latin America. In fact, the Mayan culture grew food this way at their homes on a neighborhood basis! This is one of the reasons their culture survived when others around them were collapsing.

The GROW BIOINTENSIVE method is a combination of 2 forms of horticulture practiced in Europe during the 1800s and early 1900s. *French intensive techniques* were developed in the 1700s and 1800s outside Paris. Crops were grown on 18 inches of horse manure, a fertilizer that was readily available. The crops were grown so close to each other that when the plants were

**GOAL:** *Learn from the experiences of farmers through time*

Winter lettuce growing in an 1890s cloche (bell jar). The standard diameter is 16¾ inches.

mature, their leaves would barely touch. The close spacing provided a mini-climate and a living mulch that reduced weed growth and helped hold moisture in the soil. During the winter, glass jars were placed over seedlings to give them an early start. The gardeners grew up to 9 crops each year and could even grow melon plants during the winter.

*Biodynamic techniques* were developed in the early 1920s by Rudolf Steiner, a brilliant Austrian philosopher and educator. Noting a decline in the nutritive value and yields of crops in Europe, Steiner traced the cause to the use of the newly introduced synthetic chemical fertilizers and pesticides. An increase was also noticed in the number of crops affected by disease and insect problems. These fertilizers were not complete and vital meals for the plants, but single, physical nutrients in a soluble salt form. Initially, only nitrogen fertilizers were used to stimulate growth. Later phosphorus and potassium were added to strengthen the plants and to minimize disease and insect problems. Eventually, trace minerals were added to the chemical larder to round out the plants' diet. After breaking down nutrients into their component parts for plant food, people found it necessary to recombine them in mixtures approximating a balanced diet. This attempt might have been more successful if the fertilizers had not caused chemical changes in the soil that damaged its structure, killed beneficial microbiotic life, and greatly reduced its ability to make nutrients already in the air and soil available to the plants.

Rudolf Steiner returned to the more gentle, diverse, and balanced diets of organic fertilizers as a cure for the ills brought on by synthetic chemical fertilization. He stressed the holistic growing environment for plants: their rate of growth, the synergistic balance of their environments and nutrients, their proximity to other plants, and their various companion relationships. He

Artificial fertilization.

Natural fertilization.

French gardeners at lettuce beds in the early 1900s.

initiated a movement to scientifically explore the relationships that plants have with each other. From centuries of farmer experience and from tests, it has been determined that certain flowers, herbs, weeds, and other plants can minimize insect attacks on plants. Many plants also benefit one another. Strawberries and green beans produce better when grown together. In contrast, onions stunt the growth of green beans. Some people say that tomatoes are narcissists; they prefer to be grown alone in compost made from tomato plants.

The biodynamic method also brought back raised planting beds. Two thousand years ago, the Greeks noticed that plant life thrives in landslides. The loose soil allows air, moisture, warmth, nutrients,[6] and roots to properly penetrate the soil. The curved surface area between the 2 edges of the landslide bed provides more surface area for the penetration and interaction of the natural elements than a flat surface. The simulated landslides or raised beds used by biodynamic gardeners are usually 3 to 6 feet wide and of varying lengths. In contrast, the planting rows usually made by gardeners and farmers today are only a few inches wide with wide spaces in between. The plants have difficulty growing in these rows due to the extreme penetration of air and the greater fluctuations in temperature and moisture content. During irrigation, water floods the rows, immerses the roots in water, and washes soil away from the rows and upper roots. Consequently, much of the beneficial microbiotic life around the roots and soil, which is so essential to disease prevention and to the transformation of nutrients into forms the plants can use, is destroyed and may even be replaced by harmful organisms. (About ¾ of the beneficial microbiotic life inhabits the upper 6 inches of the soil.) After the water penetrates the soil, the upper layers dry out and microbial activity is severely curtailed. The rows are then more subject to wide temperature fluctuations. Finally, to cultivate and harvest, people and machine trundle down the trough between the rows, compacting the soil and the roots, which eat, drink, and breathe—a difficult task with someone or something standing on the equivalent of your mouth and nose!

These difficulties are also often experienced at the edges of raised beds prepared in clay soils during the first few seasons. Until the soil texture becomes friable, it is necessary to level the top of the raised bed to minimize erosion (see chapter 1, Bed Preparation), and the soil on the sides of the beds is sometimes too tight for easy planting. Increased exposure to the elements occurs on the sides, and the tighter soil of the paths is nearby.

Row plants are more susceptible to soil compaction.

6. Alan Chadwick used to call these *nutriments*, the things that "nourish or promote growth and repair the natural wastage of organic life." He used the term to distinguish them from nutrients, which are merely "nourishing substances or ingredients." He did this in particular to note the importance of multinutrient organic fertilizers, which break down over a period of time and nourish microbial life growth. In contrast, chemical fertilizers generally break down rapidly and cause inefficient decomposition of organic matter. Well-decomposed organic matter is the microbial life's food source. In this book, *nutrient* has both meanings.

(*Left*) GROW BIOINTENSIVE raised bed;
(*right*) traditional rows.

The plants along the sides usually do not grow as vigorously as those further inside the bed. When raised beds are prepared in friable soil, the opposite is true. The top of the bed can now be curved and erosion will not be a problem. The soil is loose enough for plants to thrive along the sides. The edges of the beds are included in the mini-climate effect created by closely spaced plants, and the water that runs from the middle of the bed provides the extra moisture the edges need.

Between the 1920s and 1930s, Alan Chadwick, an Englishman, combined the biodynamic and French intensive techniques into the biodynamic/French intensive method. The United States was first exposed to the combination when Mr. Chadwick brought the method to the 4-acre organic Student Garden at the University of California's Santa Cruz campus in the 1960s. Chadwick, a horticultural genius, had been gardening for half a century and was also an avid dramatist and artist. He studied under Rudolf Steiner, the French gardeners, and George Bernard Shaw, and worked as a gardener for the Union of South Africa. The site he developed at Santa Cruz was on the side of a hill with poor, clayey soil. Not even "weeds" grew well there—except poison oak, which was removed with pickaxes. By hand, Chadwick and his apprentices created a good soil in 2 to 3 years. From this soil and vision, a beautiful, wondrous, and real Garden of Eden was brought into existence. Barren soil was made fertile through extensive use of compost, with its life-giving humus. The humus produced a healthy soil that grew healthy plants less susceptible to disease and insect attacks. The many nuances of the biodynamic/French intensive method—such as transplanting seedlings into a better soil each time a plant is moved and sowing by the phases of the moon—were also used. The results were beautiful flowers with exquisite fragrances and tasty vegetables of high quality. As an added bonus for all the tender loving care they received, the vegetable plants produced yields 4 times greater than those produced by commercial agriculture.

As the biodynamic/French intensive gardening method has continued to evolve and be simplified by Ecology Action, so has its name. It is now known simply as GROW BIOINTENSIVE gardening. Ecology Action is now in its 35th year of rediscovering and sharing the original principles behind the GROW BIOINTENSIVE method.

The features of GROW BIOINTENSIVE include:

- *Deep soil preparation,* which develops good soil structure. Once this structure is established, it may be maintained for several years with 2-inch-deep surface cultivation (until compaction once again necessitates deep soil preparation).
- *The use of compost* (humus) for soil fertility and nutrients.
- *Close plant spacing,* as in nature. (How surprised we would be to find natural meadows, forests, and fields growing in rows, with the area between the rows resembling long strips of desert.)
- *Synergistic planting of crop combinations* so plants that are grown together enhance each other.
- *Carbon-efficient crops*—planting approximately 60% of the growing area in dual-purpose seed and grain crops for the production of large amounts of carbonaceous material for compost and significant amounts of dietary calories.
- *Calorie-efficient crops*—planting approximately 30% of the growing area in special root crops, such as potatoes, leeks, garlic, parsnips, and Jerusalem artichokes, which produce a large amount of calories for the diet per unit of area.
- *The use of open-pollinated seeds* to preserve genetic diversity.
- *A whole, interrelated farming system.* The GROW BIOINTENSIVE food-raising method is a whole system, and its components must all be used together for the optimum effect. If all of its elements are not used together, the method's high yields can rapidly deplete the soil. In contrast, when used properly—so all wastes are recycled and enough organic matter is grown to ensure that each farm can produce enough compost to create and maintain sustainable soil fertility—*GROW BIOINTENSIVE sustainable mini-farming can create soil rapidly and maintain sustainable soil fertility.* It is *how* each one of us uses GROW BIOINTENSIVE, or other food-raising practices, that makes a living difference!

## How to Use This Book

Alan Chadwick, the horticultural genius who taught us the basis for GROW BIOINTENSIVE sustainable mini-farming practices, guided us with this advice: "Just grow one small area, and do it well. Then, once you have got it right, grow more!" One of the advantages of *How to Grow More Vegetables* is that *it describes a complete general approach to gardening.* Another is that it *lets you start small and build your skill as a gardener over the years.*

As you learn the basics of soil preparation, the simple joys of gardening will gain depth. Bed preparation, fertilization, composting, seed propagation, transplanting, watering, and weeding are performed essentially the same way for all crops. Only the seedling flat and growing-bed spacings are different from one crop to another (these are given in columns H, L1, and M2 of each section of the Master Charts beginning on page 86). *So, once you know how to grow lettuce, you know most of the basics for growing onions, tomatoes, wheat, apple trees, and even cotton!*

If you are a *beginning gardener or mini-farmer* reading *How to Grow More Vegetables,* you may want to skip most of the tables except for column H in the Master Charts, which lists plant spacings. You will probably start by growing vegetables and a few flowers and herbs, and many of these crops can be bought as seedlings from a local nursery. Starting your own seedlings requires a higher skill level, and you may want to wait to try it until your second or third year.

If you are an *intermediate gardener,* you will begin to use more of the tables and charts and to grow some compost crops, grains, and fruit trees. The bibliography and resources section (beginning on page 179) is a source of additional information on topics of interest that you may like to pursue as your skill as a mini-farmer grows.

Ten years in the garden will produce a *fully experienced food grower.* You can now draw on all of the information provided in this book as you work on growing most or all of your family's food at home, plant a mini-orchard in the front yard, begin an economic mini-farm, or teach others the skills you have already mastered.

As you begin to grow GROW BIOINTENSIVEly, be sure to grow *sustainable soil fertility crops*—which we are calling carbon-and-calorie crops (see pages 24–25)—as part of your garden. We need to grow crops that feed the soil as well as ourselves. There are many such soil fertility crops. Examples are corn, millet, wheat, oats, barley, cereal rye, and amaranth. These crops grow a lot of carbonaceous material for the compost pile, which in turn feeds the soil with humus, as well as providing a great deal of *nutritious food to eat.* Information about these *dual-purpose crops,* which provide both dietary calories and compost materials, is included in the Master Charts section beginning on page 106 of this book and in the compost crop sections of Ecology Action's Self-Teaching Mini-Series Booklets 14, 15, 25, 26, and 28.

*How to Grow More Vegetables* provides you with everything you need to create a garden symphony—from the basic techniques to advanced planning skills for a beautifully planted backyard homestead. Each of us can begin in this way to revitalize ourselves, the soil, and the Earth—one small growing area at a time. Before we know it, we will all live on a thriving, vibrant Earth consisting of many personal and community *mini-preserves,* reestablished with health as a vital, dynamic whole!

But the real excitement is that each of us will never know everything. Alan Chadwick, after he had been gardening for 50 years, said, "I am still learning!" And so are we all. In fact, while universal scientific principles operate within GROW BIOINTENSIVE sustainable mini-farming's biological systems, our gardening

"Our future security now depends . . . on developing new, more productive farming technologies."
                                          —Lester Brown

results change each time we modify our system. For example, the microbial life levels and yields differ depending on whether we prepare the soil 6 inches, 12 inches, or 24 inches deep. Why? Partly because of improved nutrient cycling and aeration. Still, we do not know *all* the reasons yet! As we explore, we will come to understand the underlying principles, and a whole new world will unfold. We will be able to make changes to improve the health, fertility, effectiveness, and sustainability of the way we farm for an even better life on this planet.

Much new material is included in this latest revision to make your job easier: key clarifications in the compost and seed propagation chapters; crop rotation information; improved techniques, understandings, and approaches; corrected and updated Master Charts and planning data; and a greatly expanded bibliography for learning more about the areas that are most important to you. That is, more information to add to your fun as you grow past the beginning stage of GROW BIOINTENSIVE mini-farming in depth and breadth! This edition represents 35 years of working with plants, soils, and people—in virtually all climates and soils around the world. The result is for your benefit.

We each have a lifetime of growing before us, and the opportunity to continually improve our understanding of the living canvas we are painting. Many more people are becoming involved in home food-raising and mini-farming as a result of peak-oil challenges, as well as from a love of nature and working with a soil teeming with life! Start now with just one raised growing bed. Self-reliance in your own "foodshed" will make all the difference in the world. Each one of us has tremendous potential to heal the Earth. Let us begin.

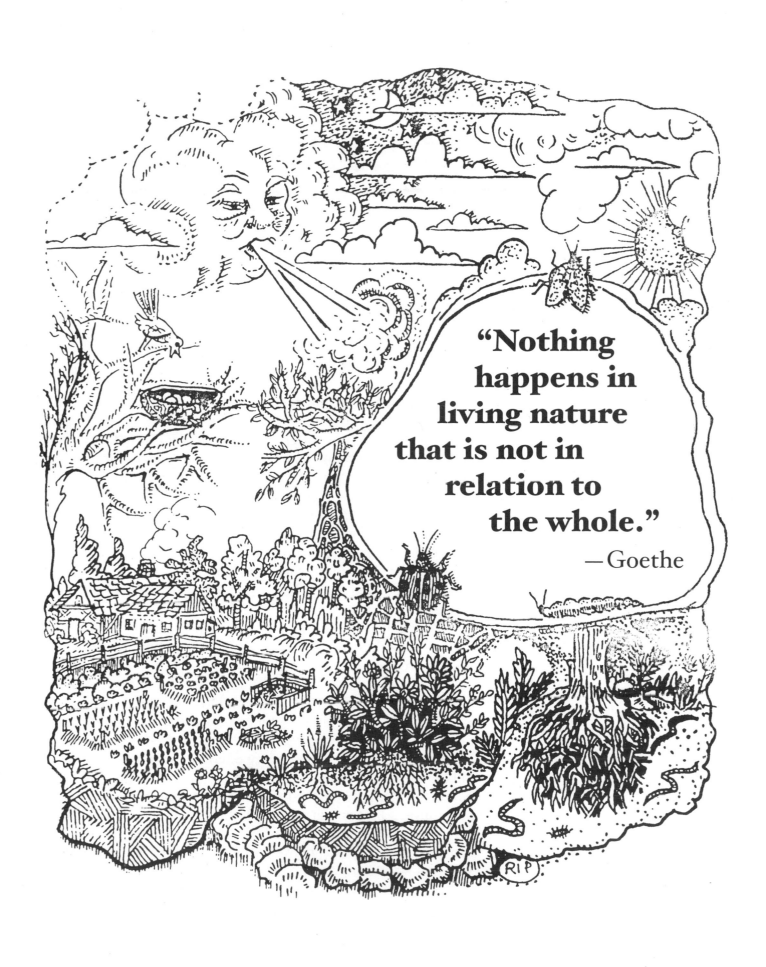

"Nothing happens in living nature that is not in relation to the whole."

— Goethe

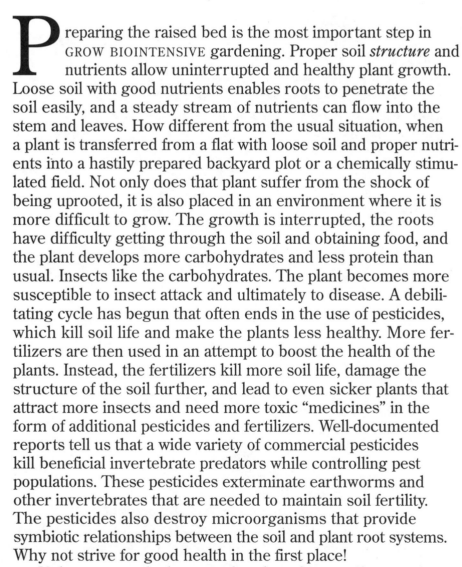

# 1
## CHAPTER ONE

# BED PREPARATION

**GOAL:** *Develop soil structure so the plants will have a "living sponge cake" in which to thrive*

Proper soil structure and nutrients allow uninterrupted and healthy plant growth.

Preparing the raised bed is the most important step in GROW BIOINTENSIVE gardening. Proper soil *structure* and nutrients allow uninterrupted and healthy plant growth. Loose soil with good nutrients enables roots to penetrate the soil easily, and a steady stream of nutrients can flow into the stem and leaves. How different from the usual situation, when a plant is transferred from a flat with loose soil and proper nutrients into a hastily prepared backyard plot or a chemically stimulated field. Not only does that plant suffer from the shock of being uprooted, it is also placed in an environment where it is more difficult to grow. The growth is interrupted, the roots have difficulty getting through the soil and obtaining food, and the plant develops more carbohydrates and less protein than usual. Insects like the carbohydrates. The plant becomes more susceptible to insect attack and ultimately to disease. A debilitating cycle has begun that often ends in the use of pesticides, which kill soil life and make the plants less healthy. More fertilizers are then used in an attempt to boost the health of the plants. Instead, the fertilizers kill more soil life, damage the structure of the soil further, and lead to even sicker plants that attract more insects and need more toxic "medicines" in the form of additional pesticides and fertilizers. Well-documented reports tell us that a wide variety of commercial pesticides kill beneficial invertebrate predators while controlling pest populations. These pesticides exterminate earthworms and other invertebrates that are needed to maintain soil fertility. The pesticides also destroy microorganisms that provide symbiotic relationships between the soil and plant root systems. Why not strive for good health in the first place!

Unless you are lucky enough to have loose soil, *preparing and planting a raised bed initially* can take a lot of time—as much as 6½ to 11 hours for a 100-square-foot bed the first time.

As you become skilled, the double-dig often takes 2 hours or less. After the first crop, however, only 4 to 6½ hours should be required on an *ongoing* basis for the whole preparing and planting process, because the soil will have better structure. Once the beds are planted, only about 30 minutes a day are required to maintain a 200-square-foot area—an area large enough to provide 1 person with vegetables 12 months a year in an area with a 4- to 6-month growing season.[1] Even less time per day and only a 100-square-foot area may be required in an area with an 8- to 12-month growing season. Beginning gardeners may require a larger area for the same yield, but we recommend a new gardener use only 100 square feet and allow the soil to gradually produce more food as his or her skills improve.

The square footage required to provide the vegetable supply for 1 person is approximate since the exact amount varies depending on whether the individual likes corn (which takes up a lot of space per pound of edible vegetable grown) or a lot of carrots, beets, potatoes, and tomatoes (which require much less area per pound of food produced). Using the tables in chapter 7, Simple Garden Plans (based on yields produced by the GROW BIOINTENSIVE method for all vegetable crops), you can determine the actual area needed for each crop. Be patient in this soil-building process. It takes 5 to 10 years to build up a good soil (and one's skills). Actually, this is very rapid. Nature often requires a period of 2,000 years or more to build a soil!

Instructions for the initial preparation of a 100-square-foot bed in a heavy clay, very sandy, or good soil are given below. Instructions for the repreparation of a bed are also given. After the soil has been initially prepared, you will find that the GROW BIOINTENSIVE method requires less work than the gardening technique you presently use. The Irish call this the "lazy bed" method of raising food. It has the added benefit of producing tasty vegetables and an average of 4 times more vegetables than your current yield! Or, if you wish to raise only the same amount of food as last year, only ¼ the area will have to be dug, weeded, and watered.

**Notes**
- 1 cubic foot = 1.5 5-gallon buckets
- 1 5-gallon bucket = 0.67 cubic feet
- The *most* cured compost that can be added per 100-square-foot area per 4- to 6-month growing season on a *sustainable* basis is probably 8 cubic feet (including 50% soil by volume). This amount has been added with good results historically in Europe. However, in various situations, 1.6 to 2.8 to 5.6 cubic feet of cured compost (that is 50% soil by volume) may be a sufficient and sustainable amount to be added the same growing season. More research is needed to determine which amounts produce the best results in different climates and soils.

## INITIAL PREPARATION PER 100 SQUARE FEET

First, perform a soil test (see "Soil Testing" in chapter 4, Fertilization), then do the following:

1. If needed, soak the area to be dug for *2 hours* with a sprinkler (for hard, dry clays).
2. Let the soil dry out partially for *2 days*.
3. Loosen 12 inches of soil with a spading fork, and remove weeds. *1 to 2 hours.*
4. Water gently by hand for *5 minutes* and let the soil rest for *1 day*.

[1]. Two hundred square feet can yield over 300 pounds of vegetables and soft fruits in a 4- to 6-month growing season at intermediate GROW BIOINTENSIVE yields. The average person in the United States consumes about 322 pounds of vegetables and soft fruits annually.

If your soil has particularly large clods, wait several extra days, and let nature help do the work. The warm sun, cool nights, wind, and water will help break down the clods. Water the bed lightly every day to aid the process.

5. At this time, sand may be added to a bed with clayey soil, or clay to a bed with sandy soil, to improve texture. Normally you should not add more than a $\frac{1}{2}$-inch layer (4 cubic feet) of sand or clay. (More sand may allow the water-soluble fertilizers to percolate down too rapidly.) Mix the sand or clay thoroughly into the loosened 12 inches of soil with a spading fork. *1 hour.*

6. Up to a $\frac{1}{2}$-inch layer (4 cubic feet or 6 5-gallon buckets) of cured compost—whatever is available—may be spread onto and incorporated with a spading fork into the surface of a bed that has good soil. You may add up to a 1-inch layer (8 cubic feet) of compost (preferably) or aged manure[2] to soil with poor (very sandy or very clayey) texture *on a one-time basis only. $\frac{1}{2}$ hour.*

7. Water gently by hand for *5 minutes,* and let the soil rest for *1 day,* if needed.

8. Remove 7, 5-gallon buckets of soil from the upper level of the first trench (assuming a 5-foot-wide growing bed; see drawing on page 6). Be sure to dig trenches across the *width* of the bed. It helps to level the soil with a rake after every 3 to 4 trenches during the digging process. Use 3 buckets of soil to make compost (these will eventually be returned to the growing beds in the form of added compost), 1 bucket of soil to make flat soil to grow seedlings in and return 3 buckets to the bed after it has been dug. Even though you have removed one upper trench of soil, there will be enough soil at the end of the double-dig process to fill in the last trench, due to the expansion of the soil's volume as air is incorporated into the soil during the dig.

9. Double-dig the soil with a flat spade and a spading fork (see pages 7–13 for double-digging instructions). Be sure to use a digging board to avoid unnecessary soil compaction. *2 to 4 hours.*

10. Level and shape the bed, filling last trench with soil. *$\frac{1}{2}$ hour.*

11. Sprinkle organic nitrogen, phosphorus, potash, calcium, and trace mineral fertilizers (such as alfalfa and kelp meals, wood ash, and eggshells) as indicated by your soil test evenly over the surface of the bed after leveling and shaping it. Include any desirable levels of pH modifiers (such as special leaf or pine needle compost to make the soil less alkaline, or lime to make the soil less acid) as indicated by your soil test. Sift in fertilizers and pH modifiers only 2 to 4 inches deep with a spading fork (2 inches if surface cultivation is being used; see page 57). After sifting in fertilizers, do no further raking to avoid disturbing the even distribution of fertilizers and compost. (If there seems to be an excess of air in your soil, tamp the soil down by placing your digging board on various sections of the bed and then standing on it. This removes excess air from the upper few inches of the bed.) *$\frac{1}{2}$ to 1 hour.*

12. Plant or transplant. *1 to 2 hours.*

Total: $6\frac{1}{2}$ to 11 hours for *initial* soil preparation, fertilization, and transplanting.

---

2. Two-year-old steer or cow manure, or 2-year-old horse manure that originally contained a lot of sawdust, or 2-month-old horse or chicken manure not containing much sawdust.

The proper tools will make the work easier and more productive.

## FOR SOIL PREPARATION

## FOR SEED PROPAGATION

Hand fork

Transplanting trowel

Dibber

D-handled flat spade

D-handled spading fork

*Note: 39-inch-long spades and forks are generally for people 5′5″ or shorter; 43-inch-long tools for people 5′6″ or taller*

Hula hoe

Bow rake (5'6" length)

*Note the difference in side views of a shovel and a spade.*

D handled spade

Standard shovel

## ONGOING PREPARATION FOR REPLANTING PER 100 SQUARE FEET—BEFORE EACH NEW CROP

1. Remove remaining vegetation, if necessary. Remove 7 5-gallon buckets of soil from the upper level of the first trench. Use 6 buckets of soil to make compost (they will eventually be returned to the growing bed in the form of added compost) and 1 bucket of soil to make flat soil.[3] Double-dig the soil. *2 to 3 hours.*

2. Level and shape the bed. *1/2 hour.*

3. Add any fertilizers and pH modifiers indicated by a soil test to the surface of the bed, and then add up to a 1/2-inch layer (4 cubic feet or 6 5-gallon buckets) of compost per 4-month growing season to the surface of the bed.[4] Sift in materials 2 to 4 inches deep with a spading fork. *1/2 to 1 hour.* (Adding the compost *after* the double-dig for *ongoing* soil preparation minimizes problems caused by water-soluble nitrogen leaching in increasingly loose soil.)

4. Plant or transplant. *1 to 2 hours.*

Total: 4 to 6 1/2 hours for *ongoing* soil preparation, fertilization, and transplanting.

3. If you are digging only 25 rather than 100 square feet, only hold out 1 3/4 5-gallon buckets of soil for making compost and flat soil, and return 5 1/4 5-gallon buckets of soil into the bed.

4. Do this at least once a year—normally at the beginning of the main growing season. Generally our practice for autumn crops is to only single-dig and to add no compost or fertilizers.

# The *Initial* Double-Dig Process

## Step-by-Step

1. Spread a layer of compost over the entire area to be dug.
2. Using a spade, remove the soil from a trench 1 foot deep and 1 foot wide across the width of the bed and put the soil into buckets or a wheelbarrow for use in making compost and flat soil. If the bed is 5 feet wide, the soil will fill 7 5-gallon buckets. (The trench is being dug across the *width* of the bed.)

Sides of the bed may be dug outward into the path.

For all-around ease, D-handled flat spades and D-handled spading forks of good temper are usually used for bed preparation. (Poor tools will wear out rapidly while you are preparing your garden area.) D-handles allow you to stand straight with the tool directly in front of you. You must frequently hold a long-handled tool to your side. This position does not allow for simple, direct posture and leverage. When digging for long periods of time, many people find the use of a D-handled tool less tiring (though it will probably take the digging of 3 beds to get used to!). However, people with back problems may need long-handled tools. In fact, people with back problems and those not in good health should check with their physician before proceeding with the physically active process of double-digging.

The flat spade has a particular advantage in that it digs equally deep all along its edge rather than in a pointed V pattern. This is especially important in the double-dig since all points in the bed should be dug to an equal depth. The blade on the flat spade also goes into the soil at less of an angle and without the usual shovel's curve. This means the sides of the bed can be dug perpendicular or even diagonally outward into the path, a plus for root penetration and water flow.

**3a.**

**4.**

You should only dig when the soil is evenly moist. It is easier and also better for the soil. Digging a hard, dry soil breaks down the structure, and it is difficult to penetrate. Wet soil is heavy and easily compacted. Compaction destroys friable structure and minimizes aeration. These conditions kill microbiotic life. The main reason for drying-out periods after watering the soil is to attain the proper moisture level and to make digging enjoyable and beneficial. Soil is too dry for digging when it is loose and will not hold its shape after being squeezed in the palm of your hand (in the cases of sands or loams) or when it cannot be penetrated by a spade (in the case of clays). Soil is too wet when it sticks to the spade as you dig.

The best time to double-dig the soil is in early morning, early evening, spring, and autumn. This is because the air temperature is cooler at these times, so less soil organic matter is lost in the process.

*Double-digging* is the term used for the process of preparing your soil 2 spades deep (about 24 inches). To begin, mark out a bed 3 to 5 feet wide and at least 3 feet long. Most people prefer a bed 5, 10, or 20 feet long, but the maximum is up to you. To double-dig, remove the soil from a trench 1 foot deep and 1 foot

3a. Loosen the soil an additional 12 inches with a spading fork by digging the tool in to its full depth and then pushing the tool handle downward so the fork tines will lever through the soil, loosening and aerating it. (See illustrations on page 8 for loosening compacted soil.)

4. Dig out the upper part of a second trench 1 foot deep and 1 foot wide. Move each spadeful of soil forward (into the first trench), mixing the soil layers as little as possible.

## 3b (i).

## 3b (ii).

3b(i). *For compacted soil:* While standing in the trench, loosen the soil an additional 12 inches with a spading fork by digging in the tool to its full depth and lifting out a tight soil section on the fork pan.

3b(ii). Then, by moving your arms upward in a small jerk, the soil will break apart as it falls downward, hits the fork tines, and falls into the hole below.

wide across the width of one end of the bed. Use a $\frac{5}{8}$-inch-thick plywood board, 2 to 3 feet long by 3 to 5 feet wide, as a "digging board" to stand on, depending on your height and the width of the bed. Place it on top of the 1-inch compost layer you spread over your bed, and advance it along the bed 1 foot at a time as you prepare to dig each new trench. Move 7 5-gallon buckets of soil from the beginning of the bed (if the bed is 5 feet wide) to a soil storage area for use in making compost and flat soil. You can also move the soil by wheelbarrow.

The goal of double-digging is to loosen the soil to a depth of 24 inches below the surface. The first year, you may only be able to reach 15 to 18 inches with reasonable effort. Be satisfied with this result. Do not strain yourself or your tools. More important than perfection the first year or two is going in the right direction. Nature, the loose soil, worms, and the plant roots will further loosen the soil with each crop, so digging will be easier each year and the depth will increase 3 to 6 inches annually.

Now, standing in the trench, dig down another 12 inches (if possible) with a spading fork, a few inches at a time if the soil is tight. Leave the fork as deep as it has penetrated, and loosen the subsoil by pushing the fork handle down and levering the tines through the soil. If the soil is not loose enough for this process, lift the chunk of soil out of the trench on the fork tines. Then throw the chunk slightly upward, and allow it to fall back on the tines so it will break apart. If this does not work, use the points of the fork tines to break the soil apart. Work from one end of the trench to the other in this manner.

Next, dig another trench behind the first one, moving each spadeful of the top 12 inches of soil forward into the first trench. When digging, make as few motions and use as little muscle as possible in this process. This will conserve your energy and involve less work. In fact, as you dig the soil, you will discover you can use an Aikido-like economy of motion and energy in which you are virtually just *shifting your balance and weight* rather than digging. (For a visual representation of this, see the *Dig It!* video carried by Ecology Action's Bountiful Gardens international mail-order service.) Sometimes you will have to work over a trench a second or third time to remove all the soil and obtain the proper trench size. Repeat the subsoil loosening process in the second trench.

Dig a third trench, and so on, until the entire bed has been double-dug. (When you are through double-digging, the aerated soil in the bed will be enough to fill in the last trench at the end of the bed, and you will add some soil to the bed in the form of cured compost.) It helps to level the soil with a rake after every 3 to 4 trenches during the digging process.

When you are sliding the soil forward from one trench into another, notice a couple of things. First, some of the compost layer you have added to the surface of the bed before beginning to dig slides 3 to 6 inches down into the trench, creating a small mound of soil or landslide. This approximates the way nature adds leaves, flower bodies, and other decaying vegetation to the top of the soil, where they break down and their essences percolate into the soil. Second, the *upper* layer of soil—the top 12 inches—should not be turned over during the double-dig and succeeding double-digs. Most of the microbiotic life lives in the upper 6 inches of the soil. Also, the natural layering of the soil that is caused by rainfall and leaching, leaf litter, temperature, gravity, and other natural forces is less disturbed when the soil is not generally mixed, even though the soil is loosened up and disturbed somewhat. Aim for a balance between nature's natural stratification and the loosened landsliding soil. (As a goal, strive not to mix the soil layers. The goal is important even though it will never be reached and significant mixing sometimes occurs. Without this goal, however, excessive disruption of the soil layers will occur.)

The U-bar (see pages 11–13).

## TYPES OF DEEP SOIL PREPARATION

*Simplified Side Views*

Ecology Action uses 4 basic types of deep soil preparation processes: the initial double-dig, the ongoing double-dig, the complete texturizing double-dig, and the U-bar dig. Following are simplified side views of each of these processes. The first 2 are described in the text.

The complete texturizing double-dig was developed to improve soil quality more rapidly and is used 1 time only. It is used usually in place of the initial double-dig, but it can be used

### **Initial** Double-Dig

1. When the soil is lightly moist, loosen the top 12 inches of the entire area to be dug with a spading fork and remove any weeds.

2. Spread a 1-inch layer of compost over the entire area to be dug (after mixing in a 1-inch layer of sand or clay 12 inches deep; optional, see page 4).

3. Remove the soil from the upper part of the first trench and place it in a soil storage area for use in making compost and flat soil.

4. Loosen the soil an additional 12 inches.

5. Dig out the upper part of the second trench and move it forward into the first trench.

6. Loosen the lower part of the second trench.

7. Continue the double-digging process (repeating steps 3, 4, 5, and 6) for the remaining trenches. Rake after each 3 to 4 trenches to ensure even bed height.

8. Shape the bed by raking it. Then evenly spread any needed fertilizers over the entire area and sift them in 2 to 4 inches deep with a spading fork. The double-dug bed is now completed.

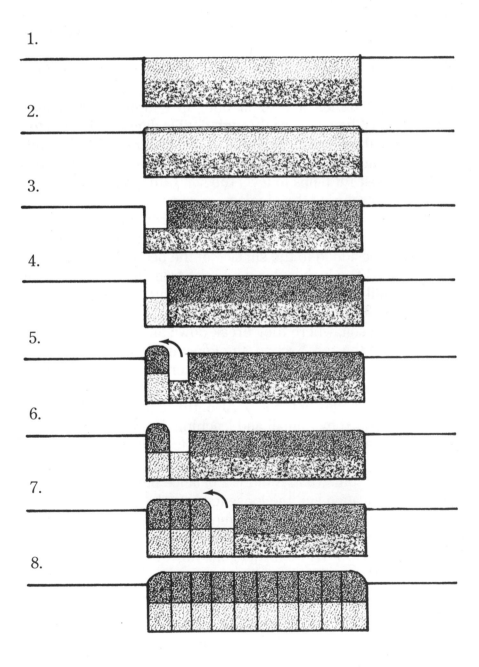

1.

2.

3.

4.

5.

6.

7.

8.

1.

2.

3.

4.

5.

6.

7.

## **Ongoing** Double-Dig

A primary difference between the ongoing and the initial double-dig is that the compost is put on *after* the digging process in the ongoing double-dig.

1. The bed is shown after harvest, with a slightly raised mound of partially recompacted soil and residual compost. Optional: When the soil is lightly moist, loosen the entire top 12 inches of the area to be dug with a spading fork and remove any weeds.

2. Remove the soil from the upper part of the first trench and place it in a soil storage area for use in making compost and flat soil.

3. Loosen the soil an additional 12 inches. (See Note below.)

4. Dig out the upper part of the second trench and move it forward into the first upper trench.

5. Loosen the lower part of the second trench.

6. Continue the double-digging process (repeating steps 4 and 5) for the remaining trenches. Rake after each 3 to 4 trenches to ensure even bed height.

7. Shape the bed by raking it. Evenly spread a 1-inch layer of compost and any needed fertilizers over the entire area. Sift in compost and any fertilizers 2 to 4 inches deep with a spading fork.

### Note

After the lower trench has been loosened, potatoes may be placed on its surface on 9-inch centers using offset spacing (see pages 59–62). The soil from the next trench's upper level may then be moved forward onto them. This is the easiest way we have found to plant potatoes. (Mark the location of the potatoes with stones or sticks in the outside paths before covering them with soil. This will indicate where potatoes should be placed on the surface of each succeeding lower trench.)

at a later point in time. We have found this soil preparation process greatly improves plant health and yields immediately in poor, compacted, and heavy soil. It is often worth the extra digging time involved. However, it does use an *insustainable* amount of organic matter.

The U-bar dig can be used as a substitute for the ongoing double-dig in soil that is in reasonably good shape. This usually means after 1 normal double-dig or more. The 18-inch-long U-bar tines (see page 9) do not prepare the soil as deeply as a spade and a spading fork used to double-dig 24 inches deep, but the lower 12 inches of the growing bed compact more slowly over time than the upper 12 inches. Also, the U-bar appears to have the advantage of mixing up the soil strata much less than double-digging with a spade and a spading fork. It aerates the soil less, however. This is an advantage in looser, sandier soil and can be a problem in tighter clays. If you use a U-bar regularly, do a normal double-dig as often as increased compaction indicates. U-barring is quicker and easier than using a spade and a

## Complete Texturizing
### Double-Dig

One time only for compacted heavy soils after the soil has been somewhat improved.

1. When the soil is lightly moist, loosen the top 12 inches of the entire area to be dug with a spading fork and remove any weeds.

2. Spread a 1-inch layer of compost over the entire area to be dug (after mixing in a 1-inch layer of sand or clay 12 inches deep; optional, see page 4).

3. Thoroughly mix in compost 12 inches deep.

4. Remove the soil from the upper part of the first trench and place it in a soil storage area for use in making compost and flat soil.

5. Loosen the soil an additional 12 inches.

6. Spread a 1-inch layer of compost on the loosened soil in the first trench.

7. Thoroughly mix the compost placed on top of the lower first trench into the soil 12 inches deep.

8. Dig out the upper part of the second trench and move it forward into the first trench.

9. Loosen the lower part of the second trench.

10. Spread a 1-inch layer of compost on the loosened soil in the second trench.

spading fork, though some knowledge of how your soil is improving, or not improving, is lost with the decreased personal contact with the soil. (For detailed plans on how to build a U-bar, see Ecology Action's *Backyard Homestead, Mini-Farm and Garden Log Book*.) At Ecology Action, we prefer to double-dig, as we learn more from it and stay more in touch with the soil.

1.

2.

3.

4.

5.

6.

7.

8.

9.

10.

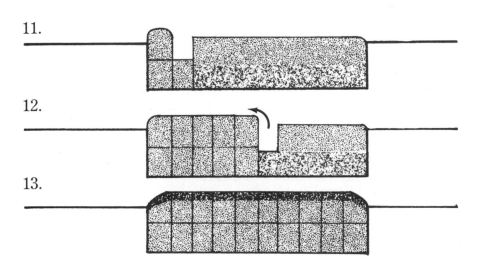

11. Thoroughly mix in the compost on the lower second trench 12 inches deep.

12. Continue the complete texturizing double-digging process (repeat steps 8 through 11) for the remaining trenches. Rake after each 3 to 4 trenches to ensure even bed height.

13. Shape the bed by raking it. Then evenly spread any needed fertilizers over the entire area and sift them in 2 to 4 inches deep with a spading fork. The complete texturizing double-dug bed is completed.

## U-Bar Dig

1. After harvest, weed the entire slightly raised bed if necessary.

2. When the soil is lightly moist, begin U-barring the soil along the length of the bed. No digging board is used. The soil will be loosened ³/₄ as deep as in the double-dig.

3. Continue U-barring until the bed is done. Two or 3 U-bar passes along the length of the bed may be necessary depending on the bed's width. The U-bar is about 2 feet wide and loosens the soil 2 to 2¹/₂ feet wide. See the drawing on page 9.

4. Break up any remaining large clumps with a spading fork. Shape the bed by raking it. Then evenly spread compost and any needed fertilizers over the entire area and sift them in 2 to 4 inches deep with a spading fork.

**Note**

See *Backyard Homestead, Mini-Farm and Garden Log Book* on the proper techniques for using a U-bar.

## SELECTED VEGETABLE ROOT SYSTEMS SHOWN IN SCALE

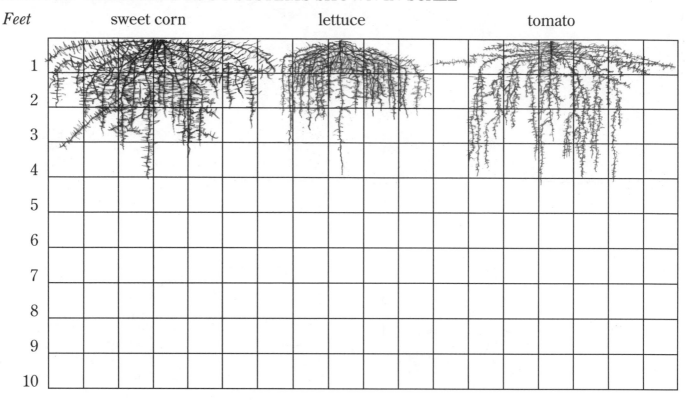

*Feet*     sweet corn        lettuce        tomato

path           bed

Soil in the path is subject to compaction; soil in the bed remains loose.

The loosened soil of the planting bed makes weeding easier.

Once the bed is prepared, you will truly appreciate its width. The distance between the tips of your fingers and your nose is about 3 feet when your arm is extended out to the side. Thus a 3- to 5-foot-wide bed can be fertilized, planted, weeded, and harvested from each side with relative ease, and insects can be controlled without walking on the bed. A 3- to 5-foot width also allows a good miniclimate to develop under closely spaced plants. You may wish to use a narrower bed, 1½ to 2½ feet wide, for plants supported by stakes, such as tomatoes, pole beans, and pole peas, for easier harvesting.

Try not to step on the growing beds once they have been prepared. To do so compacts the soil and makes it more difficult for the plants to grow. If the bed must be walked on, use the double-digging board. This will displace your weight over a large area and minimize the damage. Plants obtain much of their water and nutrients through the contact of their root hairs with the soil. If they do not develop an abundant supply of root hairs, less water and fewer nutrients are taken in. The root hairs are more numerous and vigorous in looser soil, so keep your soil loose.

When weeding, note that the entire weed root usually comes up out of loosened raised-bed soil. This is welcome weeding, and if you get all the root, you will not have to weed as often. Also, you do not need to cultivate the soil of raised beds as much as other gardens. The *living mulch* shade cover provided by mature plants helps to keep the soil surface loose. If the soil compacts between young plants before the mini-climate takes effect, you should cultivate.

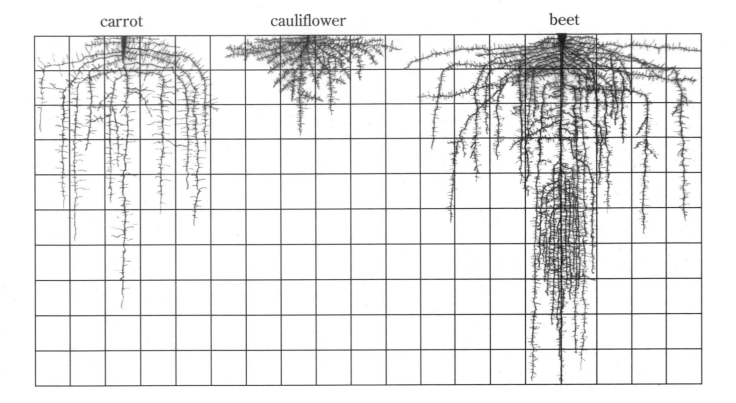

carrot          cauliflower          beet

Once this beautifully alive bed is prepared, it should be kept evenly moist until and after planting so the microbiotic life and plants will stay alive. The bed should be planted as soon as possible so the plants can take advantage of the new surge of life made possible by bringing together the soil, compost, air, water, sun, and fertilizers.

A good growing bed will often be 2 to 10 inches higher than the soil's original surface. A good soil contains 50% air space. (In fact, adequate air is one of the missing ingredients in most soil preparation processes.) Increased air space allows for increased diffusion of oxygen (which the roots and microbes depend on) into the soil, and of carbon dioxide (which the leaves depend on) out of the soil. The increased "breathing" ability of a double-dug bed is a key to improved plant health. Thus, the prepared depth will be as much as 34 inches in clayey soil. A sandy soil will probably not raise as high as clayey soil at first.

If the bed raises higher than 10 inches as you are double-digging, be sure to level it out with a rake as you go along. Otherwise you will end up with a very wide and deep trench at the end of the bed. Then you will have to move a large amount of soil from one end of the bed to the other to even it out when you are tired. This would also cause a disproportionate mis-placing of topsoil into the subsoil area. Whenever you redig a bed (after each crop or season), the 24-inch depth of the bed should be measured from the top of the bed, rather than from the path surface. We currently reprepare the soil after each

The GROW BIOINTENSIVE raised bed. A balance between nature's natural stratification and our loosened land-sliding soil

**Note**

For different types of ongoing soil culti-vation practices to use after digging, refer to the "Cultivation" information sheet in the *Gardening Techniques* information packet available from Bountiful Gardens (see page 258).

crop, except for autumn compost crops. Some people prefer to do this only once each year. As your soil improves and the large clods disappear, your bed may not raise as high as initially. Do not worry about this. It is just a sign that you and your soil are successful. The goal of double-digging is not the height of the bed, but the looseness and *good structure* of the soil.

Once a *good structure* has been established by double-digging, it may be better to use *surface cultivation* (the loosening of the upper 2 inches of the soil with a cultivating tool such as a hula hoe) for several years. In this way, the developed structure and soil organic matter are better preserved. One simple way to determine whether your soil has good structure follows. Squeeze a sample of reasonably moist soil firmly in your hand. Then open your hand. If the soil falls apart easily, it does not have good soil structure. If it holds the shape of your hand even when you press it gently with the fingers of your other hand, it does not have good soil structure. If the soil breaks apart into small clumps when you press it with your fingers, it probably has good soil structure.

When surface cultivation is used, *compost made without soil* will be used, because soil will not be removed from the bed during the soil preparation process. Whenever the lower soil becomes compacted, the bed may be double-dug again to encourage reestablishment of a well-aerated structure.

The soil's *texture* is determined by its basic ingredients: silt, clay, and sand particles. Its *structure* is the way its ingredients hold together. With your assistance, "threads" exuded by microbial life and "glue" exuded by plant roots help to loosen a clay soil and improve a sandy soil.[5] The goal is to create a sumptuous *"living sponge cake."* Bon appétit!

5. For more information on growing soil quality and soil structure, see "Table 20.1— Qualitative Soil Health Indicators," in U.S. Department of Agriculture/Agriculture Research Service, *Soil Quality Test Kit* (Washington, DC: U.S. Department of Agriculture/Agriculture Research Service, 1999); and Fred Magdoff and Harold van Es, *Building Soils for Better Crops,* 2nd ed. (Burlington, VT: Sustainable Agriculture Network, 2000).

Good soil preparation makes GROW BIOINTENSIVE fertility possible—up to 4 times the productivity per unit of area!

CHAPTER TWO

# SUSTAINABILITY

**GOAL:** *Grow and maintain sustainable soil fertility with sufficient humus in the soil while creating thriving mini-ecosystems*

"The grandfather keeps sheep, the son keeps goats, the grandson keeps nothing."
—Richard St. Barbe Baker,
*My Life, My Trees*

Sustainability means living in such a way that there are enough resources to live well in an alive, diverse, thriving environment—indefinitely.

Sustainability *is* possible—individual people, families, and communities accomplish this frequently all around the world. Yet most people find this challenging. Many of us are living on 6 times—or more—the resources that would be available to each person in the world if the resources were divided up equally!

We often think of sustainability in terms of using *nonrenewable resources* carefully. More important, however, is using *renewable resources* well. If all the Earth's agriculture became organic tomorrow, it would be wonderful and challenging. A more healthy resource-conserving, food-raising, and planetary ecosystem would be possible. However, the cost of purchasing the cured compost needed to grow food organically would be too high because the demand would exceed current supply. For that reason, we need to properly preserve, manage, and develop our renewable resources. Soil, for example, needs a given level of humus, or cured compost, in order to thrive. We each need to make sure we grow enough organic matter for our own needs.

For a garden or mini-farm to be sustainable, it must be able to produce sufficient crops to provide the gardener or farmer with what she or he needs over an indefinite period of time. This is possible *only* if the mini-farm's soil is kept fertile in a way that relies neither on nonrenewable resources, such as petroleum, nor on the nutrients or health of another soil. Most chemical fertilizers and pesticides are created in part from petroleum, which also fuels tractors, processing machinery, and transport vehicles. While organic fertilizers may seem to be a good alternative, their production relies on another farm's soil being able to produce the raw materials, such as alfalfa, cottonseed, and feed for animals that provide bone and blood meals. With these materials constantly taken away from the soil that produces them, these soils lose nutrients and eventually become depleted and infertile.

When our focus is on harvesting as much as we can from the soil, we forget to give the soil what it needs to remain fertile. We must grow *soil* in a way that is sustainable. Only then can it continue to provide us with abundant food. If we farm in a way that *does not* sustain soil fertility, the soil that is currently used to grow crops will soon be able to grow only fodder for sheep, later only scraggly weeds for goats, and then nothing at all.

## The Loss of Soil Nutrients and Humus

When soil grows crops, it loses the nutrients the crops extract as well as the humus that the soil microorganisms consume. To maintain the soil's fertility, the nutrients and humus must be replenished. Both of these requirements can be met simultaneously when the crop and all other residues from those who consumed the edible portion of the crop are composted and returned to the soil. The cured compost will have almost all of the nutrients that the crop contained and, depending on the crops that are grown, enough humus to replenish the soil's supply. (Also, see Beeby's *Future Fertility.*)

The carbon that left the soil in the form of carbon dioxide will be returned if plants that store a lot of carbon in their bodies (such as corn, amaranth, wheat, and rice) are grown and added to the soil as cured compost. These kinds of compost crops should optimally be grown on about 60% of the farm area over the course of a year in order to generate enough cured compost to maintain the soil's fertility.

## Initially Adding Nutrients and Humus to the Soil

Not all soils naturally have all of the nutrients they need for their optimum health and crop productivity. Deep-rooted crops such as alfalfa and comfrey can be grown to bring up nutrients from below the range of most roots, then composted and added to the topsoil. However, if the needed nutrients are not in the deeper regions of the soil, they will not be present in the cured compost. On the other hand, when cured compost *is* added to the soil, nutrients that were previously unavailable in the soil may be made available by the biogeologic cycle.

In the biogeologic cycle, *humic acid*—which is produced from the decomposition process and is contained in the cured compost—along with the *carbonic acid* developed around the plant's roots, can increase soil microbial activity, decompose larger minerals, and possibly alter soil pH so that previously unavailable nutrients are made available. However, if the nutrients are not in the soil in the first place, even in an unavailable form, *the cured compost made from plants grown on the nutrient-deficient soil will not contain the deficient nutrient, and the soil will still be unbalanced after the cured compost is added.* Therefore, in some cases, you may need to bring nutrients in the form of organic fertilizers into the mini-farm from the outside, but probably only once, before the mini-farm can be maintained sustainably.

You may also need to bring carbonaceous materials into the garden or mini-farm in the beginning so sufficient humus can be added to the soil. Humus is the food of soil microorganisms that are responsible for creating good soil structure and soil fertility. It also helps hold the nutrients in the soil. If there is not enough humus (about 4% to 6% organic matter in temperate regions; about 3% organic matter in tropical ones), nutrients that are returned to the soil in the form of cured compost may leach out.

## Losses = Gains?

Some nutrients will escape from the garden or mini-farm, whether from leaching, from rainfall runoff, or from the wind picking them up and carrying them away (although water and wind erosion are usually not a problem when the soil's humus supply is maintained and all of the GROW BIOINTENSIVE techniques are used). At the same time, however, nutrients are added naturally to the mini-farm through rainfall, wind, the breakdown of the soil's parental rock material, and the upsoaking of groundwater. With GROW BIOINTENSIVE sustainable gardening and mini-farming, the gain in nutrients may eventually be approximately *equal* to the loss of nutrients, and *the soil's nutrient balance may be maintained if all nutrients are recycled.*

## 100% Sustainability *Impossible*

According to the second law of thermodynamics, all systems proceed toward a state of entropy or disorder. Therefore, no system, including agriculture, can be sustained indefinitely. At the extreme, all mini-farms will cease, as will all life as we know it, when the sun burns out millions of years from now. However, until this happens, we can maintain our soils at a level close to complete sustainability (instead of close to complete *insustainability,* as is now the situation with most agricultural systems). Within a garden or mini-farm, some soil nutrients may not be replenished by natural forces, or the same natural forces may add soil nutrients in excess. In both situations, if proper soil nutrient maintenance is not pursued, the soil may cease to be able to grow significant amounts of crops in a very short period of time.

## The Need for up to "99%" Sustainability

At Ecology Action, we are looking for the quickest, most effective, most resource-conserving, and most ecologically sound ways to replenish and balance soil nutrients. Once the soil's nutrient base has been properly built and balanced, we need to learn how best to maintain those nutrients in our gardens and mini-farms. One promising approach is to grow all of our own compost materials in sufficient quantities so that the cured compost we add to the soil contains as many of the nutrients the crops removed from the soil as possible, as well as enough humus to feed the soil microbes and prevent nutrient leaching. In this way, our food-raising area becomes *a source*—rather than *a sink*—of carbon, nutrients, and fertility. (The *net* loss of carbon dioxide, or "leakage," from the system is a key concern. Worldwide, the loss of carbon from our soils—and plants in the form of harvested trees and their use for fuel—is a situation causing increasing problems.)

Keeping the nutrients within the mini-farm, as well as learning how to minimize the amount of nutrients we need to bring in from the outside, are important tasks if we are to grow all of our food, clothing, and building materials on the 9,000 square feet (or about 1/5 of an acre) that may soon be all that is available to each man, woman, and child living in developing nations (see page 249 in the appendix). Soon we simply will not have the luxury of taking nutrients from one soil to feed another.

With about 42 to 84 years' worth of topsoil remaining in the world, learning how to enrich, improve, and maintain soil— in a way that is sustainable—is of vital importance if we, as a species, are to survive. If they can only provide food for about a century before they deplete the soil, the agricultural systems that have brought us to where we are now are clearly not sustainable. Ancient civilizations sustained their soils to feed large populations for lengthy periods of time. China's soils, for example, remained productive for 4,000 years or more until the adoption of mechanized chemical agricultural techniques that have been responsible, in part, for the destruction of 15% to 33% of China's agricultural soil since the late 1950s. Many of the world's great civilizations have disappeared when their soil's fertility was not maintained. Northern Africa, for example, used to be the granary for Rome until overfarming converted it into a desert, and much of the Sahara Desert was forested until it was overcut.

## Ecology Action's Pursuit of Sustainability

When Ecology Action began the Common Ground Mini-Farm in Willits, California, the soil was so infertile that many carbonaceous compost crops did not grow well. In an effort to improve the soil so it could grow all of the carbonaceous compost material needed to provide the mini-farm with sufficient cured compost, carbonaceous compost material (straw) and nutrient-containing horse manure were imported to the mini-farm. This approach eventually did not feel appropriate because we were *importing* a significant amount of carbon. Consequently, we limited our compost building to include materials produced by the mini-farm whenever possible. However, because many crops we were testing did not contain much carbon, the mini-farm produced significantly less carbonaceous compost material than was needed to increase and maintain the soil's fertility. Without sufficient cured compost, the soil began losing the humus it had, and its ability to grow sufficient organic matter declined.

While we still chose to grow some experimental crops that did not produce a significant amount of carbonaceous compost material, we grew *more* of our own compost material than before and supplemented our supply of carbonaceous compost material with purchased straw, goat litter (primarily from outside fodder inputs), and/or straw from noncrop areas.

We have been getting closer to achieving closed-system soil humus sustainability *within the limits of the mini-farm* and are now working toward closed-system soil humus sustainability by using compost materials grown primarily *within the limits of the growing beds* that receive cured compost. In the future, we will be emphasizing the growing of an even larger percentage of the carbonaceous compost material we need each year, and will continue to do so until we are growing *all* of this material ourselves in our own growing beds. In addition, we are exploring different *levels* of maintaining sustainable soil fertility. These methods involve using different amounts of cured compost (depending on its availability), with different corresponding crop yield levels resulting.

## Current Goals of Understanding and Achieving "99%" Sustainability

Our goals are to understand how a garden or mini-farm can:
- Produce all of its own compost material initially *without having to import any straw, manure, or other carbonaceous material* for the soil's humus sustainability
- Maintain *nutrient* sustainability

Because we are not currently returning the nutrients in our human urine and manure to the mini-farm's soil, we need to import some organic fertilizers to maintain the nutrient levels and balance in the soil. However, for the future, we *are* exploring ways to safely, effectively, and legally return the nutrients in our waste to the soil from which they came.

# How to Better Sustain Your Soil's Fertility

In order to more easily sustain the fertility of your soil, you should divide your growing area as follows:

- Approximately *60%* in *carbon-and-calorie crops* that produce large amounts of carbon for compost and that also produce food in the form of significant amounts of calories. (To grow the nitrogen needed to make a good compost, legumes will need to be interplanted with these crops; for example, fava beans among wheat in winter and bush beans with corn in summer. See Ecology Action's Self-Teaching Mini-Booklet 14, *The Complete 21-Bed Biointensive Mini-Farm* and *One Basic Mexican Diet* for more details.)

- Approximately 30% in special root diet crops that produce large amounts of calories.

- A maximum of *10%* in *vegetable crops* for additional vitamins and minerals. (Up to ¾ of this area may be planted in income crops if the missing needed vitamins and minerals are provided by ¼ of the area.)

See the information on pages 24–25 for details. We hope these guidelines will make your path to sustainability easier.

In order to mini-farm sustainably, take these goals into account as you grow compost crops and apply compost:

## GOALS FOR COMPOST\* AND SUSTAINABLE SOIL FERTILITY
*per 100 sq ft per 4- to 6-month growing season*

| | Mature Material to Grow (lb/100 sq ft) | Immature Material to Grow (lb/100 sq ft) | Compost Application (including 50% soil) | | | Potential Crop Yields |
|---|---|---|---|---|---|---|
| GROW BIOINTENSIVE amount for a *beginning* level of sustainable soil fertility\*\* | 15 lb and up | 90 lb and up | 1 cu ft | 1.5 5gB\*\*\* | ⅛ inch | ~1 X (U.S. Average) |
| Ed Glenn's research for Biosphere 2 | — | — | 1.6 cu ft | 2.4 5gB | ⅕ inch | — |
| GROW BIOINTENSIVE amount for an *intermediate* level of sustainable soil fertility | 30 lb and up | 180 lb and up | 2 cu ft | 3 5gB | ¼ inch | ~2 X |
| One expert's "good" amount of compost for soil fertility and productivity | — | — | 2.8 cu ft | 4.2 5gB | ⅓ inch | — |
| GROW BIOINTENSIVE amount for a *high* level of sustainable soil fertility | 60 lb and up | 360 lb and up | 4 cu ft | 6 5gB | ½ inch | ~4 X |

\* including approximately 50% soil     \*\* some minerals still leach out because the soil still lacks sufficient organic matter     \*\*\* 5gB = 5-gallon bucket

# The GROW BIOINTENSIVE Sustainable Mini-Farm

*Approximate Crop Area Percentages for Sustainability: 60:30:10*

**Approximately 40 beds (4,000 sq ft) for 1 person (~5,000 sq ft including paths)**

**60%** carbon-and-calorie crops (e.g., grains) for maximum carbon and satisfactory calorie production *~24 beds*

**30%** high-calorie root crops (e.g., potatoes) for maximum calories *~12 beds*

**10%** vegetable crops (e.g., salad crops) for vitamins and minerals *~4 beds*

**If desired, 50% to 75% of the vegetable crops area may be used for income crops**

---

## CLARIFICATIONS AND EXAMPLES OF THE 60:30:10 DESIGN RATIO

*General Aids for Planning Your Diet*

**~60-65% of the area: "carbon-and-calorie crops"—high-carbon-producing and significant-calorie-producing (weight-efficient—see below) crops.**

- Grains: wheat, cereal rye, oats, barley, triticale, corn, sorghum, amaranth, quinoa, etc.
- Fava beans (grown to maturity for dry bean and dry biomass production)
- Sunflowers (sunflower seeds are very high in fat; maximum to avoid copper toxicity = 0.62 pound per day)
- Filberts
- Grapes (for raisins)

**~30% of the area: "high-calorie root crops"—area- and weight-efficient crops for calories.**
Crops for this category need to be both area- and weight-efficient. As defined for this worksheet, a crop is considered to be **area-efficient** if the annual area needed for total calories is 16 beds (1,600 sq ft) or less, assuming GROW BIOINTENSIVE intermediate yields; it is considered to be **weight-efficient** if the daily weight of food to be eaten for total calories is 9 pounds or less.[1]

<table>
<tr><td colspan="3" align="center">BOTH AREA- AND WEIGHT-EFFICIENT</td></tr>
<tr><td colspan="3">Potatoes (12.2 / 6.7) Maximum to avoid potassium toxicity = 2.5 lb / day</td></tr>
<tr><td>Garlic (10.8 / 3.6)*</td><td>Leeks (6.6 / 8.7)</td><td>Jerusalem artichokes (12.3 / 7.0)*</td></tr>
<tr><td>Parsnips (10.8 / 7.1)</td><td>Sweet potatoes (11.2 / 5.0)</td><td>Salsify (11.8 / 6.5)</td></tr>
<tr><td colspan="3">AREA in 100-sq-ft beds / WEIGHT in lb; e.g., it takes 12.2 beds of potatoes to produce the 2,400 calories per day needed by an average person who would have to eat 6.7 lb of potatoes per day.</td></tr>
<tr><td colspan="3">* Jerusalem artichoke and some varieties of hardneck garlic may produce significant amounts of dry biomass.</td></tr>
</table>

The crops below are *weight-efficient*, but require more area to grow and produce relatively little biomass. Therefore, they should be included in the 10% "vegetable crops" category.

| | |
|---|---|
| Peanuts (34.1 / 0.9) Very high in fat | Burdock (17.8 / 7.3) Assuming carrot yield |
| Soybeans (58.0 / 3.8) | Beans, except fava beans, (56.8 / 4.7) |
| Cassava (20.1 / 3.3) May produce modest amount of carbon | |

The following crops can be *area-efficient* if yields are high enough, but the daily weight of food exceeds the guidelines, so they should be included in the 10% "vegetable crops" category.

| | | |
|---|---|---|
| Onions, regular (12.7 / 14.0) | Turnips + tops (8.8 / 19.4) | Rutabagas (13.4 / 14.7) |
| (assuming 2 crops are possible OR yield is 2 times intermediate) | | |

**Note:** For diet diversity, you may choose crops that are *less* weight-efficient (e.g., regular onions, 14.0 pounds per day); in which case, you need to have a significant amount of food from crops that are *more* weight-efficient (e.g., filberts, 0.8 pound per day) and/or increase your design area.

Root Crops That Are Not Good Choices *for This Category:*
- Carrots (30.0 / 12.3)
- Beets or mangels, roots only (40.8 / 12.3)
- Radishes (48.1 / 26.4)

**~5% to 10% of the area: "vegetable crops"**
Low-calorie-producing, low-carbon-producing miscellaneous vegetables for vitamins and minerals.

1. In *One Circle*, by David Duhon, an "area-efficient" crop can provide total daily calories for a year with 700 sq ft or less (550 sq ft for a woman, 850 sq ft for a man); a "weight-efficient" crop can provide total daily calories for a year in 6 pounds or less for a man or 5.5 pounds or less for a woman.

The GROW BIOINTENSIVE sustainable mini-farm 60:30:10 design ratios were developed after observing the results of designs for this method by participants in workshops for about 10 years. We noted that many of the designs were in this range. We then realized that it would assist others in placing their initial designs in the right range if 60:30:10 were used as a goal within the 40-growing-bed (4,000-square-foot growing area) limit of the design process. Such a practice would make it easier and faster to obtain a good result.

Over the years, however, other participants, with different dietary preferences (e.g., more weight in grains to eat and/or a larger variety of crops to consume), have come up with other ratios that work well within the 40-bed design constraint. As a result, several standard design tradeoffs and other key information are given below. For a more detailed understanding, also see the Ecology Action publications *One Circle* by David Duhon and Booklet 31, *Designing a GROW BIOINTENSIVE® Sustainable Mini-Farm*.

- If you choose to eat more 60% crops, the weight of the food you eat will generally be less per day, but the area needed to grow your diet will generally increase.

- If you choose to eat more 30% crops, the weight of the food you eat will generally be more, but the area needed to grow your diet will generally decrease.

- If you choose to eat a diet with a large variety of crops, planning your garden/mini-farm will probably be more difficult, the phasing of crop planning and harvest will probably be more complex, and the storage of your crops will probably be more challenging.

- If you decide to increase the calories in your diet by 10% within the 40-bed goal, it may increase your area by 40% to 50%, because you will need to grow these calories with 60% crops, which have more calories per pound, but are less area-efficient for the growing of calories, instead of 30% crops, which have fewer calories per pound, but are more area-efficient for the growing of calories.

- If you grow a lot of non-interplanted legumes as part of your diet, these 10% crops, which are more weight-efficient for the growing of calories, will reduce the weight of the diet you eat, but will significantly increase the area needed for the growing of your diet, since legumes are not very area-efficient for the production of calories. In addition, if you design too many legumes into your diet, you will produce more protein than it is optimal for a person to consume.

- At intermediate yields, in many climates and soils, assuming sufficient water availability, a complete balanced diet may be grown on as few as 25 growing beds. In areas with challenging climates, soils, water availability, it may take much more than 40 growing beds. A 40-bed growing area is fairly manageable for 1 person to do part-time, once one's soil and skill are in reasonable shape. In addition, soon, many of the world's people may have only 4,000 square feet for the growing of their food and compost materials. Some already have less. The skill of being able to grow all your nutrition in such an area will be invaluable. In 1911, the Chinese were able to grow all the food for 1 person with biologically intensive techniques on an average of about this amount of farmable land.

## Sustainability Worldwide

Nature grows plants close together rather than in rows. That's why so many weeds grow between the rows in commercial agriculture. The GROW BIOINTENSIVE method of growing food takes advantage of nature's propensity to fill any void with living plants through maximizing yields by growing bountiful crops on a minimal amount of area.

The Chinese miniaturized agriculture in a similar way over 4,000 years ago! They grew food by closely spacing plants and maintaining soil fertility (using nutrient- and carbon-containing compost) for thousands of years without depleting their resources. As recently as 1890 this process enabled the Chinese to grow all the food for 1 person on about 5,800 to 7,200 square feet, including animal products used at the time. Other people in different areas of the world—Greece, Bolivia, Peru, Nepal, Guatemala, Mexico, and Japan—independently developed miniaturized forms of agriculture 2,000 years ago. How does this apply to our modern world? Recently, this kind of miniaturized crop raising has appeared in Russia, Ireland, and other parts of Europe.

Ecology Action has built on the work of the Chinese, Mayans, and others by using traditional agricultural techniques that are thousands of years old, discovering the universal scientific principles that underlie them. We have spent years making mistakes, learning and relearning, as we attempted to streamline these techniques and make them available to other people (including developing written how-to materials that are easy to understand). The worldwide results of our research and information outreach have been amazing and rewarding.

The people in Biosphere 2, a closed-system living project in Arizona during the 1990s, used techniques based on those rediscovered by Ecology Action: They raised 80% of their food for 2 years within a closed system. Their experience demonstrates that a complete year's diet for 1 person could be raised on the equivalent of just 3,403 square feet! In contrast, it currently takes commercial agriculture 15,000 to 30,000 square feet to do the same. Moreover, commercial agriculture has to bring in large inputs from other areas and soils just to make this possible, depleting other soils in the process. To raise all the food

"A [farmer] took up land [in Saskatchewan], dug a cellar and built a frame house on top of it; ploughed up the prairie and grew wheat and oats. After twenty years he decided the country was no good for farming, for eight feet of his soil had gone and he had to climb up into his house."

—Richard St. Barbe Baker, *My Life, My Trees*

for one person in a developing nation takes about 16,000 square feet, given the diets eaten and the food-raising practices used.

The Environmental Research Laboratory at the University of Arizona performed the first tests for Biosphere 2, documenting the status of the soil and crop yields over time. In the Human Diet Experiment, all crop tests involved sustainable Biointensive crop rotations including grains, legumes, and green manures, and all crop residues were returned to the soil after harvest and composting. Dr. Ed Glenn, who conducted the tests, stated: "Although funding was not available to continue these experiments for the number of years necessary to draw final conclusions, the results supported the hypothesis that sustainable food production with few or no outside inputs will not only continue to produce high yields but will improve rather than deplete the organic constituents in the soil."

In **India**, just one copy of *How to Grow More Vegetables* became the textbook for a gardening program at an alternative technologies training center, Shri AMM. Muragappa Chettiar Centre in Tamil Nadu. That program evolved over a 15-year period into preparations for a national Biointensive program. We received word that village women who have been gardening the Biointensive way on their own small plots were able not only to raise food to feed their families but also to raise an annual income by growing crops in a small area.

In all 32 states of **Mexico**, millions of people are currently using Biointensive methods to grow food for *nutrition intervention* for themselves and their families. Each year, new people are taught these processes by extension agents, universities, governmental entities, communities, and organizations, or by those already using the techniques. It is estimated that 1.6 million people are currently using these practices. In addition, many Spanish publications and videos are spreading Biointensive techniques throughout Latin America.

In **Kenya**, the Manor House Agricultural Centre has been directly and indirectly responsible for training well over 40,000 mini-farmers in just a 16-year period. The centre gives 2-year apprentice training to individuals who are sent by their villages to learn Biointensive techniques so they can go back and teach these methods to their whole village. There are also shorter training periods, and a local outreach program sends teachers out to surrounding areas on a frequent basis to educate members of the communities. The centre has now opened its training program to international students.

In the **Philippines**, Biointensive publications, conferences, and workshops given by the International Institute for Rural Reconstruction resulted in the initiation of a mandated national Biointensive educational program for all grade school and high school students.

There is also the beginning of a GROW BIOINTENSIVE network in the **United States**. Ecology Action's 3-day introductory work-

**Note**

*In order to preserve diversity on Earth*: It is important to keep at least half of the Earth's viable land as a natural preserve. GROW BIOINTENSIVE sustainable mini-farming—with its high yields and low local-resource needs—can help make this possible.

shops have drawn many people who are committed to sharing their own enthusiasm for GROW BIOINTENSIVE techniques with other people. To date, 1,457 people from 46 states, the District of Columbia, and 25 countries have been trained in these workshops. People from different parts of the country who have taken Ecology Action workshops have gone on to teach GROW BIOINTENSIVE techniques to other people. One woman's correspondence with Habitat for Humanity has developed into that organization's support of an associated project, Gardens for Humanity, which includes GROW BIOINTENSIVE practices. A group in Seattle has developed a rural community supported agriculture project to sustainably grow all the food for people in urban areas with the Biointensive method. We hear from people all over the country that they are starting to seriously use GROW BIOINTENSIVE techniques, some to produce income as well as food for their families.

Even though we are pleased that so many people and programs have adopted GROW BIOINTENSIVE practices, there is still a *challenge to be met.* Many people are successfully using GROW BIOINTENSIVE farming techniques to grow food for nutrition intervention, but few are trying to grow all their calorie food needs on a basis that *also* feeds the soil adequately. When people say they are growing all of their own food, they generally mean that they are growing 5% to 10% of their diet (the vegetables that they can produce during the growing season). *Calorie and sustainable soil fertility mini-farming and gardening* is the next step, which needs to be catalyzed by each of us! The Ecology Action publications *One Circle, The Sustainable Vegetable Garden,* and the Self-Teaching Mini-Series Booklets 14, 15, 25, 26, and 28 deal with growing a complete diet. Once this additional 90% of calorie-growing area has been established in the garden, it only takes an average of about 15 minutes or less each day *per bed* to maintain the garden!

There has been a great shift in human consciousness since Ecology Action set up its first research garden mini-farm over 30 years ago. This shift has come about because many individuals have begun to realize that although they might not be able to change the world, they can change the way they do things in their own lives. Raising food in a gentle and conscious manner is one change that has made a difference.

Being disconnected from our food base has separated us from the soil and the life of the Earth. Producing food from a small area is a strengthening, slowing-down process—a way of tuning in to the Earth's needs as we meet our own. We put life into the soil, and the soil enriches our lives.

We as humans are part of the Earth's nutrient cycle, just as the plants and animals are. The Earth welcomes us by creating what we need. The trees are a wonderful example of this: They absorb our carbon dioxide and give us back oxygen to breathe. As we become more aware of and attuned to our place in the circle of life, then *it will seem natural to plant at least 60% of our growing area in carbon-producing crops that also produce calories. In this way our crops will give life back to the Earth that has fed us.* As we become more responsible for our place in this exciting nutrient flow, we will want to grow *all* of our diet.

Despite its worldwide impact, Ecology Action has remained a small organization, believing that small is effective and human. We consider ourselves to be a catalyst: Our function is to empower people with the skills and knowledge necessary to enable them to improve their lives and thus transform the world into a garden of health and abundance. The message is to live richly in a simple manner—in a way we can all enjoy.

You can assist Ecology Action in this work by finding 5 friends and getting them involved in GROW BIOINTENSIVE sustainable mini-farming and/or other sustainable food-raising practices. Together we can make a significant difference in the world, 1 small area at a time. This is our opportunity. It is fun to be part of the *whole* picture and part of the long-term world environmental solution! A healthy soil grows healthy crops, which grow healthy people, who can grow a healthy planet and ecosystem.

# 3

# COMPOST

**GOAL:** *Maximize quality and quantity of cured compost produced per unit of compost built and maximize microbiodiversity*

## A "Natural" System

In nature, living things die, and their death allows life to be reborn. Both animals and plants die on forest floors and in meadows to be composted by time, water, microorganisms, sun, and air to produce a soil improved in structure and nutrients. Organic plant growing follows nature's example. Leaves, grass, weeds, prunings, spiders, birds, trees, and plants should be returned to the soil and reused—not thrown away. Composting is an important way to recycle such elements as carbon, nitrogen, magnesium, sulfur, calcium, phosphorus, potash, and trace minerals. These elements are all necessary to maintain the biological cycles of life that exist naturally. All too often we participate instead in agricultural strip-mining.

Composting in nature occurs in at least 3 ways: (1) in the form of manures, which are plant and animal foods composted inside an animal's body (including earthworms) and then further aged outside the animal by the heat of fermentation. Earthworms are especially good composters. Their castings are 5 times richer in nitrogen, 2 times richer in exchangeable calcium, 7 times richer in available phosphorus, and 11 times richer in available potassium than the soil they inhabit;[1] (2) in the form of animal and plant bodies that decay on top of and within the soil in nature and in compost piles; and (3) in the form of roots, root hairs, and microbial life-forms that remain and decay beneath the surface of the soil after harvesting. It is estimated that 1 cereal rye plant in good soil grows 3 miles of hairs a day, 387 miles of roots in a season, and 6,603 miles of root hairs each season![2]

Cereal rye roots grow to 6 feet deep.

1. Care must be taken to avoid overdependence on worm castings as a fertilizer; the nutrients in them are very available and can therefore be more easily lost from the soil system.

2. Helen Philbrick and Richard B. Gregg, *Companion Plants and How to Use Them* (Old Greenwich, CT: Devin-Adair Company, 1966), pp. 75–76.

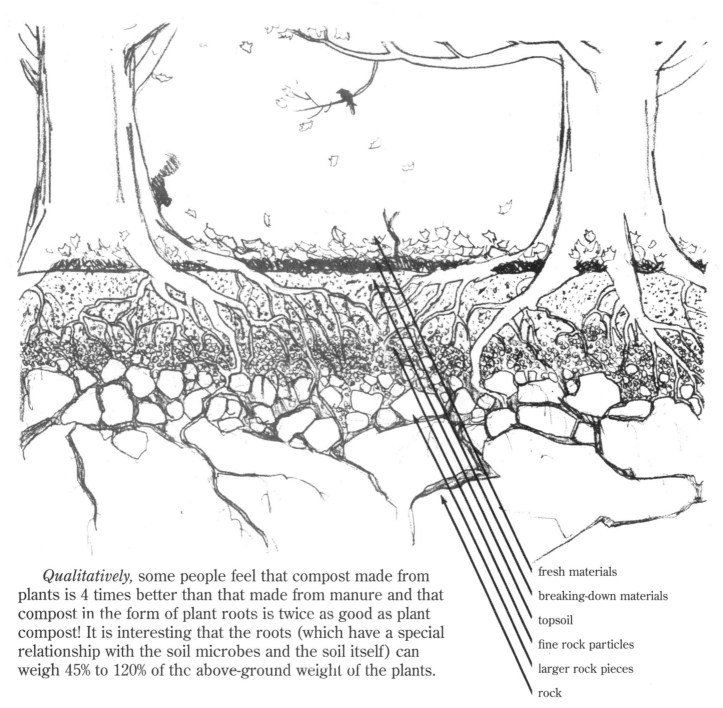

fresh materials

breaking-down materials

topsoil

fine rock particles

larger rock pieces

rock

*Qualitatively,* some people feel that compost made from plants is 4 times better than that made from manure and that compost in the form of plant roots is twice as good as plant compost! It is interesting that the roots (which have a special relationship with the soil microbes and the soil itself) can weigh 45% to 120% of the above-ground weight of the plants.

## Functions

Compost has a dual function. It improves the *structure* of the soil. This means the soil will be easier to work, will have good aeration and water-retention characteristics, and will be resistant to erosion. Compost also provides *nutrients* for plant growth, and its organic acids make nutrients in the soil more available to plants. Fewer nutrients leach out in a soil with adequate organic matter.

Improved structure and nourishment produce a healthy soil. A *healthy soil* produces healthy plants better able to resist insect and disease attacks. Most insects look for sick plants to eat. The best way to control insects and diseases in plants is with a living, healthy soil rather than with poisons that kill beneficial soil life.

Compost keeps soil at maximum health with a minimum expense. Generally, it is unnecessary to buy fertilizers to be able to grow healthy plants. At first, organic fertilizers may have to be purchased so the soil can be brought to a satisfactory level of fertility in a short period of time. Once this has been done, the soil's health can be maintained with compost, good crop rotation, and the recycling of plant residues into the compost pile.

It is important to note the difference between *fertilization* and *fertility*. There can be plenty of fertilizer in the soil, and plants still may not grow well. Add compost to the soil, and the organic acids it contains will release the hidden nutrients in a form available to the plants. This was the source of the amazing fertility of Alan Chadwick's garden at Santa Cruz.

## The Process

Compost is created from the decomposition and recombination of various forms of plant and animal life, such as leaves, grass, wood, garbage, natural-fiber clothes, hair, and bones. These materials are *organic matter.* Organic matter is only a small fraction of the total material that makes up the soil—generally between 1% and 8% by weight. Yet organic matter is absolutely essential to the sustenance of soil life and fertility. Organic matter refers to dead plant and animal residues of *all* kinds and in *all* stages of breakdown or decay. Inseparable from these decaying dead residues are the living microorganisms that decompose, or digest, them.

Microscopic life-forms (bacteria and fungi) in the soil produce the recombining process, which creates the warmth in the compost pile. Most of the decomposition involves the formation of carbon dioxide and water as the organic material is broken down. You can monitor the temperature of your compost pile with a compost thermometer. You can also do this by inserting a 1 by 1-inch piece of wood into the pile, removing it periodically and feeling the warmth with your hand. You can judge whether the latest measurement is hotter or cooler than before.

As the available energy is consumed, microbial activity slows down, their numbers diminish—and the pile cools. Most of the remaining organic matter is in the form of *humus compounds*. Humus includes the living and dead bodies of microbial life. As humus is formed, nitrogen becomes part of its structure. This stabilizes nitrogen in the soil because the humus compounds are resistant to decomposition. They are worked on slowly by soil organisms, but the nitrogen and other essential nutrients are protected from too-rapid solubility and dissipation. Organic matter includes humus and some undecomposed organic matter.

Humus also acts as a site of nutrient adsorption (accumulation of nutrients on its surface) and exchange for plants in the soil. The surfaces of humus particles carry a negative electric charge. Many of the plant nutrients—such as calcium, sodium, magnesium, potassium, and most trace minerals—carry a positive electrical charge in the soil solution and are thereby attracted to and adhere to the surface of humus. Some of the plant nutrients—such as phosphorus, sulfur, and the form of nitrogen that is available to plants—are not positively charged. Fortunately, a good supply of these nutrients becomes available to the plants through biological transformation in the compost pile and soil.

As plant roots grow through the soil in search of nutrients, they feed on the humus. Each plant root is surrounded by a halo of hydrogen ions that are a by-product of the roots' respiration. These hydrogen ions also carry a positive electric charge. The root actually "bargains" with the humus, exchanging some of its positively charged hydrogen ions for positively charged nutrient ions stuck onto the surface of the humus. An active exchange is set up between humus and roots, the plants "choosing" which nutrients they need to balance their own inner chemistry.

Therefore, humus is the most reliable plant food, and plants pull off whatever combinations of nutrients they choose from its surface. GROW BIOINTENSIVE practices rely on this natural, continual, slow-releasing biological process for nutrient release to the plants, rather than making available all the season's nutrients chemically at one time.

The beauty of humus is that it feeds plants with nutrients that the plants pick up on its surface and it also safely stores nutrients in forms that are not readily leached. The humus contains much of the remainder of the original nitrogen that was put in the compost pile in the form of grass, kitchen wastes, and so on. The humus was formed by the resynthesizing activity of numerous species of microorganisms feeding off that original "garbage."

The microorganisms in the soil then continue to feed on the humus after the finished compost is spread on the soil. As the microorganisms feed, the core nutrients in the humus are released in forms available to plant roots. Thus, the microorganisms are an integral part of the humus, and one cannot be found without the other. The only other component of the soil that holds onto and exchanges nutrients with plant roots is clay, but humus can hold onto and exchange a far greater amount of these nutrients.

"Give back to the soil as much as you have taken—and a little bit more—and Nature will provide for you abundantly!"
—Alan Chadwick

## Soil and Other Materials in the Compost Pile

It is important to add soil to your compost pile. The soil contains a good starter supply of microorganisms. It also contains some bacteria of a type that helpes stabilize nitrogen in a pile. The organisms help in several ways. Some break down complex compounds into simpler ones the plants can utilize. There are many species of free-living bacteria that fix nitrogen from the air in a form available to plants. Many microorganisms tie up nitrogen surpluses. The surpluses are released gradually as the plants need nitrogen. An excessive concentration of available nitrogen in the soil (which makes plants susceptible to disease) is therefore avoided. There are predaceous fungi that attack and devour nematodes (see page 164), but these fungi are only found in large amounts in a soil with adequate humus.

The microbial life provides a living pulsation in the soil that preserves its vitality for the plants. The microbes tie up essential nutrients in their own body tissues as they grow, and then release them slowly as they die and decompose. In this way, they help stabilize food release to the plants. These organisms are also continuously excreting a whole range of organic compounds into the soil. Sometimes described as "soil glue," these excretions contribute to the building of the soil structure. The organic compounds also contain disease-curing antibiotics and health-producing vitamins and enzymes that are integral parts of biochemical reactions in a healthy soil.

The use of soil in compost is important. It:
- Enables the pile to hold moisture better—facilitating the decomposition of the pile
- Contains microbes that enable the pile to decompose more easily
- Holds many of the nutrient-laden compost "juices"—keeping them from leaching out

Note that at least *3 different materials of 3 different textures* are used in the GROW BIOINTENSIVE method compost recipe and in many other recipes. The varied textures will allow good drainage and aeration in the pile. The compost will also have a more diverse nutrient content and greater microbial diversity. A pile made primarily of leaves or grass cuttings makes the passage of water and air through the pile difficult without frequent turning because both tend to mat. Good air and water penetration are required for proper decomposition. The layering of the materials further promotes a mixture of textures and nutrients and helps ensure even decomposition.

*Microbe diversity* is very important in the growing soil. Many microbes produce antibiotics that help plants resist diseases, and healthy plants have fewer insect challenges. Each microbe tends to have a food preference—some prefer beet refuse, others wheat straw, and so on. Therefore, a way to maximize microbe diversity in the compost pile is to build your compost pile with a large variety of materials.

## Locating the Pile

Compost piles can be built in a pit in the ground or in a pile above the ground. The latter is preferable, since during rainy periods a pit can fill up with water. A pile can be made with or without a container. We build our compost piles without using containers. They are unnecessary and use wood and metal resources.

The pile should optimally be built under a deciduous oak tree. This tree's nature provides the conditions for the development of excellent soil underneath it. And compost is a kind of soil. The second-best place for a compost pile is under any other kind of deciduous tree (with the exceptions of walnut and eucalyptus). As a last resort, you can build your pile under evergreen trees or any shady place in your backyard. The shade and windbreak provided by the trees help keep the pile at an even moisture level. (The pile should be placed 6 feet away from the tree's trunk so it will not provide a haven for potentially harmful insects.)

The least expensive type of compost container is homemade.

Some other kinds of compost piles.

Pallet type

Open pile type

Modular box type

Large wire-fabric type

For those who wish to use them, containers can help shape a pile and keep the materials looking neat. The least-expensive container is made of 12-foot-long, 3-foot-wide pieces of 1-inch mesh chicken wire with 5 3-foot-long, 1 by 2-inch boards and 2 sets of small hooks and eyes. The boards are nailed along the 2 3-foot ends of the wire and at 3-foot intervals along the length of the wire (see illustration on page 37). The hooks and eyes are attached to the 2 end boards as shown. The unit is then placed as a circle on the ground, the hooks attached to the eyes, and the compost materials placed inside. The materials hold up the circle. After the pile is built, the wire enclosure may be removed and the materials will stay in place. You may now use the enclosure to build another pile, or you may use it later to turn the first pile into if you want to speed up the decomposition process. We rarely try to accelerate this natural process.

## Size and Timing

A minimum compost pile size of 3 feet by 3 feet by 3 feet (1 cubic yard of lightly moist, built compost, weighing about 1,000 pounds) is recommended. (In colder climates, a minimum compost pile size of 4 feet by 4 feet by 4 feet will be needed to properly insulate the heat of the composting process.) Smaller piles fail to provide the insulation necessary for appropriate heating (up to 140°F) and allow too much air to penetrate. It is all right to build up piles slowly to this size as materials become available, though it is best to build an entire pile at one time. A large compost pile might be 4 feet high, 5 feet wide, and 10 feet long. A pile will cure to ⅓ to ¼ of its original size, depending on the materials used.

The best time to prepare compost is in the *spring or autumn,* when biological activity is highest. (Too much heat or cold slows down and even kills the microbial life in the pile.) The 2 high-activity periods conveniently coincide with the maximum availability of materials in the spring, as grass and other plants begin to grow rapidly, and in the autumn, as leaves fall and other plant life begins to die. Compost built at other times will simply cure more slowly.

# CROSS SECTION OF A GROW BIOINTENSIVE COMPOST PILE

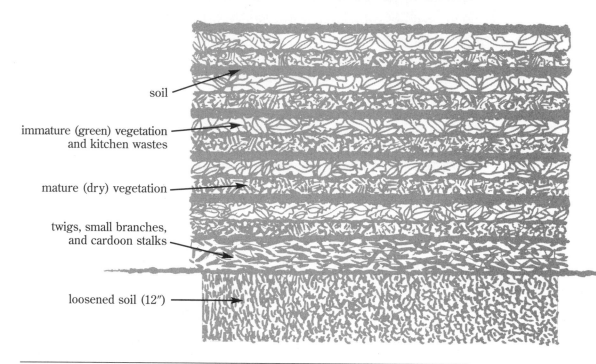

soil

immature (green) vegetation and kitchen wastes

mature (dry) vegetation

twigs, small branches, and cardoon stalks

loosened soil (12″)

## KEY ORGANIC MATTER FUNCTIONS

1. Organic matter feeds plants through nutrient exchange and through nutrient release upon its decomposition.

2. It is a continual slow-release source of nutrients for plants.

3. Organic acids in humus help dissolve minerals in the soil, making the mineral nutrients available to plants. Organic acids also increase the permeability of plant root membranes and therefore promote the plant roots' uptake of water and nutrients.

4. Organic matter is the energy source for the soil's microbial life-forms, which are an integral part of soil health. In 1 gram of humus-rich soil there are several *billion* bacteria, 1 million fungi, 10 to 20 million actinomycetes, and 800,000 algae.

5. The microbes that feed on organic matter in the soil temporarily bind the soil particles together. The fungi, with their *threadlike* mycelia, are especially important. They literally sew the soil together. The microbes secrete compounds into the soil as they live, metabolize, and ultimately decompose. Their secretions are a bacterial *glue* (polysaccharides) that holds soil particles, thus improving the soil's structure. Structure is vital to soil productivity because it ensures good aeration, good drainage, good water retention, and erosion resistance.

6. Organic matter is the key to soil structure, keeping it safe from severe erosion and keeping it in an open, porous condition for good water and air penetration.

## Building the Pile

The ground underneath the pile should be loosened to a depth of 12 inches to provide good drainage. Next, lay down roughage (brush, tree prunings, cardoon stalks, or other woody materials) 3 inches thick, if available, for air circulation.

One recipe for GROW BIOINTENSIVE compost is, **by volume**, *45% mature (dry) material, 45% immature (green) vegetation* (including *kitchen wastes*), and *10% soil*. Each layer should be watered well as it is created. This 45:45:10 recipe will give you a carbon-to-nitrogen ratio in your built compost pile of about 30 to 1, and will produce compost with a significant amount of high-quality, short-term humified carbon. The result will be a hotter (thermophilic: 113° to 149°F) pile with faster-releasing cured compost that generally releases nutrients over a 3-month to 2-year period. A lot of the carbon in this type of compost pile is lost, however, and the resulting cured compost only contains about ⅓ to ½ the cured organic matter that a *cooler* (mesophilic: 50° to 113°F) 60-to-1 compost pile will produce.

A 60-to-1 pile is built with approximately 8 parts mature material to 2 parts green vegetation (including kitchen wastes) and 1 part soil. The result of this pile will be a slower-releasing cured compost that generally releases nutrients over a 3-month to 5,000-year period—especially if the mature materials contain a large amount of lignin, such as corn and sorghum stalks. This can be a way to build up your soil fertility on a long-term basis, but the more readily available nutrients in the cured compost from a 30-to-1 pile will be important for the good growth of most vegetables. We make separate compost piles of small tree branches, since they can take 2 years or more to decompose.

The materials should optimally be added to the pile in 1- to 2-inch layers with the mature vegetation on the bottom, the immature vegetation and kitchen wastes second, and the soil third (in a ¼- to ½-inch layer). You can, however, build a pile spontaneously, adding materials daily or so, as they become available. This kind of pile will usually take a little longer to cure, but can be built more easily. Mature vegetation is high in carbon content. It is difficult for the microbes in the compost pile to digest carbon without sufficient amounts of nitrogen.

Unless you have a large household, it may be necessary to save your kitchen scraps in a tight-lidded unbreakable container for several days to get enough material for the kitchen waste layer. You may want to hold your breath when you dump them because the stronger-smelling *anaerobic* form of the decomposition process has been taking place in the closed container. The smell will disappear within a few hours after reintroducing air. All kitchen scraps may be added except meats and sizable

Soil is added to a compost pile after a layer of immature vegetation and kitchen waste.

amounts of oily salad scraps. Be sure to include bones, tea leaves, coffee grounds, eggshells, and citrus rinds. Always be sure to cover kitchen waste with soil to avoid flies and odors!

Add the soil layer immediately after the immature material and kitchen waste. It contains microorganisms that speed decomposition, keeps the smell down to a minor level, and prevents flies from laying eggs in the garbage. The smell will be difficult to eliminate entirely when waste from members of the cabbage family is added. In a few days, however, even this soil-minimized odor will disappear.

## Watering the Pile

As each layer is added, water it thoroughly so the pile is *evenly* moist—like a wrung-out damp sponge that does not give out excess water when squeezed. Sufficient water is necessary for the materials to heat and decompose properly. Too little water results in decreased biological activity, and too much simply drowns the aerobic microbial life. Water the pile, when necessary, as you water your garden. The particles in the pile should glisten. During the rainy season, some shelter or covering may be needed to prevent waterlogging and the less optimal anaerobic decomposition that occurs in a waterlogged pile. (The conditions needed for proper functioning of a compost pile and those required for good plant growth in raised beds are similar. In both cases, the proper mixture of air, soil nutrients, structure, microorganisms, and water is essential.)

## Compost Curing and Application Rates

Usually, a compost pile needs one turning to adjust the moisture level and make the mixture more homogeneous for complete breakdown. This should be done at about the 3-week point, after the *temperature* of the compost pile has *peaked and fallen*. A *decrease in moisture* usually occurs at the same time, the color begins to change to *brownish* from the original green and yellow, and the compost's odor begins to change from musty to an *earthy, freshly plowed soil aroma*. The compost will normally be ready about 2 months later.

Compost does not necessarily need to be turned. If you do not, the pile takes longer to cure, but you will probably produce more cured compost per unit of built material. This is because less oxidation may occur compared to when you turn the pile. If you turn the compost frequently, you will have cured compost faster, but may produce less cured compost per unit of built material.

Compost is ready to use when it is dark and rich looking and it crumbles in your hands. The texture should be even,

An abundant garden starts with good compost made of "waste products" such as vegetable peelings, weeds, and straw. With some knowledge and planning, the garden can produce all its needed fertilizer and organic matter.

**Notes**
- When you turn a compost pile, make the base of the new pile smaller than the original base to give the turned pile more internal volume and less surface area.
- If you are not ready to use your compost when it is fully cured, stop watering it and spread it out to dry. (See Ecology Action's booklet 32, *GROW BIOINTENSIVE® Composting and Growing Compost Materials*.)
- Compost sifted through ½-inch wire fabric is less likely to attract root hair–eating symphylans. For an easy-to-use sifter, see Ecology Action's *Backyard Homestead, Mini-Farm and Garden Log Book*.

and you should not be able to discern the original source of materials. Mature compost even smells good—like water in a forest spring! A GROW BIOINTENSIVE pile should be ready in 3 to 6 months.[3]

Parts of a regular compost pile that have not broken down completely by the end of the composting period should be placed at the bottom of a new pile. This is especially true for twigs and small branches that can use the extra protection of the pile's height to speed up their decomposition in a situation of increased warmth and moisture.

In the garden a *maximum* maintenance dressing of ½ inch of compost should be added to the soil before each crop per 4-month growing season. Guidelines for *general* maintenance dressings are a ⅛- to ½-inch layer of compost (1 to 4 cubic feet) per 100 square feet, if available.

## Composting Methods Compared

The GROW BIOINTENSIVE method of making compost differs in particular from the *biodynamic method* in that the GROW BIOINTENSIVE method is simpler, normally uses no manure, and usually uses no herbal solutions to stimulate microorganism growth.[4] Manure, used continually and in large amounts in biodynamic compost piles, is an imbalanced fertilizer, although it is a good texturizing agent because of its usual decomposed sawdust content. Rather than using herbal solutions, GROW BIOINTENSIVE practices sometimes use weeds, such as stinging nettle, and other plants, such as fava beans, as part of the ingredients in compost piles. Special compost recipes may be created in GROW BIOINTENSIVE to meet particular pH, structure, and nutrient requirements.

The GROW BIOINTENSIVE method of making compost differs from the *Rodale method;* we use little or no manure and usually

---

3. If for some reason you need compost cured quickly, there are 3 ways to speed up the decomposition rate in a compost pile—though they will probably leave you with much less *cured* compost per unit of material added to your pile originally, rather than the greatest quantity of life-enhancing compost you must seek. One way is to *increase the amount of nitrogen.* The ratio of carbon to nitrogen is critical for the breakdown rate. Materials with a high carbon-to-nitrogen ratio—such as dry leaves, grain straw, corn stalks, and small tree branches—take a long time to decompose alone since they lack sufficient nitrogen, which the bacteria depend upon for food. To boost the rate of decay in carbonaceous materials, add nitrogen-rich materials such as newly cut grass, fresh manure, vegetable wastes, green vegetation, or a fertilizer such as alfalfa meal. About 12 to 20 pounds of alfalfa meal per cubic yard of compost will fortify a compost pile with a high carbon content. Lightly sprinkle these fertilizers on each layer as you build your compost pile.

A second method is to *increase the amount of air* (aeration). Beneficial aerobic bacteria thrive in a well-aerated pile. Proper layering and periodic turning of the pile will accomplish this.

Third, you may *increase the surface area of the materials.* The smaller the size of the materials, the greater the amount of their exposed surface area. Broken-up twigs will decompose more rapidly than twigs that are left whole. We discourage the use of power shredders because nature will do the job in a relatively short time, and everyone has sufficient access to materials that will compost rapidly without resorting to a shredder. The noise from these machines is quite disturbing and spoils the peace and quiet of a garden. They also consume increasingly scarce fuel.

4. For the biodynamic method of compost preparation, see Alice Heckel (ed.), *The Pfeiffer Garden Book* (Stroudsburg, PA: Biodynamic Farming and Gardening Association, 1967), pp. 37–51.

no rock powder fertilizers or nitrogen supplements.[5] Fertilizers do not need to be added to the pile since successful compost can be made from a mixture of ingredients. The nitrogen supplements do, however, speed up the decomposition process. Both the biodynamic and Rodale methods are good ones, proven by use over a long period of time. Chadwick's Biointensive recipe seems simpler to use and equally effective.

Some people use *sheet composting,* a process of spreading uncomposted organic materials over the soil and then digging them into the soil, where they decompose. The disadvantage of this method is that the soil should not be planted for 3 months or so, until decomposition has occurred. Soil bacteria tie up the nitrogen during the decomposition process, thereby making it unavailable to the plants. Sheet composting may be beneficial if it is used during the winter in cold areas because the tie-up prevents the nitrogen from leaching out during winter rains.

Other people use *green manures*—cover crops such as vetch, clover, alfalfa, beans, peas, or other legumes, grown until the plants are at 10% to 50% flower. The nitrogen-rich plants are then dug into the soil. By using these legumes in this manner, a maximum of nitrogen is fixed in their root nodules. (The nitrogen is taken from the nodules in the seed-formation process. You can tell whether the nodules have fixed nitrogen by cutting 1 in half with a fingernail. If the inside is pink, they have fixed nitrogen.) This is a way to bring unworked soil into a better condition. These plants provide nitrogen without your having to purchase fertilizer, and they also help you dig. Their roots loosen the soil and eventually turn into humus beneath the earth. Fava beans are exceptionally good for green manuring if you plan to plant tomatoes; their decomposed bodies help eradicate tomato wilt organisms from the soil.

However, we find that green-manure crops are much more effective when used as compost materials, and their roots still have their good effect in the soil. There are several reasons for this. Due to their high nitrogen content, green manures decompose rapidly and even deplete some of the soil's humus. Another disadvantage of the green manuring process is that the land is not producing food crops during the period of cover crop growth and the 1-month period of decomposition. Additionally, green manures generally produce only about ¼ the carbon in a given area that carbonaceous compost crops do, and carbon in the form of *humus* is the most limiting and essential element in maintaining sustainable soil fertility (by serving as the energy source for microbial life and holding minerals in the soil so they cannot easily leach out of it).

The advantage of the small-scale GROW BIOINTENSIVE method is that backyard composting is easily feasible. When

5. For the Rodale method of compost preparation, see Robert Rodale (ed.), *The Basic Book of Organic Gardening* (New York: Ballantine, 1971), pp. 59–86.

you use compost crops without digging in the crop residues, the growing process will put nitrogen into the soil and make it possible to grow plants, such as corn and tomatoes, that are heavy nitrogen feeders. (See chapter 8, Companion Planting.) And the plant residues are valuable in the compost pile.

## Materials to Use Minimally or Not at All

If you need to use manures and/or less desirable materials in your compost pile, they should make up only ⅙ of your pile by volume so their less optimum effects will be minimized. Some materials should not be used in the preparation of compost, including:

- Plants infected with a disease or a severe insect attack where eggs could be preserved or where the insects themselves could survive in spite of the compost pile's heat.
- Poisonous plants, such as oleander, hemlock, and castor beans, which harm soil life.
- Plants that take too long to break down, such as magnolia leaves.
- Plants that have acids toxic to other plants and microbial life, such as eucalyptus, California bay laurel, walnut, juniper, and cypress.
- Plants that may be too acidic or contain substances that interfere with the decomposition process—such as pine needles, which are extremely acidic and contain a form of kerosene (However, special compost piles are often made of acidic materials, such as pine needles and leaves. This compost will lower the soil's pH and stimulate acid-loving plants, like strawberries.)
- Ivy and succulents, which may not be killed in the heat of the decomposition process and can regrow when the compost is placed in a planting bed.
- Pernicious weeds, such as wild morning glory and Bermuda grass, which will probably not be killed in the decomposition process and will choke out other plants when they resprout after the compost is placed in a planting.
- Cat and dog manures, which can contain pathogens harmful to infants. These pathogens are not always killed in the heat of the compost pile.

Plants infected with disease or insects and pernicious weeds should be burned to be destroyed properly. Their ashes then become good fertilizer. The ashes will also help control harmful soil insects, such as carrot worms, which shy away from the alkalinity of ashes. (Use ashes in moderate amounts.)

**Note**
In order to maintain good soil fertility, approximately 4% to 6% (by weight) organic matter is needed in temperate soils. About 3% is desirable in tropical soils. It is noteworthy that the soil organic matter level used to be measured 11 inches deep many years ago. Later, the measurement level was reduced to 6⅔ inches. Today, it has been further reduced to less than 6 inches deep.

## FUNCTIONS OF COMPOST IN THE SOIL

*Improved Structure*—Compost breaks up clay and clods and binds together sandy soil. It helps make proper aeration in clayey and sandy soil possible.

*Moisture Retention*—Compost holds 6 times its own weight in water. A soil with good organic matter content soaks up rain like a sponge and regulates the supply to plants. A soil stripped of organic matter resists water penetration, thus leading to crusting, erosion, and flooding.

*Aeration*—Plants can obtain 96% of the nutrients they need from the *air, sun, and water.* A loose, healthy soil assists in diffusing air and moisture into the soil and in exchanging nutrients. Carbon dioxide released by organic matter decomposition diffuses out of the soil and is absorbed by the canopy of leaves above in a raised bed mini-climate created by closely spaced plants.

*Fertilization*—Compost contains some nitrogen, phosphorus, potassium, magnesium, and sulfur but is especially important for trace elements. The important principle is to return to the soil, by the use of plant residues and manures, all that has been taken out of it.

*Nitrogen Storage*—The compost pile is a storehouse for nitrogen. Because it is tied up in the compost-breakdown process, water-soluble nitrogen does not leach out or oxidize into the air for a period of 3 to 6 months or more—depending on how the pile is built and maintained.

*pH Buffer*—A good percentage of compost in the soil allows plants to grow better in less-than-optimal pH situations.

*Soil Toxin Neutralizer*—Important recent studies show that plants grown in organically composted soils take up less lead, heavy metals, and other urban pollutants.

*Nutrient Release*—Organic acids dissolve soil minerals and make them available to plants. As organic matter decomposes, it releases nutrients for plant uptake and for the soil microbial population.

*Food for Microbial Life*—Good compost creates healthy conditions for organisms that live in the soil. Compost harbors earthworms and beneficial fungi that fight nematodes and other soil pests.

*The Ultimate in Recycling*—The Earth provides us with food, clothing, and shelter, and we close the cycle in offering fertility, health, and life through the shepherding of materials.

We sometimes build a compost pile on an unused growing bed so the next crop grown in that bed will pick up and utilize any nutrients leached out from the pile into the soil. The next season we build compost on another unused growing bed.

## BUILDING A COMPOST PILE STEP-BY-STEP

1. Under the pile area (9 or 16 square feet), loosen the soil to 12 inches deep with a spading fork.

2. Lay down *roughage* (brush or other woody material), 3 inches thick, if it is available, for air circulation.

3. Put down a 2-inch layer of *mature material*—dry weeds, leaves, straw, dry grass clippings, hay, and old garden wastes. Water it thoroughly.

4. Put down a 2-inch layer of *immature material and kitchen wastes*—fresh weeds, grass clippings, hedge trimmings, green cover crops, and kitchen wastes you have saved. Water well.

5. Cover lightly with a ¼- to ½-inch layer of *soil* to prevent flies and odors. Moisten the soil.

6. Add new layers of mature vegetation, immature vegetation, kitchen waste, and soil as materials become available until the pile is 3 to 4 feet high.

7. Cover the top of the pile with a ½- to 1-inch layer of soil.

8. Water the completed pile regularly until it is ready for use.

9. Let the completed pile cure 3 to 6 months while you are building a new pile. Turn the pile once for faster decomposition. For planning purposes, remember that a 4-foot-high compost pile will be 1 to 1⅓ feet high when it is ready to use.

# FERTILIZATION

## CHAPTER FOUR

**GOAL:** *Build and maintain proper levels of and balances among soil nutrients while maintaining an adequate level of humic and carbonic acids for good nutrient cycling*

The *first* goal of adding fertilizers to your soil is to build nutrients up to their proper levels and balances for your particular soil type, rainfall, climate, sun exposure, altitude, and cation-exchange capacity (a measurement of the availability of nutrients in a given soil). The *second* goal is to keep those nutrients in your food-raising area by composting properly and recycling all wastes. A *third* goal is to use *enough* nutrients, water, and compost in your growing area.

During a drought in India years ago, several women grew food using Biointensive methods. Their production was double that of others who used single-dug row cropping practices. One woman got even higher yields than other Biointensive gardeners by using her 1 unit of water, fertilizers, and seed on *1* growing area. Hoping for higher yields, the others had spread their single units of resources over 7 to 15 units of growing area. The woman with the best results got more total production in $1/7$ to $1/15$ the area. She had benefited by Alan Chadwick's observation, "Begin with 1 bed and tend it well! Then expand your growing area."

Over the years we have seen gardeners in many countries obtain excellent, good, and fair yields using GROW BIOINTENSIVE techniques, depending on the care taken with the resources and on what results individuals believed they would obtain. A good level and balance of nutrients in your soil will help your garden flourish and make it optimally healthy and productive.

## Soil Testing

A professional soil test performed by a laboratory will provide you with the most complete evaluation. Unfortunately, because of variation in soil types, climates, cultivation practices, rainfall,

## SOIL TEST

Date Performed: _____     Performed by: _____

| Test | Results | Recommendations per 100 Square Feet |
|---|---|---|
| Nitrogen | | |
| Phosphorus | | |
| Potassium | | |
| pH (6.5 or slightly acid is optimum) | | |
| Remarks (including texture) | | |

altitude, sun exposure, drainage conditions, the types of crops grown, and cation-exchange capacity, no standard added nutrient formula will work in all situations.

If you can, test your soil for major nutrients and trace minerals, as well as pH (the acidity or alkalinity level of your soil), before choosing fertilizers. The major minerals, those that plants utilize in relatively large amounts, include nitrogen, phosphorus, potassium, sulfur, magnesium, and calcium. Trace minerals—such as zinc, boron, copper, and iron—are important elements that are required in very small quantities.

For professional soil testing, we use the *Timberleaf* soil testing service.[1] It specializes in testing for organic farmers and gardeners, with an emphasis on Biointensive fertility. The service analyzes all soil and plant minerals and the soil's physical characteristics and can provide follow-up review and advice on your year's experience in the garden. If you are unable to arrange a professional soil test, purchase a home test kit. The best such kit is the *LaMotte kit*.[2] With the home kit you will be limited to testing nitrogen, phosphorus, and potassium content, and pH.

The LaMotte soil test kit is a home kit.

1. *Timberleaf,* 39648 Old Spring Road, Murieta, CA 92563-5566. (951) 677-7510.
2. LaMotte Chemical Products, Box 329, Chestertown, MD 21620: Model STH.

# NITROGEN (N), PHOSPHORUS (P), AND POTASSIUM (K)

Pounds of fertilizer to add per 100 square feet. Pounds of *pure* nutrients added are given in parentheses.
**Note:** The goal is to reduce the nutrient deficiencies in the soil slowly over time. (If you add large amounts of readily available nutrients all at once, nutrients not in short supply in the soil may become unavailable.)

| Test Rating | Nitrogen (N) | Phosphorus (P) | Potassium (K) |
|---|---|---|---|
| *Very High*[3] | **(.1)** 4.2 lbs alfalfa meal | **(.2)** 4.5 lbs phosphate rock or 9 lbs soft phosphate | **(.15)** 1.5 lbs wood ashes[4] and 1.5 lbs crushed granite[5] |
| *High*[3] | **(.2)** 8.4 lbs alfalfa meal | **(.3)** 6.8 lbs phosphate rock or 13.6 lbs soft phosphate | **(.2)** 1.5 lbs wood ashes[4] and 2.5 lbs crushed granite[5] |
| *Medium High* | **(.25)** 10.5 lbs alfalfa meal | **(.35)** 8 lbs phosphate rock or 16 lbs soft phosphate | **(.25)** 1.5 lbs wood ashes[4] and 3.5 lbs crushed granite[5] |
| *Medium* | **(.3)** 12.6 lbs alfalfa meal | **(.4)** 9 lbs phosphate rock or 18 lbs soft phosphate | **(.3)** 1.5 lbs wood ashes[4] and 4.5 lbs crushed granite[5] |
| *Medium Low* | **(.35)** 14.7 lbs alfalfa meal | **(.45)** 10.2 lbs phosphate rock or 20.4 lbs soft phosphate | **(.35)** 1.5 lbs wood ashes[4] and 5.5 lbs crushed granite[5] |
| *Low* | **(.4)** 16.8 lbs alfalfa meal | **(.5)** 11.4 lbs phosphate rock or 22.8 lbs soft phosphate | **(.4)** 1.5 lbs wood ashes[4] and 6.5 lbs crushed granite[5] |
| *Very Low* | **(.5)** 18.9 lbs alfalfa meal | **(.6)** 13.6 lbs phosphate rock or 27.2 lbs soft phosphate | **(.5)** 1.5 lbs wood ashes[4] and 8.5 lbs crushed granite[5] |

3. Addition of nutrients at these levels is optional.

4. Wood ash application should be used with care for soils with a pH above 6.5. A maximum of 1.5 lbs should be used; 1.5 lbs contains .75 lbs potassium.

5. Finely ground.

To take a soil sample from your yard, use a nonferrous trowel or a stainless steel spoon to dig a vertical soil slice from 8 inches below the surface. Take samples from 6 to 8 representative areas and mix them together well in a clean plastic bucket. Make sure you do not include residues, such as roots and surface organic litter, in the composite sample. Also, do not sample for 30 days after adding any fertilizers, manure, or compost to the area. The samples normally should be taken at the end of a growing season or just before one. You will need a total soil volume of 1 pound for professional testing or 4 heaping tablespoons for the home test kit. Remember that soil tests can save you a lot of money, since they all guard against overapplication of fertilizers, allow you to account for nutrients already available in your soil for good plant growth, and increase yields.

To use the Timberleaf service, ship your composite sample as instructed in its soil test packet without drying the soil. For a home test kit, let samples dry in a small paper bag in indirect sunlight—*not* in the sun or an oven. When you are ready to begin testing, follow the instructions included with the kit. Record home test results on a photocopy of the chart on page 48. Once you have completed the test, use the information page 49 to determine a general fertilization plan for your garden.

As you become more skilled, you may want to use John Beeby's book *Test Your Soil with Plants* to test your soil. This is how people used to learn about their soil's nutrient needs for thousands of years before chemical soil tests became available. Eventually each of us should have a *living soil test* of plants grown in a small area that is "read" to determine existing nutrient levels in the soil of that area! Until about 100 years ago, this is how farmers determined soil nutrient needs. It will take many years to fully rediscover and develop all these skills.

## ANALYSIS OF RECOMMENDED ORGANIC SOIL AMENDMENTS[6]

N, P, and K refer to 3 of the major nutrients that plants need, nitrogen, phosphorus, and potassium, respectively. According to law, any product sold as a fertilizer must provide an analysis upon request for these 3 minerals. *Nitrogen* is a key element in proteins, is a food source in compost piles, and causes green growth. *Phosphorus* gives plants energy and is necessary for the growth of flowers and seeds. *Potassium* aids in protein synthesis and the translocation of carbohydrates to build strong stems. Plants also need a good supply of *organic matter* to give them additional nitrogen, phosphorus, sulfur, copper, zinc, boron, and molybdenum, along with 8 other nutrients. Only under *ideal conditions* do native soil minerals provide these nutrients natu-

---

6. Note: GROW BIOINTENSIVE no longer uses many organic fertilizers because of problems with disease, pesticide residue, or heavy metal toxicity.

rally. Plants need a full meal of nutrients, and as good stewards of the soil we are responsible for providing them. Be aware that laboratory analysis to determine fertilizer amendments does not always show *all* of the actual needs of the soil plant system. Also, the composition may vary for products from various sources. Be sure to check the analyses on the bags.

## NITROGEN

*Alfalfa Meal*
2% to 3% N, .7% P, 2.25% K. Lasts 3 to 4 months. Use up to 19 pounds (16¾ quarts)/100 square feet. A quick-acting source of nitrogen and some potassium. (If not organic, it can contain methoxichlor pesticide residues.)

## PHOSPHORUS

*Phosphate Rock*
~11.5% to 17.5% total P. Lasts 3 to 5 years. Use up to 9 pounds (2⅔ quarts)/100 square feet. Very slow releasing.

*Soft Phosphate (Colloidal)*
~8% total P; ~2% available P. Lasts 2 to 3 years. Use up to 18 pounds (2⅔ quarts)/100 square feet. Its clay base makes it more available to plants than the phosphorus in phosphate rock, though the 2 are used interchangeably.

## POTASSIUM

*Wood Ash*
1% to 10% K. Lasts 6 months. Use a maximum of 1.5 pounds (1¾ quarts)/100 square feet. Ash from wood is high in potassium and helps repel maggots. Ash also has an alkaline effect on the soil, so use it with care if your soil pH is above 6.5. *Black* wood ash is best. Wood ash provides strength and plant essence, aids in insect control, and is a flavor enhancer for vegetables, especially lettuce and tomatoes. You can produce it with a controlled, soil-covered, slow-burning fire built during a soft drizzle or rain. This ash is higher in potassium and other minerals because they do not readily escape into the atmosphere as the wood is consumed by fire. Wood ash should be stored in a tight container until it is used; exposure to air will destroy much of its nutrient value. *Grey* wood ash from a fireplace may be used if it is from wood and not from colored or slick paper.

*Crushed Granite (Finely Ground)*
3% to 5% K. Lasts up to 10 years. Use up to 8.5 pounds (3½ quarts)/100 square feet. It is a slow-releasing source of potassium and trace minerals.

**Note**
Remember that too much nitrogen in your soil can cause the soil's all-important organic matter to break down too quickly.

## SOIL MODIFIERS

*Dolomitic Lime*
~25% Ca (calcium), ~6% to 14% Mg (magnesium). A good source of calcium and magnesium to be used when both are needed. Do not use dolomitic lime in a soil with an adequate or high level of magnesium. Do not use lime to "sweeten" the compost pile; this will result in a serious loss of nitrogen. A layer of soil will discourage flies and reduce odors. 1 quart = about 3 pounds 8 ounces.

*High-Calcium Lime (Calcite)*
A good source of calcium when magnesium levels are too high for applying dolomitic lime. Oyster shell flour lime (~34% to 36% Ca) is a good substitute. 1 quart = about 30 ounces.

*Gypsum (Calcium Sulfate)*
~23% Ca, ~19% S (sulfur) Used to correct excess levels of exchangeable sodium. Apply only when recommended by a professional soil test. 1 quart = about 1 pound 4 ounces.

*Crushed Eggshells*
High in calcium. Especially good for cabbage family crops. Eggshells help break up clay and release nutrients tied up in alkaline soils. Use up to 2 pounds (1¼ quart)/100 square feet. Dry them first.

*Manure (All Types)*
The nutrient levels in each manure will depend on proper management of the curing process and on the amount of straw or sawdust in the manure. Optimally, do not use more than .33 cubic feet per 100 square feet (½ 5-gallon bucket) of aged manure per year (about 8.3 pounds dry weight, or a ¹⁄₂₄-inch layer). It is best to use manure that contains little undecomposed sawdust. Approximately 2 cubic feet (3 5-gallon buckets) of manure (50 pounds dry weight) applied per 100 square feet can lower the pH *1* point. Composted manure is a microbial life stimulant and an animal and plant essence that has been "composted" both inside the animal and outside in a curing pile. Avoid using too much manure because manures that do not contain much sawdust or straw can contain excess salt and imbalanced ratios of nitrogen, phosphorus, and potassium. The GROW BIOINTENSIVE method uses as much (or more) phosphorus and potassium as nitrogen. This results in stronger, healthier plants. It is a difference between the GROW BIOINTENSIVE method and the French intensive approach, which depended heavily on the use of horse manure, with about 3 parts nitrogen to 1 part phosphorus to 3 parts potassium. This ratio is unbalanced in favor of nitrogen, which in time results in weak and rank plant growth more susceptible to disease and insect attack. A ratio of 1 part nitrogen to 1 part phosphorus to 1 part potassium is better. Using composted or aged manure is

recommended as an alternative to compost only when compost is not available.

## MANURES—SOLIDS
(approximate)

| | | | |
|---|---|---|---|
| Chicken—fresh | 9-15% C | 1.50% N | 1.00% P | .50% K |
| Chicken—dry | D | 4.50% N | 3.50% P | 2.00% K |
| Dairy Cow | 7.28% C | .56% N | .23% P | .60% K |
| Horse | 18.63% C | .69% N | .24% P | .72% K |
| Pig—fresh | 6.5% C | .50% N | .32% P | .46% K |
| Sheep | 19.6% C | 1.40% N | .48% P | 1.20% K |
| Steer | 11.9% C | .70% N | .55% P | .72% K |

D = Do not have data

*Compost*

Good compost is the most important part of the garden. It aerates soil, breaks up clay, binds together sand, improves drainage, prevents erosion, neutralizes toxins, holds precious moisture, releases essential nutrients, and feeds the microbiotic life of the soil, creating healthy conditions for natural antibiotics, worms, and beneficial fungi. Each 4-month growing season, use up to ½-inch of cured compost (4 cubic feet/100 square feet), which is about ⅙ of a cubic yard. (One cubic yard equals 27 cubic feet. Two cubic feet of cured compost will cover 100 square feet ¼ inch deep.) Generally, use only a maximum of 4 cubic feet of cured compost made with equal amounts by weight of mature (dry) material, immature (green) material, and soil (or 2 cubic feet of cured compost made without soil) per 100 square feet per 4- to 6-month crop to avoid using more than a sustainable amount of compost.

You should note the heavy emphasis that the GROW BIOIN-TENSIVE method places on compost. The demand for organic fertilizers is increasing while the supply available to each person in the world is decreasing. Soon, few fertilizers will be available at reasonable prices. Also, the materials used to produce chemical fertilizers are becoming less available. Materials for GROW BIOINTENSIVE compost, on the other hand, are plants and soil, which can be produced in a sustained way by a healthy garden. These compostable materials can be produced indefinitely if we take care of our soils and do not exhaust them. In fact, 96% of the total amount of nutrients needed for plant growth processes are obtained as plants use the sun's energy to work on elements already in the air and water.[7] Compost, soil, manure, wood ash, nitrogen from legumes, and nutrients from the growth of certain kinds of herbs and weeds in the beds (see chapter 8, Companion Planting) supply the 4% of a plant's diet not provided by the air and water.

**Caution**
In order to obtain a 1-inch layer of aged steer manure for use as compost on a 100-square-foot area, fodder for the animal to eat must be grown on a 500-square-foot area. This means an area 4 times as large as your growing area is being depleted of trace minerals and life-sustaining humus! Such a practice is not sustainable if used over a long period of time. When the proper *compost crops* are used instead, the compost materials for your 100-square-foot garden can be grown in just your 100-square-foot garden itself!

7. Joseph A. Cocannouer, *Farming with Nature* (Norman, OK: University of Oklahoma Press, 1954), p. 50.

GROW BIOINTENSIVE compost (see chapter 3, Compost) is high in most major and trace minerals. It also contains nitrogen and, when made properly, can be high in nitrogen. Periodically growing legumes—such as peas, beans, clover, alfalfa, and vetch—in the planting beds will provide nitrogen, too. The nitrogen that the legumes fix from the air is released when their roots, stems, and leaves decompose.

## What a Home Soil Test Will Not Tell You

A *professional soil test* is an excellent tool for analyzing deficiencies, excesses, and the relative balance of all plant nutrients in your garden's soil. A *home test kit,* however, is very limited and only points out pH level and deficiencies of nitrogen, phosphorus, and potassium. If you have difficulty growing healthy plants in your garden, a home test kit may not provide the solution. Plants grown in soil lacking any of the major or trace minerals show their deficiency in yellowed leaves, stunted growth, purple veins, or any number of other ways.

SOIL pH SCALE

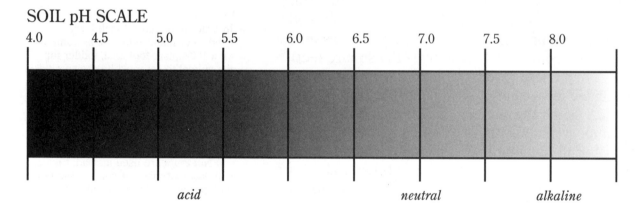

| 4.0 | 4.5 | 5.0 | 5.5 | 6.0 | 6.5 | 7.0 | 7.5 | 8.0 |

*acid*                    *neutral*        *alkaline*

## pH

A pH reading tells you the relative acidity or alkalinity of the soil water, generally called the *soil solution.* Nutrient availability for vegetable plants, soil microbial activity, and soil structure are all affected by pH. Most vegetables grow best in a slightly acidic soil with a pH of 6.8. A range of 6.0 to 7.0 is fine for most crops.

More important than the actual pH reading is the quality of the pH. This is determined by testing for the amount of plant-available potassium, magnesium, calcium, and sodium in your soil. Only a professional soil test can determine the soil's mineral balance. You should have this information before you apply pH modifiers to your soil. For instance, limestone is a common pH modifier; however, all limestones do not have the same mineral composition. An application of a dolomitic instead of a calcitic lime to a soil with a high magnesium content could disrupt your soil balance and adversely affect plant growth.

Soil-applied organic matter and manure can alter the pH over time. When adequate organic matter is used, we find crops will tolerate a wider pH range. Leaf mold, pine needles, and sawdust produce an acidic compost that can lower the pH. Manures may be alkaline and raise the pH, although they may lower the pH *1* point in some cases. Compost can be either acidic or alkaline. Using the proper limestone with the correct mineral balance is the least expensive and most practical way to increase pH. Mined sulfur, a soil nutrient deficient in many soils, is an excellent amendment to lower the pH. Although you can use organic matter to alter pH, you will need to know your soil mineral structure, the existing soil pH, and the pH of the applied material in order to apply it accurately and in an effective amount.

The "Analysis of Recommended Organic Soil Amendments," beginning on page 50, gives the mineral nutrient content of many commonly used organic fertilizers. This information will help you determine the amounts of each fertilizer to add if you are using a home test kit and are unable to have a professional soil test performed. In your calculations, it is not necessary to *subtract* the nutrients you add to the soil in the form of manure and compost. Be careful, though, about adding manure. Much aged or composted manure actually contains little nitrogen and may have a substantial amount of nitrogen-demanding sawdust. If you use a lot of manure containing large amounts of sawdust as a soil texturizer, you may want to add some additional nitrogen fertilizer, such as 4 extra pounds of alfalfa meal per 100 square feet. (Notice that the release times are different for different fertilizers.)

## Shaping the Bed

The bed should be shaped before adding fertilizers. If your soil is in good condition, use a rake to shape the bed into a *mound*. The soil will not easily wash off or erode from beds shaped in this manner once the structure of the soil is improved. While you are still improving the structure of heavy clay soils, you may want to form a *flat-topped bed* with a small lip on the outer edges of the bed (see illustration, page 56). This will minimize erosion caused by watering. The sides of the bed should have about a 30-degree slope; a sharper angle will encourage erosion. When you have shaped the bed, tamp the soil down before planting, if necessary, by placing the digging board on all parts of the bed and walking across the board. If you add a lip to the bed, do it after tamping down the soil.

## Adding Fertilizers and Compost

Add fertilizers and other amendments one at a time. Avoid windy days, and hold the fertilizer close to the bed surface when spreading. Use the different colors to help you. The soil

Broadcasting fertilizers.

is dark, so sprinkle on a light-colored fertilizer (such as oyster shell flour) first, then a darker fertilizer (such as alfalfa meal), and so on (see illustration on page 57). It is better to underapply the fertilizers because you can go back over the bed afterward to spread on any leftover, but it is difficult to pick up fertilizer if too much falls in one place. Aim for even distribution. Next, add compost. After all are applied, sift in the fertilizers and other amendments by inserting a spading fork 2 to 4 inches deep at a slant, then lifting it upward with a slight jiggling motion.

Several things should be noted about the nutrients added to the upper 2 to 4 inches of soil: (1) The nutrients are added to the upper soil layer, as occurs in nature. (2) The nutrients are relocated through the soil by the movement of larger soil organisms and when water flows downward. (3) Organic fertilizers break down more slowly than most chemical fertilizers. By utilizing natural nutrient cycles, plant-available minerals are released over an extended period of time.

## More-Sustainabile Fertilization

Each gardener should strive to use less and less fertilizer brought in from outside his or her own garden area. This will be especially true when such amendments become scarce due to the increased number of people using them. There are at least 4 ways to create a more "closed-system" garden, to which few resources are imported:

1.  Use most of the food you grow *at home,* so all the residues are returned to your soil. "Export" as little as possible of your valuable soil resource.

(*Left*) Raking soil outward from the inside for a lip; (*right*) raking the soil up from the side for a lip.

2. Grow some trees. Their deep root systems will bring up nutrients from far down in the subsoil into the topsoil and even into the tree leaves. These nutrients would not otherwise become available for use as plant food.

3. "Grow" your own fertilizers by raising plants that produce good amounts of compost material, which concentrates the nutrients required in a form that plants can use. For beginning information on plants to use, see Ecology Action's Self-Teaching Mini-Series Booklet 12, *Growing and Gathering Your Own Fertilizers* (see Ecology Action Publications, page 257), Bargyla and Gylver Rateaver's *Organic Method Primer*, and Ehrenfried Pfeiffer's *Weeds and What They Tell*. If everyone were to use organic fertilizers, there would be a worldwide shortage; eventually the key will be growing our own and recycling *all* wastes. Deep-rooted alfalfa (as deep as 125 feet) and comfrey (up to 8 feet) also help bring up leached-out and newly released nutrients from the soil strata and rocks below.

4. Maintain at least 4% to 6% organic matter by weight in at least the upper 6 inches of soil in temperate zones and 3% organic matter in tropical ones. This will encourage microbial life growth, which can keep nutrients from leaching out of the soil.

The GROW BIOINTENSIVE method has roots 4,000 years into the past in Chinese intensive agriculture, 2,000 years into the past in the Greek use of raised beds, and, more recently, in European farming. Similar practices are still used today in the native agriculture of many countries, such as Guatemala. GROW BIOINTENSIVE will extend its roots into a future where environmentally balanced resource usage is of the utmost importance.

(*Left*) Casting fertilizer onto a bed's surface; (*right*) sifting in fertilizers with a spading fork. A "twist dig" is now being used to sift in fertilizers also. It is easier on the back and does not require bending over as far. This method requires 3 motions at once: (1) a slight up-and-down motion with the left hand, (2) a twist back and forth holding onto the D-handled spade with the right hand, and (3) a slight pushing in and out of the handle through the left hand with the right hand. Develop this skill by practicing. Do not rake the bed to smooth it out after sifting in fertilizers, as this usually creates irregular concentrations of fertilizers that were previously spread evenly.

# 5

# SEED PROPAGATION

**GOAL:** *Enhanced and uninterrupted root and plant growth*

N ow that we know a little about the body and soul of our Earth, we are ready to witness the birth of seedlings. Just for a moment, close your eyes and pretend you are the seed of your favorite plant, tree, vegetable, fruit, flower, or herb. You are all alone. You can do nothing in this state. Slowly you begin to hear sounds around you. The wind, perhaps. You feel warmth from the sun, feel the ground underneath you. What do you need for good growth? Think like a seed, and ask yourself what a seed needs. It needs an entire microcosm of the world—air, warmth, moisture, soil, nutrients, and microorganisms. Plants need all these things, as do birds, insects, and animals.

Generally, the elements needed for growth fall into 2 categories: terrestrial (soil and nutrients) and celestial (air, warmth, moisture). The celestial elements cannot be completely categorized, however, since air, warmth, and moisture come from the heavens to circulate through the soil, and plants can take in air through their roots as well as through their leaves. Nutrients can also be borne upon air currents. In fact, citrus trees take in the important trace mineral zinc more readily by their leaves than by their roots. See chapter 8 for further information on the parts that other elements in the plant and animal worlds play—other plants and insects, for example.

A seed is planted at a depth equal to its thickness.

**Note**
Seeds can germinate 2 to 7 times faster in a flat mix containing compost, because of the humic acids in the compost.

## Seed Planting

Seeds should be planted at a depth equal to its thickness. Lima and fava beans may be planted on their sides. Their root systems, which emerge from an eye, can grow straight down. The seeds should be covered with humus-containing flat soil, which is similar to the soil with decomposed plant matter found over germinating seeds in nature. The compost stimulates the germination process.

8"    8"

8"

*Hexagonal spacing:*
Leaf lettuce is spaced on 8-inch centers.

Seeds, whether they are planted in beds or in flats, should be planted in a diagonally offset or hexagonal spacing pattern with an equal distance between any 2 seeds. The Master Charts later in chapter 6 tell how far apart to space different types of plants. The leaves of seedlings in the flat and of plants in the growing bed should barely touch. Appropriately spaced plants form a *living mulch,* which retards weed growth, aids in the retention of soil moisture by shading the soil, and creates the mini-climate under their leaves so essential to balanced, uninterrupted growth. When spacing seeds in flats, place the seeds far enough apart that the seedlings' leaves will barely touch when the seedlings are transplanting size. Try 1-inch to 2-inch spacings depending on the size of the seedling at its transplanting stage (see the Master Charts in chapter 6). In general, the plant spacings listed in the Master Charts for vegetables, flowers, and herbs are equal to the "within the row" spacings listed on the back of seed packets, or sometimes ¾ of this distance. *Disregard* any "between row" spacings. The Master Charts list our best spacing determinations to date for these plants.

To make the placement of seeds in planting beds or flats easier, use frames with 1-inch or 2-inch mesh chicken wire stretched across them. The mesh is built on a hexagonal pattern, so the seeds can be dropped in the center of a hexagon and be on the proper center. Or, if a center greater than 1 inch is involved and you only have 1-inch mesh, just count past the proper number of hexagons before dropping the next seed.

When transplanting or planting seeds on spacings of 3 inches or more, try using measuring sticks cut to the required length

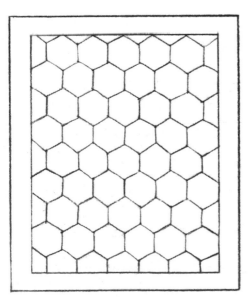

A spacing frame aids in placing seeds in flats. Place 1 seed in the center of each space.

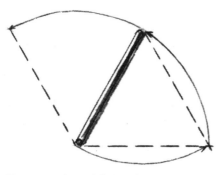

Use a spacing stick for placing seeds in beds. 3-inch to 36-inch sizes are used according to the crop planted. Triangulation is the way we plant most seeds and transplant seedlings.

Use a triangular spacing template for placing seeds in beds.

to determine where each plant should be located. Transplant or sow a seed at each point of the triangulation process. You will eventually be able to transplant with reasonable accuracy without measuring!

Once you get the feel for plant spacing, you may want to practice broadcasting seeds by hand in flats for some crops, such as lettuce and flowers. Broadcasting was the method that Alan Chadwick and his apprentices used with flats. Be sure the seeds end up ¼ to ½ inch apart in the first flat so the seeds can take advantage of their complete mini-climate for early growth stimulation and health. This method does, however, require more time to do 1 or more prick-outs. When these seedlings' leaves are barely touching, prick them out (transplant them) into other flats on 1-, 1½-, or 2-inch centers.

Cover the seeds in their flats with a layer of the flat soil mixture described later in this chapter. When broadcasting seeds onto a growing bed, gently "chop" them in afterward with a bow rake to a depth equal to their thickness (when they are lying flat on a surface). Be sure to chop the rake only up and down; do not pull it toward you. If you pull, seeds, fertilizers, and compost may concentrate irregularly over the bed rather than remain evenly spread. Or you may poke large seeds into the soil to their proper depth with your index finger. Fill the hole by pushing soil into it with your thumb and index finger.

Now that you have prepared your GROW BIOINTENSIVE bed and have spread the compost, you have a choice as to whether to sow seeds directly into the bed or to use seedlings.

Use your digging board as a planting board to minimize compaction. As you move it along the bed, reloosen the soil underneath with a hand fork.

Transplanting seedlings involves more advance planning and more time, but in a small garden, this has several advantages:

- Transplanted seedlings make better use of bed space. Seeds can take from 5 days to 12 weeks or more to reach transplanting size. If that growing is done in a flat, something else can be growing in the bed in the meantime.

- You can be reasonably sure that each transplanted seedling will grow into a healthy mature plant. Not all seeds germinate, so no matter how carefully you sow seeds directly in the bed, you can end up with gaps between plants and, therefore, bare soil that allows evaporation.

- Plants grow better if they are evenly spaced. Some seeds are sown by broadcasting, scattering them over the soil. Broadcast seeds—no matter how evenly you try to scatter them—will inevitably fall in a random pattern, with some closer and some farther apart than the optimal spacing for best plant growth. Plants that are too close together compete with each other for light, water, and nutrients. When plants are too far apart, the soil around them may become compacted, more water may evaporate, and space is wasted.

  The roots of evenly spaced transplanted seedlings can find nutrients and grow more easily, and their leaves will cover and protect the soil, creating a good mini-climate with better protection for the soil. Carbon dioxide is captured under the leaf canopy of closely spaced plants, where the plants need it for optimal growth.

A bottom view of full-sized seedling flat construction. Leave 3/16 inch between board pieces for drainage. **Note:** All measurements given are internal dimensions.

23"

14"

Seedling flats are made of redwood, or equivalent. A 3-inch-deep (internal dimension), full-sized flat with evenly moist flat soil and plants weighs about 45 pounds.

3"

The leaves are roots in the air . . .

Roots are leaves in the ground . . .

• Transplanting stimulates growth. When you transplant a seedling into a double-dug, composted bed that is fluffy, aerated, and full of nutrients, you give it a second "meal" of nutrients, air, and moisture after its first meal in the flat. If the seeds are sown directly in the bed, the soil will begin to recompact after its initial digging while the seeds are germinating and growing into seedlings. Therefore, the soil will not be as loose for the plants to grow in once the seedling stage is reached.

• Seedlings in a flat require much less water (½ gallon per day) than seedlings in a bed (10 to 20 or more gallons per 100 square feet per day).

## Flats

If you build your own flats, the standard flat size is 3 inches deep by 14 inches wide by 23 inches long (internal dimensions). For smaller home gardens, and people with less sturdy backs, half-sized flats may be more convenient. The depth is critical since an overly shallow flat allows the seedling roots to touch the bottom too soon. When this occurs, the plants believe they have reached their growth limit, and they enter a state of "premature senility." In this state the plants begin to flower and fruit even though they are only transplanting size. We have experienced this with broccoli and dwarf marigolds; the broccoli heads were the size of the nail on a little finger. The flat's length and width are not as critical. They should not become too large, however, or the flat will be hard to carry. If plants must remain in a container more than 4 to 6 weeks, use a half-sized flat that is 6 inches deep.

When planting seeds or seedlings, remember that the most important areas for the plant are the 2 inches above and the 2 inches below the surface of the flat or planting bed. The mini-climate created under the plants' leaves and the protection of the upper roots in the flat or the bed by the soil is critical. Without proper protection, the plants will develop tough necks at the point where the stem emerges from the soil. A toughened neck slows the flow of plant juices and interrupts and weakens plant growth. These few inches are also important because in a very real sense the roots are *leaves in the soil* and the leaves are *roots in the air*. The roots "breathe in" (absorb) gases in significant amounts as if they were leaves, and the leaves absorb moisture and nutrients from the air. Also, plant life activity varies above and below the ground according to monthly cycles. Root growth is stimulated more during the third quarter of each 28-day period, and leaf growth is stimulated more during the second quarter, in accordance with the phases of the moon. (See pages 68–71.)

The critical distance above and below the surface of the planting bed is not exactly 2 inches. Obviously it will be different for radishes than for corn, since their leaves begin at different heights from the soil surface and because their root systems have different depths. Generally speaking, though, the 2-inch guideline helps us develop a sensitivity to the plants' needs above and below ground. (The need for proper conditions above and below ground was also noted in the comparison between the normal use of rows in gardening and farming and the use of raised beds for growing plants, discussed on pages xvii and xviii.) In particular, this miniclimate protects feeder roots and microbial life, which are both concentrated in the upper soil.

Once you have planted a flat, there are several locations—depending on the weather—where you can place it while the seeds germinate and grow:

- In a greenhouse or miniature greenhouse if the weather is cold
- In a cold frame for 2 days when the seedlings are almost transplanting size as part of their *hardening off* (acclimatization to the cooler outside) for transplanting in cold weather
- In the open for 2 more days to complete the hardening off process before transplanting
- In the open under a 30% shade net during warm and hot weather
- In the shade to slow down their growth in hot weather

You may want to build flat covers to protect seedlings from birds and mice. An easy way to do this is to build a flat similar to the ones the seedlings will be in, but *without* the wooden bottom. We use ½-inch galvanized wire fabric on the "bottom." Then we turn the unit upside down and place it on top of the flat to protect the seeds and seedlings.

## Flat Soil

You are now ready to prepare the soil in which to grow seedlings. *A good simple flat soil mix is 1 part sifted compost and 1 part bed soil* (saved from the first trench when you double-dug) by volume. "Old" flat soil, which has been used to raise seedlings, can be stored in a bin. Although some of the nutrients will have been depleted, it will still be rich in nutrients and organic matter, so it can be used to make a new flat mix. In this case, the recipe would be 1 part old flat soil, 1 part sifted compost, and 1 part bed soil. Compost for the flat soil mix should be passed through a sieve of ½-inch or ¼-inch wire fabric. As your bed soil and your compost improve, your flat soil and seedlings also will improve.

*Remember to completely fill your flat with soil, or even mound it slightly above the edge of the flat, so the seedlings will have as much depth as possible to grow in.* If available, line the bottom

A seedling flat.

**Notes**

- Greenhouses are usually double glazed for maximum protection and are unheated or heated.
- Cold frames are single or double glazed; are open to the outside air, at least in part by being opened a little during the day; and are closed at night.

Half-sized flats are easier to carry. This shallow flat, with evenly moist flat soil and plants, weighs about 22½ pounds.

A half-sized deep flat (6 inches deep) ensures a manageable weight. This flat, with evenly moist flat soil and plants, weighs about 45 pounds. **Note:** All measurements given are internal dimensions.

Turf loam compost pile.

of the flat with a ⅛-inch layer of oak leaf mold (partially decayed oak leaves) for drainage and additional nutrients. You may place crushed eggshells above the oak leaf mold for calcium-loving plants such as carnations and members of the cabbage family. Lightly sprinkle the eggshells to cover ¼ of the total surface area.

Alan Chadwick's *classic* planting mixture for starting seeds in flats is 1 part each *by weight:* evenly moist compost (sifted, if possible), sharp (gritty) sand, and turf loam. These 3 ingredients provide a fertile, loose-textured mixture. Turf loam is made by composting sections of turf grass grown in good soil. The sections of grass are composted by alternating grass sides together and soil sides together within the pile (see the illustration, opposite). Good garden soil, from the first trench of a double-dug bed, for example, can be substituted for turf loam. Thoroughly mix the compost, sand, and garden soil or turf loam and, optionally, place them in the flat on top of oak leaf mold.

## Some Causes of Poor Germination

When seeds fail to germinate or plants hardly grow at all after germination, some common causes are:

Loose soil with good nutrients enables roots to penetrate the soil easily, and a steady stream of nutrient flows into the stem and leaves.

- Using redwood compost. This compost is widely available as a mulch or soil conditioner but contains growth inhibitors that can keep seeds from germinating or plants from growing well. (This is how redwood trees reduce competition.)
- Planting too early or too late in the season. Seeds and seedlings wait for the right temperature and length of day to start and continue growth.
- Using weed killers or soil sterilizers. Many weed killers are short-lived, but they can limit growth in a garden long after they are supposed to degrade. Some people use them to minimize or eliminate yard care, but they can continue to have an effect for 2 years. There is never any reason to use these poisons in your yard. Also, dumping used motor oil can destroy valuable growing areas. Take it to a service station for recycling.
- Using old seeds. Check your source.
- Planting in soil that is too wet. Wet soil restricts oxygen, which is required for root growth. Plants can die in fertile soils when soil oxygen is too low to sustain growth.

## Pricking Out

The GROW BIOINTENSIVE method continually seeks to foster uninterrupted plant growth. Part of this technique is embodied in the "Breakfast-Lunch-Dinner!" concept that Alan Chadwick stressed. If seedlings are raised in very good soil—with good nutrients and a good structure—only to be transplanted into an area that has few nutrients and a poor structure, the plants will suffer root shock. Results are better when seedlings are pricked out from a flat with a good planting mixture "breakfast" into a second flat with a "lunch" consisting of fresh flat soil. The plant will forget the trauma of being pricked out when it tastes the delectable new lunch treats in the second flat. This process minimizes shock and even fosters growth. Finally, a splendid GROW BIOINTENSIVE "dinner" greets the plant in the growing bed! With this kind care and stimulated healthy plant growth, there is less likelihood of insect and disease damage. In the GROW BIOINTENSIVE method, pricking out and transplanting can stimulate growth rather than slowing it down.

Seedlings from broadcasted seed are ready to be pricked out after their *cotyledons* (the first "seed leaves" that appear, although they are not true leaves) have appeared and before their roots are too long to handle easily. You should do the second pricking out (if it is called for) when the seedlings' leaves have just begun to touch each other.

To prick out seedlings, fill a 3-inch- or 6-inch-deep flat with flat soil, and mound the soil slightly (remember to fill in the corners). Use a widger or kitchen knife to loosen the soil under the seedlings so you can lift out 1 seedling at a time, holding it by its cotyledons and keeping as much soil on the roots as possible.

Place the widger or kitchen knife into the soil of a second flat at a slight backward angle, just behind where the seedling should be, and pull the widger toward you to open a hole.

Let the seedling drop into the hole, placing it a little deeper than it was in the first flat. For many crops, lettuce and the cabbage family in particular, it is optimal for the seedling to be deep enough so that its cotyledons are right at the level of the soil. Be sure not to bury the growing point.

Lift out the widger and let the soil fall around the seedling. It is often not necessary to spend time carefully pushing the soil up around the seedling; when you water the flat, the soil will settle in around the stem and roots. If soil does need to be added to the hole into which the seedling is placed, just gently sweep the soil into the hole with a widger with 1 motion. Arrange the seedlings on offset, or hexagonal, centers to maximize the space in the flat and to optimize the mini-climate that will develop around the seedlings as they grow.

Lift the first seedling out of the first flat.

Open the planting space in the new flat with a widger while . . .

. . . placing the seedling in the hole.

Gently sweep the soil into the hole.

Evenly spaced pricked-out seedlings.

Unpot a seedling correctly.

**Note**

Seedlings are transplanted when they are 2 to 3 inches high except for those marked "LG" in columns L4 and M4 of the Master Charts on pages 86–125. The LG seedlings are transplanted when they are 6 to 9 inches high.

Spread root-bound plant roots out before transplanting them into a bed.

For best bulb formation, do not plant onions too deeply; instead, plant as shown here.

# Transplanting

A Biodynamic gardener once had a row of broccoli plants. Only 2 plants had aphids, but both were quite infested. The 2 plants were dug up, and the gardener discovered that the plants had experienced root damage during transplanting. The healthy broccoli, which had experienced uninterrupted growth, were untouched by the insects, while nature eliminated the unhealthy plants.[1]

When transplanting, it is important to handle the seedlings gently and to touch them as little as possible. Plants do not like their bodies to be handled, though they do like to have human companionship and to have dead leaves removed from their stems. You should hold them only by the tips of their leaves (if the plant must be touched) or by the soil around their roots. If you have grown the seedlings in a flat, use a hand fork to gently separate a 4-inch-square section of soil and plants from the rest. Using the fork, gently lift that section from the flat and place it on the ground. Then carefully pull away 1 plant at a time from the section for transplanting. If it is particularly dry, hot, or windy, place the section on a wet towel. Always keep as much soil around the roots as possible when transplanting. If the seedling has been grown in a pot, turn the pot upside down, letting the plant stem pass between your second and third fingers, and tap firmly on the bottom of the pot with your other hand. Or tap the lip of the pot on something solid.

In all cases, if the plants are root-bound (the roots being so tightly grown together from having been kept in a starting flat or pot so long that with the soil they constitute a tight mass), gently spread the roots out in all directions. This process is important because the plant should not spend critical growth energy sending out a new, wide-ranging root system for eating and drinking when a good root system has already been produced. Instead, the plant's energy will go into the natural flow of continuous growth.

Be sure to place the seedling into a large enough hole so that the plant can be buried up to its first set of true leaves. Water the seedlings after transplanting to help settle the soil around the roots, to eliminate excess air spaces, and to provide an adequate amount of water for growth. As the soil is packed down under the pressure of watering, the final soil level will remain high enough to cover the upper roots. The plant's roots need firm contact with the soil to properly absorb water and nutrients. Press the soil firmly around the seedling, if necessary, but not too tightly. Tight packing will damage the roots and will not allow the proper penetration of water, nutrients, and air. Soil that is too loose will allow air and moisture to concentrate around the roots. This will cause root burn and decay.

1. John and Helen Philbrick, *Gardening for Health and Nutrition* (New York: Rudolph Steiner Publications, 1971), p. 93.

Transplanting seedlings up to their first true leaves prevents them from becoming top-heavy and bending over during their early growth period. (This is especially true for members of the cabbage family.) If a plant bends over, it will upright itself, but will develop a very "tough neck" that will reduce the quality and size of the plant and crop. Onions and garlic, however, do better if the bulb does not have much soil weight to push up against.

Optimally, transplanting should be done in the early evening so the seedlings get settled into their new home during more moderate weather conditions. If transplanting is performed during the day, some temporary shading may be needed. In our hot summer weather, we shade newly transplanted seedlings with 30% shade-netting or Reemay, a "row cover" cloth, for several days to minimize transplanting shock and wilt.

Transplanting is preferable to directly sowing seeds. More importantly, transplanting improves plant health. Beds become compacted as they are watered and the soil will not be as loose for a seed that is planted directly in the bed. Some compaction will have occurred by the time the seed is a "child" a month later and, in some cases, so much so after 2 months, when it is likely to be an "adolescent," that its "adulthood" may be seriously affected. If, instead, you transplant the 1-month-old "child" into the growing bed, a strong adult root system can develop during the next 2 months, and a good adult life is likely. In fact, a study at the University of California at Berkeley in the 1950s indicated that a 2% to 4% increase in root health can increase yields 2 to 4 times.[2]

## Spotting

Some newly transplanted seedlings may die for various reasons or be eaten by animals or insects. Therefore, we usually save the surplus seedlings left in the flats after transplanting. We use these seedlings during the next 10 days to fill in the holes or "spots" in the mini-climate. This process has been named "spotting."

Most vegetables should be transplanted up to their first 2 true leaves.

proper

improper

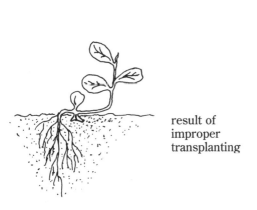

result of improper transplanting

**Tip**
When the stems of cucumbers, melons, squash, pumpkin, and gourds grow into the path, turn the stems back into the bed's growing area to keep walkways clear. The stems prefer the more humid miniclimate in the growing area and will stay there.

2. Charles Morrow Wilson, *Roots: Miracles Below—The Web of Life Beneath Our Feet* (Garden City, NY: Doubleday, 1968), p. 105.

## Planting by the Phases of the Moon

One of the most controversial aspects of the GROW BIOINTENSIVE method is Alan Chadwick's method of planting seeds and transplanting seedlings according to the phases of the moon. *Short-germinating and extra-long-germinating seeds (which take approximately 1 month to germinate)* are planted *2 days before the new moon,* when significant magnetic forces occur, and up to 7 days after the new moon. *Long-germinating seeds* are planted *at the full moon* and up to 7 days afterward. Seedlings are *transplanted* at the *opposite* time (see chart below). Both planting periods take advantage of the full sum of the forces of nature—which are greatest at the new moon—including gravity, light, and magnetism. The lunar gravitational pull that produces high tides in the oceans and water tides in the soil is very high at the new moon. And the moon, which is dark, gets progressively lighter. (See the drawings.) The exact day on which you plant or transplant is not as important as generally taking advantage of the impetus provided by nature.

If you place *short-germinating* seeds in the ground 2 days before the lunar tide forces are greatest, the seed has time to absorb water. The force exerted on the water in the seed helps create a "tide" that helps burst the seed coat in conjunction with the forces produced by the seed's swelling. No doubt you have wondered why one time beet seeds come up almost immediately and another time the germination process takes 2 weeks in the same bed under similar conditions. Temperature and moisture differences, pH changes, and humus levels may influence the seeds in each case, but the next time you note a marked difference in germination time, check your calendar to determine the phase the moon was in when you sowed the seeds. You

KEY

● New Moon

◐ First Quarter

○ Full Moon

◐ Last Quarter

+ = Increasing

– = Decreasing

## PLANTING BY THE PHASES OF THE MOON

*2 days before new moon*     *New moon*          *First 7 days*                    *Second 7 days*

Plant short- and extra-long-germinating seeds (most vegetables and herbs) in flats and/or beds and transplant seedlings germinated from long-germinating seeds.

Balanced increase in rate of root and leaf growth.

Moonlight +
Lunar gravity –

Increased leaf growth rate.

Moonlight +
Lunar gravity +

may find the moon had an influence. *Extra-long-germinating* seeds are also planted at the new moon. They then germinate about a month later.

Looking at the drawing of the moon's phases, you can see that there are both increasing and decreasing lunar gravitational and light force influences that recur periodically during the lunar month. Sometimes the forces work against each other, and sometimes they reinforce one another. When the lunar gravitational pull decreases and the amount of moonlight increases during *the first 7 days of the lunar cycle,* plants undergo a period of balanced growth. The decreasing lunar gravity (and the corresponding relative increase in Earth's gravity) *stimulates root growth.* At the same time, the increasing amount of moonlight stimulates leaf growth.

During *the second 7 days of the lunar cycle,* the lunar gravitational force reverses its relative direction, and it increases. This pull *slows down the root growth* as Earth's relative gravitational pull is lessened. The moonlight, on the other hand, continues to a peak, and *leaf growth is especially stimulated.* If root growth has been sufficient during previous periods, then the proper amounts of nutrients and water will be conveyed to the above-ground part of the plant, and balanced, uninterrupted growth will occur. This time of increasing gravitational, moonlight, and magnetic forces gives seeds that have not yet germinated a special boost. Seeds that did not germinate at the time of the new moon should do so by the full moon. Alan Chadwick said that it is during this period that seeds cannot resist coming up, and mushrooms suddenly appear overnight.

During *the third 7 days of the lunar cycle,* the amount of moonlight decreases along with the lunar gravitational pull. As

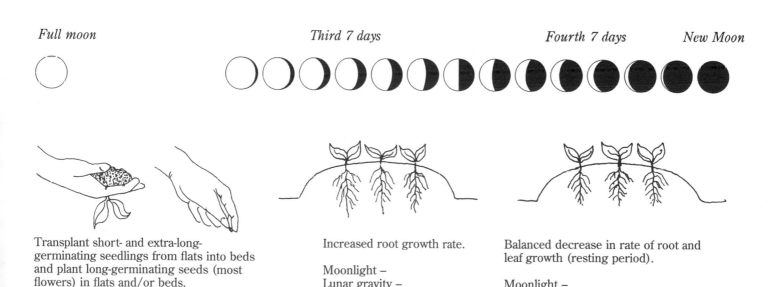

Full moon    Third 7 days    Fourth 7 days    New Moon

Transplant short- and extra-long-germinating seedlings from flats into beds and plant long-germinating seeds (most flowers) in flats and/or beds.

Increased root growth rate.

Moonlight –
Lunar gravity –

Balanced decrease in rate of root and leaf growth (resting period).

Moonlight –
Lunar gravity +

the moonlight decreases, aboveground *leaf growth slows down.* The *root growth is stimulated again,* however, as the lunar gravitational pull decreases. This is a good time to transplant, since root growth is active. This activity enables the plant to better overcome transplant shock and promotes the development of a good root system while leaf growth is slowed down. Then, 21 days later, when leaf growth is at a maximum, the plant will have a developed root system that can provide it with sufficient nutrients and water. This is also the time to plant *long-germinating* seeds that take approximately 2 weeks to germinate; they will then be ready to take advantage of the boost from the high gravitational pull of the new moon.

During *the last 7 days of the lunar cycle,* the lunar gravitational force increases, and *root growth slows down.* The amount of moonlight decreases and also *slows down leaf growth.* This period is one of a balanced decrease in growth, just as the first 7 days in the lunar month is a period of balanced increase in growth. The last 7 days, then, is a rest period that comes before the bursting forth of a period of new life. Short-, long-, and extra-long-germinating seed crops are listed in the Master Charts in chapter 6.

A planted seed bursts its seed coat around the 28th day of the lunar month and proceeds into a period of slow, balanced, and increasing growth above and below ground, passes into a period

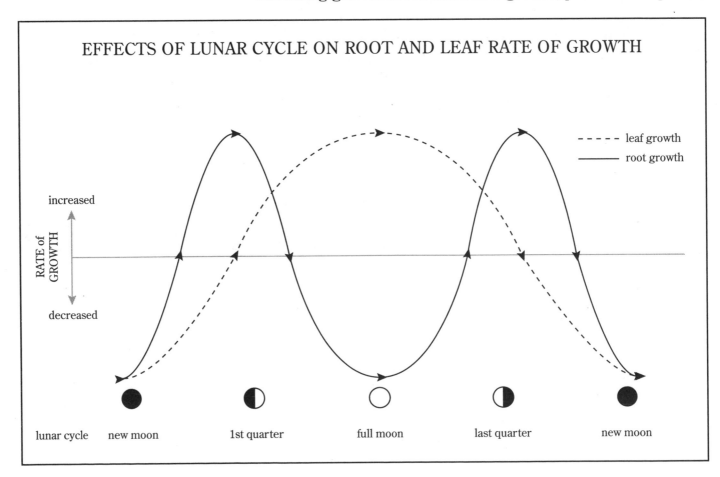

EFFECTS OF LUNAR CYCLE ON ROOT AND LEAF RATE OF GROWTH

of stimulated leaf growth, then goes into a period of stimulated root growth (getting ready for the next period of stimulated leaf growth), followed by a time of rest. This plant growth cycle repeats itself monthly. Plants germinated from short- and extra-long-germinating seeds are transplanted at the full moon so they may begin their life in the growing bed during a time of stimulated root growth to compensate for the root shock that occurs during transplanting. (It is also vital that the plant's root system be well developed so it can later provide the leaves, flowers, vegetables, fruits, and seeds with water and nutrients.) The transplanted plant then enters a time of rest before beginning another monthly cycle. The workings of nature are beautiful.

Planting by the phases of the moon is a gardening nuance that improves the health and quality of plants. If you do not follow the moon cycles, your plants will still grow satisfactorily. However, as your soil improves and as you gain experience, each gardening detail will become more important and will have a greater effect. Try this one and see.

English Haws watering can.

## Watering

When beds and flats are watered, the GROW BIOINTENSIVE method approximates rainfall as much as possible. The fine rain of water absorbs beneficial airborne nutrients as well as air, helping the growth process. For seeds and seedlings in flats, you can use a special English Haws watering can, which has fine holes in the sprinkler's "rose."[3] The rose points up so that when you water, the pressure built up in the rose first goes up into the air, where much of the pressure is dissipated as it flows through the air. The water then softly falls on the plants from above like rain, with only the force of gravity pulling the water down. When watering growing beds, you may employ the same method of spraying water into the air and letting it fall back down, using a water gun or a valve unit with a fan spray nozzle attached.[4] (If you use a water gun or a valve unit, you may need a heavy duty hose to contain the water pressure.) This gentle method of watering packs down the soil in the bed less, and the plants are not hit and damaged by a hard water spray. If you choose to point the fan downward, stand as far away from the plants as possible and/or keep the water pressure adjusted to a low point to minimize soil compaction and water damage.

Some plants, such as those in the cabbage family, like wet leaves. It is all right, and in fact beneficial, to water these plants from overhead. Other plants, such as tomatoes, peas, and members of the squash and melon families, can suffer from wilt and mildew, and their fruit may rot when their leaves are wet,

Special upward-pointing Haws watering rose.

Ross watering fan attached to a valve unit.

Ross watering fan attached to a variable water pressure gun.

3. Available by mail order from many sources, including Walter F. Nicke, P.O. Box 433, Topsfield, MA 01983.

4. A Ross No. 20 is best.

A GROW BIOINTENSIVE bed.

Watering tomato plants using a wand.

especially in foggy or humid climates. Take care when watering these plants to water only the soil around them whenever possible. (In drier climates it probably will not matter.) To avoid spraying a plant's leaves, hold the fan just above the soil and point it sideways. A better method is to use a watering wand, which will allow you to more easily direct the water under the plant's leaves.

Water the beds sufficiently each day to keep them evenly moist. Daily watering washes the dust, grime, and insects from plant leaves and creates a deliciously moist atmosphere conducive to good plant growth and thriving microbial life. (Watering may be more or less frequent when the weather is warmer or cooler than normal.)

Water mature plants in beds when the heat of the day first subsides. This is about 2 hours before sunset during the summer and earlier during the winter. However, weather conditions, especially cloud cover, may necessitate earlier watering. The soil, warmed during the day, warms the cool water from the hose so it is more temperate by the time it reaches the plant roots. The roots suffer less shock, and the soil and plants have more time to absorb water during the cooler, less windy night. Also, plants do a significant amount of their growing at night, and this ensures they will have plenty of water to do so. If you water early in the morning, much of the water will be lost in evaporation caused by the sun and wind, and the watering will be less effective. The loss will be even greater if you water at midday. If you water in the evening, the plants will be more susceptible to mildew and rust problems due to unevaporated water left on their leaves. By watering in the late afternoon, the water can percolate into the soil for 12 hours or more before the sun and wind reappear in strength. When they do, the bed will have a good reservoir of water from which the plants can draw before their next watering.

Seeds and seedlings in flats and immature plants in the growing beds may have to be watered in the morning and at noon as well as late in the afternoon. Until the living mulch effect occurs, the flats and beds dry out more rapidly. When the leaves grow closer together, less watering will be required.

To determine how much water to give a bed each day, strive for a ½- to 15-second "shiny."[5] When you first begin to water, a *shiny layer* of excess water will appear on top of the soil. If you stop watering immediately, the shiny layer will disappear quickly. You should water until the shiny layer remains for ½ to 15 seconds after you have stopped watering. The actual time involved will differ depending on your soil's texture. The

5. A simple way to estimate the amount of water a bed is receiving is to first measure the gallons delivered per minute. Turn the hose on and point the spray into a 1-gallon jar or watering can. If, for example, it takes 15 seconds to fill the jar, then you know you are delivering 4 gallons per minute to the bed. Currently, in our moderately heavy clay, we find each 5 by 20-foot bed will take anywhere from 5 to 20 gallons daily (10 gallons on the average), depending on the weather, the type of plant, the size of the plants, and the tightness of the soil.

*Watering with a wand:*
Water falls in a circular pattern on the bed, landing approximately 3 feet from the waterer at its closest point.

*Watering with a fan:*
Water falls in an oval pattern on the bed, landing approximately 10 feet away from the waterer. When watering closer, reduce the water pressure.

more clayey the texture, the longer the time will be. A newly prepared bed with good texture and structure will probably have enough water when a 1/2- to 3-second shiny is reached. A newly prepared clayey bed may indicate that it has enough water with a 3- to 5-second shiny, since a clayey soil both retains more moisture and lets the water in less rapidly. A month-old bed (which has compacted somewhat due to the watering process) may require a 5- to 8-second shiny, and beds 2 to 3 months old may require more than that.

Eventually the watering process will become automatic, and you will not have to think about when the bed has received enough water; you will know intuitively when the point has been reached. (Remember to allow for the different natures of plants. Squash plants, for instance, will want a lot of water in comparison to tomato plants.) One way to determine whether you have watered enough is to go out the next morning and poke your finger into the bed. If the soil is evenly moist for the first 2 inches and continues to be moist below this level, you are

**Note**
It is important to realize that we are *watering the soil,* so that it may thrive as a *living sponge cake.* We are not watering the plants. The soil in turn then "waters" the plants. Keeping the soil alive will help retain water and minimize the water consumed.

shiny layer established      ½ second later      1 second later      2 seconds later

A newly prepared bed is properly watered when the *shiny layer* of excess water disappears within ½ to 3 seconds after the watering stops.

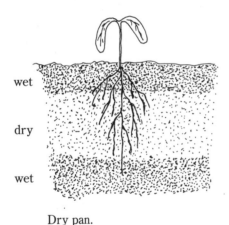

wet

dry

wet

Dry pan.

watering properly. If the soil is dry for part or all of the first 2 inches, you need more shiny. If the soil is soggy in part or all of the upper 2 inches, you need less shiny.

Remember also to adjust your watering according to the weather. A bed may lose more moisture on a cloudy, windy, *dry* day than on a hot, clear, *humid,* and still one. And there are times when the flats and beds need no water or need watering twice a day. It is important to note these differences and to become sensitive to the soil's needs. You should water for good fruit, flower, and seed production, not just so the plant will stay alive. Be sure to water the sides and ends of the growing beds more than the middle. These areas, which many people miss or underemphasize, are critical because they are subject to more evaporation than the middle of the bed. Newly dug but still unplanted beds should be watered daily so they will not lose their moisture content. A transplant in a bed that has a low moisture level (except in the recently watered upper 2 inches or so) will have difficulty growing well because of the dry pan below. If you wait until plants are wilting and drooping before you water them, they will revive but they will have suffered some permanent damage—an open invitation for pests and diseases. Slight drooping, however, is not usually a sign that you should water. Plants are just minimizing water loss (due to transpiration) when they droop on a hot day, and watering them at this time will increase water loss rather than lessen it. It will also weaken the plant through too much pampering.

## Shade Netting

After you have watered your newly planted bed, in hot weather you may want to consider covering this area with 30% shade netting from approximately 10 A.M. to 5 P.M. Use shade netting that is 1 to 3 feet wider and 3 feet longer than your growing bed, so the netting can drape down around the edges to provide shade on the sides as well as the top. We generally insert 3-foot-long pieces of 1 by 1-inch wood on a 45-degree angle into the soil at the 4 corners of the bed and every 5 feet along and perpendicular to the sides. Headless nails are hammered partway into the top end of the sticks so the shade netting can be held in place. At 5 P.M. we unhook the netting from the long eastern side of the bed and hook its edges over the nails on the other side several times to secure the netting and keep it out of the paths and the bed. We reverse this process at 10 A.M. the next day. Make sure the nails do not jut into the path where they can be a hazard to you.

We also use shade netting to protect newly transplanted grains from birds in the fall and winter. In this case, we leave the shade netting on for 10 days and use long pieces of ⅝-inch rebar to hold down the edges of the netting so birds cannot enter the growing area. We adjust the 1 by 1-inch sticks so the netting edges lie on the ground with the rebar along the edges. After 10 days, the shade netting is removed because at this point the plants are less tasty and, therefore, are not attractive to the birds.

## Mini-Greenhouses

A mini-greenhouse made from plastic sheeting and wood[6] can increase the temperature of the soil and the air surrounding plants and allow you to get an early start on the growing season in the spring and to lengthen the growing season in the autumn. Our design has double-walled construction, which can keep the inside temperature above the freezing point when the outside temperature falls as low as 20°F. This makes the unit a good season-extender for crops.

**Tip**

To conserve water, raise your seedlings in flats until transplanting size (usually for the first 2 to 4 weeks). For many crops, 1 flat, which needs only about ½ gallon of water each day, will plant a 100-square-foot growing area. When planted, this growing area will need about 10 to 20 gallons of water daily during the main growing season. The water savings in 1 month (compared with direct sowing of seeds in the growing area) is about 285 to 585 gallons of water!

SEED PROPOGATION

A mini-greenhouse.

6. For plans and instructions, see *Backyard Homestead, Mini-Farm and Garden Log Book* (Willits, CA: Ecology Action, 1993).

Sloped beds on flat ground (side view) can be used for water harvesting.

A Native American type of "bent bed" is used to capture rainfall effectively. This is a key water-harvesting technique.

**Note**

Twenty inches of rainfall over a 4-month growing season is an average of .167 inch per day.

One way to prepare a 5 by 20-foot "bent bed" for the concentration of rainwater in your growing area.

## KEY WATER FACTORS

The GROW BIOINTENSIVE method is especially important for areas with scarce water. Though much more experimentation is needed in this area, the information below should assist you.

- Seventy-five percent of the Earth's land surface where food is generally grown receives 10 inches of rainfall or more annually. About *one-half* of this rainfall can be retained in soil properly prepared for plant use. To grow a good yield, 20 inches of rain are needed annually. In an area receiving only 10 inches of rainfall, the rain a growing area receives can be increased to 20 inches in the "bent bed" examples illustrated on this page.

- The GROW BIOINTENSIVE method uses an average of 10 gallons (a 5- to 20-gallon range) per day per 100 square feet, while commercial food-raising consumes an average of 20 gallons per day for the same area. GROW BIOINTENSIVE has the potential to produce 4 times the food in the same area as commercial agricultural practices.

- Research by academic institutions has shown that soil that has organic matter as 2% of its volume in the upper 11 inches can *reduce* the rainfall or *irrigation* required for poor soils *by as much as 75%*. (Poor soils have about .5% organic matter in the upper soil area.) grow biointensive encourages maintaining more than 2% organic matter.

- Even under arid conditions, soil that is shaded can *reduce evaporation up to 63%*, depending on soil type. The *mini-climate* created by closely spaced plants provides good shading.

- *Plants transpire* water, which can be *reduced by as much as 75%* in soils that have sufficient and well-balanced nutrients in the soil water. The GROW BIOINTENSIVE method prepares the soil so it provides for a high level of fertility.

- If you combine the last 3 factors listed above, water consumption can sometimes be reduced to $\frac{1}{32}$ the level

(¼ x ½ x ¼) plants normally require. We have found that grow biointensive can reduce water consumption on average to ⅛ that of normal methods per pound of vegetable produced and to about ⅓ that of normal methods per pound of grain produced once the soil is in reasonable shape.

- Native people in some parts of Africa have been using a deeply prepared bed approach successfully with grains. They triple-dig(!) the soil, incorporating a lot of organic matter into it just before the seasonal rains. Immediately after the rains stop, they plant their seeds. No more rain falls, yet crops are harvested at the end of the season. Others in the area reportedly are unable to grow crops well during this season.

- GROW BIOINTENSIVE techniques should produce at least 4 times the yield under natural rainfall conditions (when not irri-gating) that would be obtained under the same conditions with commercial techniques. Let us know what works for you.

- Native Americans in the southwestern United States have used a number of approaches to grow food in limited rainfall areas. One method is to create large, diamond-shaped growing areas on a slight slope, with one point each being at the top and the bottom of the slope. Crops are planted in the bottom ¼ to ½ of each diamond—depending on the amount of rainfall. (More water per unit of soil area is concentrated in the bottom part of the diamond.)

  With this method, use the following information to determine how much of the diamond to plant: Well-prepared soil needs to retain approximately 10 inches of water per unit of area (623 gallons per 100 square feet) to grow 1 complete crop during a 4-month growing season. To retain this much water, the soil needs about 20 inches of rainfall (1,246 gallons per 100 square feet) per season. If only 10 inches fall, you would have only ½ the water needed, and you would plant only the bottom ½ of each diamond. If you had only 5 inches of rain, you would only have ¼ the water needed for a crop, and you would only plant the bottom ¼ of the diamond (more or less). Experimentation will be required before you have optimum success. Be careful not to overplant. A completely dry soil does not rewet or absorb water easily, which will lead to erosion. To be on the safe side, start with a small area and plant ¼ less crop than the above recom-mendations to ensure that the soil retains some moisture. Once you achieve success, you can increase the area under cultivation. Please share your experiences with us and others so this approach can be better understood.

- See John A. Widtsoe's *Dry Farming* for more information on dry farming.

## Weeding

Intensively planted raised beds do not require weeding as often as other types of gardens due to the living mulch that the plants create. Usually, our beds only need to be weeded once, about a month after the bed is planted. A bed prepared in a new area may have to be weeded more often at first, however, since many dormant seeds will be raised to a place in the soil where they can germinate readily. Over time, as the soil becomes richer and more alive, you will probably have fewer weeds, since they tend to thrive more in poor and deficient soils than in healthy ones.

There really is no such thing as a "weed." A weed is just a plant that is growing in an area where you, the gardener, do not want it to grow. In fact, many so-called weeds, such as stinging nettle, are quite beneficial to the soil and to other plants. (This will be discussed in more detail in chapter 8.) Instead of weeding indiscriminately, you should learn the natures and uses of the different weeds so you can identify and leave some of the most beneficial ones in the growing beds. Until they are removed, weeds help establish a more quickly nourishing mini-climate for your current crop. Add the weeds you pull to the compost pile. They are rich in trace minerals and other nutrients and will help grow good crops next season.

Weeds are generally hardier than cultivated plants since they are genetically closer to their parental plant stock and nearer to the origin of the plant species. They tend to germinate before broadcasted cultivated plants. You should usually wait to remove these plants from the beds until the cultured plants catch up with the weeds in height or until the cultured plants become established (about transplanting size)—whichever comes first. Weeding before this time is likely to disturb the germinating cultured plant seeds or disturb the developing new root systems, causing interrupted plant growth and weakened plants. However, be sure to remove any grass plants that develop in the beds after the first weeding. These plants put out incredibly large root systems that interfere with other plants in the competition for nutrients and water.

## Planting in Season

Vegetables, flowers, and herbs—all plants for that matter—should be planted in season. This is a good way to love your plants. If they are forced (grown out of season), much of their energy is used up straining to combat unseasonable weather in the form of cold, heat, rain, or drought. Less energy is left for balanced growth, and a plant with limited energy reserves—not unlike people—is more susceptible to disease and insect attacks. Also, for the best crop health and yields, be sure to keep your plants harvested! To determine the best time to plant various crops, see the information on pages 79–80.

Appropriate posture can make weeding easier.

# SATISFACTORY (AND OPTIMAL) PLANT-GROWING TEMPERATURE RANGES[7]

*Determine the Planting-Range Calendar for Your Area*

| Crop Season | Temperature Range | Optimal Temperature Range | Plant |
|---|---|---|---|
| *Cool-Season Crops[8]* | 30°F | | Asparagus • Rhubarb |
| | 40°–75°F | (60°–65°F) | Beet • Broad bean • Broccoli • Brussels sprouts • Cabbage • Chard • Collard • Horseradish • Kale • Kohlrabi • Parsnip • Radish • Rutabaga • Sorrel • Spinach • Turnip |
| | 45°–75°F | (60°–65°F) | Artichoke • Carrot • Cauliflower • Celeriac • Celery • Chinese cabbage • Endive • Florence fennel • Lettuce • Mustard • Parsley • Pea • Potato |
| | 45°–85°F | (55°–75°F) | Chicory • Chive • Garlic • Leek • Onion • Salsify • Shallot |
| *Warm-Season Crops* | 50°–80°F | (60°–70°F) | Bean • Lima bean |
| | 50°–95°F | (60°–75°F) | Corn • Cowpea • New Zealand spinach |
| | 50°–90°F | (65°–75°F) | Pumpkin • Squash |
| | 60°–90°F | (65°–75°F) | Cucumber • Muskmelon |
| *Hot-Season Crops* | 65°–85°F | (70°–75°F) | Sweet peppers • Tomato |
| | 65°–95°F | (70°–85°F) | Eggplant • Hot peppers • Okra • Sweet potato • Watermelon |

7. From James Edward Knott, *Handbook for Vegetable Growers* (New York: John Wiley & Sons, 1957), pp. 6–7.

8. Try these crops in shady areas in the summer. Remember, crops need *at least* 4 hours of direct sunlight to grow. Seven hours are preferred, and 11 hours are even better.

# SOIL TEMPERATURE CONDITIONS FOR VEGETABLE SEED GERMINATION[9]

| Crop | Minimum | Optimum Range | Optimum | Maximum |
|---|---|---|---|---|
| Asparagus | 50°F | 60°–85°F | 75°F | 95°F |
| Bean | 60°F | 60°–85°F | 80°F | 95°F |
| Bean, Lima | 60°F | 65°–85°F | 85°F | 85°F |
| Beet | 40°F | 50°–85°F | 85°F | 95°F |
| Cabbage | 40°F | 45°–95°F | 85°F | 100°F |
| Carrot | 40°F | 45°–85°F | 80°F | 95°F |
| Cauliflower | 40°F | 45°–85°F | 80°F | 100°F |
| Celery | 40°F | 60°–70°F | 70°F* | 85°F* |
| Chard, Swiss | 40°F | 50°–85°F | 85°F | 95°F |
| Corn | 50°F | 60°–95°F | 95°F | 105°F |
| Cucumber | 60°F | 60°–95°F | 95°F | 105°F |
| Eggplant | 60°F | 75°–90°F | 85°F | 95°F |
| Lettuce | 35°F | 40°–80°F | 75°F | 85°F |
| Muskmelon | 60°F | 75°–95°F | 90°F | 100°F |
| Okra | 60°F | 70°–95°F | 95°F | 105°F |
| Onion | 35°F | 50°–95°F | 75°F | 95°F |
| Parsley | 40°F | 50°–85°F | 75°F | 90°F |
| Parsnip | 35°F | 50°–70°F | 65°F | 85°F |
| Pea | 40°F | 40°–75°F | 75°F | 85°F |
| Pepper | 60°F | 65°–95°F | 85°F | 95°F |
| Pumpkin | 60°F | 70°–90°F | 95°F | 100°F |
| Radish | 40°F | 45°–90°F | 85°F | 95°F |
| Spinach | 35°F | 45°–75°F | 70°F | 85°F |
| Squash | 60°F | 70°–95°F | 95°F | 100°F |
| Tomato | 50°F | 60°–85°F | 85°F | 95°F |
| Turnip | 40°F | 60°–105°F | 85°F | 105°F |
| Watermelon | 60°F | 70°–95°F | 95°F | 105°F |

*Daily fluctuation to 60°F or lower at night is essential.

9. From James Edward Knott, *Handbook for Vegetable Growers* (New York: John Wiley & Sons, 1957), p. 8.

# MASTER CHARTS AND PLANNING

**CHAPTER SIX**

**GOAL:** *Maximize the effectiveness of time and space in the smallest-scale growing area.*

The Master Charts that follow should help your gardening efforts. The charts for grains, compost crops, trees, and other crops provide a picture of what you can accomplish in your own backyard or small farm-holding. (Also see Ecology Action's *Backyard Homestead, Mini-Farm and Garden Log Book.*) Additional information about special seed sources and harvesting, cleaning, grinding, storing, and preserving these crops will be included in the future. The charts are largely based on our many years of experience and are generally complete and accurate.

Ecology Action continues to study the spacings and other growing information for grains, fodder crops, fibers, bush and dwarf fruit trees, other tree crops, berries and grapes, and compost crops. As testing continues, the information is revised and the chance of error reduced. (A good explanation of the information in these charts is given in the planning section of *The Sustainable Vegetable Garden.*)

It should be noted that:

- You may not reach maximum yields in the first year. Also, 1 plant grown alone will probably not produce as large a yield as 1 plant grown among several plants under mini-climate conditions.[1]

- Seeds grown out of season will take longer to germinate and/or may decompose before they do germinate unless grown under special mini-greenhouse or shade netting conditions.

- Closer spacing may be needed during the winter to make up for slower plant growth during this period and to

**Note**

Microbial life-forms thrive and greatly increase in activity when the nighttime air temperature reaches a minimum of 60°F. The next time you go out in the morning early in the season and notice that your garden has grown a foot overnight and is a darker, lush green, check the previous night's temperature. You may be surprised!

**Other Key Air Temperatures**

| | |
|---|---|
| 32°F: | Nitrogen release begins in the soil. |
| 50°F: | Significant nitrogen release occurs in the soil. |
| 86°–95°F: | The maximum nitrogen release point is reached in the soil. |
| 90°F: | The pollination process begins to decrease. |
| 95°–104°F: | A significant decrease in nitrogen release occurs in the soil. |
| 131°F: | Nitrogen release stops in the soil |

---

1. For more information on the potential yield figures in column E of the Master Charts and how they were and are determined, see Ecology Action's "Yields" information. Available for $1.00 plus a self-addressed long envelope with 2 first-class stamps to: Ecology Action, 5798 Ridgewood Rd., Willits, CA 95490.

create a balanced winter mini-climate. (Try ¾ or ½ the usual spacing with lettuce in the winter.) Closer spacing can also promote faster, balanced growth by more rapidly creating a mini-climate. Thin extra plants to make room for larger plants. (Baby carrots and beets are a delicacy.)

- You may need wider spacings in the humid tropics during the wetter months.

One of the exciting things about the GROW BIOINTENSIVE method is its emphasis on the soil. Once you know how to prepare soil well for vegetables, a whole world of crops becomes available to you. The bed preparation, fertilization, and watering approaches remain essentially the same—only the plant spacings are different!

These charts will help you expand from growing only vegetable crops to including plants from the following broad groups:

- Grains, protein sources, and vegetable oil crops.
- Compost, organic matter, and fodder crops. Some compost crops, such as pearl millet, sorghum, and corn, can produce very high yields of biomass and should be fully recycled through composting whenever possible to minimize the potential for soil depletion.
- Energy, fiber, paper, and miscellaneous crops.
- Tree and cane food crops.

Eventually, we hope to add tree crops for fuel and building materials. If you seek more information than is contained in these detailed charts, refer to the books listed in the bibliography.

There is a convenient soil improvement succession that is good to know. Vegetables from one year improve soil for grains the next year, and this leads to soil that supports more permanent tree crops the third year. If you want to study this process more closely, see Ecology Action's *Backyard Homestead, Mini-Farm and Garden Logbook* (crop-testing chapter) for vegetable, grain, fodder, and tree crops, and read our *One Crop Test Booklet: Soybeans* (booklet 2).

The importance of the soil is especially apparent with a permanent crop-growing system. Even biological and tree cultivation systems can be environmentally unsound if improperly used. Dr. Hans Jenny, soil scientist emeritus at the University of California, Berkeley, pointed to this in *Science* magazine:

> At the turn of the century, farsighted agricultural experiment stations set up permanent cultivation plots and monitored for decades the nitrogen and carbon balances. Stirring soil and removing crops initiated profound declines in nitrogen, carbon, and humus substances and caused deterioration of soil structure. Under these circumstances water infiltration is reduced and runoff and sheet erosion are encouraged. Crop yields suffer. While applications of nitrogen fertilizers boost yields,

they have not restored the soil body. In central Europe, farmers used to remove forest litter and put it on their fields for manuring. Tree production declined markedly, documented by Aaltonen.[2] . . .

I am arguing against indiscriminate conversion of biomass and organic wastes to fuels. The humus capital, which is substantial, deserves being maintained because good soils are a national asset. The question will be raised, How much organic matter should be assigned to the soil? No general formula can be given. Soils vary widely in character and quality.

Growing crops must be approached, then, with a sensitivity to how *the way* they are being grown affects the sustainability of the soil's vitality and health. Understanding this proper relationship will take time and eventually will involve growing many different crops, including a large number of trees. Trees beneficially modify our climate, bring up and make available nutrients from deep down in the soil, protect the soil from erosion, help maintain healthy water tables, and provide us with food and building materials.

Food value columns have been added to the Master Charts for protein, calories, and calcium for each crop. These are important, but so are many other food values—including iron, vitamins, and amino acids. See the reference books listed in the bibliography if you want to pursue this further. Be sure to explore growing compost crops in between your trees to increase the soil's friability and its nitrogen and organic matter content. Try medium red clover. It has beautiful red flowers.

Increasingly, more people want to grow food. One hundred square feet of grain may yield 4, 8, 12, or more pounds of edible seed. If you are in a cooler climate and wish to grow beans for eating, try varieties such as the peanut, yellow-eye, and cranberry beans available from the Vermont Bean Seed Company. Dwarf fruit trees, if nurtured properly, can yield 50 to 100 pounds of fruit annually at maturity. Two trees on 8-foot centers in 100 square feet can have a combined yield of up to 200 pounds, and the average person in the United States eats only about 162 pounds of tree fruit per year. Fava beans may yield the greatest amount of organic matter. Alfalfa and clover are also fun to raise as nitrogen-fixing legumes to improve your soil's fertility.

Our goal with wheat is to eventually get 2 26-pound crops in an 8-month period. This would yield 1 1-pound loaf of bread for every week in the year from only 100 square feet! Then we could literally raise our own bread in our backyards. Sound impossible? Yields close to this are already occurring in some parts of the world. Our highest wheat yield to date is at the rate of about 21 pounds per 100-square-foot bed, using about 10 inches of water for the whole season, with compost we grew ourselves for fertilizer and a small amount of purchased organic fertilizer. The Zulus in South Africa use a technique similar to

**Note**

GROW BIOINTENSIVE techniques can be used to grow important protein crops. Experiments with wheat, soybeans, grains, beans, and other seeds have worked well. For information on how to grow your own open-pollinated seeds in the smallest area while preserving genetic diversity, see Ecology Action's Self-Teaching Mini-Series Booklet 13, *Growing to Seed.*

**Note**

Wheat can be threshed easily with a mini-thresher[3] made available by a public organization in your area.

2. V. T. Aaltonen, *Boden und Wald* (Berlin: Parey, 1948).
3. One good foot-treadle-powered mini-thresher is available from CeCe Co., P.O. Box 8, Ibaraki City, Osaka, Japan, or from Christy Hunt Agricultural, Ltd., Foxhills Industrial Estate, Scunthorpe, South Humberside, DN15 8QW, United Kingdom.

the GROW BIOINTENSIVE method and grow grains with natural rainfall. See what you can do! Let us know if you get to 26 pounds—and tell us how you do it!

When planning your garden, remember to look closely at *all* the factors involved. For example, sesame seeds are very high in nutrition, but they usually have low yields (compared with other protein crops), are somewhat difficult to harvest, and exhaust the soil. So on a per-square-foot, sustainable-nutrition yield basis, sesame seeds are not particularly superior to other protein sources, even though they are great nutritionally and good to eat. A large harvest of sesame seeds would also require a very large growing area. It is important to examine each crop's total *practicality*.

When you begin to produce intermediate yields, another factor to consider is the quantity of nutrients each crop takes from the soil. Many legumes, which fix nitrogen in the soil, can exhaust the soil of other nutrients over time. Soybeans are such plants, and continuous cropping of them has been demonstrated to wear out the soil. It is important to develop and work within natural sustainable cycles.

# LETTER CODES

A — Approximate germination rate as sold by seed companies. No known minimum legal germination rate. Can be higher or lower.

AA — Each "seed" contains about 3 seeds, of which half germinate.

AC — Harvest alfalfa and clover 2 to 4 inches above the growing crown (sheep shears work well for this), loosen the soil with a border fork, water the bed, and cover the growing area with shade netting cloth for 1 to 2 weeks.

B — In beds.

BB — Soak seeds overnight for best germination.

BC — Broadcast.

C — Centers.

c — Cups.

CA — Cantaloupe.

D — Do not know yet.

E — Spacing increases with warmth of climate.

EL — Extra-long-germinating seed (22 to 28 days).

F — In flats.

FA — Fall.

G — "Seed" is a seed packet of 2 to 6 seeds, of which approximately 1.62 germinate.

H — Honeydew.

I — Transplant into a 1- to 5-gallon container as appropriate. Raise sapling until 1 year old. Then transplant into soil.

J — Germination average in a laboratory.

K — Straw weight is generally 1 to 3+ times harvested and cleaned seed weight for GROW BIOINTEN-SIVEly grown grains, 1 to 2 times for grains grown with commercial agriculture (Roger Revelle, "The Resources Available for Agriculture," *Scientific American*, September 1976).

L — Long-germinating seed (8 to 21 days).

LG — Transplant seedling when larger—about 6 to 9 inches tall.

M — Cook to minimize oxalic acid, which ties up calcium.

N — Narrow bed (2 feet wide) will produce better yields due to improved pollination.

P — Perennial.

Q — Celery is pricked out into a third flat, 6 inches deep, on 2-inch centers, where it grows for a further 4 to 6 weeks until it is ready to be transplanted. The seedlings may be 4 inches tall. Overall, it takes 3 to 4 months from sowing until transplanting.

qt — Quarts.

R — Replant at points where germination fails. We call this "spotting."

S — Short-germinating seed (1 to 7 days).

SN — During hot weather, cover with shade netting cloth between approximately 10 A.M. and 5 P.M. for better results.

SP — Spring.

SU — Summer.

T — Tablespoon.

t — Teaspoon.

TO — 18 inches for cherry tomatoes; 21 inches for regular tomatoes; 24 inches for large tomatoes. Sequential information in columns D, H, and I should be used according to spacing chosen.

U — A 1-pound loaf of bread requires ⅔ pound flour (2½ cups).

V — Approximate minimum.

W — 12 or 15 inches for midget varieties; 18 inches for 5- to 7-pound varieties; 21 inches for 10- to 15-pound varieties; 24 inches for largest varieties.

WI — Winter.

Y — Estimate.

Z — Based on Ecology Action experience, half of the garlic cloves are large enough to use, on the average.

* — Digestible protein for animals.

** — Depending on variety selected.

— — Not applicable.

# — First set of figures: summer sowing in a shade netting house for fall set out or winter sowing in areas with a less cold winter and in a greenhouse for spring set out. (A shade netting house is an area generally covered with 30% shade netting to provide a cooler, more humid area for the protected raising of fall seedlings during hot weather.)

Second set of figures: winter sowing in a good greenhouse or a miniature greenhouse in areas with very cold winters for spring set out.

Harden off for 2 days outside in flat before transplanting into bed.

## — If direct sowing on centers, rather than broadcasting, plant 2 seeds per center to compensate for low germination rate.

+ — Yield may be significantly higher.

++ — Given harvest time in column O.

| PLANT A | SEED | | | YIELD | | |
|---|---|---|---|---|---|---|
| | B — Approx. No. Seeds per Ounce [4] (range: larger–smaller seed) | C — Minimum Legal Germination Rate [5] | D — Ounces / Volume Seed per 100 Square Feet (adj. for germ. rate, offset spacing, and curv. surf.) [6,7,8] | E — Possible GROW BIOINTENSIVE Yield in Pounds per 100-Square-Foot Planting [9] | F — Possible GROW BIOINTENSIVE Yield in Pounds per Plant [10,11] | G — Average U.S. Yield in Pounds per 100 Square Feet [12,13] |
| 1 Artichoke, Jerusalem | Sprouted 2 oz tuber pieces | — | 10.5 lbs / — | Tubers: 100 / 206 / 460+ Biomass, air-dry: ~7.5 / ~15 / ~30 | Tubers: 1.20–5.50+ | D |
| 2 Artichoke, Regular | From divided roots or seeds | Seeds: .70[A] | 3 roots / — | D | D | 7.2 |
| 3 Asparagus | 875–1,250 | .70 | .32 / 1 t or 159 roots | 9.5 / 19 / 38 | .06–.24 | 7.3 |
| 4 Basil | 12,000 | .60 | .09 / 1 t | 35 / 75 / 150 | .06–.24 | D |
| 5 Beans, Lima, Bush | Baby: 75–94 Regular: 25–38 | .70 | Regular: 35.5–23.3 / 6 3/16–3 3/4 c | Dry: 11.5 / 17.2 / 23 | .02–.04 | 5.9 |
| 6 Beans, Lima, Pole[N] | Baby: 35–90 Regular: 25–38 | .70 | Regular: 18.3–12 / 3 3/16–2 c | Dry: 23+ / 34.4+ / 46+ | .07+–.14+ | 11.8+ |
| 7 Beans, Snap, Bush | 100–125 | .70 | 8.8–7.0 / 1 1/2–1 1/8 c | 30 / 72 / 108 | .05–.17 | 17.6 |
| 8 Beans, Snap, Pole[N] | 100–125 | .70 | 8.8–7.0 / 1 1/2–1 1/8 c | 30+ / 72+ / 108+ | .05+–.17+ | 17.6+ |
| 9 Beets, Cylindra | 1,500–1,625 | .65[G] | 1.4–1.3 / 6 T[AA] | Roots: 110 / 220 / 540 Greens: 55 / 110 / 270 | .08–.40 .04–.20 | "68.0" D |
| 10 Beets, Regular | 1,500–1,625 | .65[G] | 1.4–1.3 / 6 T[AA] | Roots: 55 / 110 / 270 Greens: 55 / 110 / 270 | .04–.20 .04–.20 | "34.0" D |
| 11 Broccoli | 9,000 | .75 | .01 / 1/24 t | Heads: 26 / 39 / 53 Leaves: 52+ / 78+ / 106+ | .31–.63 .62–1.26 | 33.9 D |
| 12 Brussels Sprouts | 9,000 | .70 | .01 / 1/24 t | 71 / 106 / 142 | 1.34–2.68 | "36.7" |
| 13 Burdock | 1,700 | .60 | 1.3 / 4 T | 75 / 150 / 300 | .06–.22 | D |
| 14 Cabbage, Chinese | 9,000 | .75 | .03 / 1/8 t | 96 / 191 / 383 | .48–1.91 | "69.4" |
| 15 Cabbage, Regular | 9,000 | .75 | .023 / .012 / .007 / 1/24 t | 96 / 191 / 383 | .60–7.22 | "69.4" |
| 16 Carrots | 18,750–25,000 | .55 | .2 / 1 1/4 t[BB] | Roots: 100 / 150 / 400+ | .04–.16 | Fresh: 72.5/ Processing: 97.2 |
| 17 Cauliflower | 9,000 | .75 | .01 / 1/24 t | 44 / 100 / 291 | .52–3.46 | 38.5 |
| 18 Celery | 72,000 | .55 | .016 / 1/4 t | 240 / 480 / 959+ | .39–1.54 | 160.7 |
| 19 Chard, Swiss | 1,500 | .65[G] | .4 / 2 T[AA] | 200 / 405 / 810 | .62–2.53 | D |
| 20 Collards, Annual & Perennial | 9,000 | .80 | .022 / 1/8 t | 96 / 191 / 383 | .60–2.41 | D |

| | | | | BEADS/FLATS | | | | | | | | MATURITY | | FOOD NEEDED | SEED YIELD |
|---|---|---|---|---|---|---|---|---|---|---|---|---|---|---|---|
| **H** | **I** | **J** | **K** | **L1** | **L2** | **L3** | **L4** | **M1** | **M2** | **M3** | **M4** | **N** | **O** | **P** | **Q** |
| | | | | FIRST FLAT—3 INCHES DEEP | | | | SECOND FLAT | | | | | | | |
| In-Bed Spacing (inches) | MAXIMUM No. Plants per 100 Square Feet [7] | Short/Long/Extra-Long Germination Time | Plant Initially in Flats/Beds (in order of preference) | Spacing in First Flat (inches) or Broadcast | Approx. No. Plants per Flat (adj. for germ. rate) [14] | Division Factor to Determine Flats to Broadcast [15] | Approx. No. Weeks in First Flat [16] | Depth of Second Flat (inches) | Spacing in Second Flat (inches) | Approx. No. Plants per Flat [14] | Approx. No. Weeks in Second Flat [16] | Approx. No. Weeks to Maturity in Ground [17] | Approx. No. Weeks in Harvesting Period | Pounds Consumed per Year by Average Person in U.S. [13, 18] | Approx. Maximum Pounds Seed Yield per 100 Square Feet [19] |
| 15 (centers) 6 (depth) | 84 | L | F/B | Use 6-inch-deep flat. Put tubers as close as possible. | | | 3–4 | — | — | — | — | 17–26 | — | D | Tubers: 420+ |
| 72 | 3 | L | Seeds: F Roots: B | Seeds 1 | Seeds 175 | — | Seeds 3–4 | 6 | 2 | 60 | 12–16 | D, P | 8 | D | D |
| 12 | 159 | L | Seeds: F Roots: B | 1 | 175 | — | D | 6 | 2 | 60 | D | Seeds: 4 yrs. Roots: 1 yr. | 8 | 1.1 (fresh) .2 (canned) .1 (frozen) | 8.7 |
| 6 | 621 | L | F | BC | 175 | 4 | 1–2 | 3 | 1.5 | 111 | 3 | 6–8 | 12 | D | D |
| 6 | 621 | S | F | 1 | 175 | — | 1–2 | — | — | — | — | 9–11 | 12 | "1.3" | 23.0 |
| 8 | 320 | S | F | 1 | 175 | — | 1–2 | — | — | — | — | 11–13 | 12 | | 23.0+ |
| 6 | 621 | S | F | 1 | 175 | — | 1–2 | — | — | — | — | 8 | 12 | 2.0 (fresh) 3.7 (canned) 1.9 (frozen) | 17.0 |
| 6 | 621 | S | F | 1 | 175 | — | 1–2 | — | — | — | — | 8–9 | 12 | | 29.7 |
| 4 | 1,343 | S | F/B[R] | 1 | 162 | — | 3–4 | — | — | — | — | 8–9 | 4+ | "1.9" | 30.6 |
| 4 | 1,343 | S | F/B[R] | 1 | 162 | — | 3–4 | — | — | — | — | 8–9 | 4+ | | 30.6 |
| 15 | 84 | S | F | 1 | 187 | — | 2–3# 3–4 | 6 | 2 | 60 | 3–4# 5–6 LG | 8–9 | 4–6 | 5.7 (fresh) 2.6 (frozen) | 5.5 |
| 18 | 53 | S | F | 1 | 175 | — | 2–3# 3–4 | 6 | 2 | 60 | 3–4# 5–6 LG | 11–13 | 12 | ".3" | 2.8 |
| 4 | 1,343 | S | F | 1 | 150 | — | 3–4+ | — | — | — | — | Up to 42 | 8–12 | D | D |
| 10 | 201 | S | F | 1 | 187 | — | 2–3# 3–4 | 6 | 2 | 60 | 3–4# 5–6 LG | 7–11** | — | D | 6.1 |
| 12 / 15 / 18** | 159 / 84 / 53 | S | F | 1 | 187 | — | 2–3# 3–4 | 6 | 2 | 60 | 3–4# 5–6 LG | 9–16** | 2–4+ | 7.5 (fresh) 1.1 (kraut) | 3.6 |
| 3 | 2,507 | S | F/B## | BC | 137 | 3 | 3–4 | — | — | — | — | 9–11 | 4+ | 8.8 (fresh) 1.6 (canned) 1.5 (frozen) | 17.8 |
| 15 | 84 | S | F | 1 | 187 | — | 2–3# 3–4 | 6 | 2 | 60 | 3–4# 5–6 LG | 8–12** | — | 1.7 (fresh) .4 (frozen) | 1.0 |
| 6 | 621 | L/EL | F | BC | 137 | 4 | 4–6 | 3 | 1 | 250 | 4–6 Q | 12–16 | 3–4 to 26[S2] | 6.1 | 9.9 |
| 8 | 320 | S | F | 1 | 162 | — | 3–4 | — | — | — | — | 7–8 | 44 | D | 29.0 |
| 12 | 159 | S | F | 1 | 200 | — | 2–3# 3–4 | 6 | 2 | 60 | 3–4# 5–6 LG | 12 | 24 | D | D |

MASTER CHARTS

# VEGETABLES AND GARDEN CROPS

*(continued)*

| PLANT<br>AA | FOOD NEEDED<br>BB<br>*Pounds You Select* | MATERIALS NEEDED | | | | YIELDS | | MISCELLANEOUS | | |
|---|---|---|---|---|---|---|---|---|---|---|
| | | CC<br>*Approx. No. Plants You Need [20]* | DD<br>*Approx. Square Feet You Need [21]* | EE<br>*Approx. No. Flats You Need [22]* | FF<br>*Approx. Ounces Seed You Need [23]* | GG<br>*Your Actual Yield per 100 Square Feet* | HH<br>*Your Actual Yield Compared with U.S. Average [24]* | II<br>*Especially Good Varieties, Possible Seed Sources, and Remarks* | JJ<br>*Heavy Giver (HG), Light Feeder (LF), Low Nitrogen User (LNU), Heavy Feeder (HF)* | KK<br>*Time of Year to Plant (SP, SU, FA, WI)* |
| 1 Artichoke, Jerusalem | | | | | | | | Note 27 | HF | SP |
| 2 Artichoke, Regular | | | | | | | | — | HF | FA |
| 3 Asparagus | | | | | | | | — | HF | SP |
| 4 Basil | | | | | | | | — | HF | SU |
| 5 Beans, Lima, Bush | | | | | | | | — | HG | SU |
| 6 Beans, Lima, Pole[N] | | | | | | | | — | HG | SU |
| 7 Beans, Snap, Bush | | | | | | | | — | HG | SP, SU |
| 8 Beans, Snap, Pole[N] | | | | | | | | — | HG | SP, SU |
| 9 Beets, Cylindra | | | | | | | | — | LF | SP, SU, FA |
| 10 Beets, Regular | | | | | | | | — | LF | SP, SU, FA |
| 11 Broccoli | | | | | | | | Note 28 | HF | SP, FA |
| 12 Brussels Sprouts | | | | | | | | — | HF | SP, FA |
| 13 Burdock | | | | | | | | — | LF | FA |
| 14 Cabbage, Chinese | | | | | | | | — | HF | SP, FA |
| 15 Cabbage, Regular | | | | | | | | — | HF | SP, FA |
| 16 Carrots | | | | | | | | — | LF | SP, SU, FA |
| 17 Cauliflower | | | | | | | | Snow Peak [29] | HF | SP, FA |
| 18 Celery | | | | | | | | — | HF | SP, FA |
| 19 Chard, Swiss | | | | | | | | Burpee Fordhook | HF | SP, SU, FA |
| 20 Collards, Annual & Perennial | | | | | | | | Note 30 | HF | SP, FA |

| NUTRITION | | | NOTES | CROP PROCEDURES |
|---|---|---|---|---|
| **LL** | **MM** | **NN** | **OO** | **PP** |
| Protein Content per Pound in Grams (g) (454 g per pound) [25] | Calorie Content per Pound [25, 50] | Calcium Content per Pound in Milligrams (mg) [25] | | |
| 7.2 | 345 | 44 | :Raw. 31% refuse. Used in alcohol production for gasohol. Good source of organic matter. | Plant tubers 1 week after last hard frost. Try 90-day varieties. Harvest after flowers die. |
| 5.3 | 213 | 93 | :Raw. | Harvest artichokes when fully plump but before they become fibrous. Cut down stalks after they begin to dry. Resprouts from root. |
| 6.4 | 104 | 56 | :Raw. 44% refuse. | Grow from roots or seed. From seed: Let plants go to seed without harvesting first and second year, so plants build strong roots; cut down dry stalks; harvest small shoots third year; harvest full-sized shoots fourth year. From roots: Let go to seed first year, harvest second year. |
| 12 | 123 | 385 | | Transplant when seedlings have 2 sets of true leaves and a third one coming; set down to cotyledons. After approx. 6 growth nodes appear on plant or when it begins to flower, cut back to 2 nodes. Cut branches back to 1 node. |
| 92.5 | 1,533 | 327 | :Dry seeds. (Lima beans contain a small amount of cyanide.) | Transplant when seedlings have 2 true leaves but before seedlings reach 3–4 inches tall; bury up to half of stem up to cotyledons.<br><br>Snap and shell beans: Harvest regularly (every other day) for higher yields. Some varieties produce all at once; others continue to produce over a longer period. |
| 7.6 | 141 | 124 | :Raw. 12% refuse. | Dry beans: pick when beans are bulging through pods so plants will set more beans. |
| 5.1 | 195 | 51 | :Roots, raw. 33% refuse. Excellent tops often mean too much nitrogen fertilizer and poor root growth. Cylindra variety twice the weight of regular beets. | Each seed produces 1–3 seedlings. Transplant only 1 seedling from a cluster to enhance genetic diversity. |
| 5.6 | 100 | 302 M | :Greens, raw. | For optimum yield, harvest bulbs and greens when bulbs have reached maximum size without becoming fibrous and when greens are still succulent. |
| 12.7 | 127 | 364 | :Head, raw. 22% refuse. | See Cabbage for prick-out and transplanting. Heads grow very fast. Harvest before flowering begins. Can produce secondary heads for additional good harvest. |
| 13.6 | 127 | 1,189 | :Leaves, raw. Contain more nutrition than heads. | |
| 20.4 | 195 | 150 | :Raw. 8% refuse. | Does better in fertile soil. See Cabbage for prick-out and transplanting. When sprout node begins to bulge, remove leaf below it for best growth. Harvest when sprouts are at maximum plumpness, before outer leaves become fibrous and sprout becomes bitter. |
| 6.9 | 327 | 186 | Sow Watanabe in spring for summer harvest and Takinogawa in spring or fall for late summer or following spring harvest. | Harvest after about 10 months when roots have reached maximum size and before they become fibrous. |
| 5.3 | 59 | 189 | :Raw. 3% refuse. | Harvest at peak of size and succulence, before leaves begin to yellow and plants go to seed. |
| 5.3 | 113 | 200 | :Green, raw. 10% refuse. | For prick-out, set seedlings down to cotyledons. For transplant, set seedlings deep, leaving 1–3 leaves above the soil. Harvest heads before top turns yellow or top leaves begin to split. |
| 8.2 | 113 | 171 | :Red, raw. 10% refuse. | |
| 4.1 | 195 | 134 | :Raw, without tops. 18% refuse. Excellent tops often mean too much nitrogen fertilizer and poor root growth. | Transplant when seedlings have 2 true leaves, a third one coming, and a good root not more than 3 inches long; be careful to keep the root straight. Harvest at maximum diameter while they are still sweet. |
| 12.2 | 113 | 113 | :Raw. | See Cabbage for prick-out and transplanting. Cauliflower head often develops in just a few days. Harvest at full size before it begins to yellow. |
| 5.3 | 73 | 189 | :25% refuse. | Transplant when seedlings are about 4 inches tall. For maximum yield, harvest outer stalks sequentially by pulling down and twisting while holding the plant; leave a minimum of 6–8 significant stalks per plant; outer stalks will get bigger as plants mature. |
| 10.0 | 86 | 367 M | :Raw. 8% refuse. Good organic matter crop at high yields. | For transplanting, see Beets. Harvest sequentially as leaves mature, 1–2 outer stalks per plant; be sure to leave a minimum of 5 significant stalks per plant. |
| 16.3 | 136 | 921 | :Leaves and stems, raw. | For prick-out and transplanting, see Cabbage. Harvest sequentially as leaves mature, 1–2 leaves per plant; be sure to leave at least 5 significant leaves per plant/stem. |

MASTER CHARTS

| VEGETABLES AND GARDEN CROPS | SEED | | | YIELD | | | |
|---|---|---|---|---|---|---|---|
| PLANT **A** | **B** Approx. No. Seeds per Ounce [4] (range: larger–smaller seed) | **C** Minimum Legal Germination Rate [5] | **D** Ounces / Volume Seed per 100 Square Feet (adj. for germ. rate, offset spacing, and curv. surf.) [6,7,8] | **E** Possible GROW BIOINTENSIVE Yield in Pounds per 100-Square-Foot Planting [9] | **F** Possible GROW BIOINTENSIVE Yield in Pounds per Plant [10,11] | **G** Average U.S. Yield in Pounds per 100 Square Feet [12,13] | |
| 21 Corn, Sweet | 112–156 | .75 | 1.0–.72 / 2–1⅖ c | Shelled, wet: 17 / 34 / 68 Biomass, air-dry: 12 / 24 / 48 | 15" C: .20–.81 | 27.0 | |
| 22 Cucumbers | 938–1,000 | .80 | .2 / 1¼ T | 158 / 316 / 581 | 1.00–3.65 | Fresh: 39.3 Pickling: 25.0 | |
| 23 Eggplant | 6,500 | .60 | .014 / ½ t | 54 / 108 / 163 | 1.02–3.08 | "55.1" | |
| 24 Garlic | Cloves: 12 | .5 [z] | 20 lbs / 10 qt bulbs | 60 / 120 / 240+ • Hardneck: biomass, air-dry: 7.5 / 15 / 30+ | .04–.18+ | 40.9 | |
| 25 Horseradish | Live roots used | — | 159 roots / — | D | D | D | |
| 26 Kale | 9,000 | .75 | .01 / 1/24 t | 76 / 114 / 153 | .90–1.82 | "16.0" | |
| 27 Kohlrabi | 9,000 | .75 | .20 / 1/16 t | 67 / 135 / 270 | .05–.20 | D | |
| 28 Leeks | 12,500 | .60 | .1 / ³/₈ t | 240 / 480 / 960 | .39–1.55 | D | |
| 29 Lettuce, Head | 25,000 | .80 | .008 / ⅛ t | 75 / 150 / 300 | .47–1.89 | 85.8 | |
| 30 Lettuce, Leaf | 25,000 | .80 | .016 / .012 / ¼ t | 135 / 202 / 540 | 8" C: .42–1.69 9" C: .54–2.18 | 56.1 | |
| 31 Mangels | 1,600 | .65 | .41 / 3²/₅ T [AA] | Roots: 200 / 400 / 800+ Greens: 100 / 200 / 400+ | Roots: .46–1.85 Greens .23–1.11 | Roots: "68.0" Greens: D | |
| 32 Melons | 1,000–1,250 | .75 | .1–.09 / ½ t | 50 / 72 / 145 | .60–1.73 | 51.9 [H] 59.0 [CA] | |
| 33 Mustard | 15,000 | .75 | .055 / ¼ t | 180 / 225 / 270 | .29–.43 | D | |
| 34 Okra | 500 | .50 | .64 / 3½ t | 30 / 60 / 120 | .19–.75 | D | |
| 35 Onions, Bunching | 11,250–12,500 | .70 | .32–.29 / 3¾ t | 100 / 200 / 540 | .04–.21 | D | |
| 36 Onions, Regular | 8,125 | .70 | .2 / 2½ t | 100 / 200 / 540 | .07–.40 | 101.4 | |
| 37 Onions, Torpedo | 8,125 | .70 | .2 / 2½ t | 200 / 400 / 800+ | .15–.60+ | 101.4 | |
| 38 Parsley | 18,000 | .60 | .08 / 1 t | 45 / 91 / 182 (4- to 6-mo. harvest) | .05–.22 | D | |
| 39 Parsnips | 12,000 | .60 | .19 / ⅔ c | 119 / 238 / 479 | .09–.36 | D | |
| 40 Peas, Bush | 94–156 | .80 | 2–1.25 lbs / 2–1¼ c | Fresh: 25 / 53 / 106 Dry: 4 / 10 / 24 | Fresh: .01–.04 Dry: .001–.01 | Fresh: 9.2 Dry: "4.4" | |

| | BEDS/FLATS | | | | | | | | | | | MATURITY | | FOOD NEEDED | SEED YIELD |
|---|---|---|---|---|---|---|---|---|---|---|---|---|---|---|---|
| **H** | **I** | **J** | **K** | **L1** | **L2** | **L3** | **L4** | **M1** | **M2** | **M3** | **M4** | **N** | **O** | **P** | **Q** |
| | | | | FIRST FLAT—3 INCHES DEEP | | | | SECOND FLAT | | | | | | | |
| In-Bed Spacing (inches) | MAXIMUM No. Plants per 100 Square Feet [7] | Short/Long/Extra-Long Germination Time | Plant Initially in Flats/Beds (in order of preference) | Spacing in First Flat (inches) or Broadcast | Approx. No. Plants per Flat (adj. for germ. rate) [14] | Division Factor to Determine Flats to Broadcast [15] | Approx. No. Weeks in First Flat [16] | Depth of Second Flat (inches) | Spacing in Second Flat (inches) | Approx. No. Plants per Flat [14] | Approx. No. Weeks in Second Flat [16] | Approx. No. Weeks to Maturity in Ground [17] | Approx. No. Weeks in Harvesting Period | Pounds Consumed per Year by Average Person in U.S. [13,18] | Approx. Maximum Pounds Seed Yield per 100 Square Feet [19] |
| 15 | 84 | S | F | 1 | 187 | — | 3–5 days | — | — | — | — | 9–13** | — | Shelled, wet: 9.7 (fresh), 9.0 (frozen), 8.3 (canned) | 22.6 |
| 12 | 159 | S | F | 2 | 48 | — | 2–3# 3–4 | — | — | — | — | 7–10 | 7–14 | Reg: 6.1, Pickles: "4.4" (fresh) 3.6 (canned) | 4.1 |
| 18 | 53 | L / EL | F | 1 | 150 | — | 2–3 | 6 | 2 | 60 | 3–4# 5–7 LG | 10–11 | 13 | ".5" | .6 |
| 4 | 1,343 | L | B | — | — | — | — | — | — | — | — | 17–44 | — | 2.8 | Bulbs: 240 |
| 12 | 159 | L | B | — | — | — | — | — | — | — | — | 26 | — | D | D |
| 15 | 84 | S | F | 1 | 187 | — | 1–2# 3–4 | 6 | 2 | 60 | 3–4# 5–6 LG | 8–9 | 17 | D | 3.8 |
| 4 | 1,343 | S | F | 1 | 187 | — | 2–3# 3–4 | — | — | — | — | 7–8 | 4–8 | D | 20.1 |
| 6 | 621 | S | F | BC | 150 | 2 | 8–12 | — | — | — | — | 19 | 4–8 | D | 9.8 |
| 12 | 159 | S | F | BC | 200 | 4 | 1–2 | 3 | 1.5 | 111 | 2–3 | 11–13 | 1–3 | 21.4 | 1.2 |
| 8 WI / 9 SP–FA | 320 / 248 | S | F | BC | 200 | 4 | 1–(2) | 3 | 1.5 | 111 | 2–3 | 6–12**26 | 1–3 | 9.5 | 4.0 |
| 7 | 432 | S | F | 1 | 162 | — | 3–4+ | — | — | — | — | 8–12+ | 4+ | D | 20.0+ |
| 15 | 84 | S | F | 2 | 45 | — | 3–4 LG | — | — | — | — | 12–17** | 13 | 10.8 CA 2.2 H | 2.9 |
| 6 | 621 | S | F | 1 | 187 | — | 3–4 | — | — | — | — | 5–6 | 8–30 | D | 5.7 |
| 12 | 159 | L | F | 1 | 125 | — | 6–8 | 6 | 2 | 60 | 3–4 | 7–8 | 13 | D | 9.3 |
| 3 | 2,507 | S | F | BC | 175 | 2 | 6–8 | — | — | — | — | 8–17 | — | D | 39.6 |
| 4 | 1,343 | S | F | BC | 175 | 2 | 6–8# 8–10 | — | — | — | — | 14–17 | — | 19.2 | 10.3 |
| 4 | 1,343 | S | F | BC | 175 | 2 | 6–8# 8–10 | — | — | — | — | 14–17 | — | 19.2 | 10.3 |
| 5 | 833 | L / EL | F | BC | 150 | 2 | 2–3 | 6 | 2 | 60 | 6–8 | 10–13 | 17–26 | D | 24.8 |
| 4 | 1,343 | L | F | 1 | 150 | — | 3–4 | — | — | — | — | 15 | 4–8+ | D | 24.8 |
| 3 | 2,507 | S | F | 1 | 200 | — | 1–2 | — | — | — | — | 8–10 | 12 | "4.1" (fresh) 1.3 (canned) 1.9 (frozen) | 24 |

MASTER CHARTS

| PLANT AA | FOOD NEEDED BB | MATERIALS NEEDED | | | | | YIELDS | | MISCELLANEOUS | | |
|---|---|---|---|---|---|---|---|---|---|---|---|
| | Pounds You Select | Approx. No. Plants You Need [20] CC | Approx. Square Feet You Need [21] DD | Approx. No. Flats You Need [22] EE | Approx. Ounces Seed You Need [23] FF | Your Actual Yield per 100 Square Feet GG | Your Actual Yield Compared with U.S. Average [24] HH | Especially Good Varieties, Possible Seed Sources, and Remarks II | Heavy Giver (HG), Light Feeder (LF), Low Nitrogen User (LNU), Heavy Feeder (HF) JJ | Time of Year to Plant (SP, SU, FA, WI) KK |
| 21 Corn, Sweet | | | | | | | | | — | HF | SU |
| 22 Cucumbers | | | | | | | | | — | HF | SU |
| 23 Eggplant | | | | | | | | | — | HF | SU |
| 24 Garlic | | | | | | | | | — | LF | SP, FA |
| 25 Horseradish | | | | | | | | | — | LF | SP, FA |
| 26 Kale | | | | | | | | | — | HF | SP, FA |
| 27 Kohlrabi | | | | | | | | | — | LF | SP, FA |
| 28 Leeks | | | | | | | | | — | LF | SP, FA |
| 29 Lettuce, Head | | | | | | | | | SN | HF | SP, FA |
| 30 Lettuce, Leaf | | | | | | | | | SN | HF | SP, SU, FA, WI |
| 31 Mangels | | | | | | | | | Yellow Inter-mediate[33] | LF | SP, SU, FA |
| 32 Melons | | | | | | | | | Note 34 | HF | SU |
| 33 Mustard | | | | | | | | | — | HF | SP, FA |
| 34 Okra | | | | | | | | | — | HF | SU |
| 35 Onions, Bunching | | | | | | | | | Ishikura[35] | LF | SP, SU, FA |
| 36 Onions, Regular | | | | | | | | | — | LF | SP, FA |
| 37 Onions, Torpedo | | | | | | | | | Note 36 | LF | SP, FA |
| 38 Parsley | | | | | | | | | — | HF | SP, FA |
| 39 Parsnips | | | | | | | | | — | LF | SP, FA |
| 40 Peas, Bush | | | | | | | | | — | HG | SP, FA |

| NUTRITION | | | NOTES | CROP PROCEDURES |
|---|---|---|---|---|
| **LL** | **MM** | **NN** | **OO** | **PP** |
| Protein Content per Pound in Grams (g) (454 g per pound) [25] | Calorie Content per Pound [25, 50] | Calcium Content per Pound in Milligrams (mg) [25] | | |
| 8.7 | 400 | 7 | :Raw. 45% refuse (cob). | To check maturity, pull the husk open and pierce a kernel with a thumbnail. Harvest when the juice is halfway between clear and milky. Wait an additional 30 days to harvest plants for optimum compost pile biomass. |
| 3.9 | 59 | 108 | :Raw, whole. 5% refuse. | Transplant when seedlings have 3 large true leaves. Harvest when approx. 6–8 inches long; fruit should be smooth, with no ridges, just beginning to turn lighter green; cut stem about ½ inch from plant. |
| 4.4 | 118 | 44 | :Raw. 19% refuse. | Transplant when seedlings are about 6 inches tall. Harvest when fruit is beginning to soften. |
| 24.8 | 676 | 116 | :12% refuse. Contains antibiotics. Amount of seed depends on size of bulbs and cloves. | Separate bulbs into cloves; plant only the largest cloves 1–2 inches below the soil. Most bulb growth occurs in last 45 days. Harvest when plants have 6-7 green leaves. Dry well in shade. Softneck: braid or cut off stems 2 inches from bulb. Hardneck: cut off stems 2 inches from bulb. |
| 10.6 | 288 | 464 | :Raw. 27% refuse. | Transplant root pieces after last hard frost. Dig up roots after 6 months or when leaves begin to die back. Perennial in warmer climates. |
| 14.1 | 227 | 601 | :Raw leaves and stems. 26% refuse. Good vitamin and mineral content. | For prick-out and transplanting, see Cabbage. For harvest, see Chard. |
| 6.6 | 122 | 136 | :Raw. 27% refuse. | For prick-out and transplanting, see Cabbage. Harvest as soon as leaves begin to become less green and dull and bulbs stop increasing in size. |
| 5.2 | 277 | 123 | :Raw. 25% refuse. | Transplant after 8–12 weeks in flat, when seedlings are as big around as a No. 2 pencil. Harvest after approx. 5+ months. |
| 3.9 | 59 | 86 | :Raw. 5% refuse. | Transplant when seedlings are about 2–3 inches tall. Harvest in very early morning for best taste, when outer leaves are still green and shiny. |
| 3.8 | 82 | 197 | :Raw. 36% refuse. | Transplant when seedlings are about 2–3 inches tall. Harvest in very early morning for best taste, when plant is at maximum fullness and before it begins to bolt or become bitter. Winter growing in double-walled mini-greenhouse. |
| D | D | D | See Beets. | See Beets. |
| 1.6 / 2.3 | 68 / 159 | 32 / 32 | :Cantaloupe. 50% refuse. :Honeydew. 37% refuse. | Transplant when seedlings have 3 large true leaves. Harvest when the outer skin begins to change color and the blossom end begins to soften. |
| 9.5 | 118 | 73 | :Raw. 30% refuse. | Transplant when seedlings have 3–4 good true leaves. Harvest outer leaves regularly, leaving 3 good leaves in the center. |
| 9.4 | 150 | 359 | :Raw. 14% refuse. | Prick out when seedlings are 2 inches tall. Transplant when seedlings are about 6 inches tall. Harvest when the pods are succulent, before they become tough. |
| 6.5 / 1.8 | 145 / 76 | 222 / 67 | :Raw. Bulb and entire top. 4% refuse. :Raw. Bulb and white portion of top. 63% refuse. | Transplant when the seedlings are about the thickness of ordinary pencil lead. Harvest when the plants are slightly thicker than your little finger, or as desired. |
| 6.2 | 172 | 111 | :Dry. Raw. 9% refuse. | Transplant when the seedlings are about the thickness of ordinary pencil lead. Harvest: when a significant number of tops have fallen down, push down the rest and continue to water for 1 week; stop watering and let onions begin to cure in the ground for 1–2 weeks; loosen the soil under the onions and lift them out. Put them in single layer in a shady, well-ventilated area to dry thoroughly. Eat first any onions that do not dry well. |
| 6.2 | 172 | 111 | :Dry. Raw. 9% refuse. | |
| 16.3 | 163 | 921 | :Raw. | Prick out when seedlings have 1 true leaf. Transplant when seedlings are about 3 inches tall. Plants are sensitive to inappropriate handling. Choose best seedlings to transplant: white forking roots, dark green leaves. Harvest outer stalks carefully, leaving 3–5 large stalks per plant; remove inedible stalks and compost them. |
| 6.6 | 340 | 193 | :Raw. 15% refuse. | Slow to germinate and grow. Transplant when seedlings have 3–4 good true leaves. Be patient! Harvest when mature or after frost for sweetest flavor. |
| 10.9 / 109.4 | 367 / 1,542 | 45 / 290 | :Green, without pods. 62% refuse (pods). :Dry. Try sugar snap edible variety. | Timing is important: transplant approx. 1 week after last hard frost or after last soft frost in areas with a cool growing season. Harvest when seeds are bulging in the pods. |

MASTER CHARTS

| VEGETABLES AND GARDEN CROPS | SEED | | | YIELD | | |
|---|---|---|---|---|---|---|
| **PLANT**<br>A | B<br>Approx. No. Seeds per Ounce [4] (range: larger–smaller seed) | C<br>Minimum Legal Germination Rate [5] | D<br>Ounces / Volume Seed per 100 Square Feet (adj. for germ. rate, offset spacing, and curv. surf.) [6,7,8] | E<br>Possible GROW BIOINTENSIVE Yield in Pounds per 100-Square-Foot Planting [9] | F<br>Possible GROW BIOINTENSIVE Yield in Pounds per Plant [10,11] | G<br>Average U.S. Yield in Pounds per 100 Square Feet [12,13] |
| 41 Peas, Pole[N] | 94–156 | .80 | 1.1 lbs–10.7 oz / 1 1/10–2/3 c | Fresh: 25+ / 53+ / 106+<br>Dry: 4 / 10 / 24 | Fresh: .02–.08+<br>Dry: .003–.02 | Fresh: 9.2<br>Dry: "4.4" |
| 42 Peppers, Cayenne | 4,500 | .55 | .064 / 3/8 t | Dry: 5 / 10 / 20 | .03–.13 | D |
| 43 Peppers, Green | 4,500 | .55 | .064 / 3/8 t | 68 / 136 / 204 | .42–1.28 | 68.7 |
| 44 Potatoes, Irish | — | — | 31–23.25 lbs / 16–12 qt | 100 / 200 / 780 | .40–3.15 | 84.2 |
| 45 Potatoes, Sweet | — | — | 12 lbs / 6 qt | 82 / 164 / 492 | .33–1.98 | 39.5 |
| 46 Pumpkin | 94–250 | .75 | .75–.07 / 1/10 T | Whole: 48 / 96 / 191<br>Seeds without hulls: 1 / 2 / 4 | Whole: 18" C: .91–3.60 / 30" C: 3.42–13.64 / Seeds: 18" C: .02–.08 / 30" C: .07–.29 | D |
| 47 Radishes | 2,500–3,125 | .75 | 1.3–1 / 1 3/4 T | Roots: 100 / 200 / 540 | .02–.09 | D |
| 48 Rhubarb | 1,700[Y] | .60[Y] | .025 / 2/3 t | Stalks: 70 / 140 / 280 | 2.69–10.77 | D |
| 49 Rutabagas | 9,375–11,875 | .75 | .09 / 1/4 t | 200 / 400 / 800+ | .32–1.29 | "68.0+" |
| 50 Salsify | 1,900 | .75 | 1.7 / 1/2 c | 100 / 200 / 400+ | .04–.16 | D |
| 51 Shallots | 8[Y] (bulbs) | .75[Y] | 14.0 / 7 qt (bulbs) | 60 / 120 / 240+ | .04–.18+ | D |
| 52 Spinach, New Zealand, Malabar | 350 | .40 | 1.14 / 6 T | 180 / 225 / 270 | 1.13–1.70 | D |
| 53 Spinach, Regular | 2,800 | .60 | .37 / 2 t | 50 / 100 / 225 | .08–.36 | Fresh: 34.6<br>Processing: 39.0 |
| 54 Squash, Crookneck | 218–281 | .75 | .5–.4 / 2–1 1/2 T | 35 / 75 / 150 | .42–1.79 | D |
| 55 Squash, Patty Pan | 300 | .75 | .37 / 1 1/3 T | 75 / 150 / 307 | .89–3.65 | D |
| 56 Squash, Winter | 100–250+ | .75 | 12" C: 2.12–.84 / 9 1/2–3 3/4 T<br>15" C: 1.12–.45 / 5–2 T<br>18" C: .71–.28 / 3 1/5–1 1/4 T | 50 / 100 / 350 | 12" C: .31–2.20<br>15" C: .60–4.17<br>18" C: .94–6.60 | D |
| 57 Squash, Zucchini | 300 | .75 | .24 / 2 2/5 t | 160 / 319 / 478+ | 3.02–9.02 | D |
| 58 Tomatoes | 10,000–12,000 | .75 | .006 / .004 / .003 / 1 2/5 – 1/40 t | 100 / 194 / 418 | 18" C: 1.89–7.89<br>21" C: 2.89–11.94<br>24" C: 3.85–16.08 | Fresh: 67.0<br>Processing: 153.4 |
| 59 Turnips | 9,375–12,500 | .80 | .18–.13 / 2/3 t | Roots: 100 / 200 / 360<br>Greens: 100 / 200 / 360 | Roots: .07–.27<br>Greens: .07–.27 | D |
| 60 Watermelon | Small seed: 500–625<br>Large seed: 187–312 | .80 | Small seed: 12" C: .45–.36 / 3–2 3/8 t<br>18" C: .15–.12 / 1 1/8–3/4 t<br>21" C: .10–.08 / 5/8–1/2 t<br>24" C: .07–.06 / 7/16–3/8 t<br>Large seed: 12" C: 1.2–.73 / 2 3/4 T<br>18" C: .4–.24 / 2 3/8–1 3/8 t<br>21" C: .27–.16 / 1 3/4–1 1/16 t<br>24" C: .20–.12 / 1 3/8–3/4 t | 50 / 100 / 320 | .31–12.30 | 58.7 |

| | BEDS/FLATS | | | | | | | | | | | MATURITY | | FOOD NEEDED | SEED YIELD |
|---|---|---|---|---|---|---|---|---|---|---|---|---|---|---|---|
| | | | | FIRST FLAT—3 INCHES DEEP | | | | SECOND FLAT | | | | | | | |
| **H** | **I** | **J** | **K** | **L1** | **L2** | **L3** | **L4** | **M1** | **M2** | **M3** | **M4** | **N** | **O** | **P** | **Q** |
| In-Bed Spacing (inches) | MAXIMUM No. Plants per 100 Square Feet [7] | Short/Long/Extra-Long Germination Time | Plant Initially in Flats/Beds (in order of preference) | Spacing in First Flat (inches) or Broadcast | Approx. No. Plants per Flat (adj. for germ. rate) [14] | Division Factor to Determine Flats to Broadcast [15] | Approx. No. Weeks in First Flat [16] | Depth of Second Flat (inches) | Spacing in Second Flat (inches) | Approx. No. Plants per Flat [14] | Approx. No. Weeks in Second Flat [16] | Approx. No. Weeks to Maturity in Ground [17] | Approx. No. Weeks in Harvesting Period | Pounds Consumed per Year by Average Person in U.S. [13,18] | Approx. Maximum Pounds Seed Yield per 100 Square Feet [19] |
| 4 | 1,343 | S | F | 1 | 200 | — | 1–2 | — | — | — | — | 10–11 | 12 | "4.1" (fresh) 1.3 (canned) 1.9 (frozen) | 24 |
| 12 | 159 | L / EL | F | 1 | 137 | — | 2–3 | 6 | 2 | 60 | 3–4# 5–7LG | 9–11 | 17 | D | .1 |
| 12 | 159 | L / EL | F | 1 | 137 | — | 2–3 | 6 | 2 | 60 | 3–4# 5–7LG | 9–12 | 17 | 7.0 | .3 |
| 9 centers 6 to 9 depth[49] | 248 | L | Note 31 | Note 31 | — | — | — | — | — | — | — | 9–17 | — | 47.2 (fresh) 57.2 (frozen) | Tubers: 780 |
| 9 centers 6 to 9 depth[49] | 248 | L | Note 32 | Note 32 | 60 | — | 4–6 | — | — | — | — | 13–17 (3-mo var.) 26–34 (6-mo var.) | — | 4.7 | Tubers: 492 |
| 18 / 30** | 53 / 14 | S | F | 2 | 45 | — | 3–4LG | — | — | — | — | 14–16 | — | ".6" | 5.1 |
| 2 | 5,894 | S | B | — | — | — | — | — | — | — | — | 3–9** | 1 | D | 20.6 |
| 24 | 26 | L | Seeds: F Roots: B | 1 | 150 | — | D | 6 | 2 | 60 | D | Seeds: 3 yrs. / Roots: 1 yr. | D | ".03" | D |
| 6 | 621 | S | F | 1 | 187 | — | 3–4 | — | — | — | — | 13 | 4+ | D | 5.4 |
| 3 | 2,507 | S | F | 1 | 187 | — | 3–4 | — | — | — | — | 17 | 4+ | D | 27.7 |
| 4 | 1,343 | L | B | — | — | — | — | — | — | — | — | 17–26 | — | D | Bulbs: 240 |
| 12 | 159 | L | F | 2 | 24 | — | 3–4 | — | — | — | — | 10 | 42 | D | 17.2 |
| 6 | 621 | S | F | 1 | 150 | — | 3–4 | — | — | — | — | 6–7 | — | 1.7 | 10.8 |
| 15 | 84 | S | F | 2 | 45 | — | 3–4LG | — | — | — | — | 10 | 17+ | D | 6.1 |
| 15 | 84 | S | F | 2 | 45 | — | 3–4LG | — | — | — | — | 7 | 17+ | D | 6.1 |
| 12 / 15** / 18 | 159 / 84 / 53 | S | F | 2 | 45 | — | 3–4LG | — | — | — | — | 11–17** | 4+ | D | 5.7 |
| 18 | 53 | S | F | 2 | 45 | — | 3–4LG | — | — | — | — | 7–9 | 26 | D | 6.1 |
| 18 / 21 / 24 TO | 53 / 35 / 26 | S | F | 1 | 187 | — | 4–6 | 6 | 2 | 60 | 3–4LG | 8–13 | 17+ | Canned: 69.6 Fresh: 18.1 | 5.5 |
| 4 | 1,343 | S | F | 1 | 200 | — | 2–3 | — | — | — | — | 5–10** | 4+ | D | 14.7 |
| 12 / 18 / 21 / 24 W | 159 / 53 / 35 / 26 | S | F | 2 | 42 | — | 3–4LG | — | — | — | — | 10–13 | 13 | 13.8 | 2.6 |

# VEGETABLES AND GARDEN CROPS

*(continued)*

| PLANT<br><br>AA | FOOD NEEDED<br>BB<br>Pounds You Select | MATERIALS NEEDED | | | | YIELDS | | MISCELLANEOUS | | |
|---|---|---|---|---|---|---|---|---|---|---|
| | | CC<br>Approx. No. Plants You Need [20] | DD<br>Approx. Square Feet You Need [21] | EE<br>Approx. No. Flats You Need [22] | FF<br>Approx. Ounces Seed You Need [23] | GG<br>Your Actual Yield per 100 Square Feet | HH<br>Your Actual Yield Compared with U.S. Average [24] | II<br>Especially Good Varieties, Possible Seed Sources, and Remarks | JJ<br>Heavy Giver (HG), Light Feeder (LF), Low Nitrogen User (LNU), Heavy Feeder (HF) | KK<br>Time of Year to Plant (SP, SU, FA, WI) |
| 41 Peas, Pole [N] | | | | | | | | — | HG | SP, FA |
| 42 Peppers, Cayenne | | | | | | | | — | HF | SU |
| 43 Peppers, Green | | | | | | | | — | HF / LNU | SU |
| 44 Potatoes, Irish | | | | | | | | Notes 31 & 37 [SN] | "LF" | SP, SU |
| 45 Potatoes, Sweet | | | | | | | | Note 38 | LF / LNU | SU |
| 46 Pumpkin | | | | | | | | Note 39 | HF | SU |
| 47 Radishes | | | | | | | | Note 40 | LF | SP, FA |
| 48 Rhubarb | | | | | | | | — | HF | SP |
| 49 Rutabagas | | | | | | | | — | LF | SP, FA |
| 50 Salsify | | | | | | | | — | LF | SP, FA |
| 51 Shallots | | | | | | | | — | LF | SP, FA |
| 52 Spinach, New Zealand, Malabar | | | | | | | | Drought-resistant | HF | SP, SU. FA |
| 53 Spinach, Regular | | | | | | | | — | HF | SP, FA |
| 54 Squash, Crookneck | | | | | | | | Bush | HF | SU |
| 55 Squash, Patty Pan | | | | | | | | Bush | HF | SU |
| 56 Squash, Winter | | | | | | | | Bush and vine | HF | SU |
| 57 Squash, Zucchini | | | | | | | | Bush and vine | HF | SU |
| 58 Tomatoes | | | | | | | | — | HF | SU |
| 59 Turnips | | | | | | | | — | LF / LNU | SP, FA |
| 60 Watermelon | | | | | | | | Note 41 | HF | SU |

| NUTRITION | | | NOTES | CROP PROCEDURES |
|---|---|---|---|---|
| **LL**<br>Protein Content per Pound in Grams (g) (454 g per pound) [25] | **MM**<br>Calorie Content per Pound [25, 50] | **NN**<br>Calcium Content per Pound in Milligrams (mg) [25] | **OO** | **PP** |
| | | | Δ<br>Approximately 12% of the calories, 8% of the protein, and 18% of the calcium eaten worldwide is in the form of potatoes grown on 2.4% of the cropland. | |
| 10.9<br>109.4 | 367<br>1,542 | 45<br>290 | :Green, without pods. 62% refuse (pods).<br>:Dry. Try sugar snap edible-pod variety. | Timing is important: transplant approx. 1 week after last hard frost or after last soft frost in areas with a cool growing season. Harvest when seeds are bulging in the pods. |
| 45 | 1,470 | 681 | :Dry (including seeds). 4% refuse. | Transplant when seedlings are about 6 inches tall and the soil is warm. Use a mini-greenhouse or a row cover in areas with a short growing season. |
| 4.5<br>5.1 | 82<br>122 | 33<br>47 | :Green. 18% refuse.<br>:Red. 20% refuse. | Harvest when fully mature and before fruit begins to discolor. |
| 7.7 | 349 avg.<br>Red: 327<br>Russet: 358<br>White: 318 | 26 | :Raw. 19% refuse. Green parts poisonous. | See note 31. After tops die, stop watering, wait 2 weeks, dig up carefully. Put in single layer in shade to cure for 2–3 days. Store in a cool, dark, well-ventilated place. |
| 6.6<br>6.2 | 375<br>430 | 118<br>118 | :Jewel (firm).<br>:Puerto Rican (soft). } 19% refuse (peelings) } See above. Δ | See note 32. It is also possible to buy slips to plant. Harvest when tops are dead. |
| 3.2<br>131.5 | 118<br>2,454 | 67<br>231 | :Raw fruit. 30% refuse.<br>:Seeds. Hulls 30% of unhulled weight. | For transplanting, see Cucumbers. For harvest, see Winter Squash. |
| 4.1 | 91 | 122 | :Raw, without tops. 10% refuse. | Small radishes: Broadcast directly in bed (use seed amount in Col. D), or use chicken wire to space seeds 1 inch apart in the bed (will require 4 times the seed). Chop seeds in lightly with rake. Harvest after about 3–4 weeks in the ground and before the bulb becomes too hot and fibrous. Dalkon: Sow on 1-inch centers in flat (seed needed per 100 square feet: .26 = .33 ounces). Transplant when seedlings have 3–4 good true leaves, about 2 weeks after sowing. To avoid bolting, transplant after June 21. Harvest after about 2½–3 months, before seed stalk begins to form. |
| 2.3 | 95 | 374 | :Raw, without leaves. 14% refuse. Green parts poisonous. | Harvest stalks with hand-sized leaves every 5–10 days; be sure to keep 5–6 medium to medium-large shiny, newer leaves with some red on the stem on the plant. |
| 4.2 | 163 | 254 | :Raw. 15% refuse. Very flavorful when grown using GROW BIOINTENSIVE methods. | Transplant when seedlings are about 2–3 inches tall. Harvest when roots are mature (a "neck" will begin to form when the root has reached maximum size; quality will decline as neck elongates). |
| 11.4 | 372 | 185 | | For transplanting, see Carrots. Harvest after 4–5 months in ground, before leaves become dull. |
| 10.0 | 357 | 148 | :Raw. 12% refuse. | Separate bulbs; use larger bulbs for transplanting. When leaves become abundant, 10–20% can be cut for flavoring without decreasing yield of bulbs. For curing, see Onions. |
| 10.0 | 64 | 263 | :Raw. | New Zealand: see Regular Spinach, except harvest when leaves are fully mature. Malabar: see Regular Spinach. |
| 10.5 | 100 | 304 [M] | :Raw. 28% refuse. | Transplant when seedlings have 3 true leaves. Timing is crucial (see Peas). Harvest large leaves just before they become dull; leave 5 good leaves per plant. |
| 5.3 | 86 | 124 | :Raw. 2% refuse. | For transplanting, see Cucumbers. Harvest before fruit becomes dark yellow and hard. |
| 4.0 | 82 | 124 | :Raw. 2% refuse. | For transplanting, see Cucumbers. White variety: harvest when bone-white with only a tinge of green left. Colored varieties: harvest before fruit becomes dark and hard. |
| 5.2<br>4.4<br>4.2 | 152<br>171<br>117 | 107<br>102<br>57 | :Acorn, raw. 24% refuse.<br>:Butternut, raw. 30% refuse.<br>:Hubbard, raw. 34% refuse. | For transplanting, see Cucumbers. Support squash on smooth rocks to keep them off the damp soil. Harvest when stem is dry and hard; cut off with 2 inches of stem. |
| 5.2 | 64 | 121 | :Raw. 5% refuse. | For transplanting, see Cucumbers. Lightly tap open female flowers on new zucchini to push them off; if they do not come off easily, do not force them. Harvest preferably when approx. 8–10 inches long, 12–20 ounces; remove irregular and/or deformed fruit from plant. |
| 5.0 | 95 | 59 | :Raw. | Transplant when seedlings are about 6 inches tall; set plants deeper than in flat. Harvest at full color and when fruit comes off easily. |
| 3.9<br>13.6 | 122<br>127 | 152<br>1,116 | :Roots, raw.<br>:Greens, raw. | See Rutabaga. |
| 1.0 | 145 | 15 | :Raw. 54% refuse. | For transplanting, see Cucumbers. Harvest when the watermelon says "Plunk!" when you tap it with a knuckle; if it says "Plink!" or "Plank!" it is not yet mature enough. |

*Letter codes on page 85, notes on page 126*

# CALORIE, GRAIN, PROTEIN SOURCE, AND VEGETABLE OIL CROPS

For protein, also see: Beans, Lima; Buckwheat; Collards; Corn, Sweet; Garlic; Peas; Potatoes, Irish and Sweet

| A — PLANT | B — Approx. No. Seeds per Ounce[4] (range: larger–smaller seed) | C — Minimum Legal Germination Rate[5] | D — Ounces / Volume Seed per 100 Square Feet (adj. for germ. rate, offset spacing, and curv. surf.)[6,7,8] | E — Possible GROW BIOINTENSIVE Yield in Pounds per 100-Square-Foot Planting[9] | F — Possible GROW BIOINTENSIVE Yield in Pounds per Plant[10,11] | G — Average U.S. Yield in Pounds per 100 Square Feet[12,13] |
|---|---|---|---|---|---|---|
| 1 Amaranth, Grain & Leaf | 25,000–53,400 | .70[A] | .035–.017 / ⅓ –⅛ t  .009–.004 / ¹⁄₄₀ –¹⁄₈₀ t | Edible greens-type: 68 / 136 / 272+  Seed: 4 / 8 / 16+  Biomass, air-dry (stalks): 12 / 24 / 48  Biomass, wet: 53 / 132 / 317 | Greens: .08–.30  Seed: .11–.44+ | Seed: "4"  Biomass, air-dry: "6" |
| 2 Barley | 500 hulled | .70[A] | 2.4 / 6⅓ T | Seed: 5 / 10 / 24[K,U]  Biomass, air-dry: 12 / 30 / 72 | Seed: .006–.03  Biomass, dry: .01–.09 | Seed: 6.5  Biomass, dry: est. 9.7 |
| 3 Beans, Fava, Cold-Weather | 15–70 | .75 | 28.4–6.1 / 7½–1⅝ c | Dry seed: 5 / 9 / 18  Biomass, air-dry: 18 / 36 / 72  Biomass, wet: 90 / 180 / 360 | Seed: .02–.06  Biomass, dry: .06–.23 | D |
| 4 Beans, Fava, Hot-Weather | 15–70 | .75 | 55.2–11.8 / 14 ½–3 c | Dry seed: 2 / 3 / 6  Biomass, air-dry: 6 / 12 / 24  Biomass, wet: 30 / 60 / 120 | Seed: .003–.01  Biomass, dry: .01–.04 | D |
| 5 Beans, Kidney | 50 | .70[A] | 17.7 / 1⅗ c | Seed: 4 / 10 / 24 | .006–.04 | "4.0" |
| 6 Beans, Mung | 500 | .70[A] | 3.8 / 7⅝ T | Seed: 4 / 10 / 24 | .003–.02 | 3.8 |
| 7 Beans, Pinto | 70 | .70[A] | 12.7 / 2 c | Seed: 4 / 10 / 24 | .006–.04 | 3.8 |
| 8 Beans, Red Mexican & Black | 50–100 | .70[A] | 17.7–8.9 / 2¹⁄₁₀–1¹⁄₁₀ c | Seed: 4 / 10 / 24 | .006–.04 | 3.8 |
| 9 Beans, White | 90–180 | .70[A] | 9.9–4.9 / 1¾ –⅝ c | Seed: 4 / 10 / 24 | .006–.04 | 3.8 |
| 10 Cassava (Manioc/Yuca) (manihot esculenta) | — | — | D | Root: 30 / 60 / 120 | 1.67–6.67 | D |
| 11 Chickpeas (Garbanzo) | 50 | .70[A] | 38.4 / 6 c | Seed: 4 / 10 / 24 | .003–.02 | D |
| 12 Corn, Flour or Fodder, Dry | 100–200 | .70[A] | 1.2–.6 / 3–2 T | Seed: 11 / 17 / 23+  Biomass, air-dry: 24 / 48 / 96  Biomass, wet: 107 / 214 / 428 | Seed: .13–.27+ | Seed: 18.2 |
| 13 Cowpeas | 150 | .75 | 1.5 / .25 / .17  3½–1¼ T | Seed: 2.4 / 4.5 / 9  Green hay: 91 / 183 / 366 | Seed: .02–.50  Green hay: .57–20.33 | D |
| 14 Lentils | 600 | .70[A] | 3.2 / 6½ T | Seed: 4 / 6 / 8+ | .003–.006+ | "2.8" |
| 15 Millet, Japanese | 10,000 | .70[A] | .06 / ¾ t | Seed: 3 / 7 / 13+[K]  Biomass, air-dry: 12 / 30 / 72 | Seed: .002–.03+ | Seed: "3.4" |
| 16 Millet, Pearl | 2,200 unhulled | .70[A] | .3 / D | Seed: 3 / 6 / 12  Biomass, air-dry: 15 / 40 / 75  Biomass, wet: 70 / 185 / 350 | Seed: .01–.03  Biomass, dry: .03–.17 | D |
| 17 Millet, Proso | 5,000 unhulled | .70[A] | .12 / ⅖ T | Seed: 3 / 6 / 12+[K]  Biomass, air-dry: 6 / 15 / 36 | Seed: .002–.03+ | Seed: 7.1 |
| 18 Oats | 950 hulled | .70[A] | 1.25 / 3 T | Seed: 3 / 7 / 13+[K,U]  Biomass, air-dry: 12 / 30 / 72 | Seed: .004–.02  Biomass, dry: .01–.09 | Seed: 4.8  Biomass, dry: est. 7.2 |

| | BEDS/FLATS | | | | | | | | | | | MATURITY | | FOOD NEEDED | SEED YIELD |
|---|---|---|---|---|---|---|---|---|---|---|---|---|---|---|---|
| **H** | **I** | **J** | **K** | **L1** | **L2** | **L3** | **L4** | **M1** | **M2** | **M3** | **M4** | **N** | **O** | **P** | **Q** |
| | | | | FIRST FLAT—3 INCHES DEEP | | | | SECOND FLAT | | | | | | | |
| In-Bed Spacing (inches) | MAXIMUM No. Plants per 100 Square Feet [7] | Short/Long/Extra-Long Germination Time | Plant Initially in Flats/Beds (in order of preference) | Spacing in First Flat (inches) or Broadcast | Approx. No. Plants per Flat (adj. for germ. rate) [14] | Division Factor to Determine Flats to Broadcast [15] | Approx. No. Weeks in First Flat [16] | Depth of Second Flat (inches) | Spacing in Second Flat (inches) | Approx. No. Plants per Flat [14] | Approx. No. Weeks in Second Flat [16] | Approx. No. Weeks to Maturity in Ground [17] | Approx. No. Weeks in Harvesting Period | Pounds Consumed per Year by Average Person in U.S. [13,18] | Approx. Maximum Pounds Seed Yield per 100 Square Feet [19] |
| Greens: 6 Seed: 12 | 621 159 | S | F | BC | 175 | 4 | 1 | 3 | 1.5 | 111 | 3 | Greens: 6 Seed: 12 | Greens: 4+ Seed: — | D | 16+ |
| 5 | 833 | S | F | 1 or BC | 175 | 2 | 1–2 | — | — | — | — | 9–10 to 34 [47] | — | .7 | 24 |
| 8 | 320 | S | F / B[R] | 1 | 187 | — | 2 | — | — | — | — | 17–43 | — | D | 18 |
| 6 | 621 | S | F / B[R] | 1 | 187 | — | 2 | — | — | — | — | 13–17 | — | D | 6 |
| 6 | 621 | S | F | 1 | 175 | — | 1–2 | — | — | — | — | 12 | 8 | | 24 |
| 4 | 1,343 | S | F | 1 | 175 | — | 1–2 | — | — | — | — | 12 | 8 | | 24 |
| 6 | 621 | S | F | 1 | 175 | — | 1–2 | — | — | — | — | 12 | 8 | All edible dry beans: "13.5" | 24 |
| 6 | 621 | S | F | 1 | 175 | — | 1–2 | — | — | — | — | 12 | 8 | | 24 |
| 6 | 621 | S | F | 1 | 175 | — | 1–2 | — | — | — | — | 12 | 8 | | 24 |
| 36 | 18 | — | B | — | — | — | — | — | — | — | — | 26–52 | D | D | D |
| 4 | 1,343 | S | F | 1 | 175 | — | 1–2 | — | — | — | — | 9 | 8 | D | 24 |
| 15 | 84 | S | F | 1 | 175 | — | 3–5 days | — | — | — | — | 11–16 to 43 [53] | — | 25.1 (food) 86.1 (sugar and starch) | 23+ |
| 12 / 24 / 36 [E] | 159 / 26 / 18 | S | F | 1 | 187 | — | 2 | — | — | — | — | 9–12 | 8 | D | 9 |
| 4 | 1,343 | S | F | 1 | 175 | — | 1–2 | — | — | — | — | 12 | 8 | — | 8+ |
| 7 | 432 | S | F | 1 or BC | 175 | 2 | 2–4 | — | — | — | — | 6–8 | — | D | 13+ |
| 7 | 432 | S | F | 1 or BC | 175 | 2 | 2–3 | — | — | — | — | 17–21 | — | D | 12 |
| 7 | 432 | S | F | 1 or BC | 175 | 2 | 2–4 | — | — | — | — | 10–13 | — | D | 12+ |
| 5 | 833 | S | F | 1 or BC | 175 | 2 | 1–2 | — | — | — | — | 13–17 to 38 [47] | — | 4.5 | 13+ |

# CALORIE, GRAIN, PROTEIN SOURCE, AND VEGETABLE OIL CROPS

*(continued)*

| PLANT<br><br>AA | FOOD NEEDED<br>BB<br>*Pounds You Select* | MATERIALS NEEDED | | | | YIELDS | | MISCELLANEOUS | | |
|---|---|---|---|---|---|---|---|---|---|---|
| | | CC<br>*Approx. No. Plants You Need [20]* | DD<br>*Approx. Square Feet You Need [21]* | EE<br>*Approx. No. Flats You Need [22]* | FF<br>*Approx. Ounces Seed You Need [23]* | GG<br>*Your Actual Yield per 100 Square Feet* | HH<br>*Your Actual Yield Compared with U.S. Average [24]* | II<br>*Especially Good Varieties, Possible Seed Sources, and Remarks* | JJ<br>*Heavy Giver (HG), Light Feeder (LF), Low Nitrogen User (LNU), Heavy Feeder (HF)* | KK<br>*Time of Year to Plant (SP, SU, FA, WI)* |
| 1 Amaranth, Grain & Leaf | | | | | | | | Note 33 | HF | SU |
| 2 Barley | | | | | | | | Hull-less[33] | HF | SP, FA |
| 3 Beans, Fava, Cold-Weather | | | | | | | | Banner (to 10°F)[33] | HG | SP, FA |
| 4 Beans, Fava, Hot-Weather | | | | | | | | Note 42 | HG | SP |
| 5 Beans, Kidney | | | | | | | | Note 43 | HG | SU |
| 6 Beans, Mung | | | | | | | | Note 43 | HG | SU |
| 7 Beans, Pinto | | | | | | | | Note 43 | HG | SU |
| 8 Beans, Red Mexican & Black | | | | | | | | Note 42 | HG | SU |
| 9 Beans, White | | | | | | | | Note 43 | HG | SU |
| 10 Cassava (Manioc, Yuca) (manihot esculenta) | | | | | | | | — | LF | — |
| 11 Chickpeas (Garbanzo) | | | | | | | | Note 43 | HG | SU |
| 12 Corn, Flour or Fodder, Dry | | | | | | | | Note 42 | HF | SP |
| 13 Cowpeas | | | | | | | | Notes 42 & 43 | HG | SU |
| 14 Lentils | | | | | | | | Note 43 | HG | SP, SU |
| 15 Millet, Japanese | | | | | | | | Note 44 | HF | SU |
| 16 Millet, Pearl | | | | | | | | — | HF | SU |
| 17 Millet, Proso | | | | | | | | Note 45 | HF | SU |
| 18 Oats | | | | | | | | Hull-less[33] | HF | SP, FA |

| NUTRITION | | | NOTES | | CROP PROCEDURES |
|---|---|---|---|---|---|
| **LL** | **MM** | **NN** | **OO** | | **PP** |
| Protein Content per Pound in Grams (g) (454 g per pound) [25] | Calorie Content per Pound [25,50] | Calcium Content per Pound in Milligrams (mg) [25] | | | |
| 15.9<br>69.5 | 104<br>1,696 | 1,212<br>2,224 | :Greens. Good calcium source.<br>:Seed. | | Prick out when cotyledons have emerged and before first leaf emerges. Transplant when 2–3 inches tall and strong. For grain: harvest when seeds are mature and dry enough to rub out of head easily; be alert for birds. For leaves: harvest when they are large, green, and shiny and before they begin to lose their maximum green. |
| 37.2<br>43.5<br>3.2* | 1,583<br>1,579<br>224 | 73<br>154<br>145 | :Light.<br>:Pearled or scotch.<br>:Straw and chaff, dry. | Hulling of regular varieties difficult. Use hull-less varieties. | Transplant when seedlings are about 1.5–2 inches tall, before roots become unmanageable. Harvest when entire plant is 85% golden; be alert for birds. |
| 13.0<br>113.9 | 162<br>1,547 | 42<br>463 | :In pods. 66% refuse.<br>:Dry beans. | Excellent organic matter crop. Fixes up to .16+ lb nitrogen (for summer varieties) and .34 lb (for winter varieties) per 100 sq ft per year. Caution: Beans can be toxic to some people. | Transplant when seedlings are about 1 inch tall, before roots become unmanageable. For biomass, harvest when plants are at ~50% flower. |
| 13.0<br>113.9 | 162<br>1,547 | 42<br>463 | :In pods. 66% refuse.<br>:Dry beans. | | For beans, harvest all pods when first pods begin to turn black, before they shatter. |
| 102.1 | 1,510 | 499 | | | Transplant when seedlings have 2 true leaves but before seedlings reach 3–4 inches tall; bury up to half of stem up to cotyledons. |
| 109.8 | 1,574 | 535 | | | Dry beans: pick when beans are bulging through pods so plants will set more beans. Beans may shatter (fall to the ground) if left on plant too long. Fixes up to .27 lb nitrogen per 100 sq ft per year. |
| 103.9 | 1,542 | 612 | :Dry seeds, raw. | | Pinto beans: habit is often halfway between bush and pole. Ready to harvest when pods have delicate red pattern. |
| 103.9<br>102.1 | 1,583<br>1,538 | 612<br>499 | :Red Mexican.<br>:Black. | | |
| 101.2 | 1,538 | 653 | | | |
| 5.5 | 726 | 309 | :Raw. Some varieties take 104 weeks to mature. | | Transplant stem cuttings 12–18 inches long and 1–1.5 inches in diameter at beginning of rains. |
| 93.0 | 1,651 | 680 | :Dry seeds, raw. | | See Beans. |
| 40.4 | 1,656 | 100 | :Dry seeds, raw. Also produces a lot of organic matter. | | Transplant when seedlings are 1 inch tall, before roots become too long. Harvest ears as husks dry out. To speed up drying, open up husks without removing. Remove husks for final drying. Remove grain from ear when thoroughly dry, or store ears with grain and shell as needed. |
| 103.4 | 1,556 | 336 | :Dry. | | See Beans. Can harvest up to ⅓ of leaves from 21–30 days until flowering. |
| 112.0 | 1,569 | 538 | :Dry seeds, raw. | | See Beans. |
| D | 1,544 | D | | | Use 45- to 60-day varieties. Transplant when ~1.5 inches tall. Harvest when plants are 85% golden. Difficult to thresh. |
| 19.0* | 1,522 | D | :Dry. Seeds form in about 45 days when days become shorter. Yields can be 3 times higher in hot climate and good soil. | | Transplant when ~1.5 inches tall. Harvest when plants are 85% golden; be alert for shattering and birds. |
| 44.9 | 1,715 | 91 | :Dry. High in iron. | | Finger millet calories: 1,509<br>Foxtail millet calories: 1,550 |
| 64.4<br>3.2* | 1,764<br>233 | 240<br>86 | :Grain, dry.<br>:Straw and chaff, dry. | Hulling of regular varieties difficult. Use hull-less varieties. | See Barley. |

*Letter codes on page 85, notes on page 126*

MASTER CHARTS AND PLANNING  101

# CALORIE, GRAIN, PROTEIN SOURCE, AND VEGETABLE OIL CROPS

For protein, also see: Beans, Lima; Buckwheat; Collards; Corn, Sweet; Garlic; Peas; Potatoes, Irish and Sweet

| PLANT | SEED | | | YIELD | | |
|---|---|---|---|---|---|---|
| A | B — Approx. No. Seeds per Ounce[4] (range: larger–smaller seed) | C — Minimum Legal Germination Rate[5] | D — Ounces / Volume Seed per 100 Square Feet (adj. for germ. rate, offset spacing, and curv. surf.)[6,7,8] | E — Possible GROW BIOINTENSIVE Yield in Pounds per 100-Square-Foot Planting[9] | F — Possible GROW BIOINTENSIVE Yield in Pounds per Plant[10,11] | G — Average U.S. Yield in Pounds per 100 Square Feet[12,13] |
| 19 Peanuts | 20–70 unshelled 30–90 shelled | .70[A] | 11.8–3.9 / 4⅜–1½ c shelled | Seed: 4 / 10 / 24 | .02–.10 | 7.2 |
| 20 Pigeon Peas | D | .70[A] | D | Seed: 2 / 4 / 16+ | .50–4.00 | D |
| 21 Quinoa | 10,000 | .70[A] | .023 / ⅛ t | Seed: 6 / 13 / 26 Biomass, air-dry: 18 / 39 / 78 | Seed: .04–.16 | D |
| 22 Rapeseed (Canola) | 8,000 | .70[A] | .04 / 2 t | Seed: 5 / 10 / 20 | .02–.08 | 7.2 |
| 23 Rice | 1,100 unhulled | .70[A] | 1.7 / 3⅖ T | Seed: 8 / 16 / 32[K, U] Biomass, air-dry: 24 / 54 / 96 | Seed: .006–.02 Biomass, dry: .02–.07 | Seed: 15.3 Biomass, dry: est. 23.0 |
| 24 Rye, Cereal | 500 hulled | .70[A] | 2.4 / 5⅖ T | Seed: 4 / 10 / 24[K, U] Biomass, air-dry: 12 / 30 / 72 | Seed: .005–.03 Biomass, dry: .01–.09 | Seed: 3.5 Biomass, dry: est. 5.2 |
| 25 Safflower | 640 unhulled | .70[A] | 1.8 / 2⅖ c | Seed: 4 / 9 / 17+ Biomass, air-dry: 5 / 10 / 20 | Seed: .005–.02+ | Seed: 3.0 |
| 26 Sesame | 11,000 | .70[A] | .08 / ⅕ T | Seed: 1.5 / 3 / 6+ | Seed: .002–.01+ | D |
| 27 Sorghum | 1,000 | .65[A] | Reg. type: .66 / 1⅔ T Broom type: 1.9 / 6⅘ T | Seed: 8 / 16 / 24 Biomass, air-dry: 25 / 50 / 100+ Biomass, wet: 88 / 175 / 350+ | Seed: .01–.06 Biomass, dry: .06–.23 | Seed: 6.8 Biomass, wet: 52.3 |
| 28 Soybeans | 100–250 | .75 | 8.2–3.3 / 1⅛–½ c | Dry seed: 4 / 8 / 14+ | .006–.02+ | 4.6 |
| 29 Sunflowers | 650 in shell[Y] | .50+[Y] | .08 / .76 / 3–⅓ T | Seed, hulled: 24" C: 2.5 / 5 / 10 Stalks, air-dry: 9" C: 20 / 40 / 80 | Seed: 24" C: .10–.38 Stalks: 9" C: .08–.32 | Seed, hulled: 3.5 |
| 30 Wheat, Durum | 500 hulled | .70[A] | 2.4 / D | Seed: 4 / 10 / 26[K, U] Biomass, air-dry: 12 / 30 / 72 | Seed: .005–.03 Biomass, dry: .01–.09 | Seed: 4.6 Biomass, dry: est. 6.9 |
| 31 Wheat, Early Stone Age | 800 unhulled | .70[A] | 1.5 / D | Seed: 4 / 10 / 17[K, U] Biomass, air-dry: 12 / 30 / 51 | Seed: .005–.02+ Biomass, dry: .01–.06 | D |
| 32 Wheat, Hard Red Spring | 500 hulled | .70[A] | 2.4 / 6⅓ T | Seed: 4 / 10 / 26[K, U] Biomass, air-dry: 12 / 30 / 72 | Seed: .005–.03 Biomass, dry: .01–.09 | Seed: 5.4 Biomass, dry: est. 8.1 |
| 33 Wheat, Red Winter | 500 hulled | .70[A] | 2.4 / 6⅓ T | Seed: 4 / 10 / 26[K, U] Biomass, air-dry: 12 / 30 / 72 | Seed: .005–.03 Biomass, dry: .01–.09 | Seed: 6.4 Biomass, dry: est. 9.6 |
| 34 Wheat, White | 500 hulled | .70[A] | 2.4 / 6⅓ T | Seed: 4 / 10 / 24[K, U] Biomass, air-dry: 12 / 30 / 72 | Seed: .005–.03 Biomass, dry: .01–.09 | Seed: "3.7" Biomass, dry: est. 5.6 |

| | BEDS/FLATS | | | | | | | | | | | MATURITY | | FOOD NEEDED | SEED YIELD |
|---|---|---|---|---|---|---|---|---|---|---|---|---|---|---|---|
| **H** | **I** | **J** | **K** | **L1** | **L2** | **L3** | **L4** | **M1** | **M2** | **M3** | **M4** | **N** | **O** | **P** | **Q** |
| | | | | FIRST FLAT—3 INCHES DEEP | | | | SECOND FLAT | | | | | | | |
| In-Bed Spacing (inches) | MAXIMUM No. Plants per 100 Square Feet [7] | Short/Long/Extra-Long Germination Time | Plant Initially in Flats/Beds (in order of preference) | Spacing in First Flat (inches) or Broadcast | Approx. No. Plants per Flat (adj. for germ. rate)[14] | Division Factor to Determine Flats to Broadcast[15] | Approx. No. Weeks in First Flat[16] | Depth of Second Flat (inches) | Spacing in Second Flat (inches) | Approx. No. Plants per Flat[14] | Approx. No. Weeks in Second Flat[16] | Approx. No. Weeks to Maturity in Ground[17] | Approx. No. Weeks in Harvesting Period | Pounds Consumed per Year by Average Person in U.S.[13,18] | Approx. Maximum Pounds Seed Yield per 100 Square Feet[19] |
| 9 | 248 | S | F | 2 | 42 | — | 2–4 | — | — | — | — | 17 | — | ".64" | 24 |
| 60 | 4 | S | F | 1 | 175 | — | 2–3 | — | — | — | — | 22 | 26+ | D | 16+ |
| 12 | 159 | S | F | BC | 175 | 4 | 1 | 3 | 1.5 | 111 | 3 | 16 | — | D | 26 |
| 9 | 248 | S | F | BC | 175 | 2 | 1–2 | — | — | — | — | D | D | D | 20 |
| 4 | 1,343 | S | F | 1 or BC | 175 | 2 | 2 | — | — | — | — | 17 | — | 22.3 | 24 |
| 5 | 833 | S | F | 1 or BC | 175 | 2 | 1–2 | — | — | — | — | 17 to 38[47] | — | .4 | 24 |
| 5 | 833 | S | F | 1 | 175 | — | 2–3 | — | — | — | — | 17 | — | Oil: "1.0" | 17+ |
| 6 | 621 | L | F | 1 | 175 | — | 3 | — | — | — | — | 13–17 | 8 | D | 6+ |
| Reg. type: 7 Broom type: 4 | 432 1,343 | S | F | 1 or BC | 162 | 2 | 2–3 | — | — | — | — | 13 | — | D | 24 |
| 6 | 621 | S | F | 1 | 187 | — | 2 | — | — | — | — | Green: 8–9 Dry: 16–17 | 2–4 | All purposes: "467.4" | 14 |
| 24 / 9** | 26 / 248 | S | F | 1 | 125+ | — | 2–3 | — | — | — | — | 12 | — | D | 10 |
| 5 | 833 | S | F | 1 or BC | 175 | 2 | 1–2 | — | — | — | — | 16–18 to 38[47] | — | See Wheat, Hard Red Spring | 26 |
| 5 | 833 | L | F | 1 or BC | 175 | 2 | 2–3 | — | — | — | — | 16–20 to 42[47] | — | D | 17+ |
| 5 | 833 | S | F | 1 or BC | 175 | 2 | 1–2 | — | — | — | — | 16–18 to 38[47] | — | | 26 |
| 5 | 833 | S | F | 1 or BC | 175 | 2 | 1–2 | — | — | — | — | 16–18 to 38[47] | — | All purposes: 140.7 | 26 |
| 5 | 833 | S | F | 1 or BC | 175 | 2 | 1–2 | — | — | — | — | 16–18 to 38[47] | — | | 26 |

MASTER CHARTS

*(continued)*

| PLANT<br><br>AA | FOOD NEEDED<br>BB<br>*Pounds You Select* | MATERIALS NEEDED<br>CC<br>*Approx. No. Plants You Need [20]* | DD<br>*Approx. Square Feet You Need [21]* | EE<br>*Approx. No. Flats You Need [22]* | FF<br>*Approx. Ounces Seed You Need [23]* | YIELDS<br>GG<br>*Your Actual Yield per 100 Square Feet* | HH<br>*Your Actual Yield Compared with U.S. Average [24]* | MISCELLANEOUS<br>II<br>*Especially Good Varieties, Possible Seed Sources, and Remarks* | JJ<br>*Heavy Giver (HG), Light Feeder (LF), Low Nitrogen User (LNU), Heavy Feeder (HF)* | KK<br>*Time of Year to Plant (SP, SU, FA, WI)* |
|---|---|---|---|---|---|---|---|---|---|---|
| 19 Peanuts | | | | | | | | Note 45 | HG | SU |
| 20 Pigeon Peas | | | | | | | | — | HG | SU |
| 21 Quinoa | | | | | | | | — | HF | SU |
| 22 Rapeseed (Canola) | | | | | | | | Note 45 | HF | SP, SU, FA |
| 23 Rice | | | | | | | | — | HF | SU |
| 24 Rye, Cereal | | | | | | | | Note 27 | HF | FA |
| 25 Safflower | | | | | | | | Note 46 | HF | SU |
| 26 Sesame | | | | | | | | — | HF | SU |
| 27 Sorghum | | | | | | | | Note 33 | HF | SU |
| 28 Soybeans | | | | | | | | Note 27 | HG | SU |
| 29 Sunflowers | | | | | | | | — | HF | SU |
| 30 Wheat, Durum | | | | | | | | — | HF | FA |
| 31 Wheat, Early Stone Age | | | | | | | | Note 33 | HF | FA |
| 32 Wheat, Hard Red Spring | | | | | | | | Note 33 | HF | FA |
| 33 Wheat, Red Winter | | | | | | | | — | HF | FA |
| 34 Wheat, White | | | | | | | | — | HF | FA |

| NUTRITION | | | NOTES | CROP PROCEDURES |
|---|---|---|---|---|
| **LL**<br>Protein Content per Pound in Grams (g) (454 g per pound) [25] | **MM**<br>Calorie Content per Pound [25,50] | **NN**<br>Calcium Content per Pound in Milligrams (mg) [25] | **OO** | **PP** |
| 117.9 | 2,572 | 313 | :Shelled, raw. Shells 27% of unshelled weight.<br>Can be carcinogenic if not stored properly. | Transplant when ~1.5 inches tall. Harvest when leaves begin to lose their green color and become dull; check maturity by digging up a few peanuts. |
| 92.5 | 1,556 | 485 | :Dry. Hulls 61% of unhulled weight.<br>Short-lived perennial in tropical climates. | — |
| 73.5 | 1,600 | 640 | :Dry. | Prick out when cotyledons have emerged and before first leaf emerges. Transplant when 2–3 inches tall and strong. Harvest when seeds are mature and dry enough to rub out of head easily. |
| D | 1,960 | D | :Dry. Helps eradicate weeds. | Transplant when seedlings are ~1.5–2 inches tall. Harvest for seed when plants are ~85% golden; be alert for birds and/or shattering. For biomass, see Fava Beans. |
| 34.0<br>30.4<br>2.7* | 1,642<br>1,656<br>D | 145<br>109<br>86 | :Brown.<br>:White.<br>:Straw and chaff, dry. | Transplant when seedlings are about ~2 inches tall. Harvest when plants are ~85% golden; be alert for shattering and birds. |
| 54.9<br>D | 1,520<br>90 | 172<br>118 | :Dry, whole grain.  } 15% in wheat bread buffers phytates that<br>:Straw and chaff, dry.  } otherwise tie up iron. | See Barley. |
| 86.6 | 2,345 | D | :Dry, hulled. Source of organic matter and vegetable oil. Hulls 49% of unhulled weight. | Transplant when seedlings are ~1.5–2 inches tall. Harvest carefully after plant has begun to dry, when 98–100% of heads are dry, and before seeds begin to shatter. |
| 84.4 | 2,599 | 5,262 | :Dry. Very high in calcium. Seed = 40% oil. | Transplant when seedlings are ~1.5 inches tall and strong. Harvest when pods are full and plants begin losing green color, and before seeds shatter. |
| 49.9<br>15.0* | 1,538<br>351 | 127<br>154 | :Grain, dry.  } 1 gallon of sorghum syrup can be obtained<br>:Fodder, dry.  } from 100 sq ft from some varieties. | See Pearl Millet. |
| 49.9<br>154.7 | 608<br>1,887 | 304<br>1,025 | :Green.<br>:Hulled, dry. | See Beans. |
| 108.9 | 2,585 | 544 | :Dry seeds without hulls. Hulls 46% of unhulled weight. Seed = approx. 20% oil. ~.33 lb seeds required to produce 1T of oil. | Transplant when seedlings have 2 true leaves, and a third one coming. If possible, set deep enough so cotyledons are at soil surface; for leggy seedlings, set so that true leaves are 1 inch above soil surface. Harvest for seeds when "fuzz" is dry and black. May need to be protected from birds. |
| 57.6<br>1.3* | 1,538<br>100 | 168<br>95 | :Grain, dry.<br>:Straw and chaff, dry. | See Barley. |
| 83.0<br>D | D<br>D | D<br>D | :Grain, dry.  } Triticum monococcum var. Hornemanii.<br>:Straw and chaff, dry.  } Variety up to 12,500 years old.<br>} More difficult to thresh than other wheat. | See Barley. |
| 63.5<br>1.3* | 1,492<br>100 | 163<br>95 | :Grain, dry.<br>:Straw and chaff, dry. | See Barley. |
| 55.8<br>46.3<br>1.3* | 1,483<br>1,483<br>100 | 209<br>191<br>95 | :Grain, dry, hard variety.<br>:Grain, dry, soft variety.<br>:Straw and chaff, dry. | See Barley. |
| 42.6<br>1.3* | 1,551<br>100 | 163<br>95 | :Grain, dry.  } For milder, wetter climate, like the<br>:Straw and chaff, dry.  } Pacific Northwest. Not widely used. | See Barley. |

# COMPOST, CARBON, ORGANIC MATTER, FODDER AND COVER CROPS

For organic matter, also see: Artichoke, Jerusalem; Beans, Fava, Garlic

| PLANT <br> **A** | **B** Approx. No. Seeds per Ounce [4] (range: larger–smaller seed) | **C** Minimum Legal Germination Rate [5] | **D** Ounces / Volume Seed per 100 Square Feet (adj. for germ. rate, offset spacing, and curv. surf.) [6,7,8] | **E** Possible GROW BIOINTENSIVE Yield in Pounds per 100-Square-Foot Planting [9] | **F** Possible GROW BIOINTENSIVE Yield in Pounds per Plant [10,11] | **G** Average U.S. Yield in Pounds per 100 Square Feet [12,13] |
|---|---|---|---|---|---|---|
| **SEED** | | | | **YIELD** | | |
| 1 Alfalfa | 14,000 | .70^A | .085 / ¼ T | Biomass, air-dry: 37 / 69 / 103 Biomass, wet: 148 / 275 / 412, 5–6 cuttings | Dry: .04–.12 | Biomass, air-dry: 14.9; Biomass, wet: 49.9 |
| 2 Buckwheat | 1,000 | .70^A | 2.6 / ½ c | Biomass, air-dry: 2 / 4 / 6 Grain: 4 / 8 / 16+ | D | D |
| 3 Cardoon | 688 | .60 | .04 / 1½ t | Biomass, air-dry: 20 / 40 / 80 | Dry: 1.11–4.44 | D |
| 4 Clover, Alsike | 44,875 | .70^A | .55+–.3 / ⅛ t | Biomass, air-dry: 12 / 25 / 38 (6-mo. yield) | Dry: .01–.05 | Biomass, air-dry: "4.3" |
| 5 Clover, Crimson | 7,000 | .70^A | .6+ / 1¼ t | Biomass, air-dry: 15 / 30 / 45 Biomass, wet: 60 / 120 / 180 (6-mo. yield) | Dry: .02–.05 | Biomass, air-dry: "4.3" |
| 6 Clover, Medium Red | 14,500 | .70^A | .08 for hay / .72 for green manure / 2 T / 1¹⁄₁₀ c | Biomass, air-dry: 18 / 36 / 54 Biomass, wet: 90 / 180 / 270 (6-mo. yield) | Dry: .02–.09 | Biomass, air-dry: "8.7" |
| 7 Clover, Sweet, Hubam | 11,400 | .70^A | 1.1 / ⅔ t | Biomass, air-dry: 15 / 30 / 45 Biomass, wet: 68 / 136 / 204 (6-mo. yield) | Dry: .02–.05 | Biomass, air-dry: "4.3" |
| 8 Clover, White | 45,750 | .70^A | .03 / ¼ t | Biomass, air-dry: 10 / 25 / 38 Biomass, wet: 50 / 100 / 150 (6-mo. yield) | Dry: .01–.05 | Biomass, air-dry: "4.3" |
| 9 Comfrey, Russian | — | — | 53 roots | Biomass, air-dry: 10 / 20 / 30 Biomass, wet: 92 / 184 / 276 (6-mo. yield) | Dry: .06–.19 | Biomass, air-dry: "62.6" world high (12-mo. season) |
| 10 Grass, Rye, Italian | 16,875 | .70^A | 3.6 / 1⅓ c | D | D | D |
| 11 Kudzu | 2,000 | .70^A | D / D | Biomass, air-dry: 13 / 26 / 53 Biomass, wet: 53 / 105 / 211 | Propagated by seeds, cuttings, | |
| 12 Roots, General | An important hidden compost crop beneath the ground. Root matter in the soil can range from 45–120% of | | | | | |
| 13 Sainfoin | In pods: 1,560 Cleaned: 2,040 | .50^A | .82 hulled / D | Biomass, air-dry: 10 / 20 / 30 (6-mo. yield) | Dry: .01–.04 | D |
| 14 Sunn hemp, Giant | 3,000 | .70^A | .2 / 1½ t | Biomass, air-dry: 18 / 44 / 108 Biomass, wet: 79 / 198 / 475 | Dry: .04–.25 | D |
| 15 Teosinte | 440 | .70^A | .11 / ⅔ T | Grain: 2 / 4 / 6 Biomass, air-dry: 17 / 34 / 68 Biomass, wet: 88 / 166 / 232 | Dry: .48–1.94 | D |
| 16 Timothy | 82,500 | .70^A | .01 / ⅛ t | Biomass, air-dry: 18 / 35 / 51 Biomass, wet: 45 / 87 / 127 (6-mo. yield) | Dry: .02–.06 | Biomass, air-dry: "4.3" |
| 17 Vetch, Purple, Hairy, or Woolly Pod^BB | 800 | .70^A | 5.5 (.63 if interplanted) / ¾ c (1½ T) | Biomass, air-dry: 5 / 9 / 18  } planted Biomass, wet: 24 / 45 / 90  } alone | D | D |

| H | I | J | K | L1 | L2 | L3 | L4 | M1 | M2 | M3 | M4 | N | O | P | Q |
|---|---|---|---|---|---|---|---|---|---|---|---|---|---|---|---|
| **BEDS/FLATS** | | | | | | | | | | | | **MATURITY** | | **AMOUNT NEEDED** | **SEED YIELD** |
| In-Bed Spacing (inches) | MAXIMUM No. Plants per 100 Square Feet [7] | Short/Long/Extra-Long Germination Time | Plant Initially in Flats/Beds (in order of preference) | FIRST FLAT—3 INCHES DEEP | | | | SECOND FLAT | | | | Approx. No. Weeks to Maturity in Ground [17] | Approx. No. Weeks in Harvesting Period | Pounds Consumed per Year by Average Person in U.S. [13, 18] | Approx. Maximum Pounds Seed Yield per 100 Square Feet [19] |
| | | | | Spacing in First Flat (inches) or Broadcast | Approx. No. Plants per Flat (adj. for germ. rate) [14] | Division Factor to Determine Flats to Broadcast [15] | Approx. No. Weeks in First Flat [16] | Depth of Second Flat (inches) | Spacing in Second Flat (inches) | Approx. No. Plants per Flat [14] | Approx. No. Weeks in Second Flat [16] | | | | |
| 5 | 833 | S | F | BC | 175 | 4 | 8 | — | — | — | — | 12 to first cutting, 5–9 thereafter | 3–50+ years | "611.9" | 1.8+ |
| Broadcast | D | S | B | — | — | — | — | — | — | — | — | 9–13 | — | D | 16+ |
| 36 | 18 | S | F | 1 | 150 | — | 2–3 | 6 | 2 | 60 | 3–4 | Harvest when stalks mature | 1 harvest | D | D |
| 5 | 833 | S | F | BC | 175 | 4 | 8 | — | — | — | — | 17–26 | 1 cutting | | |
| 5 | 833 | S | F | BC | 175 | 4 | 8 | — | — | — | — | 17–26 | 1 cutting | | |
| 5 | 833 | S | F | BC | 175 | 4 | 8 | — | — | — | — | 17 to first cutting, 5–9 thereafter | 2–3 years | "547.5" | 2.2+ |
| 5 | 833 | S | F | BC | 175 | 4 | 8 | — | — | — | — | 17–26 | 1 cutting | | |
| 5 | 833 | S | F | BC | 175 | 4 | 8 | — | — | — | — | 17–26 | 3–5 years | | |
| 12 | 159 | S | B | — | — | — | — | — | — | — | — | 12–17 to first cutting | Years | D | D |
| Broadcast | D | S | B | — | — | — | — | — | — | — | — | D | D | D | 6.9+ |

and roots. More research needs to be performed. For some information see *The Book of Kudzu*, by Bill Shurtleff, in the bibliography.

aboveground biomass at the end of the growing season (Brady and Weil, *The Nature and Properties of Soils*, 12th ed., p. 423).

| H | I | J | K | L1 | L2 | L3 | L4 | M1 | M2 | M3 | M4 | N | O | P | Q |
|---|---|---|---|---|---|---|---|---|---|---|---|---|---|---|---|
| 5 | 833 | S | F | BC or 1 | 125 | 2 | 8 | — | — | — | — | 17 to first cutting, 9 thereafter | D | D | .46+ |
| 7 | 432 | S | F | 1 | 175 | — | 2–3 | — | — | — | — | 17+ | D | D | D |
| 21 | 35 | S | F | 1 | 175 | — | 2–3 | — | — | — | — | D | D | D | D |
| 5 | 833 | S | F | BC | 175 | 4 | 8 | — | — | — | — | 17 | D | D | .46+ |
| Broadcast | D | S | B | — | — | — | — | — | — | — | — | D | D | D | 1.1+ |

MASTER CHARTS

# COMPOST, CARBON, ORGANIC MATTER, FODDER, AND COVER CROPS

*(continued)*

| PLANT<br>AA | AMOUNT NEEDED<br>BB<br>Pounds You Select | MATERIALS NEEDED<br>CC<br>Approx. No. Plants You Need [20] | DD<br>Approx. Square Feet You Need [21] | EE<br>Approx. No. Flats You Need [22] | FF<br>Approx. Ounces Seed You Need [23] | YIELDS<br>GG<br>Your Actual Yield per 100 Square Feet | HH<br>Your Actual Yield Compared with U.S. Average [24] | MISCELLANEOUS<br>II<br>Especially Good Varieties, Possible Seed Sources, and Remarks | JJ<br>Heavy Giver (HG), Light Feeder (LF), Low Nitrogen User (LNU), Heavy Feeder (HF) | KK<br>Time of Year to Plant (SP, SU, FA, WI) |
|---|---|---|---|---|---|---|---|---|---|---|
| 1 Alfalfa | | | | | | | | Note 33, AC | HG | SP |
| 2 Buckwheat | | | | | | | | Note 33 | HF | SP, mid-SU |
| 3 Cardoon | | | | | | | | — | HF | SP |
| 4 Clover, Alsike | | | | | | | | Note 33, AC | HG | SP |
| 5 Clover, Crimson | | | | | | | | Note 33, AC | HG | SP |
| 6 Clover, Medium Red | | | | | | | | Note 33, AC | HG | SP |
| 7 Clover, Sweet, Hubam | | | | | | | | Note 45, AC | HG | SP |
| 8 Clover, White | | | | | | | | Note 33, AC | HG | SP |
| 9 Comfrey, Russian | | | | | | | | — | HF | SP |
| 10 Grass, Rye, Italian | | | | | | | | — | HF | SP |
| 11 Kudzu | | | | | | | | — | LF | D |
| 12 Roots, General | | | | | | | | — | — | — |
| 13 Sainfoin | | | | | | | | Note 46 | HG | SP |
| 14 Sunn hemp, Giant | | | | | | | | — | HG | SU |
| 15 Teosinte | | | | | | | | Notes 42 & 46 | HF | SU |
| 16 Timothy | | | | | | | | Note 45 | HF | SP |
| 17 Vetch, Purple, Hairy, or Woolly Pod[BB] | | | | | | | | Note 33 | HG | SP, FA |

| NUTRITION | | | NOTES | CROP PROCEDURES |
|---|---|---|---|---|
| **LL** | **MM** | **NN** | **OO** | **PP** |
| Protein Content per Pound in Grams (g) (454 g per pound)[25] | Calorie Content per Pound[25,50] | Calcium Content per Pound in Milligrams (mg)[25] | | |
| Air-dry: 53.1* | 411 | 667 | :Air dry at 10% bloom point. Fixes .35–.57 lb nitrogen/100 sq ft/year. | Grown as a perennial. Transplant when seedling is 2–3 months old. Can last up to 25+ years. Harvest at 10–50% flower or when leaves are dull/gray, stems are falling over, or leaves have holes. Cut back to 2 inches above growing crown. AC |
| 53.1 | 1,520 | 517 | :Dry grain. Hulling difficult. Good honeybee plant. ½ lb honey/100 sq ft. | Japanese variety may produce more dry biomass. |
| — | — | — | Flower market potential. Can become a noxious weed; do not allow seeds to disperse. | Perennial. Harvest flowers for income just as the blue is beginning to appear or for biomass before seeds begin to disperse. Harvest stalks for biomass when they become woody and the upper leaves wither. |
| 36.7* | 436 | 522 | :Dry. Fixes up to .27 lb nitrogen/100 sq ft/year. | |
| 44.5* | 391 | 558 | :Dry. Fixes up to .21 lb nitrogen/100 sq ft/year. | Annual. For harvest, see Alfalfa. |
| 51.3* | 450 | 767 | :Dry. Before bloom. Fixes up to .23–.3 lb nitrogen/100 sq ft/year. | |
| 42.6 | 355 | 567 | :Dry. | Short-lived perennial. For harvest, see Alfalfa. More productive than other clovers. |
| 42.6* | 355 | 567 | :Dry. Fixes up to .23–.3 lb nitrogen/100 sq ft/year. | Short-lived perennial. For harvest, see Alfalfa. |
| 3.4 | D | D | | Perennial. Divide roots and plant. Harvest for biomass when plants begin to flower; cut back to 2 inches. |
| 15.4* | D | — | Not good for soil. Use cereal rye to build soil and for food. | |
| 13.3 / 11.3 | D / D | D / D | :Dried root. / :Cured hay. } Plus cloth can be made from the root. Can be invasive. | |
| — | — | — | | |
| 34.0* | D | — | :Dry. Does best in slightly dry climate. Significantly less productive than alfalfa. | |
| D | D | D | Grain legume. | For harvest, see Alfalfa. Or allow to grow, and harvest seeds before they shatter. |
| 22.2* | D | D | Less productive of biomass and significantly less productive of grain than corn, but produces an extensive root system. | Harvest grain before it shatters. |
| 18.6* | D | 186 | :Dry, early bloom. | Perennial. Harvest when earliest heads are straw-colored for highest biomass yield. |
| 69.0* | D | 513 | :Dry. Fixes up to .25 lb nitrogen/100 sq ft/year. | For better germination, soak seeds overnight in warm water; mix with dry sand or soil to minimize clumping; chop seed in very lightly with rake. Harvest at 10%–50% flower. Can become weedy if seeds disperse. |

See Voisin books in the bibliography (under "Compost Crops") for ways to increase grazing yields significantly. Try 3–5 times the seeding rate for hay if growing crop seed. Roots can equal biomass weight above ground.

MASTER CHARTS

*Letter codes on page 85, notes on page 126*

# ENERGY, FIBER, PAPER, AND OTHER CROPS

| A | SEED | | | YIELD | | | |
|---|---|---|---|---|---|---|---|
| | B<br>*Approx. No. Seeds per Ounce [4] (range: larger–smaller seed)* | C<br>*Minimum Legal Germination Rate [5]* | D<br>*Ounces / Volume Seed per 100 Square Feet (adj. for germ. rate, offset spacing, and curv. surf.) [6,7,8]* | E<br>*Possible GROW BIOINTENSIVE Yield in Pounds per 100-Square-Foot Planting [9]* | F<br>*Possible GROW BIOINTENSIVE Yield in Pounds per Plant [10,11]* | G<br>*Average U.S. Yield in Pounds per 100 Square Feet [12,13]* |
| 1 Bamboo, Paper | Under research | | | | | | General: "27.5" |
| 2 Bamboo, Regular | Under research | | | | | | |
| 3 Beets, Sugar | 1,600 | .65[A] | .4[AA] / 2 T | 91 / 182 / 364 | .21–.84 | | 104.7 |
| 4 Cheese | Approx. 1 lb per gallon of milk. Heat milk to 180°F. Add ½ cup vinegar per gallon of milk. Stir. Let sit for 5 minutes. | | | | | | |
| 5 Cotton, Regular | 300 | .70[A] | .76 / varies | 1.2 / 2.4 / 4.8+ | .007–.03+ | | 1.7 |
| 6 Cotton, Tree | An African perennial variety. Under research. | | | | | | |
| 7 Eggs, Chicken | See Ecology Action's *Backyard Homestead, Mini-Farm and Garden Log Book.* | | | | | | |
| 8 Flax | 6,000 | .70[A] | Seed: .2 / ½ t<br>Fiber: .6 / 1⅔ t | seed: 2 / 4 / 8<br>biomass, air-dry: 4 / 8 / 16+ | D | | "1.4" |
| 9 Gopher Plant | For automotive oil. Under research. Also, a toxic plant for gopher control. Not to be used around young children. | | | | | | |
| 10 Gourds | 150 | .70[A] | .5 / varies | D | D | | D |
| 11 Guayule | For rubber. Under research. | | | | | | |
| 12 Jojoba | 50 | D | For oil. Under research. | | | | |
| 13 Kenaf | For newsprint, toilet paper, fiber, twine, rope. Grows up to 18 ft high. 8–10 tons of fiber yield per acre possible annually | | | | | | |
| 14 Milk, Cow | See Ecology Action's *Backyard Homestead, Mini-Farm and Garden Log Book.*<br>A cow requires about twice the fodder as a goat and produces about twice the milk. | | | | | | |
| 15 Milk, Goat | | | | | | | |
| 16 Sprouts, Alfalfa | To be developed. Nutritious, but a large area is required for the production of the seed. | | | | | | |
| 17 Sprouts, Wheat | | | | | | | |

| | BEDS/FLATS | | | | | | | | | | | MATURITY | | AMOUNT NEEDED | SEED YIELD |
|---|---|---|---|---|---|---|---|---|---|---|---|---|---|---|---|
| **H** | **I** | **J** | **K** | **L1** | **L2** | **L3** | **L4** | **M1** | **M2** | **M3** | **M4** | **N** | **O** | **P** | **Q** |
| | | | | FIRST FLAT—3 INCHES DEEP | | | | SECOND FLAT | | | | | | | |
| In-Bed Spacing (inches) | MAXIMUM No. Plants per 100 Square Feet [7] | Short/Long/Extra-Long Germination Time | Plant Initially in Flats/Beds (in order of preference) | Spacing in First Flat (inches) or Broadcast | Approx. No. Plants per Flat (adj. for germ. rate) [14] | Division Factor to Determine Flats to Broadcast [15] | Approx. No. Weeks in First Flat [16] | Depth of Second Flat (inches) | Spacing in Second Flat (inches) | Approx. No. Plants per Flat [14] | Approx. No. Weeks in Second Flat [16] | Approx. No. Weeks to Maturity in Ground [17] | Approx. No. Weeks in Harvesting Period | Pounds Consumed per Year by Average Person in U.S. [13, 18] | Approx. Maximum Pounds Seed Yield per 100 Square Feet [19] |
| | | | | | | | | | | | | | | All paper and paperboard: "699" | |
| | | | | | | | | | | | | | | | |
| 7 | 432 | L | F | 1 | 162 | — | 3–4 | — | — | — | — | 12 | — | All sugars: "67.1 lbs" All syrups: "10+ gal" | "30.6" |

Pour through cheesecloth lining a colander. Let drain until excess moisture is gone. Result: soft cheese.

| | | | | | | | | | | | | | | | |
|---|---|---|---|---|---|---|---|---|---|---|---|---|---|---|---|
| 12 | 159 | L | F | 1 | 175 | — | 3–4 | — | — | — | — | 17–26 | — | D | 22.7 |
| | | | | | | | | | | | | | | | |
| | | | | | | | | | | | | | | Eggs: "240 (30 lb)" | |
| Seed: 5 Fiber: 3 | 833 2,507 | S | F | 1 | 175 | — | 2–3 | — | — | — | — | 12–14 | — | D | D |
| | | | | | | | | | | | | | | | |
| 18 | 53 | S | F | 2 | 42 | — | 3–4 | — | — | — | — | 16 | — | D | D |
| | | | | | | | | | | | | | | | |
| | | | | | | | | | | | | | | | |

(5 times the pulp per acre compared with wood).

| | | | | | | | | | | | | | | | |
|---|---|---|---|---|---|---|---|---|---|---|---|---|---|---|---|
| | | | | | | | | | | | | | | Fluid milk and cream: 207.0 lbs (25.9 gal) | |
| | | | | | | | | | | | | | | D | |
| | | | | | | | | | | | | | | | |
| | | | | | | | | | | | | | | | |

MASTER CHARTS

# ENERGY, FIBER, PAPER, AND OTHER CROPS
*(continued)*

| AA | AMOUNT NEEDED BB — Pounds You Select | MATERIALS NEEDED CC — Approx. No. Plants You Need [20] | DD — Approx. Square Feet You Need [21] | EE — Approx. No. Flats You Need [22] | FF — Approx. Ounces Seed You Need [23] | YIELDS GG — Your Actual Yield per 100 Square Feet | HH — Your Actual Yield Compared with U.S. Average [24] | MISCELLANEOUS II — Especially Good Varieties, Possible Seed Sources, and Remarks | JJ — Heavy Giver (HG), Light Feeder (LF), Low Nitrogen User (LNU), Heavy Feeder (HF) | KK — Time of Year to Plant (SP, SU, FA, WI) |
|---|---|---|---|---|---|---|---|---|---|---|
| 1 Bamboo, Paper | | | | | | | | — | — | — |
| 2 Bamboo, Regular | | | | | | | | — | — | — |
| 3 Beets, Sugar | | | | | | | | Note 45 | LF | SP, SU, FA |
| 4 Cheese | | | | | | | | — | — | — |
| 5 Cotton, Regular | | | | | | | | Note 42 | HF | SU |
| 6 Cotton, Tree | | | | | | | | — | — | SU |
| 7 Eggs, Chicken | | | | | | | | — | — | — |
| 8 Flax | | | | | | | | Note 46 | HF | SP |
| 9 Gopher Plant | | | | | | | | — | — | — |
| 10 Gourds | | | | | | | | — | HF | SU |
| 11 Guayule | | | | | | | | — | — | — |
| 12 Jojoba | | | | | | | | — | — | — |
| 13 Kenaf | | | | | | | | — | — | — |
| 14 Milk, Cow | | | | | | | | — | — | — |
| 15 Milk, Goat | | | | | | | | — | — | — |
| 16 Sprouts, Alfalfa | | | | | | | | — | — | All year |
| 17 Sprouts, Wheat | | | | | | | | — | — | All year |

| NUTRITION | | | NOTES | CROP PROCEDURES |
|---|---|---|---|---|
| **LL** | **MM** | **NN** | **OO** | **PP** |
| Protein Content per Pound in Grams (g) (454 g per pound) [25] | Calorie Content per Pound [25, 50] | Calcium Content per Pound in Milligrams (mg) [25] | Δ Probably any abundant local species, reasonably priced, may be used. Better grades of paper are made from young and still leafless culms; older, mature culms are too lignified for easy processing but can be used for coarse, dark-fibered paper. 40% paper yield. For wrapping paper, newsprint, and book-quality paper. Paper can also be made from many fibrous plants, including cabbage. | |
| — | — | — | See above. Δ | |
| — | — | — | Building materials, piping. | Use clumping bamboo to minimize spreading; roots may need to be restrained. For building, furniture, and pipeline, harvest after 3 years of growth. |
| D | 1,746 | D | ~5.2 lb of sugar beets are required to produce 1 T of sugar. | |
| 36.3 | 1,696 | 281 | :Cream cheese. Add parsley, dill seeds, chives for flavor. | |
| — | — | — | Minimum clothes replacement rate per year: 2.5 lbs. Thousands of years ago in India, people placed a mineral in the soil with the cotton plants, and colored fibers resulted! | Harvest when seeds are fully developed. |
| — | — | — | | |
| 52.1 | 658 | 218 | :11% refuse. | |
| 89 | 2,419 | 1,115 | | For seed, harvest before seeds shatter. For fiber, harvest when seeds are beginning to turn color from green to brown and bottom of plant is beginning to turn yellow. |
| — | — | — | | |
| — | — | — | | For transplanting, see Cucumbers. Support gourds on smooth rocks to keep them off the damp soil. Harvest when stem is dry and hard; cut off with 2 inches of stem. |
| — | — | — | | |
| | | — | | |
| — | — | — | For more information on kenaf, write to the American Kenaf Society, PMB 440, 1001 South 10th Street, Ste G, McAllen, TX 78501. | |
| 15.9 | 299 | 531 | :3.7% fat. | |
| 14.5 | 304 | 585 | Has only ⅓ the vitamin $B_{12}$ that cow's milk has. | |
| Nutritive amounts given for sprouts differ. | | | | |

MASTER CHARTS

| TREE AND CANE CROPS | SEED | | | YIELD | | |
|---|---|---|---|---|---|---|
| | **B** | **C** | **D** | **E** | **F** | **G** |
| **PLANT**<br>**A** | Approx. No. Seeds per Ounce [4] (range: larger–smaller seed) | Minimum Legal Germination Rate [5] | Approx. No. Plants per Acre | Possible GROW BIOINTENSIVE Yield in Pounds per 100-Square-Foot Planting [9] | Possible GROW BIOINTENSIVE Yield in Pounds per Plant [10, 11] | Average U.S. Yield in Pounds per 100 Square Feet [12, 13] |
| 1 Almond | 12–15 | D | 160 | Shelled: 1.4 / 2.8 / 4.2+ | 3.8–11.4 | 7.2 |
| 2 Apple, Dwarf | 600–1,000 | D | 681 | 50 / 75 / 100 | 32–64 | 51.4 |
| 3 Apple, Regular | 600–1,000 | .65^ | 27 | 50 / 75 / 100 | 800–1,600 | 51.4 |
| 4 Apple, Semidwarf | 600–1,000 | D | 194 | 50 / 75 / 100 | 112–225 | 51.4 |
| 5 Apricot, Dwarf | 18–20 | D | 681 | 25 / 50 / 100 | 25–100 | 25.1 |
| 6 Apricot, Regular | 18–20 | .90^ | 70 | 25 / 50 / 100 | 156–625 | 25.1 |
| 7 Apricot, Semidwarf | 18–20 | D | 303 | 25 / 50 / 100 | 36–144 | 25.1 |
| 8 Avocado, Tall / Dwarf | D | D | 302–193 / 681 | 9 / 18 / 36 | 13–81 / 6–23 | 16.0 |
| 9 Banana, Tall / Dwarf | — | D | 302–193 / 681 | 27 / 60 / 92+ | 39–208 / 12–59 | 38.3 |
| 10 Blackberries | 10,000 | — | 2,723 | 24 / 36 / 48+ | 3.8–7.6+ | 15.0 |
| 11 Blueberries, Low Bush / High Bush | — | — | 10,890 / 2,723 | 19 / 37 / 75 | .76–3.0 / 3.0–12.0 | D |
| 12 Boysenberries | — | — | 681 | 26 / 39 / 52+ | 16.6–33+ | "25.7" |
| 13 Cherry, Sour, Bush | D | D | 4,840 | 8 / 17 / 34 | .8–3.0 | D |
| 14 Cherry, Sour, Dwarf | 200–250 | .80^ | 681 | 17 / 34 / 51 | 11–32.6 | 14.0 |
| 15 Cherry, Sour, Regular | 200–250 | D | 1,089 | 17 / 34 / 51 | 68–204 | 14.0 |
| 16 Cherry, Sweet, Bush | D | D | 4,840 | 8 / 17 / 34 | .8–3.0 | D |
| 17 Cherry, Sweet, Dwarf | 150–160 | D | 681 | 17 / 34 / 51 | 11–32.6 | 15.0 |
| 18 Cherry, Sweet, Regular | 150–160 | .75^ | 481 | 17 / 34 / 51 | 153–459 | 15.0 |
| 19 Chestnut | 1 | .72^ | 27 | In shell: 3.5 / 7 / 15 | 56–240 | D |

| | BEDS/FLATS | | | | | | MATURITY | | FOOD NEEDED | SEED YIELD |
|---|---|---|---|---|---|---|---|---|---|---|
| **H** In-Bed Spacing (feet) | **I** Square Feet Required per Plant | **J** Short/Long/Extra-Long Germination Time | **K** Plant Initially in Flats/Beds (in order of preference) | **L** Flats spacing for First Flat and Second Flat (inches) | **M** Approx. No. Plants per Flat (adj. for germ. rate)[14] | **N** Approx. No. Weeks in Flats[16] | **O** Approx. No. Years to Bearing and Approx. No. Years to Max. Bearing | **P** Approx. No. Weeks in Harvesting Period and Possible Bearing Years | **Q** Pounds Consumed per Year by Average Person in U.S.[13,18] | **R** Approx. Maximum Pounds Seed Yield per 100 Square Feet[19] |
|---|---|---|---|---|---|---|---|---|---|---|
| 16.5 | 272 | L | F | 4 / I | D / — | D / D | 3–4 / D | D / D | ".4" | In shell: 8.4 |
| 8 | 64 | EL | F | 2 / I | D / — | D / D | 3 / D | D / D | | D |
| 40 | 1,600 | EL | F | 2 / I | 39 / — | D / D | 5 / 10 | D / 35–50 | "16.0" | D |
| 15 | 225 | EL | F | 2 / I | D / — | D / D | 4 / 10 | D / D | | D |
| 8 | 64 | L | F | 4 / I | D / — | D / D | 2 / D | D / D | | D |
| 25 | 625 | L | F | 4 / I | 14 / — | D / D | 3 / D | D / D | ".17" | D |
| 12 | 144 | L | F | 4 / I | D / — | D / D | 3 / D | D / D | | D |
| 12–15 / 8 | 144–225 / 64 | D | F | 4 / I | D / — | D / D | D / D | D / D | "1.3" | D |
| 12–15 / 8 | 144–225 / 64 | D | F | 4 / I | D / D | D / D | D / D | D / D | D | — |
| 4 | 16 | D | Deep flat | 6 / I | D / — | D / D | 2 / D | D / 6–25 | D | — |
| 2 / 4 | 4 / 16 | D | D | — / — | M / D | D / D | 3–4 / D | 6–7 / 10–15 | ".12" | — |
| 8 | 64 | D | Deep flat | 6 / I | D / — | D / D | 2 / D | D / 6–10 | D | — |
| 3 | 9 | L | F | 3 / I | D / — | D / D | 3 / D | D / D | | D |
| 8 | 64 | L | F | 3 / I | 22 / — | D / D | 3 / D | D / D | | D |
| 20 | 400 | L | F | 3 / I | D / — | D / D | 4 / 10–20 | D / D | ".62" | D |
| 3 | 9 | L | F | 3 / I | D / — | D / D | 3 / D | D / D | | D |
| 8 | 64 | L | F | 3 / I | D / — | D / D | 3 / D | D / D | | D |
| 30 | 900 | L | F | 3 / I | 20 / — | D / D | 4 / 10–20 | D / D | | D |
| 40 | 1,600 | D | Deep flat | 6 / I | 5 / — | D / D | D / D | D / D | D | In shell: 15.0 |

*Letter codes on page 85, notes on page 126*

MASTER CHARTS

# TREE AND CANE CROPS
*(continued)*

| PLANT<br><br>AA | FOOD NEEDED<br><br>BB<br><br>*Pounds You Select* | MATERIALS NEEDED | | | | YIELDS | | MISCELLANEOUS | | |
|---|---|---|---|---|---|---|---|---|---|---|
| | | CC<br><br>*Approx. No. Plants You Need* [20] | DD<br><br>*Approx. Square Feet You Need* [21] | EE<br><br>*Approx. No. Flats You Need* [22] | FF<br><br>*Approx. Ounces Seed You Need* [23] | GG<br><br>*Your Actual Yield per 100 Square Feet* | HH<br><br>*Your Actual Yield Compared with U.S. Average* [24] | II<br><br>*Especially Good Varieties, Possible Seed Sources, and Remarks* | JJ<br><br>*Heavy Giver (HG), Light Feeder (LF), Low Nitrogen User (LNU), Heavy Feeder (HF)* | KK<br><br>*Time of Year to Plant (SP, SU, FA, WI)* |
| 1 Almond | | | | | | | | — | HF | Early SP |
| 2 Apple, Dwarf | | | | | | | | — | HF | Early SP |
| 3 Apple, Regular | | | | | | | | — | HF | Early SP |
| 4 Apple, Semidwarf | | | | | | | | — | HF | Early SP |
| 5 Apricot, Dwarf | | | | | | | | — | HF | Early SP |
| 6 Apricot, Regular | | | | | | | | Manchurian | HF | Early SP |
| 7 Apricot, Semidwarf | | | | | | | | — | HF | Early SP |
| 8 Avocado, Tall Dwarf | | | | | | | | — | HF | Early SP |
| 9 Banana, Tall Dwarf | | | | | | | | — | HF | Early SP |
| 10 Blackberries | | | | | | | | — | HF | Early SP |
| 11 Blueberries, Low Bush High Bush | | | | | | | | — | HF | Early SP |
| 12 Boysenberries | | | | | | | | — | HF | Early SP |
| 13 Cherry, Sour, Bush | | | | | | | | 2 varieties for pollination | HF | Early SP |
| 14 Cherry, Sour, Dwarf | | | | | | | | — | HF | Early SP |
| 15 Cherry, Sour, Regular | | | | | | | | — | HF | Early SP |
| 16 Cherry, Sweet, Bush | | | | | | | | — | HF | Early SP |
| 17 Cherry, Sweet, Dwarf | | | | | | | | — | HF | Early SP |
| 18 Cherry, Sweet, Regular | | | | | | | | — | HF | Early SP |
| 19 Chestnut | | | | | | | | — | HF | Early SP |

| NUTRITION | | | NOTES | CROP PROCEDURES |
|---|---|---|---|---|
| **LL** | **MM** | **NN** | **OO** | **PP** |
| Protein Content per Pound in Grams (g) (454 g per pound) [25] | Calorie Content per Pound [25,50] | Calcium Content per Pound in Milligrams (mg) [25] | | For varietal and other information, see (HPW) *Western Fruit, Berries and Nuts: How to Select, Grow and Enjoy*, by Lance Walheim and Robert L. Stebbins (under Fruits, Berries, and Nuts in Bibliography), and/or (DW) Dave Wilson Nursery catalog (under Seed Catalogs in Bibliography), or (HPC) *Citrus: How to Select, Grow and Enjoy*, by Richard Ray and Lance Walheim (under Fruits, Berries, and Nuts in Bibliography). |
| 84.4 | 2,713 | 1,061 | :Shelled. Shells 49% of unshelled weight. | HPW, DW. |
| .8 | 242 | 29 | :Raw. 8% refuse. Spur-type yields higher. Thin to 6 to 8 in. | (1) Harvest according to varietal maturation time. Also, harvest before first frost, before significant drop occurs, and before or as bird damage begins to occur. Optimum harvest time will vary from year to year depending on climatic conditions. |
| .8 | 242 | 29 | :Raw. 8% refuse. Thin to 6 to 8 in. | (2) Consider grafting several varieties on 1 tree for harvest during a significant part of the growing season, depending on climate. |
| .8 | 242 | 29 | :Raw. 8% refuse. Thin to 6 to 8 in. | (3) Note that one full-sized tree at maturity can produce approximately 3 lb of apples per day, at intermediate yields. You do not need many fruit trees to have enough fruit. Consider doing a few trees well. It takes less time! 1.5 gallons of apple cider or apple cider vinegar can be obtained per 100 sq ft. |
| 4.3 | 217 | 72 | :Raw. 6% refuse. A fall-yielding variety also exists. | See (1) and (2) under Apples. HPW, DW. |
| 4.3 | 217 | 72 | :Raw. 6% refuse. 30 ft high. | |
| 4.3 | 217 | 72 | :Raw. 6% refuse. | |
| 7.1 | 568 | 34 | :25% refuse. | HPW |
| 3.4 | 262 | 25 | :Yellow.         32% refuse | HPW |
| 3.7 | 278 | 31 | :Red. | |
| 5.3 | 264 | 145 | :Raw. | Propagated by cuttings. Beds 2–3 ft wide. Some people use 2-ft centers. See (1) under Apples. HPW. |
| 2.9 | 259 | 63 | :Raw. 8% refuse. | Propagated by cuttings in late SP. Remove blossoms for first 2 years. Use bird netting. See (1) under Apples. HPW, DW. |
| 3.2 | 163 | 86 | :Canned. 8% refuse. Bearing season: Logan (midsummer); Young (midsummer); Olallie (late summer). | Propagated by cuttings. 2-ft-wide beds. 4–8 canes/center. See Blackberries. |
| 5.0 | 242 | 92 | :Raw. 8% refuse. | See (1) under Apples. HPW, DW. |
| 5.0 | 242 | 92 | :Raw. 8% refuse. | |
| 5.0 | 242 | 92 | :Raw. 8% refuse. | |
| 3.6 | 195 | 68 | :Canned, without pits. | |
| 3.6 | 195 | 68 | :Canned, without pits. One self-pollinating variety exists. | |
| 3.6 | 195 | 68 | :Canned, without pits. | |
| 30.4 | 1,710 | 236 | :Dried and shelled: 18% of unshelled weight. Problems with blight. | HPW, DW. |

MASTER CHARTS

# TREE AND CANE CROPS

| PLANT A | SEED Approx. No. Seeds per Ounce [4] (range: larger-smaller seed) B | SEED Minimum Legal Germination Rate [5] C | SEED Approx. No. Plants per Acre D | YIELD Possible GROW BIOINTENSIVE Yield in Pounds per 100-Square-Foot Planting [9] E | YIELD Possible GROW BIOINTENSIVE Yield in Pounds per Plant [10, 11] F | YIELD Average U.S. Yield in Pounds per 100 Square Feet [12, 13] G |
|---|---|---|---|---|---|---|
| 20 Coconut | — | D | 48 | 3 / 6 / 13 | 27–118 | D |
| 21 Currants, Black | — | — | 2,723 | D | D | D |
| 22 Dates | 40 | — | 48 | 23 / 46 / 70 | 207–630 | 14.2 |
| 23 Fig | — | — | 194 | Raw: 12 / 24 / 36++ | 27–81++ | 17.1 |
| 24 Filbert | 10–20 | — | 194 | Shelled: 7 / 15 / 30 | 15.7–67.4 | 6.2 |
| 25 Grapefruit | 150–200 | D | 76 | 63 / 95 / 126 | 362–724 | 73.7 |
| 26 Grapes, Raisin | — | — | 681 | Fresh, for drying: 45 / 67 / 90 | 29–58 | "45.4" |
| 27 Grapes, Table | — | — | 681 | 45 / 67 / 90 | 29–58 | 31.2 |
| 28 Grapes, Wine | — | — | 681 | 32 / 48 / 64 | 20.5–41 | "31.6" |
| 29 Guava | D | D | 303 | D | D | 28.9 |
| 30 Hickory | 1–5 depends on variety | .55–.80 j depends on variety | 27 | D | D | D |
| 31 Honey Locust | 180 | .50 j | 27 | Pods and beans: 6 / 13 / 26+ | 128–320 | D |
| 32 Lemon | 200–300 | D | 76 | 75 / 112 / 150 | 432–864 | 76.2 |
| 33 Lime | 300–400 | D | 194 | D | D | "32.3" |
| 34 Mango | D | D | 48 | D | D | D |
| 35 Mesquite | D | D | 109 | Seeds: D  Pods: D | D  D | D |
| 36 Nectarine, Dwarf | D | D | 681 | 40 / 60 / 80 | 25.6–51+ | "29.0" |
| 37 Nectarine, Regular | D | D | 194 | 40 / 60 / 80 | 90–180+ | "29.0" |
| 38 Olive | D | D | 27 | 8 / 17 / 35 | 129–564 | 15.0 |

| H | I | J | K | L | M | N | O | P | Q | R |
|---|---|---|---|---|---|---|---|---|---|---|
| **BEDS/FLATS** | | | | | | | **MATURITY** | | **FOOD NEEDED** | **SEED YIELD** |
| In-Bed Spacing (feet) | Square Feet Required per Plant | Short/Long/Extra-Long Germination Time | Plant Initially in Flats/Beds (in order of preference) | Flats spacing for First Flat and Second Flat (inches) | Approx. No. Plants per Flat (adj. for germ. rate)[14] | Approx. No. Weeks in Flats[16] | Approx. No. Years to Bearing and Approx. No. Years to Max. Bearing | Approx. No. Weeks in Harvesting Period and Possible Bearing Years | Pounds Consumed per Year by Average Person in U.S.[13,18] | Approx. Maximum Pounds Seed Yield per 100 Square Feet[19] |
| 30 | 900 | D | F | 4 / I | D / — | D / D | D / D | D / D | D | D |
| 4 | 16 | D | Deep flat | 6 / I | D / — | D / D | 3 / D | D / D | D | — |
| 30 | 900 | D | Deep flat | 9 / I | D / — | D / D | 5–6 / 10–15 | D / D | D | D |
| 15 | 225 | D | Deep flat | 9 / I | D / — | D / D | D / D | D / 17 | D | D |
| 15 (18–25) | 225 | D | Deep flat | 9 / I | D / — | D / D | D / D | D / D | ".07" | In shell: 55.0 |
| 24 | 576 | L | F | 3 / I | D / — | D / D | 3 / D | D / D | "6.7" | D |
| 8 | 64 | D | F | 6 / I | D / — | D / D | 3 / D | D / D | Dry: "2.0" | D |
| 8 | 64 | D | F | 6 / I | D / — | D / D | 3 / D | D / D | "4.6" | D |
| 8 | 64 | D | F | 6 / I | D / — | D / D | 3 / D | D / D | "20.4" | D |
| 12 | 144 | D | F | 2 / I | D / — | D / D | D / D | D / D | FOOD | D |
| 40 | 1,600 | D | F | 4 / I | 8–12 / — | D / D | D / D | D / 25–350 | D | D |
| 40 | 1,600 | D | F | 4 / I | 8 / — | D / D | D / D | D / 10 100 | D | In shell: 13.0 |
| 24 | 576 | D | F | 2 / I | D / — | D / D | 3 / D | D / 50+ | "3.8" | D |
| 15 | 225 | D | F | 2 / I | D / — | D / D | 3 / D | D / D | ".3" | D |
| 30 | 900 | D | F | 2 / I | D / — | D / D | D / D | D / D | ".02" | D |
| 20 | 400 | D | F | 2 / I | D / — | D / D | D / D | D / D | D | D |
| 8 | 64 | D | Sapling: B | — | — | — | 3–4 / 8–12 | D / D | "1.8" | D |
| 15 | 225 | D | F | 4 / I | D / — | D / D | D / D | D / D | "1.8" | D |
| 40 | 1,600 | D | F | 2 / I | D / — | D / D | D / D | D / D | D | D |

MASTER CHARTS

# TREE AND CANE CROPS

*(continued)*

| PLANT | FOOD NEEDED | MATERIALS NEEDED | | | | YIELDS | | MISCELLANEOUS | | |
| | BB | CC | DD | EE | FF | GG | HH | II | JJ | KK |
| AA | Pounds You Select | Approx. No. Plants You Need [20] | Approx. Square Feet You Need [21] | Approx. No. Flats You Need [22] | Approx. Ounces Seed You Need [23] | Your Actual Yield per 100 Square Feet | Your Actual Yield Compared with U.S. Average [24] | Especially Good Varieties, Possible Seed Sources, and Remarks | Heavy Giver (HG), Light Feeder (LF), Low Nitrogen User (LNU), Heavy Feeder (HF) | Time of Year to Plant (SP, SU, FA, WI) |
|---|---|---|---|---|---|---|---|---|---|---|
| 20 Coconut | | | | | | | | — | HF | Early SP |
| 21 Currants, Black | | | | | | | | — | HF | Early SP |
| 22 Dates | | | | | | | | — | HF | Early SP |
| 23 Fig | | | | | | | | — | HF | Early SP |
| 24 Filbert | | | | | | | | — | HF | Early SP |
| 25 Grapefruit | | | | | | | | — | HF | Early SP |
| 26 Grapes, Raisin | | | | | | | | — | HF | Early SP |
| 27 Grapes, Table | | | | | | | | — | HF | Early SP |
| 28 Grapes, Wine | | | | | | | | — | HF | Early SP |
| 29 Guava | | | | | | | | — | HF | Early SP |
| 30 Hickory | | | | | | | | — | HF | Early SP |
| 31 Honey Locust | | | | | | | | — | HF | Early SP |
| 32 Lemon | | | | | | | | — | HF | Early SP |
| 33 Lime | | | | | | | | — | HF | Early SP |
| 34 Mango | | | | | | | | — | HF | D |
| 35 Mesquite | | | | | | | | — | HF | Early SP |
| 36 Nectarine, Dwarf | | | | | | | | — | HF | Early SP |
| 37 Nectarine, Regular | | | | | | | | — | HF | Early SP |
| 38 Olive | | | | | | | | — | HF | Early SP |

| NUTRITION | | | NOTES | CROP PROCEDURES |
|---|---|---|---|---|
| **LL** | **MM** | **NN** | **OO** | **PP** |
| Protein Content per Pound in Grams (g) (454 g per pound) [25] | Calorie Content per Pound [25,50] | Calcium Content per Pound in Milligrams (mg) [25] | | For varietal and other information, see (HPW) *Western Fruit, Berries and Nuts: How to Select, Grow and Enjoy*, by Lance Walheim and Robert L. Stebbins (under Fruits, Berries, and Nuts in Bibliography), and/or (DW) Dave Wilson Nursery catalog (under Seed Catalogs in Bibliography), or (HPC) *Citrus: How to Select, Grow and Enjoy*, by Richard Ray and Lance Walheim (under Fruits, Berries, and Nuts in Bibliography). |
| 8.3<br>15.9 | 816<br>1,569 | 31<br>59 | :Fresh. 48% refuse<br>:Meat | D |
| 7.6 | 240 | 267 | :Raw. 2% refuse. | 2-foot-wide beds. See (1) under Apples. HPW. Propagated by cuttings. |
| 10.0 | 1,243 | 268 | :Dry and pitted. Pits: 13% of dried weight. | 1 male to 100 female plants for pollination. Propagated by cuttings. |
| 5.4<br>19.5 | 363<br>1,243 | 159<br>572 | :Raw. Drying ratio 3:1.<br>:Dried. 23% moisture. | See (1) under Apples. HPW, DW. Propagated by cuttings. |
| 57.2 | 2,876 | 948 | :Shelled: 54% of unshelled weight. 46% refuse. | See (1) under Apples. HPW, DW. Propagated by cuttings. |
| 1.0 | 84 | 33 | :Raw. 55% refuse. | HPC |
| 11.3 | 1,311 | 281 | :Dry. 18% moisture. Drying ratio 4.3:1. | See (1) under Apples. HPW, DW. Propagated by cuttings. |
| 2.4 | 270 | 48 | :Raw. 11% refuse. | Propagated by cuttings. |
| 3.7 | 197 | 46 | :Raw. 37% refuse. | Propagated by cuttings. |
| 3.5 | 273 | 101 | :Raw. 35% refuse. 15 ft high. | HPW |
| 59.9 | 3,053 | Trace | :Shelled: 65% of unshelled weight. | See (1) under Apples. |
| 72 | D | D | Can make a flour from the beans. Pods and beans a good fodder. A very important tree. *Gleditsia trianconti*. | See *Forest Farming*, by J. Sholto Douglas and Rebecca Hart and/or *Tree Crops*, by J. Russell Smith (in Bibliography under Trees). |
| 3.3 | 82 | 79 | :33% refuse. | HPW, HPC. |
| 2.7 | 107 | 126 | :16% refuse. | HPW, HPC. |
| 2.1 | 201 | 30 | :33% refuse. 90 ft high at maturity. | HPW. Propagated by seed or grafting. |
| 17.0<br>76.2 | D<br>D | 260<br>D | :Seed.<br>:Pod. | |
| 2.5 | 267 | 263 | :8% refuse. 8 ft high. Thin to 6 to 8 in (10 in for early varieties). | See (1) under Apples. HPW, DW. |
| 2.5 | 267 | 263 | :8% refuse. 25 ft high. Thin to 6 to 8 in (10 in for early varieties). | |
| 5.3<br>8.0 | 442<br>1,227 | 232<br>— | :Green. 16% refuse.    Pasquale, up to 40% oil.<br>:Ripe. 20% refuse.    All others, 16.5–21.8% oil. | |

*Letter codes on page 85, notes on page 126*

MASTER CHARTS AND PLANNING 121

# TREE AND CANE CROPS

| PLANT | SEED | | | YIELD | | | |
|---|---|---|---|---|---|---|---|
| **A** | **B** Approx. No. Seeds per Ounce [4] (range: larger–smaller seed) | **C** Minimum Legal Germination Rate [5] | **D** Approx. No. Plants per Acre | **E** Possible GROW BIOINTENSIVE Yield in Pounds per 100-Square-Foot Planting [9] | **F** Possible GROW BIOINTENSIVE Yield in Pounds per Plant [10, 11] | **G** Average U.S. Yield in Pounds per 100 Square Feet [12, 13] | |
| 39 Orange, Sweet | 200–300 | D | 97 76 | Navel: 32 / 48 / 64 Valencia: 42 / 63 / 84 | 155–310 242–484 | 67.0 | |
| 40 Peach, Dwarf | 610 | D | 681 | Clingstone: 60 / 90 / 120 | 38–76 | "60.3" | |
| 41 Peach, Regular | 610 | D | 194 | Clingstone: 60 / 90 / 120 Freestone: 39 / 59 / 78 | 135–270 88–176 | "53.4" 39.7 | |
| 42 Pear, Dwarf | 750 | D | 681 | 36 / 72 / 108 | 23–70 | 66.6 | |
| 43 Pear, Regular | 750 | D | 170 | 36 / 72 / 108 | 92–276 | 66.6 | |
| 44 Pecan | 6 | .50 [J] | 27 | In shell: 6 / 12 / 25+ | 96–400+ | D | |
| 45 Persimmon | 74 | D | 134 | 8 / 16 / 32+ | 26–103 | D | |
| 46 Pistachio | In shell: 28 | D | 109 | D | D | 3.1 | |
| 47 Plum, Bush | D | D | 4,840 | 9.5 / 19 / 38 | .85–3.4 | D | |
| 48 Plum, Regular | 50–55 | D | 134 | Regular: 19 / 38 / 57 Dry prune: 18 / 36 / 72 | 61–184 59–234 | 26.7 36.8 | |
| 49 Pomegranate | D | D | 435 | 50 / 75 / 100 | 50–100 | D | |
| 50 Raspberries | — | — | 2,723 | Berries: 12 / 18 / 24 Biomass, air-dry: 50 / 100 / 255+ | Berries: .95–3.8+ | "12.3" | |
| 51 Strawberries | 40,000 | D | 43,560 | 40 / 80 / 160 | .4–1.6 | 102.4 | |
| 52 Tangelo | 200–300 | D | 109 | D | D | 53.3 | |
| 53 Tangerine | 300–400 | D | 109 | D | D | 47.9 | |
| 54 Walnut, Eastern, Black | 3 | .50 [A] | 27 | In shell: 5 / 7.5 / 10+ | 80–160+ | 7.0 | |
| 55 Walnut, English (Persian) | 2 | .80 [A] | 27 | In shell: 5 / 7.5 / 10+ | 80–160+ | 7.0 | |
| 56 Walnut, No. Calif. Black | 3 | .40 [A] | 27 | In shell: 5 / 7.5 / 10+ | 80–160+ | 7.0 | |

| | BEDS/FLATS | | | | | | MATURITY | | FOOD NEEDED | SEED YIELD |
|---|---|---|---|---|---|---|---|---|---|---|
| **H** In-Bed Spacing (feet) | **I** Square Feet Required per Plant | **J** Short/Long/Extra-Long Germination Time | **K** Plant Initially in Flats/Beds (in order of preference) | **L** Flats spacing for First Flat and Second Flat (inches) | **M** Approx. No. Plants per Flat (adj. for germ. rate)[14] | **N** Approx. No. Weeks in Flats[16] | **O** Approx. No. Years to Bearing and Approx. No. Years to Max. Bearing | **P** Approx. No. Weeks in Harvesting Period and Possible Bearing Years | **Q** Pounds Consumed per Year by Average Person in U.S.[13,18] | **R** Approx. Maximum Pounds Seed Yield per 100 Square Feet[19] |
| 22 / 24 | 484 / 576 | D | F | 2 / I | D / — | D / D | 3 / D | D / 50+ | "17.2" | D |
| 8 | 64 | D | Sapling: B | — | — | — | 3 / D | D / D | "2.6" | D |
| 15 | 225 | D | F | 4 / I | D / — | D / D | 3–4 / 8–12 | D / 8–12 | | D |
| 8 | 64 | D | Sapling: B | — | D / — | D / D | 3 / D | D / D | "3.4" | D |
| 16 (−20) | 256 | EL | F | 1 / I | D / — | D / D | 4 / D | D / 50–75 | "3.4" | D |
| 40 (−70) | 1,600 | L | F | 4 / I | 8 / — | D / D | D / D | D / 150 | ".4" | In shell: 25.0+ |
| 18 | 324 | D | F | 1 / I | D / — | D / D | 2–3 / D | D / 20–300 | D | D |
| 20 | 400 | D | F | 2 / I | D / — | D / D | D / D | D / 30–50 | D | D |
| 3 | 9 | D | Sapling: B | — | — | — | 3 / D | D / D | "2.0" | D |
| 18 (−24) | 324 | D | F | 4 / I | D / — | D / — | 4 / D | D / 20–25 | | D |
| 10 | 100 | D | F | 2 / I | D / D | D / — | D / D | D / D | D | D |
| 4 | 16 | D | Deep flat | 6 / I | D / — | D / — | 2 / D | D / 6–10 | D | — |
| 1 | 1 | D | F | 1 / 2 | — / 60 | D / D | 2 / D | D / 4 | "3.3" | D |
| 20 | 400 | D | F | 1 / I | D / — | D / D | 3 / D | D / D | ".34" | D |
| 20 | 400 | D | F | 1 / I | D / — | D / D | 3 / D | D / D | ".7" | D |
| 40 | 1,600 | EL | F | 4 / I | 6 / — | D / D | D / D | D / D | | In shell: 10.0+ |
| 40 | 1,600 | L | F | 4 / I | 12 / — | D / D | D / D | D / D | "4.6" | In shell: 10.0+ |
| 40 | 1,600 | EL | F | 4 / I | 8 / — | D / D | D / D | D / D | | In shell: 10.0+ |

# TREE AND CANE CROPS

*(continued)*

| AA PLANT | FOOD NEEDED BB — Pounds You Select | MATERIALS NEEDED CC — Approx. No. Plants You Need [20] | DD — Approx. Square Feet You Need [21] | EE — Approx. No. Flats You Need [22] | FF — Approx. Ounces Seed You Need [23] | YIELDS GG — Your Actual Yield per 100 Square Feet | HH — Your Actual Yield Compared with U.S. Average [24] | MISCELLANEOUS II — Especially Good Varieties, Possible Seed Sources, and Remarks | JJ — Heavy Giver (HG), Light Feeder (LF), Low Nitrogen User (LNU), Heavy Feeder (HF) | KK — Time of Year to Plant (SP, SU, FA, WI) |
|---|---|---|---|---|---|---|---|---|---|---|
| 39 Orange, Sweet | | | | | | | | — | HF | Early SP |
| 40 Peach, Dwarf | | | | | | | | — | HF | Early SP |
| 41 Peach, Regular | | | | | | | | — | HF | Early SP |
| 42 Pear, Dwarf | | | | | | | | — | HF | Early SP |
| 43 Pear, Regular | | | | | | | | — | HF | Early SP |
| 44 Pecan | | | | | | | | — | HF | Early SP |
| 45 Persimmon | | | | | | | | — | HF | Early SP |
| 46 Pistachio | | | | | | | | — | HF | Early SP |
| 47 Plum, Bush | | | | | | | | — | HF | Early SP |
| 48 Plum, Regular | | | | | | | | — | HF | Early SP |
| 49 Pomegranate | | | | | | | | — | HF | Early SP |
| 50 Raspberries | | | | | | | | — | HF | Early SP |
| 51 Strawberries | | | | | | | | — | HF | Early SP |
| 52 Tangelo | | | | | | | | — | HF | Early SP |
| 53 Tangerine | | | | | | | | — | HF | Early SP |
| 54 Walnut, Eastern, Black | | | | | | | | — | HF | Early SP |
| 55 Walnut, English (Persian) | | | | | | | | — | HF | Early SP |
| 56 Walnut, No. Calif. Black | | | | | | | | — | HF | Early SP |

| NUTRITION | | | NOTES | CROP PROCEDURES |
|---|---|---|---|---|
| **LL** | **MM** | **NN** | **OO** | **PP** |
| Protein Content per Pound in Grams (g) (454 g per pound) [25] | Calorie Content per Pound [25, 50] | Calcium Content per Pound in Milligrams (mg) [25] | | For varietal and other information, see (HPW) *Western Fruit, Berries and Nuts: How to Select, Grow and Enjoy*, by Lance Walheim and Robert L. Stebbins (under Fruits, Berries, and Nuts in Bibliography), and/or (DW) Dave Wilson Nursery catalog (under Seed Catalogs in Bibliography), or (HPC) *Citrus: How to Select, Grow and Enjoy*, by Richard Ray and Lance Walheim (under Fruits, Berries, and Nuts in Bibliography). |
| 4.0<br>4.1 | 157<br>174 | 123<br>136 | :Navels (winter-bearing). 32% refuse.<br>:Valencia (summer-bearing). 25% refuse. | HPW, HPC. |
| 2.4 | 150 | 36 | :13% refuse. 8 ft high. Thin to 6 to 10 in (10 in for early varieties). | See (1) under Apples. HPW, DW. |
| 2.4 | 150 | 36 | :13% refuse. 25 ft high. Thin to 6 to 10 in (10 in for early varieties). | |
| 2.9 | 252 | 33 | :9% refuse. 8 ft high. | See (1) under Apples. HPW, DW. |
| 2.9 | 252 | 33 | :9% refuse. 30–40 ft high. | |
| 41.7 | 3,116 | 331 | :Shelled. 47% of unshelled weight. | See (1) under Apples. HPW, DW. |
| 2.6 | 286 | 22 | :18% refuse. 30 ft high. | See (1) under Apples. HPW, DW. |
| 87.5 | 2,694 | 594 | :Shelled. 50% of unshelled weight. 30 ft high. | See (1) under Apples. HPW, DW. |
| 2.1 | 272 | 74 | :9% refuse. 3 ft high. Thin to 4 to 6 in. | See (1) under Apples. HPW, DW. |
| 2.1<br>3.4 | 272<br>320 | 74<br>51 | :Damson. 9% refuse.<br>:Prune. 6% refuse. } Thin to 4 to 6 in. | |
| 1.3 | 160 | 8 | :44% refuse. | HPW, DW. |
| 6.6<br>5.3 | 321<br>251 | 132<br>97 | :Black.<br>:Red. Also yellow and purple varieties. } 3% refuse. | Prune to 2–8 canes/ft of row. Beds 2–3 ft wide. Some people plant on 2-ft centers. See (1) under Apples. HPW. Propagated by cuttings. |
| 3.0 | 161 | 91 | :4% refuse. Bear well second through fourth year. | Use new plants on end of runners to renew bed by fifth year. Plant initially in fall for a better first-year crop. Usually propagated by runner rather than seed, except for Alpine variety. See (1) under Apples. HPW. |
| 1.3 | 104 | D | :44% refuse. 30 ft high. | HPW, HPC. |
| 2.7 | 154 | 134 | :26% refuse. 30 ft high. | HPW, HPC. |
| 67.1 | 2,953 | Trace | :Shelled. 78% refuse. Up to 150 ft high.<br>A good tree to plant for your great-great-grandchildren! | |
| 93.0 | 2,849 | 449 | :Shelled. 55% refuse. Up to 60 ft high. | |
| D | D | D | 30–60 ft high. | See (1) under Apples. HPW, DW. |

MASTER CHARTS

# NOTES

4. From Donald N. Maynard and George J. Hochmuth, *Knott's Handbook for Vegetable Growers* (New York: John Wiley & Sons, 1999), pp. 97–98; and other reference sources.

5. Ibid., p. 460; and other reference sources.

6. Column I ÷ Column B ÷ Column C.

7. The number of plants you will need may vary. The rise of a curved bed surface (approximate 10-inch rise) adds up to 10% to the planting surface, and a "flat-topped" raised bed (see p. 55) adds up to 20% to the planting surface. Also, the hexagonal "offset" spacing uses up less space than spacing where plants are lined up opposite each other. Up to 159 plants fit in 120 square feet of curved surface on 12-inch (1-foot) centers, rather than fewer plants. You will probably have more plants ready than you need when using Column I to plan, so use the best plants first and save the rest for "spotting" areas that lose plants, or give the extras to friends. To calculate the distance between rows on offset spacing, multiply the spacing by 0.87. To calculate the number of plants on offset spacing in a *flat* bed, first calculate the number of plants on "square" spacing, then multiply by 1.13.

8. Less seed may be necessary if the seed of a given variety is particularly small and/or if there is not much rise to the bed.

9. Estimates based on our experience and research. Use lowest figure if you are a beginning gardener; middle if a good one; highest if an excellent gardener with a good soil and climate. (The testing and development process requires a long time and has involved many failures. Its direction, however, has been encouraging over the years, as the soil, our skills, and yields have improved, and as resource-consumption levels have decreased. There is still much left to be done.)

10. The approximate plant yield averages in some instances are much lower than one would expect. For example, a beginning gardener will get carrots much larger than the .04 lb noted, but all of their carrots will probably not germinate as well as a good or excellent gardener's will and they will probably not be as large. Therefore, it is estimated that the average weight of each carrot would be .04 lb, assuming the bed produces 2,507 carrots.

11. Column E × Column I × 0.01.

12. From U.S. Department of Agriculture, *Agricultural Statistics—2005,* 2003 data (Washington, DC: U.S. Government Printing Office, 2000; see the index at the end of the volume); and other reference sources.

13. Numbers in quotes are approximations from other data, because official data are not available for this crop.

14. Assumes flat with *internal* dimensions of 13 inches by 21 inches (or 273 square inches) for both 3-inch- and 6-inch-deep flats, in which at least 250 plants fit on 1-inch centers and 60 plants on 2-inch centers; *if half-sized flats are used,* 125 plants fit on 1-inch centers and 30 plants on 2-inch centers.

15. When seeds are broadcast into a flat, it is possible to reduce the number of flats used. To calculate the number of flats needed for broadcast seed, determine the number of plants you need, divide by the number in Column L², then divide by the number in Column L³. Broadcast the needed amount of seed evenly into the number of flats just calculated.

16. From Donald N. Maynard and George J. Hochmuth, *Knott's Handbook for Vegetable Growers* (New York: John Wiley & Sons, 1999), p. 51; and from our experience and research.

17. The Approximate Weeks to Maturity in Ground generally remains the same whether seeds are started in a flat or in a bed because the number of weeks to maturity indicated on the seed packet assumes optimal growing conditions that are rarely present.

18. From U.S. Department of Agriculture, *Agricultural Statistics—2005,* 2003 data (Washington, DC: U.S. Government Printing Office, 2000; see the index at the end of the volume); and other sources.

19. Based in part on standard field figures from James Edward Knott, *Handbook for Vegetable Growers* (New York: John Wiley & Sons, 1975), pp. 198–199, in combination with a multiplier factor based on our research and experience; and other reference sources. The result, however, is preliminary, for your guidance, and very experimental. If growing seed, remember to adjust for the germination rate when determining the amount to grow for your use.

20. Column BB ÷ Column F.

21. Column BB ÷ Column E × 100. Use the lowest figure in Column E if you are a beginning gardener; middle if a good one working with good soil; highest if an excellent gardener working with excellent soil.

22. Column CC ÷ Column L² or M³.

23. Column DD × Column D × .01.

24. Column GG ÷ Column G.

25. From U.S. Department of Agriculture, *Composition of Foods* (Washington, DC: U.S. Government Printing Office, 1963) and other reference sources, and from USDA food search website: http://www.nal.usda.gov/fnic/foodcomp/search/index.html.

26. 6 to 8 weeks in warm weather and/or with a good mini-greenhouse; 9 to 12 weeks in cooler weather outdoors without a mini-greenhouse.

27. Johnny's Selected Seeds (see p. 227).

28. Smaller secondary and tertiary heads may also be used and may double the yield.

29. The Redwood City Seed Company carries an interesting tropical variety, Snow Peak, which heads only in the summer. A good variety with small heads for out-of-season growing.

30. Produces 4 times the general protein (not amino acids) and 8 times the calcium (free of oxalic acid) per unit of area compared to the milk produced by a cow or a goat fed on an equal area of alfalfa.

31. Be sure to obtain "seed" Irish potatoes; many potatoes in stores have been treated to retard sprouting. Sprout without soil in a 3-inch-deep flat or box with small air spaces between the tubers in a warm, dry, airy location in indirect light for up to 1 month, until sprouts are about ¼ inch long. Caution: Avoid conditions of 90% humidity and 70°F, or more, for a period of 24 hours; they can encourage blight. Use pieces of potato weighing at least 1.5 to 2 ounces. Each potato piece should optimally have 2 or 3 sprouted eyes. For planting purposes, tubers are in dormancy for 5 to 20 weeks after harvest. For planting procedure, see note on p. 11.

32. Be sure to obtain "seed" sweet potatoes; many potatoes in stores have been treated to retard sprouting. Sprout in wide-mouth canning jars with water. Insert toothpicks into sweet potatoes around their outside to hold the upper half out of the water. Roots form on the portion in the water, and small plantlets grow from the eyes on the upper portion. Each 8-ounce sweet potato will make 3 to 4 of these "starts." When a shoot is about 1 to 1½ inches long, nick it off along with a very small piece of the sweet potato where it is attached, and plant it in a 3-inch-deep flat on 2-inch centers so only the last set of leaves is above the surface of the flat soil. Whole sweet potatoes may also be sprouted side by side in a flat; approximately 4 to 8 flats are needed for a 100-square-foot bed. When the seedlings are 7 to 9 inches tall, transplant them into the growing bed so at least 6 inches of the stem is beneath the soil.

33. Bountiful Gardens (see p. 226).

34. Use the French variety (Vilmorin's Cantalun—orange-fleshed) or the Israeli variety (Haogen—green-fleshed). Both have a smooth exterior without netting. This minimizes rotting.

35. Stokes Seeds (see p. 229). Specify untreated seeds.

36. Try the torpedo onion. Its long shape is particularly suited to intensive raised-bed gardening and farming, and it can produce twice the yield per unit of area.

37. Irish potatoes. Place your order for the entire year in January in order to ensure availability. Specify *untreated* seed and delivery date(s) desired (1 month before planting, so sprouts can develop properly). Irish Eyes (see p. 227) is a good source.

38. Sweet potatoes: Jewel, Centennial, Garnett, and Jersey varieties. Order in September *untreated,* number 2 size, for the following summer in 40-pound boxes, to ensure availability. Joe Alvernaz, P.O. Box 474, Livingston, CA 95334, is a good source, although not organic. Ask for prices and include a stamped, self-addressed envelope.

39. Burpee's Triple Treat variety with hull-less seeds. No shelling of nutritious and tasty seeds!

40. Burpee's Sparkler variety: red top with white bottom half. Good-looking.

41. Burpee's New Hampshire Midget variety.

42. Native Seeds/SEARCH (see p. 228).

43. Vermont Bean Seed Co. (see p. 230).

44. Fedco Seeds (see p. 226).

45. R. H. Shumway Seed (see p. 228).

46. J. L. Hudson, Seedsman (see p. 227).

47. If overwintering.

48. In some tropical regions.

49. Six inches deep in areas with cooler nights.

50. Some calorie values determined from USDA website.

51. Including for fodder.

52. Longer harvest period is for sequential harvesting of separate stalks on each plant as stalks become mature.

53. As high as 43 weeks in some other countries in the world.

# NOTES ON THE PLANNING CHARTS

# FLOWER SPACING CHART

Spacings vary for flowers depending on the variety and how the flowers are used. The following will help you start out with the most common flowers.

| Annuals—Replant each year in spring from seed | | | | | | |
|---|---|---|---|---|---|---|
| | Height | Inches Apart* | | | Height | Inches Apart* |
| African daisy | 4–6″ | 12 | Pansy | | 6–9″ | 8–10 |
| Aster | 1–3′ | 10–12 | Petunia | | 12–16″ | 12 |
| Calendula*** | 1½–2′ | 12 | Phlox (*Phlox drummondii*)** | | 6–18″ | 9 |
| California poppy*** | 9–12″ | 12 | Portulaca | | 6″ | 6–9 |
| Columbine | 2–3′ | 12 | Scarlet sage (*Salvia splendens*) | | 1–1½′ | 12 |
| Cosmos*** | 2–3′ | 12–18 | Schizanthus | | 1½–2′ | 12–18 |
| Echinacea | 1′ | 18–24 | Shirley poppy | | 1½–2′ | 12–18 |
| Flowering tobacco | 2–3′ | 18–24 | Snapdragons | | 1½–3′ | 12 |
| Hollyhock*** | 4–6′ | 12 | Stocks | | 1–2½′ | 12 |
| Marigold, African | 2–4′ | 12–24 | Strawflower | | 2–3′ | 12–18 |
| Marigold, French | 6–18″ | 8–12 | Sweet peas | | Climbing | 12 |
| Nasturtium, climbing*** | Trailing | 10 | Zinnia | | 1–3′ | 12–18 |
| Nasturtium, dwarf*** | 1′ | 8 | | | | |

| Perennials—Need a permanent space in the garden | | | | | | |
|---|---|---|---|---|---|---|
| | Height | Inches Apart* | | | Height | Inches Apart* |
| Alyssum (*Lobularia maritima*) | 4–6″ | 10–12 | Iceland poppy | | 1′ | 12 |
| Aubrieta | Trailing | 12–15 | Jacob's ladder (*Polemonium caeruleum*) | | 6″–3′ | 12–15 |
| Baby's breath | 3–4′ | 14–16 | Marguerite | | 2½–3′ | 18–24 |
| Bachelor's button | 2′ | 12 | Oriental poppy | | 2½–3′ | 12–14 |
| Carnation | 1′ | 12 | Painted daisy | | 3′ | 12 |
| Chrysanthemum | 2–3′ | 18–24 | Peony | | 2′ | 14–16 |
| Coral bells (*Heuchera sanguinea*) | 2′ | 12 | Pinks (*Dianthus*) | | 1′ | 12 |
| Coreopsis | 2′ | 9–18 | Scabiosa | | 2′ | 12 |
| Delphinium | 1–5′ | 24 | Sea pink (*Armeria*) | | 4–6″ | 10–12 |
| Foxglove | 3′ | 12 | Shasta daisy | | 2½–3′ | 12 |
| Gaillardia | 2–3′ | 12 | Sweet William | | 1–2′ | 12 |
| Gazania | 6–12″ | 10 | | | | |

**Note**
Most flowers have long-germinating seeds (8 to 21 days).

* Spacings for standard-sized plants. For smaller varieties, reduce the spacings in proportion to the reduced plant size.

** Botanical Latin names prevent possible confusion.
*** Reseed themselves easily by dropping many seeds on the ground.

# HERB SPACING CHART

## *Annuals*—Plant seed in spring for late summer harvest

| | Height | Inches Apart* | | Height | Inches Apart* |
|---|---|---|---|---|---|
| Anise | 2′ | 8 | Coriander | 1–1½′ | 6 |
| Basil, sweet | 1–2′ | 6 | Cumin | 1′ | 18 |
| Borage | 1½′ | 15 | Dill | 2½′ | 8 |
| Caraway | 2½′ | 6 | Fennel | 3–5′ | 12 |
| Chamomile (*Matricaria recutita*) | 2½′ | 6–10 | Parsley | 2½′ | 5 |
| Chervil | 1½′ | 4 | Savory, summer | 1½′ | 6 |
| Cilantro | 1–1½′ | 5 | | | |

## *Perennials*††—Need a permanent space in the garden

| | | Height | Inches Apart* | | Height | Inches Apart* |
|---|---|---|---|---|---|---|
| Angelica | | 4–6′ | 36 | Marjoram | 1′ | 12 |
| Bee balm† | | 3′ | 30 | Oregano† | 2′ | 18–24 |
| Burnet | | 15″ | 15 | Peppermint | 2½′ | 12# |
| Catnip | | 2–3′ | 15# | Pineapple sage† | 4′ | 24–36 |
| Chamomile, Roman (*Chamaemelum nobile*)† | | 3–12′ | 12 | Rosemary | 3–4′ | 18–24 |
| Chives | | 10–24″ | 5 | Rue | 3′ | 18 |
| Comfrey† | | 15–36″ | 12 | Sage | 2′ | 18 |
| Costmary | | 2–6′ | 12 | Santolina | 2′ | 30 |
| Feverfew | | 1–3′ | 10–15 | Savory, winter | 1′ | 12 |
| Geraniums, scented† | Apple | 10″ | 18 | Southernwood | 3–5′ | 30 |
| | Coconut | 8–12″ | 18 | Spearmint† | 2–3′ | 15# |
| | Lemon | 2–3′ | ## | Stevia | 1–1½′ | 12 |
| | Lime | 2′ | 18 | Stinging nettle | 4–6′ | 24# |
| | Peppermint | 2′ | 48 | St. Johns wort | 2′ | 8 |
| | Rose | 3′ | 30 | Tansy | 4′ | 30 |
| Good King Henry | | 1′ | 16 | Tarragon | 2′ | 12–18 |
| Horehound | | 2′ | 9# | Thyme | 1′ | 6–12 |
| Hyssop | | 2′ | 12 | Valerian | 4′ | 18 |
| Lavender | | 3′ | 18 | Woodruff† | 6–10″ | 8–12# |
| Lemon balm | | 3′ | 12# | Wormwood | 3–5′ | 12–24 |
| Lemon verbena | | 10′ | 24 | Yarrow, common (*Achillea millefolium*) | 3–5′ | 12–18 |
| Lovage | | 6′ | 3 | Yarrow, white-, red-, or pink-flowered† | 2½–3′ | 12 |

**Note**
Many herbs have extra-long-germinating seeds (22 to 28 days).

† Generally based on our experience. Others are from the Herb Chart by Evelyn Gregg, Biodynamic Farming and Gardening Association, Wyoming, Rhode Island.

†† Normally started from cuttings or root divisions, they often take 1 to 4 years to reach full size from seed.

# Spreads underground; keep it contained or plant where it can keep going.

## Unknown.

PLANNING

Use this space to record your favorite flowers and herbs that are not included in the preceding spacing charts. *Use within-the-row spacings given on the back of the seed packets.*

# 7

# SAMPLE GARDEN PLANS

**GOAL:** *Make your daily garden tasks easier and more effective through coordinated garden planning.*

Now we come to the art of putting the theory into a garden plan. No book can make gardening foolproof. If growing plants did not involve real learning and *experimentation,* it would not be nearly so satisfying. The plans that follow illustrate some of the considerations that make a garden successful. They are based on what the average American consumes each year, but do not take the precise amounts too seriously. Everyone has different tastes and your "average American diet" will change rapidly when you have abundant fresh vegetables to eat. You will probably want to eat many more fresh fruits and vegetables than you do now.

Before you start, you will need some local information. Talk to your neighbors who garden, check with the county agricultural agent, or ask at the local nursery. You want to know:

- Which vegetables grow well in your area?
- When does the main planting season start?
- When are your first and last frosts?
- When are your periods with and without rains?
- What are the special requirements of your specific soil?
- Are there any special climatic conditions to be aware of, such as heavy winds, hot dry spells, or excessive rains?
- How do people usually plan for this?

The first sample plan is for a generic simple mini-garden. Following is a plan for a 1-person mini-garden. Plans are included for each of the first 4 years. The first year includes the easiest crops to grow in 100 square feet based on yields expected of a good gardener. The second year, *the square footage doubles* and more-difficult crops are added. The third and fourth years, trees, herbs, strawberries, and asparagus are included—permanent plantings that are placed in soil that has now been worked and improved for 2 years—and a third bed is added. After 3 or 4 years, with improved gardening skills, the vegetable crop can be condensed from 200 square feet to 100 square feet, leaving 100 square feet of improved soil for protein crops (wheat, rye, peanuts, lentils, soybeans, and rice), fiber crops (cotton or flax), or special interest crops (chicken, goat, or bee forage; grapes; blueberries; bamboo; herbs; nut trees; and so on).

Lastly, a garden plan for a family of 4 is shown. We rec-ommend using a similar 3- to 4-year progression, starting with approximately 300 square feet for the first year, and adding 300 more square feet each year until the entire garden is developed.

Buying seeds for a backyard garden easily runs up a $10 to $20+ bill. At our garden supply store in Palo Alto, we purchase seeds in bulk and sell them out in jars like penny candy, using teaspoons and tablespoons to measure. You can easily buy seeds for 6 months of vegetables in our store for less than $2. You can take advantage of the same low prices by having your favorite local co-op grocery store order bulk seeds for you.

Consider spacing and maturation when you develop your plan. If you have extra plants, plant the best ones and give any extras to a friend or save them in case of damage to first trans-plants. Leaf lettuce matures sooner than head lettuce. Planting both ensures a continuous harvest. Similarly, half of the toma-toes should be an early variety (maturing in 65 days) for con-tinuous harvesting. Save space by tying tomatoes up to stakes. Pumpkins take up a lot of space. Plant them at the edge of the garden where they can sprawl over uncultivated areas. Corn is pollinated by the wind; a square block of 4 corn plants in each direction (not a row), for a total of 16 plants, is the minimum for adequate pollination. In small plantings you may want to hand-pollinate corn so all the ears fill out optimally. (See Suzanne Ashworth's *Seed to Seed* in the bibliography.)

When choosing a site for your garden, take into considera-tion the amount of available direct sunlight. *Optimally,* your garden area should have 11 hours of sunlight or more; 7 hours may allow plants to grow acceptably, and in some instances, 4 hours may work for cool season crops (see page 79). Experi-mentation will probably be needed if you plan to garden in soil that receives less than 11 hours of sun.

# THE GARDEN YEAR

## Winter
- ☐ Plan the garden.
- ☐ Order *open-pollinated*, untreated seeds (allow 2 months for delivery if ordering by mail).
- ☐ Make flats, trellises, mini-greenhouses, and shade-netting units.[1]

## Spring
- ☐ Plant flats so seedlings can mature while the soil is being prepared.
- ☐ Start new compost piles with weeds, grass clippings, and compost crops.
- ☐ Harvest compost crops, dig garden beds, and spread cured fall/winter compost.
- ☐ Plant cool-weather crops in early spring and warm- and hot-weather crops in late spring and early summer.

## Summer
- ☐ Plant summer crops.
- ☐ Keep the garden watered and weeded.
- ☐ Harvest and enjoy the fruits of your work.
- ☐ In mild-winter areas, plant fall gardens of cool-weather crops at the end of summer.

## Fall
- ☐ Start additional compost piles with plentiful leaves and garden waste.
- ☐ Harvest summer crops.
- ☐ Plant fall/winter compost crops.

---

1. See Ecology Action's *Backyard Homestead, Mini-Farm and Garden Log Book* for miniature mini-greenhouse and shade-netting house plans.

# SIMPLE MINI-GARDEN, 6-MONTH GROWING SEASON
## 100–140+ SQUARE FEET

*As early as possible in spring, plant (optional):*
bare root
   dwarf fruit tree     —     1 tree     40.0+ sq ft

### 6 weeks before last spring frost _____
(date)

*Start seedlings in flats:*
head lettuce     —     4 seeds Ⓢ
leaf lettuce     —     8 seeds Ⓢ
parsley     —     2 seeds

### 5 weeks before last frost _____
(date)

*Start seedlings in flats:*
carrots     —     58 seeds

*Prick out seedlings into flats:*
head lettuce     —     3 seedlings Ⓢ
leaf lettuce     —     6 seedlings Ⓢ

### 4 weeks before last frost _____
(date)

*Sprout:*
potatoes
   (65 days to maturity)     —     9.5 lbs tubers

*Start seedlings in flat:*
chard     —     2 seeds

### 3 weeks before last frost _____
(date)

*Start seedlings in flats:*
bush peas     —     230 seeds

*Prick out seedlings into flat:*
parsley     —     1 seedling

### 2 weeks before last frost _____
(date)

*Start seedlings in flats:*
bunching onions
   (60 days to maturity)     —     10 seeds
cherry tomatoes     —     10 seeds

*Transplant:*
bush peas     —     184 seedlings     10.0 sq ft
carrots     —     32 seedlings
head lettuce     —     4 seedlings Ⓢ     2.0 sq ft
leaf lettuce (9″)     —     2 seedlings Ⓢ     2.0 sq ft

*Plant:*
radishes     —     10 seeds

### On last frost _____
(date)

*Start seedlings in flats:*
cantaloupes     —     10 seeds
cucumbers     —     3 seeds
dwarf marigolds     —     3 seeds
New Hampshire midget
   watermelons (12″)     —     16 seeds
sunflowers     —     4 seeds

*Transplant:*
potatoes**     —     75 sprouted
                             pieces     30.0 sq ft

### 1 week after last frost _____
(date)

*Start seedlings in flat:*
early corn     —     20 seeds

### 2 weeks after last frost _____
(date)

*Sprout:*
potatoes     —     9.5 lbs tubers

*Start seedlings in flats:*
acorn winter squash     —     2 seeds
pumpkins     —     3 seeds
zucchini     —     2 seeds

*Prick out seedlings into flat:*
cherry tomatoes     —     7+ seedlings

*Transplant:*
chard     —     1 seedling Ⓣ
early corn     —     15 seedlings     20.0 sq ft
sunflowers     —     2 seedlings Ⓣ

### 3 weeks after last frost _____
(date)

*Transplant:*
cantaloupes     —     7 seedlings     10.0 sq ft
cucumbers     —     2 seedlings Ⓣ
dwarf marigolds     —     2 seedlings Ⓣ
New Hampshire midget
   watermelons (12″)     —     11 seedlings     10.0 sq ft

### Notes
- Numbers given are for the approximate number of seeds and seedlings that should be required for each crop for the area involved.
- To improve the soil fertility and increase the sustainability of your garden/mini-farm, additionally grow 200 to 300 square feet of carbon-and-calorie crops, described on pages 24–25.

Ⓢ = Stagger planting for a more continuous harvest.
Ⓣ = Transplant seedlings on edge of bed; see plan, opposite.
\* = Spot additional seeds later where seeds do not germinate.
\*\* = See note with potato planting instructions on page 11.

## SIMPLE MINI-GARDEN

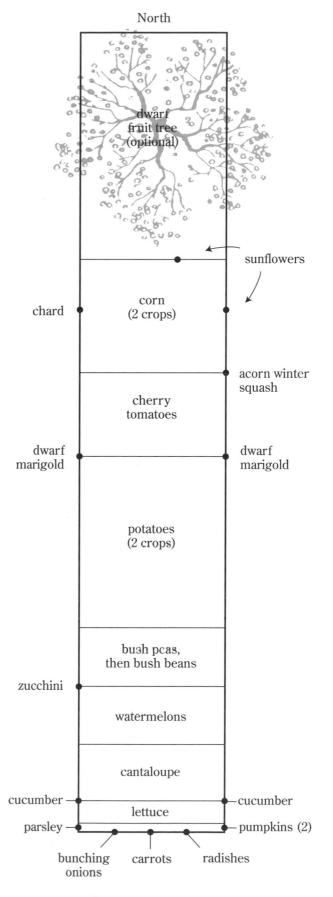

North

**6 weeks after last frost** _____
(date)

*Transplant:*

| | | | |
|---|---|---|---|
| acorn winter squash | — | 1 seedling⊤ | |
| bunching onions (3″) | — | 7 seedlings | |
| cherry tomatoes (18″) | — | 7 seedlings | 15.0 sq ft |
| pumpkins | — | 2 seedlings⊤ | |
| zucchini | — | 1 seedling⊤ | |

**8 weeks after last frost** _____
(date)

*Start seedlings in flats:*

| | | |
|---|---|---|
| head lettuce | — | 3 seedsⓈ |
| leaf lettuce | — | 11 seedsⓈ |

*As first planting comes out, transplant:*

| | | | |
|---|---|---|---|
| parsley | — | 1 seedling⊤ | |
| potatoes** | — | 75 sprouted pieces | 30.0 sq ft |

**13 weeks before first fall frost** _____
(date)

*Start seedlings in flats:*

| | | |
|---|---|---|
| bush beans | — | 65 seeds |
| carrots | — | 17 seeds |

**11 weeks before first frost** _____
(date)

*Start seedlings in flats:*

| | | |
|---|---|---|
| early corn | — | 20 seeds |

*Prick out seedlings into flats:*

| | | |
|---|---|---|
| head lettuce | — | 2+ seedlings |
| leaf lettuce | — | 9+ seedlings |

*Transplant:*

| | | | |
|---|---|---|---|
| bush beans | — | 46 seedlings | 10.0 sq ft |

**10 weeks before first frost** _____
(date)

*Transplant:*

| | | | |
|---|---|---|---|
| carrots | — | 9 seedlings | .5 sq ft |
| early corn | — | 15 seedlings | 20.0 sq ft |

**8 weeks before first frost** _____
(date)

*Transplant:*

| | | | |
|---|---|---|---|
| head lettuce | — | 2 seedlingsⓈ | 2.0 sq ft |
| leaf lettuce (8″) | — | 9 seedlingsⓈ | 2.0 sq ft |

**7 weeks before first frost** _____
(date)

*Plant:*

| | | | |
|---|---|---|---|
| radishes | — | 5 seeds | .125 sq ft |

Scale: 5/16 inch = 1 foot. Growing bed is 100 square feet (5 by 20 feet).

# 1-PERSON MINI-GARDEN, *FIRST* YEAR, 6-MONTH GROWING SEASON
## 100 SQUARE FEET

**6 weeks before last spring frost** _____
(date)

*Start seedlings in flats:*

| | | |
|---|---|---|
| broccoli | — | 3 seeds |
| cabbage | — | 6 seeds |
| cylindra beets | — | 15 seeds |
| head lettuce | — | 3 seedsⓈ |
| leaf lettuce | — | 8 seedsⓈ |

**5 weeks before last frost** _____
(date)

*Prick out seedlings into flats:*

| | | |
|---|---|---|
| head lettuce | — | 2+ seedlingsⓈ |
| leaf lettuce | — | 6+ seedlingsⓈ |

**4 weeks before last frost** _____
(date)

*Sprout:*

| | | |
|---|---|---|
| potatoes (65 days to maturity)— | | 10.9 lbs tubers |

*Start seedlings in flat:*

| | | |
|---|---|---|
| carrots | — | 100 seeds |

**3 weeks before last frost** _____
(date)

*Start seedlings in flat:*

| | | |
|---|---|---|
| bush peas | — | 215 seeds |

*Prick out seedlings into flats:*

| | | |
|---|---|---|
| broccoli | — | 2+ seedlings |
| cabbage | — | 4+ seedlings |

**2 weeks before last frost** _____
(date)

*Start seedlings in flats:*

| | | |
|---|---|---|
| cucumbers | — | 12 seeds |
| green peppers | — | 12 seeds |
| regular tomatoes | — | 10 seeds |
| sweet basil | — | 2 seeds |
| zinnias | — | 6 seeds |

*Transplant:*

| | | | |
|---|---|---|---|
| bush peas | — | 172 seedlings | 9.0 sq ft |
| carrots | — | 55 seedlings | 3.0 sq ft |
| cylindra beets | — | 10 seedlings | 1.0 sq ft |
| head lettuce | — | 2 seedlingsⓈ | 2.0 sq ft |
| leaf lettuce (9″) | — | 6 seedlingsⓈ | 3.0 sq ft |

*Plant:*

| | | | |
|---|---|---|---|
| onions (purchased) | — | 95 sets | 3.8 sq ft |
| radishes | — | 10 seeds | .25 sq ft |

**On last frost** _____
(date)

*Start seedlings in flats:*

| | | |
|---|---|---|
| pumpkins | — | 2 seeds |
| zucchini | — | 2 seeds |

*Prick out seedlings into flats:*

| | | |
|---|---|---|
| green peppers | — | 5+ seedlings |
| regular tomatoes | — | 5+ seedlings |

*Transplant:*

| | | | |
|---|---|---|---|
| cucumbers | — | 6 seedlings | 4.0 sq ft |
| potatoes** | — | 87 sprouted pieces | 35.0 sq ft |
| sweet basil | — | 1 seedling | 1.0 sq ft |
| zinnias | — | 3 seedlings | 3.0 sq ft |

**1 week after last frost** _____
(date)

*Transplant:*

| | | | |
|---|---|---|---|
| broccoli | — | 2 seedlings | 3.2 sq ft |
| cabbage | — | 4 seedlings | 6.7 sq ft |

**4 weeks after last frost** _____
(date)

*Start seedlings in flats:*

| | | |
|---|---|---|
| cosmos | — | 2 seeds |

*Transplant:*

| | | | |
|---|---|---|---|
| green peppers | — | 4 seedlings | 4.0 sq ft |
| pumpkins | — | 2 seedlings | 6.0 sq ft |
| regular tomatoes (24″)— | | 4 seedlings | 15.0 sq ft |
| zucchini | — | 1 seedling | 2.0 sq ft |

**6 weeks after last frost** _____
(date)

*Start seedlings in flat:*

| | | |
|---|---|---|
| bush lima beans | — | 59 seeds |

**7 weeks after last frost** _____
(date)

*Start seedlings in flat:*

| | | |
|---|---|---|
| early corn (65 days to maturity)— | | 20 seeds |

**8 weeks after last frost** _____
(date)

*Transplant:*

| | | | |
|---|---|---|---|
| bush lima beans | — | 41 seedlings | 9.0 sq ft |
| cosmos | — | 1 seedlingⓉ | 1.0 sq ft |
| early corn | — | 15 seedlings | 20.0 sq ft |

**Note**

Numbers given are for the approximate number of seeds and seedlings that should be required for each crop for the area involved.

Ⓢ = Stagger planting for a more continuous harvest.

Ⓣ = Transplant seedlings on edge of bed; see plan, page 138.

\* = Spot additional seeds later where seeds do not germinate.

\*\* = See note with potato planting instructions on page 11.

**12 weeks after last frost** _____
(date)

*Start seedlings in flat:*
bush green beans     —     55 seeds

**13 weeks after last frost** _____
(date)

*Start seedlings in flat:*
corn     —     24 seeds

**14 weeks after last frost** _____
(date)

*After potatoes come out, transplant:*

| | | | |
|---|---|---|---|
| bush green beans | — | 46 seedlings | 10.0 sq ft |
| corn | — | 18 seedlings | 25.0 sq ft |

**13 weeks before first fall frost** _____
(date)

*Start seedlings in flat:*
broccoli     —     2 seeds

**12 weeks before first frost** _____
(date)

*Start seedlings in flats:*

| | | |
|---|---|---|
| carrots | — | 112 seeds |
| head lettuce | — | 4 seeds ⑤ |
| leaf lettuce | — | 17 seeds ⑤ |

**11 weeks before first frost** _____
(date)

*Start seedlings in flats:*

| | | |
|---|---|---|
| calendulas | — | 8 seeds |
| chard | — | 2 seeds |
| stocks | — | 8 seeds |

*Prick out seedlings into flats:*

| | | |
|---|---|---|
| broccoli | — | 1 seedling |
| head lettuce | — | 3+ seedlings ⑤ |
| leaf lettuce | — | 14+ seedlings ⑤ |

**9 weeks before first frost** _____
(date)

*Start seedlings in flat:*
bush peas     —     156 seeds

**8 weeks before first frost** _____
(date)

*As early corn and bush lima beans come out, transplant:*

| | | | |
|---|---|---|---|
| broccoli | — | 1 seedling | 1.6 sq ft |
| bush peas | — | 125 seedlings | 6.8 sq ft |
| calendulas | — | 6 seedlings | 5.0 sq ft |
| carrots | — | 62 seedlings | 2.7 sq ft |
| chard | — | 1 seedling | .25 sq ft |
| head lettuce | — | 3 seedlings ⑤ | 2.7 sq ft |
| leaf lettuce | — | 14 seedlings ⑤ | 5.3 sq ft |
| stocks | — | 6 seedlings | 5.0 sq ft |

*Plant:*

| | | | |
|---|---|---|---|
| radishes | — | 10 seeds | .25 sq ft |

See page 138 for plan of 1-Person Mini-Garden, First Year.

**Notes**
- Numbers given are for the approximate number of seeds and seedlings that should be required for each crop for the area involved.
- To improve the soil fertility and increase the sustainability of your garden/mini-farm, additionally grow 200 to 300 square feet of carbon-and-calorie crops, described on pages 24–25.

⑤   = Stagger planting for a more continuous harvest.
\*   = Spot additional seeds later where seeds do not germinate.
\*\*   = See note with potato planting instructions on page 11.

SAMPLE GARDEN PLANS   137

# 1-PERSON MINI-GARDEN, *FIRST* YEAR

*Spring*
(Bed 1)

cucumber

pumpkin

peppers

basil

regular
tomatoes

zinnias

zucchini

potatoes

onions

carrots

cabbage

radishes →

beets

peas

broccoli

lettuce

*Summer*
(Bed 1)

bush
beans

corn

early corn—
first planting

bush
beans

cosmos

*Fall*
(Bed 1)

peas

← radishes

lettuce

stocks

carrots

broccoli
and chard

calendulas

Scale: 5/16 inch = 1 foot. Growing bed is 100 square feet (5 by 20 feet).

# 1-PERSON MINI-GARDEN, *SECOND* YEAR, 6-MONTH GROWING SEASON
## 240 SQUARE FEET (including path)

**6 weeks before last spring frost** _____
(date)

*Start seedlings in flats:*

| | | |
|---|---|---|
| broccoli | — | 3 seeds |
| brussels sprouts | — | 2 seeds |
| cabbage | — | 5 seeds |
| cauliflower | — | 2 seeds |
| celery | — | 20 seeds |
| head lettuce | — | 3 seeds Ⓢ |
| leaf lettuce | — | 15 seeds Ⓢ |
| parsley | — | 2 seeds |
| regular tomatoes | — | 10 seeds |

**5 weeks before last frost**_____
(date)

*Start seedlings in flats:*

| | | |
|---|---|---|
| carrots | — | 90 seeds |
| cylindra beets | — | 16 seeds |

*Prick out seedlings into flats:*

| | | |
|---|---|---|
| head lettuce | — | 2+ seedlings |
| leaf lettuce | — | 12+ seedlings |

**4 weeks before last frost**_____
(date)

*Sprout:*

| | | |
|---|---|---|
| potatoes | | |
| (65 days to maturity)— | | 12.5 lbs tubers |

*Prick out seedlings into flat:*

| | | |
|---|---|---|
| parsley | — | 1+ seedlings |

**3 weeks before last frost**_____
(date)

*Start seedlings in flats:*

| | | |
|---|---|---|
| bush peas | — | 156 seeds |
| spinach | — | 17 seeds |

*Prick out seedlings into flats:*

| | | |
|---|---|---|
| broccoli | — | 2+ seedlings |
| brussels sprouts | — | 1+ seedlings |
| cabbage | — | 4+ seedlings |
| cauliflower | — | 1+ seedlings |

**2 weeks before last frost**_____
(date)

*Start seedlings in flats:*

| | | |
|---|---|---|
| dill | — | 2 seeds |
| eggplant | — | 2 seeds |
| green peppers | — | 10 seeds |

*Prick out seedlings into flat:*

| | | |
|---|---|---|
| celery | — | 12 seedlings |

*Transplant:*

| | | | |
|---|---|---|---|
| broccoli | — | 2 seedlings | 2.6 sq ft |
| brussels sprouts | — | 1 seedling | 2.3 sq ft |
| bush peas | — | 125 seedlings | 6.8 sq ft |
| cabbage | — | 4 seedlings | 5.2 sq ft |
| carrots | — | 50 seedlings | 2.7 sq ft |
| cauliflower | — | 1 seedling | 1.3 sq ft |
| cylindra beets | — | 10 seedlings | 1.0 sq ft |
| head lettuce | — | 2 seedlings Ⓢ | 2.0 sq ft |
| leaf lettuce (9″) | — | 12 seedlings Ⓢ | 6.0 sq ft |
| spinach | — | 10 seedlings | 2.2 sq ft |

*Plant:*

| | | | |
|---|---|---|---|
| garlic | — | 2 cloves | .3 sq ft |
| onions (purchased) | — | 39 sets | 3.8 sq ft |
| radishes | — | 25 seeds | .8 sq ft |

**On last frost** _____
(date)

*Sprout:*

| | | |
|---|---|---|
| sweet potatoes | — | .5 lb tubers |

*Start seedlings in flats:*

| | | |
|---|---|---|
| cantaloupes | — | 7 seeds |
| cosmos | — | 4 seeds |
| cucumbers | — | 6 seeds |
| honeydew melons | — | 7 seeds |
| New Hampshire | | |
|   midget watermelons— | | 26 seeds |
| sweet basil | — | 2 seeds |

*Prick out seedlings into flats:*

| | | |
|---|---|---|
| celery | — | 11+ seedlings |
| regular tomatoes | — | 7+ seedlings |

*Transplant:*

| | | | |
|---|---|---|---|
| parsley | — | 1 seedling | .2 sq ft |
| potatoes** | — | 100 sprouted pieces | 40.2 sq ft |

**2 weeks after last frost** _____
(date)

*Start seedlings in flats:*

| | | |
|---|---|---|
| bush green beans | — | 86 seeds |
| bush lima beans | — | 59 seeds |
| early corn | | |
|   (65 days to maturity)— | | 24 seeds |

*Prick out seedlings into flat:*

| | | |
|---|---|---|
| celery | — | 12 seedlings |

**3 weeks after last frost** _____
(date)

*Transplant:*

| | | | |
|---|---|---|---|
| early corn | — | 18 seedlings | 25.0 sq ft |

**Note**

Numbers given are for the approximate number of seeds and seedlings that should be required for each crop for the area involved.

Ⓢ = Stagger planting for a more continuous harvest.

\* = Spot additional seeds later where seeds do not germinate.

\*\* = See note with potato planting instructions on page 11.

## 4 weeks after last frost _____
(date)

*Sprout:*
potatoes
(65 days to maturity)— 12.5 lbs tubers

*Start seedlings in flats:*
| | | |
|---|---|---|
| pumpkins | — | 2 seeds |
| zucchini | — | 2 seeds |

*Transplant:*
| | | | |
|---|---|---|---|
| bush green beans | — | 64 seedlings | 14.0 sq ft |
| bush lima beans | — | 41 seedlings | 9.0 sq ft |
| cantaloupes | — | 5 seedlings | 7.0 sq ft |
| celery | — | 11 seedlings | 2.5 sq ft |
| cosmos | — | 3 seedlings⊤ | 3.0 sq ft |
| cucumbers | — | 5 seedlings | 4.0 sq ft |
| dill | — | 1 seedling⊤ | .4 sq ft |
| honeydew melons | — | 5 seedlings | 7.0 sq ft |
| New Hampshire midget watermelons | — | 18 seedlings | 16.0 sq ft |
| regular tomatoes (21″) | — | 7 seedlings | 20.0 sq ft |
| sweet basil | — | 1 seedling | 1.0 sq ft |
| sweet potatoes | — | 20 sprouted pieces | 4.5 sq ft |
| zinnias | — | 3 seedlings⊤ | 3.0 sq ft |

## 5 weeks after last frost _____
(date)

*Prick out seedlings into flats:*
| | | |
|---|---|---|
| eggplant | — | 1+ seedlings |
| green peppers | — | 5+ seedlings |

## 6 weeks after last frost _____
(date)

*Start seedlings in flat:*
| | | |
|---|---|---|
| chard | — | 5 seeds |

*Transplant:*
| | | | |
|---|---|---|---|
| celery | — | 12 seedlings | 2.5 sq ft |
| pumpkin | — | 1 seedling | 6.3 sq ft |
| zucchini | — | 1 seedling | 2.3 sq ft |

## 8 weeks after last frost _____
(date)

*As first planting comes out, transplant:*
| | | | |
|---|---|---|---|
| potatoes** | — | 100 sprouted pieces | 40.2 sq ft |

## 9 weeks after last frost _____
(date)

*Transplant:*
| | | | |
|---|---|---|---|
| eggplant | — | 1 seedling | 2.3 sq ft |
| green peppers | — | 5 seedlings | 4.0 sq ft |

## 14 weeks before first fall frost _____
(date)

*Start seedlings in flats:*
| | | |
|---|---|---|
| broccoli | — | 2 seeds |
| cabbage | — | 5 seeds |
| calendulas | — | 6 seeds |
| stocks | — | 6 seeds |

## 13 weeks before first frost _____
(date)

*Start seedlings in flats:*
| | | |
|---|---|---|
| corn (65 days to maturity) | — | 25 seeds |
| head lettuce | — | 5 seeds⑤ |
| leaf lettuce | — | 25 seeds⑤ |

*Transplant:*
| | | | |
|---|---|---|---|
| chard | — | 3 seedlings | 1.0 sq ft |

## 12 weeks before first frost _____
(date)

*Prick out seedlings into flats:*
| | | |
|---|---|---|
| head lettuce | — | 5+ seedlings⑤ |
| leaf lettuce | — | 20+ seedlings⑤ |

*As first potatoes come out, transplant:*
| | | | |
|---|---|---|---|
| corn | — | 18 seedlings | 25.0 sq ft |

## 11 weeks before first frost _____
(date)

*Start seedlings in flats:*
| | | |
|---|---|---|
| bush peas | — | 156 seeds |
| carrots | — | 90 seeds |
| spinach | — | 17 seeds |

*Prick out seedlings into flats:*
| | | |
|---|---|---|
| broccoli | — | 1+ seedlings |
| cabbage | — | 4+ seedlings |

## 9 weeks before first frost _____
(date)

*Transplant:*
| | | | |
|---|---|---|---|
| bush peas | — | 125 seedlings | 6.8 sq ft |
| chard | — | 3 seedlings | 1.0 sq ft |

## 8 weeks before first frost _____
(date)

*Transplant:*
| | | | |
|---|---|---|---|
| broccoli | — | 1 seedling | 1.3 sq ft |
| cabbage | — | 4 seedlings | 5.2 sq ft |
| calendulas | — | 4 seedlings | 4.0 sq ft |
| carrots | — | 50 seedlings | 2.7 sq ft |
| head lettuce | — | 3 seedlings⑤ | 2.7 sq ft |
| leaf lettuce (8″) | — | 20 seedlings⑤ | 7.8 sq ft |
| spinach | — | 10 seedlings | 2.2 sq ft |
| stocks | — | 4 seedlings | 4.0 sq ft |

*Plant:*
| | | | |
|---|---|---|---|
| radishes | — | 10 seeds | .25 sq ft |

### Notes
- Numbers given are for the approximate number of seeds and seedlings that should be required for each crop for the area involved.
- To improve the soil fertility and increase the sustainability of your garden/mini-farm, additionally grow 475 square feet of carbon-and-calorie crops, described on pages 24–25.

⑤ = Stagger planting for a more continuous harvest.

⊤ = Transplant seedlings on edge of bed; see plan, page 141.

\* = Spot additional seeds later where seeds do not germinate.

\*\* = See note with potato planting instructions on page 11.

# 1-PERSON MINI-GARDEN, *SECOND* YEAR

*Early Spring–Early Summer* (Bed 1)

zinnias

peppers eggplant

celery

zucchini

regular tomatoes

cucumbers

sweet potatoes

beans

lettuce

peas

brassicas: broccoli, brussels sprouts, cabbage, and cauliflower

spinach

carrots

beets parsley

radishes basil

onions and garlic

(Bed 2)

cosmos

dill

potatoes

cantaloupes, honeydew melons, and watermelons

pumpkins

early corn

cosmos

cosmos

*Summer–Late Summer* (Bed 1)

unchanged from late spring to early summer

potatoes

(Bed 2)

corn

peas

stocks

carrots

cantaloupes, honeydew melons, and watermelons (continued)

calendulas

lettuce

chard

radishes spinach cabbage broccoli

Scale: 5/16 inch = 1 foot. Growing bed is 100 square feet (5 by 20 feet).

**Note**

By the second year, the curved bed surface gives you up to 120 square feet of planting area in each 100 square feet of bed.

# 1-PERSON MINI-GARDEN, *THIRD* YEAR, 6-MONTH GROWING SEASON
## 380 SQUARE FEET (including path)

*As early as possible in spring, plant:*

| | | | |
|---|---|---|---|
| asparagus | — | 13 roots | 8.0 sq ft |
| bare root | | | |
|   dwarf fruit trees | — | 1 tree | 64.0 sq ft |
| strawberries | — | 32 seedlings | 20.0 sq ft |

**6 weeks before last spring frost** _____
*(date)*

*Start seedlings in flats:*

| | | |
|---|---|---|
| broccoli | — | 3 seeds |
| brussels sprouts | — | 2 seeds |
| cabbage | — | 6 seeds |
| cauliflower | — | 2 seeds |
| celery | — | 18 seeds |
| head lettuce | — | 3 seedsⓈ |
| leaf lettuce | — | 5 seedsⓈ |
| parsley | — | 2 seeds |
| regular tomatoes | — | 10 seeds |

**5 weeks before last frost** _____
*(date)*

*Start seedlings in flats:*

| | | |
|---|---|---|
| carrots | — | 90 seeds |
| cylindra beets | — | 16 seeds |

*Prick out seedlings into flats:*

| | | |
|---|---|---|
| head lettuce | — | 2+ seedlingsⓈ |
| leaf lettuce | — | 4+ seedlingsⓈ |

**4 weeks before last frost** _____
*(date)*

*Sprout:*

| | | |
|---|---|---|
| potatoes | | |
|   (65 days to maturity)— | 15.5 lbs tubers | |

*Prick out seedlings into flat:*

| | | |
|---|---|---|
| parsley | — | 1+ seedlings |

**3 weeks before last frost** _____
*(date)*

*Start seedlings in flats:*

| | | |
|---|---|---|
| bush peas | — | 100 seeds |
| spinach | — | 16 seeds |

*Prick out seedlings into flats:*

| | | |
|---|---|---|
| broccoli | — | 2+ seedlings |
| brussels sprouts | — | 1+ seedlings |
| cabbage | — | 4+ seedlings |
| cauliflower | — | 1+ seedlings |

**2 weeks before last frost** _____
*(date)*

*Start seedlings in flats:*

| | | |
|---|---|---|
| dill | — | 2 seeds |
| eggplant | — | 2 seeds |
| green peppers | — | 10 seeds |
| tomatoes | — | 14 seeds |

*Transplant:*

| | | | |
|---|---|---|---|
| broccoli | — | 2 seedlings | 2.6 sq ft |
| brussels sprouts | — | 1 seedling | 2.3 sq ft |
| bush peas | — | 70 seedlings* | 6.8 sq ft |
| cabbage | — | 4 seedlings | 5.2 sq ft |
| carrots | — | 50 seedlings | 2.7 sq ft |
| cauliflower | — | 1 seedling | 1.3 sq ft |
| cylindra beets | — | 10 seedlings | 1.0 sq ft |
| head lettuce | — | 2 seedlingsⓈ | 2.0 sq ft |
| leaf lettuce (9″) | — | 4 seedlingsⓈ | 2.0 sq ft |
| spinach | — | 10 seedlings | 2.2 sq ft |

*Plant:*

| | | | |
|---|---|---|---|
| garlic | — | 3 cloves | .3 sq ft |
| onions (purchased) | — | 39 sets | 3.8 sq ft |
| radishes | — | 10 seeds | .25 sq ft |

**On last frost** _____
*(date)*

*Sprout:*

| | | |
|---|---|---|
| sweet potatoes | — | .5 lb tubers |

*Start seedlings in flats:*

| | | |
|---|---|---|
| cantaloupes | — | 6 seeds |
| cosmos | — | 7 seeds |
| cucumbers | — | 6 seeds |
| honeydew melons | — | 7 seeds |
| New Hampshire | | |
|   midget watermelons | — | 26 seeds |
| sweet basil | — | 2 seeds |
| zinnias | — | 7 seeds |

*Prick out seedlings into flats:*

| | | |
|---|---|---|
| celery | — | 10+ seedlings |
| regular tomatoes | — | 7+ seedlings |

*Transplant:*

| | | | |
|---|---|---|---|
| parsley | — | 1 seedling | .2 sq ft |
| potatoes | — | 124 sprouted | |
| | |   pieces | 50.0 sq ft |

**2 weeks after last frost** _____
*(date)*

*Start seedlings in flats:*

| | | |
|---|---|---|
| early corn | — | 49 seeds |

*Prick out seedlings into flats:*

| | | |
|---|---|---|
| tomatoes | — | 10 seedlings |

*Transplant:*

| | | | |
|---|---|---|---|
| dill | — | 1 seedling | .2 sq ft |

**Note**

Numbers given are for the approximate number of seeds and seedlings that should be required for each crop for the area involved.

Ⓢ = Stagger planting for a more continuous harvest.

\* = Spot additional seeds later where seeds do not germinate.

\*\* = See note with potato planting instructions on page 11.

**3 weeks after last frost** _____
                                              (date)

_Start seedlings in flats:_
bush green beans — 96 seeds
bush lima beans — 62 seeds

_Transplant:_
early corn — 35 seedlings 30 sq ft

**4 weeks after last frost** _____
                                              (date)

_Sprout:_
potatoes — 9.3 lbs tubers

_Prick out seedlings into flats:_
celery — 10+ seedlings

_Transplant:_
bush green beans — 68 seedlings* 14.0 sq ft
bush lima beans — 43 seedlings* 9.0 sq ft
cantaloupes — 4 seedlings 5.0 sq ft
celery — 9 seedlings 2.0 sq ft
cosmos — 5 seedlings 5.0 sq ft
cucumbers — 5 seedlings 4.0 sq ft
honeydew melons — 5 seedlings 7.5 sq ft
New Hampshire
   midget watermelons — 18 seedlings 16.0 sq ft
regular tomatoes (21″) — 7 seedlings 20.0 sq ft
sweet basil — 1 seedling 1.0 sq ft
sweet potatoes — 20 seedlings 4.5 sq ft
zinnias (12″) — 5 seedlings 5.0 sq ft

_Start seedlings in flats:_
pumpkins — 2 seeds
zucchini — 2 seeds

**5 weeks after last frost** _____
                                              (date)

_Prick out seedlings into flats:_
eggplant — 1+ seedlings
green peppers — 5+ seedlings

**6 weeks after last frost** _____
                                              (date)

_Transplant:_
pumpkin — 1 seedling 6.3 sq ft
tomatoes — 10 seedlings 30 sq ft
zucchini — 1 seedling 2.3 sq ft

**8 weeks after last frost** _____
                                              (date)

_As first planting comes out, transplant:_
celery — 9 seedlings 2.0 sq ft
potatoes** — 75 sprouted
                 pieces 30.0 sq ft

**Notes**
- Numbers given are for the approximate number of seeds and seedlings that should be required for each crop for the area involved.
- To improve the soil fertility and increase the sustainability of your garden/mini-farm, additionally grow 665 square feet of carbon-and-calorie crops, described on pages 24–25.

**9 weeks after last frost** _____
                                              (date)

_Transplant:_
eggplant — 1 seedling 2.3 sq ft
green peppers — 5 seedlings 4.0 sq ft

**13 weeks before first fall frost** _____
                                              (date)

_Start seedlings in flats:_
broccoli — 2 seeds
cabbage — 8 seeds

**11 weeks before first frost** _____
                                              (date)

_Start seedlings in flats:_
calendulas — 6 seeds
carrots — 90 seeds
chard — 11 seeds
head lettuce — 4 seeds ⓢ
leaf lettuce — 25 seeds ⓢ
spinach — 17 seeds
stocks — 6 seeds

_Prick out seedlings into flats:_
broccoli — 1+ seedlings
cabbage — 4+ seedlings
head lettuce — 3+ seedlings ⓢ
leaf lettuce — 20+ seedlings ⓢ

**9 weeks before first frost** _____
                                              (date)

_Start seedlings in flat:_
bush peas — 156 seeds

**8 weeks before first frost** _____
                                              (date)

_As first potatoes come out, transplant:_
broccoli — 1 seedling 1.3 sq ft
bush peas — 125 seedlings* 6.8 sq ft
cabbage — 4 seedlings 5.2 sq ft
calendulas — 4 seedlings 4.0 sq ft
carrots — 49 seedlings 2.7 sq ft
chard — 7 seedlings 2.7 sq ft
head lettuce — 3 seedlings ⓢ 2.7 sq ft
leaf lettuce (8″) — 20 seedlings ⓢ 7.8 sq ft
spinach — 10 seedlings 2.2 sq ft
stocks — 4 seedlings 4.0 sq ft

_Plant:_
radishes — 10 seeds .25 sq ft

_See page 144 for plan of 1-Person Mini-Garden, Third Year._

ⓢ = Stagger planting for a more continuous harvest.

\* = Spot additional seeds later where seeds do not germinate.

\*\* = See note with potato planting instructions on page 11.

# 1-PERSON MINI-GARDEN, *THIRD* YEAR

*Spring*
(Bed 1)

zinnias | cosmos | regular tomatoes | celery | cantaloupes, honeydew melons, and watermelons | strawberries | dwarf fruit tree | strawberries

*Spring*
(Bed 2)

early corn | sweet potatoes | peppers | eggplant | beans | cucumbers | zucchini | asparagus

*Spring*
(Bed 3)

pumpkin | brussels sprouts | peas | cabbage | potatoes | cauliflower | onions | carrots | spinach | beets | broccoli | lettuce

radishes
parsley
dill
basil
garlic

*followed by potatoes in early summer*

*Early Fall*
(Bed 2)

cabbage and broccoli
peas
stocks | calendulas
lettuce
chard | carrots | radishes

Scale: 5/16 inch = 1 foot. Growing beds are 100 square feet (5 by 20 feet).

# 1-PERSON MINI-GARDEN, *FOURTH* YEAR, 6-MONTH GROWING SEASON
## 380 SQUARE FEET (including paths)

*As soon as possible in spring, plant:*
bare root

| | | | |
|---|---|---|---|
| dwarf fruit tree | — | 1 tree | 64.0 sq ft |
| chives (purchased) | — | 3 seedlings | .5 sq ft |
| lavender (purchased) | — | 1 seedling | 4.0 sq ft |
| marjoram (purchased) | — | 1 seedling | 1.0 sq ft |
| sage (purchased) | — | 1 seedling | 2.3 sq ft |
| strawberries | | | |
| (relocated; see plan) | — | 32 seedlings | 20.0 sq ft |

*or whatever herbs are desired*

## 6 weeks before last spring frost _____
(date)

*Start seedlings in flats:*

| | | |
|---|---|---|
| broccoli | — | 3 seeds |
| brussels sprouts | — | 2 seeds |
| cabbage | — | 5 seeds |
| cauliflower | — | 2 seeds |
| celery | — | 18 seeds |
| head lettuce | — | 3 seeds Ⓢ |
| leaf lettuce | — | 13 seeds Ⓢ |
| parsley | — | 2 seeds |
| regular tomatoes | — | 9 seeds |

## 5 weeks before last frost _____
(date)

*Start seedlings in flats:*

| | | |
|---|---|---|
| carrots | — | 90 seeds |
| cylindra beets | — | 16 seeds |

*Prick out seedlings into flats:*

| | | |
|---|---|---|
| head lettuce | — | 2+ seedlings Ⓢ |
| leaf lettuce | — | 10+ seedlings Ⓢ |

## 4 weeks before last frost _____
(date)

*Sprout:*

| | | |
|---|---|---|
| potatoes | — | 12.5 lbs tubers |

*Prick out seedlings into flat:*

| | | |
|---|---|---|
| parsley | — | 1+ seedlings |

## 3 weeks before last frost _____
(date)

*Start seedlings in flat:*

| | | |
|---|---|---|
| bush peas | — | 156 seeds |

*Prick out seedlings into flats:*

| | | |
|---|---|---|
| broccoli | — | 2+ seedlings |
| brussels sprouts | — | 1+ seedlings |
| cabbage | — | 4+ seedlings |
| cauliflower | — | 1+ seedlings |

## 2 weeks before last frost _____
(date)

*Start seedlings in flats:*

| | | |
|---|---|---|
| dill | — | 2 seeds |
| eggplant | — | 2 seeds |
| green peppers | — | 8 seeds |

*Prick out seedlings into flat:*

| | | |
|---|---|---|
| celery | — | 9+ seedlings |

*Transplant:*

| | | | |
|---|---|---|---|
| broccoli | — | 2 seedlings | 2.6 sq ft |
| brussels sprouts | — | 1 seedling | 2.3 sq ft |
| bush peas | — | 125 seedlings | 6.8 sq ft |
| cabbage | — | 4 seedlings | 5.2 sq ft |
| carrots | — | 50 seedlings | 2.7 sq ft |
| cauliflower | — | 1 seedling | 1.3 sq ft |
| cylindra beets | — | 10 seedlings | 1.0 sq ft |
| head lettuce | — | 2 seedlings Ⓢ | 2.0 sq ft |
| leaf lettuce (9″) | — | 10 seedlings Ⓢ | 6.0 sq ft |

*Plant:*

| | | | |
|---|---|---|---|
| garlic | — | 3 cloves | .3 sq ft |
| onions (purchased) | — | 39 sets | 3.8 sq ft |
| radishes | — | 15 seeds | .25 sq ft |

## On last frost _____
(date)

*Start seedlings in flats:*

| | | |
|---|---|---|
| cantaloupes | — | 4 seeds |
| cucumbers | — | 6 seeds |
| honeydew melons | — | 4 seeds |
| New Hampshire midget watermelons | — | 41 seeds |
| pumpkins | — | 3 seeds |
| sweet basil | — | 2 seeds |

*Prick out seedlings into flats:*

| | | |
|---|---|---|
| celery | — | 9+ seedlings |
| regular tomatoes | — | 7+ seedlings |

*Transplant:*

| | | | |
|---|---|---|---|
| parsley | — | 1 seedling | .15 sq ft |
| potatoes | — | 99 sprouted pieces | 40.0 sq ft |

## 2 weeks after last frost _____
(date)

*Start seedlings in flats:*

| | | |
|---|---|---|
| bush green beans | — | 86 seeds * |
| bush lima beans | — | 59 seeds * |
| early corn (65 days to maturity) | — | 25 seeds |

*Prick out seedlings into flat:*

| | | |
|---|---|---|
| celery | — | 9+ seedlings |

## Note
Numbers given are for the approximate number of seeds and seedlings that should be required for each crop for the area involved.

Ⓢ = Stagger planting for a more continuous harvest.

\* = Spot additional seeds later where seeds do not germinate.

\*\* = See note with potato planting instructions on page 11.

**3 weeks after last frost** _____
_____(date)_____

*Transplant:*

| | | | |
|---|---|---|---|
| early corn | — | 18 seedlings | 25.0 sq ft |
| regular | | | |
|   tomatoes (21″) | — | 7 seedlings | 20.0 sq ft |

**4 weeks after last frost** _____
_____(date)_____

*Transplant:*

| | | | |
|---|---|---|---|
| bush green beans | — | 64 seedlings* | 14.0 sq ft |
| bush lima beans | — | 41 seedlings* | 9.0 sq ft |
| cantaloupes | — | 3 seedlings | 5.0 sq ft |
| cucumbers | — | 5 seedlings | 4.0 sq ft |
| honeydew melons | — | 3 seedlings | 5.0 sq ft |
| New Hampshire | | | |
|   midget watermelons | — | 23 seedlings | 20.0 sq ft |
| pumpkins | — | 2 seedlings | 6.3 sq ft |
| sweet basil | — | 1 seedling | .25 sq ft |

**5 weeks after last frost** _____
_____(date)_____

*Prick out seedlings into flats:*

| | | |
|---|---|---|
| eggplant | — | 1+ seedlings |
| green peppers | — | 5+ seedlings |

**6 weeks after last frost** _____
_____(date)_____

*Transplant:*

| | | | |
|---|---|---|---|
| celery | — | 9 seedlings | 2.0 sq ft |

**7 weeks after last frost** _____
_____(date)_____

*Sprout:*

| | | |
|---|---|---|
| potatoes | — | 12.5 lbs tubers |

*Transplant:*

| | | | |
|---|---|---|---|
| eggplant | — | 1 seedling | 2.3 sq ft |
| green peppers | — | 5 seedlings | 4.0 sq ft |

**8 weeks after last frost** _____
_____(date)_____

*As first planting comes out, transplant:*

| | | | |
|---|---|---|---|
| potatoes** | — | 99 sprouted | |
| | | pieces | 40.0 sq ft |

**16 weeks before first fall frost** _____
_____(date)_____

*Start seedlings in flat:*

| | | |
|---|---|---|
| chard | — | 3 seeds |

**14 weeks before first frost** _____
_____(date)_____

*Start seedlings in flats:*

| | | |
|---|---|---|
| broccoli | — | 2 seeds |
| cabbage | — | 4 seeds |
| calendulas | — | 7 seeds |
| head lettuce | — | 4 seeds Ⓢ |
| leaf lettuce | — | 25 seeds Ⓢ |
| stocks | — | 7 seeds |

**13 weeks before first frost** _____
_____(date)_____

*Prick out seedlings into flats:*

| | | |
|---|---|---|
| head lettuce | — | 3+ seedlings Ⓢ |
| leaf lettuce | — | 20+ seedlings Ⓢ |

*Transplant:*

| | | | |
|---|---|---|---|
| chard | — | 2 seedlings | 1.0 sq ft |

**11 weeks before first frost** _____
_____(date)_____

*Start seedlings in flats:*

| | | |
|---|---|---|
| bush peas | — | 156 seeds |
| carrots | — | 90 seeds |
| spinach | — | 17 seeds |

*Prick out seedlings into flats:*

| | | |
|---|---|---|
| broccoli | — | 1+ seedlings |
| cabbage | — | 3+ seedlings |

**10 weeks before first frost** _____
_____(date)_____

*Transplant:*

| | | | |
|---|---|---|---|
| bush peas | — | 125 seedlings | 6.8 sq ft |
| head lettuce | — | 3 seedlings Ⓢ | 2.7 sq ft |
| leaf lettuce (8″) | — | 20 seedlings Ⓢ | 7.8 sq ft |

**9 weeks before first frost** _____
_____(date)_____

*Start seedlings in flats:*

| | | |
|---|---|---|
| bush peas | — | 156 seeds |
| corn | | |
|   (65 days to maturity) | — | 24 seeds |

**8 weeks before first frost** _____
_____(date)_____

*As first potatoes comes out, transplant:*

| | | | |
|---|---|---|---|
| broccoli | — | 1 seedling | 1.3 sq ft |
| bush peas | — | 125 seedlings | 6.8 sq ft |
| cabbage | — | 3 seedlings | 5.2 sq ft |
| calendulas | — | 5 seedlings | 5.0 sq ft |
| carrots | — | 50 seedlings | 2.7 sq ft |
| corn | — | 18 seedlings | 25.0 sq ft |
| spinach | — | 10 seedlings | 2.2 sq ft |
| stocks | — | 5 seedlings | 5.0 sq ft |

**Notes**

- Numbers given are for the approximate number of seeds and seedlings that should be required for each crop for the area involved.
- To improve the soil fertility and increase the sustainability of your garden/mini-farm, additionally grow 570 square feet of carbon-and-calorie crops, described on pages 24–25.

Ⓢ  = Stagger planting for a more continuous harvest.

\*  = Spot additional seeds later where seeds do not germinate.

\*\* = See note with potato planting instructions on page 11.

# 1-PERSON MINI-GARDEN, *FOURTH* YEAR

*Spring*
(Bed 1)

potatoes | eggplant | green peppers | sweet potatoes | cucumbers | strawberries | dwarf fruit tree | strawberries

*Spring*
(Bed 2)

basil
beets
dill
garlic
parsley
radishes

lettuce | peas | cauliflower | cabbage | carrots | broccoli | onions | brussels sprouts | optional | corn | regular tomatoes | lavender | sage | chives | marjoram | asparagus

*Spring*
(Bed 3)

celery | beans | pumpkin | melons | dwarf fruit tree | strawberries (relocated)

*Summer–
Early Fall*
(Bed 1)

corn | spinach | calendulas | broccoli cabbage

Scale: 5/16 inch ≅ 1 foot. Most growing beds are
100 square feet (5 by 20 feet).

*Summer–
Early Fall*
(Bed 2)

potatoes | lettuce | peas | carrots | chard | radishes | stocks

# 4-PERSON FAMILY FOOD GARDEN, 6-MONTH GROWING SEASON
## 1,302 SQUARE FEET (including paths)

*As soon as possible in spring, plant:*
bare root
   dwarf fruit trees — 7 trees    448.0 sq ft

## 6 weeks before last spring frost _____
(date)

*Start seedlings in flats:*
broccoli — 16 seeds
brussels sprouts — 8 seeds
cabbage — 32 seeds
cauliflower — 8 seeds
celery — 96 seeds
head lettuce — 56 seeds⑤
leaf lettuce — 96 seeds⑤
parsley — 16 seeds
regular tomatoes — 35 seeds

## 5 weeks before last frost _____
(date)

*Start seedlings in flats:*
carrots — 86 seeds
cylindra beets — 36 seeds
spinach — 61 seeds

*Prick out seedlings into flats:*
head lettuce — 28+ seedlings⑤
leaf lettuce — 48+ seedlings⑤

## 4 weeks before last frost _____
(date)

*Prick out seedlings into flat:*
parsley — 4+ seedlings

## 3 weeks before last frost _____
(date)

*Start seedlings in flats:*
bush peas — 1,880 seeds

*Prick out seedlings into flats:*
broccoli — 8+ seedlings
brussels sprouts — 4+ seedlings
cabbage — 16+ seedlings
cauliflower — 4+ seedlings

## 2 weeks before last frost _____
(date)

*Sprout:*
sweet potatoes — 1.5 lbs tubers

*Start seedlings in flats:*
chard — 16 seeds
dill — 8 seeds
eggplant — 8 seeds
green peppers — 36 seeds
spinach — 61 seeds

*Prick out seedlings into flats:*
celery — 53+ seedlings
regular tomatoes — 26+ seedlings

*Transplant:*
broccoli — 8 seedlings   45.6 sq ft
brussels sprouts — 4 seedlings   45.6 sq ft
bush peas — 1,500 seedlings   68.0 sq ft
cabbage — 16 seedlings   45.6 sq ft
carrots — 43 seedlings   2.7 sq ft
cauliflower — 4 seedlings   45.6 sq ft
cylindra beets — 36 seedlings   4.0 sq ft
head lettuce — 28 seedlings⑤   31.2 sq ft
leaf lettuce (9″) — 48 seedlings⑤   31.2 sq ft

*Plant:*
garlic — 3 cloves   .3 sq ft
onions (purchased) — 39 sets   3.8 sq ft
radishes — 10 seeds   .25 sq ft

## On last frost _____
(date)

*Start seedlings in flats:*
cantaloupes — 17 seeds
cosmos — 17 seeds
cucumbers — 23 seeds
honeydew melons — 17 seeds
New Hampshire
  midget watermelons — 17 seeds
pumpkins — 6 seeds
sweet basil — 8 seeds
zinnias — 14 seeds
zucchini — 10 seeds

*Prick out seedlings into flat:*
parsley — 9+ seedlings⑤   1.5 sq ft

*Transplant:*
potatoes** — 546 sprouted
               pieces   220.0 sq ft

## 2 weeks after last frost _____
(date)

*Start seedlings in flats:*
bush green beans — 299 seeds
bush lima beans — 206 seeds
early corn
  (65 days to maturity) — 98 seeds
sunflowers — 8 seeds

*Prick out seedlings into flat:*
celery — 53+ seedlings

*Transplant:*
chard — 16 seedlings   4.0 sq ft
spinach — 36 seedlings   9.0 sq ft

## Note
Numbers given are for the approximate number of seeds and seedlings that should be required for each crop for the area involved.

⑤ = Stagger planting for a more continuous harvest.

\* = Spot additional seeds later where seeds do not germinate.

\** = See note with potato planting instructions on page 11.

**3 weeks after last frost** _____
                                          (date)

*Transplant:*
early corn                —      73 seedlings      100.0 sq ft
regular tomatoes (21″)—        28 seedlings       80.0 sq ft

**4 weeks after last frost** _____
                                          (date)

*As early brassicas, onions, and lettuce come out, transplant:*
bush green beans     —      224 seedlings      56.0 sq ft
bush lima beans      —      144 seedlings      36.0 sq ft
sweet potatoes       —       27 seedlings       6.0 sq ft

*Transplant:*
cosmos (*after potatoes
  are harvested*)     —       12 seedlings      10.0 sq ft
cucumbers            —       18 seedlings      16.0 sq ft
dill                 —        4 seedlings       1.6 sq ft
pumpkins             —        4 seedlings      25.2 sq ft
sunflowers (24″)     —        4 seedlings      15.0 sq ft
sweet basil          —        4 seedlings       4.0 sq ft
zinnias (*after potatoes
  are harvested*)     —       10 seedlings      10.0 sq ft
zucchini             —        7 seedlings       9.2 sq ft

**5 weeks after last frost** _____
                                          (date)

*Prick out seedlings into flats:*
eggplant             —        4+ seedlings
green peppers        —       18+ seedlings

**6 weeks after last frost** _____
                                          (date)

*Sprout:*
potatoes             —      31 lbs tubers

*Prick out seedlings into flat:*
parsley              —        3+ seedlings

*As peas and carrots come out, replant bed with:*
cantaloupes          —       12 seedlings
honeydew melons      —       12 seedlings       50.0 sq ft
New Hampshire midget
  watermelons (12″)  —       12 seedlings

*Transplant:*
celery               —       50 seedlings       15.0 sq ft

**7 weeks after last frost** _____
                                          (date)

*Transplant:*
eggplant             —        4 seedlings        9.2 sq ft
green peppers        —       18 seedlings       16.0 sq ft

**Notes**
• Numbers given are for the approximate number of seeds
  and seedlings that should be required for each crop for
  the area involved.
• To improve the soil fertility and increase the sustainability of
  your garden/mini-farm, additionally grow 1,562 square feet
  of carbon-and-calorie crops, described on pages 24–25.

**8 weeks after last frost** _____
                                          (date)

*Transplant:*
parsley              —        3 seedlings       __sq ft

**10 weeks after last frost** _____
                                          (date)

*As first corn planting comes out, transplant:*
potatoes**           —      248 sprouted
                                 pieces      100.0 sq ft

**13 weeks before first frost** _____
                                          (date)

*Start seedlings in flats:*
broccoli             —        5 seeds
cabbage              —       20 seeds
calendulas           —       14 seeds
head lettuce         —       14 seeds⑤
leaf lettuce (8″)    —       69 seeds⑤
stocks               —       14 seeds

**12 weeks before first frost** _____
                                          (date)

*Prick out seedlings into flats:*
head lettuce         —       11+ seedlings⑤
leaf lettuce         —       55+ seedlings⑤

**11 weeks before first frost** _____
                                          (date)

*Start seedlings in flats:*
chard                —       15 seeds
spinach              —       61 seeds

*Prick out seedlings into flats:*
broccoli             —        1+ seedlings
cabbage              —       15+ seedlings

**10 weeks before first frost** _____
                                          (date)

*Transplant:*
head lettuce         —       11 seedlings⑤     10.0 sq ft
leaf lettuce         —       55 seedlings⑤     21.2 sq ft

**8 weeks before first frost** _____
                                          (date)

*As last potatoes comes out, transplant:*
broccoli             —        1 seedling        1.3 sq ft
cabbage              —       15 seedlings       20.8 sq ft
calendulas           —       10 seedlings       10.0 sq ft
chard                —       10 seedlings        4.0 sq ft
spinach              —       37 seedlings        8.0 sq ft
stocks               —       10 seedlings       10.0 sq ft

*Plant:*
radishes             —       41 seeds           1.0 sq ft

*See pages 150 and 151 for plan of Four-Person Family
Food Garden.*

⑤ = Stagger planting for a more continuous harvest.

\* = Spot additional seeds later where seeds do not germinate.

** = See note with potato planting instructions on page 11.

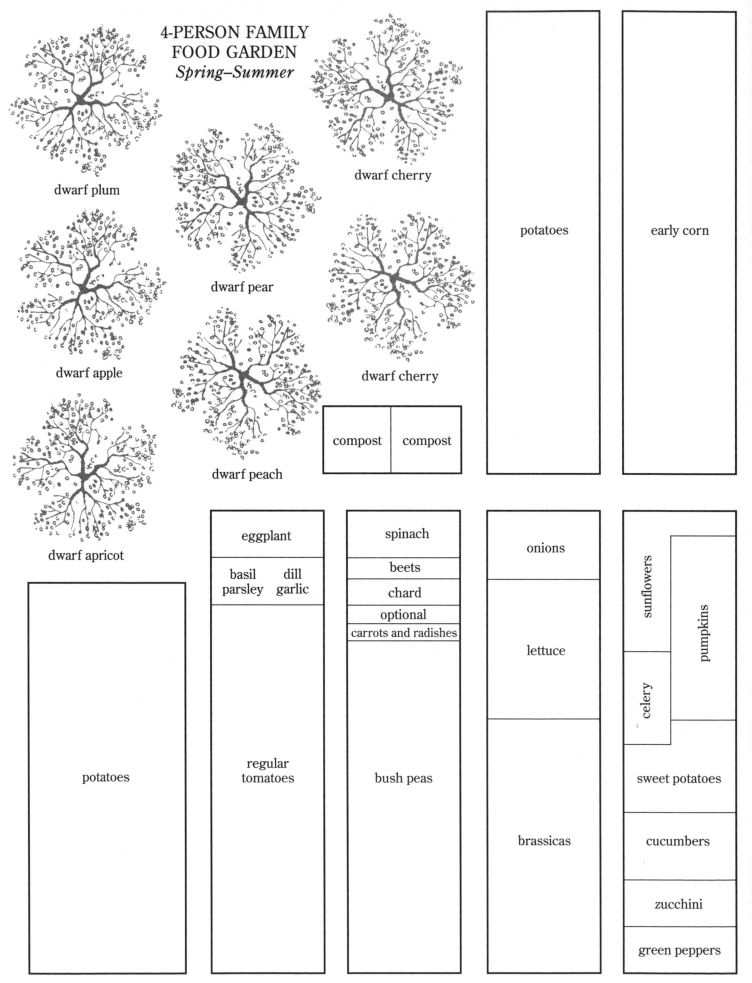

# 4-PERSON FAMILY FOOD GARDEN
## *Spring–Summer*

dwarf plum

dwarf pear

dwarf cherry

dwarf apple

dwarf cherry

dwarf peach

dwarf apricot

| compost | compost |

potatoes

early corn

| eggplant |
| basil dill |
| parsley garlic |
| regular tomatoes | potatoes |

| spinach |
| beets |
| chard |
| optional |
| carrots and radishes |
| bush peas |

onions

lettuce

brassicas

sunflowers

pumpkins

celery

sweet potatoes

cucumbers

zucchini

green peppers

Scale: ¼ inch ≅ 1 foot. Most growing beds are 100 square feet (5 by 20 feet).

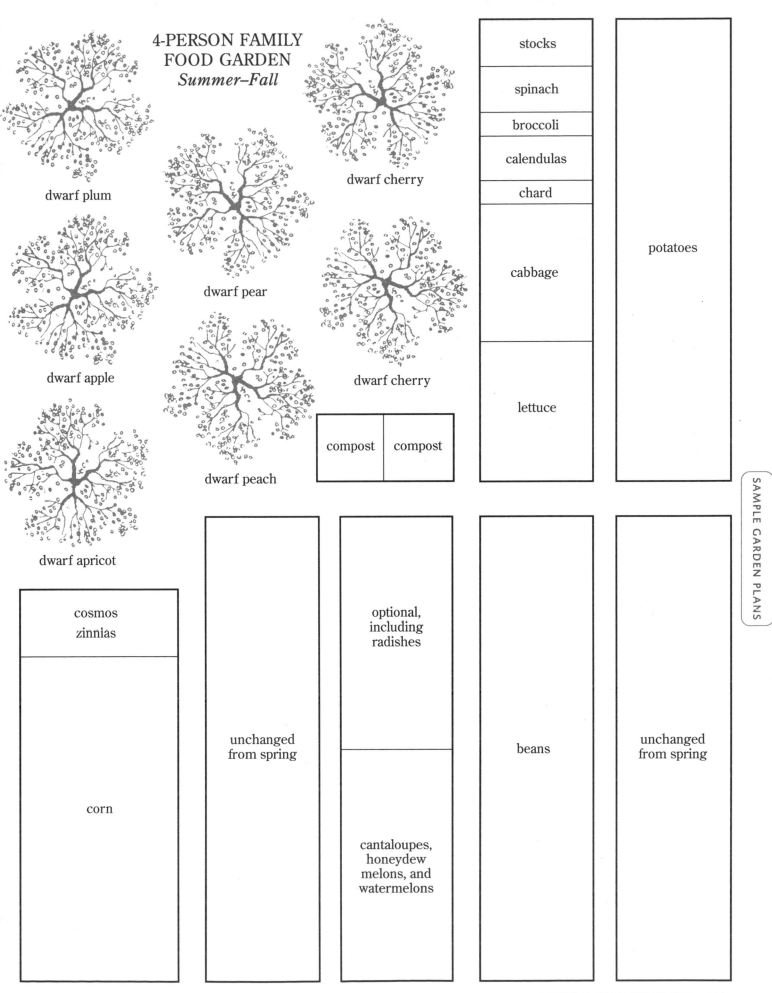

4-PERSON FAMILY
FOOD GARDEN
*Summer–Fall*

dwarf plum

dwarf cherry

dwarf pear

dwarf apple

dwarf cherry

dwarf peach

dwarf apricot

stocks

spinach

broccoli

calendulas

chard

cabbage

lettuce

potatoes

compost | compost

cosmos
zinnias

corn

unchanged
from spring

optional,
including
radishes

cantaloupes,
honeydew
melons, and
watermelons

beans

unchanged
from spring

# COMPANION PLANTING

## CHAPTER EIGHT

**GOAL:** *Focus on the **whole** garden to create a thriving mini-ecosytem that has beneficial interrelationships*

Like people in relationships, certain plants like or dislike each other, depending on the specific natures involved. Seedlings of transplanting size begin to relate more and more with the plants around them. These relationships become especially important as adult plants develop distinct personalities, essences, and aromas. Green beans and strawberries, for example, thrive better when they are grown together than when they are grown separately. To get really good-tasting Bibb lettuce, 1 spinach plant should be grown for every 4 Bibb lettuce plants.

In contrast, no plants grow well near wormwood due to its toxic leaf and root excretions. However, wormwood tea repels black fleas, discourages slugs, keeps beetles and weevils out of grain, and combats aphids. So wormwood is not a totally noxious herb. Few plants are. Instead, they have their place in the natural order of things.

Weeds are often specialists and doctors in the plant community. They take very well to sick soil that needs to be built up and almost seem to seek it out. Where cultivated garden plants cannot manage, weeds are able to draw phosphorus, potash, calcium, trace minerals, and other nutrients out of the soil and subsoil and concentrate them in their bodies. Plants seem to have uncanny instincts.

Weeds can be used to concentrate nutrients for future fertilization or to withdraw noxious elements, such as unwanted salts, from the growing area. A deficient soil is often enriched by adding weeds to man-made compost or by returning their dead bodies to the soil as nature does.

Companion planting is the constructive use of plant relationships by gardeners, horticulturists, and farmers. A scientific definition of companion planting is "The placing together of plants having complementary physical demands." A more accurate, living, and spiritual description is "The growing together of all those elements and beings that encourage *life* and *growth;* the creation of a microcosm that includes vegetables, fruits, trees, bushes, wheat, flowers, weeds, birds, soil, microorganisms, water, nutrients, insects, toads, spiders, and chickens."

Companion planting is still an experimental field in which much more research needs to be performed. The age of the plants involved and the percentage of each of the types of plants grown together can be critical, as can be their relative proximity to one another. Companion planting should, therefore, be used with some caution and much observation. You may want to study the causes of some of these beneficial relationships. Are they due to root excretions, plant aroma, or the pollen of composite flowers that attracts certain beneficial insects? Companion planting is a fascinating field.

Some of the companion planting techniques you might try and experience are for health, crop rotation, nutrition, physical complementarity, and weed, insect, and animal relationships.

## Health

*Better Growth*—Growing green beans and strawberries together, and Bibb lettuce and spinach, has already been mentioned. On the other end of the spectrum, onions, garlic, chives, and shallots seriously inhibit the growth of peas and beans. In between the extremes, *bush* beans and beets may be grown together with no particular advantage or disadvantage to either plant. *Pole* beans and beets, however, do not get along well. The nuances are amazing. What is the difference between bush and pole beans? No one appears to know the scientific reason yet for this difference in behavior, but it can be observed.

Ehrenfreid Pfeiffer developed a method known as "crystallization," from which one can predict whether or not plants will be good companions. In this technique, part of a plant is ground up and mixed with a chemical solution. After the solution dries, a crystalline pattern remains. Different plants have distinct, representative patterns. When 2 plant solutions are mixed, the patterns increase, decrease, or stay the same in strength and regularity. Sometimes both patterns improve, indicating a reciprocal, beneficial influence. Or both patterns may deteriorate in a reciprocal negative reaction. One pattern may improve while another deteriorates, indicating a one-sided advantage. Both patterns may remain the same, indicating no particular companion advantage or disadvantage. And one plant pattern may increase or decrease in quality while the other undergoes no change. Two plants that suffer a decrease in quality on a 1-to-1 basis may show an increase in strength in a 1:10 ratio.

Stinging nettle and tomatoes are good garden companions.

**Note**

Lemon balm, marjoram, oregano, dandelion, chamomile, stinging nettle, and valerian are perennials. They are traditionally planted in a section along an end of the bed so they need not be disturbed when the bed is replanted.

*Spacing for Better Companions*—Using GROW BIOINTENSIVE spacing with the plant leaves barely touching allows good companions to be better friends.

*All-Around Beneficial Influence*—Certain herbs and a tree have a beneficial influence on all of the plant community. These plants and their characteristics are:[1]

- Lemon balm (*Melissa officinalis*): Creates a beneficial atmosphere around itself and attracts bees. Part of the mint family.
- Marjoram (*Origanum majorana*): Has a "beneficial effect on surrounding plants."
- Oregano (*Origanum vulgare*): Has a "beneficial effect on surrounding plants."
- Stinging nettle (*Urtica dioica*): "Helps neighboring plants to grow more resistant to spoiling." Increases the essential oil content in many herbs. "Stimulates humus formation." Helps stimulate fermentation in compost piles. As a tea, it promotes plant growth and helps strengthen plants. Concentrates sulfur, potassium, calcium, and iron in its body.
- Valerian (*Valeriana officinalis*): "Helps most vegetables." Stimulates phosphorus activity in its vicinity. Encourages health and disease resistance in plants.
- Chamomile (*Chamaemelum nobile*): A lime specialist. "Contains a growth hormone which . . . stimulates the growth of yeast." In a 1:100 ratio, it helps the growth of wheat. As a tea, it combats diseases such as damping off in young plants. Concentrates calcium, sulfur, and potash in its body.
- Dandelion (*Taraxacum officinale*): Increases the "aromatic quality of all herbs." "In small amounts" it helps most vegetables. Concentrates potash in its body.
- Oak tree (*Quercus spp.*): Concentrates calcium in its bark (bark ash is 77% calcium). In a special tea, it helps plants resist harmful diseases. The oak tree provides a beneficial influence around it that helps create excellent soil underneath its branches. This is a great place to build a compost pile for the same reason, but keep the pile at least 6 feet from the tree trunk so the environment near the tree will not be conducive to disease or attractive to harmful insects.

*Soil Life Stimulation*—Stinging nettle helps stimulate the microbial life, and this helps plant growth.

1. Helen Philbrick and Richard B. Gregg, *Companion Plants and How to Use Them* (Old Greenwich, CT: Devin-Adair Company, 1966), pp. 16, 57, 58, 60, 65, 84, 85, 86, 92; and Rudolf Steiner, *Agriculture—A Course of Eight Lectures* (London: Biodynamic Agricultural Association, 1958), pp. 93–95, 97, 99, 100.

*Soil Improvement*—Sow thistle (*Sonchus oleraceus*) brings up nutrients from the subsoil to enrich a depleted topsoil. After years of dead sow thistle bodies have enriched the topsoil, heavier-feeding grasses return. This is part of nature's recycling program, in which leached-out nutrients are returned to the topsoil, and it is a natural method for raising new nutrients to the upper layers of the soil. It has been estimated that *1* cereal rye plant grown in good soil produces an average of 3 miles of roots per day; that is 387 miles of roots and 6,603 miles of root hairs during a season. Plants are continuously providing their own composting program underground. In 1 year, plants put 800 to 1,500 pounds of roots per acre into the soil in a small garden, and red clover puts 1,200 to 3,850 pounds of roots into the soil in the same period of time.[2]

Plant root systems improve the topsoil by bringing up nutrients from the subsoil.

## Rotations

For many years Ecology Action often followed a heavy giver, heavy feeder, light feeder, low nitrogen lover type of crop rotation approach. However, we discovered that this process, while it was good for organizing 1 type of rotation program, was complicated and did not take everything into account. One example is potatoes, which are a "light feeder" crop according to the definitions involved, yet they, along with tomatoes, are in reality among the heaviest "heavy feeders."

Eventually, we began to research rotations and discovered that many rotation programs exist. However, it was difficult to find a repeating pattern in almost all of them. In addition, it has been observed that biologically intensive food raising, because of the diversity of crops it uses, produces genetically diverse compost piles. The use of the cured compost from these piles throughout the growing area, in turn, is itself a kind of "rotation." As a result of this and a lot of experience, we have developed the following simpler rotation guidelines:

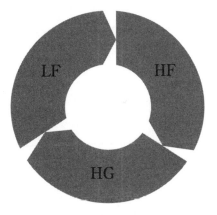

*Agricultural recycling:*
To preserve the soil's nutrients, plant heavy feeders, then heavy givers, then light feeders.

- For **main-season crops**, with few exceptions, we try not to grow the same crop, or a member of the same family, in the same growing bed 2 years in a row. In areas where 2 or more crops can be grown in the same growing bed during the year, we do not grow the same crop, or a member of the same family, in that bed a second time during the year. In addition, we try to grow a quick-maturing 60+-day "catch crop" after the main-season crop whenever possible. Fast-maturing bean and amaranth varieties are examples of this. (A list of plant families is given on page 158.)

- In addition, **for non-main-season crops planted in the fall**, there are 3 possible approaches: a 3-year rotation and 2 types of 2-year rotations.

2. Helen Philbrick and Richard B. Gregg, *Companion Plants and How to Use Them* (Old Greenwich, CT: Devin-Adair Company, 1966), pp. 75–76.

There are some points to be noted in these 3 approaches. All 3 begin with a planting for nitrogen accumulation to build up the soil before grains are grown to maturity. The second rotation system does this with a legume only and, therefore, provides the most nitrogen for the soil. The first rotation system has a third part, which grows a legume to maturity in order to provide a period of soil resting.[3]

You may want to experiment with different combinations, depending on the quality of your soil and the type of climate you have. The important thing is to develop a combination that provides the nitrogen you need and that grows sufficient mature biomass and immature biomass to produce enough cured compost to maintain sustainable soil fertility while you grow food for yourself.

In tropical areas, you will need to substitute warmer-weather crops that provide the same functions.

| 1. A 3-YEAR ROTATION | |
| --- | --- |
| Year 1 | Immature Grain and Legume Combination for Nitrogen Accumulation in the Crop Biomass and Nodules |
| Year 2 | Mature Grain for Calories and Mature Biomass |
| Year 3 | Mature Legume for Soil Nitrogen Resting[3] |

**Year 1:** The growing of a compost crop **interplanted mixture** (see Self-Teaching Mini-Series Booklet 14) **with double the amount of seed of cold-weather grains** broadcasted (wheat or hull-less barley or hull-less oats or triticale, and cereal rye) **and legumes** (broadcasted vetch and a sown cold-weather fava bean). The entire crop is harvested when it is immature so a main-season crop can be planted in time to go to maturity. (Inoculation of the legumes with the relevant nitrogen-fixing bacteria for the crops involved will be needed if the soil does not already contain these microbes.)

**Year 2:** The transplanting of a **cold-weather grain** (wheat or hull-less barley or hull-less oats or cereal rye or triticale), with the entire crop being harvested at maturity. In areas with a *long* main growing season, a main-season hot-weather crop is planted afterward to go to maturity. In areas with a *short* main growing season, we try to grow a quick-maturing 60+-day "catch crop" after the grain harvest whenever possible. Fast-maturing bean varieties are examples of this. Or an immature compost crop, such as pearl millet, may be grown at this point.

---

3. Legumes fix atmospheric nitrogen in nodules on their roots during the first part of their growth. As the legume begins to flower and set seed, all of this nitrogen is transferred through the plant and goes into the seed to form protein. In this way, the growing of mature legumes provides a period of "soil nitrogen resting," since nitrogen in the soil is not needed for their growth, provided the appropriate bacteria are present in the soil.

**Year 3:** The transplanting of a **legume** (a cold-weather fava bean variety), with the entire crop being harvested at maturity. In addition, we try to grow a quick-maturing 60+-day "catch crop" after the legume harvest whenever possible. Amaranth is an example of this. Or an immature compost crop, such as pearl millet, may be grown at this point.

| 2. A 2-YEAR ROTATION | |
|---|---|
| Year 1 | Immature Legume for Nitrogen Accumulation in the Crop Biomass and Nodules |
| Year 2 | Mature Grain for Calories and Mature Biomass |

**Year 1:** The transplanting of a **legume** (a cold-weather fava bean variety), with the entire crop being harvested when it is at 10% to 50% flower, so a main-season crop can be planted in time to go to maturity. (Inoculation of the legume with the relevant nitrogen-fixing bacteria for the crop involved will be needed if the soil does not already contain these microbes.)

**Year 2:** The transplanting of a **cold-weather grain** (wheat or hull-less barley or hull-less oats or cereal rye or triticale), with the entire crop being harvested at maturity. In areas with a *long* main growing season, a main-season hot-weather crop is planted afterward to go to maturity. In areas with a *short* main growing season, we try to grow a quick-maturing 60+-day "catch crop" after the grain harvest whenever possible. Fast-maturing bean varieties are examples of this. Or an immature compost crop, such as pearl millet, may be grown at this point.

| 3. ANOTHER TYPE OF 2-YEAR ROTATION | |
|---|---|
| Year 1 | Immature Grain and Legume Combination for Crop Biodiversity and Nitrogen Accumulation in the Crop Biomass and Nodules |
| Year 2 | Mature Grain for Calories and Immature Legume Combination for Nitrogen Accumulation in the Crop Biomass and Nodules |

**Year 1:** The growing of a compost crop **interplanted mixture** (see Self-Teaching Mini-Series Booklet 14) **with double the amount of seed of cold-weather grains** broadcasted (wheat or hull-less barley or hull-less oats or triticale, and cereal rye) and **legumes** (broadcasted vetch and a sown cold-weather fava bean). The entire crop is harvested when it is immature, so a main-season crop can be planted in time to go to maturity. (Inoculation of the legumes with the relevant nitrogen-fixing bacteria for the crops involved will be needed, if the soil does not already contain these microbes.)

**Year 2:** The growing of a compost crop **interplanted mixture** (see Self-Teaching Mini-Series Booklet 14) **of**

**legumes** (broadcasted vetch and a sown cold-weather fava bean) **with** transplanted **cold-weather** grains—a different grain from the one grown in Year 1, and cereal rye. The vetch and fava bean crops are removed when they are at 10% to 50% flower, and the entire grain crop is harvested when it is mature. In addition, we try to grow a quick-maturing 60+-day "catch crop" after the grain harvest whenever possible. Fast-maturing bean varieties are examples of this. Or an immature compost crop, such as pearl millet, may be grown at this point.

**Additional years:** The same cycling as Year 1 and Year 2 above, with a different grain being used with cereal rye in each succeeding cycle.

## PLANT FAMILIES (FOR PLANNING ROTATIONS)
*Avoid planting members of the same family in subsequent years.*

| BEET FAMILY (Chenopodiaceae) | PARSLEY FAMILY (Umbelliferae, Apiaceae) | SUNFLOWER FAMILY (Compositae, Asteraceae) |
|---|---|---|
| beets / mangels<br>spinach / chard<br>orache<br>quinoa | carrots / parsnips<br>celery / parsley<br>fennel<br>coriander / cilantro | lettuce / endive<br>sunflower / salsify<br>artichoke / cardoon<br>Jerusalem artichoke |
| ONION FAMILY (Amaryllidaceae, Alliaceae) | GRASS FAMILY (Gramineae, Poaceae) | TOBACCO FAMILY (Solanaceae) |
| garlic<br>onions<br>leeks<br>chives | corn / rice<br>barley / wheat<br>oats / rye<br>millet / sorghum | tomatoes<br>potatoes<br>peppers<br>eggplant |
| PEA FAMILY (Fabaceae, Leguminosae) | SQUASH FAMILY (Cucurbitaceae) | COLE FAMILY (Brassicaceae) |
| beans / peas<br>fava beans<br>runner beans<br>cowpeas / lentils<br>garbanzos<br>peanuts | cucumbers<br>gourds<br>melons, incl. watermelon<br>summer squash<br>winter squash<br>pumpkins | broccoli / cabbage<br>cauliflower / kohlrabi<br>kale / collards<br>radish / rutabaga<br>turnip / mustard |
| MINT FAMILY (Labiatae, Lamiaceae) | MORNING GLORY FAMILY (Convulvulaceae) | MALO FAMILY (Malvaceae) |
| basil | sweet potatoes | okra |
| AMARANTH FAMILY (Amaranthaceae) | LILY FAMILY (Liliaceae) | BUCKWHEAT FAMILY (Polygonaceae) |
| amaranth | asparagus | buckwheat / rhubarb |

## Nutrition

*Over Time*—Companion planting "over time" has been known for years as "crop rotation." A major form of this is given in the preceding pages. Another approach used by some is described below.

After properly preparing the soil, heavy feeders are planted. These are followed by heavy givers and then by light feeders. This is a kind of *agricultural recycling* in which people and plants participate to return as much to the soil as has been taken out.

Heavy feeders—most of the vegetables we like and eat (including corn, tomatoes, squash, lettuce, and cabbage)—take large amounts of nutrients, especially nitrogen, from the soil. In the GROW BIOINTENSIVE method, after harvesting heavy feeders you can return phosphorus and potassium to the soil in the form of compost.

To return nitrogen to the soil, grow heavy givers. Heavy givers are nitrogen-fixing plants or legumes, such as peas, beans, alfalfa, clover, and vetch. Fava beans are also good for this purpose. Not only do they bring large amounts of nitrogen into the soil, they also excrete substances that help eradicate tomato wilt–causing organisms. (*Caution:* Some people of Mediterranean descent are *fatally allergic* to fava beans, even though the beans are very popular and widely eaten in that area. People on certain medications experience the same reaction. Check with your physician first.)

After heavy givers, plant light feeders (all root crops) to give the soil a rest before the next heavy feeder onslaught. Three vegetables are low nitrogen lovers: turnips (a light feeder), sweet potatoes (a light feeder), and green peppers (a heavy feeder of nutrients other than nitrogen). The 2 light feeders would normally be planted after heavy givers, which put a lot of nitrogen into the soil. You may find it useful to have them follow a heavy feeder instead. It would also be good to have green peppers follow a heavy feeder. (They normally come after a heavy giver and a light feeder.)[4] You should experiment with these out-of-sequence plantings.

*In Space*—Companion planting of heavy feeders, heavy givers, and light feeders can be done in the same growing area, or space, at the same time. For example, corn, beans, and beets can be intermingled in the same bed. Just as with companion planting over time, you should proceed with care. In this combination, the beans must be bush beans, since pole beans and beets do not grow well together. Also, pole beans have been reported to pull the ears off corn stalks. Sometimes pole beans have been grown successfully with corn, however, and a

---

4. This way of looking at crops was developed many years ago. It is based on how much nitrogen crops generally consume or produce. Actually, it is not always accurate. For example, potatoes, a root crop and therefore a light feeder, consume some of the largest amounts of nitrogen. As a result, they are functionally a heavy feeder. Nonetheless, this system can be a way to organize crop rotation. See: Chaboussou, Francis. *Healthy Crops*, Charlbury, England: Jon Carpenter Publishing, Alder House, Ox7-3PH, 2004. 234pp.

vegetable such as carrots may be substituted for the beets so you can use the tall beans. When different plants are grown together, you sacrifice some of the *living mulch* advantage to companion planting "in space" because of the different plant heights. One way to determine the spacing for different plants grown together is to add their spacing together and divide by 2. If you grow corn and beets together, add 15 inches and 4 inches for a total of 19 inches. Divide by 2 and you get a per-plant spacing of 9½ inches. The beets, then, would be 9½ inches from each corn plant and vice versa. Each corn plant will be 19 inches from each corn plant and most beet plants will be 9½ inches from the other beet plants nearest to them. In the drawing below, note that each corn plant gets the 7½ inches in each direction that it requires for a total growing area with a diameter of 15 inches. Each beet plant, at the same time, gets the 2 inches it requires in each direction for a growing space with a 4-inch diameter.

## 2-CROP COMPANION PLANTING
*Circles show average root growth diameters.*

C = Corn (15″ C)
B = Beets (4″ C)

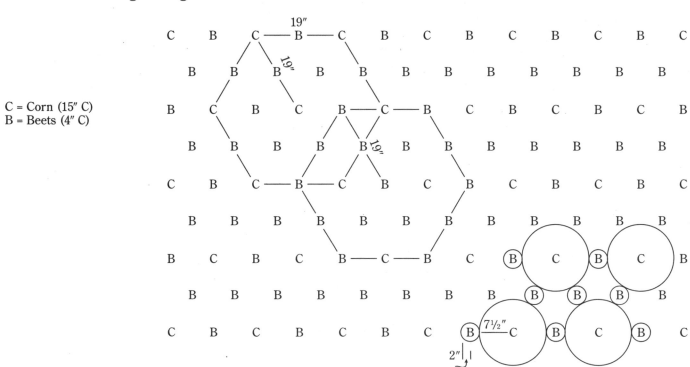

## MULTICROP COMPANION PLANTING IN SPACE

| corn | bush beans | beets | corn | bush beans | beets |
|------|-----------|-------|------|-----------|-------|
|      |           |       |      |           |       |

A spacing example for 3 crops grown together—corn (a heavy feeder), bush beans (a heavy giver), and beets (a light feeder)—is given on page 162. You should note that this approach to companion planting in space uses more bush bean and beet plants than corn plants. Be sure to plant the corn and beet seedlings 2 weeks before the beans, or the beans will retard the others' growth.

An easier, and probably just as effective, method of companion planting in space is to divide your planting bed into separate sections (or beds within a bed) for each vegetable. In this method, a grouping of corn plants would be next to a group of bush beans and a group of beets. In reality, this is a kind of companion planting over time, since there are heavy feeder, eavy giver, and light feeder sections within a bed. Roots extend 1 to 4 feet around each plant, so it is also companion planting in space. *We recommend you use this approach.* Additional spacing patterns no doubt exist and will be developed for companion planting in space.

*Compromise and Planning*—You can see by now that companion planting involves selecting the combination of factors that works best in your soil and climate. Fortunately, the myriad details fall into a pattern of simple guidelines. Within the guidelines, however, there are so many possible combinations that the planning process can become quite complex. Be easy on yourself. Do only as much companion planting as is reasonable for you and comes naturally. What you learn this year and become comfortable with can be applied next year, and so on. An easy place to start is with salad vegetables, since these are generally companions. Also, it is easier to companion plant over time rather than in space. Since you probably will not have enough area to use an entire bed for each crop, you might create several heavy feeder, heavy giver, and light feeder sections within each bed. You may want to grow a preponderance of crops from 1 group, such as the heavy feeders. (It is unlikely that you will want to grow ⅓ of each crop type.) Therefore, you will need to make adjustments, such as adding extra fertilizer and compost, when you follow one heavy feeder with another. Because of lack of space, you may have to grow some plants together that are

**Note**
When interplanting corn with other crops (e.g. beans and squash), transplant the corn 2 weeks before the other crops, so the corn has time to establish itself first.

## 3-CROP COMPANION PLANTING
*Circles show average root growth diameters.*

C  = Corn (15″ C)
B  = Beets (4″ C)
Ⓑ = Bush beans (6″ C)

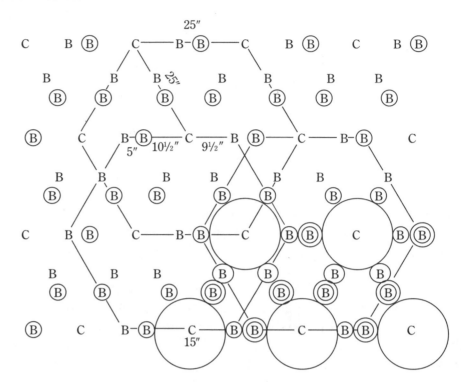

**Note**

Using the sun and shade technique is one way to make the most of your plants' physically complementary characteristics.

Lettuce plants can be nestled among other, larger plants for the partial shade they need.

Corn can provide the shade that cucumbers enjoy.

not companions. If so, you may need to be satisfied with lower yields, lower-quality vegetables, and less-healthy plants. Or you might try to alter your diet so that it is still balanced but more in line with the balances of nature. At any rate, you can see it is useful to plan your garden in advance. You will need to know how many pounds of each vegetable you want during the year, how many plants are needed to grow the weight of vegetables you require, when to plant seeds in flats and in the ground, when and how to rotate your crops, and when to raise and transplant herbs so they will be at the peak of their own special influence. Use the Master Charts in chapter 6 to assist in this work. Herb plants should be reasonably mature when transplanted into a bed for insect control or general beneficial influence to have their optimum effect as companions. Try to plan your garden 12 months at a time, and always at least 3 months in advance.

## Physical Complementarity

*Sun/Shade*—Many plants have special needs for sunlight or a lack of it. Cucumbers, for example, are very hard to please. They like heat, moisture, a well-drained soil, and some shade. One way to provide these conditions is to grow cucumbers with corn. The corn plants, which like heat and sun, can provide partial shade for the cucumber plants. Having lettuce or carrot plants nestle among other plants for partial shade is another example. Sunflowers, which are tall and like lots of sun, should be planted at the north side of the garden. There they will receive enough sun for themselves but will not shade other plants.

*Shallow/Deep Rooting*—One example is shallower-rooting beans interplanted with deeper-rooting corn. A dynamic process of improved soil structure occurs over time as plants with root systems of differing depths and breadths work different areas of soil in the planting bed.[5]

*Fast/Slow Maturing*—The French intensive gardeners were able to grow as many as 4 crops in a growing bed at a time due to the staggered growth and maturation rates of different vegetables. The fact that the edible portions of the plants appeared in different vertical locations also helped. Radishes, carrots, lettuce, and cauliflower were grown together in 1 combination used by the French to take advantage of these differences.

*Vertical Location of the Plant's Edible Portion*—See Fast and Slow Maturing.

## Weed, Insect, and Animal Relationships

*"Weed" Control*—The growth of beets, members of the cabbage family, and alfalfa is slowed down significantly by the presence of weeds. To minimize the weed problem for sensitive plants, you can grow other plants during the previous season that discourage "weed" growth in the soil in the current season. Two such plants are kale and rape. Another example is the Mexican marigold (*Tagetes minuta*).[6] "In many instances it has killed even couch grass, convolvulus (wild morning glory), ground ivy, ground elder, horsetail, and other persistent weeds that defy most poisons. Its lethal action works only on starch roots and has no effect on woody ones like roses, fruit bushes, and shrubs. Where it had grown, the soil was enriched as well as cleansed, its texture was refined, and lumps of clay were broken up."[7] Some care should be taken when using this marigold, however, since it might also kill vegetable crops and it does give off toxic excretions. Tests need to be performed to determine how long the influence of these excretions stays with the soil. But to cleanse a soil of pernicious weeds and thereby get it ready for vegetables, *Tagetes minuta* appears to be a useful plant.

*Insect and Pest Control*—At least 2 elements are important in companion planting for insect control. First is the use of older plants with well-developed aroma and essential oil accumulations. You want the insects to know the plant is there.

Sow thistle grows with lettuce in one example of shallow/deep rooting symbiosis. Their roots do not compete with each other.

An example of using fast/slow maturing to advantage is to interplant carrots with radishes.

5. Also see Emanuel Epstein, "Roots," *Scientific American,* May 1973, pp. 48–58.

6. Illegal in California, where it is considered a noxious weed that aggressively takes over cattle lands and prevents fodder from growing. It is probably also toxic to cattle.

7. Audrey Wynne Hatfield, *How to Enjoy Your Weeds* (New York: Sterling Publishing, 1971).

Second, it is important to use a large variety of herbs. Five different herbs help discourage the cabbageworm butterfly, although one herb may work better than another in your area. Testing several herbs will help you determine the ones that work best for you. The more "unpleasant" plants there are in the garden, the sooner harmful insects will get the idea that your garden is not a pleasant place to eat and propagate. Using a large number of herbs also fits in with the diversity of plant life favored by nature. Much more research needs to be performed to determine the optimum ages for control plants and the number of control plants per bed. Too few plants will not control an insect problem, and too many may reduce your yields. Some insect controls are:

- Whiteflies: Marigolds—but not pot marigolds (calendula)—and flowering tobacco. The first are supposed to excrete substances from their roots that the other plants absorb. When the whiteflies suck on the other plants, they think they are on a strong-tasting marigold and leave. The flowering tobacco plant has a sticky substance on the underside of its leaves to which whiteflies stick and die when they come for a meal.

- Ants: Spearmint, tansy, and pennyroyal. Mint often attracts whiteflies, so you may want to grow a few marigolds for control, but not so many as to possibly impair the taste of the mint, and certainly not one of the more poisonous marigolds. This is another area for compromise. A few insects are probably less of a problem than mint with a strange taste.

- Nematodes and root pests: Mexican marigold (*Tagetes minuta*) "eliminates all kinds of destructive eelworms . . . wireworms, millipedes and various root-eating pests from its vicinity." The French marigold (*Tagetes patula*) eliminates some "plant-destroying nematodes . . . at up to a range of three feet . . . The beneficial . . . eelworms which do not feed on healthy roots were not affected."[8]

- Aphids: *Yellow* nasturtiums are a *decoy* for black aphids. They may be planted at the base of tomatoes for this purpose. Remove the plants and aphids before the insects begin to produce young with wings. Spearmint, stinging nettle, southernwood, and garlic help repel aphids.

- Tomato worms: Borage reportedly helps repel tomato worms and/or serves as a decoy. Its blue flowers also attract bees.

8. Ibid., p. 17.

*Gophers*—Elderberry cuttings placed in gopher holes and runs reportedly repel these animals. Daffodils, castor beans, and gopher plant (*Euphorbia lathyrus*) are all poisonous to gophers. Be careful with the latter 2, however, as they are also *very* toxic to children, especially infants.

*Birds, Bees, and Other Animals*—Sow thistle attracts birds. Some birds are vegetarian, and some are omnivorous. The omnivorous birds may stay for a main course of insects after a seed snack. If you are having trouble with birds eating the berries in your berry patch, you could erect a wren house in the middle of it. Wrens are insectivores, and they will not bother the berries. But they will attack any bird, however large, that comes near their nest.

Hummingbirds are attracted to red flowers. They especially like the tiny, red, torchlike flowers of the pineapple sage in our garden. Bees may be attracted by hyssop, thyme, catnip, lemon balm, pot marjoram, sweet basil, summer savory, borage, mint, and *blue* flowers. Once in the garden they help pollinate.

Animals are good for the garden, too. Their manures can be used as fertilizers. Chickens are one of the few reliable controllers of earwigs, sow bugs, pill bugs, snails, grasshoppers, and maggots, though you may have to protect young seedlings from chickens pecking tasty plant morsels.

Birds and plants can work together. The *Sonchus* plant seeds attract the finch, which afterward eats aphids from the cabbage.

Companion planting in all its aspects can be a complex and often mind-boggling exercise—if you worry too much about the details. Nature is complex. We can only assist and approximate her in our creations. If we are gentle in relation to her forces and balances, she will correct our errors and fill in for our lack of understanding. As you gain more experience and develop a sensitivity and feeling for gardening, more companion planting details will become clear naturally. Do not let too much planning spoil the fun and excitement of working with nature!

# A LIST OF COMMON GARDEN VEGETABLES, THEIR COMPANIONS, AND THEIR ANTAGONISTS[9]

|  | Companions | Antagonists |
|---|---|---|
| Asparagus | Tomatoes, parsley, basil | |
| Beans | Potatoes, carrots, cucumbers, cauliflower, cabbage, summer savory, most other vegetables and herbs | Onions, garlic, gladiolus, chives |
| Beans, bush | Potatoes, cucumbers, corn, strawberries, celery, summer savory | Onions |
| Beans, pole | Corn, summer savory, sunflowers | Onions, beets, kohlrabi, cabbage |
| Beets | Onions, kohlrabi | Pole beans |
| Cabbage family (cabbage, cauliflower, kale, kohlrabi, broccoli) | Aromatic plants, potatoes, celery, dill, chamomile, sage, peppermint, rosemary, beets, onions | Strawberries, tomatoes, pole beans |
| Carrots | Peas, leaf lettuce, chives, onions, leeks, rosemary, sage, tomatoes | Dill |
| Celery | Leeks, tomatoes, bush beans, cauliflower, cabbage | |
| Chives | Carrots, tomatoes | Peas, beans |
| Corn | Potatoes, peas, beans, cucumbers, pumpkins, squash | |
| Cucumbers | Beans, corn, peas, radishes, sunflowers, lettuce | Potatoes, aromatic herbs |
| Eggplant | Beans, potatoes | |
| Leeks | Onions, celery, carrots | |
| Lettuce | Carrots and radishes (lettuce, carrots, and radishes make a strong team grown together), strawberries, cucumbers, onions | |
| Onions (and garlic) | Beets, strawberries, tomatoes, lettuce, summer savory, leeks, chamomile (sparsely) | Peas, beans |

9. From *Organic Gardening and Farming*, February 1972, p. 54.

| | **Companions** | **Antagonists** |
|---|---|---|
| Parsley | Tomatoes, asparagus | |
| Peas | Carrots, turnips, radishes, cucumbers, corn, beans, most vegetables and herbs | Onions, garlic, gladiolus, potatoes, chives |
| Peppers | Basil, okra | |
| Potatoes | Beans, corn, cabbage, horse-radish (should be planted at the corners of the patch), marigolds, eggplant (as a lure for the Colorado potato beetle) | Pumpkins, squash, cucumbers, sunflowers, tomatoes, raspberries |
| Pumpkins | Corn | Potatoes |
| Radishes | Peas, nasturtiums, lettuce, cucumbers | |
| Soybeans | Grows with anything, helps everything | |
| Spinach | Strawberries | |
| Squash | Nasturtiums, corn | Potatoes |
| Strawberries | Bush beans, spinach, borage, lettuce (as a border), onions | Cabbage |
| Sunflowers | Cucumbers | Potatoes |
| Tomatoes | Chives, onions, parsley, asparagus, marigolds, nasturtiums, carrots | Kohlrabi, potatoes, fennel, cabbage |
| Turnips | Peas | |

## A COMPANIONATE HERBAL FOR THE ORGANIC GARDEN[10]

*A list of herbs, their companions, and their uses, including some beneficial weeds and flowers.*

| | |
|---|---|
| Basil | Companion to tomatoes; dislikes rue intensely; improves growth and flavor; repels flies and mosquitoes. |
| Bee balm | Companion to tomatoes; improves growth and flavor. |
| Borage | Companion to tomatoes, squash, and strawberries; deters tomato worms; improves growth and flavor. |
| Caraway | Plant here and there; loosens soil. |

10. From *Organic Gardening and Farming*, February 1972, pp. 52–53.

| | |
|---|---|
| Catnip | Plant in borders; deters flea beetles. |
| Chamomile | Companion to cabbage and onions; improves growth and flavor. |
| Chervil | Companion to radishes; improves growth and flavor. |
| Chives | Companion to carrots; improves growth and flavor. |
| "Dead" nettle | Companion to potatoes; deters potato bugs; improves growth and flavor. |
| Dill | Companion to cabbage; dislikes carrots; improves growth and health of cabbage. |
| Fennel | Plant away from gardens; most plants dislike it. |
| Flax | Companion to carrots and potatoes; deters potato bugs; improves growth and flavor. |
| Garlic | Plant near roses and raspberries; deters Japanese beetles; improves growth and health. |
| Henbit | General insect repellent. |
| Horseradish | Plant at the corners of a potato patch to deter potato bugs. |
| Hyssop | Deters cabbage moths; companion to cabbage and grapes. Keep away from radishes. |
| Lamb's-quarters | This edible weed should be allowed to grow in moderate amounts in the garden, especially in corn. |
| Lemon balm | Sprinkle throughout the garden. |
| Lovage | Improves flavor and health of plants if planted here and there. |
| Marigolds | The workhorse of the pest deterrents. Plant throughout the garden; discourages Mexican bean beetles, nematodes, and other insects. |
| Marjoram | Plant here and there in the garden; improves flavor. |
| Mint | Companion to cabbage and tomatoes; improves health and flavor; deters white cabbage moths. |
| Mole plant | Deters moles and mice if planted here and there. |
| Nasturtium | Companion to radishes, cabbage, and cucurbits[11]; plant under fruit trees; deters aphids, squash bugs, and striped pumpkin beetles; improves growth and flavor. |

11. Plants in the gourd family.

| | |
|---|---|
| Peppermint | Planted among cabbages, it repels white cabbage butterflies. |
| Petunia | Protects beans. |
| Pigweed | One of the best weeds for pumping nutrients from the subsoil; good for potatoes, onions, and corn; keep weeds thinned. |
| Pot marigold (calendula) | Companion to tomatoes, but plant elsewhere in the garden, too; deters asparagus beetles, tomato worms, and general garden pests. |
| Purslane | This edible weed makes good ground cover among corn. |
| Rosemary | Companion to cabbage, beans, carrots, and sage; deters cabbage moths, bean beetles, and carrot flies. |
| Rue | Keep it far away from sweet basil; plant near roses and raspberries; deters Japanese beetles. |
| Sage | Plant with rosemary, cabbage, and carrots; keep away from cucumbers; deters cabbage moth and carrot fly. |
| Southernwood | Plant here and there in the garden; companion to cabbage; improves growth and flavor; deters cabbage moths. |
| Sow thistle | This weed in moderate amounts can help tomatoes, onions, and corn. |
| Summer savory | Plant with beans and onions; improves growth and flavor; deters bean beetles. |
| Tansy | Plant under fruit trees; companion to roses and raspberries; deters flying insects, Japanese beetles, striped cucumber beetles, squash bugs, and ants. |
| Tarragon | Good throughout the garden. |
| Thyme | Plant here and there in the garden; deters cabbage worms. |
| Valerian | Good anywhere in the garden. |
| Wild morning glory[12] | Allow it to grow in the corn. |
| Wormwood | As a border, it keeps animals from the garden. |
| Yarrow | Plant along borders, paths, and near aromatic herbs; enhances essential oil production. |

12. We discourage growing wild morning glory anywhere in your garden since it is a pernicious weed. Cultured morning glory is fine, however. *This information was collected from many sources, most notably the Bio-Dynamic Association and the Herb Society of America.*

# A BALANCED NATURAL BACKYARD ECOSYSTEM AND ITS INSECT LIFE

## CHAPTER NINE

**GOAL:** *Grow a mini-ecosystem thriving with life*

Insects and people are only part of the complex, interrelated world of life. Both are important, integral parts of its living dynamism. Insects are an important part of the diet for many birds, toads, and frogs, and for some insects in nature's complex food chain. The GROW BIOINTENSIVE method reminds you that every time you relate to an insect you are relating to the whole system of life, and that if you choose to dominate the insect population, rather than work in harmony with it, part of the system dies. For example, we depend on insects to pollinate many of our vegetables, fruits, flowers, herbs, fibers, and cover crops. When we choose dominating, death-oriented control, then the scope and depth of our lives become narrower and smaller. We are actually detracting from our lives rather than adding to them. In trying to isolate an insect and deal with it separately out of relation to the ecosystem in which it lives, we work against nature, which in turn works against us in counter-productive results.

When an excess of insects appears in a garden, nature is indicating that a problem exists in the life of that garden. In each case, we need to become sensitive to the source of the imbalance. Observation and gentle action will produce the best results. In contrast, when a heavy-handed approach is taken and poisons are used, beneficial predators are killed as well as the targeted harmful insects. Spraying trees to eliminate worms or beetles often results in a secondary outbreak of spider mites or aphids because ladybugs and other predators cannot reestablish themselves as quickly as the destructive species.

Paying attention to the soil and to plant health, planning a varied environment, and leaving a few wild spaces for unexpected benefactors minimize pest losses more effectively than the use of poison. Also, in order to have beneficial insects in your food-producing area, you must provide food for them—which may be some of the harmful insects! If there are no harmful insects to feed them, then there will be few, if any, beneficial insects around to act as friendly guardians for your garden. This seeming paradox—the need for both kinds of insects for the most healthy garden—is symbolic of nature's balances. Not too much moisture, but enough. Not too much aeration, but enough. Not too many harmful insects, but enough. You find the need for these balances everywhere—in the compost pile, in the soil, in the mini-climate, and in the backyard microcosm as a whole.

In a small backyard garden ecosystem or mini-farm, it is especially important to welcome all life-forms as much as possible. Ants destroy fruit fly and housefly larvae and keep the garden cleared of rotting debris. Have you ever squashed a snail and watched how the ants come to whisk the remains away almost within a day? Earwigs are carnivorous and prey on other insects. Tachinid flies parasitize caterpillars, earwigs, tomato worms, and grasshoppers by laying their eggs in them. We've found cabbage worms immobilized and bristling with cottony white torpedoes the size of a pinhead—larvae of the braconid wasp, which will hatch and go in search of more cabbage worms. Toads eat earwigs, slugs, and other pests. Chickens control earwigs, sowbugs, and flies. Even the ancient and fascinating snails have a natural predator: humans!

The first step in insect control is to cultivate strong, vigorous plants by cultivating a healthy place where they can grow. Normally (about 90% of the time), insects only attack unhealthy plants. Just as a healthy person who eats good food is less susceptible to disease, so are healthy plants on a good diet less susceptible to plant disease and insect attack. The insect is *not* the source of the problem, but rather an unhealthy soil is. The soil needs your energy, not the insect. The uninterrupted growth that the GROW BIOINTENSIVE method stresses is also important to maintaining plant health. We are shepherds providing the conditions our plants need for healthy, vigorous growth.

Here are some elements to consider when caring for your garden's health:

- Did you dig the soil properly?
- Are the proper plant nutrients available in the soil?
- Did you use enough compost?
- Is the soil pH within reasonable limits for the plant being grown?
- Did you transplant the seedlings properly?
- Are you watering the plants properly?
- Are you weeding effectively?
- Are you maintaining the soil in a way that will enable it to retain moisture and nutrients?

- Are the plants receiving enough sun?
- Are you growing the plants in season?

Another factor that aids plant health and minimizes insect and disease problems is keeping a correct balance of phosphorus and potash in the soil in relation to the amount of nitrogen present. The optimal ratio among these elements is still to be determined. Research also needs to be completed to determine the *minimum* amounts of these elements (in pounds per 100 square feet) that should be in the soil. (Smaller amounts of organic fertilizer elements are required in comparison with soluble synthetic chemical fertilizers, since they break down more slowly and remain available to the plants for a longer period of time.)

Properly planning the garden can eliminate many insect and disease problems!

- Use seeds that grow well in your climate and soil.
- Use plant varieties that are weather hardy, insect resistant, and disease resistant. New strains, especially hybrids (whether developed for higher yields, disease resistance, or other reasons), should usually be avoided. Some hybrids produce foods of lower nutritive value in comparison with older strains, and often use up nutrients from the soil at a more rapid rate than a living soil can sustain over time. Hybrids also tend to be very susceptible to a few diseases even when they are greatly resistant to many prevalent ones.
- Companion plant. Grow vegetables and flowers together that grow well with each other.
- Avoid putting the same vegetable in the same growing bed each year. This practice invites disease.
- Rotate your crops; follow heavy feeders with heavy givers and then light feeders.

## Natural Predators

Encourage natural insect control by enlisting the aid of nature.

*Birds*—Some are vegetarians. Others are omnivorous. A bird that stops for a seed snack may remain for an insect dinner. A house wren feeds 500 spiders and caterpillars to her young in an afternoon; a brown thrasher consumes 6,000 insects a day; a chickadee eats 138,000 cankerworm eggs in 25 days; and a pair of flickers eats 5,000 ants as a snack. A Baltimore oriole can consume 17 hairy caterpillars in a minute. You can encourage the presence of birds with moving water, by planting bushes for their protection, by planting sour berry bushes for food, and by growing plants that have seeds they like to eat.

*Toads, Snakes, and Spiders*—They also eat insects and other garden pests. Toads eat as many as 10,000 insects in 3 months, including cutworms, slugs, crickets, ants, caterpillars, and squash bugs.

*Ladybugs*—These beetles are good predators in your garden since they eat a single particular pest, aphids, and do not eat beneficial insects. Ladybugs eat 40 to 50 insects per day, and their larvae eat even more.

*Praying Mantids*—These predators should only be used in infestation emergencies, since they eat beneficial as well as harmful insects. They are not selective and even eat each other.

*Trichogramma Wasps*—They lay their eggs in hosts, such as moth and butterfly larvae, that eat leaves. When they hatch, the wasp larvae parasitize the host larvae, which fail to reach maturity. Up to 98% of the hosts are rendered useless in this way.

*Tachinid Flies*—These parasites help control caterpillars, Japanese beetles, earwigs, gypsy moths, brown-tail moths, tomato worms, and grasshoppers.

*Syrphid Flies*—These parasites prey upon aphids and help pollinate crops.[1]

After you have done everything possible to provide a healthy, balanced garden for your plants, you may still have insect problems. If so, you should approach the unwanted insects with the idea of *living control* rather than elimination. If there is a problem, identify the pest and try to determine whether an *environmental change* can solve the problem. In our research garden, we have minimized (not eliminated, though) gophers by introducing gopher snakes.

The pocket Golden Guides *Insects* and *Insect Pests* are invaluable guides for getting to know the creatures that inhabit your garden. Out of the 86,000 species of insects in the United States, 76,000 are considered beneficial or friendly.[2] So, be careful! An insect that looks ugly or malicious may be a friend. If you can't seem to find an obvious culprit for your problem, try exploring at night with a flashlight. Many predators are active then.

Ask yourself whether the *damage* is *extensive* enough to warrant a "policing" effort. During 1972, we grew bush beans in one of our test beds. The primary leaves were almost entirely destroyed by the 12-spotted cucumber beetle. But in most cases the damage was not so rapid as to prevent the development of healthy secondary leaves. The less tender secondary leaves were ultimately attacked and quite heavily eaten. About 80% of

1. Beatrice Trum Hunter, *Gardening Without Poisons* (New York: Berkeley Publishing Corp., 1971), pp. 31, 37, 42, 43, 48.
    2. Ibid., p. 28.

the secondary leaf area remained, however, and we harvested very tasty, unblemished beans. The yield in pounds was still 3.9 times the United States average! Recent tests have shown that leaf damage of up to 30% by insects can actually increase the yield in some crops. You may decide to sacrifice some yield for beauty; many destructive caterpillars become beautiful butterflies. To get the yield you want and/or to encourage the presence of butterflies, you can plant extra plants of the crops they like.

We often underestimate the ability of plants to take care of themselves. The damage done by insects often affects only a very small percentage of the edible crop. Because of this, many GROW BIOINTENSIVE gardeners plant a little extra for the insect world to eat. This practice is beautiful, mellow, and in keeping with life-giving forms of insect control. Furthermore, extensive research has shown that beneficial organisms found in soil and ocean environments can withstand stress, in the form of temperature, pressure, pH, and nutrient fluctuations, to a much greater degree in an organically fertilized medium than in a synthetically fertilized medium. I suspect researchers will come to a similar conclusion about plant resistance to insect attack.

Any time an insect or other pest invades your garden, there is an opportunity to learn more about nature's cycles and balances. Learn why they are there and find a *living control*. Look for controls that will affect only the harmful insect. Protect new seedlings from birds and squirrels with netting or chicken wire, trap earwigs in dry dark places, wash aphids off with a strong spray of water, or block ants with a sticky barrier of Vaseline, Tanglefoot Pest Barrier, or a tack trap. While you are doing this, continue to strive for a long-term natural balance in your growing area.

At our Common Ground Research Garden, only 3 pest problems have taken a lot of our energy: snails, slugs, and gophers. The first few years we primarily trapped gophers. A lot of time was spent checking and resetting traps and worrying about them, yet the gophers probably only damaged about 5% of our crop. We later found that, in addition to gopher snakes, they really do not like certain things placed in their holes (sardines, garlic juice, fish heads, male urine, and dead gophers). The gophers may also be blocked with strips of daffodils. Daffodils contain arsenic in their bulbs and can discourage them. Gopher snakes, of course, prevent a population explosion. A combination of approaches and gentle persistence paid off.

We have a simple routine for snails and slugs. At the end of the spring rains we go out at night with flashlights and collect gallons of them. We drop the snails in buckets of soapy water, which kills them. If we use soap that is quick to degrade, we can dump them on the compost pile the next day. We catch most of them in the first 3 nights. Going out occasionally over the next 2 weeks, we can catch new ones that were too small to get in the first sweep or that have just hatched from eggs laid in the soil. Such a concentrated cleanup can be effective for several months. The red-bellied snake eats large numbers of slugs. A sorghum mulch is reported to repel slugs as well.

Another kind of problem has been solved through observation. For example, one year a cherry tomato bed was wilting. Several people, including a graduate student studying insects, told us it was caused by nematodes. When we dug down into the soil to look for the damage, we discovered the real source. The soil was bone dry below the upper 8 inches. A good soaking took care of the problem, and we learned not to take gardening advice on faith, but to always check it out for ourselves— as we hope you will.

## Other Initiatives

Here are some other living control approaches to try:

*Hand-picking*—You can pick the insects from plants once you are certain the insect involved is *harmful* and is the source of the problem. Consult a book such as Fichter's *Insect Pests* (see page 217 of the bibliography), which has color drawings of insects in their several stages (nymph, larva, and adult). Some insects are only harmful in one stage and can even be beneficial in other stages.

*Spraying*—In general, insects may be divided into 2 categories— those that chew and bite plants and those that suck juices from them. *Chewing or biting insects* include caterpillars, flea beetles, potato bugs, cankerworms, cutworms, and grasshoppers. *Aromatic and distasteful* substances such as garlic, onion, and pepper sprays can discourage them. *Sucking insects* include aphids, thrips, squash bug nymphs, flies, and scale insects. Soap solutions (not detergents, which would damage the plant and soil as well as the insects), clear miscible oil solutions, and other solutions that asphyxiate the insects by coating their tender bodies and preventing respiration through body spiracles or breathing holes help control these insects.

*Traps*—Some traps, such as shredded newspaper in clay pots turned upside down on sticks in the garden, will attract earwigs during daylight hours. Snails, slugs, sowbugs, and symphylans can be trapped under damp boards or sweet potatoes cut in half lengthways. They retreat to these places in the heat and light of the day.

*Barriers*—The sticky commercial Tanglefoot substance will catch some insects crawling along tree trunks during part of their life cycle. Catching insects in this manner often prevents infestation of the tree in a later season. (Tanglefoot barriers must be applied to apple tree trunks in July to catch codling moth larvae leaving the tree. This will minimize codling moth infestation the following spring. Plan ahead!) You can also use plant barriers and decoys. Grow a vegetable or flower preferred by a particular insect away from the garden to attract it to another location. Place repellent plants near a vegetable or flower that needs protection.

*Companion Plants*—You may also wish to plant some herbs in your bed for insect control. The age and number of plants used per 100 square feet determine the herb's effectiveness. A young plant does not have an aroma or root exudate strong enough to discourage harmful insects or to attract beneficial ones. Similarly, too few herbs will not control a pest or attract a needed predator. But too many herbs may retard vegetable growth and yield. Composite flowers, such as pot marigolds (calendulas) and sunflowers, are excellent attractants for predatory insects because their large supplies of pollen serve as predator food sources. A few (2 to 4) plants per 100-square-foot bed will probably suffice. We have not done many experiments with them yet, since accurate testing can take 2 to 3 years for 1 herb grown with 1 food plant to control 1 insect. You may wish to try some of these biodynamic observations, though. It's a lot of fun to try to see for yourself!

Probably the most important form of insect control with plants is just diverse cropping. The GROW BIOINTENSIVE method we use utilizes diverse cropping, and we have only experienced 5% to 10% crop loss due to pests. Biodynamic gardeners and farmers also use diverse cropping and have suggested planting 10% more area to make up for crop losses. In contrast, the monocropped acreage of today's commercial agriculture provides an ideal uniform habitat for widespread attack by pests that favor a single crop. Pesticides have been used to counteract the problem inherent in monocropping. Yet the Environmental Protection Agency estimated that in 1940, "American farmers used 50 million pounds of pesticides and lost 7 percent of their crop before harvest," and that by 1970, 12 times more pesticides were used, "yet the percentage of crops lost before harvest has almost doubled."[3] Today, about 30 times more pesticides are used than in 1940, and the percentage of crops lost to insects has been estimated to be as high as 37 percent. In fact, many pesticides targeted for a single pest species actually cause increases in numbers of nontargeted pests. By their action on the physiology of the plant, pesticides can make a plant more nutritionally favorable to insects, thereby increasing the fertility and longevity of feeding pests.[4]

3. James S. Turner, *A Chemical Feast: Report on the Food and Drug Administration* (Ralph Nader Study Group Reports) (New York: Grossman, 1970). Cited in Frances Moore Lappe and Joseph Collins, *Food First* (Boston: Houghton Mifflin Company, 1977), p. 49.

4. Francis Chaboussou, *Healthy Crops: A New Agricultural Revolution* (Charlsbury, UK: John Carpenter Publishing for The Gaia Foundation, 2004).

## INSECT PESTS AND PLANT CONTROLS[5]

| Insect Pest | Plant Control |
|---|---|
| Ants | Spearmint, tansy, pennyroyal |
| Aphids | Nasturtium, spearmint, stinging nettle, southernwood, garlic |
| Black flea beetle | Wormwood, mint |
| Blackfly | Intercropping, stinging nettle |
| Cabbageworm butterfly | Sage, rosemary, hyssop, thyme, mint, wormwood, southernwood |
| Colorado potato beetle | Eggplant, flax, green beans |
| Cutworm | Oak leaf mulch, tanbark |
| Flies | Nut trees, rue, tansy, spray of wormwood and/or tomato |
| Japanese beetle | White geranium, datura |
| June bug grub | Oak leaf mulch, tanbark |
| Malaria mosquito | Wormwood, southernwood, rosemary |
| Mexican bean beetle | Potatoes |
| Mosquito | Legumes |
| Moths | Sage, santolina, lavender, mint, stinging nettle, herbs |
| Plant lice | Castor bean, sassafras, pennyroyal |
| Potato bugs | Flax, eggplant |
| Slugs | Oak leaf mulch, tanbark |
| Squash bugs | Nasturtium |
| Striped cucumber beetle | Radish |
| Weevils | Garlic |
| Woolly aphids | Nasturtium |
| Worms in goats | Carrots |
| Worms in horses | Tansy leaves, mulberry leaves |

5. Helen Philbrick and Richard B. Gregg, *Companion Plants and How to Use Them* (Old Greenwich, CT: Devon-Adair Company, 1966), pp. 52–53. This book and others should be consulted for the proper use and application rates of these plant remedies. Improper use or application can cause problems and could be harmful to you, your plants, and animals.

It is evident that pesticides are not an effective solution for crop losses due to pests. *Diverse* cropping without pesticides may be able to reduce total pest losses more than monocropping with pesticides, even in large-scale agriculture. Using standard agricultural practices, Cornell University researchers, in a 5-year study completed in 1970, found that without pesticides the insect population could be cut in half when only 2 crops were grown together.[6] You can do this when you grow a diversity of plants in your backyard with life-giving techniques!

This introduction to insect control has emphasized philosophy and general approaches. Philbrick's *Companion Plants and How to Use Them,* Hunter's *Gardening Without Poisons,* and Philbrick's *The Bug Book* (see pages 188, 217, and 218 of the bibliography) have already vigorously explored the spectrum of organic insect control in detail. These books provide companion planting combinations, recipes for insect control solutions, and addresses for buying predatory insects.

I hope each person who reads this book will plant at least one small, 3 by 3-foot GROW BIOINTENSIVE bed. You will find the experience fun and exciting beyond your wildest expectations!

---

6. See Jeff Cox, "The Technique That Halves Your Insect Population," *Organic Gardening and Farming,* May 1973, pp. 103–104.

# BIBLIOGRAPHY AND RESOURCES

Ecology Action's Bountiful Gardens mail order service offers numerous books. You can write to them at 18001 Shafer Ranch Rd., Willits, CA 95490 for a free catalog for current prices, and to inquire about other titles. Ecology Action has numerous publications on the GROW BIOINTENSIVE® method as well as books, booklets, and information on gardening, mini-farming, and related topics (see page 254). You can use the books listed here to develop your own mini-course(s) for study of those areas that interest you most. Publications followed by "**BL**," "**IL**," or "**AL**" are particularly recommended for, respectively, a basic-level, intermediate-level, or advanced-level library. Publications preceded with an asterisk (*) are particularly recommended for a given topic.

### Alan Chadwick

*Bronson, William. "The Lesson of a Garden." *Cry California,* Winter 1970: 4–17.

Cuthbertson, Tom. *Alan Chadwick's Enchanted Garden.* New York: Dutton, 1978. 199 pp. Captures the flavor of working with Alan Chadwick.

Mulligan, Jim, and John de Graaf. *Gardensong.* Oley, PA: Bullfrog Films (Box 149, Oley, PA 19547). Video.

National Video Portrait Library (1869 Kirby Rd., McLean, VA 22101). 55-minute, black-and-white, ¾-inch videocassette of a spontaneous philosophical interview with the late Alan Chadwick. Send 2 stamps for a response when inquiring.

Singh, Tara. *Awakening a Child from Within.* Los Angeles: Life Action Press (P.O. Box 48932, Los Angeles, CA 90048), 1991: 333–334.

### Animals

American Rabbit Breeders Association. *A Practical Beginning to Successful Rabbit Raising.* Bloomington, IL: ARBA, 1975. 64 pp.

Ash, William J. *Raising Ducks. Farmers' Bulletin No. 2215.* Washington, DC: U.S. Dept. of Agriculture, 1969. 14 pp.

Bardach, John E., et al. *Aquaculture: The Farming and Husbandry of Freshwater and Marine Organisms.* New York: John Wiley & Sons, 1972. 868 pp.

Belanger, Jerome. "A Basic Guide to Goatkeeping." *Countryside Magazine* 65, 12 (1981): 20–31.

Bell, F. R. *Green Food for Rabbits & Cavies.* Yorkshire, Great Britain: Watmoughs Limited, 1971. 92 pp.

Bement, C. U. *The American Poulterer's Companion.* New York: Harper, 1871. 304 pp.

Bennett, Bob. *Raising Rabbits the Modern Way.* Charlotte, VT: Garden Way Publishing, 1975. 158 pp.

Booth, Barbara. "Birds in the Farm." *Biodynamics,* Fall 1992: 6–33.

British Goat Society. *Goat Feeding.* Devon, UK: British Goat Society, n.d. 36 pp.

Bryant, Paul, et al. *Backyard Fish Farming.* Dorchester, Dorset, UK: Prism Press, 1980. 170 pp.

Bull and Carroll. *Principles of Feeding Farm Animals.* New York: Macmillan, 1937. 395 pp.

*Calf Rearing.* Zero Grazing Series. Vol. 3. Nairobi, Kenya: Ministry of Livestock Development, National Dairy Development Project (P.O. Box 34188, Nairobi, Kenya). 16 pp.

Colby, Byron E., et al. *Dairy Goats: Breeding/Feeding/Management.* Spindale, NC: American Dairy Goat Assoc. (P.O. Box 186, Spindale, NC 28160), 1972. 79 pp.

Coutant, Frank R. *The ABC of Goat Dairying.* Columbia, MO: Dairy Goat Journal, 1946. 127 pp.

Cowley, W. O. *How to Produce Broilers for Show.* College Station: Texas A&M University, PS. 141, 1975. 6 pp.

Craig, John A., and F. R. Marshall. *Sheep Farming.* New York: Macmillan, 1913. 302 pp.

Cuthbertson, David. *The Nutrient Requirements of Farm Livestock.* Vol. 2, *Ruminants.* London: Agricultural Research Council, 1965. 264 pp.

*Dairy Goat Journal.* P.O. Box 1908, Scottsdale, AZ 85252. January 1976, Vol. 54, No. 1 Focus on LaManchas. March 1976, Vol. 54, No. 3 Focus on Nubians. April 1976, Vol. 54, No. 4 Focus on Housing, Fencing & Equipment. July 1976, Vol. 54, No. 7 Focus on Toggenburgs. September 1976, Vol. 54, No. 9 Focus on National Spotlight Sale Catalog.

de Baïracle Levi, Juliette. *Herbal Handbook for Farm and Stable.* Emmaus, PA: Rodale Press, 1976. 320 pp. **BL**

Devendra, C., and Marcia Burns. *Goat Production in the Tropics.* Farnham Royal, Bucks, UK: Commonwealth Agricultural Bureaux, 1970. 177 pp.

Dillon, Olan Jr., et al. *Warm-Water Fishponds. Farmers' Bulletin 2250.* Washington, DC: U.S. Dept. of Agriculture, 1971. 14 pp.

Ecology Center. *How to Raise Rabbits & Chickens in an Urban Area.* Berkeley, CA: Ecology Center, 1976. 44 pp.

Ernst, Ralph A. *One-Sheet Answers: Peafowl.* Agricultural Extension, Univ. of California, 1973.

Ernst, Ralph A., and Stanley W. Coates. *Raising Geese.* Leaflet 75-LE/2225. Division of Agricultural Sciences, Univ. of California, n.d. 4 pp.

Farr, Marion M. *Intestinal Coccidiosis of Chickens: How to Control It.* Leaflet 402. Washington, DC: U.S. Dept. of Ag., 1956. 2 pp.

*The Feeding of the Dairy Cow.* Zero Grazing Series. Vol. 5. Nairobi, Kenya: Ministry of Livestock Development, National Dairy Development Project (P.O. Box 34188, Nairobi, Kenya). 15 pp.

*The Fertility of the Dairy Cow.* Zero Grazing Series. Vol. 4. Nairobi, Kenya: Ministry of Livestock Development, National Dairy Development Project (P.O. Box 34188, Nairobi, Kenya). 12 pp.

Fowler, J. C., et al. *The Home Broiler Flock.* Fact Sheet L-1247. College Station: Texas A&M University, n.d. 4 pp.

Gould, James L., and Carol Grant Gould. *The Animal Mind.* New York: Scientific American Library, 1999. 236 pp.

Grizzell, Roy A. *Catfish Farming: A New Farm Crop. Farmers' Bulletin 2244.* Washington, DC: U.S. Dept. of Agriculture, 1969. 22 pp.

Hart, S. A., et al. *Light and Temperature Controlled Housing for Poultry. Circular 526.* Division of Agricultural Sciences, Univ. of California, 1964. 12 pp.

Hawthorne, Ronald, et al. *Snails as Food . . . Escargot. Leaflet 75-LE/2222.* Division of Agricultural Sciences, Univ. of California, n.d. 4 pp.

Hetherington, L. U. *Home Goat Keeping.* West Yorkshire, UK: EP Publishing Limited, 1979. 71 pp.

*In Practice.* Bimonthly publication of the Center for Holistic Management.

Jordan, Whitman H. *The Feeding of Animals.* New York: Macmillan, 1903. 450 pp.

Juhre, Robert G. *Preventing Deer Damage.* Kettle Falls, WA: Robert G. Juhre, 1996. 54 pp.

Laurie, Duncan Forbes. *Poultry Foods and Feeding.* New York: Cassell and Co., 1912. 188 pp.

Leach, Carol A. *Aids to Goatkeeping.* Scottsdale, AZ: Dairy Goat Journal, 1975. 277 pp.

Lucas, L. M., et al. *Lighting Poultry Houses. Farmers' Bulletin 2229.* Washington, DC: U.S. Dept. of Agriculture, 1968. 12 pp.

Luttmann, Rick and Gail. *Chickens in Your Backyard.* Emmaus, PA: Rodale Press, 1976. 157 pp.

Mackenzie, David. *Goat Husbandry.* London: Faber and Faber, 1970. 336 pp. **BL**

*Marketing Eggs. Farmers' Bulletin 1378.* Washington, DC: U.S. Dept. of Agriculture, 1954. 46 pp.

McNulty, Robert W., et al. *Your Dairy Goat.* Agricultural Extension, Univ. of California, 4-H-Ag26, 1972. 16 pp.

Miller, Madeline. *Bunnies as Pets: A Guide to the Selection, Care and Breeding of Rabbits.* Jersey City, NJ: T.F.H. Publications, 1955. 24 pp.

Miller, Robert, and John R. Dunbar. *A Practical Guide to Swine Nutrition.* Agricultural Extension, Univ. of California, 1914. 8 pp.

Nordell, Anne and Eric. "Work Hogs and Manure." *Small Farmers Journal,* 15, 2: 46–47.

Oxen Culture Demonstration Farm (Tillers International, 5239 S. 24th St., Kalamazoo, MI 49002).

Pegler, H. S. Holmes. *Goat Keeping for Amateurs.* London: Bazaar, Exchange & Mart, 1950. 101 pp.

Podems, Marc. "Coturnix Quail Challenges the Chicken." *Organic Farming and Gardening Magazine.* June 1975: 36–41.

Potash and Phosphate Institute. "Phosphorus for Agriculture." *Better Crops with Plant Food,* Spring 1978. Atlanta, GA: Potash & Phosphate Inst., 1978. 39 pp.

*Raising Guinea Fowl.* Washington, DC: Animal Husbandry Research Division, Agricultural Research Service, 1963. 8pp.

*Raising Livestock on Small Farms. Farmers' Bulletin 2224.* Washington, DC: U.S. Dept. of Agriculture, 1972. 22 pp.

Richardson, Berthier Warren. *The Hygienic Box Stall System for Dairy Goats.* Worcester, MA: Berthier W. Richardson, 1950. 50 pp.

Rollin, Bernard E. *The Frankenstein Syndrome: Ethical and Social Issues in the Genetic Engineering of Animals.* New York: Cambridge University Press, 1995. 241 pp.

Roth, Charles E., and Joseph R. Froehlich. *The Farm Book.* New York: Harper & Row, 1975. 95 pp.

Salsbury Laboratories. *Salsbury Manual of Poultry Diseases.* Charles City, IA: Salsbury Laboratories, 1971. 48 pp.

Savory, Allan. *The Complete Holistic Management™ Planning and Monitoring Guide.* Albuquerque, NM: The Center for Holistic Management (1010 Tijeras NW), 2000. Looseleaf binder. 158 pp.

———. *Grazing Plan & Control Chart Livestock/Wildlife/Crops/Other Uses).* The Center for Holistic Management, 1997.

———. *Holistic Management: A New Framework for Decision Making.* Covelo, CA: Island Press, 1999. 616 pp.

———. *Holistic Resource Management.* Covelo, CA: Island Press, 1988. 564 pp.

Schell, Orville. *Modern Meat: Antibiotics, Hormones and the Pharmaceutical Farm.* New York: Vintage Books, 1985. 343 pp.

Schreib, Andrea. "All About Moles." *BackHome Magazine* March/April 2004: 38–39.

Shields, Joan and Harry. *The Modern Dairy Goat.* London: C. Arthur Pearson, 1949. 172 pp.

Sibley, David Allen. *National Audubon Society: The Sibley Guide to Birds.* New York: Knopf, 2000. 544 pp.

Sunset Editors. *Attracting Birds to Your Garden.* Menlo Park, CA: Sunset Books, 1974. 96 pp.

Sweeny, Sedley. *Looking at Livestock and Some of the More Common Diseases of Farm Animals and Their Symptoms.* Suffolk, UK: Soil Association, 1977. 22 pp.

Taylor, John G, and J. M. Stanley. *Brooding Chicks with Infrared Lamps. Leaflet 397.* Washington, DC: U.S. Dept. of Ag., 1955. 3 pp.

Teller, Walter Magnes. *Starting Right with Sheep.* Charlotte, VT: Garden Way Publishing, 1973. 34 pp.

Templeton, George S. *Domestic Rabbit Production.* Danville, IL: The Interstate Printers & Publishers, 1968. 213 pp.

Tewalt, Will L. *Improved Milk Goats: A Guide for Breeders, Dairymen and Exhibitors.* New York: Orange Judd Publishing, 1946. 145 pp.

Thomas, Steven. *Backyard Lifestock.* Taftsville, VT: The Countryman Press, 1976. 264 pp.

Van Riet, William J. *Small-Scale Pork Production.* Univ. of California Agricultural Extension in Stanislaus County, 1974. 20 pp.

Vivian, John M., ed. "Raising Ducks on the Small Place." *Bulletin G.* Charlotte, VT: Garden Way Publishing, 1975. 22 pp.

Wales, J. H. *Trout of California.* Sacramento: State of California Dept. of Fish and Game, 1957. 55 pp.

Watson, George C. *Farm Poultry.* New York: Macmillan, 1901.

Wehr, Everett E. *Cecal Coccidiosis of Chickens: How to Control It.* Washington, DC: U.S. Dept. of Agriculture, 1955.

Williams, Ann. *Backyard Rabbit Farming.* Dorchester, UK: Prism Press, 1978. 123 pp.

*Wolf, Tom. "Bucking Tradition: Moving toward Sustainable Ranching—The Gospel According to Pete Tatschl—An Environmentalist Questions Whether Cows Belong in the Southwest, and Gets in Response a Healthy Dose of Holistic Range Management." *High Country News* (P.O. Box 1090, Paonia, CO 81428), March 1990: 25–27.

Woll, F. W. *Lippincott's Farm Manuals: Productive Feeding of Farm Animals.* Philadelphia, PA: J. B. Lippincott, The Washington Square Press, 1916. 385 pp.

## Appropriate Technologies

*101 Technologies from the South for the South.* Ottawa, Canada: International Development Research Centre (P.O. Box 8500, Ottawa, ON K1G 3H9, Canada), 1992. 231 pp.

Allen, Hugh. *The Kenya Ceramic Jiko: A Manual for Stovemakers.* Croton-on-Hudson, NY: International Technology Development Group of North America (The Bootstrap Press, P.O. Box 337, Croton-on-Hudson, NY 10520), 1991. 99 pp.

Appropriate Technology Project. Volunteers in Asia. P.O. Box 4543, Stanford, CA 94309. A nonprofit research organization that makes information about key appropriate technology publications available to others.

Ap-Tech. Appropriate Technology Development Association (P.O. Box 311, Gandhi Bhawan, Lucknow-226001, U.P. India). Occasional papers on topics related to appropriate technology.

Barmann, Dan, and Dan Fink. "Build a Wind Turbine from Scratch (Part II)." *BackHome Magazine* March/April 2005: 28–31.

Bielenberg, Carl, and Hugh Allen. *How to Make and Use the Treadle Irrigation Pump.* London: Intermediate Technology Publications, 1995. 77 pp.

Brace Research Institute, Faculty of Engineering (P.O. Box 900, Macdonald College of McGill University, Ste. Anne de Bellevue, Quebec H9X 3V9, Canada). Appropriate technology publications focusing on small communities in rural areas.

"Building the Outdoor Oven." *Countryside and Small Stock Journal.* Vol. 78, No. 4 (July/August 1994).

*Darrow, Ken. *Appropriate Technology Source Book.* Stanford, CA: Volunteers in Asia (P.O. Box 4543, Stanford, CA 94305), 1986. 799 pp. **BL**

Denzer, Kiko. *Build Your Own Earth Oven.* Blodgett, OR: Hand Print Press, 2000. 114 pp.

Edholm, Steven, and Tamara Wilder. "Hand Drill Fire Making." 1994. 5 pp.

———. "Cordage." 1995. 5 pp.

Elpel, Thomas. *Participating in Nature: Thomas J. Elpel's Field Guide to Primitive Living Skills,* 4th ed., rev. Pony, MT: HOPS Press, 1999. 158 pp.

*Evans, Ianto. *Lorena Stoves.* Stanford, CA: Volunteers in Asia (P.O. Box 4543, Stanford, CA 94305), 1981. 144 pp.

*The Hay Box—The Energy Saving Cooker.* Eugene, OR: The Aprovecho Institute (359 Polk St., Eugene, OR 97402), 1939. 20 pp.

Hazeltine, Barrett, and Christopher Bull, eds. *Field Guide to Appropriate Technology.* San Diego, CA: Academic Press, 2003. 874 pp.

Hill, Jack. *Country Chair Making.* Devon, UK: David & Charles, 1997. 152 pp.

Joseph, Stephen, et al. *Wood-Conserving Cookstoves: A Design Guide.* Mount Rainer, MD: Volunteers in Technical Assistance, 1981. 111 pp.

Kaufman, Marcus. *From Lorena to a Mountain of Fire: A Case Study of Yayasan Dian Desa's Fuel Efficient Stove Program (1978–1983).* Bulaksumer, Yogyadarta, Indonesia: Yayasan

Dian Desa (P.O. Box 19), 1983.
52 pp.

Ludwig, Art. *Principles of Ecological Design: Integrating Technology, Economics and Ecology.* Santa Barbara, CA: Oasis Design, 2003. 18 pp.

Proske. Frank. "Masonry Heaters." *BackHome Magazine,* March/April 2003: 36–39

*Rohde, Eleanour S. *Haybox Cookery.* London: George Routledge & Sons (Broadway House, 68–74 Carter Ln., E.C., England), 1939. 108 pp.

Schaeffer, John, ed. *Alternative Energy Sourcebook.* Hopland, CA: Real Goods Trading Corp. (13771 S. Hwy. 101, Hopland, CA), 1992. 518 pp.

*Village Technology Handbook.* Arlington, VA: Volunteers in Technical Assistance (1815 N. Lynn St., Arlington, VA 22209), 1988. 422 pp.

Wescott, David, ed. *Primitive Technology II: Ancestral Skills.* Layton, UT: Gibbs Smith Publisher, 2001. 248 pp.

### Arid Regions/Dryland Farming

Adams, L. H., and E. S. Goff. *Reports on Oats, Barley, and Potatoes for 1889. Bulletin No. 22.* Madison, WI: University of Wisconsin, January 1890. 12 pp.

Anderson, Edward F. *The Cactus Family.* Portland, OR: Timber Press, 2001.

Appropriate Technology Development Association. "Water Harvesting," *ApTech Newsletter* (P.O. Box 311, Gandhi Bhawan, Lucknow-226001, U.P. India). 776 pp.

*Arid Land Newsletter.* Center for People, Food, and Environment (344 S. 3rd Ave., Tucson, AZ 85701).

Arnon, I. *Crop Production in Dry Regions.* 2 Vols. London: Leonard Hill, 1972. 649 pp., 682 pp.

Atkinson, Alfred. "Crop Growing Suggestions to Dry-Land Farmers." *Circular 45.* Bozeman, MT: Montana Agricultural College

Experiment Station, February 1915: 121–140.

Atkinson, Alfred, and N. C. Donaldson. "Dry Farm Grain Tests in Montana." *Bulletin No. 110.* Bozeman, MT: Montana Agricultural College Experiment Station, February 1916: 167–218.

Atkinson, Alfred, and J. B. Nelson. "Dry Farming Investigations in Montana." *Bulletin No. 74.* Bozeman, MT: Montana Agricultural College Experiment Station, December 1908: 63–89.

Aune, Beyer. *Suggestions to Settlers on the Belle Fourche Irrigation Project.* Circular No. 83. Washington, DC: USDA Bureau of Plant Industry, July 24, 1911. 14 pp.

Bainbridge, David A. "Pitcher Irrigation," *Drylander.* Vol. II, No. 1 (1988): 3.

———. "Using Trees to Maintain Groundwater," *Drylander,* Vol. I, No. 2 (1987): 3.

Baylor, Byrd. *The Desert Is Theirs.* New York: Macmillan, 1975.

Briggs, Lyman J., and J. O. Belz. *Dry Farming in Relation to Rainfall and Evaporation. Bulletin No. 188.* Washington, DC: USDA Bureau of Plant Industry, November 5, 1910. 71 pp.

Bromfield, Louis. *Malabar Farm.* New York: Harper & Row, 1948. 405 pp. **BL**

Brookbank, George. *Desert Gardening: The Complete Guide.* Tucson, AZ: Fisher Books, 1991. 282 pp.

Buffum, B. C., *Crop Report for 1893. Cost and Profit of Growing Wheat, Sugar Beets, Garden Vegetables and Tobacco. Progress Report on Fruits and Trees. Meteorology for 1893. Notes on Climate. Bulletin No. 17.* Laramie, WY: University of Wyoming, March 1894. 45 pp.

Buffum, B. C., and Aven Nelson. *Growing and Preparing Agricultural Crops for Exhibition. Bulletin No. 58.* Laramie, WY: University of Wyoming, April 1903. 12 pp.

Cardon, P. V. "Minor Dry Land Crops at the Nephi Experiment Farm." *Bulletin 132.* Logan, UT: Utah Agricultural College Experi-

ment Station, March 1914: 349–378.

*Cleveland, David A., and Daniela Soleri. *Food from Dryland Gardens: An Ecological, Nutritional and Social Approach to Small-Scale Household Food Production.* Tucson, AZ: Center for People, Food, and Environment (344 S. 3rd Ave., Tucson, AZ 85701), 1991. 387 pp. **BL**

Clothier, R. W. "Dry-Farming in the Arid Southwest." *Bulletin No. 70.* Tucson, AZ: University of Arizona Agricultural Experiment Station, February 1, 1913: 725–798.

Connell, J. H., et al. "Field Experiments at College Station with Corn, Cotton, and Forage Plants." *Bulletin No. 40.* College Station, TX: Texas Agricultural Experiment Station, September 1896: 851–874.

———. "Field Experiments at McKinnley Sub-Station and Wichita Falls Sub-Station with Wheat, Corn, Cotton, Grasses and Manures." *Bulletin No. 34.* College Station, TX: Texas Agricultural Experiment Station, February 1895: 523–592.

Cook, O. F. *Vegetation Affected by Agriculture in Central America. Bulletin No. 145.* Washington, DC: USDA Bureau of Plant Industry, April 10, 1909. 30 pp.

Cooley, F. S. *Suggestions to the Dry Farmer. Circular 19.* Bozeman, MT: Montana Agricultural College Experiment Station, May 1912. 52 pp.

Cottrell, H. M. *Dry Land Farming in Eastern Colorado. Bulletin 145.* Fort Collins, CO: Colorado Agricultural College Experiment Station, December 1909. 32 pp.

Critchley, Will. *Looking After Our Land: New Approaches to Soil and Water Conservation in Dryland Africa.* Oxford, UK: OXFAM, 1991. 84 pp.

Critchley, Will, et al. *Water Harvesting for Plant Production.* Vol. 2. Washington, DC: World Bank, 1992. 134 pp.

Cromell, Cathy, Linda A. Guy, and Lucy K. Bradley. *Desert Gardening for Beginners.* Phoenix, AZ: Master Gardener Press, 1999. 100 pp.

*Crop Management in the Semi-Arid Tropics.* Silang, Cavite, Philippines and Bangalore, India: Indian Rural Reconstruction Movement and International Institute of Rural Reconstruction. 14 pp.

"Cross Ridging Holds Precious Rainwater on the Land." *Developing Countries Farm Radio, Package No. 14.* Toronto: Developing Countries Farm Radio (c/o Massey Ferguson, 595 Bay St., Toronto, Canada), 1988. 5 pp.

Dillman, Arthur C. *Breeding Drought-Resistant Forage Plants for the Great Plains Area. Bulletin No. 196.* Washington, DC: USDA Bureau of Plant Industry, December 1910. 40 pp.

Ebeling, Walter. *Handbook of Indian Foods and Fiber of Arid America.* Berkeley, CA: University of California Press, 1986. 971 pp.

Ellison, A. D., et al. "Dry-Farming in Utah." *Circular No. 21.* Lehi Sun Print, 1916: 2–35.

Fargher, John. *Arid Landwater Harvesting.* Orange, MA: John Fargher, 1985. 8 pp.

Foaden, George P. *Notes on Egyptian Agriculture. Bulletin No. 62.* Washington, DC: USDA Bureau of Plant Industry, July 9, 1904. 61 pp.

Forbes, R. H. "Agriculture of Sulphur Spring Valley Arizona." *Bulletin No. 72.* University of Arizona, June 30, 1913: 214–224.

Fraps, G. S. *Observations of European Agriculture. Bulletin No. 143.* College Station, TX: Texas Agricultural Experiment Station, December 1911. 35 pp.

Friends of the Arboretum. *Desert Plants.* Tucson, AZ: Friends of the Arboretum (P.O. Box 3607, Tucson, AZ 85722).

Goldstein, W. *Alternative Crops, Rotations and Management Systems for the Palouse.* Pullman, WA: Washington State University, 1986. 333 pp.

Goldstein, Walter A., and Douglas L. Young. "An Agronomic and Economic Comparison of a Conventional and a Low-Input Cropping System in the Palouse." *American Journal of Alternative Agriculture,* Spring 1987: 51–56.

Gore, Rick. "No Way to Run a Desert." *National Geographic,* June 1985: 694–719.

Granatstein, David. *Dryland Farming in the Northwestern United States.* Pullman, WA: College of Agriculture and Home Economics Research Center, Washington State University, 1992. 31 pp.

Hall, A. E. *Agriculture in Semi-Arid Environments.* New York: Springer-Verlag, 1979. 340 pp.

Harrington, H. H. "Grasses and Forage Plants: A Study of Composition and Value; Texas Grains: Composition; Ash Analyses, Grasses and Grains." *Bulletin No. 20.* College Station: Texas Agricultural Experiment Station, 1892: 170–190.

Harris, Frank S., et al. "Variety Tests of Field Crops in Utah." *Bulletin 131.* Logan, UT: Utah Agricultural College, March 1914: 317–346.

Harsch, Jonathon. "Dryland Farming May Return as Ground Water Levels Drop." *Christian Science Monitor* July 19, 1980: 10.

Hartley, Carl. "Injury by Disinfectants to Seeds and Roots in Sandy Soils." *Bulletin No. 169.* Washington, DC: USDA Bureau of Plant Industry, February 20, 1915: 2–35.

Hilgard, E. W., et al. *The Conservation of Soil Moisture and Economy in the Use of Irrigation Water. Bulletin 121.* Berkeley, CA: University of California Agricultural Experiment Station, August 1898. 15 pp.

Hugalle, N. R. "Tied Ridges Improve Semi-Arid Crop Yields." *International Ag-Sieve* Vol. 1, No. 2 (1988): 4.

Hutchison, C. B., et al. "Experiments with Farm Crops in Southwest Missouri." *Bulletin No. 123.*

Columbia, MO: University of Missouri, January 1915: 163–185.

Indian Agricultural Research Institute. *A New Technology for Dryland Farming.* New Delhi: Indian Agricultural Research Institute, 1970. 189 pp.

Kezer, Alvin. *Dry Farming in Colorado. Bulletin 227.* Fort Collins, CO: Colorado Agricultural College Experiment Station, April 1917. 40 pp.

Letteer, C. R. *Experiments in Crop Production of Fallow Land at San Antonio. Bulletin No. 151.* Washington, DC: USDA Bureau of Plant Industry, September 19, 1914. 10 pp.

McClelland, C. K. "Variety Work with Corn and Cotton." *Bulletin 113.* Experiment, GA: Georgia Experiment Station, January 1915: 252–256.

Merriam, Hart C. *Life Zones and Crop Zones of the United States. Bulletin No. 10.* Washington, DC: USDA Division of Biological Survey, June 20, 1898. 79 pp.

Mooers, Charles. "Experiments with Fertilizers and Field Crops on Important Soil Types of Middle Tennessee." *Bulletin No. 92.* Knoxville, TN: University of Tennessee, June 1911: 27–95.

———. "Experiments with Soils, Fertilizers, and Farm Crops." *Bulletin No. 86.* Knoxville, TN: University of Tennessee, April 1909: 35–88.

Nehrling, Arno, et al. *Easy Gardening with Drought-Resistant Plants.* New York: Dover, 1968. 320 pp.

Nyhuis, Jane. *Desert Harvest.* Tuscon, AZ: Meals for Millions (Box 42622, Tucson, AZ 85733), 1982. 63 pp.

Oklahoma Agricultural Experiment Station. *Field Crops, 1899. Bulletin No. 44.* Stillwater, OK: Oklahoma Agricultural Experiment Station, December 1899. 12 pp.

Paddock, Wendell, and Orville B. Whipple. *Fruit Growing in Arid Regions.* Boston, MA: Macmillan, 1913. 395 pp.

Payne, J. E. "The Plains." *Bulletin 123*. Fort Collins, CO: Colorado Agricultural College Experiment Station, January 1908: 4–32.

"Quantitative Phenology of Warm Desert Legumes: Seasonal Growth of Six *Prosopis* Species at the Same Site." *Journal of Arid Environments*, 1991: 299–311.

Reij, Chris, et al. *Water Harvesting for Plant Production*. Vol. 1. Washington, DC: World Bank, 1988. 123 pp.

Riddle, R. "Drought-Resistant Fruit and Nuts for the Water-Efficient Landscape." *CFRG Journal,* 1989: 8–19.

Rodale, J. I. *Stone Mulching in the Garden*. Emmaus, PA: Rodale Press, 1949. 164 pp.

Saunders, D. A. *Drought Resistant Forage Experiments. Bulletin 74*. Brookings, SD: South Dakota Agricultural College Experiment Station, March 1902. 16 pp.

———. "Drought Resistant Forage Experiments at Highmore, South Dakota, 1900." *Bulletin 70*. Brookings, SD: South Dakota Agricultural College Experiment Station, February 1901: 57–73.

Shepard, James H. "Drought-Resisting Forage Plants at the Co-Operative Range Experiment Station, Highmore, South Dakota." *Bulletin 66*. Brookings, SD: South Dakota Agricultural College Experiment Station, March 1900, 35–52.

Snyder, W. P. *Crop Production in Western Nebraska. Principles of Cultivation. Bulletin 109*. Lincoln, NE: University of Nebraska Agricultural Experiment Station. 56 pp.

Snyder, W. P., and W. W. Burr. *Growing Crops in Western Nebraska. Bulletin No. 7*. Lincoln, NE: University of Nebraska Agricultural Experiment Station, February 15, 1911. 69 pp.

Snyder, W. P., and W. M. Osborn. *Rotations and Tillage Methods in Western Nebraska. Bulletin No. 155*. Lincoln, NE: University of Nebraska Agricultural Experiment Station, June 1, 1916. 48 pp.

Soule, Andrew M., and John R. Fain. *Crops for the Silo. Bulletin 1*. Knoxville, TN: University of Tennessee, January 1904. 24 pp.

Stephens, D. E., and C. E. Hill. *Dry Farming Investigations at the Sherman County Branch Experiment Station. Station Bulletin 144*. Moro, OR: Oregon Agriculture College Experiment Station, April 1917. 48 pp.

Stewart, Robert. *The Nitrogen and Humus Problem in Dry-Land Farming. Bulletin No. 109*. Logan, UT: Utah Agricultural College Experiment Station, August 1910. 73 pp.

Sunset Editors. *Desert Gardening*. Menlo Park, CA: Sunset Books, 1967. 96 pp.

———. *Waterwise Gardening: Landscaping Ideas, Watering Systems and Unthirsty Plants*. Menlo Park, CA: Sunset Books, 1989. 96 pp.

"Sustainable Living in Drylands." *Journal of Arid Lands Permaculture* (Southwest Regional Permaculture Institute, P.O. Box 27371, Tucson, AZ 85726-7371), Fall 1989.

Swingle, Walter T. A., et al. *Miscellaneous Papers. Circular No. 129*. Washington, DC: USDA Bureau of Plant Industry, June 17, 1913. 32 pp.

Thatcher, R. W. *The Nitrogen and Humus Problem in Dry Farming. Bulletin No. 105*. Pullman, WA: State College of Washington Agricultural Experiment Station, June 1912. 16 pp.

Thom, C. C., and H. F. Holz. *Dry Farming in Washington. Popular Bulletin No. 69*. Pullman, WA: State College of Washington Agricultural Experiment Station, April 1, 1914. 31 pp.

Thysell, John, et al. "Dry Farming Investigations in Western North Dakota." *Bulletin No. 110*. Agricultural College, ND: North Dakota Agricultural Experiment Station, February 1915, 159–207.

Tonge, Peter. "Twice the Yield, Half the Work." *Christian Science Monitor,* January 12, 1988: 23.

Towar, J. D. *Dry Farming in Wyoming. Bulletin No. 80*. Laramie, WY: University of Wyoming Agricultural College Department, March 1909. 29 pp.

"Trench Composting: A Model for Africa." *Organic Gardening and Farming,* January 1976: 14–150.

*Trench Composting for Arid Regions*. International Federation of Organic Agricultural Movements (R.D. 1, Box 323, Kutztown, PA 19530), June 1976. Newsletter.

UNICEF. "Some Sources of Nutrition from the Dry Season Garden." New York: UNICEF. 1 p.

University of Arizona. "Timely Hints for Farmers." *Bulletin No. 57*. Tuscon: University of Arizona, June 20, 1908: 247–287.

Voorhees, J. F. "Relation of Temperature and Rainfall to Crop Systems and Production." *Bulletin No. 91*. Knoxville, TN: University of Tennessee, January 1911: 3–23.

"What an Inch of Rain Is Worth." *Successful Farming,* January 1974: 79.

Whitney, Milton. *Fertilizers on Soils Used for Oats, Hay, and Miscellaneous Crops. Bulletin No. 67*. Washington, DC: USDA Bureau of Soils, June 8, 1910. 73 pp.

*Widtsoe, John A. *Dry Farming*. New York: Macmillan, 1919. 445 pp. An important basic work. **BL**

———. "The Nature of the Dry Farm Soils of Utah." *Bulletin No. 122*. Salt Lake City, UT: Utah Agricultural College Experiment Station, January 1913: 270–288.

———. "The Storage of Winter Precipitation in Soils." *Bulletin No. 104*. Logan, UT: Agricultural College of Utah Experiment Station, October 1908: 282–316.

## Bamboo

Bell, Michael. *The Gardener's Guide to Growing Temperate Bamboos*. Portland, OR: Timber Press, 2000. 159 pp.

Cusack, Victor. *Bamboo Rediscovered.* Trentham, Victoria, Australia: Earth Garden Books, 1997. 95 pp.

Guardiani, Nunzia. *Construccion de Viviendas Con Bambu.* Santo Domingo: ENDA-Caribe, 1991. 47 pp.

Judziewicz, Emmet J., Lynn G. Clark, Ximena Londono, and Margaret J. Stern. *American Bamboos.* Washington, DC: Smithsonian Institution Press, 1999. 392 pp.

Meeker, John. "Backyard Bamboo." *Organic Gardening,* October 1980: 88–99.

Meredith, Ted Jordan. *Bamboo for Gardens.* Portland, OR: Timber Press, 2001. 406 pp.

Ueda, Dr. Koichiro. *Studies on the Physiology of Bamboo.* Japan: Resources Bureau, Science and Technics Agency, Prime Minister's Office, 1960. 167 pp.

van den Heuvel, Kick. *Wood and Bamboo for Rural Water Supply.* Delft, The Netherlands: Delft University Press, 1981. 76 pp.

Whittaker, Paul. *Hardy Bamboos: Taming the Dragon.* Portland, OR: Timber Press, 2005. 300 pp.

Young, Robert A., and Joseph R. Haun. *Bamboo in the United States: Description, Culture, and Utilization.* Washington, D.C.: U.S. Dept. of Agriculture, Superintendent of Documents, U.S. Government Printing Office, 1961. 74 pp.

## Biodynamics

Biodynamic Farming and Gardening Association. Bldg. 1002B, Thoreau Center, The Presidio, San Francisco, CA 94120.

*Bio-Dynamic Gardening: A How-To Guide.* Canoga Park, CA: Rudolf Steiner Research Foundation (BOKAJO Enterprises, 20959 Elkwood St., Canoga Park, CA 91304), 1988. Video. 58:30 mins.

*Biodynamics: Farming and Gardening for the 21st Century.* Biodynamic Farming and Gardening Association. Bimonthly journal.

Bockemuhl, Jochen. *In Partnership with Nature.* Wyoming, RI: Bio-Dynamic Literature, 1981. 84 pp.

Booth, Barbara. "Birds in the Farm." *Biodynamics,* Fall 1992: 6–33.

Brinton, William F., Jr. "The End of Reductionism: Science and the 21st Century." *Biodynamics,* March/April 1997: 20–23.

———. "Living Compost, Living Carbon." *Biodynamics,* January/February 1998: 1–3.

Carpenter-Boggs, Lynne A. *Effects of Biodynamic Preparations on Compost, Crop, and Soil Quality.* Washington State University Doctoral Dissertation, 1997. 164 pp.

Childs, Gilbert. *Rudolf Steiner: His Life and Work.* Hudson, NY: Anthroposophic Press, 1995. 94 pp.

*Ehrenfried Pfeiffer Himself.* Metairie, LA: Acres U.S.A. Masters of Eco-Agriculture Series (P.O. Box 8800, Metairie, LA 70011). 8 audiotapes.

Gregg, Evelyn S. *Herb Chart.* Wyoming, RI: Biodynamic Farming and Gardening Association. Detailed cultural notes. Available from BDFGA.

Groh, Trauger, M., and Steven S. H. McFadden. *Farms of Tomorrow: Community-Supported Farms, Farm-Supported Communities.* Kimberton, PA: Biodynamic Farming and Gardening Association, 1990. 169 pp.

Heckel, Alice, ed. *The Pfeiffer Garden Book: Biodynamics in the Home Garden.* Stroudsburg, PA: Bio dynamic Farming and Gardening Association, 1967. 199 pp. **IL**

Joly, Nicolas. *Wine, from Sky to Earth: Growing and Appreciating Biodynamic Wine.* Austin, TX: Acres U.S.A., 1999. 168 pp.

*Koepf, Herbert H. *The Biodynamic Farm.* Hudson, NY: Anthroposophic Press, 1989. 245 pp. Available from BDFGA.

———. *Compost.* Wyoming, RI: Biodynamic Farming and Gardening Association, 1966. 18 pp. Short, detailed pamphlet. Available from BDFGA. **AL**

———. *Ehrenfried Pfeiffer: Pioneer in Agriculture and Natural Science.* Kimberton, PA: Biodynamic Farming and Gardening Association, 1991. 31 pp. Available from BDFGA.

———. *Research in Biodynamic Agriculture Methods and Results.* Kimberton, PA: Biodynamic Farming and Gardening Association, 1993. 78 pp. Available from BDFGA.

*Koepf, Herbert H., B. D. Peterson, and Wolfgang Schauman. *Biodynamic Agriculture: An Introduction.* Spring Valley, NY: Anthroposophic Press, 1976. 429 pp. **IL**

Lovel, Hugh. *A Biodynamic Farm for Growing Wholesome Food.* Kansas City, MO: Acres U.S.A., 1994. 215 pp. Available from BDFGA.

Marshall, Anne E. *Index to Bio-Dynamics 1941–1975.* San Francisco: Biodynamic Farming and Gardening, 1976. 108 pp.

Pauli, F. W. *Soil Fertility: A Biodynamic Approach.* London: Adarn Hilger (98 St. Pancras Way, London NW1, England), 1976. 204 pp.

Pfeiffer, Ehrenfried. "Applied Biodynamics." *Newsletter of the Josephine Porter Institute,* Spring 1999: 122–136.

———. *Biodynamic Farming and Gardening: Soil Fertility Renewal and Preservation.* New York: Anthroposophic Press, 1943. 240 pp.

———. *Biodynamic Farming—Articles 1942–1962.* Wyoming, RI: Biodynamic Farming and Gardening Association. 150 pp.

———. *Chromatography Applied to Quality Testing.* Wyoming, RI: Biodynamic Literature, 1984. 44 pp. Available from BDFGA.

———. *The Compost Manufacturer's Manual.* Philadelphia, PA: The Pfeiffer Foundation, 1956. 137 pp.

*———. *Sensitive Crystallization Processes.* Spring Valley, NY: Anthroposophic Press, 1936. 59 pp.

*Philbrick, John and Helen. *Gardening for Health and Nutrition.* Blauvelt, NY: Rudolf Steiner Publications, 1971. 93 pp. **BL**

Podolinksy, Alex. *Biodynamic Agriculture: Introductory Lectures.* 2 vols. Sydney, Australia: Gavemer, 1988. 190 pp; 173 pp. Available from BDFGA.

Sattler, Friedrich, and Eckard V. Wistinghausen. *Bio-Dynamic Farming Practice.* Sturbridge, England: Bio-Dynamic Agricultural Association, 1989. 333 pp.

Soper, John. *Bio-Dynamic Gardening.* London: Souvenir Press, 1996. 210 pp.

———. *Studying the Agriculture Course.* London: Bio-Dynamic Agricultural Association, 1976. 88 pp. **AL**

*Steiner, Rudolf. *Agriculture—A Course of Eight Lectures.* London: Bio-Dynamic Agricultural Association, 1958. 175 pp. The basis of the biodynamic movement. **AL**

*Storl, Wolf. *Culture and Horticulture.* Wyoming, RI: Biodynamic Farming and Gardening Association, 1979. Biodynamics and organic agricultural history simply explained. Available from BDFGA.

Thun, Maria. *Gardening for Life—The Biodynamic Way.* Gloucestershire, UK: Hawthorn Press, 1999. 127 pp.

*The Voice of Demeter—Newsletter of the Demeter Association for Certification of Biodynamic Agriculture.* Aurora, NY: The Demeter Association for Certification of Agriculture. Newsletter.

## Bioextensive

Nordell, Anne and Eric. "Cultivating Questions: Concerning the Bioextensive Market Garden." *Small Farmers Journal* Vol. 21, No. 3: 28–31.

## Biointensive

(see also GROW BIOINTENSIVE)

*Agricultura Bio-Intensiva Sostenible en el Minifundio Mexicano.* Universidad Autonoma Chapingo (Departmento de Suelos, Chapingo, Texcoco, Mexico).

*B.I.G. Biointensive Gardening Cebuano.* Silang, Cavite, Philippines: International Institute of Rural Reconstruction, n.d. Vol. 3, No. 5. *B.I.G. Biointensive Gardening Tagalog.* Silang, Cavite, Philippines: International Institute of Rural Reconstruction, n.d. 32 pp. (2 languages)

*The Biointensive Approach to Family Food Gardens.* International Institute of Rural Reconstruction (1775 Broadway, New York, NY 10019). Information packet.

*The Biointensive Approach to Small-Scale Household Food Production.* Silang, Cavite, Philippines: The International Institute of Rural Reconstruction, 1991.

*Biointensive Mini-Farming Information—Mexico. Ecopol. Av. Centenario, Edif. H10-1-2, Col. Lomas de Plateros, D.F. C.P. 01480, Mexico. Specializes in training. Excellent.

*Burck, Doug, and Sandra Mardigian. *A Journey in Kenya—Visiting Biointensive Farmers and Manor House Agricultural Centre.* Video.

Centre for Biointensive Agriculture. *Training and Demonstration Syllabus.* Kitale, Kenya: Manor House Agricultural Centre, 1996. 49 pp.

International Institute of Tropical Agriculture. 133 Dharmapala Mawatha, Columbo 7, Sri Lanka.

Martinez Valdez, Juan Manuel, and Dr. Francisco Alarcón Navarro. *Huertos Familiares.* Mexico: Academia de Investigacion en Demografía Médica (Edif H10-1-2, Col. Lomas de Plateros, D.F. C.P. 01480, Mexico), 1988. 116 pp. plus 24 slides. Very good.

*Seshadri, C. V. *Biodynamic Gardening: Monograph Series on Engineering of Photosynthetic Systems.* Vol. 4. Tharamani, Madras, India: Shri AMM Murugappa Chettiar Research Center, 1980. 38 pp. Available from Ecology Action.

Sunset Editors. "Getting Started with the French Intensive Method." *Sunset,* September 1972: 168.

## Biosafety

Sunshine Project. *Biosafety, Biosecurity and Bioweapons: Three Agreements on Biotechnology, Health and the Environment, and Their Potential Contribution to Biological Weapons Control.* Austin, TX: The Sunshine Project, 2003. 50 pp.

## Botany

Buhner, Stephen Harold. *The Lost Language of Plants.* White River Junction, VT: Chelsea Green Publishing, 2002. 325 pp.

Elpel, Thomas. *Botany in a Day: Thomas J. Elpel's Herbal Field Guide to Plant Families,* 4th ed. Pony, MT: HOPS Press, 2000. 204 pp.

Galston, Arthur W. *The Life of the Green Plant.* Foundations of Modern Biology Series. Englewood Cliffs, NJ: Prentice-Hall, 1961. 118 pp.

Tompkins, Peter, and Christopher Bird. "Love Among the Cabbages." *Harper's,* November 1972: 136–141.

———. *The Secret Life of Plants.* New York: Harper & Row, 1973. 402 pp.

## Calorie/Diet Crops

Beard, Benjamin H. "The Sunflower Crop." *Scientific American,* May 1981: 150–161.

Cox, Jeff. "The Sunflower Seed Huller and Oil Press." *Organic Gardening,* April 1979: 58–61.

Eames-Sheavly, Marcia. *The Great American Peanut.* Ithaca, NY: Cornell University Cooperative Extension, 1994. 20 pp.

Eames-Sheavly, Marcia, and Tracy Farrell. *The Humble Potato: Underground Gold.* Cornell University Cooperative Extension, 1995. 40 pp.

Flores, Barbara. *The Great Sunflower Book.* Berkeley, CA: Ten Speed Press, 1997. 130 pp.

Graff, E. *Beet-Root Sugar and Cultivation of the Beet.* New York: Cornhill Press, 1880. 158 pp.

Harris, F. S. *The Sugar Beet in America.* New York: Macmillan, 1919.

Heiser, Charles B., Jr. *The Sunflower.* Norman, OK: University of Oklahoma Press, 1976. 198 pp.

Hurt, E. F. *Sunflower for Food, Fodder and Fertility.* London: Faber and Faber, 1946. 155 pp.

Kay, Daisy K. *Food Legumes.* Kent, UK: Natural Resource Institute (Central Ave., Chatherm, Maritime, Kent ME4 4TB, UK), 1979. 435 pp.

Pustovoit, V. S. *Handbook of Selection and Seed Growing of Oil Plants.* Jerusalem: Israel Program for Scientific Translations, 1973. 304 pp. Translated from Russian.

Willis, Harold. *How to Grow Super Soybeans.* Austin, TX: Acres U.S.A. (P.O. Box 91299, Austin, TX 78709), 1989. 48 pp.

## Children's Books

Barrett, Judith. *Old MacDonald Had an Apartment House.* New York: Atheneum, 1969. 32 pp.

Baylor, Byrd. *The Desert Is Theirs.* New York. Macmillan, 1975. 32 pp.

Begley, Evelyn M. *The Little Red Hen.* Racine, WI: Western Publishing Co., 1966. 24 pp.

Brown, Marc. *Your First Garden Book.* Boston: Little, Brown and Company, 1981. 48 pp.

Fryer, Lee, and Leigh Bradford. *A Child's Organic Garden.* Washington, DC: Acropolis Books, 1989. 88 pp.

*Ichikawa, Satomi, and Elizabeth Laird. *Rosy's Garden—A Child's Keepsake of Flowers.* New York. Putnam and Grosset, 1990. 48 pp. Excellent.

Katzen, Mollie, and Ann Henderson. *Pretend Soup and Other Real Recipes.* Berkeley, CA: Tricycle Press, 1994. 95 pp. Cookbook for preschoolers and up.

Krauss, Ruth. *The Carrot Seed.* New York: Harper Festival, 1993. 22 pp.

Main, Jody. *The Children's Garden (An Organic Gardening Primer).* Woodside, CA: The Woodside School and Jody Main (333 B Albion, Woodside, CA 94602), 1996. 53 pp.

Moore, Eva. *Johnny Appleseed.* New York: Scholastic Book Services, 1964. 48 pp.

Ocone, Lynne. *Guide to Kids' Gardening.* New York: John Wiley & Sons. 148 pp.

Paladino, Catherine. *One Good Apple: Growing Our Food for the Sake of the Earth.* Boston, MA: Houghton Mifflin, 1999. 48 pp.

Partridge, Jenny. *Lop Ear.* New York: Holt, Rinehart and Winston, 1981.

Rose, Deborah. *The People Who Hugged the Trees.* Niwot, CO: Roberts Rinehart, 1990. 32 pp

Seymour, John. *John Seymour's Gardening Book (for Children).* London: G. Whizzard (105 Great Russell St., London WC1, England), 1978. 61 pp.

## Climate

Dauncey, Guy, and Patrick Mazza. *Stormy Weather: 101 Solutions to Global Climate Change.* Gabriola Isl., BC, Canada: New Society Publishers, 2001. 271 pp.

Goldman, M. C. "Stop That Frost—Cold!" *Organic Gardening,* November/December 2001: 36.

Thompson, Tim. "Where Have All the Clouds Gone?" *Southern Hemisphere,* Fall 1992: 40–43.

## Communities

*1995 National Directory of Conservational Land Trusts.* Washington DC: Land Trust Alliance, 1995. 238 pp.

Bouvard, Marguerite. *The Intentional Community Movement: Building a New Moral World.* Port Washington, NY: National University Publications, Kennikat Press, 1975. 207 pp.

Caneff, Denny. *Sustaining Land, People, Animals, and Communities.* Washington, DC: Midwest Sustainable Agriculture Working Group (110 Maryland Ave., NE, Box 76, Washington, DC 20020), 1993. 26 pp.

"Cohousing." *Communities,* Spring 2000. Communities. (Rte. 1, Box 155-CM, Rutledge MO 63563). Magazine.

*Communities Directory: A Guide to Intentional Communities and Cooperative Living, 2000 Edition.* Rutledge, MO: Fellowship for International Community (R.R. 1, Box 156-D, Rutledge, MO 63563), 2000. 456 pp.

*Exchange.* Washington, DC: The Land Trust Alliance (900 17th St. NW, Ste. 410, Washington, DC 20006-2596).

Gaia Trust and Context Institute. *Eco-Villages & Sustainable Communities.* Bainbridge Island, WA: Context Institute (P.O. Box 11470, Bainbridge Island, WA 98110), 1991. 213 pp.

Gaia Trust and Findhorn Foundation. *Eco-Villages and Sustainable Communities.* Scotland: Findhorn Press, 1996. 95 pp.

Hanson, Chris. *The Cohousing Handbook.* Pt. Roberts, WA: Hartley and Marks Publishers (P.O. Box 147, Pt. Roberts, WA 98281), 1996. 278 pp.

Henderson, Elizabeth, and Robyn Van En. *Sharing the Harvest: A Guide to Community Supported Agriculture.* White River Junction, VT: Chelsea Green Publishing, 1999. 254 pp.

International Independence Institute. *The Community Land Trust: A Guide to a New Model for Land Tenure in America.* Ashby, MA: Center for Community Economic Development, 1972. 117 pp.

Kinkade, Kathleen. *A Walden Two Experiment: The First Five Years of Twin Oaks Community.* New York: William Morrow, 1973. 271 pp.

Malakoff, David. *What Good Is Community Greening?* Philadelphia: American Community Gardening Association (100 N. 20th St., 5th Floor, Philadelphia, PA), 1995. 23 pp.

*McCamant, Kathryn, and Charles Durrett. *Cohousing.* Berkeley, CA: Ten Speed Press, 2003. 208 pp.

Morehouse, Ward, ed. *Building Sustainable Communities.* New York: The Bootstrap Press (Intermediate Technology Development

Group of North America, Ste. 3C, 777 United Nations Plaza, New York, NY), 1997. 218 pp.

Norwood, Ken, and Kathleen Smith. *Rebuilding Community in America: Housing for Ecological Living, Personal Empowerment, and the New Extended Family.* Berkeley, CA: Shared Living Resource Center (2375 Shattuck Ave., Berkeley, CA 94704), 1995. 432 pp.

Payne, Karen, and Deborah Fryman. *Cultivating Community: Principles and Practices for Community Gardening as a Community-Building Tool.* Philadelphia: American Community Gardening Association (100 N. 20th St., 5th Floor, Philadelphia, PA), 2001. 56 pp.

Powell, G. Harold. *Co-Operation in Agriculture.* New York: Macmillan, 1918. 327 pp.

*Starting a Land Trust.* Washington, DC: The Land Trust Alliance, 1990. 175 pp.

## Companion Planting/ Rotations

Allardice, Pamela. *A–Z of Companion Planting.* Pymble, Australia: Angus and Robertson, 1993. 208 pp.

*Carr, Anna. *Good Neighbors: Companion Planting for Gardeners.* Emmaus, PA: Rodale Press, 1985. 379 pp. A useful compilation of tradition, research, and practical gardening advice. **BL**

Eames-Sheavly, Marcia. *The Three Sisters: Exploring an Iroquois Garden.* Ithaca, NY: Media Services (Cornell University), 1993. 20 pp.

Flowerdew, Bob. *Good Companions: A Guide to Gardening with Plants That Help Each Other.* New York: Summit Books, 1991. 96 pp.

Franck, Gertrud. *Companion Planting: Successful Gardening the Organic Way.* Wellingborough, Northamptonshire, England: Thorsons, 1983. 128 pp. Interesting systematic approach.

Ingels, Chuck A., et al., eds. *Cover Cropping in Vineyards: A Grower's Handbook, Publication 3338.* Oakland, CA: University of California, Agriculture and Natural

Resources, Communication Services, 1998. 162 pp.

Kohli, Ravinder K., et al., eds. *Allelopathy in Agroecosystems.* Binghamton, NY: Food Products Press, 2001. 447 pp. A scientific text.

Matthias, Stelly, ed. *Multiple Cropping.* ASA Special Publication No. 27. Madison, WI: American Society of Agronomy, 1976. 378 pp.

*Philbrick, Helen, and Richard B. Gregg. *Companion Plants and How to Use Them.* Old Greenwich, CT: Devin-Adair, 1966. 113 pp. **BL**

Ruttle, Jack. "The Tomato and Vetch Connection." *National Gardening,* July/August 1994: 44–47.

University of California Agriculture and Natural Resources. *Overseeding and Companion Cropping in Alfalfa.* Oakland, CA: Communication Services (6701 San Pablo Ave., 2nd Floor, Oakland, CA). 2000. 31 pp.

Watts, Mag T. *Reading the Landscape of America.* New York: Collins Books, 1975. 354 pp.

## Compost/Carbon/Fodder/ Organic Matter/Cover Crops

Ahlgren, Gilbert H. *Forage Crops.* New York: McGraw-Hill, 1942. 418 pp.

Anderson, Simon, et al. *Cover Crops in Smallholder Agriculture: Lessons from Latin America.* Southampton Row, London: ITDG, 2001. 136 pp.

Awang, D. V. C. "Herb Report: Comfrey." *American Herb Association Newsletter,* 1989: 6–7.

Ball, Carleton R. *The History and Distribution of Sorghum.* Washington, DC: Government Printing Office, 1910. 63 pp.

Biological Sciences Communication Project of the George Washington University. *Sorghum: A Bibliography of the World Literature.* Metuchen, NJ: The Scarecrow Press, 1967. 301 pp.

Buckles, D., et al., eds. *Cover Crops in West Africa Contributing to Sustainable Agriculture.* Ottawa: International Development

Research Centre (P.O. Box 8500, Ottawa, ON, Canada), 1998. 291 pp.

Buckles, Daniel, Bernard Triomphe, and Gustavo Sain. *Cover Crops in Hillside Agriculture: Farmer Innovation with Mucuna.* Ottawa: International Development Research Centre, 1998. 218 pp.

Bunch, Roland. *The Use of Green Manures by Villager Farmers: What We Have Learned to Date.* CIDICCO Technical Report, July 1995. 8 pp.

CIDICCO. *Cover Crops News.* Miscellaneous articles. No. 3, 1991. 4 pp. Tegucigalpa, Honduras: Centro Internacional de Informacion sobre Cultivos de Cobertura (Apartado Postal 3385, Tegucigalpa, M.D.C., Honduras, C.A.). Quarterly newsletter.

———. *Lablab Bean Use.* No. 4, 1995. 4 pp.

———. *Management Practices to Work with Velvetbean.* No. 5, 1995. 6 pp.

———. *The Use of Legume Cover Crops in Orchards.* No. 7. February 1994. 6 pp.

———. *The Utilization of Legumes in Traditional High Altitude Farming Systems.* No. 6. August 1993. 8 pp.

Clark, George. H., and M. Oscar Malte. *Fodder and Pasture Plants.* Ottawa: Department of Agriculture, 1913. 143 pp.

Clark, Wilson. "China's Green Manure Revolution." *Science 80,* September/October 1980.

*Clover vs. Alfalfa for Milk Production. Bulletin 327.* Wooster, Ohio: Ohio Agricultural Experiment Station, July 1918. 36 pp.

Coburn, F. D. *The Book of Alfalfa.* New York: Orange Judd, 1907. 344 pp.

"Cover Crops as Miracle Workers," *Sunset Magazine,* October 1989: 196-D.

*Dickinson's Alfalfa Facts: Useful Guide for Growing Alfalfa.* Chicago: Albert Dickinson Co., 1913. 48 pp.

Duggar, John. *Southern Forage Crops.* New York: Macmillan, 1925. 283 pp.

Evans, Ianto. *A Gardener's Guide to Fava Beans.* Eugene, OR: Fava Project/Gardeners Guide (549 Van Buren St.), 1992–1999. 58 pp.

Folmer, H. D. *Alfalfa on Wildwood Farm.* Columbus, OH: Nitschke Brothers, Printers. 1911. 105 pp.

Foster, Steven. "Comfrey—A Fading Romance." *The Herbal Companion,* February/March 1992: 50–55.

Fussell, Betty. *The Story of Corn.* Albuquerque, NM: Univ. of New Mexico Press, 1992. 356 pp.

*Grain Sorghum Date of Planting and Spacing Experiments.* College Station, TX: Texas Agricultural Experiment Station, 1931. 71 pp.

Graves, Walter. *Legumes, Inoculation and Nitrogen Fixation: Understanding the Relationship.* San Diego: Cooperative Extension (University of California, Bldg. 4, 5555 Overland Ave., San Diego, CA 92123), July 1986.

Graves, Walter L., William A. Williams, and Craig D. Thomsen. *Berseem Clover: A Winter Annual Forage for California Agriculture.* Oakland, CA: Publication 21536, University of California Communication Services—Publications, Division of Agriculture and Natural Resources (6701 San Pablo Ave., 2nd Floor), 1996. 12 pp.

Henry, W. A. *Feeds and Feeding: A Hand-Book for the Student and Stockman.* Madison, WI: Published by the author, 1910. 613 pp.

Hills, Lawrence D. *Comfrey.* New York: Universe, 1976. 253 pp.

Hitchcock, A. S. *Rape as a Forage Crop. Farmers' Bulletin No. 164.* Washington, DC: U.S. Department of Agriculture, Farmers' Bulletin No. 164, Government Printing Office, 1903. 16 pp.

Hodgson, Harlow J. "Forage Crops." *Scientific American,* February 1976: 60–75.

Howard, Albert, and Yeshwant D. Wad. *The Waste Products of Agriculture.* New York: Humphrey Milford Oxford University Press, 1931. 167 pp.

Hughes, H. D., Maurice E. Heath, and Darrel Metcalfe. *Forages.* Ames, IA: Iowa State College Press, 1951. 724 pp.

Hunter, Peter J. P. *Hunter's Guide to Grasses, Clovers, and Weeds.* Chester, England: James Hunter, 1970. 80 pp.

Jeavons, John, and Bill Bruneau. "Green Manure Crops." *Mother Earth News,* September/October 1986: 42–45.

Knowles, Paul F., and Milton D. Miller. *Safflower. Circular 532.* Davis, CA: California Agricultural Extension Services, 1965. 51 pp.

Koepf, Herbert H., Scott M. Schreiber, and Michael Fields Agricultural Institute. *Forage Based Farming, Manure Handling and Farm Composting. Bulletin No. 4.* East Troy, WI: Michael Fields Agricultural Institute (W2493 County Rd. ES, East Troy, WI 53120), 1993. 48 pp.

Kuepper, George. *Sweet Sorghum—Production and Processing.* Poteau, OK: Kerr Center for Sustainable Agriculture, 1994. 95 pp.

Lewis, Rebecca, et al. *Making Pastures Produce.* Emmaus, PA: Rodale Press, 1980. 43 pp.

*The Management of Napier Grass.* Zero Grazing Series Vol. 3. Nairobi, Kenya: Ministry of Livestock Development, National Dairy Development Project (P.O. Box 34188, Nairobi, Kenya). 18 pp.

*Managing Cover Crops Profitably.* Beltsville, MD: Sustainable Agriculture Network, 1998. 212 pp.

McLeod, Edwin. *Feed the Soil.* Graton, CA: Organic Agriculture Research Institute, 1982. 209 pp.

*Morrison, Frank B. *Feeds and Feeding,* 22nd ed. Ithaca, NY: Morrison, 1957. 1,165 pp.

*Murphy, Bill. *Greener Pastures on Your Side of the Fence: Better Farming with Voisin Grazing Management.* Colchester, VT: Arriba, 1991. 298 pp.

Orloff, Steve B., and Harry L. Carlson, eds. *Intermountain Alfalfa Management.* Oakland, CA: Publication 3366, University of California Communication Services—Publications, Division of Agriculture and Natural Resources (6701 San Pablo Ave., 2nd Floor, Oakland, CA), 1997. 138 pp.

Paterson, William G.R., ed. *Farm Crops.* Vol. 3, *Pastures and Hay.* London, England: The Gresham Publishing Co., 1925. 307 pp.

Piper, Charles V. *Forage Plants and Their Culture.* New York: Macmillan, 1924. 671 pp.

Rather, Howard C. *Field Crops.* New York: McGraw-Hill, 1942. 454 pp.

Sarrantonio, Marianne. *Soil-Improving Legumes, Methodologies for Screening.* Kutztown, PA: Rodale Institute, 1991. 312 pp.

Schmid, Otto, et al. *Green Manuring, Principles and Practice.* Mt. Vernon, ME: Woods End Agricultural Institute (RFD 1, Box 4040, Mt. Vernon, ME 04357), 1984. 50 pp.

Shaw, Thomas. *Clovers and How to Grow Them.* New York: Orange Judd, 1922. 349 pp.

Sheaffer, Craig, et al. *Forage Legumes: Clovers, Birdsfoot Trefoil, Cicer Milkvetch, Crownvetch, Sainfoin, and Alfalfa.* St. Paul, MN: University of Minnesota Agricultural Experiment Station, 1993. 40 pp.

Shurtleff, William, and Akiko Aoyagi. *The Book of Kudzu: A Culinary and Healing Guide.* Wayne, NJ: Avery, 1985. 102 pp.

Smith, Sally. *Comfrey for Gardeners.* Coventry, England: Henry Doubleday Research Association Publishing, 2003. 16 pp.

Snook, Laurence C. *Tagasaste (Tree Lucerne): High Production Fodder Crop.* Shepparton, New Zealand: Night Owl, 1986. 102 pp. Temperate "living terracing" crop.

U.S. Department of Agriculture. *Farmers' Bulletin No. 1126, Sudan Grass.* Washington, DC: U.S. Government Printing Office, 1940. 24 pp.

———. *Farmers' Bulletin No. 1539, High-Grade Alfalfa Hay.* Washington, DC: U.S. Government Printing Office, 1939. 29 pp.

———. *Farmers' Bulletin No. 1731, Alfalfa Varieties in the United States.* Washington, DC: U.S. Government Printing Office, 1940. 13 pp.

———. *Farmers' Bulletin No. 1770, High-Grade Timothy and Clover Hay.* Washington, DC: U.S. Government Printing Office, 1937. 16 pp.

———. *Technical Bulletin No. 352, Sudan Grass as Hay, Silage, and Pasture for Dairy Cattle.* Washington, DC: U.S. Government Printing Office, 1933. 28 pp.

———. *Technical Bulletin No. 506, Identification, History, and Distribution of Common Sorghum Varieties.* Washington, DC: U.S. Government Printing Office, 1936. 102 pp.

Vinall, H. N., J. C. Stephens, and J. H. Martin. *U.S. Department of Agriculture Technical Bulletin No. 506. Identification, History, and Distribution of Common Sorghum Varieties.* Washington, DC: U.S. Government Printing Office, July 1936.

*Voisin, Andre. *Better Grassland Sward.* London: Crosby Lockwood & Son (26 Old Brompton Rd., London SW7, England), 1960. 340 pp. A unique approach to greatly increased fodder production. **IL**

*———. *Grass Productivity.* New York: Philosophical Library (15 E. 40th St., New York, NY 10016), 1959. 353 pp. **IL**

Willis, Harold. *How to Grow Great Alfalfa.* Madison, WI: A-R Editions, 1983. 42 pp.

Wrightson, John. *Fallow and Fodder Crops.* London: Chapman & Hall, Limited, 1989. 276 pp.

## Composting

Alther, Richard, and Richard O. Raymond. *Improving Garden Soil with Green Manures.* Charlotte, VT: Garden Way, 1974. 44 pp. Contains a good 2-page chart.

Brinton, William F., Jr. *Earth, Plant and Compost.* San Francisco: Biodynamic Farming and Gardening Association, 2002. 73 pp.

———. "Sustainability of Modern Composting: Intensification Versus Costs & Quality." *Biodynamics,* 1997.

Cox, Jeff. "What You Should Know about Nitrogen." *Organic Gardening and Farming,* June 1972: 69–94. See also insert on page 68.

Damon, Gretchen. "From Organic Matter to Gray Matter." *Back-Home Magazine* May/June 2003: 14–15.

Darwin, Charles. *Darwin on Humus and the Earthworm.* London: Faber and Faber, 1945. 153 pp.

*Denison, William C. "Life in Tall Trees." *Scientific American,* June 1973: 75–80.

Dougherty, Mark, ed. *Field Guide to On-Farm Composting.* Ithaca, NY: Natural Resources, Agriculture, and Engineering Services (NRAES), Cooperative Extension, 1999. 118 pp.

Gershuny, Grace. *Compost, Vermicompost and Compost Tea: Feeding the Soil on the Organic Farm.* Anthol, MA: Highland Press, 2004. 89 pp.

Golueke, Clarence G. *Composting: A Study of the Process and Its Principles.* Emmaus, PA: Rodale Press, 1972. 110 pp. For those with an advanced interest.

Gotaas, Harold B. *Composting, Sanitary Disposal and Reclamation of Organic Wastes.* Geneva, Switzerland: World Health Organization, 1956. 205 pp.

Harrison, Ellen Z. *Hygienic Implications of Small-Scale Composting in New York State: Final Report of the Cold Compost Project.* Ithaca, NY: Cornell Waste Management Institute, 2004. 71 pp.

*"Is Too Much Compost Harmful?" in *The Complete Book of Composting.* Emmaus, PA: Rodale Press, 1960: 386–392. **BL**

Martin, Deborah L., and Grace Gershuny, eds. *The Rodale Book of Composting: Easy Methods for Every Gardener.* Emmaus, PA: Rodale Press, 1992. 278 pp.

McGarey, Michael G., and Jill Stainforth, eds. *Compost, Fertilizer, and Biogas Production from Human and Farm Wastes in the People's Republic of China.* Ottawa: International Development Research Centre, 1978. 94 pp.

Minnich, Jerry, et al. *The Rodale Guide to Composting.* Emmaus, PA: Rodale Press, 1979. 405 pp.

Putnam, Cynthia, et al., eds. *Easy Composting.* San Ramon, CA: Ortho Books, 1992. 96 pp.

Raabe, Robert D. *The Rapid Composting Method.* Berkeley, CA: California Cooperative Extension Service, 1981. 4 pp.

Rynk, Robert, et al. *On Farm Composting Handbook.* Ithaca, NY: Northeast Regional Agricultural Engineering Service (152 Riley-Robb Hall, Cooperative Extension, Ithaca, NY 14853-5701), 1992. 186 pp.

Soucie, Gary. "How You Gonna Keep It Down on the Farm." *Audubon,* September 1972: 112–115.

*Urban Home Composting, Rodent-Resistant Bins, and Environmental Health Standards.* Vancouver, Canada: City Farmer, Canada's Office of Urban Agriculture (318 Homer St., Ste. 801, Vancouver, BC V6B 2V3, Canada), 1991. 36 pp.

## Container Gardening

Burke, Ken, ed. *Container Gardening.* Mount Vernon, VA: The American Horticultural Society, 1974. 144 pp.

Franklin, Candace Conard, ed. *Growing Plants in Containers: Indoors & Out.* Birmingham, AL: Oxmoor House, 1976. 96 pp.

McGee, Rose Marie Nichols, and Maggie Stuckey. *The Bountiful Container.* New York: Workman, 2002. 432 pp.

*Newcomb, Duane. *The Apartment Farmer: The Hassle-Free Way to Grow Vegetables Indoors, on Balconies, Patios, Roofs, and in Small Yards.* New York: Avon Books, 1976. 154 pp. Excellent. **BL**

Nordell, Anne and Eric. "Composting with Pigs." *Small Farmer's Journal,* Vol. 22, No. 2: 23–29.

Staff of Sunset Books. *Gardening in Containers.* Menlo Park, CA: Lane Book Co., 1959. 112 pp.

Stevens, Elaine. *The Creative Container Gardener.* Berkeley, CA: Ten Speed Press, 1995. 216 pp.

## Cookbooks

Adams, Margaret Byrd. *American Wood Heat Cookery.* Seattle, WA: Pacific Search Press, 1984. 250 pp.

Brotman, Juliano, with Erika Lenkert. *Raw: The Uncook Book.* New York: Harper Collins, 1999. 288 pp.

Brown, Edward Espe. *The Tassajara Bread Book.* Boston: Shambhala Books, 1986. 146 pp.

Costenbader, Carol W. *Mustards, Ketchups and Vinegars.* Pownal, VT: Storey, 1996. 96 pp.

Courter, Gay. *The Beansprout Book.* New York: Simon & Schuster, 1973. 96 pp.

Creasy, Rosalind. *Cooking from the Garden.* San Francisco: Sierra Club Books, 1988. 547 pp.

Crowhurst, Adrienne. *The Weed Cookbook.* New Jersey: Lancer Books, 1973. 198 pp.

———. *The Flower Cookbook.* New York: Lancer Books, 1973. 198 pp.

Diamond, Marilyn. *The American Vegetarian Cookbook.* New York: Warner Books, 1990. 422 pp.

Drückler, Sabine. *Grain Food for Sustainable Living Power.* Kaiwaka, New Zealand: Pukahukahu Press (Otamatea Eco Village RD 2, Kaiwaka, Northland, New Zealand). 63 pp. Good beginning for grain-based diets.

Editorial Staff at Ortho Books. *When the Good Cook Gardens.* San Francisco: Ortho Books, 1974. 96 pp.

Fabricant, Florence. *Elizabeth Berry's Great Bean Book.* Berkeley, CA: Ten Speed Press, 1999. 129 pp.

Gerras, Charles, ed. *Rodale's Basic Natural Foods Cookbook.* New York: Simon & Schuster, 1989. 899 pp.

Graf, Emma. *Cooking with Grains.* Stroud, UK: InterActions, 1996. 128 pp.

Greene, Bert. *The Grains Cookbook.* New York: Workman, 1988. 410 pp.

Hagler, Louise, and Dorothy R. Bates. *The Farm Vegetarian Cookbook.* Summertown, TN: Book Publishing Co., 1978. 219 pp.

———. *The New Farm Vegetarian Cookbook.* Summertown, TN: Book Publishing Co., 1988. 219 pp.

Haynes, Linda. *The Vegetarian Lunchbasket.* Willow Springs, MO: Nucleus Publications, 1990. 198 pp.

Hewitt, Jean. *The New York Times Natural Foods Cookbook.* New York: Avon Books, 1971. 434 pp.

*Homemade Olive Oil.* Leaflet #2789. University of California: Division of Agricultural Sciences, 1977.

Hurd, Frank J. *Ten Talents.* Collegedale, TN: College Press, 1985. 368 pp.

Jason, Dan. *The Whole Organic Food Book.* Vancouver, BC, Canada: Raincoast Books, 2000. 244 pp.

Jason, Dan, and Paul Ingraham. *Salt Spring Seeds Garlic Book.* Salt Spring Island, BC, Canada: Lightning Press, 1996. 87 pp.

Katz, Sandor Ellix. *Wild Fermentation.* White River Junction, VT: Chelsea Green Publishing, 2004. 187 pp.

Katzen, Mollie. *The Enchanted Broccoli Forest.* Berkeley, CA: Ten Speed Press, 1982. 320 pp.

———. *The Moosewood Cookbook.* Berkeley, CA: Ten Speed Press, 1977. 240 pp. Tasty recipes for lots of fresh vegetables.

———. *Still Life with Menu.* Berkeley, CA: Ten Speed Press, 1988. 350 pp.

McCarty, Meredith. *Fresh: From a Vegetarian Kitchen.* Eureka, CA: Turning Point Publications, 1989. Unique cookbook of vegetarian whole foods.

*McDougall, John A. and Mary A. *The McDougall Plan.* Clinton, NJ: New Win (P.O. Box 5159, Clinton, NJ 08809), 1983. 340 pp.

McKay, G. L., and C. Larsen. *Principles and Practice of Butter-Making.* New York: John Wiley & Sons, 1908. 351 pp.

Moosewood Staff. *New Recipes from Moosewood Restaurant.* Berkeley, CA: Ten Speed Press, 1987. 302 pp.

Morash, Marian. *The Victory Garden Cookbook.* New York: Knopf, 1982. 374 pp. **IL**

Munroe, Esther. *Sprouts to Grow and Eat.* Brattleboro, VT: The Stephen Greene Press, 1974. 119 pp.

Nearing, Helen. *Simple Food for the Good Life.* White River Junction, VT: Chelsea Green, 1999. 309 pp.

Niethammer, Carolyn J. *The Tumbleweed Gourmet: Cooking with Wild Southwestern Plants.* Tucson, AZ: The University of Arizona Press, 1987. 229 pp.

Pickarski, Ron. *Friendly Foods.* Berkeley, CA: Ten Speed Press, 1991. 277 pp.

Proulx, Annie, and Lew Nichols. *Cider: Making, Using & Enjoying Sweet & Hard Cider.* Pownal, VT: Storey, 1997. 219 pp.

Robertson, Laurel, et al. *The Laurel's Kitchen Bread Book.* New York: Random House, 1984. 447 pp. **BL**

———. *New Laurel's Kitchen.* Berkeley, CA: Ten Speed Press, 1986. 512 pp. **BL**

Rodriquez, Barbara. "Pickles." *Organic Gardening,* August/September 2004: 26–29.

Saltzman, Joanne. *Amazing Grains: Creating Vegetarian Main Dishes with Whole Grains.* Novato, CA: New World Library (14 Pamaron Way, Novato, CA 94948), 1990. 202 pp.

Santa Clara County Planned Parenthood. *Zucchini Cookbook.* Santa Cruz, CA: Planned Parenthood (421 Ocean St., Santa Cruz, CA 95060), 1974.

*Sass, Lorna J. *Recipes from an Ecological Kitchen.* New York: William Morrow, 1992. 492 pp.

Shurtleff, William, and Akiko Aoyagi. *The Book of Miso.* New York: Ballantine Books, 1976. 618 pp.

———. *The Book of Tempeh,* 2nd ed. Berkeley, CA: Ten Speed Press, 1979. 173 pp.

Sibbett, G. Steven, and Joseph Connell. *Producing Olive Oil in California.* Butte & Tulare Co. Farm Advisors, 1991. 19 pp.

Simmons, Paula. *Zucchini Cookbook.* Seattle, WA: Pacific Search, 1974. 127 pp.

Stepaniak, Joanne. *The Nutritional Yeast Cookbook.* Summertown, TN: Book Publishing Co., 1997. 143 pp.

Stowe, Sally and Martin. *The Brilliant Bean.* New York: Bantam, 1988. 276 pp.

Tucker, Eric, Bruce Enloe, and Amy Pearce. *The Artful Vegan.* Berkeley, CA: Ten Speed Press, 2003. 232 pp.

Turner, Kristina. *The Self Healing Cookbook,* 4th ed. Vashon Island, WA: Earthtones Press (P.O. Box 411, Vashon Island, WA 98070), 1989. Excellent, simple introduction to natural foods cooking and healing.

Wagner, Lindsey, and Ariane Spade. *The High Road to Health.* New York: Simon & Schuster, 1994. 287 pp.

Wasserman, Debra. *Simply Vegan: Quick Vegetarian Meals.* Baltimore: The Vegetarian Resource Group (P.O. Box 1463, Baltimore, MD 21203), 1991. 224 pp.

Waters, Alice. *Chez Panisse Vegetables.* New York: Harper Collins Publishers, 1996. 344 pp.

Wing, Daniel, and Alan Scott. *The Bread Builders: Hearth Loaves and Masonry Ovens.* White River Junction, VT: Chelsea Green, 1999. 253 pp.

Woodruff, Sandra. *Secrets of Fat-Free Baking.* Garden City Park, NY: Avery, 1994. 232 pp.

## Crafts

Bliss, Anne. *North American Dye Plants.* Boulder, CO: Juniper House, 1986. 288 pp.

Brill, Edith. *Cotswold Crafts.* Exeter, Great Britain: A. Wheaton, 1977. 184 pp.

Buchanan, Rita. *A Dyer's Garden: From Plant to Pot, Growing Dyes for Natural Fibers.* Loveland, CO: Interweave Press, 1995. 112 pp.

Cary, Mara. *Useful Baskets.* Boston: Houghton Mifflin, 1977. 132 pp.

Daugherty, Robin Taylor. *Splint-woven Basketry.* Loveland, CO: Interweave Press, 1986. 160 pp.

Dyer, Anne, Lettice Sandford, and Zena Edwards. *Country Crafts.* London: Book Club Associates, 1979. 133 pp.

Editors of the American Agriculturist. *Broom-Corn and Brooms.* New York: Orange Judd, 1906. 59 pp.

Hiebert, Helen. *Papermaking with Plants.* Pownal, VT: Storey, 1998. 107 pp.

———. *The Papermaker's Companion: The Ultimate Guide to Making and Using Handmade Paper.* Pownal, VT: Storey, 2000. 219 pp.

Hill, Jack. *Country Chair Making.* David & Charles, 1997. 151 pp.

Hunt, Ben W. *Ben Hunt's Big Indian-craft Book.* New York: Bruce Publishing, 1945.

Jenkins, J. Geraint. *Traditional Country Craftsmen.* Boston, MA: Routledge & Kegan Paul, 1978. 253 pp.

———. *Traditional Country Craftsmen.* London: Routledge & Kegan Paul Limited, 1965. 236 pp.

Jensen, Elizabeth. *Baskets from Nature's Bounty.* Loveland, CO: Interweave Press, 1991. 197 pp.

Keville, Kathi. "Soap—What It Is and How to Make It." *Vegetarian Times/Well-Being Magazine,* 1981, No. 52.

———. "How to Make Tooth Powder, Toothpaste and Mouthwash." *Vegetarian Times/Well-Being Magazine,* 1981, No. 53.

Langsner, Drew. *Country Woodcraft.* Emmaus, PA: Rodale Press, 1978. 304 pp.

———. *Green Woodworking.* Asheville, NC: Lark Books, 1995. 176 pp.

Langsner, Drew and Louise. *Handmade.* New York: Harmony Books, 1974. 192 pp.

Long, Jim. *Making Bentwood Trellises, Arbors, Gates and Fences.* Pownal, VT: Storey, 1998. 155 pp.

Mack, Daniel. *Making Rustic Furniture.* New York: Sterling, 1992. 160 pp.

Montgomery, David. *Native American Crafts & Skills.* Guilford, CT: The Lyons Press, 2000. 215 pp.

Newsholme, Christopher. *Willows: The Genus Salix.* London: B. T. Batsford (4 Fitzhardinge St., London W1H OAH, England), 1992. 224 pp.

Oppenheimer, Betty. *The Candlemaker's Companion: A Complete Guide to Rolling, Pouring, Dipping, and Decorating Your Own Candles.* Pownal, VT: Storey Books, 1997. 169 pp.

———. *Gifts for Herb Lovers.* Pownal, VT: Storey, 1997. 123 pp.

Owens-Celli, Morgyn Geoffry. *The Book of Wheat Weaving and Straw Craft.* Asheville, NC: Lark Books, 1997. 143 pp.

Richards, Llynne, and Ronald J. Tyrl. *Dyes from American Native Plants: A Practical Guide.* Portland, OR: Timber Press, 2005. 339 pp.

Rudge, Geraldine. *Garden Crafts: A Practical Guide to Creating Hand-Crafted Features for Your Garden.* New York: The Lyons Press, 1999. 144 pp.

Ruoff, Abby. *Making Twig Furniture.* Roberts, WA: Hartley & Marks Publishers, 1991. 243 pp.

Seymour, John. *The Forgotten Crafts: A Practical Guide to Traditional Skills.* New York: Random House, 1984. 192 pp.

Stiles, David and Jeanie. *Garden Retreats: A Build-It-Yourself Guide.* Pownal, VT: Storey, 1999. 155 pp.

Tabor, Raymond. *Traditional Woodland Crafts.* 583 Fulham Road, London SW6 5BY, UK, 1997. 160 pp.

Tod, Osma Gallinger. *Earth Basketry.* New York: Crown Publishers, 1972. 169 pp.

Van Straten, Trudy. *Indigo, Madder, and Marigold—A Portfolio of Colors from Natural Dyes.* Loveland, CO: Interweave Press, 1993. 127 pp.

Verdet-Fierz, Bernard and Regula. *Willow Basketry.* Loveland, CO: Interweave Press, 1993. 355 pp.

White, Elaine C. *Super Formulas Arts and Crafts.* Brandon, MS: Quail Ridge Press (P.O. Box 1223, Brandon, MS), 1993. 114 pp.

*Woodwork Magazine.* 42 Digital Dr., #5, Novato, CA 94949.

## Development

*Alternatives to the Peace Corps: A Guide to Global Volunteer Opportunities,* 11th ed. Oakland, CA: Food First Books, 2005. 116 pp. **BL**

Altieri, Miguel A. *Latin American Institutions Conducting Research, Training, and Development Activities in Sustainable Agriculture.* Albany, CA: University of California (Division of Biological Control, 1050 San Pablo Ave., Albany, CA 94706). 46 pp.

*Amigos Handbook.* Houston, TX: Amigos de las Americas (5618 Star Lane, Houston, TX 77057), 1970s.

Arbab, Farzam. *Rural University: Learning about Education and Development.* Ottawa, Canada: International Development Research Center (Box 8500, Ottawa, Canada), 1984. 71 pp.

Benor, Daniel, and James Q. Harrison. *Agricultural Extension: The Training and Visit System.* Washington, DC: World Bank, 1977. 55 pp.

Bradfield, D. J. *Guide to Extension Training.* Rome, Italy: Food and Agriculture Organization of the United Nations, 1966. 176 pp.

Brusko, Michael, ed. *Proceedings of Workshop on Resource-Efficient Farming Methods for Tanzania.* Emmaus, PA: Rodale Press, 1983. 128 pp.

*Bunch, Roland. *Two Ears of Corn: A Guide to People-Centered Agricultural Improvement.* Oklahoma City: World Neighbors (5116 N. Portland, Oklahoma City, OK 73112), 1982. 251 pp. **BL**

Chapman, Duane, and Randy Barker. *Resource Depletion, Agricultural Research, and Development.* U.S. National Academy of Sciences and Czechoslovak Academy Sciences Workshop on Agricultural Development and Environmental Research, April 6–16, 1987. 34 pp.

Clark, Colin, and Margaret Haswell. *The Economics of Subsistence Agriculture.* Glasgow, UK: The University Press, 1970. 267 pp.

CODEL. *Integration of Programs for Managing Renewable Natural Resources for Human Development.* Report on Workshop Seminar, San Jose de Ocoa, D.R., January 29–February 3, 1984. Environment and Development Program, 1984. 47 pp. Also available in Spanish.

———. *People's Participation in Development and the Management of Natural Resources.* Report on the Caribbean Regional Workshop in Vieux Fort, St. Lucia, April 15–19, 1985. Environment and Development Program, 1985. 42 pp.

*Darrow, Ken, et al. *Trans-Cultural Study Guide.* Stanford, CA: Volunteers in Asia (Box 4543, Stanford, CA 94305), 1981. 155 pp. **BL**

*Edwards, Michael. *Arriving Where We Started.* London: Voluntary Service Overseas (9 Belgrave Square, London, England), 1983. 208 pp. **BL**

*Fantini, Alvino E., ed. *Cross-Cultural Orientation.* Brattleboro, VT: The Experiment in International Living (P.O. Box 676, Brattleboro, VT 05301), 1984. 115 pp. **BL**

Gliessman, Stephen, and Robert Grantham. "Agroecology: Reshaping Agricultural Development," in Suzanne Head and Robert Heinzman, eds., *Lessons of the Rainforest,* Sierra Club Books, 1990, 196–207 and 266.

IMSS. *Catálogo de actividades de acción comunitaria.* Mexico City, Mexico: Instituto Mexicano del Seguro Social (Paseo de la Reforma 476, D.F. C.P. 0600, Mexico), 1984. 386 pp.

Kann, Peter R. "The Food Crisis." *The Wall Street Journal,* November 18, 1974: 1, 14.

Kohr, Leopold. *Development Without Aid: The Translucent Society.* New York: Schocken, 1973. 226 pp.

Office of Technology Assessment Workshop November 24–25, 1980. *Background Papers for Innovative Biological Technologies for Lesser Developed Countries.* Washington, DC: U.S. Government Printing Office, 1981. 511 pp.

Pradervand, Pierre. *Listening to Africa: Developing Africa from the Grassroots.* New York: Praeger Publishers, 1989. 229 pp.

Roberts, Glyn. *Handbook for Development Workers Overseas.* Alverstoke, Hampshire, UK: The Alver Press, 1978. 43 pp.

Rosset, Peter, and Medea Benjamin, eds. *The Greening of the Revolution: Cuba's Experiment with Organic Agriculture.* San Francisco: Global Exchange (2017 Mission St., Rm. 303, San Francisco, CA 94110), 1995.

Sachs, Wolfgang, ed. *The Development Dictionary: A Guide to Knowledge as Power.* Atlantic Highlands, NJ: Zed Books, 1992. 306 pp.

Seymour, John. *La Vida en al Campo y e Horticultur Autosuficiente.* Barcelona: Libro Blume, 1976. 256 pp.

Slider, Ronald J. *Rich Christians in an Age of Hunger.* Downers Grove, IL: Inter-Varsity Press, 1980. 249 pp.

Smith, Marney. *Growing Your Own Food.* Westport, CT: Save the Children Federation (48 Wilton Rd., Westport, CT 06880), 1980. 35 pp.

Toledo, Victor Manuel. *Ecologia y Autosuficiencia Alimentaria.* Mexico, Spain, Argentina, Colombia: Siglo Veintiuno Editores, 1985. 118 pp.

United Nations Development Programme. *Human Development Report—1990.* New York: Oxford University Press, 1990. 189 pp.

———. *Sustainable Human Development and Agriculture.* New York: UNDP Bureau for Program Policy and Evaluation, 1994. 92 pp.

*van den Bor, Wout. *The Art of Beginning.* Pudoc, Wageningen, Netherlands: Centre for Agricultural Publishing and Documentation, 1983. 174 pp. **BL**

*Wade, Isabel. *City Food: Crop Selection in Third World Cities.* San Francisco: Urban Resource Systems (783 Buena Vista W., San Francisco, CA 94117), 1986. 54 pp.

*"Wasteful North," *World View Magazine,* Spring 1992: 17.

Weisman, Alan. *Gaviotas: A Village to Reinvent the World.* White River Junction, VT: Chelsea Green, 1998. 227 pp.

Winblad, Uno. *The Productive Homestead: A Report of a Study Tour.* Stockholm: Winblad Konsult AB (Pataholm 5503, 384 92 ALEM, Sweden), 1992. 16 pp.

*World Neighbors.* Oklahoma City: World Neighbors (54127 NW 122 St., Oklahoma City, OK 73120-8869).

## Education

Bear, John B., and Mariah P. Bear. *Bears' Guide to Earning Degrees Nontraditionally.* El Cerrito, CA: Degree.net Books, 1999. 410 pp.

Bolles, Richard Nelson. *The What Color Is Your Parachute Workbook.* Berkeley, CA: Ten Speed Press, 1998. 47 pp.

Gates, Jane Potter. *Educational and Training Opportunities in Sustainable Agriculture,* 3rd ed. Beltsville, MD: Alternative Farming Systems, 1990. 15 pp.

UCSC. *Teaching Organic Farming and Gardening.* Santa Cruz, CA: CASFS. 2003.

## Energy

Barbour, Erwin Hinkley. *The Home-made Windmills of Nebraska.* Occidental, CA: The Farallones Institute (Reprint from the Agricultural Experiment Station Bulletin of 1899), 1976. 78 pp.

Bener, Martin H. "Energy in Agriculture: Lessons from the Sunshine Project." *The Land Institute Journal,* July 2003.

Box, Dan, et al. "The End of Cheap Oil: The Consequences." *The Ecologist,* October 2005: 46–53.

Center for Renewable Energy and Sustainable Technology. *Energy Stories.* Washington, DC: Crest, 1999. CD-ROM.

Clark, Wilson. *Energy for Survival.* New York: Anchor Doubleday, 1974. 652 pp.

———. "U.S. Agriculture Is Growing Trouble as Well as Crops." *Smithsonian,* January 1975. **BL**

Crea, Dominic. "The Trouble With Hydrogen (Part I)." *BackHome Magazine,* January/February 2006: 44–47.

Dazhong, W., and D. Pimentel. "Energy Flow through an Organic Agroecosystem in China." *Agriculture, Ecosystems and Environment* Vol. 11, 1984, 145–160.

———. "Energy Use in Crop Systems in Northeastern China," in *Food and Energy Resources,* D. Pimentel and C. W. Hall, eds. New York: Academic Press, 1984: 91–120.

*Energy Primer.* Menlo Park, CA: Portola Institute, 1974. 200 pp.

*Energy Primer: Updated and Revised.* Menlo Park, CA: Delta, 1978. 256 pp.

Hemenway, Toby. "Cities, Peak Oil, and Sustainability." *Urban Permaculture,* November 2005: 5–8.

Kunstler, James Howard. "Global Oil Production Peak." *BackHome Magazine,* March/April 2005: 17–19.

MacPherson, George. *Home-Grown Energy from Short-Rotation Coppice.* Ipswich, UK: Farming Press, 1995. 214 pp.

*Odum, Howard T. and Elisabeth C. *Energy Basis for Man and Nature.* New York: McGraw-Hill, 1976. 297 pp. **IL**

"Oil Dependence," *The Ecologist,* October 2005: 45.

Pahl, Greg. "Biodiesel: Homegrown Oil." *Mother Earth News,* February/March 2006: 65–71.

Panel on Methane Generation. *Methane Generation from Human, Animal, and Agricultural Wastes.* Washington, DC: National Academy of Sciences, 1977. 131 pp.

*Perelman, Michael J. *Efficiency and Agriculture.* Chico, CA: Economics Department, Chico State College.

*———. "Farming with Nature." *Environment,* Vol. 14, No. 8 (1972). **BL**

*———. "Farming with Petroleum." *Environment,* October 1972: 8–13. **BL**

*Perelman, Michael J., and Kevin P. Shea. "The Big Farm." *Environment,* December 1972: 10–15. **BL**

Pimentel, David, et al. "Energy and Land Constraints in Food Protein Production." *Science,* Vol. 190 (November 1975): 754–761.

Pimentel, David, and E. Heichel. "Energy Efficiency and Sustainability of Farming Systems," in *Soil Management for Sustainability,* R. Lal and F. J. Pierce, eds. Ankeny, IA: Soil and Water Conservation Society (7515 NE Ankeny Rd., Ankeny, IA 50021), 1991: 113–123.

———. "Energy Flow in Agroecosystems," in *Agricultural Ecosystems: Unifying Concepts,* R. Lawrance, et al., eds. New York: John Wiley & Sons, 1984: 121–132.

———. "Energy Flow in the Food System," in *Food and Energy Resources,* D. Pimentel and C. W. Hall, eds. New York: Academic Press, 1984: 1–24.

———. "Energy Use in Cereal Grain Production," in *Energy Use Management,* Vol. 1, R. A. Fazzoare and C. B. Smith, eds. New York: Permagon Press, 1977: 759–767.

Pimentel, David, and E. C. Terhune. "Energy Use in Food Production."

———. "Energy and Food." *Annual Review of Energy,* 1977: 171–195.

Savinar, J. D. *The Oil Age Is Over.* Kearney, NE: Morris Publishing, 2004. 181 pp.

## *Farming*

Ableman, Michael. *On Good Land: The Autobiography of an Urban Farm.* San Francisco: Chronicle Books, 1998. 144 pp.

Ashley, John. *Food Crops and Drought.* London and Basingstoke, UK: Macmillan Education, 1999. 133 pp.

Bailey, L. H. *Principles of Agriculture.* New York: Macmillan, 1909. 336 pp.

Bromfield, Louis. *Malabar Farm.* New York: Ballantine Books, 1970. 470 pp.

Cavigelli, M. A., et al., eds. *Michigan Field Crop Ecology: Managing Biological Processes for Productivity and Environmental Quality.* Michigan State University Extension Bulletin E-2646, 1998. 92 pp.

Cocannouer, Joseph A. *Farming with Nature.* Norman, OK: University of Oklahoma Press, 1954. 147 pp.

Cox, Joseph F., and Lyman Jackson. *Field Crops and Land Use.* New York: John Wiley & Sons, 1942. 473 pp.

Dorf, P. *Liberty Hyde Bailey: An Informal Biography.* Ithaca, NY: Cornell University Press, 1956. 257 pp.

"Down on the Farm." *NOVA* #1106 (transcript). Boston: WGBH. 1984. 24 pp.

Ernst, Matt. "Picking at the Peak," *Organic Gardening,* August/September 2004: 20–24.

"Facing the Farm Crisis." *The Ecologist,* Special Supplement. June 2000.

Gliessman, Stephen R., et al. *Agroecology.* New York: Springer-Verlag, 1990. 380 pp.

Gregson, Bob and Bonnie. *Rebirth of the Small Family Farm: A Handbook for Starting a Successful Organic Farm Based on the Community Supported Agriculture Concept.* Vashon Island, WA: IMF Associates (P.O. Box 2542, Vashon Island, WA 98070), 1996. 63 pp.

Hainsworth, P. H. *Agriculture—The Only Right Approach.* Pauma Valley, CA: Bargyla and Gylver Rateaver, 1976. 238 pp.

Hallberg, Milton C. *Economic Trends in U.S. Agriculture and Food Systems Since World War II.* Ames, Iowa: Iowa State University Press, 2001. 179 pp.

Halweil, Brian. *Home Grown: The Case for Local Food in a Global Market.* Worldwatch Paper 163. Washington, DC: Worldwatch Institute, 2002. 83 pp.

Harmond, Paul, ed. *The Farmstead Book.* Seattle: Cloudburst, 1978. 258 pp.

Haystead, Ladd, and Gilbert C. Fite. *The Agricultural Regions of the United States.* Norman, OK: University of Oklahoma Press, 1955. 288 pp.

Humphrey, Shirley, et al., eds. *Small Farm Handbook.* Oakland, CA: University of California, 1994. 170 pp.

Imhoff, Daniel. *Farming with the Wild: Enhancing Biodiversity on Farms and Ranches.* San Francisco: Sierra Club Books, 2003. 182 pp.

Kinsey, Neal. *Hands-On Agronomy.* Austin, TX: Acres U.S.A. (P.O. Box 91299, Austin, TX 78709), 1993. 352 pp.

Kral, David M., ed. *Organic Farming: Current Technology and Its Role in a Sustainable Agriculture.* American Society of Agronomy Special Publication Number 46. Madison, WI: ASA, 1984. 192 pp. Proceedings of a symposium held in Atlanta, GA, November 29–December 3, 1981, sponsored by ASA and Soil Science Society of America.

Lampkin, Nicolas. *Organic Farming.* Ipswich, UK: Farming Press, 1998. 715 pp.

*Living the Good Life with Helen and Scott Nearing.* Olney, PA: Bullfrog Films. Excellent film on Helen and Scott Nearing and their For-est Farm homestead in Vermont. Video. **BL**

Logsdon, Gene. *The Contrary Farmer.* White River Junction, VT: Chelsea Green, 1994. 237 pp.

Lyson, Thomas A. *Civic Agriculture: Reconnecting Farm, Food, and Community.* Medford, MA: Tufts Univ. Press, 2004. 136 pp.

Masumoto, David Mas. *Harvest Son.* New York: W. W. Norton, 1998. 302 pp.

Medvedev, Zhores. *Soviet Agriculture.* New York: W. W. Norton, 1987. 464 pp.

*Multiple Cropping Systems.* Groenken, The Netherlands: AME Foundation, 1985. 19 pp.

Mutsaers, H. J. W., et al. *A Field Guide for On-Farm Experimentation.* Ibadan, Nigeria: International Institute of Tropical Agriculture, 1997. 235 pp.

Myase, Ann D. *Sustainable Farming Systems: A Guide to the Transition.* Davis, CA: Sustainable Agriculture Research and Education Program (1 Shields Ave., University of CA, Davis, CA), 1997. 81 pp.

*Organic Farming in Kenya.* Nairobi, Kenya: Kenya Institute of Organic Farming (P.O. Box 34972, Nairobi, Kenya) and CODEL, 1990. 80 pp.

Paterson, William G. R., ed. *Farm Crops.* Vol. 4, *Miscellaneous Crops.* London: The Gresham Publishing Co., 1925. 316 pp. Covers tobacco, buckwheat, mustard, hemp, flax, fruits and vegetables, and more.

Pesek, John, ed. *Agronomy: Science in Action.* Madison, WI: American Society of Agronomy, 1979. 40 pp.

Pettersson, B. D., and E. V. Wistinghausen. *Organic, Biodynamic and Conventional Cropping Systems: A Long Term Comparison.* Trans. William F. Brinton, Jr. Mt. Vernon, ME: Woods End Laboratory, 1988.

Pimentel, David. *Agriculture and EcoTechnology.* Ithaca, NY: Department of Entomology, Cornell University, 1989.

———. *Agriculture, Technology, and Natural Resources.* Ithaca, NY: Department of Entomology, Cornell University.

Poincelot, Raymond P. *Toward a More Sustainable Agriculture.* Westport, CT: AVI Publishing Company, 1986. 241 pp.

Pretty, Jules N. *Regenerating Agriculture.* Washington, DC: Joseph Henry Press, 1995. 320 pp.

Reijntjes, Coen, Bertus Haverkort, and Ann Waters-Bayer. *Farming for the Future.* Leusden, The Netherlands: ILEIA, 1992. 250 pp.

*Revelle, Roger. "The Resources Available for Agriculture." *Scientific American,* September 1976: 165–176.

Robinson, Ed and Carolyn. *The "Have-More" Plan—"A Little Land—A Lot of Living": How to Make a Small Cash Income into the Best and Happiest Living Any Family Could Want.* Pownal, VT: Garden Way Publishing, 1943, 1973. 70 pp.

Schafer, Kristin S., ed. *Learning from the BIOS Approach.* Davis, CA: World Resources Institute. 35 pp.

Singles in Agriculture. P.O. Box 7, Pearl City, IL 61062.

*Small Farm Today.* 3903 W. Ridge Trail Road, Clark, MO 65243-9525. Magazine.

Soule, Judith D., and Jon K. Piper. *Farming in Nature's Image.* Covelo, CA: Island Press, 1992. 286 pp.

Strange, Marty. *Family Farming: A New Economic Vision.* Lincoln, NE: University of Nebraska Press, 1988. 311 pp.

Streeter, John Williams. *The Fat of the Land.* New York: The Macmillan Company, 1918. 406 pp.

The Sustainable Agriculture Network (SARE). *Transitioning to Organic Production: Part 1. Introduction to Organic Farming.* Burlington, VT: University of Vermont, Sustainable Agriculture Publications.

Sykes, Friend. *Food, Farming and the Future.* Emmaus, PA: Rodale Press, 1951. 293 pp.

———. *Humus and the Farmer.* Emmaus, PA: Rodale Press, 1949. 392 pp.

Thomas Jefferson Agricultural Institute, 601 West Nifong Boulevard, Suite 1D, Columbia, MO 65203. A nonprofit organization that conducts education, research, and market development in support of small farms. Also publishes a wide variety of topical crop papers.

U.S. Department of Agriculture. *Report and Recommendations on Organic Farming.* Washington, DC: Office of Governmental and Public Affairs, USDA, 1980. 94 pp.

———. *A Time to Act: A Report of the USDA National Commission on Small Farms.* Washington, DC: USDA, 1998. 121 pp.

U.S. Department of Agriculture National Commission on Small Farms. *A Time to Act.* Washington, DC: USDA, 1998. 121 pp.

Volin, Lazar. *A Survey of Soviet Russian Agriculture.* Washington, DC: U.S. Department of Agriculture, 1951. 194 pp.

Walters, Charles, Jr., and C. J. Fenzau. *Eco-Farm: An Acres U.S.A. Primer.* Austin, TX: Acres U.S.A. (P.O. Box 91299, Austin, TX 78709), 1996. 447 pp.

Warren, G. F. *Farm Management.* New York: Macmillan, 1922. 590 pp.

Wilken, Gene C. *Good Farmers.* London: University of California Press, 1987. 302 pp.

Williams, Allan N., and Neville Graham. *The Small Farmers' Guide to Alternative Farming Techniques.* Belmont, Port of Spain, Trinidad and Tobago, and Roseau, Commonwealth of Dominica: ACT Press, 1998. 61 pp.

Wittwer, Sylvan, et al. *Feeding a Billion: Frontiers of Chinese Agriculture.* East Lansing, MI: Michigan State University Press, 1987. 462 pp.

Wortman, Sterling. "Food and Agriculture." *Scientific American,* September 1976: 31–39.

Zimmer, Gary F. *The Biological Farmer.* Austin, TX: Acres U.S.A., 2000. 352 pp.

## *Fertilizer*

American Society of Agronomy. *The Role of Phosphorus in Agriculture.* Madison, WI: ASA, 1980. 910 pp.

Bunch, Roland. "Nutrient Quantity or Nutrient Access? A New Understanding of How to Maintain Soil Fertility in the Tropics." *ECHO Development Notes,* January 2002: 1–7.

*Chemical Periodic Table, Permachart.* Concord, Canada: Papertech Marketing Group (163 Buttermill Ave., Unit 12, Concord, ON L4K 3X8, Canada), 1999. Helpful for better understanding of soil nutrient exchange.

Engelstad, Orvis P., ed. *Nutrient Mobility in Soils: Accumulation and Losses.* Madison, WI: Soil Science of America, Inc., 1970. 81 pp.

Ingham, Elaine R. "Brewing Compost Tea." *Kitchen Gardener,* October/November 2000: 16–19.

Kilmer, V. J., et al., eds., *The Role of Potassium in Agriculture.* Madison, WI: American Society of Agronomy, Inc., 1968. 509 pp. Proceedings of a symposium held in Mussel Shoals, Alabama, June 18–19, 1968.

Mengel, K., and E. A. Kirkby. *Principles of Plant Nutrition.* Worblaufen-Bern, Switzerland: International Potash Institut, 1978. 593 pp.

Mortvedt, J. J., ed. *Micronutrients in Agriculture.* Madison, WI: Soil Science Society of America, Inc., 1972. 666 pp. Proceedings of a symposium held in Mussel Shoals, Alabama, April 20–22, 1971.

Munson, Robert D., ed. *Potassium in Agriculture.* Madison, WI: American Society of Agronomy, Inc., 1985. 1223 pp. Proceedings of an international symposium held in Atlanta, Georgia, July 7–10, 1985.

National Academy of Sciences. *Accumulation of Nitrate.* Washington, DC: National Academy of Sciences, 1972. 106 pp.

The New Farm Staff, eds. *The Farmer's Fertilizer Handbook.*

Emmaus, PA: Rodale Institute, 1986. 208 pp.

Norman, Cynthia, "Dung Ho." *National Gardening,* May 1987, 28–30.

*Organic Soil Amendments and Fertilizers.* Publications Division of Agriculture and Natural Resources, University of California (6701 San Pablo Ave., Oakland, CA 94608-1239), 1992. 36 pp.

Pettersson, B. D., and E. V. Wistinghausen. *Effects of Organic and Inorganic Fertilizers on Soils and Crops.* Temple, ME: Woods End Agricultural Institute (Orchard Hill Rd., Temple, ME 04984), 1979. 44 pp. **AL**

Shirley, Christopher, and The New Farm Staff, eds. *What Really Happens When You Cut Chemicals?* Emmaus, PA: Rodale Institute, 1993. 156 pp.

Smith, Edward G., et al. *Impacts of Chemical Use Reduction on Crop Yields and Costs.* College Station, TX: Agricultural and Food Policy Center, Dept. of Agricultural Economics, Texas A&M Univ. System, n.d. 103 pp.

Tandon, H. L. S. *Fertilizer Management in Rainfed Dryland Agriculture—A Guidebook.* New Delhi: Fertiliser Development and Consultation Organisation (204-204A Bhanot Corner, 1-2 Pamposh Enclave, New Delhi-110048, India), 1993. 103 pp.

Tisdale, Samuel L., and Werner L. Nelson. *Soil Fertility and Fertilizers.* New York: Macmillan, 1956. 634 pp.

United States Salinity Laboratory Staff. *Diagnosis and Improvement of Saline and Alkali Soils.* Ag. Handbook No. 60, U.S. Dept. of Ag., 1969. 160 pp.

Van Slyke, Lucius. *Fertilizers and Crop Production.* New York: Orange Judd, 1932. 193 pp.

### Fiber Crops

Baines, Patricia. *Linen: Hand Spinning and Weaving.* London: B. T. Batsford, 1989. 208 pp.

Buchanan, Rita. *A Weaver's Garden.* Loveland, CO: Interweave Press, 1987. 230 pp. **IL**

Chandler, Deborah. *Learning to Weave.* Loveland, CO: Interweave Press, 1995.

Davidson, Marguerite Porter. *A Handweaver's Pattern Book.* Swarthmore, PA: Marguerite P. Davison (P.O. Box 263, Swarthmore, PA 19081), 1944.

Dempsey, James M. *Fiber Crops.* Gainesville, FL: The University Presses of Florida, 1975. 457 pp.

Eaton, Frank M. "Early Defloration as a Method of Increasing Cotton Yields and the Relation of Fruitfulness to Fiber and Boll Characters." *Journal of Agricultural Research,* April 15, 1931: 447–462.

Fryxell, Paul A. *The Natural History of the Cotton Tribe.* College Station, TX: Texas A & M University Press.

Jarman, Cyril. *Plant Fibre Processing: A Handbook.* London: Intermediate Technology Publications, 1998. 52 pp.

The Jefferson Institute. "Flax: A Crop from America's Past with Renewed Potential." Alternative Crop Guide. Columbia, MO: The Jefferson Institute, 2002.

Linder, Olive and Harry. *Handspinning Flax.* Phoenix, AZ: Bizarre Butterfly, 1986.

Myers, Dorothy, and Sue Stolton. *Organic Cotton: From Field to Final Product.* London: Intermediate Technology Publications, 1999. 267 pp.

### Flowers

Anderson, E. B., et al. *The Oxford Book of Garden Flowers.* New York: Oxford University Press, 1963. 207 pp.

Armitage, Allan M. *Specialty Cut Flowers.* Portland, OR: Timber Press, 1995. 372 pp.

Arnosky, Pamela and Frank. "Specialty Cut Flowers: How to Get Long Stems and High-Quality Flowers." *Growing for Market,* September 1998: 15–17.

———. *We're Gonna Be Rich!: Growing Specialty Cut Flowers for Market.* Lawrence, KS: Fairplain Publications, 1999. 168 pp.

*Arranging Cut Flowers.* San Francisco: Ortho Books, 1985. 96 pp.

Babcock, Mary Reynolds. *First Aid for Flowers.* New York: Farrar, Straus & Giroux, 1954. 55 pp.

Ball, Jeff. *Rodale's Flower Garden Problem Solver.* Emmaus, PA: Rodale Press, 1990. 422 pp.

Black, Penny. *The Book of Pressed Flowers.* New York: Simon & Schuster, 1988. 120 pp. Excellent ideas, plants, and colors. Good information on tools, equipment, and how to press flowers.

Blamey, Marjorie. *Flowers of the Countryside.* New York: William Morrow, 1980. 224 pp.

Brennan Georgeanne, and Kathryn Kleinman. *Flowerkeeping: The Time-Honored Art of Preserving Flowers.* Berkeley, CA: Ten Speed Press, 1999. 142 pp.

Byczynski, Lynn. *The Flower Farmer.* White River Junction, VT: Chelsea Green, 1997. 208 pp.

———. "Grow Flowers for Cash." *Mother Earth News,* December/January 2003: 20–25.

Cavagnaro, David. "A Seed Saver's Guide to Flowers." *National Gardening,* August 1988: 39–45.

Christopher, Thomas. *In Search of Lost Roses.* New York: Summit Books, 1989.

Crockett, James Underwood. *Annuals.* New York: Time-Life Books, 1971. 176 pp.

———. *Bulbs.* New York: Time-Life Books, 1971. 160 pp.

———. *Crockett's Flower Garden.* New York: Little, Brown, 1981. 311 pp.

———. *Perennials.* New York: Time-Life Books, 1972. 160 pp.

———. *Roses.* New York: Time-Life Books, 1971. 160 pp.

Curless, Chris. "Renovating a Perennial Bed: How to Give an Old Border a New Lease on Life." *Fine Gardening,* Vol. 37.

Daar, Sheila. "Rose Diseases: New, Less Toxic Controls." *Common*

BIBLIOGRAPHY

*Sense Pest Control Quarterly,* Winter/Spring 1985: 4–10.

DeWolf, Gordon P., Jr., et al. *Taylor's Guide to Bulbs.* New York: Houghton Mifflin, 1961. 463 pp.

Duthie, Pam. *Continuous Bloom.* Batavia, IL: Ball Publishing, 2000. 328 pp.

Easton, Valerie. "A Cutting Garden for All Seasons." *Fine Gardening,* May/June 1998.

Evelegh, Tessa. *Lavender: Practical Inspirations for Natural Gifts, Country Crafts and Decorative Displays.* New York: Lorenz Books, 1996. 128 pp.

*Foster, Catharine O. *Organic Flower Gardening.* Emmaus, PA: Rodale Press, 1975. 305 pp. Excellent!

Gips, Kathleen M. *Flora's Dictionary: The Victorian Language of Herbs and Flowers.* Chagrin Falls, OH: Village Herb Shop (26 S. Main St., Chagrin Falls, OH 44022), 1990. 199 pp.

Hatfield, Audrey W. *Flowers to Know and Grow.* New York: Scribner's, 1950. 174 pp.

Hawks, Kim. "Starting Native Perennials from Seeds: Tips on Collection, Storage, and Germination." *Fine Gardening,* July/August 1991.

Hillier, Malcolm. *The Book of Fresh Flowers.* New York: Simon & Schuster, 1986. 252 pp.

Hillier, Malcolm, et al. *The Book of Dried Flowers.* New York: Simon & Schuster, 1986. 192 pp.

Horn, Elizabeth L. *Sierra Nevada Wildflowers.* Missoula, MT: Mountain Press, 1998. 215 pp.

*Huxley, Anthony, ed. *Garden Annuals and Bulbs.* New York: Macmillan, 1971. 208 pp.

*———. *Garden Perennials and Water Plants.* New York: Macmillan, 1971. 216 pp.

Jacobs, Betty E. M. *Flowers That Last Forever.* Pownal, VT: Storey, 1988. 222 pp.

James, Theodore, Jr. *The Potpourri Gardener.* New York: Macmillan, 1990. 148 pp.

Karel, Leonard. *Dried Flowers: From Antiquity to the Present.* Metuchen, NJ: Scarecrow Press, 1973.

*Kasperski, Victoria R. *How to Make Cut Flowers Last.* New York: William Morris, 1975. 191 pp. **IL**

Kramer, Jack. *The Old-Fashioned Cutting Garden.* New York: Macmillan, 1979. 160 pp.

Larson, Roy A., ed. *Introduction to Floriculture.* San Diego, CA: Academic Press, 1992. 636 pp.

Lovejoy, Ann. *The Year in Bloom.* Seattle, WA: Sasquatch Books, 1987. 264 pp.

MacNicol, Mary. *Flower Cookery.* New York: Collier Books, 1967. 262 pp.

Madison, Mike. *Growing Flowers for Market.* Winters, CA: Yolo Press, 1998. 257 pp.

Martin, Laura C. *Wildflower Meadow Book: A Gardener's Guide.* Chester, CT: The Globe Pequot Press, 1990. 320 pp.

Martin, Orin. *An Organic Approach to Rose Selection and Care: Rose Primer.* Santa Cruz, CA: Friends of UCSC Farm & Garden and the Center for Agroecology & Sustainable Food Systems, 2005. 40 pp.

Normand Eyre, Suzanne, ed. *Sunset Western Garden Annual.* Menlo Park, CA: Sunset Publishing Corp., 2001. 416 pp. Growing flowers.

Nowak, Joanna, and Ryszard M. Rudnicki. *Postharvest Handling and Storage of Cut Flowers, Florist Greens, and Potted Plants.* Portland, OR: Timber Press, 1990. 210 pp. **IL**

*Perennials (Eyewitness Garden Handbooks).* New York: DK Publishing, 1996. 352 pp. A reference guide to more than 1,000 plants.

Phillips, Ellen, and C. Colston Burrell. *Illustrated Encyclopedia of Perennials.* Emmaus, PA: Rodale Press, 1993. 533 pp.

Poncavage, Joanna. *Totally Sunflowers.* Berkeley, CA: Celestial Arts, 1996. 94 pp.

Powell, Eileen. *The Gardener's A–Z Guide to Growing from Seed to Bloom.* North Adams, MA: Storey Publishing, 2004. 528 pp.

Proctor, Rob. *The Cutting Garden: Plants for Gorgeous Blooms All Year Long.* New York: Houghton Mifflin Co., 2000. 122 pp.

Quarles, William. "Disease Resistant Roses." *Common Sense Pest Control Quarterly,* Spring 1998: 4–6.

———. "Non-Toxic Fungicides for Roses." *Common Sense Pest Control Quarterly,* Spring 1998: 7–14.

———. "Protecting Gardens from Deer Damage." *Common Sense Pest Control Quarterly,* Spring 1994: 4–15.

Remes, Shirley. "The Comeback Kids." *Organic Gardening,* February/March 2006: 24–29.

Sala, Orietta. *The Mitchell Beazley Pocket Guide to Old-Fashioned Roses.* London: Mitchell Beazley, 1995. 164 pp.

Sanchez, Janet H. *Perennials.* Menlo Park, CA: Sunset Books, 2000. 128 pp.

*Schneider, Alfred F. *Park's Success with Bulbs.* Greenwood, SC: George W. Park Seed Co., 1981. 173 pp. **IL**

Squires, M. *The Art of Drying Plants and Flowers.* New York: Bonanza, 1958. 258 pp.

Stevenson, Violet. *Successful Flower Marketing.* London: W. H. & L. Collingridge, 1952. 164 pp.

Sturdivant, Lee. *Flowers for Sale.* Friday Harbor, WA: San Juan Naturals (P.O. Box 642, Friday Harbor, WA 98250), 1992. 197 pp.

Swiadon, Laurie, and William Quarles. "Organic Control of Rose Insect and Mite Pests." *Common Sense Pest Control Quarterly,* Spring 1998: 15–19.

Sunset Editors. *Garden Colors: Annuals and Perennials.* Menlo Park, CA: Sunset Books, 1981. 96 pp.

Taylor, Ronald J. *Desert Wildflowers of North America.* Missoula, MT: Mountain Press, 1998. 349 pp.

Thorpc, Patricia. *Everlastings: The Complete Book of Dried Flowers.* New York: Facts on File Publications, 1985. 144 pp.

Verey, Rosemary. *The Flower Arranger's Garden.* New York: Little, Brown, and Co., 1989. 144 pp.

Verner, Yvette. *The Blooming Lawn: Creating a Flower Meadow.* White River Junction, VT: Chelsea Green, 1998. 144 pp.

White, Edward A. *The Principles of Floriculture.* New York: Macmillan, 1931. 467 pp.

Whitelaw, Mark. "Growing Roses the Natural Way." *National Gardening,* May/June 1996: 62–65.

Wickson, Edward J. *California Garden Flowers—Shrubs, Trees & Vines.* San Francisco: Pacific Rural Press, 1929. 255 pp.

Wilder, Louise B. *The Fragrant Garden.* New York: Dover, 1974. 407 pp.

## Food and Nutrition

(see also Solar Cooking)

*Agricultural Research Service, U.S. Department of Agriculture. *Composition of Foods. Agriculture Handbook No. 8.* Washington, DC: U.S. Government Printing Office, 1963. 190 pp. **BL**

Aihara, Herman. *Acid and Alkaline.* Oroville, CA: George Ohsawa Macrobiotic Foundation (1511 Robinson St., Oroville, CA 95965), 1986. 121 pp.

———. *Basic Macrobiotics.* Tokyo, Japan: Japan Publications, 1985. Introduction to holistic living with good details.

Alamgir, Mohiuddin, and Poonam Arora. *Providing Food Security for All.* New York: University Press, 1990. 269 pp.

Balch, James F. and Phyllis A. *Prescription for Nutritional Healing.* Garden City Park, NY: Avery, 1990. 368 pp.

Balch, Phyllis A. *Prescription for Herbal Healing: An Easy-to-Use A–Z Reference to Hundreds of Common Disorders and Their Herbal Remedies.* New York: Avery, 2002. 352 pp.

Board of Directors. "Position Paper on the Vegetarian Approach to Eating." *The American Dietetic Association Reports,* July 1980: 61–69.

Comité Interdepartmental de Nutrición para la Defensa Nacional, et al. *Tabla de Composicion de Alimentos Para Uso en America Latina.* Bethesda, MD: National Institutes of Health, 1961. 157 pp. Also available in English.

Cousens, Gabriel. *Conscious Eating.* Berkeley, CA: North Atlantic Books, 2000. 850 pp.

de Selincourt, Kate. *Local Harvest.* London: Lawrence & Wishart, 1997. 229 pp.

*Duhon, David, and Cindy Gebhard. *One Circle: How to Grow a Complete Diet in Less Than 1000 Square Feet.* Willits, CA: Ecology Action, 1984. 200 pp. Excellent. **BL/IL/AL**

Elliot, Rose. *Vegetarian Mother and Baby Book.* New York: Pantheon Books, 1986. 261 pp.

Ferré, Carl. *Pocket Guide to Macrobiotics.* Freedom, CA: Crossing Press, 1997. 126 pp.

*Flores, Marina, et al. *Valor Nutrivo de los Alimentos para Centro America y Panama.* Guatemala: Investigaciones Dietaticas—Nutrición Aplicada, 1971. 15 pp.

*Food Composition Table for Use in Africa.* U.S. Department of Health, Education, and Welfare, Public Health Service, Health Services and Mental Health Administration. Bethesda, MD: National Center for Chronic Disease Control, Nutrition Program, 1968. 306 pp.

*Food Composition Table for Use in East Asia.* Rome: Food and Agriculture Organization of the United Nations, 1972. 334 pp.

Freeman, John A. *Survival Gardening.* Rock Hill, SC: John's Press, 1982. 84 pp.

Glenn, E., et al. *Sustainable Food Production for a Complete Diet.* Tucson, AZ: Environmental Research Laboratory, 1989. 25 pp.

Gussow, Joan. *The Feeding Web.* Palo Alto, CA: Bull Publishing, 1978. 457 pp.

Halweil, Brian. *Eat Here.* New York: Norton, 2004. 236 pp.

*Heritage, Ford. *Composition and Facts about Foods.* Mokelumne Hill, CA: Health Research, 1971. 121 pp. Very useful!

The Hunger Project. *Ending Hunger: An Idea Whose Time Has Come.* New York: Praeger, 1985. 430 pp.

Hur, Robin. *Food Reform: Our Desperate Need.* Austin, TX: Heidelberg Publishers, 1975. 260 pp.

IMSS. *Programa de Autosuficiencia Alimentaria a Nivel Familiar (Ecoalimentacion) y Conservacion de Alimentos.* Mexico: IMSS Promotoras Voluntarias, 1992.

Jack, Alex. *America's Vanishing Nutrients: Decline in Fruit and Vegetable Quality Poses Serious Health and Environmental Risks.* Becket, MA: Amberwaves, 2005. 18 pp.

Kapuler, Alan M., and Sarangamat Gurusiddiah. "The Amino Acids Precursory to Proteins Are Primary Human Food: Proline, Glutamine, and Arginine Found Free in the Juices of Common Vegetables and Herbs." *Journal of Medicinal Food* Vol. 1, No. 2 (1988): 97–115.

*Kirschmann, John D. *Nutrition Almanac.* New York: McGraw-Hill, 1979. 313 pp.

Knight, Jonathan. "The Nutrition Garden Project." *The Cultivar* (Newsletter of the Center for Agroecology and Sustainable Food Systems, University of California at Santa Cruz), Winter 1997. 7 pp.

Knorr, Dietrich W., and Tom R. Watkins, ed. *Alterations in Food Production.* New York: Van Nostrand Reinhold Co., 1984. 241 pp.

Kushi, Michio. *The Macrobiotic Way.* Wayne, NJ: Avery, 1985. Introduction to holistic living.

Kushi, Michio, and Alex Jack. *The Macrobiotic Path to Total Health.* New York: Ballantine Books, 2003. 546 pp.

Lappé, Frances M. *Diet for a Small Planet.* New York: Ballantine Books, 1984. 496 pp.

Linder, Maria C. "A Review of the Evidence for Food Quality." *Biodynamics,* Summer 1973, 1–11.

Lockeretz, William, ed. *Agricultural Production and Nutrition: Proceedings of an International Conference, Boston, Massachusetts, March 19–21, 1997.* Medford, MA: School of Nutrition Science and Policy, Tufts University, 1997. 213 pp.

Mainland, Rowena S., and W. E. Hauver, Jr. *Egg Buying Guides for Consumers.* Washington, DC: U.S. Dept. of Ag., 1954. 8 pp.

Metz, Edwin T., ed. *Quality Protein Maize.* St. Paul, MN: American Association of Cereal Chemists, 1992. 294 pp.

Minnich, Jerry. *Gardening for Maximum Nutrition.* Emmaus, PA: Rodale Press, 1983. 220 pp.

Muñoz de Chávez, et al. *Tablas de valor nutritivo de los alimentos de mahor consumo en México.* Mexico: Editorial Pax México (Libreria Carlos Césarman, S.A., Av. Cuauhtémoc 1430, Col. Sta. Cruz Atoyac, Mexico), 1996. 330 pp.

Nabham, Gary Paul, and Rood Sashley. *Renewing America's Food Traditions: Bringing Cultural and Culinary Mainstays from the Past into the New Millennium.* Tucson: Center for Sustainable Environments, 2004. 82 pp.

*National Academy of Sciences. *Recommended Dietary Allowances,* 8th ed. Washington, DC: NAS, 1974. 129 pp. IL

Peavy, William, and Warren Peary. *Super Nutrition Gardening: How to Grow Your Own Power-Charged Foods.* Garden City Park, NY: Avery, 1993. 236 pp.

*Pennington, Jean A. T. *Bowes and Church's Food Values of Portions Commonly Used.* Philadelphia, PA: Lippincott-Raven, 1998. 481 pp.

Petrini, Carlo. *Slow Food: The Case for Taste.* New York: Columbia Univ. Press, 2001. 155 pp.

*Postharvest Food Losses in Developing Countries.* Washington, DC: National Academy of Sciences, 1978. 205 pp.

Pothukuchi, Kami, et al. *What's Cooking in Your Food System?* Venice, CA: Community Food Security Coalition, 2002. 123 pp.

Riebel, Linda, and Ken Jacobsen. *Eating to Save the Earth.* Berkeley, CA: Celestial Arts, 2002. 94 pp.

Robbins, John. *Diet for a New America.* Walpole, NH: Stillpoint Publishing, 1987. 423 pp.

———. *Diet for a New World.* New York: Avon Books, 1992. 415 pp.

———. *The Food Revolution: How Your Diet Can Help Save Your Life and the World.* Berkeley, CA: Conari Press, 2001. 449 pp.

Rodale, J. I., and staff, eds. *The Complete Book of Food and Nutrition.* Emmaus, PA: Rodale Books, 1961. 1,054 pp.

*Root, Waverly. *Food: An Authoritative and Visual History and Dictionary of the Foods of the World.* New York: Simon & Schuster, 1980. 602 pp. **BL**

Runyon, Linda. *From Crabgrass Muffins to Pine Needle Tea: A National Wild Food Field Guide.* Shiloh, NJ: Wild Food Company, 2002. 268 pp.

———. *Survival Guide: 50 Nationwide Wild Foods & Medicines.* Pomeroy, WA: Health Research, 1985. 42 pp.

Safron, Jeremy A. *The Raw Truth.* Berkeley, CA: Celestial Arts, 2003. 186 pp.

Schaeffer, Severen L. *Instinctive Nutrition.* Berkeley, CA: Celestial Arts, 1987. 223 pp.

Schmidt, Gerhard. *The Dynamics of Nutrition.* Wyoming, RI: Biodynamic Literature, 1980. 243 pp.

Smith, Bob. "Organic Foods vs. Supermarket Foods: Element Levels." *Journal of Applied Nutrition,* Vol. 45, No. 1 (1993): 35–39.

Swezey, Lauren Bonar, with Linda Lau Anusasananan. "From Seed to Bread: Kids Gain Hands-On Experience with the Staff of Life." *Sunset,* November 1993: 88–91.

Szekely, Edmond Bordeaux. *Scientific Vegetarianism.* International Biogenic Society, 1991. 48 pp.

U.S. Department of Agriculture. *Organically Produced Foods: Nutritive Content.* Beltsville, MD: Agriculture Research Service, National Agricultural Library, Alternative Farming Systems Information Center, 2000. 21 pp. Bibliography.

Walford, Roy L. *The 120-Year Diet.* New York: Simon & Schuster, 1986. 432 pp.

———. *How to Double Your Vital Years.* New York: Simon & Schuster, 1986. 432 pp.

Williams, Roger J. *Nutrition against Disease.* Huntington Beach, CA: International Institute of Natural Health Sciences. 259 pp.

Willett, Walter C. *Eat, Drink, and Be Healthy.* New York: Free Press, 2001. 299 pp.

Wood, Rebecca. *The New Whole Foods Encyclopedia.* New York: Penguin Group, 1999. 426 pp.

Yepsen, Roger B., Jr., ed. *Home Food Systems.* Emmaus, PA: Rodale Press, 1981. 475 pp.

## Food Preservation and Storage

Arnold, Robyn. *Root Cellars.* ASPI Technical Series TP-24. Livingston, KY: ASPI Publications, 1993. 6 pp.

Axtell, Barrie. *Drying Food for Profit: A Guide for Small Businesses.* London: ITDG Publishing, 2002. 120 pp.

Axtell, Barrie, and Alex Bush. *Case Study—Try Drying It!* London: Intermediate Technology Publications, 1991. 63 pp.

Bachmann, Janet. *Small-Scale Oilseed Processing.* Fayetteville, AR: Appropriate Technology Transfer for Rural Areas, National Center for Appropriate Technology, University of Arkansas, Fayetteville, 1998. 9 pp.

*Bubel, Mike and Nancy. *Root Cellaring: Natural Cold Storage of Fruit and Vegetables.* Pownal, VT: Storey, 1991. 304 pp.

*Cornell Extension Bulletin No. 22. Construction and Management of Root Storage Cellars.* Ithaca, NY: New York State College of Agriculture at Cornell University, 1917.

Costenbader, Carol W. *The Big Book of Preserving the Harvest.* Pownal, VT: Storey, 1997. 348 pp.

———. *Preserving Fruits and Vegetables.* Pownal, VT: Storey, 1996. 96 pp.

De Long, Deanna. *How to Dry Foods.* Tucson, AZ: H. P. Books, 1979. 160 pp.

Esterly, Lindsay. "The Latest Addition: A Root Cellar." *Nature's Spirit Newsletter,* Vol. 3, No. 2 (1999): 2 and 13.

Freeman, Hazel. "All About Maple Syrup." *BackHome Magazine,* March/April 2005: 36–38.

———. "The Basics of Making Maple Syrup." *BackHome Magazine,* January/February 2006: 25–27.

Gardeners and Farmers of Terre Vivante. *Keeping Food Fresh.* White River Junction, VT: Chelsea Green, 1999. 197 pp.

Hamilton, Eric. "No-Root-Cellar Root Cellaring." *BackHome Magazine,* Fall 1991: 58–60.

Hertzberg, Ruth, et al. *Putting Food By.* New York: Bantam Books, 1973. 565 pp.

Hobson, Phyllis. *Making and Using Dried Foods.* Pownal, VT: Storey, 1994. 82 pp.

Howard, L. R., et al. "Antioxidant Capacity and Phenolic Content of Spinach as Affected by Genetics and Growing Season." *Journal of Agricultural and Food Chemistry,* Vol. 50, no. 21: 5891–5896.

*Hupping, Carol, and staff of the Rodale Food Center. *Stocking Up III.* Emmaus, PA: Rodale Press, 1986. 627 pp.

Kimball, Herrick C. *The Complete Guide to Making Great Garlic Powder.* Maravia, NY: Whizbang Books, 2003. 39 pp.

Kline, Jeff. *How to Sun Dry Your Food.* Las Trampas, NM: Self-Reliance Foundation (Box 1, Las Trampas, NM 87576), 1983. 100 pp.

Macmaniman, Gen. *Dry It.* Fall City, WA: Living Food Dehydrators, 1973. 58 pp.

McClure, Susan. *Preserving Summer's Bounty.* Emmaus, PA: Rodale Press, 1998. 372 pp.

Miller, Martin W. *Drying Foods at Home.* Leaflet 2785. Division of Agricultural Sciences, Univ. of California (Ag. Extension, 215 N. 1st Street, San Jose, CA 95113), 1975. 20 pp.

*Root Cellars.* Mt. Vernon, KY: ASPI Publications (50 Lair St., Mt. Vernon, KY). Video.

Serafini, Mauro, et al. "Effect of Acute Ingestion of Fresh and Stored Lettuce (*Lactuca sativa*) on Plasma Total Antioxidant Levels in Human Subjects." *British Journal of Nutrition* 88 (2002): 615–623.

Shaffer, Marcella. "Build a Stacked-Timber Root Cellar." *BackHome Magazine,* September/October 1998: 24–27.

"Storage of Organic Apples and Pears," *Agroforestry News,* November 2005: 37–40.

*Twelve Months' Harvest.* San Francisco: Ortho Books Division (Chevron Chemical Co., San Francisco, CA), 1975. 96 pp. Covers canning, freezing, smoking, drying, cheese, cider, soap, and grinding grains. Many good tips.

Vaughn, Reese. *Home Pickling of Olives. Publication 2758.* Oakland, CA: University of California, Division of Agriculture and Natural Resources, 1998. 11 pp.

Walk, Larisa. *A Pantry Full of Sunshine.* Winona, MN: Seldom Scene Productions (Rte. 3, Box 163A), 1997. 61 pp.

Yurk, George K. *Homemade Olive Oil. Publication 2789.* Oakland, CA: University of California, Division of Agriculture and Natural Resources, 1996.

## Fruits, Berries, and Nuts

*Agroforestry News—Peaches.* Devon, UK: Agroforestry Research Trust (46 Hunters Moon, Dartington, Totnes, Devon, TQ96JT, UK).

Bailey, L. H., Jr. *The Apple Tree.* New York: Macmillan, 1922. 117 pp.

———. *Field Notes on Apple Culture.* New York: Orange Judd, 1906. 90 pp.

———. *The Principles of Fruit-Growing.* New York: Macmillan, 1897. 516 pp.

*Baker, Harry. *The Fruit Garden Displayed.* London: Cassell Educational Limited for the Royal Horticultural Society, 1991. 223 pp. Excellent.

Bowling, Barbara L. *The Berry Grower's Companion.* Portland, OR: Timber Press, 2000. 284 pp.

Brickell, Christopher. *Fruit.* New York: Simon & Schuster, 1980. 96 pp.

Brooks, Reid, and Claron Hesse. *Western Fruit Gardening.* Berkeley, CA: University of California Press, 1953. 287 pp. Old but still good.

Chaplin, Lois Trigg. "Sing a Song of Blueberries." *Organic Gardening,* March 1992: 83–89.

"Chestnut Variety Trial Results: 2005." *Agroforestry News,* November 2005: 7–12.

Childers, Norman F., and Paul Eck. *Blueberry Culture.* New Brunswick, NJ: Rutgers University Press, 1966. 378 pp.

Christensen, L. Peter, ed. *Raisin Production Manual.* Oakland, CA: University of California Division of Agriculture and Natural Resources, 2000. 295 pp.

Coble, Parker C. "The Eastern Black Walnut." *White Paper Series.* Gettysburg, PA: Pennsylvania Nut Growers Association (717-334-6876), 2000. 28 pp.

Coit, J. Eliot. *Citrus Fruits.* New York: Macmillan, 1917. 520 pp.

Cord, Fred W. *Bush Fruits.* New York: Macmillan, 1909. 537 pp.

Cox, Jeff. *From Vines to Wines: The Complete Guide to Growing Grapes and Making Your Own Wine.* Pownal, VT: Storey, 1999. 235 pp.

Crandall, Perry C. *Bramble Production: The Management and Marketing of Raspberries and Blackberries.* Binghamton, NY: Food Products Press, an imprint of the Haworth Press, 1995. 213 pp.

Downing, A. J. *The Fruits and Fruit Trees of America.* New York: John Wiley & Sons, 1862. 760 pp.

Edwards, Linda. *Organic Tree Fruit Management.* Keremeos, Canada: Similkameen Okanagan Organic Producers Association (SOOPA, formerly Certified Organic Associations of British Columbia, Box 577, Keremeos, BC V0H 1N0, Canada), 1998. 240 pp.

Eisen, Gustav, Ph.D. *The Fig: Its History, Culture, and Curing.* Washington, DC: Government Printing Office, 1901. 317 pp.

Ferguson, Louise, et al., eds. *Olive Production Manual.* Oakland, CA: University of California, Division of Agriculture and Natural Resources, 1994. 156 pp.

Flores, Barbara Jeanne. *The Great Book of Pears.* Berkeley, CA: Ten Speed Press, 2000. 163 pp.

Fraser, Samuel. *The Strawberry.* New York: Orange Judd, 1926. 120 pp.

Garner, R. J. *The Grafter's Handbook.* New York: Oxford University Press, 1979. 319 pp.

Gould, H. P. *Peach-Growing.* New York: Macmillan, 1918. 426 pp.

Hartmann, Hudson T., et al. *Propagation of Temperate-Zone Fruit Plants.* Davis, CA: University of California Cooperative Extension Service, 1979. 63 pp.

Hemmelgam, Melissa. *NUTrition and Your Health: Missouri Black Walnuts.* Columbia, MO: University of Missouri Center for Agroforestry, n.d. 6 pp.

———. *NUTrition and Your Health: Missouri Chestnuts.* Columbia, MO: University of Missouri Center for Agroforestry, n.d. 6 pp.

———. *NUTrition and Your Health: Missouri Pecans.* Columbia, MO: University of Missouri Center for Agroforestry, n.d. 6 pp.

Hendrickson, A. H. *Prune Growing in California, Bulletin 328.* Berkeley, CA: University of California Press, 1923. 38 pp.

Hendrickson, Robert. *The Berry Book.* Garden City, NY: Doubleday, 1981. 259 pp.

Hessayon, D. G. *The Fruit Expert.* London: Transworld Publishers, 1995. 128 pp.

Huber, Hank. "The Hanging Grapes of Buffalo." *BackHome Magazine,* March/April 2005: 24–25.

Hume, H. H. *The Cultivation of Citrus Fruits.* New York: Macmillan, 1954. 561 pp.

Hunt, Ken, et al. *Growing Chinese Chestnuts in Missouri.* Agroforestry in Action series. Columbia: University of Missouri Center for Agroforestry, 2005. 12 pp.

IMSS. *La Participacion Comunitaria en SALUD.* Mexico: IMSS, 1997. 299 pp.

*James, Theodore, Jr. *How to Select, Grow and Enjoy Fruit, Berries and Nuts in the East and Midwest.* Tucson, AZ: H. P. Books, 1983. 144 pp.

*Kiwifruit Enthusiasts Journal.* Tonasket, WA: Friends of the Trees (P.O. Box 1064, Tonasket, WA 98855), 1992.

Koch, Frank D. *Avocado Grower's Handbook.* Bonsall, CA: Bonsall Publications, 1983. 273 pp.

Kourik, Robert. "Fabulous Figs." *National Gardening,* July/August 1996: 35–40.

Kraft, Ken and Pat. *Fruits for the Home Garden.* New York: Morrow, 1968. 287 pp.

———. *Grow Your Own Dwarf Fruit Trees.* New York: Walker, 1974. 218 pp.

Krautwurst, Terry. "Overwintering Fruit Trees." *BackHome Magazine,* Winter 1996–1997: 62–63.

La Rue, James H., and R. Scott Johnson, eds. *Peaches, Plums and Nectarines: Growing and Handling for Fresh Market.* Oakland, CA: University of California, Division of Agriculture and Natural Resources, 1989. 246 pp.

Logsdon, Gene. *Organic Orcharding: A Grove of Trees to Live In.* Emmaus, PA: Rodale Press, 1981. 415 pp.

Martin, R. Sanford. *How to Prune Fruit Trees.* Published by the author (10535 Las Lunitas Ave., Tujunga, CA 91042), 1978. 90 pp. Best and simplest book on pruning for West Coast gardeners.

McClure, Susan. *Rodale's Successful Organic Gardening: Fruits and Berries.* Emmaus, PA: Rodale Press, 1996. 160 pp.

McEachern, George, and Larry Stein. *Planting and Establishing Pecan Trees.* College Station, TX: Texas Agricultural Extension Service, Texas A&M University System, n.d.

Micke, Warren C., ed. *Almond Production Manual.* Oakland, CA: University of California Division of Agriculture and Natural Resources, 1996. 289 pp.

Miller, G. "Grape Growing Under Glass." *Journal of the Royal Horticultural Society,* February 1963: 85–91.

Moore, S. W. *Practical Orcharding on Rough Lands.* Akron, OH: New Werner, 1911. 289 pp.

*North American Fruit Explorer's Quarterly.* (Henry Converse, 2317 Seneca Ln., Paducah, KY 42001.) Magazine.

Ocean, Suellen. *Acorns and Eat 'Em.* Willits, CA: Ocean-House (28970 Sherwood Rd., Willits, CA 95490), 1993. 86 pp.

Ortho Books Editorial Staff. *All about Citrus and Subtropical Fruits.* Des Moines, IA: Meredith Corporation Ortho Books, 1985. 96 pp.

Otto, Stella. *The Backyard Orchardist: A Complete Guide to Growing Fruit Trees in the Home Garden.* Grawn, MI: Otto Graphics (6893 Sullivan Rd., Grawn, MI 49637), 1993. 250 pp.

Paddock, Whipple. *Fruit Growing in Arid Regions.* New York: Macmillan, 1913. 395 pp.

"Passiflora: Passion Flowers and Passion Fruits." *Agroforestry News,* November 2005: 15–19.

Phillips, Michael. *The Apple Grower: A Guide for the Organic Orchardist.* White River Junction, VT: Chelsea Green Publishing, 2005. 343 pp.

———. "Growing Apples . . . Naturally." *National Gardening,* March/April 1999: 46–50.

Ramos, David E., ed. *Walnut Production Manual.* Oakland, CA: University of California, Division of Agriculture and Natural Resources, 1998. 317 pp.

*Ray, Richard, and Lance Walheim. *Citrus: How to Select, Grow, and Enjoy.* Tucson, AZ: H. P. Books, 1980. 176 pp.

Reed, Brenda H. "How to Grow Grapes." *BackHome Magazine,* March/April 2005: 20–23.

Reich, Lee. "Peewee Kiwis and Other Sweet Delights." *Mother Earth News,* June/July 2004: 74–80.

Reid, William. *Growing Pecans in Missouri.* Agroforestry in Action series. Columbia: MO: University of Missouri Center for Agroforestry, 2000. 14 pp.

———. *Propagating Pecan and Black Walnut in Missouri.* Agroforestry in Action series. University of Missouri Center for Agroforestry, 2001. 10 pp.

Rivers, Thomas. *The Miniature Fruit Garden.* New York: Orange Judd, 1866. 133 pp.

Robinson, J. C. *Bananas and Plantains.* Wallingford, Oxon, UK: CAB International, 1996. 238 pp.

Salloum, Habeeb. "The Versatile Avocado: Mexico's Nutritious Gift to the World," *Countryside and Small Stock Journal,* January/February 2006: 56–58.

Sanders, Rosanne. *The Apple Book.* New York: Philosophical Library, 1988. 142 pp.

Simms, Clive. *Nutshell Guide to Growing Blueberries, Cranberries and Lingonberries.* Woodhurst, UK: Orchard House Books, 2005. 36 pp.

Sunset Books Editorial Staff. *Citrus.* Menlo Park, CA: Sunset Books, 1996. 96 pp.

Swezey, Sean L., et al. *Organic Apple Production Manual.* Oakland, CA: University of California, Division of Agriculture and Natural Resources, 2000. 72 pp.

Taylor, Judith M. *The Olive in California: History of an Immigrant Tree.* Berkeley, CA: Ten Speed Press, 2000. 316 pp.

Thompson, Bruce. *Black Walnuts for Fun and Profit.* Beaverton, OR: Timber Press, 1976. 285 pp.

Tufts, Warren P. *Pruning Deciduous Fruit Trees. Circular 112.* California Agricultural Ext. Service, 1941. 63 pp.

Tukey, Harold Bradford. *Dwarfed Fruit Trees.* Ithaca, NY: Cornell University Press, 1964. 562 pp. Definitive work on the subject.

University of California Extension Service. *Avocado Care in the Home Orchard.* 1975. 3 pp.

Waldo, George F., and Cecil O. Rawlings. *Black Raspberry Growing. Extension Bulletin 750.* Corvallis, OR: Federal Cooperative Extension Service, Oregon State College, 1955. 21 pp.

*Walheim, Lance, and Robert L. Stebbins. *Western Fruit, Berries and Nuts: How to Select, Grow and Enjoy.* Tucson, AZ: H. P. Books (P.O. Box 5367, Tucson, AZ 85703), 1981. 192 pp. Excellent. Worth several lifetimes of experience. Good for all tree raisers—not just Western ones.

Watson, Ben. *Cider Hard and Sweet.* Woodstock, VT: The Countryman Press, 1999. 231 pp.

Waugh, F. A. *Plums and Plum Culture.* New York: Orange Judd, 1910. 371 pp.

*Whealy, Kent, ed. *Fruit, Berry and Nut Inventory,* 3rd ed. Decorah, IA: Seed Savers Exchange, 2001. 560 pp.

Williams, S. R. *Compost Fruit Growing.* London: W. Foulsham, 1961. 126 pp.

Wilson, C. P. H. *Bush Peaches.* Forest Hill, NY: Transatlantic Arts, 1958. 140 pp.

Yepsen, Roger. *Apples.* New York: W. W. Norton, 1994. 255 pp.

## Fukuoka Culture

*Fukuoka, Masanoubu. *The Natural Way of Farming: The Theory and Practice of Green Philosophy.* Tokyo and New York: Japan Publications, 1985. 280 pp.

———. *The One-Straw Revolution.* Emmaus, PA: Rodale Press, 1978. 181 pp. Natural farming from a Japanese philosopher/farmer. One of the few to address a sustainable grain culture.

———. *The Road Back to Nature.* Tokyo and New York: Japan Publications, 1987. 377 pp.

## Gardening

(see also Container Gardening)

Abraham, Doc and Katy. *Green Thumb Wisdom: Garden Myths Revealed!* Pownal, VT: Storey, 1996. 152 pp.

Agate, Elizabeth. *Footpaths.* The Eastern Press, 1994. 192 pp.

Bailey, Liberty H. *The Garden Lover.* Norwood, MA: Macmillan, 1928. 154 pp.

———. *The Horticulturist's Rule-Book.* New York: Macmillan, 1909. 312 pp.

———. *Manual of Gardening.* New York: Macmillan, 1914. 541 pp.

Beard, Henry, et al. *Gardening: A Gardener's Dictionary.* New York: Workman, 1982. 95 pp.

Benjamin, Joan, and Deborah L. Martin, eds. *Great Garden Formulas.* Emmaus, PA: Rodale Press, 1998. 342 pp.

Bieny, D. R. *The Why and How of Home Horticulture.* San Francisco: W. H. Freeman, 1980. 513 pp.

Bradley, Fern Marshall, and Barbara W. Ellis. *Rodale's All-New Encyclopedia of Organic Gardening.* Emmaus, PA: Rodale Press, 1992. 690 pp.

Brenzel, Kathleen Norris, ed. *Sunset Western Garden Book.* Menlo Park, CA: Sunset Books, 2001.

BIBLIOGRAPHY

768 pp. Indispensable descriptions and cultural directions for flowering plants, trees, and landscaping. For West Coast gardeners. Not organic.

Brown, Marc. *Your First Garden Book.* Boston, MA: Little, Brown, and Co., 1991. 48 pp.

Bruce, Hank, and Tomi Jill Folk. *Global Gardening.* Winter Springs, FL: Winner Enterprises, 2001. 288 pp. Growing plants from around the world, issues of hunger, and how to help.

Bubel, Nancy. *52 Weekend Garden Projects.* Emmaus, PA: Rodale Press, 1992. 354 pp.

Campbell, Stu. *Mulch It! A Practical Guide to Using Mulch in the Garden and Landscape.* Pownal, VT: Storey, 2001. 123 pp.

Carr, Anna, et al. *Rodale's Chemical-Free Yard and Lawn.* Emmaus, PA: Rodale Press, 1991. 456 pp.

Carroll, Steven B., and Steven D. Salt. *Ecology for Gardeners.* Portland, OR: Timber Press, 2004. 328 pp.

Creasy, Rosalind. *The Complete Book of Edible Landscaping.* San Francisco: Sierra Club Books, 1982. 379 pp.

———. *The Edible Asian Garden.* Boston, MA: Periplus Editions (HK), 2000. 106 pp.

———. *The Edible French Garden.* Boston, MA: Periplus Editions (HK), 1999. 106 pp.

Dahl, Jurgen. *The Curious Gardener.* Portland, OR: Timber Press, 2004. 264 pp.

Dean, Heather, and Tom Benevento. *Gardening for the Earth and Soul,* Elgin, IL: Brethren Press, 2004. 180 pp.

Denckla, Tanya. *Gardening at a Glance.* Franklin, WV: Wooden Angel Publishing (Wooden Angel Farm, Bldg. 1-A, P.O. Box 869, Franklin, WV 26807), 1991. 272 pp.

———. *The Organic Gardener's Home Reference: A Plant-by-Plant Guide to Growing Fresh, Healthy Food.* Pownal, VT: Garden Way, 1994. 273 pp.

DiSabato-Aust, Tracy. *The Well-Tended Perennial Garden: Planting and Pruning Techniques.* Portland, OR: Timber Press, 1998. 269 pp.

Faust, Joan Lee. *The New York Times Book of Vegetable Gardening.* New York: Quadrangle/The New York Times Book Co., 1975. 282 pp.

*Fine Gardening.* (Rodale Press, 33 E. Minor St., Emmaus, PA 18049.) Magazine.

Fisher, Joe and Dennis. *The Homebrewer's Garden.* Pownal, VT: Storey, 1998. 187 pp.

Foster, Catharine Osgood. *Building Healthy Gardens.* Pownal, VT: Storey, 1989. 279 pp.

*———. *The Organic Gardener.* New York: Random House, 1972. 234 pp. Excellent, chatty, experienced. New England area especially.

Gibson, Eric. *The Grower's Green Book.* Carmichael, CA: New World, 1992. 224 pp.

*Greenprints.* (P.O. Box 1355, Fairview, NC 28730.) Quarterly publication about gardening experiences.

*Growth Point Magazine.* (Horticultural Therapy, Goulds Ground, Vallis Way, Frome, Somerset BA11 3DW, England.) Gardening magazine for the physically handicapped.

Hale, Gill. *The Feng Shui Garden.* Pownal, VT: Storey, 1998. 128 pp.

Hill, Lewis. *Successful Cold-Climate Gardening.* Pownal, VT: Storey, 1987. 308 pp.

*Horticulture.* (Horticulture Association, 755 Boyleston St., Boston, MA 02116.) Magazine.

*HortIdeas.* (750 Black Lick Rd., Gravel Switch, KY 40328.) A monthly report on the latest gardening research, methods, tools, plants, books, and so on. Excellent.

Jobb, Jamie. *My Garden Companion.* San Francisco: Sierra Club Books, 1977. 35 pp. Especially for beginners.

King, Tim. "Garden Early, Harvest Longer." *BackHome Magazine,* March/April 2004: 49–51.

Kraft, Ken, and P. Kraft. *Growing Food the Natural Way.* New York: Doubleday, 1973. 292 pp. California-area orientation.

Langer, Richard W. *Grow It!* New York: Saturday Review Press, 1972. 395 pp.

Leach, Helen. *1,000 Years of Gardening in New Zealand.* Wellington, New Zealand: A. H. & A. W. Reed, 1984. 157 pp.

Loewer, Peter. *Tough Plants for Tough Places.* Emmaus, PA: Rodale Press, 1992. 247 pp.

Marshall, Fern, et al. *The Experts' Book of Garden Hints.* Emmaus, PA: Rodale Press, 1993. 346 pp.

Merrill, Richard, and Joe Ortiz. *The Gardeners' Table: A Guide to Natural Vegetable Growing and Cooking.* Berkeley, CA: Ten Speed Press, 2000. 468 pp.

Morse, Harriet K. *Gardening in the Shade.* Portland, OR: Timber Press, 1962. 242 pp.

Neal, Bill. *Gardener's Latin.* Chapel Hill, NC: Algonquin Books (P.O. Box 2225, Chapel Hill, NC 27515).

Nuñez, Vera K. *Household Gardens: Theoretical Considerations on an Old Survival Strategy.* Report 1. Potatoes in Food Systems Research Series. Lima, Peru: International Potato Center, Training and Communications Department, 1985. 41 pp.

*OG.* (Wiveliscombe, Taunton, UK) Magazine.

Olwell, Carol. *Gardening from the Heart—Why Gardeners Garden.* Berkeley, CA: Antelope Island Press, 1990: 144–152.

*Organic Gardening.* (Rodale Press, 33 E. Minor St., Emmaus, PA 18049.) Magazine.

Patent, Dorothy Hinshaw, and Diane Bilderback. *The Harrowsmith Country Life Book of Garden Secrets.* Charlotte, VT: Camden House, 1991. 349 pp.

Peplow, Elizabeth and Reginald. *In a Monastery Garden.* North Pomfret, VT: David & Charles, 1988. 182 pp.

Perry, Robert L. *Basic Gardening in Florida Sand.* Largo, FL: Florida

Gardening Companion (P.O. Box 896, Largo, FL 33540), 1977. 72 pp.

Pettinger, April, with Brenda Costanzo. *Native Plants in the Coastal Garden: A Guide for Gardeners in the Pacific Northwest.* Portland, OR: Timber Press, 2002. 232 pp.

Pettinger, Dennis R., ed. *California Master Gardener Handbook.* University of California Agricultural and Natural Resources Community Services Publication No. 3382. Oakland, CA: University of California, 2002. 702 pp.

Pleasant, Barbara. *Warm-Climate Gardening.* Pownal, VT: Storey, 1993. 204 pp.

Rahn, James J. *Making the Weather Work for You: A Practical Guide for Gardener and Farmer.* Charlotte, VT: Garden Way, 1979. 205 pp.

Rateaver, Bargyla, and Gylver Rateaver. *The Organic Method Primer Update,* special edition. Published by the authors (P.O. Box 26567, San Diego, CA 92196-0567), 1993. 257 pp. Packed with detailed information, much of it very good.

Reader's Digest. *Ideas for Your Garden.* Pleasantville, NY: The Reader's Digest Association, 1995. 335 pp.

Rickett, Harold W. *Botany for Gardeners.* New York: Macmillan Co., 1957. 236 pp.

Rodale, Robert, ed. *The Basic Book of Organic Gardening.* New York: Ballantine Books, 1971. 377 pp. Condensed information includes 14-day compost and nationwide planting dates.

*———, ed. *The Encyclopedia of Organic Gardening.* Emmaus, PA: Rodale Press, 1959. 1,145 pp.

*———. *How to Grow Fruits and Vegetables by the Organic Method.* Emmaus, PA: Rodale Press. 1961. 926 pp. Two excellent references. Many prefer the encyclopedia format, but we find the second to be more complete.

*Salisbury, E. J. *The Living Garden (or The How and Why of Garden Life).* London: G. Bell & Sons, 1946. 232 pp. An excellent book.

*Seymour, John. *The Self-Sufficient Gardener.* London: Faber and Faber, 1978. 256 pp. Coffee-table size. Seymour has long been a popular back-to-the-land advocate in England, both doing it and writing about it in his own humorous style. His new "productions" are gorgeously illustrated, accurate, and uncluttered.

Smith, Edward C. *The Vegetable Gardener's Bible.* Pownal, VT: Storey, 2000. 309 pp.

Smith, J. Robert, with Beatrice S. Smith. *The Prairie Garden (70 Native Plants).* Madison, WI: University of Wisconsin Press, 1980. 218 pp.

Smith, Marney. *Gardening with Conscience.* New York: Seabury Press, 1981. 86 pp.

Smith and Hawken Books. *The Book of Outdoor Gardening.* New York: Workman, 1996. 513 pp.

Sneed, Dave. "Alaskan Gardening Tips." *Countryside and Small Stock Journal,* January/February 2006: 64.

Sobkoviak, Don and Lois. *The Food Mission: Sustainable Food Production—A Manual of Sustainable Methods of Plant Production Helpful in Meeting Food Needs Everywhere.* Bartlesville, OK: Sand Institutes International. 80 pp.

Solomon, Steve. *Growing Vegetables West of the Cascades: The Complete Guide to Natural Gardening.* Seattle, WA: Sasquatch Books, 2000. 356 pp.

Spedding, Colin and Geoffrey. *The Natural History of the Garden.* Portland, OR: Timber Press, 2003. 245 pp.

Sperry, Neil. *Neil Sperry's Complete Guide to Texas Gardening.* Dallas, TX: Taylor, 1991. 388 pp.

Staff of Successful Gardening. *Successful Gardening.* 2 Vols. Stamford, CT: 1988. Numerous garden crop studies organized into 16 sections.

Sunset Editors. *Vegetable Gardening.* Menlo Park, CA: Sunset Books, 1998. 128 pp.

Tenenbaum, Frances, ed. *Taylor's Guide to Shade Gardening.* Boston: Houghton Mifflin, 1994. 501 pp.

Tiedjens, Victor A. *The Vegetable Encyclopedia and Gardener's Guide.* New York: New Home Library, 1943. 215 pp. Important cultural detailings.

Vasil'yev, I. M. *Wintering of Plants.* Washington, DC: Royer and Royer, 1961. 300 pp.

Vickery, Deborah and James. *Intensive Vegetable Gardening for Profit and Self-Sufficiency.* Washington, DC: U.S. Peace Corps, Information Collection and Exchange, 1981. 158 pp. In English and Spanish.

Wasowski, Sally and Andy. *Native Gardens for Dry Climates.* New York: Clarkson Potter, 1995. 176 pp.

Watkins, Norma. *How to Grow More Vegetables Organically in South Florida.* Miami, FL: Environmental Demonstration Center, Life Lab Division (Miami Dade Community College), 1979. 8 pp. Visit www.mdcc.edu/wolfson/departments/environethics/eehomepage.html and click on Resources.

Wright, Richardson. *The Story of Gardening.* New York: Dodd, Mead & Co., 1934. 475 pp.

Yang, Linda. *Plants for Problem Places: How to Turn Any Difficult Site into a Beautiful Easy-Care Garden.* New York: Houghton Mifflin Co., 1997. 122 pp.

*Year-Round Gardening.* Mt. Vernon, KY: ASPI Publications (50 Lair St., Mt. Vernon, KY 40456). Video.

Yeoman, John. *Gardening Secrets That Time Forgot.* Leighton Buzzard, UK: The Village Guild Ltd., 2004. 293 pp.

Young, Carol L. *What Grows Where?* Published by the author (229 Peninsula Dr., Lake Almanor, CA 96137), 1987. 187 pp.

## General

Rheingold, Howard, ed. *The Millennium Whole Earth Catalog: Access to Tools and Ideas for the Twenty-First Century.* San Francisco: HarperSan Francisco, 1994. 384 pp.

## Global Perspective

Akin, Wallace E. *Global Patterns—Climate, Vegetation and Soils.* Norman, OK: University of Oklahoma Press, 1991. 370 pp.

Anderson, Sarah, ed. *Views from the South: The Effects of Globalization and the WTO on Third World Countries.* Oakland: Food First Books, 2000. 195 pp.

Bennett, Charles F., Jr. *Man and Earth's Ecosystems.* New York: John Wiley & Sons, 1975. 331 pp.

*Brown, Lester R. *State of the World—1990.* New York: W. W. Norton, 1990. 253 pp. Excellent resource tool. Also see this publication for other years. **AL**

———. *The Twenty-Ninth Day.* New York: W. W. Norton, 1978. 363 pp.

Brown, Lester R., Janet Larson, and Bernie Fischlowitz-Roberts. *The Earth Policy Reader.* New York: W. W. Norton & Co., 2002. 304 pp.

———. *Eco-Economy: Building an Economy for the Earth.* New York: W. W. Norton & Co., 2001. 334 pp.

Camp, Sharon L., ed. "The International Human Suffering Index." Washington, DC: Population Crisis Committee, 1987. Glossy chart handout.

Carley, Michael, and Philippe Spapens. *Sharing the World, Sustainable Living and Global Equity in the 21st Century.* New York: St. Martin's Press, 1998. 208 pp.

Carson, Rachel. *Silent Spring.* Boston: Houghton Mifflin. 1962.

Coleman, Alice, et al. *Land-Use Perspectives.* London: The Land Decade Educational Council, 1979. 147 pp.

Conniff, Richard. "Counting Carbons." *Discover,* August 2005: 54–61.

Conservation Foundation. *Agriculture and the Environment in a Changing World Economy.* Washington, DC: The Conservation Foundation, 1986. 66 pp.

Cox, George W., and Michael D. Atkins. *Agricultural Ecology—An Analysis of World Food Production Systems.* San Francisco: W. H. Freeman, 1964. 72 pp.

Dahlberg, Kenneth A. *Beyond the Green Revolution: The Ecology and Politics of Global Agricultural Development.* New York: Plenum Press, 1979. 256 pp.

"Farming a Shrinking Planet." *Christian Science Monitor,* October 28, 1992: 9–12.

*Food and Agriculture Organization of the United Nations. *FAO Production Yearbook—1994.* Rome: FAO, 1995. 243 pp.

Gelbspan, Ross. *The Heat Is On: The Climate Crisis, the Cover-Up, the Prescription.* Cambridge, MA: Perseus Books, 1997, 1998. 278 pp.

Gever, John, et al., eds. *Beyond Oil: The Threat to Food and Fuel in the Coming Decades.* Cambridge, MA: Ballinger Publishing Co., 1986. 306 pp.

Johnson, D. Gale. *World Agriculture in Disarray.* London: Fontana, 1973. 304 pp.

Kendall, Henry, and David Pimentel. "Constraints on the Expansion of the Global Food Supply." *Ambio,* Vol. 23, No. 3, 1994: 198–205.

Knickerbocker, Brad. "Living with the Planet in Mind." *The Christian Science Monitor,* March 3, 1992.

Madeley, John. *Food for All: The Need for a New Agriculture.* New York: Palgrave/St. Martin's Press, 2002. 191 pp.

Mason, Colin. *The 2030 Spike: Countdown to Global Catastrophe.* Sterling, VA: Earthscan Publications, 2003. 250 pp.

Meadows, Donella H. "Population, Poverty, and Planet Earth." *Context,* No. 31 (Spring 1992): 32–35.

*Meadows, Donella H., Dennis L. Meadows, and Jorgen Randers. *Beyond the Limits.* Post Mills, VT: Chelsea Green, 1992. 300 pp.

Nixon, Will. "Can Talking Heads Save an Ailing Planet?" *E Magazine,* May/June 1992: 37–42.

Parson, Edward A. *Protecting the Ozone Layer: Science and Strategy.* New York: Oxford University Press, 2003. 377 pp.

Pimentel, David. *Competition for Land: Development, Food and Fuel.* Boca Raton, FL: Technologies for a Greenhouse-Constrained Society, 1992, 325–348.

———. "Environmental and Economic Benefits of Sustainable Agriculture." In *Socio-Economic and Policy Issues for Sustainable Farming Systems.* Padova, Italy: Cooperativa Amicizia S.r.l., 1993, 4–19.

———. *Food and the Energy Crisis.* Vol. 54, No. 12 (1973: 11.)

———. *Food, Energy, and Climate Change.* 1981, 303–323.

———. *Food, Energy and the Environment.* Vol. 31, 1981, 85–100.

———. "Perspectives on Ecological Integrity," chapter 15 in *The Global Population, Food, and the Environment.* Kluwer Academic Publishers, 1995: 239–253.

———. *World Food, Energy, Man and Environment.* 1975, 5–16.

Pimentel, David, and Marcia Pimentel. *Food, Energy, and Society.* Niwot, CO: University Press of Colorado, 1996. 363 pp.

Rodale, Robert, and Mike McGrath. *Save Three Lives: A Plan for Famine Prevention.* San Francisco: Sierra Club Books, 1991.

Shiva, Vandana. *Biopiracy: The Plunder of Nature and Knowlege.* Boston, MA: South End Press, 1997. 148 pp.

———. *Monocultures of the Mind: Perspectives on Biodiversity and Biotechnology.* New York and London: Zed Books, 1993. 184 pp.

———. *Stolen Harvest: The Hijacking of the Global Food Supply.* Cambridge, MA: South End Press, 2000. 146 pp.

The Sierra Club. *The Case Against the Global Economy.* San Francisco: Sierra Club, 1996. 549 pp.

*Stopping the Coming Ice Age.* Berkeley, CA: Institute for a Future (2000 Center St., Berkeley, CA 94704). 60-minute video.

Thrupp, Lori Ann. *Bittersweet Harvests for Global Supermarkets: Challenges in Latin America's Agricultural Export Boom.* Washington, DC: World Resources Institute, 1995. 202 pp.

*Timeline.* (Palo Alto, CA: The Foundation for Global Community.) Bimonthly publication.

Vogtmann, Hartmut, Engelhard Boehncke, and Inka Frick, eds. *The Importance of Biological Agriculture in a World of Diminishing Resources: Proceedings of the 5th IFOAM International Scientific Conference at the University of Kassel (Germany) August 27–30, 1984.* Witzenhausen, Germany: Verlagsgruppe Weiland, Happ, Burkhard, 1986. 448 pp.

Watt, Kenneth E. F. *Taming the Future: A Revolutionary Breakthrough in Scientific Forecasting.* Davis, CA: The Contextured Web Press, 1992. 233 pp.

World Resources Institute. *World Resources—1990–91.* New York: Oxford University Press, 1990. 383 pp. Also see this publication for other years.

Worldwatch Institute. *The Dispossessed of the Earth: Land Reform and Sustainable Development.* Worldwatch Paper 30. Washington, DC: Worldwatch Institute, 1979. 48 pp.

———. *Vital Signs 2003: The Trends That Are Shaping Our Future.* New York: W.W. Norton & Co., 2003. 153 pp.

WSSA. *For All Generations: Making World Agriculture More Sustainable.* Glendale, CA: OM Publishing, 1997. 642 pp.

## Gourds

Bailey, L. H. *The Garden of Gourds.* New York: Macmillan, 1937. 134 pp.

Bubel, Nancy. "Hordes of Gourds." *Horticulture,* November 1993: 59–64.

*Consumer Tips.* Cooperative Extension, University of California, Vol. 1, No. 4. (November/December 1985).

*The Gourd Book.* Mt. Gilead, OH: Ohio Gourd Society (Box 274, Mt. Gilead, OH 43338), 1979.

Heiser, Charles. *The Gourd Book.* Norman, OK: University of Oklahoma Press, 1979. 248 pp.

Pleasant, Barbara. "Goodness! Gracious! Great Gobs of Gourds!" *Organic Gardening,* March 1992: 32–36.

Rood, Mary Ann. "Growing and Crafting Gourds." *Fine Gardening,* November/December 1991.

## Grains

Bailey, Liberty H., ed. *The Small Grains.* Norwood, MA: Macmillan, 1920. 699 pp.

Basey, Marieta F. "The Grain, the Whole Grain and Nothing but the Grain . . ." *Mother Earth News,* December/January, 2005: 77–83.

Beaven, E. S. *Barley: Fifty Years of Observation and Experiment.* London: Duckworth, 1947. 394 pp.

Board on Science and Technology for International Development, National Research Council. *Lost Crops of Africa,* Vol. 1, *Grains.* Washington, DC: National Academy Press, 1996. 383 pp.

Cavagnaro, David. "Amaranths: Ancient and Modern." *National Gardening,* May/June 1998: 36–40, 74.

Cole, John N. *Amaranth.* Emmaus, PA: Rodale Press, 1979. 311 pp.

Creasy, Rosalind. "The Bread Garden." *Harrowsmith,* September/October 1986: 89–90, 92–96.

Dondlinger, Peter Tracy. *The Book of Wheat: An Economic History and Practical Manual of the Wheat Industry.* New York: Orange Judd, 1919. 369 pp.

Finrock, Dwight C., and Milton D. Miller. *Wild Rice. Division of Agricultural Sciences, Leaflet No. 116.* Davis, CA: University of California, Division of Agricultural Sciences, 1959.

Gorman, Marion. "Gardener's Bread." *Organic Gardening,* December 1988: 53–54.

Granatstein, David. *Amber Waves.* Pullman, WA: College of Agriculture and Home Economics Research Center, Washington State University, 1992. 82 pp.

Hunt, Thomas F. *The Cereals in America.* New York: Orange Judd, 1912. 421 pp.

Jarde, Auguste. *Les Céréales dans l'Antiquité Grecque.* Paris: E. De Boccard, 1925. 237 pp.

The Jefferson Institute. "Buckwheat: A Versatile Short-Season Crop." *Alternative Crop Guide.* Columbia, MO: The Jefferson Institute, 2002.

———. "Pearl Millet: A New Crop Option for Sandy Soils or Other Moisture-Limited Conditions." *Alternative Crop Guide.* Columbia, MO: The Jefferson Institute, 2002.

Leonard, Thom. "Staff of Life." *Organic Gardening,* December 1988: 46–51.

*Leonard, Warren H., and John H. Martin. *Cereal Crops.* New York: Macmillan, 1963. 824 pp. **AL**

**The Living Land.* Palo Alto, CA: Foundation for Global Community, 1999. Video. **BL**

*Logsdon, Gene. *Small-Scale Grain Raising.* Emmaus, PA: Rodale Press, 1977. 305 pp. **BL**

Mangelsdorf, Paul C. *Corn: Its Origin, Evolution and Improvement.* Cambridge, MA: The Belknap Press of Harvard University Press, 1974. 262 pp.

Mangelsdorf, P. C., and R. G. Reeves. *The Origin of Indian Corn and Its Relatives.* College Station, TX: Texas Agricultural Experiment Station, 1939. 315 pp.

Manning, Edna. "Ancient Grains Revisited." *BackHome Magazine* January/February 2004: 52–53.

Montgomery, E. G. *The Corn Crops.* New York: Macmillan, 1916. 347 pp.

Paterson, William G. R., ed. *Farm Crops: Grain Crops.* Vol. 1,

London: The Gresham Publishing Co., Ltd., 1925. 356 pp.

Piper, Jon K., ed. "A Grain Agriculture Fashioned in Nature's Image: The Work of the Land Institute." *Great Plains Research,* Vol. 3, No. 2, (1993): 249–272.

———. *The Land Institute Research Report, Summary of Work to Develop Mixtures of Perennial Seed Crops Using the Prairie Ecosystem as Standard.* Salina, KS: The Land Institute (2440 E. Water Well Rd., Salina, KS 67401). 39 pp.

———. "Soil Water and Nutrient Change in Stands of Three Perennial Crops." *Soil Science Society of America Journal* (677 S. Segoe Rd., Madison, WI 53711), Vol. 57, No. 2 (March–April 1993).

Rachie, Kenneth, and J. V. Majmudar. *Pearl Millet.* University Park, PA: Pennsylvania State University Press, 1980. 307 pp.

Rodale, Robert. *Amaranth Round-Up.* Emmaus, PA: Rodale Press, 1977. 48 pp.

Schaller, Lorenz K. *What's Up with Triticale?* Ojai, CA: Kusa Seed Research Foundation (P.O. Box 761, Ojai, CA), 2000. 9 pp.

Swezey, Lauren Bonar. "From Seed to Bread." *Sunset,* November 1993: 88–91.

USDA. *Classification of American Wheat Varieties.* Washington, DC: Government Printing Office, 1922. 238 pp.

USDA. *The Basis for the Improvement of American Wheats.* Washington, DC: Government Printing Office, 1900. 87 pp.

Wallace, Henry A., and Earl N. Bressman. *Corn and Corn Growing.* New York: John Wiley & Sons, 1937. 436 pp.

Willis, Harold. *How to Grow Top Quality Corn.* Madison, WI: A-R Editions, 1984. 58 pp.

## Grasses

Barnes, Robert F., et al., eds. *Forages: An Introduction to Grassland Agriculture.* Vol. 1. Ames, IA: Iowa State Press, 2003. 556 pp.

Fe, John. *The Encyclopedia of Ornamental Grasses.* Emmaus, PA: Rodale Press, 1992. 186 pp.

Hitchcock, A. S. *Manual of the Grasses of the United States.* Washington, DC: U.S. Department of Agriculture, Government Printing Office, 1935. 1,040 pp.

Hopkins, Alan, ed. *Grass, Its Production and Utilization.* Oxford, England: Blackwell Science, 2000. 440 pp.

Ondra, Nancy J. *Grasses: Versatile Partners for Uncommon Garden Design.* North Adams, MA: Storey Publishing, 2002. 143 pp.

Packard, Stephen, and Cornelia Mutel, eds. *The Tallgrass Restoration Handbook.* Covelo, CA: Island Press, 1997. 463 pp.

Shaw, Thomas. *Grasses and How to Grow Them.* St. Paul, MN: Webb Publishing Co., 1903.

Shirley, Shirley. *Restoring the Tallgrass Prairie: An Illustrated Manual for Iowa and the Upper Midwest.* Iowa City, IA: University of Iowa Press, 1994. 330 pp.

Soil Conservation Society of America. *Warm-Season Grasses: Balancing Forage Programs in the Northeast and Southern Corn Belt.* Ankeny, IA: Soil and Water Conservation Society (7515 NE Ankeny Rd., Ankeny, IA 50021), 1986. 35 pp.

Staten, H. W. *Grasses and Grassland Farming.* New York: Devin-Adir, 1958. 319 pp.

*U.S. Department of Agriculture. *Grass: The Yearbook of Agriculture 1948.* Washington, DC: U.S. Government Printing Office, 1948. 892 pp.

## Greenhouse Culture

Abraham, George and Katy. *Organic Gardening Under Glass.* Emmaus, PA: Rodale Press, 1975. 308 pp.

Anderson, Phyllis. "Gardening Under a Roomy Tent You Make with Shadecloth or Plastic over PVC Pipe." *Sunset* (Southern California edition), March 1980: 200–201.

*Antill, David. *Gardening Under Protection.* Wakefield, England: EP Publishing, 1978. 72 pp.

Aquatias, A. *Intensive Culture of Vegetables.* Harrisville, NH: Solar Survival Press (Harrisville, NH 03450), 1978. 129 pp. Reprint from 1913 on raising food under glass.

Arthurs, Kathryn L. *Greenhouse Gardening.* Menlo Park, CA: Lane Publishing Co., 1976. 96 pp.

Bailey, L. H. *The Forcing Book.* New York: Macmillan, 1903. 259 pp.

———. *The Nursery Manual.* New York: Macmillan, 1923. 456 pp.

Chase, J. L. H. *Cloche Gardening.* London: Faber and Faber, 1948. 195 pp. A classic.

Colebrook, Binda. *Winter Gardening in the Maritime Northwest.* Arlington, WA: Tilth Association (Rte. 2, Box 190-A, Arlington, WA 98223), 1977. 128 pp.

Coleman, Eliot. "The All-Season Covered Garden." *Country Journal* September/October 1992: 37–51.

———. *Four-Season Harvest.* White River Junction, VT: Chelsea Green, 1999. 234 pp.

———. *The New Organic Grower's Four-Season Harvest.* Post Mills, VT: Chelsea Green, 1992. 212 pp.

Fisher, Rick, and Bill Yanda. *The Food and Heat Producing Solar Greenhouse.* Santa Fe, NM: John Muir Publications, 1976. 161 pp. Detailed.

Frazier, Jack. *Green Winters: The Solar-Heated Walk-In Season Extender Construction Manual.* Theodosia, MO: Ozark Exotica (Rte. 3, Box 500, Theodosia, MO 65761), 1990. 13 pp.

Hodgson, Larry. "The Greenhouse Effect." *Organic Gardening,* January/February 2001: 40–48.

Lawrence, William J. C. *Better Glasshouse Crops.* London: Allen & Unwin, 1949. 57 pp.

———. *Science and the Glasshouse.* London: Oliver & Boyd, 1950. 175 pp.

Mansouri, Thomas, and Alain Guinebault. "Passive Solar Architecture for Mountain Agriculture,"

*LEISA Magazine,* March 2005: 22–23.

McCullagh, James C., ed. *The Solar Greenhouse Book.* Emmaus, PA: Rodale Press, 1978. 328 pp.

Moore, Steve. *Passive Solar Greenhouse: Design, Construction and Operation.* Spring Grove, PA: Harmony Essentials, 2003. 72 pp.

Moore, Steve and Carol. "Inside a Passive Solar Greenhouse, Crops Thrive Both Winter and Summer." *Growing for Market,* December 1999: 10–12.

*Nearing, Helen and Scott. *Building and Using Our Sun-Heated Greenhouse: Grow Vegetables All Year Round.* Charlotte, VT: Garden Way, 1977. 148 pp.

Nelson, Kennard S. *Flower and Plant Production in the Greenhouse.* Danville, IL: Interstate Publishers, 1991. 220 pp.

Poisson, Leandre, and Gretchen Vogel. *Solar Gardening: Growing Vegetables Year-Round the American Intensive Way.* White River Junction, VT: Chelsea Green, 1994. 267 pp.

Rieke, Paul E., and Darryl D. Warncke. *Greenhouse Soils.* Chestertown, MD: LaMotte Chemical Products Co., 1975. 36 pp.

## GROW BIOINTENSIVE
(see also Biointensive)

Belsie, Laurent. "Future Farms: Bigger, and Possibly Better, Food Suppliers. Intensive 'Micro-Farming' May Help Fill Tables in Third World." *The Christian Science Monitor,* October 16, 1987.

Griffin, J. M., et al. *Growing and Gathering Your Own Fertilizers.* Willits, CA: Ecology Action, 1988. 140 pp. See Appendix D for information on night soil composting.

Jeavons, John C. "New Ways from Old." *Cry California,* Winter 1973–74.

MacFadyne, J. Tevere, "The Call to Dig." *Horticulture,* March 1985: 38.

"Mulching, Living Mulch and Double Digging." Willits, CA: Ecology Action, 1999. Information sheet. 2 pp. **BL**

"Roots in the Soil." Willits, CA: Ecology Action, 1997. Information sheet. **BL**

Stone, Pat. "John Jeavons: Digging Up the Future." *Mother Earth News,* January/February 1990: 45.

Tonge, Peter. "Feeding the World." *The Christian Science Monitor,* October 16, 1987.

## *Health*

Balch, James F. and Phyllis A. *Prescription for Nutritional Healing.* Garden City, NY: Avery, 1990. 368 pp.

Barbieri, Terry. "Protecting Your Home from Mold." *BackHome Magazine,* May/June 2003: 37–39.

Batmanghelidj, F. *Water: For Health, for Healing, for Life.* New York: Warner Books, 2003. 284 pp.

———. *Your Body's Many Cries for Water.* Falls Church, VA: Global Health Solutions, 1995. 182 pp.

Buhner, Stephen Harrod. *Herbal Antibiotics: Natural Alternatives for Treating Drug-Resistant Bacteria.* Pownal, VT: Storey Books, 1999. 135 pp.

Burns, A. August, et al. *Donde No Hay Doctor para Mujeres: Un Manual para la Salud de la Mujer.* Berkeley, CA: The Hesperian Foundation, 1999. 581 pp.

———. *Where Women Have No Doctor: A Health Guide for Women.* Berkeley, CA: The Hesperian Foundation, 1997. 583 pp.

Chevallier, Andrew. *The Encyclopedia of Medicinal Plants.* New York: DK Publishing, 1996. 336.

DesMaisons, Kathleen. *Potatoes Not Prozac.* New York, NY: Fireside, 1998. 252 pp.

Dickson, Murray. *Donde No Hay Dentista.* Berkeley, CA: Hesperian Foundation, 2005. 320 pp.

———. *Where There Is No Dentist.* Berkley, CA: Hesperian Foundation, 2004. 238 pp.

D'Orazio, Veronica. *Gardener's Yoga.* Seattle: Sasquatch Books, 2006. 63 pp.

Finnegan, John. *The Facts about Fats.* Berkeley, CA: Celestial Arts, 1993. 130 pp.

Garcia, Hernán, Antonio Sierra, and Gilberto Balám. *Wind in the Blood: Mayan Healing and Chinese Medicine.* Berkeley, CA: North Atlantic Books, 1999. 283 pp.

*The Gerson Therapy.* Bonita, CA: The Gerson Institute (P.O. Box 430, Bonita, CA 91908). Information brochure.

Haas, Elson M. *Staying Healthy with Nutrition,* revised ed. Berkeley, CA: Celestial Arts, 2006. 1,140 pp.

———. *Staying Healthy with the Seasons.* Berkeley, CA: Celestial Arts, 1981. 242 pp.

Haas, Elson M., and Eleonora Manzolini. *A Cookbook for All Seasons.* Berkeley, CA: Celestial Arts, 1995. 251 pp.

*Healing Newsletter.* Bonita, CA: The Gerson Institute (P.O. Box 430, Bonita, CA 91908), 1989. Vol. 5, No. 2.

The Hesperian Foundation, P.O. Box 11577, Berkeley, CA 94712-2577. Publications on self-help medical approaches.

Howard, Albert. *Farming and Gardening for Health or Disease.* London: Faber and Faber, 1945. 282 pp.

Keville, Kathi. "How to Make Poultices and Compresses." *Vegetarian Times/Well-Being Magazine,* No. 48.

Klein, Susan. *A Book for Midwives: A Manual for Traditional Birth Attendants and Community Midwives.* Berkeley, CA: The Hesperian Foundation, 1995. 520 pp.

———. *Un Libro para Parteras: Una Guia para Comadronas y Parteras Tradicionales.* Berkeley, CA: The Hesperian Foundation, 1998. 508 pp.

Kneipp, Sebastian. *The Kneipp Cure.* New York: The Nature Cure Publishing Co., 1949.

*The Life Science Health System: Part XIV. Common Illnesses and Diseases and How Hygienic Living*

*Can Help.* Austin, TX: Life Science Institute, 1986: 1,509–1,524.

Mars, Brigitte. *Natural First Aid.* Pownal, VT: Storey Books, 1999. 137 pp.

Ogren, Thomas Leo. *Allergy-Free Gardening: The Revolutionary Guide to Healthy Landscaping.* Berkeley, CA: Ten Speed Press, 2000. 267 pp.

Pitchford, Paul. *Healing with Whole Foods: Oriental Traditions and Modern Nutrition.* Berkeley, CA: North Atlantic, 1993. 705 pp.

Pizzorno, Joseph, *Total Wellness.* Rocklin, CA: Prima, 1996. 419 pp.

Poxiletik, Syunal. *Plantas Medicinales.* Mexico: Instituto Mexicano del Seguro Social, 1992. 73 pp.

Prevention Magazine Health Books. *The Complete Book of Cancer Prevention.* Emmaus, PA: Rodale Press, 1988. 562 pp.

Roberts, Wayne, Rod MacRae, and Lori Stahlbrand. *Real Food for a Change.* Random House of Canada, 1999. 243 pp.

Ross, Julia. *The Mood Cure.* New York: Viking, 2002. 387 pp.

Schwarzbein, Diana. *The Schwarzbein Principle: The Truth about Losing Weight, Being Healthy, and Feeling Young.* Deerfield Beach, FL: Health Communications, 1999. 364 pp.

Sears, Barry. *Enter the Zone: A Dietary Road Map.* New York: Regan Books, 1995. 286 pp.

Sehnert, Keith W. *How to Be Your Own Doctor . . . Sometimes.* New York: Putnam, 1985.

Simpson, Harold N. *Unhealthy Food = Unhealthy People.* Chicago: Peter Jon Simpson, 1994. 117 pp.

Szekely, Edmond Bordeaux. *The Essene Way: Biogenic Living.* Matsqui, Canada: I.B.S. International, 1989. 184 pp.

———. *Search for the Ageless.* Vol. 1, *My Unusual Adventures on the Five Continents in Search for the Ageless.* Nelson, Canada: International Biogenic Society (P.O. Box 849, Nelson, BC V1L 6A5, Canada), 1977. 211 pp.

Tourles, Stephanie. *Natural Foot Care.* Pownal, VT: Storey, 1998. 187 pp.

Voisin, André. *Soil, Grass and Cancer.* Austin, TX: Acres U.S.A., 1999. 370 pp.

Walker, N. W. *Fresh Vegetable and Fruit Juices.* Prescott, AZ: Norwalk Press (P.O. Box 12260, Prescott, AZ 86304-2260), 1970. 118 pp.

Warburg, Otto. *The Prime Cause and Prevention of Cancer.* Trans. Dean Burk. Bethesda, MD: National Cancer Institute, 1969. 15 pp.

*Werner, David. *Donde no Hay Doctor: Una Guia para los Campesinos Que Viven Lejos de los Centros Médicos.* Berkeley, CA: The Hesperian Foundation, 1995. 455 pp.

———. *Where There Is No Doctor: A Village Health Care Handbook.* Berkeley, CA: The Hesperian Foundation, 1992. 446 pp. **BL**

*———. *Helping Health Workers Learn.* Palo Alto, CA: The Hesperian Foundation (Box 1692, Palo Alto, CA 94302), 1982. 573 pp. **BL**

## Hedges

*Brooks, Alan. *Hedging: A Practical Handbook,* 3rd ed. Wallingford, UK: British Trust for Conservation Volunteers, 1988. 120 pp. Excellent book on the practical techniques needed to establish living fences.

Dowdeswell, W. H. *Hedgerows and Verges.* London: Allen and Unwin, 1987. 190 pp.

Elliott, Charles. "The Age of Hedges." *Horticulture,* August/September 1993.

Hart, Edward. *Hedge Laying and Fencing—The Countryman's Art Explained.* Wellingborough, Northamptonshire, England: Thorsons, 1981. 128 pp.

Kuchelmeister, Guido. *Hedges for Resource-Poor Land Users in Developing Countries.* Eschborn, Germany: Deutsche Gesellschaft für Technische Zusammenarbeit (Postfach 5180, D-65726 Eschborn), 1989. 256 pp.

*White, John T. *Hedgerow.* New York: William Morrow, 1980. 46 pp.

## Herbs

Adam, Katherine L. *Lavender Production, Products, Markets, and Entertainment Farms: Value Added Processing Guide.* Fayetteville, AR: ATTRA, 2004. 13 pp.

Barclay, Gwen, and Madalene Hill. "Hold That Flavor." *The Herb Companion,* October/November 2000: 34–37.

Bass, Ruth. *Herbal Breads.* Pownal, VT: Storey, 1996. 63 pp.

———. *Herbal Salads.* Pownal, VT: Storey, 1996. 63 pp.

———. *Herbal Soups.* Pownal, VT: Storey, 1996. 63 pp.

———. *Herbal Sweets.* Pownal, VT: Storey, 1996. 63 pp.

———. *Mushrooms Love Herbs.* Pownal, VT: Storey, 1996. 63 pp.

———. *Onions Love Herbs.* Pownal, VT: Storey, 1996. 63 pp.

———. *Peppers Love Herbs.* Pownal, VT: Storey, 1996. 63 pp.

———. *Tomatoes Love Herbs.* Pownal, VT: Storey, 1996. 63 pp.

Bender, Richard W. *Herbal Bonsai: Practicing the Art with Fast-Growing Herbs.* Mechanicsburg, PA: Stackpole Books, 1996. 100 pp.

Blose, Nora, and Dawn Cusick. *Herb Drying Handbook.* New York: Sterling, 1993. 96 pp.

Bremness, Lesley. *Herbs: The Visual Guide to More Than 700 Herb Species from around the World.* New York: DK Publishing, 1994. 304 pp.

Brown, Deni. *New Encyclopedia of Herbs and Their Uses.* London: DK, 2001. 448 pp.

Byers, Dorie. *Herbal Remedy Gardens.* Pownal, VT: Storey, 1999. 219 pp.

Castleman, Michael. *The Healing Herbs: The Ultimate Guide to the Curative Power of Nature's Medicines.* Emmaus, PA: Rodale Press, 1991. 436 pp.

Cech, Richo. *Making Plant Medicine.* Williams, OR: Horizon Herbs, 2000. 282 pp.

Davies, Jill Rosemary. *Milk Thistle.* Boston, MA: Element Books, 2000. 57 pp.

DeBaggio, Thomas. "Growing Herbs from Seed." *The Herb Companion,* October/November 1988: 9–13.

Elliott, Brook. "Make Your Own Herbal Medicines." *Mother Earth News,* June/July 2004: 82–85.

*Foster, Gertrude B., et al. *Park's Success with Herbs.* Greenwood, SC: George W. Park Seed Co., 1980. 192 pp.

Foster, Steven. *Echinacea: Nature's Immune Enhancer.* Rochester, VT: Healing Arts Press, 1991. 150 pp.

———. *Herbs for Your Health.* Loveland, CO: Interweave Press, 1996. 121 pp.

Foster, Steven, and Varro E. Tyler. *Tyler's Honest Herbal.* New York: Haworth Press, 1999. 442 pp.

Grieve, M. *A Modern Herbal.* London: Tiger, 1994. 912 pp.

Hartung, Tammi. *Growing 101 Herbs That Heal.* Pownal, VT: Storey, 2000. 250 pp.

*The Herb Companion.* (243 E. 4th St., Loveland, CO 80537.) Magazine.

Herzberger, Heidi. "Liquid Herbs." *The Herb Companion,* April/May 1998: 52–54.

Hobbs, Christopher. *Ginkgo: Elixir of Youth.* Santa Cruz, CA: Botanica Press, 1995. 80 pp.

———. *Milk Thistle: The Liver Herb.* Loveland, CO: Botanica Press, 1984. 32 pp.

———. *St. John's Wort: The Mood Enhancing Herb.* Loveland, CO: Botanica Press, 1997. 176 pp.

———. *Usnea: The Herbal Antibiotic and Other Medicinal Lichens.* Capitola, CA: Botanica Press, 1990. 20 pp.

———. *Valerian: The Relaxing and Sleep Herb.* Capitola, CA: Botanica Press, 1993. 71 pp.

Hoffmann, David L. *The Herb User's Guide.* Rochester, VT: Thorsons, 1987. 240 pp.

———. *The New Holistic Herbal.* Rockport, MA: Element, 1992. 284 pp.

Hollis, Joe. "Chinese Medicinal Herbs." *The Permaculture Activist,* June 1996: 22–24.

Hylton, William H., ed. *The Rodale Herb Book.* Emmaus, PA: Rodale Press, 1974. 653 pp.

Keville, Kathy. "A Guide to Harvesting." Part 2 in the Herbal Craftsman. Herb Farm (14648 Pear Tree Ln., Nevada City, CA 95959), n.d. 3 pp.

———. "Herbal Help for the Respiratory Tract." *Vegetarian Times Magazine,* February 1988.

———. "Herbal Tinctures, Everything You Wanted to Know . . ." *Vegetarian Times/Well Being,* No. 49.

———. "Herbs for the Immune System." *Herbs! Magazine,* 13–16.

———. *The Illustrated Herb Encyclopedia.* Mallard Press, 1991. 224 pp.

———. "Make Your Herbal First Aid Kit." *Well-Being Magazine,* No. 30, 1978.

———. "Salves—Making and Keeping Your Own." *Vegetarian Times/Well Being,* No. 47. (Or write to Herb Farm, 14684 Pear Tree Ln., Nevada City, CA 95959).

———. "Say Goodbye to Colds and Flu." *Vegetarian Times Magazine,* February 1988.

Kowalchick, Claire, et al. *Rodale's Encyclopedia of Herbs.* Emmaus, PA: Rodale Press, 1987. 545 pp.

Lima, Patrick. *The Harrowsmith Illustrated Book of Herbs.* Camden East Ontario, Canada: Camden House, 1986. 175 pp.

Mabey, Richard. *The New Age Herbalist.* New York: Collier Books, 1988. 288 pp.

Mackin, Jeanne. *The Cornell Book of Herbs and Edible Flowers.* Ithaca, NY: Cornell Cooperative Extension, 1993. 104 pp.

Maine, Sandy. *Creating an Herbal Bodycare Business.* Pownal, VT: Storey, 1999. 155 pp.

Marcin, Marietta Marshall. *Herbal Tea Gardens: 22 Plans for Your Enjoyment and Well-Being.* Pownal, VT: Storey, 1999. 187 pp.

McClure, Susan. *The Herb Gardener.* Pownal, VT: Storey, 1996. 236 pp.

McLeod, Judith A. *Lavender, Sweet Lavender.* Kenthurst, Australia: Kangaroo Press, 1989. 120 pp.

McNaughton, Virginia. *Lavender: The Grower's Guide.* Portland, OR: Timber Press, 2000. 180 pp.

Miller, Amy Bess. *Shaker Medicinal Herbs.* Pownal, VT: Storey, 1998. 215 pp.

Mowrey, Daniel B. *Proven Herbal Blends: A Rational Approach to Prevention and Remedy.* Lehi, UT: Cormorant Books (P.O. Box 386, Lehi, UT 84043), 1986. 46 pp.

Nuzzi, Debra. *Pocket Herbal Reference Guide.* Santa Cruz, CA: The Crossing Press, 1992. 138 pp.

Ody, Penelope. *Healing with Herbs.* Pownal, VT: Storey, 1999. 160 pp.

Oppenheimer, Betty. *Gifts for Herb Lovers.* Pownal, VT: Storey, 1997. 123 pp.

Oster, Maggie. *Herb Mixtures and Spicey Blends.* Pownal, VT: Storey, 1996. 156 pp.

Phillips, Harriet Flannery. "Herbal Ground Covers: Useful plants for Problem Areas." *The Herb Companion,* June/July 1997: 36–41.

Phillips, Roger, and Nicky Foy. *The Random House Book of Herbs: How to Grow or Gather Herbal Plants and Use Them for Cooking.* New York: Random House, 1990. 192 pp.

Pilarski, Michael. *Resource Guide to Sustainable Wildcrafting and Medicinal Herbs in the Pacific Northwest.* Bellingham, WA: Friends of the Trees Society, 2000. 82 pp.

Proctor, Peter. *Grasp the Nettle.* New Zealand: Random House New Zealand, 1997. 176 pp.

Romm, Aviva, and Tracy Romm. *ADHD Alternatives.* Pownal, VT: Versa Press, 2001. 149 pp.

Shores, Sandie. *Growing and Selling Fresh-Cut Herbs.* Pownal, VT: Storey, 1999. 453 pp.

Smith, Ed. *Therapeutic Herb Manual: The Therapeutic Administration of Medicinal Herb*

BIBLIOGRAPHY

*Compounds.* Williams, OR: Herb Farm (20260 Williams Hwy, Williams, OR), 1997. 65 pp.

St. Clare, Debra. *The Herbal Medicine Cabinet: Preparing Natural Remedies at Home.* Berkeley, CA: Celestial Arts, 1997. 150 pp.

Sturdivant, Lee, and Tim Blakley. *Medicinal Herbs in the Garden, Field and Marketplace.* Friday Harbor, WA: San Juan Naturals, 1999. 323 pp.

Sunset Editors. *How to Grow Herbs.* Menlo Park, CA: Sunset Books, 1974. 80 pp.

Tierra, Lesley. *The Herbs of Life: Health and Healing Using Western and Chinese Techniques.* Freedom, CA: The Crossing Press, 1992. Food as medicine, natural living, and herbs from East and West.

Tierra, Michael. *Planetary Herbology.* Santa Fe, NM: Lotus Press, 1988. 485 pp.

———. *The Way of Herbs.* New York: Pocket Books, 1990. Excellent guide to herbal health and lifestyle.

Tolley, Emelie, et al. *Herbs, Gardens, Decorations and Recipes.* New York: Crown, 1985. 244 pp.

Tourles, Stephanie. *The Herbal Body Book.* Pownal, VT: Storey, 1994. 122 pp.

Tyler, Varro E., and James E. Robbers. *Tyler's Herbs of Choice.* New York: Haworth Press, 1999. 287 pp.

van Wyk, Ben-Erik, and Michael Wink. *Medicinal Plants of the World.* Portland, OR: Timber Press, 2004. 480 pp.

Vickers, Lois. *The Scented Lavender Book.* Dawsonville, GA: Little Brown, 1991. 80 pp.

Wallis, Gail. "Herbal Skin Care." *The Herb Companion,* April/May 1992.

Wright, Robert R. "Ginseng and Goldenseal." *Countryside and Small Stock Journal,* March/April 1996: 28–29.

## High-Altitude Food Raising

Allen, Judy. "Endless Summer." *National Gardening,* October 1989: 36–39, 50–51.

———. "A Mountain Legend." *National Gardening,* November 1987: 24–27.

———. "Mountain Top Gardening." *National Gardening,* September 1985: 14–18.

———. "Seedlings Under Snow." *National Gardening,* November 1986: 12–13.

———. "Undercover Report." *National Gardening,* September 1986: 18–19.

Coleman, Clara. "My Rocky Mountain Winter Garden." *Mother Earth News,* December/January 2004: 24–25.

Jodha, N. S., M. Banskota, and Teg Partap. *Sustainable Mountain Agriculture.* Vol. 1, *Perspectives and Issues.* Mohan Primlani for Oxford & IBH (Pvt. Ltd., 66 Janpath, New Delhi 110 001, India), 1992. 389 pp.

———. *Sustainable Mountain Agriculture.* Vol. 2, *Farmers' Strategies and Innovative Approaches.* New Delhi, India: Mohan Primlani for Oxford and IBH, 1992. 389 pp.

*Mountain Agriculture.* Vol. 4, No. 1 (March 1988). Information for low external input agriculture (P.O. Box 64, 3830 AB Leusden, The Netherlands). An excellent magazine. 24 pp.

*Rocky Mountain Gardener.* (403 N. Pine, Gunnison, CO 81230.) Quarterly.

Weinberg, July. *Growing Food in the High Desert.* Santa Fe, NM: Sunstone Press, 1985. 91 pp.

## History

Bender, Barbara. *Farming in Prehistory.* London: John Baker, 1975.

Buchanan, Keith. *Transformation of the Chinese Earth.* New York: Praeger, 1970. 335 pp.

Burrill, George C., and James R. Nolfi. *Land, Bread, and History: A Research Report on the Potential for Food Self-Sufficiency in Vermont.* Burlington, VT: Center for Studies in Food Self-Sufficiency, Vermont Institute of Community Involvement, 1976. 93 pp.

Dazhong, Wen, and David Pimentel. "Seventeenth Century Organic Agriculture in China: I. Cropping Systems in Jiaxing Region." *Human Ecology,* Vol. 14, No. 1 (1986): 1–14.

———. "Seventeenth Century Organic Agriculture in China: II Energy Flows through an Agroecosystem in Jiaxing Region." Vol. 14, No. 1, 1986, 15–28.

Doherty, Catherine de Hueck. *Apostolic Farming.* Combermere, Canada: Madonna House Publications (Combermere, ON K0J 1L0, Canada), n.d. 22 pp.

Fenton, Carroll Lane, and Herminie B. Kitchen. *Plants That Feed Us: The Story of Grains and Vegetables.* New York: John Day, 1956. 95 pp.

Hanson, Victor Davis. *Fields Without Dreams.* New York: Free Press, 1997. 289 pp.

———. *The Other Greeks: The Family Farm and the Agrarian Roots of Western Civilization.* Berkeley, CA: University of California Press, 1999. 566 pp.

———. *Warfare and Agriculture in Classical Greece.* Berkeley, CA: University of California Press, 1998. 281 pp.

Huxley, Anthony. *An Illustrated History of Gardening.* New York: Paddington Press, 1978. 352 pp.

*King, F. H. *Farmers of Forty Centuries.* Emmaus, PA: Rodale Press, 1972. 441 pp. **IL**

MacNeish, Richard S. *The Origins of Agriculture and Settled Life.* Norman, OK: University of Oklahoma Press, 1992. 433 pp.

Mann, Albert Russell. *Beginnings in Agriculture.* New York: Macmillan, 1926.

Matheny, Ray T., and Deanne L. Gurr. "Variation in Prehistorical Agricultural Systems of the New World." *Annual Review of Anthropology* 12, 1983: 79–103.

Miller, Naomi, and Kathryn Gleason. *The Archaeology of Garden and Field.* Philadelphia: University of Pennsylvania Press, 1994. 221 pp.

Nabham, Gary Paul. *Cultures of Habitat: On Nature, Culture, and Story.* Washington, DC: Counterpoint, 1997. 338 pp.

Needham, Joseph. *Science and Civilization in China.* Vol. VI:2, *Biology and Biological Technology: Agriculture.* Cambridge, UK: Cambridge University Press, 1984. 724 pp.

Ponting, Clive. *A Green History of the World: The Environment and the Collapse of Great Civilizations.* New York: Penguin, 1991. 430 pp.

Rasmussen, Wayne D. *Agriculture in the United States: A Documentary History.* New York: Random House, 1975. 365 pp.

Reed, Charles A., ed. *Origins of Agriculture.* The Hague, The Netherlands: Mouton, 1977. 1,013 pp.

*Steinbeck, John. *The Grapes of Wrath.* New York: Penguin, 1992. 619 pp.

Strueur, Stuart. *Prehistoric Agriculture.* Garden City, NY: Natural History Press, 1971. 733 pp.

"Traditional Agriculture in Sri Lanka." *The Ecologist,* October 1982: 209-216. Edward Goldsmith interviews Mudiyanse Tenakoon on agriculture in poor countries.

Waln, Nora. *The House of Exile.* New York: Blue Ribbon Books, 1933. 337 pp.

Weatherford, Jack. *Indian Givers.* New York: Random House, 1988. 272 pp.

Weaver, William Woys. *100 Vegetables and Where They Came From.* Chapel Hill, NC: Algonquin, 2000. 316 pp.

Wilson, Gilbert L. *Buffalo Bird Woman's Garden.* St. Paul, MN: Minnesota Historical Society, 1987. 129 pp.

## Homesteading

*BackHome Magazine.* (P.O. Box 370, Mountain Home, NC 28758.) Excellent urban and rural "homesteading" skills periodical.

Bacon, R. M. *The Yankee Magazine Book of Forgotten Arts.* New York: Simon & Schuster, 1978. 219 pp.

Bakule, Paula Dreifus, ed. *Rodale's Book of Practical Formulas: Easy-to-Make, Easy-to-Use Recipes for Hundreds of Everyday Activities and Tasks.* Emmaus, PA: Rodale Press, 1991. 456 pp.

Blankenship, Bart and Robin. *Earth Knack: Stone Age Skills for the 21st Century.* Layton, UT: Gibbs-Smith, 1996. 192 pp.

Bromfield, Louis. *Out of the Earth.* New York: Harper & Brothers Publishers, 1950. 305 pp.

Burns, Deborah, ed. *Storey's Basic Country Skills.* Pownal, VT: Storey, 1999. 564 pp.

Burns, Scott. *The Household Economy.* Boston: Beacon House, 1974.

Byler, Emma (Jonas Em). *Plain and Happy Living: Amish Recipes and Remedies.* Cleveland, Ohio: Goosefoot Acres Press, 1991. 156 pp.

Cameron, Brenda and Brian. *Making Bent Willow Furniture.* Pownal, VT: Storey, 1998. 139 pp.

*Dry Stone Walling.* London: British Trust for Conservation Volunteers (Zoological Gardens, Regents Park, London NW1 4RY, England), 1977. 120 pp.

Dwyer, C. P. *The Homestead Builder: Practical Hints for Handy-Men: A Classic Guide to Building Cabins and Houses from Scratch,* 10th ed. New York: The Lyons Press, 1998. 145 pp.

Emery, Carla. *The Encyclopedia of Country Living: An Old-Fashioned Recipe Book.* Seattle: Sasquatch Books, 1994. 858 pp.

Emptor, C. "Buying Country Property." *BackHome Magazine,* September/October 1997: 18–19.

Farallones Institute. *The Integral Urban House: Self-Reliant Living in the City.* San Francisco: Sierra Club Books, 1979. 494 pp.

*Farm Conveniences and How to Make Them.* New York: The Lyons Press, 1998. 256 pp.

Gussow, Joan Dye. *This Organic Life: Confessions of a Suburban Homesteader.* White River Junction, VT: Chelsea Green, 2001. 273 pp.

Halweil, Brian. *Eat Here: Reclaiming Homegrown Pleasures in a Global Supermarket.* New York: Norton, 2004. 236 pp.

Higginbothan, Pearl, and Mary Ellen Pinkham. *Mary Ellen's Best of Helpful Hints: Fast/Easy/Fun Ways of Solving Household Problems.* New York: Warner, 1979. 119 pp.

*The Home Workplace.* Compiled by the editors of *Organic Gardening and Farming.* Emmaus, PA: Rodale Press, 1979. 127 pp.

Jason, Dan. *Living Lightly on the Land: Self-Reliance in Food and Medicine.* Salt Spring Island, Canada: Barnyard Grafix (Box 444, Ganges, Salt Spring Island, BC V8K 2W1, Canada), 1998. 142 pp.

Keiley, Lynn. "Choosing Safe Lumber." *Mother Earth News,* February/March 2003: 104–106.

Lawrence, James, ed. *The Harrowsmith Reader: The Best from Canada's Award Winning Magazine of Country Life and Alternatives to Bigness.* Camden East, Ontario, Canada: Camden House Publishing, 1978. 287 pp.

Lyle, David. *The Book of Masonry Stoves.* White River Junction, VT: Chelsea Green, 1997. 192 pp.

Mack, Norman, ed. *Back to Basics: How to Learn and Enjoy Traditional American Skills.* Pleasantville, NY: Reader's Digest, 1981. 456 pp.

Marks, Vic, and Michael Kovacsics, eds. *The Farmstead Book.* Seattle, WA: Cloudburst, 1978. 258 pp.

Martin, George A. *Fences, Gates, and Bridges and How to Build Them.* New York: The Lyons Press, 1999. 192 pp.

McRaven, Charles. *Stonework Techniques and Projects.* Pownal, VT: Storey, 1997. 183 pp.

Nearing, Helen. *Loving and Leaving the Good Life.* White River Junction, VT: Chelsea Green, 1992. 194 pp.

BIBLIOGRAPHY

HOMESTEADING • HOUSEPLANTS • HOUSING

*Nearing, Helen and Scott. *Continuing the Good Life.* New York: Schocken, 1979. 194 pp.

*———. *Living the Good Life.* New York: Schocken, 1970. 213 pp.

Neese, Harvey C. *The Almanac of Rural Living: The Illustrated Do-It-Yourself Library of Rural Living.* Troy, ID: N & N Resources, 1976. 483 pp.

Orem, Howard and Susan. *Country Land and Its Uses.* Healdsburg, CA: Naturegraph Publishers, 1974. 310 pp.

Philippe-Johnson, L. Kevin and Donna. "How We Went from $42,000 to $6,500 and Lived to Tell about It!" *Countryside and Small Stock Journal* November/December 2005: 47–50.

Preston, Edward. *How to Buy Land Cheap.* Port Townsend, WA: Loompanics Unlimited (P.O. Box 1197, Port Townsend, WA 98368), 1991. 141 pp.

Proulx, Earl. *Make It Last.* Dublin, NH: Yankee, 1997. 394 pp.

Roy, Rob. *Mortgage Free! Radical Strategies for Home Ownership.* White River Junction, VT: Chelsea Green, 1998. 353 pp.

The Rural Institute and the Ukiah Community Center. *Simple Living: Proceedings of Second Annual Simple Living Workshops.* Ukiah, CA: The Rural Institute, 1977. 121 pp.

Savage, D. S. *Self-Sufficient Country Living.* New York: St. Martin's Press, 1978. 304 pp.

Schaeffer, John. *Real Goods Solar Living Source Book.* White River Junction, VT: Chelsea Green Publishing, 2001. 590 pp. Includes land, shelter, water, heating, electricity, and more.

*Scher, Les and Carol. *Finding and Buying Your Place in the Country,* 4th ed. Chicago: Real Estate Education Co., 1996. 414 pp.

*Seymour, John. *The Complete Book of Self-Sufficiency.* London: Faber and Faber, 1976. 256 pp. Coffee-table size. Includes grains, livestock, energy, and skills such as

spinning, metalwork, and thatching. IL

———. *The Guide to Self-Sufficiency.* New York: Popular Mechanics Books, 1976. 256 pp.

———. *La Vida en el Campo y El Horticultor Autosuficiente.* Barcelona: Blume, 1991. 256 pp.

Seymour, John and Sally. *Farming for Self-Sufficiency: Independence on a 5-acre Farm.* New York: Schocken Books, 1973. 249 pp.

———. *Self-Sufficiency: The Science and Art of Producing and Preserving Your Own Food.* London: Faber and Faber, 1973. 250 pp. Includes information on food storage and farming.

Slay, Israel. *Homesteaders Handbook: A Guide to Raising, Growing, Preparing and Preserving Foodstuffs . . . and a Few Side Trips.* San Francisco: Homesteader's Handbook, 1975. 318 pp.

Stein, Matthew. *When Technology Fails.* Santa Fe, NM: Clear Light Publishers, 2000. 405 pp.

Storey Books Editors. *Country Wisdom and Know-How: Everything You Need to Know to Live Off the Land.* New York: Workman Publishing, 2004. 480 pp. A real treasure trove of information.

Sun Bear, Wabun, Nimimosha, and the Tribe. *The Bear Tribe's Self Reliance Book.* Spokane, WA: 1977. 144 pp.

Tresemer, David. *Splitting Firewood.* Brattleboro, VT: Hand and Foot, 1981. 142 pp.

Turnipseed, Jane. "Heat-Saving Window Shades." *BackHome Magazine,* January/February 2006: 38–39.

*United Country Magazine.* (United National Real Estate 4700 Belleview, Ste. 200, Kansas City, MO 64112.) Good source for farm real estate listings.

Vivian, John. *Building Stone Walls.* Charlotte, VT: Garden Way, 1978. 109 pp.

———. *The Manual of Practical Homesteading.* Emmaus, PA: Rodale Press, 1975. 340 pp.

———. *Wood Heat.* Emmaus, PA: Rodale Press, 1978. 428 pp.

*Wells, Kenneth McNeil. *The Owl Pen Reader.* New York: Doubleday, 1969. 445 pp.

Zwinger, Ann. *Beyond the Aspen Grove.* New York: Random House, 1970. 368 pp.

## Houseplants

Arthurs, Kathryn L., ed. *How to Grow African Violets.* Menlo Park, CA; Lane Publishing Co., 1977. 80 pp.

Jacobsen, Pamela D. "Make Your Own Houseplant Fertilizers." *BackHome Magazine,* January/February 2006: 33–35.

March, Ken. *Houseplants for Free: A Step-by-Step Guide to the Propagation of Healthy Houseplants.* Secaucus, NJ: Chartwell Books, 1988. 127 pp.

## Housing

Alexander, Christopher, Sara Ishikawa, and Murray Silverstein. *A Pattern Language.* New York: Oxford University Press, 1977. 1,171 pp.

Bainbridge, David. *Plastered Straw Bale Construction.* Canelo, AZ: The Canelo Project (HCR Box 324, Canelo, AZ 85611), 1992. 44 pp.

Baldwin, J., and Stewart Brand. *Soft-Tech.* New York: Penguin Books, 1978. 175 pp.

Beard, D. C. *Shelters, Shacks and Shanties.* Berkeley, CA: Ten Speed Press, 1992. 243 pp.

Beaudoin, Edna. "The Stenman Paper House." *BackHome Magazine,* November/December 2000: 45.

Bee, Becky. *The Cob Builder's Handbook.* Murphy, OR: Groundworks (P.O. Box 381, Murphy, OR 97553), 1997. 173 pp.

Billett, Michael. *Thatching and Thatched Buildings.* London: Robert Hale Limited, 1979. 208 pp.

Broadstreet, Jim. *Building with Junk and Other Good Stuff: A Guide to Home Building and Remodeling Using Recycled Materials.* Port

214  BIBLIOGRAPHY AND RESOURCES

Townsend, WA: Loompanics Unlimited (P.O. Box 1197, Port Townsend, WA 98368), 1990. 162 pp.

Burnham, Richard. *Housing Ourselves: Creating Affordable, Sustainable Shelter.* New York: McGraw Hill, 1998. 196 pp.

Chiras, Daniel D. *The Natural House.* White River Junction, VT: Chelsea Green, 2000. 468 pp.

Cruz, William. *Will's Guide to Building the $9,000 House.* Santa Cruz, CA: Unity Press, 1978. 176 pp.

Easton, David. *The Rammed Earth Experience.* Wilseyville, CA: Blue Mountain Press, 1982. 71 pp.

Eccli, Eugene, ed. *Low-Cost, Energy-Efficient Shelter for the Owner and Builder.* Emmaus, PA: Rodale, 1976. 408 pp.

Evans, Ianto, Michael G. Smith, and Linda Smiley. *The Hand-Sculpted House: A Practical and Philosophical Guide to Building a Cob Cottage.* White River Junction, VT: Chelsea Green Publishing, 2002. 346 pp.

Foreman, Patricia, and Andy Lee. *A Tiny Home to Call Your Own.* Buena Vista, VA: Good Earth Publications, 2005. 208 pp.

Grady, Wayne. *Green Home Planning and the Environmentally Advanced House.* Buffalo, NY: Camden House, 1993. 208 pp.

Gray, Alan T., and Anne Hall, eds. *Strawbale Homebuilding.* White River Junction, VT: Chelsea Green Publishing, 2000. 156 pp.

Gray, Virginia, and Alan Macrae. *Mud Space and Spirit: Handmade Adobes.* Santa Barbara, CA: Capra Press, 1976. 93 pp.

Hunton, Linda Mason. *The Natural Home Handbook.* Emmaus, PA: Rodale Press, 1991. 39 pp.

Jeswald, Peter. *Homework: Ten Steps to Foolproof Planning Before Building.* Berkeley, CA: Ten Speed Press, 1995. 294 pp.

Jones, Barbara. *Building with Straw Bales: A Practical Guide for the UK and Ireland.* White River Junction, VT: Chelsea Green, 2002. 125 pp.

Kern, Ken. *The Owner-Built Home.* Oakhurst, CA: Ken Kern Drafting (P.O. Box 550, Oakhurst, CA 93644), 1972. 274 pp.

Khalili, Nader. *Ceramic Houses: How to Build Your Own.* San Francisco: Harper & Row, 1986. 221.

———. *Racing Alone: A Visionary Architect's Quest for Houses Made with Earth and Fire.* New York: Harper & Row, 1983. 241 pp.

*The Last Straw: The Grass Roots Journal of Straw-Bale and Natural Building* (HC 66, Box 9, Hillsboro, NM 88042). Periodical.

Leckie, Jim, et al. *More Other Homes and Garbage: Designs for Self-Sufficient Living.* San Francisco: Sierra Club Books, 1981. 374 pp.

MacDonald, S. O. *A Visual Primer to Straw-Bale Construction.* Gila, NM: Appropriate Development Project, UGWA (P.O. Box 383, Gila, NM), 1999. 22 pp.

MacDonald, S. O. and Orien. *A Straw-Bale Primer.* Self-published (P.O. Box 58, Gila, NM 88038), 1992. 24 pp.

Magwood, Chris, et al. "Expert Advice on Straw Bale Building." *Mother Earth News,* February/March 2006: 58–64.

Middleton, G. F. *Build Your House of Earth.* Melbourne, Australia: Compendium Pty, 1975. 110 pp.

Myhrman, Matts. *Build It with Bales: Version 2.* Tucson, AZ: Out On Bale, (un)limited, 1997.

Niemeir, Randy and Donna. *Montana Log Cabin, Rugged and Rustic, $12,000.* Helmville, MT: Randy and Donna Niemeir (P.O. Box 69, Helmville, Montana 59843), n.d. 37 pp.

Norton, John. *Building with Earth: A Handbook.* Rugby, UK: Intermediate Technology Development Group (Myson House, Railway Terrace, Rugby CV21 3HT, UK), 1986. 68 pp.

Oehler, Mike. *The $50 and Up Underground House Book.* Bonners Ferry, ID: Mole, 1997. 115 pp.

Pearson, David. *The Natural House Book.* New York: Simon & Schuster, 1989. 287 pp.

Roberts, Carolyn. *A House of Straw: A Natural Building Odyssey.* White River Junction, VT: Chelsea Green Publishing, 2002. 238 pp.

Roy, Rob. *Mortgage Free! Radical Strategies for Home Ownership.* White River Junction, VT: Chelsea Green, 1998. 353 pp.

Smith, Michael G. *The Cobber's Companion: How to Build Your Own Earthen Home.* Cottage Grove, OR: Cob Cottage Co., 2000: 134 pp.

Solberg, Gordon. "Papercrete and Fibrous Adobe." *BackHome Magazine,* November/December 2000: 40–44.

Vélez, Simón, et al. *Grow Your Own House, Simón Vélez and Bamboo Architecture.* Weil am Rhein, Germany: Vitra Design Museum, 2000. 255 pp.

Walker, Lester. *Tiny, Tiny Houses.* Woodstock, NY: The Overlook Press, 1986. 220 pp.

Wells, Malcolm. *How to Build an Underground House.* Brewster, MA: Malcolm Wells (673 Satucket Rd., Brewster, MA 02631), 1991. 96 pp.

Whitefield, Patrick. *Tipi Living.* White River Junction, VT: Chelsea Green Publishing, 1987. 43 pp.

Wojciechowska, Paulina. *Building with Earth: A Guide to Flexible-Form Earthbag Construction.* White River Junction, VT: Chelsea Green Publishing, 2001. 163 pp.

### Human Waste

Beeby, John. *Future Fertility: Transforming Human Waste into Human Wealth.* Willits, CA: Ecology Action, 1998. 164 pp.

Chy, Viet. *Human Faeces, Urine and Their Utilization.* Bangkok, Thailand: Environmental Sanitation Information Center (Asian Institute of Technology, P.O. Box 2754, Bangkok, Thailand), 1978.

Clayton, Doug, and Dave Jacke. *The Gap Mountain Permaculture Mouldering Toilet.* Jaffrey, NH: Gap Mountain Permaculture, 1992. 32 pp.

Del Porto, David, and Carol Steinfeld. *The Composting Toilet System Book.* Concord, MA: The Center for Ecological Pollution Prevention (CEPP, P.O. Box 1330, Concord, MA), 1999. 234 pp.

Feachem, R. G., et al. *Appropriate Technology for Water Supply and Sanitation.* Vol. 3, *Health Aspects of Excreta and Sullae Management—A State of the Art Review.* Washington, DC: World Bank, 1981. 80 pp.

Harper, Peter. *Fertile Waste: Managing Your Domestic Sewage.* Machynlleth, UK: The Centre for Alternative Technology, 1994. 26 pp.

Harper, Peter, and Louise Halestrap. *Lifting the Lid: An Ecological Approach to Toilet Systems.* Machynlleth, UK: The Centre for Alternative Technology, 1999. 153 pp.

Huggins, Geoffrey. "Building and Using a Composting Privy." *BackHome Magazine,* May/June 1999: 41–43.

Jenkins, Joseph. *The Humanure Handbook: A Guide to Composting Human Manure,* 3rd ed. White River Junction, VT: Chelsea Green Publishing, 2005. 255 pp. **AL**

Kahn, Lloyd, Blair Allen, and Julie Jones. *The Septic System Owner's Manual.* Bolinas, CA: Shelter Publications, 2000. 161 pp.

Shuval, H. L., et al. *Appropriate Technology for Water Supply and Sanitation.* Vol. 10, *Nightsoil Composting.* Washington, DC: World Bank, 1981. 81 pp.

Steinfeld, Carol. *Liquid Gold: The Lore and Logic of Using Urine to Grow Plants.* Sheffield, VT: Green Frigate Books, 2004. 88 pp.

*Stoner, C. H., ed. *Goodbye to the Flush Toilet.* Emmaus, PA: Rodale Press, 1977.

*Van der Ryn, Sim. *The Toilet Papers.* Santa Barbara, CA: Capra Press, 1978. 124 pp.

### Hydroponics

Douglas, Sholto. *Hydroponics: The Bengal System with Notes on Other Methods of Soil-less Cultivation.* Bombay: Oxford University Press, 1959. 185 pp.

Grotzke, Heinz. "Can Food Plants Grown Hydroponically Be Considered Organically Grown?" *The Voice of Demeter* (Newsletter of the Demeter Association, Inc. for Certification of Biodynamic Agriculture), Summer 1999: 10.

Haq, A. H. M. Rezaul, Tapan Kumar Ghosal, and Pritam Ghosh. "Cultivating Wetlands in Bangladesh," *LIESA,* December 2004: 18–20.

### Income

Adams, Barbara Berst. *Micro Eco-Farming: Prospering from Backyard to Small Acreage in Partnership with the Earth.* Auburn, CA: New World Publishing, 2004. 174 pp.

Byczynski, Lynn. *Marketing Your Produce: Ideas for Small-Scale Farmers.* Auburn, KS: Fairplain Publications, 1997. 112 pp.

DeVault, George. "City Farm Grosses $238,000 on 1/2 Acre." *The New Farm,* July/August 1990: 12–15.

Gibson, Eric. "Big Bucks from Small Acres." *Income Opportunities,* July/August 1988: 54–56.

———. *Sell What You Sow!* Carmichael, CA: New World, 1994. 302 pp.

Harlan, Michael and Linda. *Growing Profits: How to Start and Operate a Backyard Nursery.* Citrus Heights, CA: Moneta, 1997. 205 pp.

Henderson, Peter. *Gardening for Profit.* Chillicothe, IL: American Botanist Booksellers (P.O. Box 532, Chillicothe, IL 61523). 243 pp.

Lee, Andrew. *Backyard Market Gardening: The Entrepreneur's Guide to Selling What You Grow.* Burlington, VT: Good Earth Publications (P.O. Box 4352, Burlington, VT 05406-4352), 1993. 351 pp.

Olson, Michael. *MetroFarm: The Guide to Growing for Big Profit on a Small Parcel of Land.* Santa Cruz, CA: TS Books (P.O. Box 1244, Santa Cruz, CA 95061), 1994. 498 pp.

Osgood, William. *How to Earn a Living in the Country (Without Farming).* Charlotte, VT: Garden Way Publishing, 1974. 111 pp.

Platt, Ellen Spector. *How to Profit from Flower and Herb Crafts.* Mechanicsburg, PA: Stackpole Books, 1996. 202 pp.

*Profitable Farming Now!* Emmaus, PA: Regenerative Agriculture Association, 1985. 100 pp.

"Salad: Fresh from 4th Street." *Berkeley Ecology Center Newsletter,* March 1986: 2.

*Specialty and Minor Crops Handbook,* 2nd ed. Oakland, CA: University of California, Division of Agriculture and Natural Resources, 1998. 184 pp. Useful for economic mini-farming.

*Spring Newsletter.* Kona Kai Farms (1824 5th St., Berkeley, CA 94710), March 1988. 4 pp.

Sturdivant, Lee. *Herbs for Sale: Growing and Marketing Herbs, Herbal Products and Herbal Know-How.* Friday Harbor, WA: San Juan Naturals, 1994. 246 pp.

———. *Profits from Your Backyard Herb Garden.* Friday Harbor, WA: San Juan Naturals (P.O. Box 642, Friday Harbor, WA 98250), 1988. 118 pp.

Taylor, T. M. *Secrets to a Successful Greenhouse and Business.* Melbourne, FL: Green Earth, 1998. 279 pp.

Van En, Robyn. *Basic Formula to Create Community-Supported Agriculture.* Great Barrington, MA: CSA Indian Line Farm (R.R. 3, Box 85, Great Barrington, MA 02130), 1988. 80 pp.

Whatley, Booker. *How to Make $100,000 Farming 25 Acres.* Chillicothe, IL: The American Botanist, 1987. 180 pp.

Yepsen, Roger B., Jr. *Growing for Market.* Emmaus, PA: Rodale Press, 1978. 301 pp. Ideas for market gardeners.

## Insect Life and Balance/Plant Health

*Attracting Butterflies to Your Garden.* Emmaus, PA: Rodale Press, 1992. 32 pp.

Ball, Jeff. *Rodale's Garden Problem Solver.* Emmaus, PA: Rodale Press, 1988. 556 pp.

Barclay, Leslie W., et al. *Insect and Disease Management in the Home Orchard.* Berkeley, CA: California Cooperative Extension Service, 1981. 39 pp.

Brinton, William F. "The Control of Plant Pathogenic Fungi by Use of Compost Teas." *Biodynamics,* January/February 1995: 12–15.

Buchmann, Stephen L., and Gary Paul Nabhan. *The Forgotten Pollinators.* Washington, DC: Island Press, 1996. 292 pp.

Carr, Anna. *Rodale's Color Handbook of Garden Insects.* Emmaus, PA: Rodale Press, 1979. 241 pp.

Cavigelli, M. A., et al., eds. *Michigan Field Crop Pest Ecology and Management.* Michigan State University Extension Bulletin E-2704. Lansing: Michigan State University, 2000. 108 pp.

Chaboussou, Francis. *Healthy Crops: A New Agricultural Revolution.* Charlbury, UK: Jon Carpenter Publishing for the Gaia Foundation, 2004. 234 pp.

Christie, Jesse R. *Plant Nematodes: Their Bionomics and Control.* Jacksonville, FL: H. & W. B. Drew, 1959. 256 pp.

Cranshaw, Whitney. *Garden Insects of North America.* Princeton, NJ: Princeton University Press, 2004. 656 pp.

Curtis, Jennifer, et al. *Harvest of Hope: The Potential for Alternative Agriculture to Reduce Pesticide Use.* New York: Natural Resources Defense Council, 1991. 124 pp.

Dean, Molly. "Butterflies: Invite Them into Your Garden with These Easy-Care Shrubs." *National Gardening,* July/August 1994: 38–41.

Edwards, Clive A., ed. *Earthworm Ecology.* Boca Raton, FL: CRC Press, 2004. 441 pp.

Edwards, C. A., and P. J. Bohlen. *Biology and Ecology of Earthworms.* Chapman and Hall, 1996.

*Ellis, Barbara W., and Fern Bradley, eds. *The Organic Gardener's Handbook of Natural Insect and Disease Control.* Emmaus, PA: Rodale Press, 1996. 534 pp. Good color insect photos.

Fichter, George S. *Insect Pests.* New York: Golden Press, 1966. 160 pp.

Fish and Wildlife Service, U.S. Department of the Interior. *Attracting and Feeding Birds. Conservation Bulletin No. 1.* Washington, DC: U.S. Government Printing Office, revised 1973. 10 pp.

Flint, Mary Louise. *Pests of the Garden and Small Farm.* University of California Publications, 1990.

Flint, Mary Louise, and Steve H. Dreistadt. *Natural Enemies Handbook: The Illustrated Guide to Biological Pest Control.* Berkeley, CA: University of California Press, 1998. 154 pp.

Free, J. B. *Insect Pollination of Crops.* New York: Academic Press, 1970. 544 pp.

Fuglie, Lowell J. *Producing Food Without Pesticides: Local Solutions to Crop Pest Control in West Africa.* Dakar, Senegal: Church World Service, 1998. 158 pp.

Gilkeson, Linda, Pam Peirce, and Miranda Smith. *Rodale's Pest and Disease Problem Solver.* Emmaus, PA: Rodale Press, 1996. 384 pp.

Gordh, G., and D. H. Headrick. *A Dictionary of Entomology.* New York: CABI Publishing, 2001. 1032 pp.

Gordon, David George. *The Western Society of Malacologists: Field Guide to the Slug.* Seattle, WA: Sasquatch Books (1008 Western Ave., Seattle, WA 98104), 1994. 48 pp.

Grainger, Janette, and Connie Moore. *Natural Insect Repellents.* Austin, TX: The Herb Bar (200 W. Mary, Austin, TX 78704), 1991. 152 pp.

Griffin, Brian L. *The Orchard Mason Bee.* Bellingham, WA: Knox Cellars Publishing, 1993. 69 pp.

Grissell, Eric. *Insects and Gardens.* Portland, OR: Timber Press, 2001. 343 pp.

Grossman, Joel, and Helga Olkowski. "Stopping Slugs and Snails." *Common Sense Pest Control Quarterly,* Winter 1990: 7–18.

Hart, Rhonda Massingham. *Bugs, Slugs and Other Thugs.* Pownal, VT: Storey, 1991. 214 pp.

———. *Squirrel Proofing Your Home and Garden.* Pownal, VT: Storey, 1999. 153 pp.

Headrick, George and David. *A Dictionary of Entomology.* New York: CABI Publishing, 2001. 1032 pp.

Helyer, Neil, Kevin Brown, and Nigel D. Cattlin. *A Color Handbook of Biological Control in Plant Protection.* Portland, OR: Timber Press, 2003. 126 pp.

Hess, Lilo. *The Amazing Earthworm.* New York: Charles Scribner's Sons, 1979. 48 pp.

Hoffmann, Michael P. *Natural Enemies of Vegetable Insect Pests.* Ithaca, NY: Resource Center (7 Business/Technology Park, Cornell University, Ithaca, NY 14850), 1993. 63 pp.

Howes, F. N. *Plants and Beekeeping.* London: Faber and Faber, 1945. 224 pp.

*Hunter, Beatrice Trum. *Gardening without Poisons.* New York: Berkeley Publishing, 1971. 352 pp. Comprehensive survey of insect control methods.

Hunter, Charles D. *Suppliers of Beneficial Organisms in North America.* Sacramento, CA: California Environmental Protection Agency (Department of Pesticide Regulation, Environmental Monitoring and Pest Management), 1992. 31 pp.

*Insect Life.* San Francisco: Pesticide Action Network (49 Powell St., Ste. 500, San Francisco, CA 94102). Computer disk (TAPP database).

*Insect Pest Management Guidelines for California Landscape Ornamentals.* University of California Pub. No. 3317, 1987.

Keville, Kathi. "Herbal Bug Repellents." *Well-Being Magazine,* July 1982.

Khambata, S. R., and J. V. Bhat. "A Contribution to the Study of the Intestinal Microflora of Indian Earthworms." *Archiv für Mikrobiologie,* Bd. 28, S., 1957: 69–80.

Klein, Hilary Dole, and Adrian M. Wenner. *Tiny Game Hunting.* New York: Bantam, 1991. 278 pp.

Larch, W. *Physiological Plant Ecology.* Berlin-Heidelberg: Springer-Verlag, 1980. 303 pp.

*Least-Toxic Pest Management Publications Catalog.* Berkeley, CA: The Bio-Integral Resource Center (P.O. Box 7414, Berkeley, CA 94707), April 1990. 11 pp.

Levi, Herbert W. *Spiders.* New York: Golden Press, 1968. 160 pp.

Maeterlinck, Maurice. *The Life of the Bee.* New York: Dodd, Mead, 1916. 427 pp.

Maltas, Michael. *Orchard Pest Management and Spray Schedule.* Kimberton, PA: Biodynamic Farming and Gardening, 1987. 27 pp. Available from BDFGA.

*McClure, Susan, and C. Colston Burrell. *Rodale's Successful Organic Gardening: Controlling of Pests and Diseases.* Emmaus, PA: Rodale Press, 1992.

*McGregor, S. E. *Insect Pollination of Cultivated Crop Plants.* Washington, DC: Agricultural Research Service, U.S. Department of Agriculture, 1976. 411 pp. Excellent.

Mellon, Margaret, and Jane Rissler, eds. *Now or Never: Serious New Plans to Save a Natural Pest Control.* Cambridge, MA: Union of Concerned Scientists, 1998. 149 pp.

Metcalf, C. L., and W. Flint, revised by R. L. Metcalf. *Destructive and Useful Insects—Their Habits and Control.* New York: McGraw-Hill, 1951.

Milne, Lorus, and Margery Milne. *The Audubon Society Field Guide to North American Insects and Spiders.* New York: Knopf, 1980. 1,008 pp. Small format. Excellent color photographs!

Minnich, Jerry. *The Earthworm Book.* Emmaus, PA: Rodale Press, 1977. 372 pp.

*Mitchell, Robert T. *Butterflies and Moths.* New York: Golden Press, 1962. 160 pp. **BL**

Newman, L. Hugh. *Create a Butterfly Garden.* Kingswood, England: World's Work (Kingswood, Fodworth, Surrey, England), 1969. 115 pp.

Olkowski, Helga. "Coping with Imported Fire Ants." *Common Sense Pest Control Quarterly,* Spring 1989: 8–17.

———. "Learning to Welcome Beneficial Spiders in the Garden." *Common Sense Pest Control Quarterly,* Summer 1991: 5–11.

Olkowski, William and Helga. "Carpenter Ants." *Common Sense Pest Control Quarterly,* Spring 1985: 11–16.

———. "Carpenter Bees," *Common Sense Pest Control Quarterly,* Spring 1985: 17–19.

Olkowski, William, Helga Olkowski, and Shiela Daar. "Managing Ticks, the Least-Toxic Way." *Common Sense Pest Control Quarterly,* Spring 1990: 4–16.

Peairs, Leonard Marion. *Insect Pests of Farm, Garden, and Orchard,* 4th ed. New York: John Wiley.

*Pesticide Action Network (49 Powell St., Ste. 500, San Francisco, CA 94102). Worldwide information clearinghouse on pesticide dangers.

*Pesticide Perspectives.* Santa Cruz, CA: Agroecology Program, University of California, 1990. 11 pp. Information brochure.

Philbrick, John and Helen. *The Bug Book.* Charlotte, VT: Garden Way, 1974. 126 pp. **BL**

Pimentel, David. "Reducing Pesticide Use through Alternative Agricultural Practices: Fungicides and Herbicides," in *Pesticide Interactions in Crop Production: Beneficial and Deleterious Effects,* J. Altman, ed. Boca Raton, FL: CRC Press, 1993: 435–448.

Pimentel, David, et al. "Environmental and Economic Costs of Pesticide Use." *BioScience,* November 1992: 750–760.

Pleasant, Barbara. "Organic Pest Control." *Mother Earth News,* February/March 2006: 46–51.

Proctor, Michael, Peter Yeo, and Andrew Lack. *The Natural History of Pollination.* Portland, OR: Timber Press, 1996. 479 pp.

Quarles, William. "Baiting Pharaoh or Argentine Ants." *Common Sense Pest Control Quarterly,* Fall 1995: 5–13

———. "Fly Repellants." *Common Sense Pest Control Quarterly,* Summer 1997: 13–19.

———. "Fly Traps." *Common Sense Pest Control Quarterly,* Summer 1997: 5–12.

———. "Garlic as a Pesticide." *Common Sense Pest Control Quarterly,* Fall 1999: 4–12.

———. "Grow Pesto for Your Pests!" *Common Sense Pest Control Quarterly,* Fall 1999: 13–19.

———. "Least-Toxic Termite Baits." *Common Sense Pest Control Quarterly,* Spring 1995: 5–17.

———. "Least-Toxic Termite Control." *Common Sense Pest Control Quarterly,* Winter 1993: 5–14.

———. "Managing Pest Rabbits in Gardens and Fields." *Common Sense Pest Control Quarterly,* Winter 1994: 5–14.

———. "Managing Tree Squirrels." *Common Sense Pest Control Quarterly,* Fall 1995: 14–17.

———. "Protect Your Garden with Aspirin and Salicylate." *Common Sense Pest Control Quarterly,* Spring 1996: 16–18.

———. "The Truth About Horsetails or Natural Plant Disease Protection from Silica." *Common Sense Pest Control Quarterly,* Spring 1995: 18.

Quarles, William, and Laurie Swiadon. "Gophers and Moles: Under-ground Thugs and Blind Bandits." *Common Sense Pest Control Quarterly,* Spring 1996: 5–15.

Rincon-Vitova Insectories (P.O. Box 95, Oak View, CA 93022). Predatory insect source.

Schwartz, P. H., Jr. *Control of Insects on Deciduous Fruits and Tree Gnats in the Home Orchard—Without Insecticides.* Hyattsville, MD: U.S. Department of Agriculture Research Service, 1975. 36 pp.

Smith, Miranda, et al. *Rodale's Garden Insect, Disease and Weed Identification Guide.* Emmaus, PA: Rodale Press, 1979. 328 pp.

Smittle, Delilah, ed. *Rodale's Complete Garden Problem Solver.* Emmaus, PA: Rodale Press, 1997. 346 pp.

Starcher, Allison Mia. *Good Bugs for Your Garden.* Chapel Hill, NC: Algonquin, 1995. 54 pp.

Stein, Dan. *Least Toxic Home Pest Control.* Eugene, OR: Hulogosi, 1991. 88 pp.

Swiadon, Laurie, and Tanya Drik. "Managing Pest Yellowjackets." *Common Sense Pest Control Quarterly,* Winter 1998: 5–14.

Swiadon, Laurie, and William Quarles. "Integrated Rat Management." *Common Sense Pest Control Quarterly,* Winter 1996: 5–15.

"Talking Plants." *Discover,* April 2002: 46–51.

Tanem, Bob. *Deer List: 1982 Update.* San Rafael, CA: Santa Venetia Nursery (273 N. San Pedro Rd., San Rafael, CA 94903). 2 pp.

———. *Deer Resistant Plant Books.* Brochure.

Thurston, H. David. *Sustainable Practices for Plant Disease Management in Traditional Farming Systems.* Ithaca, NY: Cornell University (Department of Plant Pathology, 330 Plant Sciences Bldg., Ithaca, NY 14853), 1991. 300 pp.

Thurston, H. David, and Jeanne M. Parker. *Raised Field and Plant Disease Management.* Ithaca, NY: Department of Plant Pathology, Cornell University. 21 pp.

Troetschler, Ruth, et al. *Rebugging Your Home and Garden: A Step by Step Guide to Modern Pest Control.* Los Altos, CA: PTF Press, 1996. 256 pp.

Van Den Bosch, Robert. *The Pesticide Conspiracy.* Berkeley, CA: University of California Press, 1978. 223 pp.

Vivian, John. *Keeping Bees.* Charlotte, VT: Williamson, 1986. 238 pp.

"A Whole Farm Approach to Managing Pests." Beltsville, MD: The Sustainable Agriculture Network (SARE)

Wiles, Richard and Christopher Campbell. *Washed, Peeled, Contaminated: Pesticide Residues in Ready-to-Eat Fruits and Vegetables.* Washington, DC: Environmental Working Group, 1994. 32 pp.

Woodward, Penny. *Pest-Repellent Plants.* Flemington, Victoria, Australia: Hyland House Publishing Pty Ltd, 1997. 128 pp.

Yarborough, Alice. "Gardening for Butterflies." *National Gardening,* July/August 1996: 30–33.

Yepson, Roger B., Jr. *The Encyclopedia of Natural Insect and Disease Control.* Emmaus, PA: Rodale Press, 1984. 490 pp.

———. *Organic Plant Protection.* Emmaus, PA: Rodale Press, 1976. 688 pp.

The Xerces Society. *Pollinator Conservation Handbook: A Guide to Understanding, Protecting, and Providing Habitat for Native Pollinator Insects.* Portland, OR: The Xerces Society, 2003. 145 pp.

Zim, Herbert S. *Insects.* New York: Golden Press, 1956. 160 pp.

## Intensive Gardening

Bonnefons, Nicholas de. *The French Gardener: Instructing How to Cultivate All Sorts of Fruit Trees and Herbs for the Garden.* St. Paul's Church-Yard, England: John Crooke, 1658. 294 pp.

Borie, Victor. "The Parisian Market-Gardeners." *Revue Horticole,* Series IV, Vol. 5 (1956): 374–376.

Broad, William J. "Too Rich a Soil: Scientists Find the Flaw That Undid the Biosphere." *New York Times,* October 5, 1993, Section B.

Bronson, William. "The Lesson of a Garden." *Cry California,* Winter 1970–71: 4–6.

Coe, Michael D. "The Chinampas of Mexico." *Scientific American* 211, July 1964: 90–98, 144.

Cook, Jonathan. "Revolutionary Plots: With Limited Access to Fuel and Pesticides, Cuba Has Turned to Organic Urban Agriculture to Feed Its People." *Orion,* March/April 2003: 62–69

*Courtois-Gérard, M. *Manuel Pratique de Culture Maraîchère.* Paris: J. Hetzel et Cie, 1845. 336 pp.

Crews, Timothy E., and Stephen R. Gliessman. "Raised Field Agriculture in Tlaxcala, Mexico: An Ecosystem Perspective on Maintenance of Soil Fertility." *American Journal of Alternative Agriculture,* November 1991: 9–16.

Doscher, Paul, et al. "History," in *Intensive Gardening Round the Year.* Brattleboro, VT: Stephen Greene Press, 1981. 144 pp.

*Duhon, David. *A History of Intensive Food Gardening.* Willits, CA: Ecology Action, 1984. 136 pp.

Erickson, Clark L. *An Archeological Investigation in the Lake Titicaca Basin of Peru.* Unpublished Ph.D. dissertation, Department of Anthropology, University of Illinois, Champagne-Urbana, 1988. See chapter 4, "Experiments in Raised Field Agriculture": 205–221.

———. "Raised Field Agriculture in the Lake Titicaca Basin: Putting Ancient Agriculture Back to Work." *Expedition,* Vol. 30, No. 3 (1989).

Erickson, Clark L., and Kay L. Candler. "Raised Fields and Sustainable Agriculture in the Lake Titicaca Basin of Peru," *Fragile Lands of Latin America: Strategies for Sustainable Development,* John O. Browder, ed. Boulder, CO: Westview Press, 1988.

BIBLIOGRAPHY

Ferrell, J. E. "Andes Indians Use Agricultural Methods of Their Ancestors." *The Cleveland Plain Dealer,* February 20, 1992: 6-C.

———. "A Return to Ancient Ways." *The Cleveland Plain Dealer,* February 20, 1992.

Macself, A. J. *French Intensive Gardening on Money-Making Lines.* London: W. H. & L. Collingridge, circa 1930. 128 pp.

Marx, Gary. "Bolivia Sows Ancient Fruits." *Chicago Tribune,* September 2, 1990: Section 1, 5.

McKay, C. D. *The French Garden— A Diary and Manual of Intensive Cultivation.* London: Associated Newspapers, Carmelite House, 1908. 62 pp.

Moseley, Michael E. *Archeology and the Quest for Higher Yields.* Chicago: Field Museum of Natural History, n.d. 9 pp.

Mullen, William. "Secrets of Tiwanaku—How Ingenious Farmers Built an Empire That Inspired the Incas and Rivaled Rome." *Chicago Tribune Magazine,* November 23, 1986: 1–19, 23–27, and 29–32.

*O'Brien, R. Dalziel. *Intensive Gardening.* London: Faber and Faber, 1956. 183 pp. Useful for potential mini-farmers. Veganic approach. **BL/IL**

Painter, James. "Archeology Makes Edible Impact—Revival of Ancient Agricultural Techniques Make Bolivian Raised Bed Potato Project Pay." *Christian Science Monitor,* October 9, 1991: 12–13.

Pigorsch, Susan S. "Lost Horizons." *Wisconsin Alumni,* May/June 1988: 12–17.

Poisson, Leandre, and Gretchen Vogel. *Solar Gardening: Growing Vegetables Year-Round the American Intensive Way.* White River Junction, VT: Chelsea Green Publishing, 1994. 267 pp.

Quarrell, C. P. *Intensive Salad Production.* London: Crosby Lockwood & Sons, 1945. 250 pp.

Robineau, Maryvonne and Bruno. "The Bolivian Andes: Farming on the Roof of the World," *Maine Organic Farmer and Gardener,* January/February 1994: 16–17.

Smith, Thomas. *French Gardening.* London: Utopia Press, 1909. 128 pp.

Stanhill, G. "An Urban Agro-Ecosystem: The Example of Nineteenth Century Paris." *Agro-Ecosystems,* 3 (1977): 269–284.

Stevens, William K. "Scientists Revive a Lost Secret of Farming—Ancient Peruvian Fields Yield Inexpensive Technology." *New York Times,* c. 1988 C-1, C-15.

Weathers, John. *Commercial Gardening.* Vols. 1–4. London: Gresham, 1913. 230 pp., 235 pp., 240 pp., 239 pp.

———. *French Market Gardening.* London: John Murray, 1909. 225 pp.

## Language and Travel

Amery, Heather, et al. *The First 1,000 Words in Spanish.* London: Usborne Publishing, 1979. 62 pp.

Bourke, Desmond O'Donnell. *French-English Horticultural Dictionary with English-French Index.* Wallingford, UK: C.A.B. International, 1989. 240 pp.

———. *Spanish-English Horticultural Dictionary.* Wallingford, UK: C.A.B. International, 1987. 148 pp.

Cody, Anna. *Latin American Spanish Phrasebook.* Oakland, CA: Lonely Planet, 1991. 173 pp.

Hamilton, Gevase. *A Health Handbook for the Tropics.* London: Voluntary Service Overseas (9 Belgrave Square, London SW1X 8PW, England), 1982. 111 pp.

Harpstrite, Pat, and Georgia Montrouil. *Spanish/English Glossary of Terms Used in "How to Grow More Vegetables."* Willits, CA: Ecology Action, 1987. 30 pp.

MacKay, Susan E. *Field Glossary of Agriculture Terms in French and English—Emphasis: West Africa.* Lafayette, IN: Purdue Research Foundation, 1984. 197 pp.

Pavick, Alan M. *First Travel: Meds for Injuries and Illness.* Timonium, MD: Publishing Corporation of America, 1986. 138 pp. Compact.

Peace Corps. *A Glossary of Agricultural Terms: Spanish/English–English/Spanish.* Washington, DC: American Language Center, the American University, 1976. 107 pp.

Rice, Robert P., Jr. *Thomson's English/Spanish–Spanish/English Illustrated Agricultural Dictionary.* Fresno, CA: Thomson Publications (P.O. Box 9335, Fresno, CA 93791), 1993. 160 pp.

Schroeder, Dirk. *Staying Healthy in Asia, Africa and Latin America.* Stanford, CA: Volunteers in Asia, 1988. 168 pp.

The Sybervision Foreign Language Series. (7133 Koll Center Parkway, Pleasanton, CA 94566.) 647 pp. Excellent audio learning tapes with manual.

Wilkes, Angela. *Spanish for Beginners.* Lincolnwood, IL: National Textbook Co., 1988. 50 pp.

## Learning/Teaching

Bailey, Liberty H. *The Nature Study Idea.* New York: Doubleday, Page, 1903. 159 pp.

Bailey, L. H., ed. *Cornell Nature Study Leaflets.* Albany, NY: J. B. Lyon, 1904. 607 pp.

———. *The Outlook to Nature.* Norwood, MA: Macmillan, 1915. 195 pp.

———. *The Training of Farmers.* New York: Macmillan, 1909. 263 pp.

Bear, John. *Bear's Guide to Earning Non-Traditional College Degrees.* Berkeley, CA: Ten Speed Press, 1988. 323 pp.

Brown, Marc. *Your First Garden Book.* Boston, MA: Little, Brown, 1981. 48 pp.

Call, Leland E., and E. G. Schafer. *A Laboratory Manual of Agriculture for Secondary Schools.* New York: Macmillan, 1920. 344 pp.

Center for Ecoliteracy. *The Edible Schoolyard.* Berkeley, CA: Learning in the Real World (2522 San Pablo Ave., Berkeley, CA 94702), 1999. 90 pp.

*The Common Roots Program: Education So Real You Can See It Growing. Montpelier, VT: Food Works (64 Main St., Montpelier, VT 05602). Excellent innovative hands-on teaching/learning program for kindergarten through grade 6.

Composite Growing Systems. (P.O. Box 343, Skyline Blvd., La Honda, CA 94020.) La Honda, CA: Learning Boxes. Four-tiered microcosm of garden beds for teachers.

Gibson, William G. Eye Spy. New York: Harper, 1899. 264 pp.

Guy, Linda A., Cathy Cromell, and Lucy K. Bradley. Success with School Gardens: How to Create a Learning Oasis in the Desert. Phoenix, AZ: Arizona Master Gardener Press, 1996. 140 pp.

Hayes, Marion. Project Management from Idea to Implementation. Oakville, Canada: Reid Publishing (P.O. Box 7267, Oakville, ON L6J 6L6, Canada), 1989. 85 pp.

Hilgard, E. W., and W. J. V. Osterhout. Agriculture for Schools of the Pacific Slope. New York: Macmillan, 1927. 428 pp.

Ingles, Andrew W., et al. The Participatory Process for Supporting Collaborative Management of Natural Resources: An Overview. Rome, Italy: Food and Agriculture Org. of the United Nations, 1999. 84 pp.

Jeetze, Hartmut von. "In Defense of Old-Fashioned Training." Biodynamics. (Biodynamic Farming and Gardening Association, P.O. Box 550, Kimberton, PA 19442), Vol. 122 (Spring 1977): 7–11; Vol. 123 (Summer 1977): 23–26.

Jurenka, Nancy Allen, and Rosanne Blass. Beyond the Bean Seed: Gardening Activities for Grades K–6. Englewood, CO: Teacher Ideas Press, 1996. 195 pp.

Kiefer, Joseph, and Martin Kemple. Digging Deeper: Integrating Youth Gardens Into Schools and Communities. Montpelier, VT: Food Works Common Roots Press, 1998. 141 pp.

*Life Lab Science Curriculum. (1156 High St., Santa Cruz, CA 95060.) A good curriculum for high school students.

Lovejoy, Ann. Sunflower Houses. Loveland, CO: Interweave Press, 1991. 144 pp.

Luhrs, Janet. "Building Bridges of Peace in Pakistan." Simple Living Oasis, Spring 2000: 8–10.

MacLatchie, Sharon. Gardening with Kids. Emmaus, PA: Rodale Press, 1977. 207 pp.

Ocone, Lynn, and Eve Pranis. The National Gardening Association Guide to Kid's Gardening: A Complete Guide for Teachers, Parents and Youth Leaders. New York: John Wiley & Sons, 1990.

Osterhout, W. J. V. Experiments with Plants. New York: Macmillan, 1911. 492 pp.

Raftery, Kevin, and Kim Gilbert. Kids Gardening. Palo Alto, CA: Klutz Press, 1989. 92 pp., plus seeds for 13 kinds of crops.

Resources for Teaching Sustainable Agriculture. Mt. Horeb, WI: WRDC/CIAS Resource Guide, 1992. 26 pp.

Rivera, William M., and Daniel J. Gustafson. Agriculture Extension: Worldwide Institutional Evolution and Forces for Change. New York: Elsevier Science, 1991. 312 pp.

Sampson, H. O. Effective Farming: A Text-Book for American Schools. New York: Macmillan, 1919. 490 pp.

Smith, Marny, and June Plecan. School Garden Manual. Westport, CT: Save the Children (54 Wilton Rd., Westport, CT 06880), 1989. 84 pp.

Teaching Peace through Gardening. Seattle, WA: Seattle Tilth (4649 Sunnyside Ave. N., Rm. 1, Seattle, WA). Children's education.

Toward a Sustainable Agriculture: A Teacher's Guide. Madison, WI: The Sustainable Agriculture Curriculum Project, University of Wisconsin Center for Integrated Agriculture Systems (240 Ag Hall, Madison, WI 53706), 1991. 151 pp.

Wooliever, Mary Avery. Tres Semillas para Una Mejor Alimentacion: Un Manual de Agricultura Familiar. San Ysidro, CA: Los Ninos (7065 Marconi Dr., Ste. 105, San Ysidro, CA 92703), 1990. 171 pp.

## "Living Farm" Museums

The Accokeek Foundation, 3400 Bryant Point Rd., Accokeek, MD 20607.

Howell Living Farm, Titusville, NJ.

## Marketing

Horowitz, Shel. Grassroots Marketing: Getting Noticed in a Noisy World. White River Junction, VT: Chelsea Green, 2000. 306 pp.

Macher, Ron. Making Your Small Farm Profitable. North Adams, MA: Storey Publishing, 1999. 273 pp.

Nordell, Anne and Eric. "Designing the Market Garden with Work Horses in Mind." The Natural Farmer, Summer 1998: 26–27.

Rutherford, Pat. "Profits from Asparagus." BackHome Magazine, January/February 2003: 44–47.

## Mushrooms

Arora, David. Mushrooms Demystified. Berkeley, CA: Ten Speed Press, 1979. 668 pp.

Hall, Ian R., et al. Edible and Poisonous Mushrooms of the World. Portland, OR: Timber Press, 2003. 371 pp.

Stamets, Paul. Growing Gourmet and Medicinal Mushrooms. Berkeley, CA: Ten Speed Press, 2000. 574 pp. Excellent and thorough, for those with serious interest.

———. Mycelium Running: How Mushrooms Can Help Save the World. Berkeley, CA: Ten Speed Press, 2005. 339 pp.

## Native Americans

Bingham, Sam and Janet. Navajo Farming. Logan, UT: Utah State University, 1979. 122 pp.

Bruchac, Joseph, and Michael J. Caduto. Native American Gardening: Stories, Projects and

BIBLIOGRAPHY

*Recipes for Families.* Golden, CO: Fulcrum, 1996. 158 pp.

Buchanan, Carol. *Brother Crow, Sister Corn.* Berkeley, CA: Ten Speed Press, 1997. 124 pp.

Grant, Bruce. *Concise Encyclopedia of the American Indian.* New York: Wings Books, 1994. 352 pp.

Sturtevant, William C., and Robert F. Heizer, eds. *Handbook of North American Indians, California.* Washington, DC: Smithsonian Institution, 1978. 800 pp.

Sturtevant, William C., and Alfonso Ortiz, eds. *Handbook of North American Indians, Southwest.* Washington, DC: Smithsonian Institution, 1983. 868 pp.

Suttles, Wayne, ed. *Handbook of North American Indians, Northwest Coast.* Washington, DC: Smithsonian Institute, 1990. 777 pp.

Yanovsky, Ellas. *Food Plants of the North American Indians.* Misc. Publications No. 237. Washington, DC: U.S. Dept. of Ag., n.d. 83 pp.

## Oil Crops

The Jefferson Institute. "Canola: An Emerging Oilseed Alternative." Alternative Crop Guide. Columbia, MO: The Jefferson Institute, 2002. 4 pp.

———. "Sunflower: A Native Oilseed with Growing Markets." Alternative Crop Guide. Columbia, MO: The Jefferson Institute, 2002. 4 pp.

## Out-of-Print Book Sources

The American Botanist. P.O. Box 532, Chillicothe, IL 61523.

Calendula Horticultural Books. 160 SW Alfred St., Chehalis, WA 98532.

Fertile Ground Books. 3912 Vale Ave., Oakland, CA 94619-2222, (530) 298-2060, books@agribooks.com.

Hortulus. 101 Scollard St., Toronto, ON M5R 1G4, Canada.

Hurley Books. R.R. 1, Box 160, Westmoreland, NH 03467.

Interloc, P.O. Box 5, Southworth, WA 98386.

Old Library Shop. (610) 838-2790.

Robert Gear. Box 1137, Greenfield, MA 01302.

## Permaculture

Baxter, Kay. *Design Your Own Orchard: Bringing Permaculture Design to the Ground in Aotearoa.* Maungaturoto, New Zealand: Koanga Gardens, n.d. 80 pp.

Bell, Graham. *The Permaculture Way.* London: HarperCollins, 1992. 240 pp.

"Cities and Their Regions." *The Permaculture Activist,* December 1995.

Holmgren, David. *"Melliodora," Hepburn Permaculture Gardens: 10 Years of Sustainable Living.* Victoria, Australia: Holmgren Design Services, 1995. 61 pp.

———. *Permaculture: Principles & Pathways Beyond Sustainability.* Victoria, Australia: Holmgren Design Services, 2002. 286 pp.

Jacke, Dave, and Eric Toensmeier. *Edible Forest Gardens: Ecological Vision and Theory for Temperate Climate Permaculture.* Vol. 1, *Vision and Theory.* White River Junction, VT: Chelsea Green Publishing, 2005. 378 pp.

*Mollison, Bill. *Permaculture: A Designers' Manual.* Tyalgum, Australia: Tagari Publications, 1996. 276 pp.

———. *Permaculture: A Practical Guide for a Sustainable Future.* Covelo, CA: Island Press, 1990. 579 pp.

Mollison, Bill, and David Holmgren. *Permaculture One.* Ealing, England: Corgi Books (TransWorld Publishers, Century House, 61–61 Uxbridge Rd., Ealing W5 5SA, England), 1978. 128 pp.

———. *Permaculture Two.* Tasmania: Tagari Books (P.O. Box 96, Stanley, Tasmania 7331, Australia), 1979.

Mollison, Bill, with Remy Mia Slay. *Introduction to Permaculture.* Tyalgum, Australia: Tagari Publications, 1994. 213 pp.

*The Permaculture Activist.* (Rte. 1, Box 38, Primm Springs, TN 38476.) Magazine.

*Permaculture Resources.* (56 Farmersville Rd., Caliton, NJ 07830, (800) 832-6285.) Magazine.

Weber, Don. Coppicing Workshops. (Box 1322, Mendocino, CA 95460.)

"Where Is Permaculture?" *The Permaculture Activist,* No. 49 (December 2002). Profiles on 10 North American permaculture sites plus the "Best in the World."

Whitefield, Patrick. *Permaculture in a Nutshell.* Hampshire, England: Permanent Publications, 2000. 84 pp.

## Philosophy

Adams, George, and Olive Whicher. *The Plant Between Sun and Earth.* Boulder, CO: Shambhala, 1980. 224 pp.

*Agriculture, Food and Human Values.* (100 E. Normal St., Kirksville, MO 63501-4211.) Quarterly journal.

*All-Consuming Passion: Waking Up from the American Dream.* Seattle, WA: New Road Map Foundation (P.O. Box 15981, Seattle, WA 98115), 1993. 23 pp.

Amidon, Elias, and Elizabeth Roberts, eds. *Earth Prayers from around the World: 365 Prayers, Poems, and Invocations for Honoring the Earth.* New York: Harper Collins, 1991. 451 pp.

Bailey, L. H. *The Harvest of the Year to the Tiller of the Soil.* New York: Macmillan, 1927.

———. *The Holy Earth.* New York: New York State College of Agriculture and Life Sciences, 1980. 112 pp.

Berry, Thomas. *The Dream of the Earth.* San Francisco: Sierra Club Books, 1988. 247 pp.

*Berry, Wendell. *The Unsettling of America: Culture and Agriculture.* San Francisco: Sierra Club Books, 1977. 226 pp. Eloquent and passionate view of the sociological aspects of farming.

Blix, Jacqueline, and David Heitmiller. *Getting a Life.* New York: Viking, 1997. 363 pp.

Boice, Judith L. *At One with All Life.* Moray, Scotland: Findhorn Press, 1989. 273 pp.

Boldt, Laurence G. *Zen and the Art of Making a Living.* New York: Penguin, 1999. 640 pp.

Bortoft, Henri. *The Wholeness of Nature.* Hudson, NY: Lindisfarne Press, 1996. 407 pp.

Bullfrog Films. *Sowing for Need or Sowing for Greed?* Oley, PA: Bullfrog Films. 58-minute video.

Burch, Mark A. *Simplicity.* Philadelphia, PA: New Society Publishers, 1995. 130 pp.

Calder, Ritchie. *After the Seventh Day.* New York: Simon & Schuster, 1961. 448 pp.

Capra, Fritjof. *The Turning Point: Science, Society, and the Rising Culture.* New York: Bantam Books, 1982. 464 pp.

*Christensen, Carl. *The Green Bible.* Ben Lomond, CA: Johnny Publishing (P.O. Box 624, Ben Lomond, CA 95005), 1990. 81 pp. Excellent.

deGraaf, John, David Wann, and Thomas H. Naylor. *Affluenza: The All-Consuming Epidemic.* San Francisco: Berrett-Koehler Publishers, 2001. 268 pp.

DeVault, George, ed. *Return to Pleasant Valley: Louis Bromfield's Best from Malabar Farm and His Other Country Classics.* Chillicothe, IL: The American Botanist, 1996. 318 pp.

*Dominguez, Joe, and Vicki Robin. *Your Money or Your Life: Transforming Your Relationship with Money and Achieving Financial Independence.* New York: Penguin, 1992. 350 pp.

Duesing, Bill and Suzanne. *Living on the Earth: Eclectic Essays for a Sustainable and Joyful Future.* East Haven, CT: Long River Books (140 Commerce St., East Haven, CT 06512), 1993. 222 pp.

Dull, Christine and Ralph. *Soviet Laughter, Soviet Tears.* Englewood, OH: Stillmore Press (7000 Stillmore Dr., Englewood, OH 45322), 1992. 370 pp.

Durning, Alan. *How Much Is Enough?* New York: W. W. Norton, 1992. 200 pp.

*The Earth Summit.* San Francisco: U.S. Citizens Network on UNCED (300 Broadway, Ste. 39, San Francisco, CA 94133), 1991. 44 pp. An introductory guide to the Earth Summit (June 1–12, 1992; Rio de Janeiro, Brazil).

Ehrlich, Gretel. *John Muir: Nature's Visionary.* Washington, DC: National Geographic Society, 2000. 240 pp.

*Faulkner, Edward H. *Plowman's Folly.* Norman, OK: University of Oklahoma Press, 1943. 155 pp.

Food and Agriculture Organization of the United Nations. *Report of the Panel of Eminent Experts on Ethics in Food and Agriculture.* First Session, September 2000. Rome: FAO. 26 pp.

Gillies, Douglas. *Prophet: The Hatmaker's Son: The Life of Robert Muller.* Santa Barbara, CA. East Beach Press, 2003. 282 pp.

*Goering, Peter, Helena Norberg Hodge, and John Page. *From the Ground Up: Rethinking Industrial Agriculture.* Atlantic Highlands, NJ: Zed Books/International Society for Ecology and Culture, 1993. 130 pp.

Gowdy, John, ed. *Limited Wants, Unlimited Means: A Reader on Hunter-Gatherer Economics and the Environment.* Washington, DC: Island Press, 1998. 342 pp.

*Gray, Charles. *Toward a Nonviolent Economics.* Eugene, OR: Charles Gray (888 Almaden, Eugene, OR 97402), 1989. 143 pp.

Gussow, Joan Dye. *Chicken Little, Tomato Sauce and Agriculture.* New York: Bookstrap Press, 1991. 150 pp.

Harlan, Jack R. *Crops and Man.* Madison, WI: American Society of Agronomy, Crop Science Society of America (677 S. Segoe Rd., Madison, WI 53711), 1992. 284 pp.

Hillel, Daniel. *Out of the Earth.* Berkeley, CA: University of California Press, 1992. 321 pp.

Howard, Louise E. *The Earth's Green Carpet.* Emmaus, PA: Rodale Press, 1947. 258 pp.

Hudson, Lois Phillips. *The Bones of Plenty.* St. Paul, MN: Minnesota Historical Press, 1984. 439 pp.

Illich, Ivan. *The Wisdom of Leopold Kohr.* Great Barrington, MA: E. F. Schumacher Society, 1996. 24 pp.

Kotke, William. H. *The Final Empire: The Collapse of Civilization.* Portland, OR: Arrow Point Press, 1993. 401 pp.

Luhrs, Janet. *The Simple Living Guide.* New York: Broadway Books, 1997. 444 pp.

*Mander, Jerry. *In the Absence of the Sacred.* San Francisco: Sierra Club Books (730 Polk St., San Francisco, CA 94109), 1992. 446 pp.

Maté, Ferenc. *A Reasonable Life: Toward a Simpler, Secure, More Humane Existence.* New York: W. W. Norton, 1993. 259 pp.

McRobie, George. *Small Is Possible.* New York: Harper & Row, 1980. 331 pp.

Merkel, Jim. *Radical Simplicity: Small Footprints on a Finite Earth.* Gabriola Island, BC, Canada: New Society Publishers, 2003. 248 pp.

Merrill, Richard, ed. *Radical Agriculture.* New York: Harper & Row, 1976. 459 pp. Philosophical and political aspects of food production.

*Millman, Dan. *Way of the Peaceful Warrior: A Book That Changes Lives.* Tiburon, CA: H. J. Kramer (P.O. Box 1082, Tiburon, CA 94920), 1984. 210 pp.

Quinn, Daniel. *Ishmael.* New York: Bantam, 1992. 262 pp.

*Return to the Earth.* Penang, Malaysia: The Third World Network (87 Cantonment Rd., 10250 Penang, Malaysia), 1990. 570 pp.

Richardson, William N., and Thomas Stubbs. *Plants, Agriculture, and Human Society.* Menlo Park, CA: W.A. Benjamin, Inc., 1978. 353 pp.

Rifkin, Jeremy. *Entropy.* New York: Bantam Books, 1981. 302 pp.

Roberts, Wayne, et al. *Get A Life!* Toronto: Get a Life Publishing House, 1993. 127 pp.

Rodale, Robert. *Sane Living in a Mad World: A Guide to the Organic Way of Life.* Emmaus, PA: Rodale Press, 1972. 270 pp.

Rosset, Peter, and Medea Benjamin, et al. *Two Steps Backward, One Step Forward.* San Francisco: Global Exchange, 1993. 67 pp.

Sahlins, Marshall. *Stone Age Economics.* New York: Aldine de Gruyter, 1972. 348 pp.

Sampson, R. Niel. *Farmland or Wasteland.* Emmaus, PA: Rodale Press, 1981. 422 pp.

Savage, Scott. *The Plain Reader.* New York: Ballantine, 1998. 241 pp.

Schumacher, E. F., et al. *The Collected Writings of Hazel Henderson—Creating Alternative Futures.* New York: Berkeley Publishing (200 Madison Ave., New York, NY 10016), 1978. 403 pp.

———. *An Economics of Peace.* Great Barrington, MA: E. F. Schumacher Society, 2001. 30 pp.

*———. *Good Work.* New York: Harper & Row, 1979. 223 pp.

*———. *Small Is Beautiful.* New York: Harper & Row, 1973. 305 pp.

Seymour, John. *I'm a Stranger Here Myself.* London: Faber and Faber, 1978. 140 pp. Absorbing personal account.

Teale, Edward Way, ed. *The Wilderness World of John Muir.* Boston: Houghton Mifflin, 1964. 332 pp.

Thomas, William L., Jr. *Man's Role in Changing the Face of the Earth.* 2 vols. Chicago: University of Chicago Press, 1956. 1,193 pp.

Thompson, Paul B. *The Spirit of the Soil: Agriculture and Environmental Ethics.* New York: Routledge, 1995. 196 pp.

Vandenbroeck, Goldian. *Less Is More.* Rochester, VT: Inner Traditions (One Park St., Rochester, VT 05767), 1991. 316 pp.

Willers, Bill. *Learning to Listen to the Land.* Washington, DC: Island Press, 1991. 283 pp.

## Plant Names

Bailey, L. H. *How Plants Got Their Names.* New York: Dover, 1963. 181 pp.

Healey, B. J. *A Gardener's Guide to Plant Names.* New York: Scribner's, 1972. 284 pp.

Johnson, A. F., and H. A. Smith. *Plant Names Simplified.* Bromyard, England: Landsman Bookshop (Buckenhill, Bromyard, Herefordshire, England), 1972. 120 pp.

## Plant Nutrient Indicators

Bear, Firman E. *Hunger Signs in Crops.* Washington, DC: The American Society of Agronomy and the National Fertilizer Assoc., 1949. 390 pp.

Clement, Frederic. *Plant Indicators: The Relation of Plant Communities to Process and Practice.* Stanford, CA: Carnegie Institute of Washington, 1920. 388 pp.

Dale, Hugh M. "Weed Complexes on Abandoned Pastures as Indicators of Site Characteristics." *Canadian Journal of Botany,* Vol. 44: 11–17.

Dale, Hugh M., P. J. Harrison, and G. W. Thomson. "Weeds as Indicators of Physical Site Characteristics in Abandoned Pastures." *Canadian Journal of Botany,* Vol. 43: 1,319–1,327.

Gershuny, Grace, and Joseph Smillie. *The Soul of Soil.* St. Johnsbury, VT: Gaia Services, 1986. 174 pp.

Hill, Stuart, and Jennifer Ramsey. "Weeds as Indicators of Soil Conditions." *Macdonald Journal,* Vol. 38, No. 3 (March 1939).

Pfeiffer, Ehrenfried. *Weeds and What They Tell.* Stroudsburg, PA: Biodynamic Farming and Gardening Assn., 1970. 96 pp. Reading soil conditions by weeds.

Sampson, Arthur W. "Plant Indicators—Concept and Status." *Botanical Review,* Vol. 5, No. 3 (March 1939).

Shantz, Homer Leroy. *Natural Vegetation as an Indicator of the Capabilities of Land for Crop Production in the Great Plains Area.* Washington, DC: U.S. Department of Agriculture, 1911. 100 pp.

## Pruning

Bailey, L. H. *The Pruning Manual.* New York: Macmillan, 1954. 320 pp. Constantly revised for 50 years and now out of print.

Brickell, Christopher. *Fruit.* New York: Simon & Schuster, 1980. 96 pp.

*———. *Pruning.* New York: Simon & Schuster, 1980. 96 pp.

Brickell, Christopher, and David Joyce. *Pruning and Training.* New York: DK, 1996. 336 pp.

DiSabato-Aust, Tracy. "Pruning Perennials in Midseason." *Fine Gardening,* May/June 1998: 55–59.

Hill, Lewis. *Pruning Simplified.* Pownal, VT: Storey, 1986. 208 pp.

Lorette, Louis. *The Lorette System of Pruning.* London: Martin Hopkinson, 1925. 164 pp. Practiced by Alan Chadwick. Fruit trees are gently pinched and trained during summer.

Stebbins, Robert L., and Michael MacCaskey. *Pruning: How-To Guide for Gardeners.* Los Angeles: HP Books, 1983. 160 pp.

Sunset Editors. *Pruning Handbook.* Menlo Park, CA: Sunset Books, 1976. 96 pp.

Turnbull, Cass. *Cass Turnbull's Guide to Pruning.* Seattle: Sasquatch Books, 2004. 226 pp.

## Reference

*Bailey, L. H. *Cyclopedia of American Agriculture in Four Volumes.* New York: Macmillan, 1907. 2,675 pp., including many illustrations. Excellent. See Vol. 2, *Crops,* especially.

———. *The Farm and Garden Rule-Book.* New York: Macmillan, 1915. 586 pp.

———. *The Standard Cyclopedia of Horticulture in Three Volumes.* New York: Macmillan, 1944. 4,056 pp., including 4,000+ engravings and other illustrations.

Bailey, Liberty Hyde, and Ethel Zoe. *Hortus Third: A Concise Dictionary of Plants Cultivated in the United States and Canada.* New York: Macmillan, 1976. 1,290 pp.

Bullfrog Films. (Department F., Oley, PA 19547.) Good selection of films on food, farming, land use, and the environment, including *Gardensong,* a PBS special on Alan Chadwick and the Biointensive method, and *Circle of Plenty,* a PBS-TV special on Ecology Action's work and a key Biointensive mini-farming project in Mexico. Send 2 stamps for a catalog.

Chittenden, Fred J., ed. *Dictionary of Gardening in Three Volumes,* 2nd edition. Oxford, England: Royal Horticulture Society, Clarendon Press, 1977. 2,316 pp.

Creasy, Rosalind. *Van Patten's Organic Gardener's Edible Plants.* Chicago, IL: Login Publishers Consortium, 1993. 222 pp.

DeMuth, Suzanne. *Vegetables and Fruits: A Guide to Heirloom Varieties and Community-Based Stewardship.* 3 vols.: Annotated Bibliography, Resource Organizations, Historical Supplement. Beltsville, MD: U.S. Department of Agriculture, Special Reference Briefs Series 98–05, 1998. 135 pp., 72 pp., 78 pp.

Department of Agronomy and Range Science, University of California, Davis, CA. Bulletins, Crop Production, 80 B. Various bulletins from 1890s through early 1900s.

Els, David, et al., eds. *The National Gardening Association Dictionary of Horticulture.* New York: Penguin Books, 1994. 830 pp.

*Erichsen-Brown, Charlotte. *Medicinal and Other Uses of North American Plants.* New York: Dover, 1989. 512 pp. Originally called *The Use of Plants for the Past 500 Years.*

Fern, Ken. *Plants for a Future: Edible and Useful Plants for a Healthier World.* East Meon, Hampshire, England: Permanent Publications, Hyden House, The Sustainability Centre, 2000. 300 pp.

Hickman, James C. ed., *The Jepson Manual: Higher Plants of California.* Berkeley, CA: University of California Press, 1993. 1,400 pp.

Montgomery, E. G. *Lippincott's Farm Manuals: Productive Farm Crops.* Philadelphia, PA: J. B. Lippincott, 1916. 501 pp.

*Past Worlds: The Times Atlas of Archeology.* Maplewood, NJ: Hammond, 1988. 319 pp.

Pratt, Anne. *Flowering Plants, Grasses, Sedges and Ferns of Great Britain.* 4 vols. London: Frederick Warne, 1905. 215 pp., 279 pp., 269 pp., 258 pp.

Raven, Peter H., Ray F. Evert, and Susan E. Eichhorn. *Biology of Plants.* New York: Worth, 1992. 791 pp.

Schery, Robert W. *Plants for Man.* Englewood Cliffs, NJ: Prentice-Hall, 1972. 657 pp.

*Seagfer, Joni, ed. *The State of the Earth Atlas.* New York: Simon & Schuster, 1990. 127 pp.

*Source Book of Sustainable Agriculture.* Burlington, VT: University of Vermont, Sustainable Agriculture Publications, 1997. 136 pp. A guide to books, newsletters, conference proceedings, bulletins, videos, and more.

*Sustainable Agriculture Directory of Expertise—1993.* Burlington, VA: Sustainable Agriculture Publications (Hills Bldg., Rm. 12, University of Vermont, Burlington, VT 05405-0082), 1993.

Synge, Patrick M., ed. *Dictionary of Gardening,* 2nd ed. supplement. Oxford, England: Royal Horticultural Society, Clarendon Press, 1979. 554 pp.

## Roots

Epstein, Emanuel. "Roots." *Scientific American,* May 1973: 48–58.

Hill, Madalene, and Gwen Barclay. "It's Not Your Mother's Tapioca [Cassava]." *Herb Companion,* July 2005: 38–42.

Paterson, William G. R., ed. *Farm Crops.* Vol.2, *Root Crops.* London: The Gresham Publishing Co., 1925. 306 pp.

*Weaver, John E. *Prairie Plants and Their Environment.* Lincoln, NE: University of Nebraska Press, 1968. 276 pp. **IL**

*———. *Root Development of Field Crops.* New York: McGraw-Hill, 1926. 291 pp. **IL**

*———. *Root Development of Vegetable Crops.* New York: McGraw-Hill, 1927. 351 pp. Excellent diagrams of root systems. **IL**

*Wilson, Charles M. *Roots: Miracles Below.* New York: Doubleday, 1968. 234 pp.

## Seed and Gardening Catalogs

Abundant Life Catalog. P.O. Box 157, Saginaw, OR 97472. Open-pollinated and heirloom seeds; books.

AgroForester Tropical Seeds. P.O. Box 428, Holualoa, HI 96725.

Agroforestry Research Trust—Plants, Seeds, Books & Sundries. 46 Hunters Totnes, Devon, TQ9 6JT, UK.

Always Summer Herbs. 199 Magill Rd., Slippery Rock, PA 16057.

American Bamboo Co. 345 W. 2nd St., Dayton, OH 45402.

American Willow Growers Network. RFD Box 124-A, S. New Berlin, NY 13843.

Anderson Valley Nursery. P.O. Box 504, Boonville, CA 95415. Perennials, shrubs, and trees.

*The Antique Rose Emporium. Rte. 5, Box 143, Brenham, TX 77833. Excellent. $5 for catalog.

Applesource. Rte. 1, Chapin, IL 62628. Apple trees.

Archia's Seed. 106–108 E. Main St., Sedalia, MO 65301. Seeds; garden and greenhouse supplies.

Baker Creek Heirloom Seeds. 2278 Naker Creek Rd., Mansfield, MO 65704. An excellent source of a wide variety of heirloom seeds.

Bakker of Holland. U.S. Bulb Reservation Center, Louisiana, MO 63350. Bulbs and perennials.

The Banana Tree. 715 Northampton St., Easton, PA 18042. Rare seeds.

Bear Creek Nursery. P.O. Box 411, Northport, WA 99157. Trees, tools, and books.

BIBLIOGRAPHY

Biologische Tuinzaden. 83 De Bolster, 9605 PL, Kielwindeweer, Germany. Vegetable seeds.

*Bountiful Gardens. 18001 Shafer Ranch Rd., Willits, CA 95490. Ecology Action's international mail order service for vegetable, grain, compost crop, flower, and herb seeds in growing area–sized packets; key gardening books and supplies; and all Ecology Action publications.

Breck's. 6523 N. Galena Rd., Peoria, IL 61632. Bulbs, wildflowers, and lilies.

Brittingham's Plant Farms. P.O. Box 2538, Salisbury, MD 21801. Berries, grapes, and asparagus.

Burpee Seed Co. Warminster, PA 18974. Large, well-known company with wide selection of vegetables and flowers. Separate catalog of heirloom seeds.

California Conservation Corps. P.O. Box 329, Yountville Center, Yountville, CA 94599. Trees.

California Gardener's Seed Co. 904 Silver Spur Rd., Ste. 414, Rolling Hills Estates, CA 90274. Seeds and garden supplies.

Caprilands Herb Farm. 534 Silver St., Coventry, CT 06238.

Carroll Gardens. P.O. Box 310, Westminster, MD 21158. Seeds.

Catnip Acres Farm. Christian St., Oxford, CT 06483. Herbs and flowers.

Charles H. Mueller. River Rd., New Hope, PA 18938. Flowers, lilies, and bulbs.

Cherfas, Jeremy. *The Fruit and Veg Finder.* Coventry, England: Henry Doubleday Research Association, 1995. 367 pp.

Chestnut Hill Nursery. 15105 NW 94 Ave., Alachua, FL 32615. Chestnuts, persimmons, and figs.

Clyde Robin Seed Co. P.O. Box 2366, Castro Valley, CA 94546. Wildflower seeds.

Comfrey Roots. Machado Farms, P.O. Box 655, Sun City, CA 92586.

Companion Plants. 7247 N. Coolville Ridge Rd., Athens, OH 45701. Herbs.

Comstock. 263 Main St., Wethersfield, CT 06109. Seeds and supplies.

Cook's Garden. P.O. Box 535, Londonderry, VT 05148. Seeds and supplies.

Country Heritage Nursery. P.O. Box 5, Hartford, MI 49057. Berries, grapes, roots, and hedges; fruit, nut, ornamental, shade, and evergreen trees.

Country Hills Greenhouse. Rte. 2, Corning, OH 43710. Plants.

Crimson Sage Nursery. P.O. Box 83, Orleans, CA 95556.

Crocket Seed Co. P.O. Box 327, Metamora, OH 43540. Seeds.

Cruikshank's. 1015 Mount Pleasant Rd., Toronto, ON M4P 2M1, Canada. Seeds, bulbs, books, and supplies.

Dave Wilson Nursery. 19701 Lake Rd., Hickman, CA 95323. Good fruit trees. Wholesale only.

Davidson-Wilson Greenhouses. R.R. 2, Crawfordsville, IN 47933. Familiar, flowering, and exotic tropical houseplants, and mini and standard violets.

De Bolster. Pieter Venmakade 61, 9605 PL Kielwindeweer, Netherlands. Biodynamic vegetable, herb, and flower seeds.

De Giorgi Co. 6011 N St., Omaha, NE 68117-1634.

De Grandchamp's Nursery. 15575 77th St., South Haven, MI 49090. Blueberries.

Dean Swift Seed Co. P.O. Box B, Jaroso, CO 81138. Bulk tree seeds.

*Deep Diversity. P.O. Box 15700, Santa Fe, NM 87506-5700. Wide variety of organically grown, open-pollinated seeds and related publications. Excellent.

Di Giorgi Co. 1411 3rd St., Council Bluffs, IA 51501. Forage crops, old-fashioned lettuce and other vegetables, and open-pollinated corn.

Dr. Yoo Farm. P.O. Box 90, College Park, MD 20740. Oriental vegetable seeds.

Earl May Seed and Nursery. Shenandoah, IA 51603. Fertilizers, berries, grapes, vines, hedges, shrubs, roses, and seeds; fruit and nut trees.

Early Seed and Garden Center. 2615 Lorne Ave., Saskatoon, SK S7J 0S5, Canada. Grain, fodder, and cover crops.

Ed Hume Seeds. P.O. Box 1450, Kent, WA 98035. Seeds and tools.

Edible Landscapes. P.O. Box 77, Afton, VA 22920. Trees, berries, grapes, and vines.

Elixir Farm Botanicals. Brixey, MO 65618. Chinese and indigenous medicinal plants, seeds, and garlic.

Environmental Seed. P.O. Box 5904, El Monte, CA 91734. Wildflower seeds.

Epicure Seeds. Avon, NY 14414. Choice varieties from gourmet seed houses of Europe.

Essence of Old Gardeners. P.O. Box 407, Redkey, IN 47373. Seeds.

Evergreen Y. H. Enterprises. P.O. Box 17538, Anaheim CA 92817. An extensive selection of Oriental vegetable seeds.

Exotica Seed Company and Rare Fruit Nursery. P.O. Box 160, Vista, CA 92083. Rare fruits, vegetables, and vines; nuts, palms, and flowering trees.

Facciola, Stephen. *Cornucopia II— A Source Book of Edible Plants.* Vista, CA: Kampong Publications (1870 Sunrise Dr., Vista, CA 92084), 1998. 713 pp. A listing of seeds carried by many catalogs and sources in the United States and other countries.

Fedco Seeds. P.O. Box 520, Waterville, ME 04903-0520. A growers' cooperative with an extensive listing, including Japanese millet (not food quality).

Filaree Farm. 182 Conconully Hwy., Okanogan, WA 98840. Lots of organically grown garlic varieties.

Fisher's Seeds. P.O. Box 236, Belgrade, MT 59714. Vegetable and flower seeds for high altitudes and short growing seasons. Not all open-pollinated.

Forest Farm. 990 Tethrow Rd., Williams, OR 97544-9599. Plants, trees, and books.

Fox Hill Farm. 440 W. Michigan Ave., Box 9, Parma, MI 49269. Flowers and herbs.

Fox Hollow Herb and Heirloom Seed Co. P.O. Box 148, McGrann, PA 16236.

Fragrant Fields. 2460 Swan Pond Rd., Dangola, IL 62926.

Frey Nurseries. 14000 Tomki Rd., Redwood Valley, CA 95470. Plants.

*Friends of the Trees Society. P.O. Box 1064, Tonasket, WA 98855. Books. Excellent.

Fungi Perfecti. P.O. Box 7634, Olympia, WA 98507. Mushroom-growing supplies and books.

Future Forests Nursery and Design. P.O. Box 428, Holualoa, HI 96725. Sustainable reforestation and agroforestry.

G. S. Grimes Seeds. 201 W. Main St., Smethport, PA 16749. Seeds, bulbs, and perennials.

Garlic King Farms. Dean and Mary Sue Sedinger, 833 Baxter Rd., Vineland, CO 81006.

George W. Park Seed Co. 1 Parkton Ave., Greenwood, SC 29647-0001. The best selection of flowers. Gorgeous full-color catalog available free.

Goodwin Creek Gardens. P.O. Box 83, Williams, OR 97544. (800) 846-7359.

The Gourmet Gardener. 8650 College Blvd., Oakland Park, KS 66210. Imported and domestic herb, vegetable, and flower seed.

Great Northern Botanicals Association. P.O. Box 362, Helena, MT 59624. Northern Rockies specialty crops and plant information.

Gurney's Seed and Nursery. 110 Capital St., Yankton, SD 57079. Seeds, vines, berries, ground covers, hedges, shrubs, bulbs, perennials, roses, and houseplants; fruit, nut, shade, and flowering trees; and supplies.

Harmony Farm Supply. P.O. Box 460, Graton, CA 95444. Plants, berries, and fruit and nut trees.

Hart Seed Co. P.O. Box 9169, Wethersfield, CT 06109. Largest selection of old-fashioned and nonhybrid vegetables. Many hard-to-find varieties available on request.

Hartmann's Nursery. P.O. Box 100, Lacota, MI 49063-0100.

The Heirloom Gardener. P.O. Box 70, Mansfield, MO 65704-0700. Quarterly periodical focusing on heirloom vegetables, fruits, and seeds.

Heirloom Seed Project. 2451 Kissel Hill Rd., Lancaster, PA 17601. Seeds.

*Henry Doubleday Research Association—Ryton Gardens— The National Centre for Organic Gardening. Ryton-on-Dunsmore, Coventry CV8 3LG, England. Vegetable, flower, herb, and green manure seeds, organic fertilizer, safe pesticides, comfrey products, educational materials, books, and attractant plants. Excellent group.

Henry Field's Seed and Nursery. 415 N. Burnett, Shenandoah, IA 51602. Seeds, ground cover, vines, berries, roses, lilies, perennials, and Oriental grasses; fruit, nut, and flowering trees; and supplies.

Henry Leuthardt. Montauk Hwy., East Moriches, Long Island, NY 11940. Specializes in old-fashioned varieties of apple trees, pear trees, and grapes.

Henry Morton—Old Fashioned Apples. Rte. 1, Box 203, Gatlinburg, TN 37738. Old Appalachian Mountain varieties.

The Herb Cottage. 442 CR 233, Hallettsville, TX 77964.

Herbst Brothers. 1000 N. Main St., Brewster, NY 10509. Seeds, annuals, perennials, trees, and bulbs; greenhouse and nursery supplies.

Heritage Roses. 40340 Wilderness Rd., Branscomb, CA 95417. Roses.

Hidden Springs Nursery. Rte. 14, Box 159, Cookeville, TN 38501. Edible landscaping plants, herbs, and tree crops.

High Altitude Gardens. P.O. Box 4619, Ketchum, ID 83340. Vegetable, wildflower, and herb seeds; native grasses and supplies.

A High Country Garden. 2909 Rufina St., Santa Fe, NM 87505-2929. Drought-hardy, perennial plants for Western gardens.

High Mowing Seeds. 813 Brook Rd., Wolcott, VT 05680. Open-pollinated and heirloom varieties for the Northeast.

Hillier Nurseries, Ltd. Ampfield, Ramsey, Hants S05 9PA, England. Excellent tree and plant supplier.

Hilltop Herb Farm. Box 866, Cleveland, TX 77327. Herb plants.

Holland Bulb Farms. P.O. Box 220, Tatamy, PA 18085-0220. Bulbs.

Horizon Herbs. P.O. Box 69, Williams, OR 97544-0069. 62 pp.

Horus Botanicals. 341 Mulberry, Salem, AR 72576. Heirloom grains and other seeds from all over the world.

Hurov's Tropical Seeds. P.O. Box 1596, Chula Vista, CA 92012. Tropical seeds and indoor exotics.

Indiana Berry and Plant Company. 5218 West 500 South, Huntingburg, IN 47542.

Irish Eyes. P.O. Box 307, Ellensburg, WA 98926. Potatoes and garlic.

J. H. Judkins and Sons Tree Nursery. Rte. 4, Smithville, TN 37166. Hedges, shrubs, ground cover, vines, and fruit trees.

*J. L. Hudson, Seedsman. Star Rte. 2, Box 337, LaHonda, CA 94020. Vegetable, flower, and herb seeds; books. Excellent selection.

Johnny's Selected Seeds. Foss Hill Rd., R.R. 1, Box 2580, Albion, ME 04910-9731. Small seed company with integrity. Carries Native American crops, select Oriental vegetables, grains, short-maturing soybeans, and supplies.

Kester's Wild Game Nurseries. Box 516, Omro, WI 54963. Grain, vegetable, and grass seeds; publications.

*KUSA Seed Foundation. Box 761, Ojai, CA 93023. Key seed crop seeds and literature. Excellent.

Landreth Seed Co. 650 N. North Point Rd., Baltimore, MI 21237.

Larner Seeds. P.O. Box 60143, 445 Monroe Dr., Palo Alto, CA 94306. Vegetable, flower, grass, shrub, vine, and tree seeds. Specializes in California and New England native seeds.

*Legume Seed Source Directory.* Kutztown, PA: Rodale Institute Research Center (611 Siegfriedale Rd., Kutztown, PA 19530), 1992. 23 pp.

Lingle's Herbs. 2055 N. Lomiona Ave., Long Beach, CA 90815

Living Tree Center. P.O. Box 797, Bolinas, CA 94924. Seeds and trees.

Lockhart Seeds. P.O. Box 1361, Stockton, CA 95205. Vegetable seeds.

Lost Prairie Herb Farm. 805 Kienas Rd., Kalispell, MT 59901. Plants, supplies, and books.

Machado Farms. P.O. Box 655, Sun City, CA 92586. Comfrey roots. Send a self-addressed, stamped envelope for more information.

Maine Seed Saving Network. P.O. Box 126, Penobscot, ME 04476.

McClure and Zimmerman. P.O. Box 368, 108 W. Winnebago, Friesland, WI 53935. Bulbs and books.

Mellinger's. 2310 W. South Range Rd., North Lima, OH 44452-9731. Unusual imported vegetable, herb, flower, and grass seeds; berries and vines. Wide variety of familiar and unusual trees, plants, and roses. Mushrooms, tools, supplies, books, and greenhouse equipment.

Messelaar Bulb Co. P.O. Box 269, Ipswich, MA 01938. Bulbs.

Michigan Bulb Co. 1950 Waldorf, Grand Rapids, MI 49550. Grapes, berries, roses, plants, flowers, and fruit trees.

Mongold, Susan and Rex. HCR 15, Dyer, NV 89010. Seed potatoes.

Moon Mountain. P.O. Box 34, Morro Bay, CA 93442. Wildflower seeds.

Moose Grower's Supply. P.O. Box 520, Waterville, ME 04903. Seed potatoes, onion sets, Jerusalem artichokes, cover crop seeds, organic fertilizers, and books.

Mountain Maples. 5901 Spy Rock Rd., Laytonville, CA 95454-1329. Variety of maples, bonsai, and dwarf conifers.

Mountain Valley Growers. 38325 Pepperweed Road, Squaw Valley, CA 93675.

Mulberry Creek Herb Farm. 3312 Bogart Rd., Huron, OH 44839.

*Native Seeds and Plants.* Ankeny, IA: Soil and Water Conservation Society (7515 NE Ankeny Rd., Ankeny, IA 50021). 36 pp.

*Native Seeds/SEARCH. 526 N. 4th Ave., Tucson, AZ 85705. Herbs, books, dyes, and baskets. Excellent cotton and tobacco seeds, drought-tolerant corn, beans, and vegetables.

New England Strawberry Nursery. S. Deerfield, MA 01373. Strawberries.

Nichols Garden Nursery. 1190 Old Salem Rd. NE, Albany, OR 97321-4580. Unusual specialties: elephant garlic, luffa sponge, winemaking supplies, and herbs.

No Thyme Productions. 8321 S.E. 61st St., Mercer Island, WA 98040.

North Central Comfrey Products. P.O. Box 195, Glidden, WI 54527. Comfrey and comfrey products.

North Star Gardens. 19060 Manning Trail N., Marine-on-St. Croix, MN 55047-9723. Raspberries— northern, western, and southern stock.

Nourse Farms, Inc. 41 River Rd., South Deerfield, MA 01373. Strawberry, raspberry, asparagus, and rhubarb starts.

Oikos Tree Crops. P.O. Box 19425, Kalamazoo, MI 49019-0425.

One Green World. 28696 S. Cramer Rd., Molalla, OR 97038-8576. Fruit trees and ornamentals.

Oregon Exotics Nursery. 1065 Messinger Rd., Grants Pass, OR 97527.

P. de Jager and Sons. P.O. Box 100, Brewster, NY 10509. Bulbs and lilies.

Papa Geno's. 6005 W. Roca Rd., Martell, NE 68404.

Peace Seeds. 2385 SE Thompson St., Corvallis, OR 97333.

Perennial Vegetable Seed Co. P.O. Box 608, Belchertown, MA 01007.

Phoenix Seeds. P.O. Box 9, Stanley, Tasmania 7331. Organic seed varieties.

Plants of the Southwest. Agua Fria, Rte. 6, Box 11A, Santa Fe, NM 87501. Products for a healthy planet.

Possum Creek Herb Farm. 528 Nature Trail, Soddy-Daisy, TN 37379.

Prairie Moon Nursery. 31837 Bur Oak Lane, Winona, MN 55987-4219. Native plants and seeds for wetland, prairie, savanna, and woodland.

R. H. Shumway Seed Company. 334 W. Stroud St., Randolph, WI 53956. Vegetable, flower, herb, grass, grain, fodder, and cover crop seeds; roses, berries, and fruit trees; and supplies.

Raintree Nursery. 391 Butts Rd., Morton, WA 98356. Berries, plants, fruit and nut trees, books, and supplies.

Ramsey Seed. P.O. Box 351, 205 Stockton St., Manteca, CA 95336. Wide variety of seeds, including those for compost crops.

Redwood City Seed Co. P.O. Box 361, Redwood City, CA 94064. Basic selection of nonhybrid, untreated vegetable and herb seeds. Expert at locating various tree seeds, including redwoods.

Reliable Seeds. 3862 Carlsbad Blvd., Carlsbad, CA 92008. Seeds.

Richters—Canada's Herb Specialist. 357 Hwy. 47, Goodwood, ON L0C 1A0, Canada. Herb, vegetable, and flower seeds. Plants, supplies, potpourri, natural medicines, and books.

Rocky Mountain Seed Services. Box 215, Golden, BC V0A 1H0, Canada. British Columbia native seeds, including hard-to-find varieties.

Rohrer Seeds. P.O. Box 250, Smoketown, PA 17576. Vegetable and flower seeds plus some cover crops and grains.

Ronniger Potato Farm. 20094 N. State Highway 149, Powderhorn, CO 81243. Organic potato and garlic seeds.

Roses of Yesterday and Today. 802 Brown's Valley Rd., Watsonville, CA 95076-0398. Old, rare, unusual, and modern roses.

Russell Graham. 4030 Eagle Crest Rd. NW, Salem, OR 97304. Bulbs, flowers, perennials, ferns, and Oriental grasses.

Salt Spring Seeds. P.O. Box 444, Ganges, Salt Spring Island, BC V8K 2W1, Canada. Organic open-pollinated grains, beans, and vegetables.

Sanctuary Seeds. 1913 Yew St., Vancouver, BC V6K 3G3, Canada. Seeds, companion plants, and medicinals.

Sand Hill Preservation Center. 1878 230th St., Calamus, IA 52729. Heirloom seeds and poultry. 90-day sweet potato varieties.

Sandy Mush Herb Nursery. 316 Surrett Cove Rd., Leicester, NC 28748-9622. Seeds, plants, herbs, and books.

Sassafras Farms. P.O. Box 1007, Topanga, CA 90290. Two dozen organically grown vegetable varieties and miscellaneous roots.

*Seed Saver's Exchange. 3076 North Winn Rd., Decorah, IA 52101. Exchange listings published yearly for $2. Good source of heirloom varieties. Listing includes seed saving guide. Excellent.

*————. *Fruit, Berry and Nut Inventory*, 3rd ed. Seed Saver's Exchange, 3076 North Winn Rd., Decorah, IA 52101, 2001. 560 pp.

*————. *Garden Seed Inventory*, 5th ed. Seed Saver's Exchange, 3076 North Winn Rd., Decorah, IA 52101, 2001. 560 pp. Excellent listing of all open-pollinated vegetable seed varieties sold in the United States.

*Seeds of Change. P.O. Box 15700, Santa Fe, NM 87592-1500. Organic seeds.

Self-Reliance Seed Co. P.O. Box 96, Stanley, Tasmania 7331. Vegetable, annual, herb, and tree seeds.

Setropa. P.O. Box 203, 1400, A. E. Bussum, Holland. Seeds for forestry and environmental conservation.

Shady Acres Herb Farm. 7815 Hwy. 212, Chaska, MN 55318.

Shepherd's Garden Seeds. 30 Irene St., Torrington, CT 06790-6658. Special vegetable, flower, and herb seeds; supplies and books.

Shoulder to Shoulder Farms. P.O. Box 1509, Philomath, OR 97370.

Sonoma Antique Apple Nursery. 4395 Westside Rd., Healdsburg, CA 95448. Fruit trees.

Sourcepoint Organic Seeds. 26422 Moss Park Rd., Hotchkiss, CO 81419. Organic cereal grains, vegetables, and other seeds from many parts of the world.

Southern Exposure Seed Exchange. P.O. Box 460, Mineral, VA 23117. Apple, vegetable, and flower seeds; supplies and books. Mostly open-pollinated seeds.

Southmeadow Fruit Gardens. Lakeside, MI 49116. Large selection of fruit trees.

Spring Hill Nurseries. 110 W. Elm St., Tipp City, OH 45371. Perennial plants and flowers.

St. Lawrence Nurseries. 325 State Hwy. 345, Potsdam, NY 13676. Berries and vines; fruit and nut trees.

Stark Brothers Nurseries and Orchards Co. P.O. Box 510, Louisiana, MO 63353-0510. Fruit tree and landscaping catalog. Hedges, shrubs, vines, berries, ground covers, and roses; fruit, nut, shade, and ornamental trees; supplies and books. Specializes in fruit trees, especially dwarf and semidwarf varieties, including many developed by Luther Burbank.

Steele Plant Co. Gleason, TN 38229. Sweet potato starts; onion, cauliflower, cabbage, brussels sprouts, and broccoli seeds.

*Stokes Seeds. P.O. Box 548, Buffalo, NY 14240-0548. Carries excellent varieties of many vegetables, especially carrots. Be sure to specify untreated seeds.

Suffolk Herbs. Sawyer's Farm, Little Cornard, Sudbury, Suffolk C010 0NY, England. Wide variety of seeds and herbs.

Sunnyboy Gardens. 3314 Earlysville Rd., Earlysville, VA 22936. Herb catalog.

Sunnybrook Farms Nursery. 9448 Mayfield Rd., Chesterland, OH 44026. Scented geranium source.

Suttons Seeds. Hele Rd., Torquay, Devon TQ2 7QJ, England. Catalog available only in England. Use catalog for information only. Order seeds through Garden Import, P.O. Box 760, Thornhill, ON L3T 4A5, Canada.

Synergy Seeds. P.O. Box 787, Somes Bar, CA 95556. Open-pollinated, some wildcrafted. Unusual grains.

Taylor Herb Gardens. 1535 Lone Oak Rd., Vista, CA 92084. Herb seeds and plants by mail.

Territorial Seed Co. P.O. Box 157, Cottage Grove, OR 97424-0061. Seeds, tools, and supplies.

Thompson and Morgan. P.O. Box 1308, Jackson, NJ 08527-0308. Wide variety of seeds.

Thunderfoot Earthworks—Sunny-land Seeds. John Munk, P.O. Box 385, Paradox, CO 81429.

The Thyme Garden. 20546 Alsea Hwy., Alsea, OR 97324.

Tillinghast Seed Co. P.O. Box 738, LaConner, WA 98257.

Tolowa Nursery. P.O. Box 509, Talent, OR 97540. Berries, grapes, and fruit, nut, woodlot, and ornamental trees.

Tomato Growers Supply. P.O. Box 2237, Fort Myers, FL 33902. Tomato and pepper seeds; supplies, books, and cooking equipment.

Tradewinds Bamboo Nursery. 28446 Hunter Creek Loop, Gold Beach, OR 97444. Plants, books, hard goods, and bamboo products.

True Seed Exchange. R.R. 1, Princeton, MO 64673. Exchange for home-grown seed. To join (i.e., to list your seeds for exchange and to receive listings in return), send $2.

Turtle Tree Seeds. Camphill Village, Copake, NY 12516. Biodynamic, open-pollinated seeds.

Underwood Gardens. Grandma's Garden, 1414 Zimmerman Rd.,

Woodstock, IL 60098. Open-pollinated and heirloom seeds.

Valley Seed Service. P.O. Box 9335, Fresno, CA 93791. Specialty seeds for research.

Van Bourgondien. P.O. Box A, 245 Farmingdale Rd., Babylon, NY 11702. Bulbs, ground cover seeds, and rare perennials.

Van Engelen. 23 Tulip Dr., Bantam, CT 06750. Bulbs and lilies.

Vandenberg. Black Meadow Rd., Chester, NY 10918. Bulbs, indoor plants, lilies, perennials, and wildflowers.

Vermont Bean Seed Co. 334 W. Stroud St., Randolph, WI 53956. All kinds of beans for those who want to start growing more protein crops.

Vesey's Seeds for Short Seasons. P.O. Box 9000, Calais, ME 04619-6102. Vegetable and flower seeds, supplies, tools, books, and natural pest control.

Victory Garden Plants. P.O. Box 867, Mendocino, CA 95460. Landscaping plants.

Vilmorin. 6104 Yorkshire Terr., Bethesda, MD 20814. Vegetable seeds.

Vilmorin Andrieux. 4, quai de la Megisserie, 75001 Paris, France. Old, respected seed house specializing in high-quality gourmet vegetables. Catalog in French. Expensive minimum order.

Volkman/North Coast Seed Co. P.O. Box 5875, Portland, OR 97228. Grass, pasture, and bird seed.

Wayside Gardens. 1 Garden Ln., Hodges, SC 29695-0001. Trees, vines, shrubs, plants, supplies, and books.

Well-Sweep Herb Farm. 317 Mount Bethel Rd., Port Murray, NJ 07865. Herbs, supplies, and books.

Western Native Seed. P.O. Box 188, Coaldale, CO 81222. Native plant seeds for the Rockies and Great Plains.

White Flower Farm. Litchfield, CT 06759-0050. Plants, flowers, tools, supplies, and books.

Willhite Seed Co. P.O. Box 23, Poolville, TX 76076. Vegetable seeds.

Wilson Brothers Floral Co. Roachdale, IN 46172. Scented geranium source.

Winterthur. Winterthur, DE 19735. Rare plants.

Wolf River Nurseries. Rte. 67, Buskirk, NY 12028. Vines, berries, and trees.

Wood Prairie Farm. 49 Kinney Rd., Bridgewater, ME 04735. Organic seed potatoes.

Yates Vegetable Seed Catalog for Commercial Growers. P.O. Box 616, Toowoomba, Queensland, Australia 4350. Specializes in tropical varieties suitable for the southern hemisphere. Free international seed catalog.

*Yerba Buena Nursery. 19500 Skyline Blvd., Woodside, CA 94062. Native California plants. Excellent.

## Seed Saving

Almekinders, Conny, and Niels Louwaars. *Farmers' Seed Production: New Approaches and Practices.* London: Intermediate Technology Publications, 1999. 291 pp.

*Ashworth, Suzanne. *Seed to Seed.* Decorah, IA: Seed Savers Publications (3076 North Winn Rd., Decorah, IA 52101), 1991. 222 pp.

Bubel, Nancy. "Saving Seeds." *Mother Earth News,* September/October 1987: 58–63.

Department of Agronomy. *Seed Saving Project News* (U.C. Davis), Winter/Spring 1991. 13 pp.

Deppe, Carol. *Breed Your Own Vegetable Varieties.* White River Junction, VT: Chelsea Green, 2000. 367 pp.

Dremann, Craig. *Vegetable Seed Production.* Redwood City, CA: Redwood City Seed Co. (P.O. Box 360, Redwood City, CA 94064), 1974. 6 pp.

Gately, Barbara. *Plant Pollination Instructional Manual.* Berkeley, CA: U.C. Instructional Laboratory, Graduate School of Education.

George, Raymond A. T. *Vegetable Seed Production,* 2nd edition. New York: CABI Publishing, 1999. 328 pp.

Horizon Herbs, P.O. Box 69, Williams, OR 97544. Seed cleaning screens.

Jason, Dan. *Save Our Seeds, Save Ourselves.* Salt Spring Island, Canada: Salt Spring Seeds (P.O. Box 444, Ganges, Salt Spring Island, BC V8K 2W1, Canada). 23 pp.

Johnston, Robert, Jr. *Growing Garden Seeds.* Albion, ME: Johnny's Selected Seeds (Albion, ME 04910), 1976. 32 pp. Culture of plants for saving seed.

Justice, Oren L., and Louis N. Bass. *Principles and Practices of Seed Storage.* Agriculture Handbook No. 506. Washington, DC: U.S. Government Printing Office, 1978. 289 pp.

Loewer, Peter. *The Definitive Guide to Growing Seeds: History & Lore.* Portland, OR: Timber Press, 1995. 229 pp.

McCormack, Jeffrey H. *Bean Seed Production: An Organic Seed Production Manual for Seed Growers in the Mid-Atlantic and Southern U.S.* Pittsboro, NC: Carolina Farm Stewardship Assn., 2004. 14 pp.

———. *Isolation Distances: Principles and Practices of Isolation Distances for Seed Crops: An Organic Seed Production Manual for Seed Growers in the Mid-Atlantic and Southern U.S.* Pittsboro, NC: Carolina Farm Stewardship Assn., 2004. 21 pp.

———. *Seed Processing and Storage: Principles and Practices of Seed Harvesting, Processing, and Storage: An Organic Seed Production Manual for Seed Growers in the Mid-Atlantic and Southern U.S.* Pittsboro, NC: Carolina Farm Stewardship Assn., 2004. 28 pp.

———. *Tomato Seed Production: An Organic Seed Production Manual for Seed Growers in the Mid-Atlantic and Southern U.S.* Pittsboro, NC: Carolina Farm Stewardship Assn., 2004. 15 pp.

Miller, Douglas C. *Vegetable and Herb Seed Growing for the Gardener and Small Farmer.* Hersey, MI: Bullkill Creek Publishing, 1977. 46 pp. A good book to start with.

Nabham, Gary Paul. *Enduring Seeds: Native American Agriculture and Wild Plant Conservation.* Berkeley, CA: North Point Press (850 Talbon Ave., Berkeley, CA 94706), 1989. 225 pp.

"New Isn't Necessarily Better." *Harrowsmith Country Life,* January/February 1994.

Roberts, E. H., ed. *Viability of Seeds.* Syracuse, NY: Syracuse University Press, 1972. 448 pp.

*Rogers, Marc. *Saving Seeds: The Gardener's Guide to Growing and Storing Vegetable and Flower Seeds.* Pownal, VT: Storey, 1990. 185 pp.

"Seeds for Life." *ILEIA Newsletter,* March 1994.

Stickland, Sue. *Back Garden Seed Saving: Keeping Our Seed Heritage Alive.* Bristol, UK: Eco-logic books, 2001. 199 pp.

U.S. Department of Agriculture. *Seeds: The Yearbook of Agriculture, 1961.* Washington, DC: U.S. Government Printing Office, 1961. 591 pp.

### Seeds/Diversity

Cromwell, Elizabeth, and Steve Wiggins. *Sowing beyond the State: NGOs and Seed Supply in Developing Countries.* London: Overseas Development Institute (Regent's College, Inner Circle, Regent's Park, London NWI 4NS, England), 1993. 143 pp.

*"Crop Genetic Erosion in the Field." *The Seed Map* (RAFI, P.O. Box 655, Pittsboro, NC 27312), 1992. Large chart.

Duffus, Carol, and Colin Slaughter. *Seeds and Their Uses.* Chichester, UK: John Wiley & Sons, 1980. 154 pp.

Fowler, Cary, and Pat Mooney. *Shattering: Food, Politics, and the Loss of Genetic Diversity.* Tucson, AZ: University of Arizona Press, 1990. 278 pp.

"Grain—Genetic Resources Action International." *Grain Publications List,* Summer 1992.

Guillet, Dominique. *The Seeds of Kokopelli.* Avignon, France: Les Presses de Provence, 2002. 440 pp. Available from Kokopelli Seed Foundation, 59 Westland Ave., Boston, MA 02115.

"Plants and Seeds as Intellectual Property." *The Seedhead News,* Winter 1994.

Shand, Hope. *Human Nature: Agricultural Biodiversity and Farm-Based Food Security.* Ottawa: RAFI, 1997. 94 pp.

von Elsakker, Boudewijn. *Benefits of Diversity: An Incentive toward Sustainable Agriculture.* New York: United Nations Development Program, 1992. 209 pp.

### Seeds/GMOs

"Are Gene-Altered Plants an Ecological Threat? Test Is Devised." *New York Times–Science,* June 22, 1993.

Belsie, Laurent. "Calling Poirot: Bizarre Case of Cross-Border 'Super Corn.'" *The Christian Science Monitor,* March 20, 2002: 5.

*Biotechnology: An Activists' Handbook.* Montpelier, VT: The Vermont Biotechnology Working Group (Rural Vermont, 15 Barre St., Montpelier, VT 05602), 1991. 47 pp.

"The Conflict Between Farmers' Rights and Breeders' Rights." *RAFI Action,* Spring 1993: 4–5.

"Flaws in the Tailoring." *Christian Science Monitor,* March 21, 1994.

Gendel, Steven M., et al. *Agricultural Bioethics: Implications of Agricultural Biotechnology.* Ames, IA: Iowa State University Press, 1990. 357 pp.

Goldberg, Rebecca, et al. *Biotechnology's Bitter Harvest.* Biotechnology Working Group, 1990. 73 pp.

"High-Tech Farming Sows Misery in the Philippines." *Utne Reader,* October/November 1986, 104–105.

Ho, Mae-Wan, et al. *The Case for a GM-Free Sustainable World.*

London: Institute of Science in Society.

———. *Gene Technology in the Etiology of Drug-Resistant Diseases.* Penan, Malaysia: Third World Network, 1998. 102 pp.

———. *Slipping Through the Regulatory Net: "Naked" and "Free" Nucleic Acids.* Penan, Malaysia: Third World Network, 2001. 26 pp.

Ho, Mae-Wan, and Ricarda A. Steinbrecher. *Fatal Flaws in Food Safety Assessment: Critique of the Joint FAO/WHO Biotechnology & Food Safety Report.* Penan, Malaysia: Third World Network, 1998. 60 pp.

Kneen, Brewster. *Farmageddon: Food and the Culture of Biotechnology.* Gabriola Island, BC, Canada: New Society Publishers, 1999. 231 pp.

Rissler, Jane, and Margaret Mellon. *The Ecological Risks of Engineered Crops.* Cambridge, MA: MIT Press, 1996. 168 pp.

Smith, Jeffrey M. *Seeds of Deception.* Fairfield, IA: Yes! Books, 2003. 288 pp.

"A Storm Is Breaking Down on the Farm," *Science and Technology,* December 14, 1992, 98–101.

Tappeser, Beatrix, Manuela Jager, and Claudia Eckelkamp. *Survival, Persistence, Transfer: An Update on Current Knowledge on GMOs and the Fate of Their Recombinant DNA.* Penan, Malaysia: Third World Network, 1999. 44 pp.

Wolf, Edward C. *Beyond the Green Revolution: New Approaches for Third World Agriculture.* Worldwatch Paper 73. Washington, DC: Worldwatch Institute, 1986. 46 pp.

### Seeds/Green Revolution

"Green Revolution." *The Elements* (1901 Q St. NW, Washington, DC 20009), June 1975: 1, 14–16.

"Green Revolution #2." *Dollars and Sense Magazine,* December 1985.

"Green Revolution Hits Double Trouble." *U.S. News & World Report,* July 28, 1980: 37, 40.

BIBLIOGRAPHY

"Green Revolution Is Not Enough, Study Finds." *New York Times–Science,* September 6, 1994.

Horne, James E., and Maura McDermott. *The Next Green Revolution: Essential Steps to a Healthy, Sustainable Agriculture.* Binghamton, NY: Food Products Press, 2001. 312 pp.

"How Green Is the Green Revolution?" *Enfo* (Box 761, Berkeley, CA 94701), September 1973, 1–2.

Johnson, Stanley. *The Green Revolution.* New York: Harper & Row, 1972. 218 pp.

Lipton, Michael, and Richard Longhurst. *New Seeds and Poor People.* Baltimore, MD: Johns Hopkins University Press, 1989. 464 pp.

Merrill, Richard. *Ecology of the Green Counter-Revolution.* Santa Barbara, CA: Community Environmental Council, 1973.

Mullen, William. "The Green Revolution: Can the World Salvage It?" *San Francisco Examiner and Chronicle,* December 14, 1975: A-13.

Shiva, Vandana. *The Violence of the Green Revolution: Third World Agriculture, Ecology and Politics.* London: Zed Books, 1991. 264 pp.

"Tanzania Corn Taller, Greener but Costlier." *The Oregonian,* February 24, 1993.

"The U.S. Won't Be Shielded in the Event of a Bio-Crisis." *Christian Science Monitor,* November 23, 1994.

Wallace, James N. "Is the Green Revolution Over?" *San Francisco Examiner and Chronicle,* August 17, 1980.

Wilkes, H. Garrison, and Susan Wilkes. "The Green Revolution." *Environment,* October 1972: 32–39.

"The Withering Green Revolution." *Natural History,* March 1973: 20–21.

### Seeds/Plant Propagation

Brickell, Christopher, ed. *Plant Propagation.* New York: Simon & Schuster, 1979. 96 pp.

Connolly, Bryan. *The Wisdom of Plant Heritage: Organic Seed Production and Saving.* Athol, MA: Highland Press, 2004. 111 pp.

Food and Agricultural Organization of the United Nations. *The Plant: The Flower.* Rome: FAO, 1976. 29 pp. In the United States: UNIPUB, 1180 Ave. of the Americas, New York, NY 10036.

———. *The Plant: The Living Plant; the Root.* Rome: FAO, 1976. 29 pp.

———. *The Plant: The Stem; the Buds; the Leaves.* Rome: FAO, 1976. 30 pp.

Fyfe, Agnes. *Moon and Planet.* Arlesheim, Switzerland: Society for Cancer Research, 1975. 94 pp.

Hartmann, Hudson T., et al. *Plant Propagation: Principles and Practices,* 5th ed. Englewood Cliffs, NJ: Prentice Hall, 1990. 647 pp.

Hawthorn, Leslie, and Leonard H. Pollard. *Seed Production.* New York: Blakiston, 1954. 626 pp. A classic.

Heiser, Charles B., Jr. *Seed to Civilization.* San Francisco: W. H. Freeman, 1973. 243 pp.

Hill, Lewis. *Secrets of Plant Propagation: Starting Your Own Flowers, Vegetables, Fruits, Berries, Shrubs, Trees, and Houseplants.* Pownal, VT: Garden Way Publishing, 1985.

Hofstetter, Robert. *Overseeding Research Results, 1982–1984.* Kutztown, PA: Agronomy Department, Rodale Institute Research Center, 1984. 30 pp.

Lawrence, William J. C., and J. Newell. *Seed and Potting Composts.* London: Allen & Unwin, 1941. 136 pp.

Lorenz, Oscar A., and Donald N. Maynard. *Knott's Handbook for Vegetable Growers,* 3rd ed. New York: John Wiley & Sons, 1988. Useful charts for small farmers. Strong chemical orientation.

Powell, Eileen. *From Seed to Bloom.* Pownal, VT: Storey, 1995. 312 pp.

*Reilly, Ann. *Park's Success with Seeds.* Greenwood, SC: George W.

Park Seed Co. (Greenwood, SC 29647), 1978. 364 pp.

Robinson, Raoul A. *Return to Resistance: Breeding Crops to Reduce Pesticide Dependence.* Davis, CA: agAccess, 1996. 480 pp.

*Sutton and Sons. *The Culture of Vegetables and Flowers from Seeds and Roots.* London: Simpkin, Marshall. Hamilton, Kent, 1898. 427 pp. Excellent.

### Soil

Albrecht, William A. *The Albrecht Papers: Enter Without Knocking.* Austin, TX: Acres U.S.A., 1992. 315 pp.

———. *The Albrecht Papers.* Vol. 3, Austin TX: Acres U.S.A., 1989. 401 pp.

———. *The Other Side of the Fence.* Austin, TX: Acres U.S.A., 1996. 25-minute video.

American Society of Agronomy, Crop Science Society of America, Soil Science Society of America. "Crop Tolerance to Suboptimal Land Conditions." Proceedings of a symposium, November–December 1976. Madison, WI: American Society of Agronomy, Crop Science Society of America, Soil Science Society of America, 1978. 343 pp.

———. "The Role of Phosphorus in Agriculture." Proceedings of a symposium held June 1976. Madison, WI: American Society of Agronomy, Crop Science Society of America, Soil Science Society of America, 1980. 910 pp.

Balfour, Lady E. B. *The Living Soil and the Haughley Experiment.* London: Faber and Faber, 1975. 383 pp.

Bear, Firman E. *Soils and Fertilizers,* 4th ed. New York: John Wiley & Sons, 1959. 420 pp.

Beatty, Marvin T. *Soil Science at the University of Wisconsin–Madison: A History of the Department, 1889–1989.* Madison, WI: University of Wisconsin, 1991. 141 pp.

Berkelaar, Edward. "The Effect of Aluminum in Acidic Soils on Plant Growth." *ECHO Development*

*Notes* (17391 Durrance Rd., North Myers, FL 33917), April 2001: 1–3.

*Biofuels, Development and Soil Productivity.* Sacramento, CA: Office of Appropriate Technology (1600 9th St., Sacramento, CA 95814), 1982. 109 pp.

Black, C. A. *Soil-Plant Relationships.* Ames, IA: Dept. of Agronomy, Iowa State Univ. and John Wiley and Sons, 1968. 792 pp.

Bowers, Wilbur O. *Water-Holding Characteristics of California Soils.* Oakland, CA: University of California, 1989. 92 pp.

*Brady, Nyle. *The Nature and Properties of Soils,* 10th ed. New York: Macmillan, 1990. 621 pp.

Brown, Kirk W., et al. *Sustaining Our Soils and Society.* Alexandria, VA: American Geological Institute, 1999. 64 pp.

Brown, Vinson, David Allen, and James Stark. *Rocks and Minerals of California.* Happy Camp, CA: Naturegraph Publishers, 1991. 200 pp.

Buol, S. W., et al. *Soil Genesis and Classification.* Ames, IA: Iowa State University Press, 1997. 527 pp.

Carter, Martin R., ed. *Soil Sampling and Methods of Analysis.* Boca Raton, FL: Lewis, 1993. 823 pp.

*Carter, Vernon G., and Tom Dale. *Topsoil and Civilization.* Norman, OK: University of Oklahoma Press, 1955. 292 pp. Describes how flourishing civilizations have fallen into decay by not maintaining their agricultural health and soil.

Chapman, Homer. *Diagnostic Criteria for Plants and Soils.* Riverside, CA: University of California, Division of Agricultural Sciences, 1966. 793 pp.

Coleman, David C., and D. A. Crossley, Jr. *Fundamentals of Soil Ecology.* San Diego, CA: Academic Press, 1996. 205 pp.

Crozier, Carl. *Soil Conservation Techniques for Hillside Farms: A Guide for Peace Corps Volunteers.* Springfield, VA: National Technical Information Service (Peace Corps Information Collection & Exchange, Office of Training and Program Support, 806 Connecticut Ave., NW, Washington, DC 20526), 1986. 97 pp.

Dalla Rosa, Karl R. "Building Soils on Pacific Atolls." *Nitrogen Fixing Tree News* (Nitrogen Fixing Tree Assoc., Morrilton, AR), January–March 1993.

Dindal, Daniel L. and Matthew R. Werner. *Impact of Conversion to Organic Agricultural Practices on Soil Invertebrate Ecosystems.* Syracuse, NY: SUNY College of Environmental Science and Forestry, 1988. 207 pp.

Donahue, Roy L., et al. *Soils: An Introduction to Soils and Plant Growth.* Englewood Cliffs, NJ: Prentice-Hall, 1971. 587 pp.

Doran, John W., and Alice J. Jones. *Methods for Assessing Soil Quality.* Madison, WI: Soil Science Society of America, 1996. 410 pp.

Ducerf, Gérard, and Camille Thiry. Les Plantes Bio-indicatrices: Guide de Diagnostic des Sol. Briant, France: Eds. Promonature, 2003. 2008 pp.

Farb, Peter. *Living Earth.* New York: Harper Colophon, 1959. 175 pp. Easy-to-read peek at the life under the soil.

Faulkner, Edward H. *Plowman's Folly.* Norman, OK: University of Oklahoma Press, 1943. 155 pp. Classic.

———. *Soil Development.* Norman, OK: University of Oklahoma Press, 1952. 232 pp.

Fenzau, C. J. *An Acres U.S.A. Primer.* Austin, TX: Acres U.S.A., 1979. 435 pp.

Ford, Brian J. *Microbe Power.* New York: Stein and Day, 1976. 181 pp.

Gardner, Gary. *Shrinking Fields: Cropland Loss in a World of Eight Billion.* Worldwatch Paper 131. Washington, DC: Worldwatch Institute, 1996. 56 pp.

Gershuny, Grace, and Smillie, Joseph. *Soul of Soil: A Guide to Ecological Soil Management.* Davis, CA: agAccess, 1995. 174 pp.

Gilman, Steve. *Organic Soil Fertility Management.* White River Junction, VT: Chelsea Green Publishing, 2002. 60 pp.

Glanz, James. *Saving Our Soil: Solutions for Sustaining Earth's Vital Resource.* Boulder, CO: Johnson Books, 1995. 182 pp.

Godderham, P. T. "The Effect on Soil Conditions of Mechanized Cultivation at High Moisture Content and of Loosening by Hand Digging." *Journal of Agricultural Science,* No. 976: 567–571.

Grimshaw, Richard G., and Larisa Helfer, eds. *Vetiver Grass for Soil and Water Conservation, Land Rehabilitation and Embankment Stabilization.* World Bank Technical Paper No. 273. Washington, DC: World Bank, 1995. 281 pp.

Hall, A. D. *The Soil—An Introduction to the Scientific Study of the Growth of Crops.* New York: E. P. Dutton, 1920. 252 pp.

*Handbook on Soils.* Brooklyn, NY: Brooklyn Botanic Garden, 1956. 81 pp. Some photos of root systems in the soil.

*Hans Jenny. Soil Scientist, Teacher, and Scholar.* Berkeley, CA: Regional Oral History Office (386 Library, University of California, Berkeley, CA 94720), 1989. 372 pp.

Harpstead, Milo I., Thomas J. Sauer, and William F. Bennett. *Soil Science Simplified.* Ames, IA: Iowa State University Press, 1997. 210 pp.

Havlin, John L., et al. *Soil Fertility and Fertilizers,* 6th ed. Upper Saddle River, NJ: Prentice Hall, 1999. 499 pp.

*Hensel, Julius. *Bread from Stones.* Austin, TX: Acres U.S.A., 1991. 102 pp.

Hillel, Daniel. *Out of the Earth: Civilization and the Life of the Soil.* Berkeley and Los Angeles: University of California Press, 1992. 321 pp.

Hopkins, Cyril. *Agricultural Experiment Station, How Not to Treat Illinois Soils.* Urbana, IL: University of Illinois, 1915. 31 pp.

BIBLIOGRAPHY

Hopkins, Donald P. *Chemicals, Humus, and the Soils.* London: Faber and Faber Limited, 1945. 278 pp.

Howard, Albert. *An Agricultural Testament.* New York: Oxford University Press, 1943. 253 pp.

*———. *The Soil and Health.* New York: Devin-Adair, 1956. 307 pp. A cornerstone of the organic movement.

*Hyams, Edward. *Soil and Civilization.* New York: Harper & Row, 1976. 312 pp. Reprint from 1952.

Ingham, Elaine. "Life in the Soil—Understanding the Foodweb." *Acres, U.S.A.,* January 1997: 18–23.

Ingham, Elaine R., Andrew R. Moldenke, and Clive A. Edwards. *Soil Biology Primer.* Ankeny, IA: Soil and Water Conservation Society (7515 NE Ankeny Rd., Ankeny, IA 50021), 2000. 48 pp.

*Introduction to Soil and Water Conservation Practices.* Oklahoma City, OK: World Neighbors (International Headquarters, 5116 N. Portland, Oklahoma City, OK 73112), 1985. 33 pp.

Jenny, Hans. *Factors of Soil Formation: A System of Quantitative Pedology.* New York: Dover, 1994. 281 pp.

———. *The Soil Resource: Origin and Behavior.* New York: Springer-Verlag, 1980. 377 pp.

King, F. H. *The Soil.* New York: Macmillan, 1895. 303 pp.

Kohnke, Helmut. *Soil Science Simplified,* 3rd ed. Prospect Heights, IL: Waveland Press, 1966. 78 pp.

Kruckeberg, Arthur R. *California Serpentines: Flora, Vegetation, Geology, Soils, and Management Problems.* Berkeley, CA: University of California Press, 1984. 180 pp.

Krupenikov, I. A. *History of Soil Science: From Its Inception to the Present.* New Delhi, India: Oxonian Press Pvt., 1992. 352 pp. Translated from Russian.

Larkcom, Joy. "Deep Cultivation." Subsection of "Soil and Soil Pests." *Journal of the Royal Horticultural Society* 104, Part 6, June 1979: 252–256.

Lewandowski, Ann. Minnesota Soil Management Series: *Soil Management* (21 pp.), *Compaction* (17 pp.), *Manure Management* (17 pp.), *Organic Matter Management* (17 pp.), and *Soil Biology and Soil Management* (17 pp.). St. Paul, MN: Minnesota Institute for Sustainable Agriculture, University of Minnesota Extension Service (405 Coffey Hall, 1420 Eckles Ave., St. Paul, MN 55108-6068), 2000. For large-scale agriculture; very good information also applicable on smaller scales.

Lewis, Trevor. *Institute of Arable Crops Research.* Rothamsted Experimental Station, Harpenden, UK: Agriculture and Food Research Council, n.d. 14 pp. A brochure about the council and its work at three prominent research stations.

———. *One Hundred and Fifty Years of Agricultural Research Rothamsted 1843–1993.* Rothamsted Experimental Station, Harpenden, UK: Agriculture and Food Research Council.

Lindert, Peter H. *Shifting Ground: The Changing Agricultural Soils of China and Indonesia.* Cambridge, MA: MIT Press, 2000. 351 pp.

Logsdon, Gene. *The Gardener's Guide to Better Soil.* Emmaus, PA: Rodale Press, 1975. 246 pp.

Lord, Russell. *The Care of the Earth: A History of Husbandry.* New York: The New American Library, 1962. 384 pp.

Lowdermilk, W. C. *Conquest of the Land through Seven Thousand Years. Agricultural Information Bulletin No. 99.* Washington, DC: U.S. Government Printing Office, 1975. 30 pp.

Lyon, T. Lyttleton, et al. *The Nature and Properties of Soils,* 5th ed. New York: Macmillan, 1952. 591 pp.

———. *Soils: Their Properties and Management.* New York: Macmillan, 1915. 764 pp.

Lyon, T. Lyttleton, and Harry O. Buckman. *The Nature and Properties of Soils.* New York: Macmillan, 1929. 428 pp. 1st edition only for more organic treatment.

Magdoff, Fred, and Harold van Es. *Building Soils for Better Crops.* Burlington, VT: Sustainable Agriculture Network, Sustainable Agriculture Publications (Hills Bldg., Rm. 10), University of Vermont, 2000. 230 pp.

Magdoff, Fred, and Ray R. Weil, eds. *Soil Organic Matter in Sustainable Agriculture.* Boca Raton, FL: CRC Press, 2004. 398 pp.

Morgan, Sampson. *Clean Culture—The New Soil Science: An Original and Scientific Treatise on Clean Culture, the Mineralized-Humus Method of Soil Fertilization Without the Use of Animal Manure.* 1908.

Nierenberg, Danielle. "Toxic Fertility." *World Watch,* March/April 2001: 30–38.

*No-Digging Report No. 1.* Essex, England: Henry Doubleday Research Association, 1972. Reprint. 40 pp.

Nordell, Eric. "A Few Long Furrows on Horsedrawn Tillage." *Small Farmer's Journal* Vol. 17, No. 2: 17–23.

Nordell, Eric, et al. "The Ridge-Till Trails." *Organic Farms, Folks & Foods,* May/June 1998: 12–13.

Ortloff, Stuart H., and Henry B. Raymore. *A Book about Soils for the Home Gardener.* New York: M. Barrows, 1962. 189 pp.

*Parnes, Robert. *Fertile Soil: A Grower's Guide to Organic and Inorganic Fertilizers.* Davis, CA: agAccess, 1990. 194 pp.

Paul, E. A., et al., eds. *Soil Organic Matter in Temperate Agroecosystems.* Boca Raton, FL: CRC Press, 1997. 414 pp.

Pearce, Fred. "An Ordinary Miracle." *New Scientist,* February 3, 2001: 16–17.

Pellant, Chris. *Rocks and Minerals: The Most Accessible Recognition Guides.* New York: Dorling

Kindersley Handbooks, 1992. 256 pp.

Pfeiffer, Ehrenfried. "Organic Matter Rebuilt in Pure Sand." *Biodynamics,* Spring 1951: 2–8. **AL**

———. *Soil Fertility: Renewal and Preservation.* East Grinstead, Sussex, England: Lanthorn Press, 1983. 199 pp.

Pimentel, David, ed. *World Soil Erosion and Conservation.* Cambridge, UK: Cambridge University Press, 1993. 349 pp.

Ridzon, Leonard, and Charles Walters. *The Carbon Cycle.* Kansas City, MO: Acres U.S.A., 1994. 150 pp.

*Robert Parnes Speaks on the Science and Necessity of Organic Residues in the Soil.* Gates Mills, OH: Griesinger Films, 1991. 60-min Video. **IL**

Rosemeyer, M., et al. *Applied Soil Ecology: A Section of Agriculture, Ecosystems & Environment.* New York: Elsevier Science, 2000. 59 pp.

*Rothamsted Experimental Station.* Rothamsted Experimental Station, Harpenden, UK: Agriculture and Food Research Council, n. d. A large brochure about this organization.

———. *Rothamsted Experimental Station Guide.* Harpenden: UK: Lawes Agricultural Trust, n.d. 77 pp. Descriptions of experiments and work of the departments.

Russell, E. J. *The Fertility of the Soil.* London: Cambridge University Press, 1913. 128 pp.

Russell, E. John, rewritten by E. Walter Russell. *Soil Conditions and Plant Growth.* New York: Longmans, Green, 1950. 635 pp.

*Sachs, Paul D. *Edaphos: Dynamics of a Natural Soil System,* 2nd ed. Newbury, VT: Edaphic Press, 1999. 201 pp. Excellent for understanding the soil ecosystem.

Shaxson, T. F. *Land Husbandry: A Framework for Soil and Water Conservation.* Ankeny, IA: Soil and Water Conservation Society (7515 NE Ankeny Rd., Ankeny, IA 50021), 1989. 64 pp.

Singer, Michael J., and Donald N. Munns. *Soils: An Introduction.* Upper Saddle River, NJ: Prentice Hall, 1996. 480 pp.

Smith, William C. *How to Grow 100 Bushels of Corn per Acre on Worn Soil.* Delphi, IN: Smith, 1910. 111 pp.

*Soil Quality Test Kit Guide.* Washington, DC: U.S. Department of Agriculture, Agriculture Research Service, Natural Resources Conservation Service, Soil Quality Institute, 1999. 82 pp. **IL/AL**

Soil Science Society of America, American Society of Agronomy. "Field Soil Water Regime." Proceedings of a symposium held on August 16, 1971. Madison, WI: Soil Science Society of America, American Society of Agronomy, 1973. 212 pp.

———. "Soil Fertility and Organic Matter as Critical Components of Production Systems." Proceedings of a symposium sponsored by Division S-4, S-2, S-3, and S-8 of the Soil Science Society of America in Chicago, December 3, 1985. Madison, WI: Soil Science Society of America, American Society of Agronomy, 1987. 166 pp.

———. "Soils for Management of Organic Wastes and Waste Waters." Proceedings of a symposium held March 1975. Madison, WI: Soil Science Society of America, 1977. 650 pp.

Soil Survey Staff. *Soil Survey Manual. Handbook No. 18.* Washington, DC: U.S. Dept. of Ag., August 1951. 503 pp.

*Soils and the Greenhouse Effect.* Sussex, England: John Wiley & Sons, 1990. 575 pp.

Stelly, Matthias, ed. *Soil Testing: Correlating and Interpreting the Analytical Results. ASA Special Publication Number 29.* Madison, WI: American Society of Agronomy, 1977. 117 pp.

Storey, P. J. *The Conservation and Improvement of Sloping Land.* 3 vols. Enfield, NH: Science Publishers, 2002.

Sylvia, David M., et al., eds. *Principles and Applications of Soil Microbiology.* Upper Saddle River, NJ: Prentice Hall, 1999. 550 pp.

Terry, D. L., and C. B. McCants. *The Leaching of Ions in Soils.* North Carolina Agricultural Experiment Station, Tech. Bul. No. 184. Raleigh, NC: Agricultural Experiment Station, 1968. 16 pp.

Tompkins, Peter, and Christopher Bird. *Secrets of the Soil.* New York: Harper & Row, 1989. 444 pp.

Univ. of California Agriculture and Natural Resources. *Emerging Soil Management Options for California.* Davis, CA: U.C. and U.S.D.A., 1998. 67 pp. Proceedings of a conference, April 22–23, 1998.

*U.S. Department of Agriculture. *Soils and Men:The Yearbook of Agriculture, 1938.* Washington, DC: U.S. Government Printing Office, 1938. 1,232 pp.

*The Vanishing Soil.* Kimberton, PA: Biodynamic Farming and Gardening Association (P.O. Box 550, Kimberton, PA 19442). Video.

Veldkamp, Tom. *AGRODOK 2, Soil Fertility.* Wagenigen, The Netherlands: Agromisa (P.O. Box 41, 6700 AA Wagenigen, The Netherlands), 1992. 25 pp. Chemical orientation; can be modified for biointensive and organic use.

"The Vetiver System: A Proven Solution." Arlington, VA: The Vetiver Network (3601 N. 14th St., Arlington, VA 22201). Pamphlet.

Waksman, Selam A. *Humus.* Baltimore, MD: Williams and Wilkins, 1938. 526 pp.

———. *Soil Microbiology.* New York: John Wiley & Sons, 1952. 356 pp.

Westerman, R. L., ed. *Soil Testing and Plant Analysis.* Madison, WI: Soil Science Society of America, 1990. 784 pp.

Wildman, William E., et al. *Soil: Physical Environment and How It Affects Plant Growth.* Leaflet No. 2280. Davis, CA: University of California, Division of Agricultural Sciences, June 1975. 10 pp.

## Solar Cooking

*Como Hacer y Usar Una Caja Solar para Cocinar.* Sacramento, CA: Solar Cookers International (1919 21st St., #101, Sacramento, CA 95814), n.d. 27 pp.

Kerr, Barbara Prosser. *The Expanding World of Solar Box Cookers.* Taylor, AZ: Kerr-Cole Solar Box Cookers (P.O. Box 576, Taylor, AZ 85939), 1991. 79 pp.

Kerr Enterprises. (P.O. Box 27417, Tempe, AZ 85281.) A very good solar box cooker. Send $4 for plans and other material.

*The Solar Box Cooker Manual: How to Make, Use and Teach Others about Them.* Sacramento, CA: Solar Cookers International (1919 21st St., #101, Sacramento, CA 95814), May 1990. 66 pp. $10.

*Solar Cookers International. (1919 21st St., #101, Sacramento, CA 95814.) A nonprofit organization with excellent solar oven plans, recipes, and cooking information. Write for publications list.

Still, Dean, and Jim Kness. *Capturing Heat: Five Earth-Friendly Cooking Technologies and How to Build Them.* Cottage Grove, OR: Aprovecho Research Center (80574 Hazelton Rd., Cottage Grove, OR 97424), 1996. 35 pp.

Still, Dean, Mike Hatfield, and Peter Scott. *Capturing Heat Two: Fuel-Efficient Cooking Stoves with Chimneys, A Pizza Oven, and Simple Water Heaters: How to Design and Build Them.* Cottage Grove, OR: Aprovecho Research Center (80574 Hazelton Rd., Cottage Grove, OR 97424), 2000. 48 pp.

## Supply Catalogs

Bozeman Bio-Tech. P.O. Box 3146, 1612 Gold Ave., Bozeman, MT 59772. Long-term insect pest control.

*Catalog for Cooks.* Williams-Sonoma. P.O. Box 7456, San Francisco, CA 94120. Cooking utensils.

Coast Dry Flowers and Baskets. Box 10, San Francisco, CA 94101. Dry flowers, bouquets, baskets, and floral supplies.

Cotton Clouds. Rte. 2, Desert Hills #16, Safford, AZ 85546. Cotton yarn.

Countryside General Store. 103 N. Monroe St., Waterloo, WI 53595.

Cumberland General Store. Rte. 3, P.O. Box 81, Crossville, TN 38555. Old-time general merchandise.

De Van Koek Dutch Trader. 3100 Industrial Terr., Austin, TX 78759. Garden tools.

*Down to Earth Dist. Garden Products Catalog.* P.O. Box 1419, Eugene, OR 97440. Wholesale fertilizers, tools, etc. Minimum order $100.

Dramm. P.O. Box 528, Manitowoc, WI 54220. Professional watering tools.

Duluth Trading Company. 8300 Highland Dr., Wausau, WI 54401, (877) DTC-2345. Sells gel knee pads.

The Earth Store. P.O. Box 2286, Bellaire, TX 77402. Organic products.

Environmental Concerns. 9051-E Mill Station Rd., Sebastopol, CA 95472. Products for a safer, cleaner world, including biodegradable soaps and recycled paper.

*Fertile Ground Books. P.O. Box 2008, Davis, CA 95617-2008, books@agribooks.com. Excellent books.

Florist Products Horticultural Supplies. 2242 N. Palmer Dr., Schaumburg, IL 60195. Supplies and tools.

*Gardener's Supply, 128 Intervale Rd., Burlington, VT 05401. Garden tools, greenhouses, and supplies.

*Gardens for Growing People. P.O. Box 630, Pt. Reyes Sta., CA 94956. Children's gardening supplies.

*The Garrett Wade Tool Catalog.* 161 Avenue of the Americas, New York, NY 10013. Good tool source, especially Japanese saws.

Gohn Bros. Box 1110 Middlebury, IN 46540. Amish clothing.

Good Books Catalog. P.O. Box 419, Intercourse, PA 17534.

*Great Lakes IPM Catalog of Insect Monitoring Systems for the Profes-sional Grower.* 10220 Church Rd. NE, Vestaburg, MI 48891.

Jacobs Brothers Co. 8928 Sepulveda Blvd., Sepulveda, CA 91343. Fifteen-year shade and pest net-ting in various percentages of shading capacity.

Magic Garden Supply. P.O. Box 68, Redway, CA 95560. Supplies.

Mountain Rose Herbs. P.O. Box 50220, Eugene, OR 97405.

Nasco Farm and Ranch. P.O. Box 901, Fort Atkinson, WI 53538. Farm and ranch supplies.

New England Cheesemaking Supply Company. P.O. Box 85, Ashfield, MA 01330. Supplies and books.

Nitragin, Inc. 3101 W. Custer Ave., Milwaukee, WI 53209. Source of many kinds of inocula for seeds, so you can maximize the fixing of nitrogen in the soil by legumes and obtain higher yields and higher protein content.

Northeast Carry Trading Company. 110 Water St., Hallowell, ME 04347.

Ohio Earth Food. 13737 Duquette Ave. NE, Hartville, OH 44632. Mail-order organic fertilizers.

*Peaceful Valley Farm Supply. P.O. Box 2209, Grass Valley, CA 95945. Fertilizers, supplies, seeds, and books. Excellent source.

Pratt, Doug, ed. *Real Goods Solar Living Source Book: The Complete Guide to Renewable Energy Technologies and Sustainable Living,* 10th edition. White River Junction, VT: Chelsea Green, 1999. 561 pp. A directory of equipment.

Precision Meters. 9495 Delgate Drive, Orlando, FL, 32837. 407-851-4470. Contact for the name of a local distributor. Sells PMM Multi-Jet 5/8-inch meter for measuring the amount of water used in the garden.

Real Goods. 13771 S. Hwy. 101, Hopland, CA 95449. Renewable energy.

*Real Goods Renewables: Utility Intertie Systems: How to Sell Power to Your Electric Utility Company (and Get Yours for Free!).* 1031 N. State St., Ukiah, CA 95482-3413.

Rocket Chef. P.O. Box 4525, Pacoima, CA 91331. (800) 544-4099. Non-electric food processor.

*SelfCare Catalog.* 349 Healdsburg Ave., Healdsburg, CA 95448. Products for self-help health care, including key books.

Seven Springs Farm. 426 Jerry Lane NE, Check, VA 24072. Organic farming and gardening supplies.

Seventh Generation. Colchester, VT 54460.

Silica Gel Dessicant Products Co. 5601 W. Slauson Ave, Suite 260, Culver City, CA 90230-6598.

Smith and Hawken. Box 6900, Florence, KY 41022-6900. Tools, clothes, bulbs, and books.

Snow Pond Farm Supply. P.O. Box 70, Salem, MA 01970. Soil-building seed, soil amendments, and fertilizers; natural pest controls; and tools.

Sun Day Afternoons Sun Protective Hats & Clothing. 716 South Pacific Hwy., Talent, OR 97540.

Timber Press. 9999 SW Wilshire, Portland, OR 97225. Books.

VJ Growers Supply. 500 W. Orange Blossom Trail, Apopka, FL 32703. Six-year clear vinyl 6-ml plastic film for constructing mini-greenhouses. Available in 54-inch-wide, 100-foot-long rolls only.

*Walt Nicke's Garden Talk.* P.O. Box 433, Topsfield, MA 01983. Supplies and tools. Good catalog.

Wild Weeds. P.O. Box 88, Redway, CA 95560. Herbal solutions for all purposes, seeds, and books.

## Sustainable Agriculture

Andersen, Arden B. *Life & Energy in Agriculture.* Kansas City, MO: Acres U.S.A., 1989. 115 pp.

———. *Science in Agriculture: Advanced Methods for Sustainable Farming.* Austin, TX: Acres U.S.A., 2000. 376 pp.

*Appropriate Technology Transfer for Rural Areas (ATTRA). Sustainable Agriculture Directory of Expertise.* Burlington, VT: Sustainable Agriculture Network, Sustainable Agriculture Publica-

tions, University of Vermont, 1996.

Brockman, Henry. *Organic Matters.* Congerville, IL: TerraBooks, 2001. 24 pp. Discusses the importance of *small-scale* organic farming.

Clark, Robert, ed. *Our Sustainable Table.* San Francisco: North Point Press, 1990. 176 pp.

Enriquez, Laura J. *Cuba's New Agricultural Revolution: The Transformation of Food Crop Production in Contemporary Cuba.* Oakland, CA: Food First—Institute for Food and Development Policy (398 60th St., Oakland, CA 94618), 2000. 29 pp.

Funes, Fernando, et al. *Sustainable Agriculture and Resistance: Transforming Food Production in Cuba.* Oakland, CA: Food First Books, 2002. 307 pp.

Gates, Jane Potter. *Tracing the Evolution of Organic/Sustainable Agriculture.* Beltsville, MD: National Agricultural Library, 1988. 20 pp.

Gliessman, Stephen R. *Agroecology: Ecological Processes in Sustainable Agriculture.* Boca Raton, FL: Lewis, 2000. 357 pp.

———. *Agroecosystem Sustainability: Developing Practical Strategies.* Boca Raton, FL: CRC Press, 2000.

Haney, Wava G., et al. *Sustainable Agriculture Research Sourcebook: A Compilation of Current Activities on Sustainable Agriculture at U.S. Universities.* Black Earth, WI: Wisconsin Rural Development Ctr., 1986. 56 pp.

International Institute of Rural Reconstruction. *Sustainable Agriculture Extension Manual for Eastern and Southern Africa.* Nairobi: IIRR, 1998. 241 pp.

Jackson, Wes. *New Roots for Agriculture.* San Francisco: Friends of the Earth, 1980. 155 pp. Addresses the importance of developing sustainable agricultural systems, including perennial seed-producing plants.

Jason, Dan. *Greening the Garden: A Guide to Sustainable Growing.*

Philadelphia, PA: New Society Publishers, 1991. 196 pp.

Kirschenmann, Frederick. *Switching to a Sustainable System.* Windsor, ND: Northern Plants Sustainable Agriculture Society (R.R. 1, Box 73, Windsor, ND 58424), 1988. 18 pp.

Kolisko, E., and L. Kolisko. *Agriculture of Tomorrow.* Bournemouth, England: Kolisko Archive Publications, 1975. 322 pp.

Lockeretz, William, ed. *Environmental Enhancement through Agriculture.* Medford, MA: Tufts University, 1995. 334 pp.

*Looking after Our Land.* Oxford, UK: Oxfam Publications (274 Banbury Rd., Oxford 0X2 7DZ, UK). 20-minute video.

Lowrance, Richard, Benjamin R. Stinner, and Garfield J. House, eds. *Agricultural Ecosystems: Unifying Concepts.* New York: John Wiley & Sons, 1984. 233 pp.

National Research Council. *Alternative Agriculture.* Washington, DC: National Academy Press, 1989. 448 pp.

———. *Sustainable Agriculture and the Environment in the Humid Tropics.* Washington, DC: National Academy Press, 1993. 702 pp.

Peet, Mary. *Sustainable Practices for Vegetable Production in the South.* Newburyport, MA: Focus Publishing (P.O. Box 369, Newburyport, MA 01950), 1996. 174 pp.

Pereira, Winin. *Tending the Earth: Traditional, Sustainable Agriculture in India.* Bombay, India: Earthcare Books (2 Anand, 17 Carmichael Rd., Bombay 400 026, India), 1993. 315 pp.

Petersen, Cass, Laurie E. Drinkwater, and Peggy Wagoner. *The Rodale Institute Farming Systems Trial: The First 15 Years.* Kutztown, PA: The Rodale Institute, 1999. 40 pp.

Pretty, Jules. *The Living Land.* London: Earthscan Publications, 1998. 324 pp.

*Resourceful Farming: A Primer for Family Farmers.* Hartington, NE:

The Small Farm Resources Project, 1987. 118 pp.

Schriefer, Donald L. *Agriculture in Transition.* Austin, TX: Acres U.S.A., 2000. 238 pp.

*Sustainable Agriculture for California.* Pub. 3349. Oakland, CA: Division of Agriculture and Natural Resources, University of California (6701 San Pablo Ave., Oakland, CA 94608-1239), 1991. 197 pp.

Sustainability of California Agriculture—A Symposium. Davis, CA: U.C. Cooperative Extension, U.C. Davis College of Agricultural and Environmental Sciences, U.C. Santa Cruz Agroecology Program, U.C. Agricultural Experiment Station, American Society of Agronomy California Chapter, n.d. 317 pp.

*Sustainable Farming.* Quebec, Canada: REAP (Box 125, Glenaladale House, Ste.-Anne-de-Bellevue, Quebec H9X 1C0, Canada). Quarterly magazine.

*Towards Sustainable Agriculture.* Langenbruck, Switzerland: Agroecol Development (c/o Oekozentrum Langenbruck, CH-4438 Langenbruck, Switzerland). *Information of Low-External Input Agriculture* (P.O. Box 64, 3830 AB Leusden, The Netherlands), 1988. Two-part series.

*The Transition Document: Toward an Environmentally Sound Agriculture.* Portland, OR: Oregon Tilth Research and Education Committee, 1989. 77 pp.

*What Is Sustainable Agriculture?* Davis, CA: University of California, Sustainable Agriculture Research and Education Program, 1991. 5 pp.

United Nations Development Programme (UNDP). *Urban Agriculture—Food, Jobs and Sustainable Cities.* New York: UNDP, 1996. 302 pp.

## Terracing

Copijn, A. N. *A-Frames and Other Levelling Instruments.* Leusden, The Netherlands: ETC Foundation, AME Programme (P.O. Box 64, 3830 AB Leusden, The Netherlands), 1986. 13 pp.

———. *Soil Protection.* Leusden, The Netherlands: ETC Foundation, AME Programme, 1987. 16 pp.

*How to Farm Hilly Lands.* Forestry for People Series. The Philippines: Bureau of Forest Development. 15 pp.

"Kenyans Shore Up Hopes and Topsoil with Terraces." *Christian Science Monitor,* May 9, 1988.

*Vetiver Grass: A Thin Green Line Against Erosion.* Washington, DC: National Research Council, National Academy Press, 1993. 171 pp. "Living terracing" crop.

Wenner, Carl G. *An Outline of Soil Conservation in Kenya.* Nairobi, Kenya: Kenya Ministry of Agriculture, Soil Conservation Extension Unit. 57 pp.

———. *Trees in Erosion and Soil Conservation.* Nairobi, Kenya: Nairobi Ministry of Agriculture, Farm Management Branch Project and Evaluation Division, 1980. 26 pp.

World Bank. *Vetiver Grass: The Hedge Against Erosion.* Washington, DC: World Bank, 1990. 78 pp.

## Testing

Chapman, Homer D., and Parker F. Pratt. *Methods of Analysis for Soils, Plants, and Waters.* Riverside, CA: University of California, Division of Agricultural Sciences, 1961. 309 pp.

*International Conference on the Assessment and Monitoring of Soil Quality.* Emmaus, PA: Rodale Institute, 1991. 38 pp.

Kiehl, Elmer R. *Some Considerations for Interpretation of Soil Test for Phosphorus and Potassium. Research Bulletin 1007.* Columbia, MO: Univ. of Missouri–Columbia College of Ag., Ag. Experiment Station, 1974. 36 pp.

National Testing Laboratory. 6555 Wilson Mills Rd., Ste. 102, Cleveland, OH 44143. Water testing.

*Timberleaf Soil Testing Service. 39648 Old Spring Rd., Murrieta, CA 92563-5566. (951) 677-7510. Excellent. Send for information on services and prices. The basic and trace mineral tests are highly recommended.

Wallace, T. M. C. *The Diagnosis of Mineral Deficiencies in Plants.* Long Ashton, Bristol: University of Bristol Agricultural and Horticultural Research Station, 1944. 164 pp.

*Watercheck. 6555 Wilson Mills Rd., Cleveland, OH 44123. (800) 458-3330. Excellent water testing laboratory. Write for information.

## Tools

Arts Machine Shop. Harrison at Oregon Trail, American Falls, ID 83211. Good-quality soil corers.

Blackburn, Graham. *Woodworking Handtools.* New York: Simon & Schuster, 1974. 238 pp.

Bradley, Fern M., and Christine Bucks, ed. *Great Garden Gadgets.* Emmaus, PA: Rodale, 2001. 168 pp. Using recycled material to help with seed starting, composting, tool organizing, and more.

Branch, Diana S. *Tools for Homesteaders, Gardeners, and Small-Scale Farmers.* Emmaus, PA: Rodale Press, 1978. 512 pp.

The C. S. Bell Co. 170 W. Davis St., Tiffin, OH 44883. Grain mills and shellers.

Carruthers, Ian, and Marc Rodriquez. *Tools for Agriculture: A Guide to Appropriate Equipment for Smallholder Farmers.* Nottingham, UK: Russell Press, 1992. 238 pp.

Cobleigh, Rolfe. *Handy Farm Devices and How to Make Them.* New York: The Lyons Press, 1996. Reprint. 284 pp.

Happy Valley Ranch. P.O. Box 9153, Yakima, WA 98909. Cider, fruit, and wine presses.

Hida Tool Co. 1333 San Pablo Ave., Berkeley, CA 94702.

Hylton, William H., ed. *Build It Better Yourself.* Emmaus, PA: Rodale Press, 1977. 942 pp.

J. A. Cissell Co. Aqunkum-Yellowbrook Rd., Farmingdale, NJ 07727. Five- to ten-year bird netting.

Jackson, Albert, and David Day. *Tools and How to Use Them.* New York: Knopf, 1979. 252 pp.

Jones, Bernard E., ed. *The Complete Woodworker.* Berkeley, CA: Ten Speed Press, 1980. 408 pp.

Logan, William Bryant. *The Tool Book: A Compendium of Over 500 Tools for the Well-Tended Garden.* New York: Workman, 1997. 302 pp.

*McCullagh, James C. *Pedal Power: In Work, Leisure and Transportation.* Emmaus, PA: Rodale Press, 1977. 133 pp.

McRobie, George, ed. *Tools for Organic Farming.* London: Intermediate Technology Publications, 1990. 77 pp.

R. Hunt & Co. Ltd. Atlas Works. Earls Colne Colchester, Essex, England CO6 2EP. Manufacturers of mechanical power transmission equipment agricultural machinery, e.g., chaff cutters, winnowers, groundnut decorticators, and grinding mills.

*Seymour Hardware Catalog.* Seymour Manufacturing Co., 500 N. Broadway, Seymour, IN 47274.

Stratoflex, Inc. 220 Roberts Cut-Off, P.O. Box 10398, Fort Worth, TX 76114. Excellent heavy-duty water hoses. We like the #230-12.

*Tresemer, David. *The Scythe Book: Mowing Hay, Cutting Weeds, and Harvesting Small Grains with Hand Tools.* Brattleboro, VT: Hand and Foot, 1981. 120 pp.

Volunteers in Technical Assistance. 3206 Rhode Island Ave., Mt. Rainier, MD 20822. Appropriate technology materials information sheets.

———. *Village Technology Handbook.* Croton-on-Hudson, NY: Bootstrap Press, 1988. 422 pp.

Wells, Malcolm. *Recovering America—A More Gentle Way to Build.* Brewster, MA: Malcolm Wells (673 Satucket Rd., Brewster, Cape Cod, MA), 1999. 143 pp.

Wright, Philip. *Old Farm Implements.* London: The Country Book Club, 1963. 95 pp.

## Traditional Agriculture

Conklin, Harold. *Hanundoo Agriculture: A Report on an Integral System of Shifting Cultivation in the Philippines.* Rome: Food and Agriculture Organization of the United Nations, 1957. 154 pp.

Gliessman, Stephen R., et al. "The Ecology and Management of Traditional Farming Systems," from Altieri, M., and S. Hecht, eds., *Agroecology and Small Farm Development,* 1990, 13–17.

———. *Un Enfoque Agro-ecologico en el Estudio de la Agricultura Tradicional.* Santa Cruz, CA: Agroecology Program, University of California at Santa Cruz, 1984. 10 pp.

*Information for Low External Input Agriculture. Understanding Traditional Agriculture.* The Netherlands: ILEIA (P.O. Box 64, 3830 AB Leusen, The Netherlands), 1987. 144 pp. Bibliography.

Mountjoy, Daniel C., and Stephen R. Gliessman. "Traditional Management of a Hillside Agroecosystem in Tlaxcala, Mexico: An Ecologically Based Maintenance System." *American Journal of Alternative Agriculture,* Winter 1988: 3–10.

Sattaur, Omar. "The Lost Art of the Waru Waru." *New Scientist,* May 12, 1988: 50–51.

Stevens, William K. "An Eden in Ancient America? Not Really." *New York Times,* March 30, 1993.

## Trees

Agroforestry Research Trust. "Akebia." *Agroforestry News* Vol. 10, No. 1. (October 2001): 40 pp. Includes peaches, basketry plants, pecans, apples, and pears.

Allen, William. *Green Phoenix: Restoring the Tropical Forests of Guanacaste, Costa Rica.* New York: Oxford University Press, 2001. 310 pp.

Association for Temperate Agroforestry. *Agroforestry in the United States: Research and Technology Transfer Needs for the Next Millennium.* Columbia, MO: ATA, 2000. 23 pp.

Ayensu, Edward S., et al. *Firewood Crops.* Washington, DC: National Academy of Sciences, 1980. 237 pp.

Bailey, L. H. *The Cultivated Conifers in North America.* New York: Macmillan, 1933. 404 pp.

Baker, Richard St. Barbe. *Among the Trees.* London: Man of the Trees, 1935. 96 pp.

———. *The Brotherhood of the Trees.* London: Adelphi, n.d. 64 pp.

———. *Caravan Story and Country Notebook.* Wolverton, Bucks, England: McCorquodale, 1979. 71 pp.

———. *Dance of the Trees.* London: Oldbourne Press (121/128 Fleet St., London EC4, England), 1956. 192 pp.

———. *Famous Trees of New Zealand.* Wellington, New Zealand: A. H. and A. W. Reed, 1965. 150 pp.

———. *Green Glory.* New York: A. A. Wyn, 1949. 253 pp.

———. *I Planted Trees.* London: Lutterworth Press, 1952. 262 pp.

———. *Kabongo—The Story of a Kikuyu Chief.* New York: A. S. Barnes, 1955. 127 pp.

———. *Kamiti.* New York: Duell, Sloan and Pearce, 1958. 117 pp.

———. *Men of the Trees.* New York: Dial Press, 1931. 283 pp.

———. *My Life, My Trees.* Forres, Scotland: Findhorn Publications, 1970. 167 pp.

———. *The Redwoods.* London: Lindsay Drummond (2 Guilford Place, London WC1, England), 1945. 95 pp.

———. *Sahara Challenge.* London: Lutterworth Press, 1954. 152 pp. Important book.

———. *Trees: A Book of the Seasons.* London: Lindsay Drummond, 1940. 113 pp.

———. *Trees in the Environment—Selected Writings of Richard St. Barbe Baker.* Saskatchewan, Canada: University of

Saskatchewan Archives. 153 pp. Unpublished manuscript.

*Balancing Ecology and Economics: A Start-Up Guide for Forest Owner Cooperation.* Madison, WI: Cooperative Development Services (30 W. Mifflin St., Ste. 401, Madison, WI), University of Wisconsin Center for Cooperatives (230 Taylor Hall, 427 Lorch St., Madison, WI), Community Forestry Resource Center, Institute for Agriculture & Trade Policy (2105 First Ave. S., Minneapolis, MN), 2000. 107 pp. plus appendices.

Board on Science and Technology for International Development. *Firewood Crops: Shrubs and Tree Species for Energy Production,* Vol. 2. Washington DC: National Research Council, 1984. 92 pp.

Brinkman, Willemine, ed. *Why Natural Forests Are Linked with Nutrition: Health and Self Reliance of Villagers in Northeast Thailand—A Collection of Papers.* Phu Wiang, Khon Kaen Province: Royal Forest Department, Ministry of Agriculture and Cooperatives (United National Development Programme, Food and Agriculture Organization of the United Nations. Phu Wiang, Khon Kaen Province, Thailand), 1989. 86 pp.

Broad, Ken. *Caring for Small Woods.* London: Earthscan, 1999. 233 pp.

Brooks, Alan. *Woodlands: A Practical Handbook,* revised ed. Wallingford, UK: British Trust for Conservation Volunteers, 1988. 173 pp.

Bruce, John W. *Legal Bases for the Management of Forest Resources as Common Property.* Rome, Italy: Food and Agriculture Organization of the United Nations, 1999. 133 pp.

Buck, Louise E., ed., et al. *Agroforestry in Sustainable Agriculture Systems.* Boca Raton, FL: CRC Press, 1999. 416 pp.

Burkhardt, Hans J. *Maximizing Forest Productivity.* Willits, CA: Burkhardt Books (P.O. Box 117, Willits, CA 95490), 1994. 140 pp.

Camp, Orville. *The Forest Farmer's Handbook: A Guide to Natural Selection Forest Management.* Ashland, OR: Sky River Press, 1990. 72 pp.

Carter, Jane. "Alley Farming: Have Resource-Poor Farmers Benefited?" *Agroforestry Today,* April–June 1996: 5–7.

Cheyney, E. G. *Farm Forestry.* New York: Macmillan.

Cheyney, E. G., and J. P. Wentling. *The Farm Woodlot.* New York: Macmillan, 1919. 343 pp.

Clark, F. B. *Planting Black Walnut for Timber.* Washington, DC: U.S. Department of Agriculture Forest Service, 1976. 10 pp.

Coe, Richard. "Through the Looking Glass: 10 Common Problems in Alley-Cropping Research." *Agroforestry Today,* January–March 1994: 9–11.

Collingwood, G. H., and Warren D. Brush. *Knowing Your Trees.* Washington, DC: American Forestry Association, 1978. 389 pp.

Crawford, Martin. *Chestnuts.* Dartington, Totnes, Devon, UK: Agroforestry Research Trust, 1995. 52 pp.

———. *Hazelnuts.* Dartington, Totnes, Devon, UK: Agroforestry Research Trust, 1995. 28 pp.

———. *Walnuts.* Dartington, Totnes, Devon, UK: Agroforestry Research Trust, 1995. 28 pp.

Elevitch, Craig R., and Kim M. Wilkinson, eds. *The Overstory Book: Cultivating Connections with Trees.* Holualoa, HI: Permanent Agriculture Resources, 2001. 416 pp. Accompanied by a CD of the same title.

*Establishing a Hedgerow.* Communications Services, University of California, Davis, CA 95616. Video.

Evans, D. O., and L. T. Szott. *Nitrogen-Fixing Trees for Acid Soils.* Morrilton, AR: Winrock International Nitrogen Fixing Tree Association, 1995. 328 pp.

Farris, Cecil W. *The Hazel Tree.* East Lansing, MI: Northern Nut Growers Association, Department of Botany and Plant Pathology, Michigan State University, 2000. 74 pp.

Food and Agriculture Organization of the United Nations. *Forest Tree Seed Directory.* New York: United Nations, 1975. 283 pp.

———. *Proceedings of the International Workshop on Community Forestry in Africa.* Rome, Italy: FAO (Viale Delle Terme di Caracalla, 00100 Rome, Italy), 2000. 423 pp.

Forest, Farm, and Community Tree Network (FACT Net). *Nitrogen-Fixing Trees for Fodder Production.* Morrilton, AR: Winrock International, 1996. 125 pp.

*Forestry and Nutrition: A Reference Manual.* Bangkok, Thailand: Regional Forestry Officer (FAO Regional Office for Asia and the Pacific, Maliwan Mansion, Phra Atit Rd., Bangkok, Thailand), 1989. 114 pp.

*Forests, Trees and Food.* Rome: Community Forestry Unit (Forestry Department, Forestry Policy and Planning Division, FAO, Via delle Terme di Carcalla 00100 Rome, Italy), 1992. 26 pp.

Foster, Ruth. *Landscaping That Saves Energy Dollars.* New York: David McKay, 1978.

Friends of the Trees. *1988 International Green Front Report.* Chelan, WA: Friends of the Trees, 1988. 97 pp.

Friends of the Trees Society. P.O. Box 474, Hood River, OR 97031. Good tree information.

Garrett, H. E., W. J. Rietveld, and R. F. Fisher, eds. *North American Agroforestry: An Integrated Science and Practice.* Madison, WI: American Society of Agronomy, 2000. 402 pp.

*Giono, Jean. *The Man Who Planted Hope and Grew Happiness.* Brooksville, ME: Friends of Nature, 1967. 17 pp. Account of a 1-man tree planting program. Inspirational.

The Greenwood Trust—Woodland Courses. Station Rd., Coalbrookdale, Telford, Shropshire TF8 7DR, England. Courses include coppicing. A rare opportunity.

*Gridley, Karen, ed. *Man of the Trees: Selected Writings of Richard St. Barbe Baker.* Willits, CA: Ecology Action, 1989. 144 pp.

Hammond, Herb. *Seeing the Forest Among the Trees: The Case for Wholistic Forest Use.* Vancouver, Canada: Polestar Press, 1991. 309 pp.

Hart, Robert A. de J. *Forest Gardening.* Bideford, England: Green Books (Ford House, Hartland, Bideford, Devon EX39 6EE, England), 1991. 212 pp.

Hartmann, Hudson T., and Karl W. Opitiz. *Olive Production in California.* Berkeley, CA: University of California Agricultural Publications (207 University Hall, Berkeley, CA 94720), 1966. 63 pp.

*The Harvard Forest Models.* Cambridge, MA: Harvard College, 1941. 48 pp.

Hilliers and Sons. *Hilliers' Manual of Trees and Shrubs,* 4th ed. Newton Abbot, England: David and Charles, 1977. 575 pp. A key publication.

Hilts, Stewart, and Peter Mitchell. *The Woodlot Management Handbook.* Buffalo, NY: Firefly Books, 1999. 282 pp.

*How to Grow Your Own Firewood.* Publication 21484. Cooperative Extension (University of California, Division of Agriculture and Natural Resources), 6 pp.

Hutchinson, F. *A Guide to the Richard St. Barbe Baker Papers.* Saskatchewan, Canada: University of Saskatchewan Archives, 1988. 26 pp.

Huxley, Anthony, ed. *Deciduous Garden Trees and Shrubs.* New York: Macmillan, 1973. 216 pp.

———. *Evergreen Garden Trees and Shrubs.* New York: Macmillan, 1973. 216 pp.

Institute for Sustainable Forestry. *Landowner Resource Guide.* Redway, CA: Institute for Sustainable Forestry (P.O. Box 1580, Redway, CA 95560), June 2000.

"An Integration of Land Use Practices." *Agroforestry.* Columbia, MO: University of Missouri Center for Agroforestry, 2000.

International Institute of Rural Reconstruction. *Agroforestry Technology Information Kit.* Silang, Philippines: IIRR, 1998. 650 pp. 6 booklets.

Johnson, Dave. *The Good Woodcutter's Guide: Chain Saws, Portable Mills, and Woodlots.* White River Junction, VT: Chelsea Green, 1998. 215 pp.

Johnson, Hugh. *The International Book of Trees.* New York: Bonanza Books, 1980. 288 pp. Good background.

Josiah, Scott, et al. *Agroforestry in Minnesota: A Guide to Resources and Demonstration Sites.* St. Paul, MN: Center for Integrated Natural Resource and Agricultural Management, University of Minnesota, 1999. 132 pp.

Kang, B. T., A. N. Atta-krah, and L. Reynolds. *Alley Farming.* London: Macmillan, 1999. 110 pp.

Kang, B. T., et al. *Alley Cropping: A Stable Alternative to Shifting Cultivation.* Ibadan, Nigeria: IITA, 1984. 22 pp.

Kinro, Gerald. "The Bark Graft." *BackHome Magazine,* March/April 2005: 49–51.

Koppell, Carla R. R., et al. *Guidelines for Integrating Nutrition Concerns into Forestry Projects.* Rome: Community Forestry Unit (Forestry Department, Food & Agriculture Organization, Via delle Germe di Caracalla, 00100 Rome, Italy), 1991. 41 pp.

*Kyle, H. R., et al. *CCC Forestry.* Washington, DC: U.S. Department of the Interior, Office of Education, 1937. 334 pp.

Lambert, F. *Tools and Devices for Coppice Crafts.* Chatham, UK: Mackay, 1957. (Available from the Centre for Alternative Technology, Machynlleth, Powys SY20-9AZ, Wales, UK) 48 pp.

Lansky, Mitch, ed. *Low Impact Forestry: Forestry as if the Future Mattered.* Hallowell, ME: Maine

Environmental Policy Institute, 2002. 171 pp.

Law, Ben. *The Woodland Way: A Permaculture Approach to Sustainable Woodland Management.* White River Junction, VT: Chelsea Green Publishing, 2001. 231 pp.

*Leucaena: Forage Production and Use.* Waimanalo, HI: Nitrogen-Fixing Tree Association, 1985. 39 pp.

*Leucaena: Promising Forage and Tree Crop for the Tropics.* Washington, DC: National Academy of Sciences, 1977. 102 pp.

*Leucaena: Wood Production and Use.* Waimanalo, HI: Nitrogen Fixing Tree Association, 1985. 50 pp.

*Leucaena-Based Farming.* Oklahoma City, OK: World Neighbors, 1986. 29 pp.

Lindstrom, Jan, and Rose Kingamkono. *Foods from Forests, Fields and Fallows.* Uppsala, Sweden: Swedish University of Agricultural Sciences (International Rural Development Centre, Box 7005, S-750 07 Uppsala, Sweden), 1991. 133 pp.

Longhurst, Richard. *Dependency on Forestry and Tree Foods for Food Security.* Upsala, Sweden: Swedish University of Agricultural Sciences, 1991.

MacDicken, K., and N. Vergara. *Agroforestry: Classification and Management.* New York: John Wiley & Sons, 1990. 382 pp.

*Man of the Trees.* Redway, CA: Music for Little People (P.O. Box 1460, Redway, CA 95560). Video. **BL**

*The Man Who Planted Trees.* Los Angeles: Direct Cinema (P.O. Box 69799, Los Angeles, CA 90069). Video. Excellent animated adaptation of Jean Giono's classic story. In English and French. Academy Award, 1987. **BL**

Mann, Rink. *Backyard Sugarin'.* Woodstock, VT: Countryman Press, 1978. 78 pp.

Martz, Jeff. "Multi-Story Cropping System for the Dominican Republic." *The Permaculture Activist,* November 1988: 14–15.

Men of the Trees. *Richard St. Barbe Baker, 1889–1972: A Keepsake Book for All Ages and Generations.* Perth, Australia: Men of the Trees, 1989. 72 pp.

Mitchell, Alan. *The Trees of North America.* New York: Facts on File, 1979. 280 pp.

Mulawarman, et al. *Tree Seed Management: Seed Sources, Seed Collection and Seed Handling: A Field Manual for Field Workers and Farmers.* Bogor, Indonesia: International Centre for Research in Agroforestry, SEA Regional Research Programme, Winrock International, 2003. 54 pp.

Nearing, Helen and Scott. *The Maple Sugar Book.* White River Junction, VT: Chelsea Green, 2000. 305 pp.

*Neem: A Tree for Solving Global Problems.* Washington, DC: National Academy Press, 1992. 141 pp.

Nitrogen Fixing Tree Association. *Nitrogen Fixing Tree Research Report,* Vol. 11, 1993. Morrilton, AR: NFTA, 1993. 140 pp.

*On the Edge of the Forest.* Olney, PA: Bullfrog Films. Excellent video of Dr. E. F. Schumacher, author of *Small Is Beautiful.* A key perception about agroforestry and trees, 1977. **BL**

Pavlik, Bruce, et al. *Oaks of California.* Los Olivos: Cachuma Press (P.O. Box 560, Los Olivos, CA 93441), 1991. 184 pp.

Perry, David A. *Forest Ecosystems.* Baltimore, MD: The Johns Hopkins University Press, 1994. 649 pp.

Pilarski, Michael, ed. *Restoration Forestry: An International Guide to Sustainable Forestry Practices.* Durango, CO: Kivaki Press (585 E. 31st St., Durango, CO 81301), 1994. 525 pp.

Read, Helen J., and Mark Frater. *Woodland Habitats.* New York: Routledge, 1999. 177 pp.

Reich, Lee. "Making a Whip Graft." *Horticulture Magazine,* February 1994: 58–59.

"Riparian Forest Buffers: An Agroforestry Practice." Columbia, MO: University of Missouri Center for Agroforestry.

Roshetko, J. M., ed. *Agroforestry Species and Technologies.* Morrilton, AR: Winrock International, 2001. 232 pp.

Schubert, Gilbert H., and Ronald S. Adams. *Reforestation Practices for Conifers in California.* Sacramento, CA: Department of Conservation, Division of Forestry, 1971. 359 pp.

Sheat, W. G. *Propagation of Trees, Shrubs, and Conifers.* New York: Macmillan, 1957.

*Sholto Douglas, J., and Roberta A. de J. Hart. *Forest Farming.* London: Intermediate Technology Publications, 1984. 207 pp. Excellent.

*Short Rotation Forestry.* Oley, PA: Bullfrog Films (P.O. Box 149, Oley, PA 19547), 1982. 29-minute video.

*Smith, J. Russell. *Tree Crops: Key to a Permanent Agriculture.* Old Greenwich, CT: Devin-Adair, 1953. 408 pp. Classic work on an important concept.

Smith, Michael, and Michael Pilarski. *Friends of the Trees: Third World Resource Guide.* Tonasket, WA: Friends of the Trees Society (P.O. Box 1064, Tonasket, WA 98855), May 1993.

Sudworth, George B. *Forest Trees of the Pacific Slope.* New York: Dover, 1967. 455 pp.

Sunset Editors. *Garden Trees.* Menlo Park, CA: Sunset Books, 1975. 96 pp.

Titmuss, F. H. *A Concise Encyclopedia of World Timbers.* New York: Philosophical Library, 1949. 156 pp.

Tree People. *The Simple Act of Planting a Tree: Healing Your Neighborhood, Your City, and Your World.* Los Angeles: Jeremy P. Tarcher, 1990. 236 pp.

USDA, Institute for Sustainable Forestry. *Landowner Resource Guide.* Washington DC: USDA, 2000.

U.S. Department of Agriculture. *Trees: The Yearbook of Agriculture, 1949.* Washington, DC: U.S. Government Printing Office, 1949. 944 pp.

Utah Community Forest Council. *Shigo on Trees: The Video.* Spotlight Visual Communications. Video.

*Weiner, M. A. *Plant a Tree.* New York: Macmillan, 1975. 277 pp. Excellent.

Whitefield, Patrick. *How to Make a Forest Garden.* East Meon, Hampshire, England: Hyden House, The Sustainability Centre, 1998. 168 pp.

Wijewardene, Ray, et al. *Conservation Farming.* Sri Lanka: Marga Publications (61, Isipathana Mawatha, Colombo 5, Sri Lanka).

"Windbreaks: An Agroforestry Practice." Columbia, MO: University of Missouri Center for Agroforestry.

Yepsen, Roger B., Jr. *Trees for the Yard, Orchard, and Woodlot.* Emmaus, PA: Rodale Press, 1976. 305 pp.

## *Tropics*

*Ackland, J. D. *East African Crops.* London: Longman Group, 1980. 252 pp. Very good.

Appert, Jean. *The Storage of Food Grains and Seeds.* London: Macmillan, 1987. 146 pp.

Asian Vegetable Research and Development Center. P.O. Box 42, Shanhua, Tainan 741, Taiwan ROC. A nonprofit research organization for vegetables.

Atkins, George. *Growing Crops on Mounds in Low Wetlands.* The Developing Countries Farm Radio Network (595 Bay St., Toronto, ON M5G 2C3, Canada). 8 pp.

Beets, Willem C. *Raising and Sustaining Productivity of Smallholder Farming Systems in the Tropics.* Alkmaar, Holland: AgBé Publishing (P.O. Box 9125, 1800 GC Alkmaar, Holland), 1990. 738 pp.

Bernhardt, Ed. *Home Gardening in Costa Rica.* San Jose, CA: The Tico Times (P.O. Box 4632, San Jose, Costa Rica), 1985. 88 pp.

Brandjes, Pieter, Peter van Dongen, and Anneke van der Veer. *Green Manuring and Other Forms of Soil Improvement in the Tropics.* Wageningen, The Netherlands: CTA (P.O. Box 380, 6700 AJ Wageningen, The Netherlands), 1989. 49 pp.

Bunch, Roland. "An Odyssey of Discovery." *ILEIA Newsletter* Vol. 7, No. 3 (1995): 18–19. Published in Tegucigalpa, Honduras.

CIDICCO. *Technical Report No. 1. The Use of Velvetbean by Village Farmers of Honduras to Produce Corn.* Tegucigalpa, Honduras: CIDICCO, August 1993. 4 pp.

———. *Technical Report No. 2. The Use of Lablab Bean by Traditional Farmers in Honduras.* Tegucigalpa, Honduras: CIDICCO, August 1993. 4 pp.

———. *Technical Report No. 7. The Use of Velvetbean as Cover Crop in Citrus Plantations.* Tegucigalpa, Honduras: CIDICCO, March 1992. 4 pp.

———. *Technical Report No. 8. The Utilization of Velvetbean as a Source of Food.* Tegucigalpa, Honduras: CIDICCO, February 1993. 4 pp.

*Composting for the Tropics.* Bocking, England: Henry Doubleday Research Association, 1963. 288 pp. Useful pamphlet for humid areas.

Dupriez, Hugues, and Philippe De Leneer. *African Gardens and Orchards.* Wageningen, The Netherlands: CTA (P.O. Box 380, 6700 AJ Wageningen, The Netherlands), 1988. 294 pp.

———. *Agriculture in African Rural Communities.* Wageningen, The Netherlands: CTA (P.O. Box 380, 6700 AJ Wageningen, The Netherlands), 1988. 294 pp.

*Dynamics of Soil Organic Matter in Tropical Ecosystems.* Honolulu, Hawaii: NifTAL Project, University of Hawaii, 1989. 249 pp.

ECHO (Educational Concerns for Hunger Organization). 17391 Durrance Rd., North Fort Myers, FL 33917. A nonprofit organiza-tion that provides key seeds to development projects.

Ecology Action Staff. *A Preliminary Guide to Tropical Biointensive Food Raising.* Palo Alto, CA: Ecology Action, 1982. 31 pp. Includes a large bibliography.

Enoch, Ivan, and R. E. Holttum. *Gardening in the Tropics.* Singapore: Times Editions, 1991. 384 pp.

*Gardening Nutritious Vegetables.* Shanhua, Taiwan: The Asian Vegetable Research and Development Center (Shanhua, Taiwan, R.O.C.), 1988. 136 pp.

Garner, R. J. *Tropical Propagation of Fruit Trees. Part One: Materials and Methods.* Farnham Royal, Slough, UK: Commonwealth Agricultural Bureau, 1976. 556 pp.

Gibson, D., and A. Pain. *Crops of the Drier Regions of the Tropics.* Singapore: Longman Singapore, 1985. 157 pp.

Gliessman, Stephen R., et al. "The Ecological Basis for the Application of Traditional Agricultural Technology in the Management of Tropical Agro-Ecosystems." *Agro-Ecosystems* Vol.7, 1981: 173–185.

———. "Ecological Basis of Traditional Management of Wetlands in Tropical Mexico: Learning from Agroecosystem Models," in *Biodiversity—Culture, Conservation and Ecodevelopment,* Margery Oldfield and Janis B. Alcorn, eds. Boulder, CO: Westview Press, 1991: 211–229.

———. "Local Resource Use Systems in the Tropics: Taking Pressure Off the Forests," in *Tropical Rainforests,* Frank Almeda and Catherine Pringle, eds. San Francisco: California Academy of Sciences, 1988: 53–70.

———. "Understanding the Basis of Sustainability for Agriculture in the Tropics: Experiences in Latin America," in *Sustainable Agricultural Systems* C. A. Edwards et al., eds. Ankeny, IA: Soil and Water Conservation Society (7515 NE Ankeny Rd., Ankeny, IA 50021), n.d.: 378–390.

Goeltenboth, Friedholm, ed. *Subsistence Agriculture Improvement: Manual for the Humid Tropics.* Lanham, MD: Unipub, 1990. 228 pp.

Hill, D. S., and J. M. Waller. *Pests and Diseases of Tropical Crops.* Vol. 1, *Principles and Methods of Control.* Harlow, Essex, England: Longman, 1990. 175 pp.

Hodges, R. D., ed. *Composting in Tropical Agriculture.* Ipswich, England: International Institute of Biological Husbandry, 1979. 32 pp.

*Honey Bee: A Voice of Creative Farmers, Artisans, Pastoralists and Other Grassroots Innovators.* Ahnedbad, India: Society for Research and Initiatives for Sustainable Technologies and Institutions, Indian Institute of Management. Periodical.

*ILEIA Newsletter.* (Centre for Information for Low External Input and Sustainable Agriculture, P.O. Box 64, 3830 AB Leusden, The Netherlands.) An excellent magazine.

Institute for Tropical Agriculture. University of Florida, Box 13533, Gainesville, FL 32604.

International Institute of Rural Reconstruction. 1775 Broadway, New York, NY 10019. Also: Silang, Cavite, Philippines. Has specialized in Biointensive mini-farming. Information packet on agricultural technologies).

International Institute of Tropical Agriculture. 133 Dharmapala Mawatha, Columbo 7, Sri Lanka.

Irvine, F. R. *West African Crops.* Oxford, England: Oxford University Press, 1969. 272 pp.

Janzen, Daniel. "Tropical Agroecosystems." *Science,* Vol. 182 (1973): 1,212–1,219.

*MacKay, Susan E. *Alley Farming in the Humid and Subhumid Tropics. Proceedings of an International Workshop Held at Ibadan, Nigeria.* Ottwawa, Canada: IDRC (P.O. Box

8500, Ottawa, ON K1G 3H9, Canada), March 1986. 251 pp.

Manor House Agricultural Centre. Private Bag, Kitale, Kenya, East Africa. A nonprofit organization that specializes in Biointensive mini-farming training.

Martin, Franklin W. *Forages for the Small Farm.* N. Ft. Myers, FL: ECHO (17430 Durrance Rd., N. Ft. Myers, FL 33917-2200), n.d. 24 pp.

———. *Handbook of Tropical Food Crops.* Boca Raton, FL: CRC Press, 1984. 296 pp.

———. *Primer on Plants and Techniques for Agriculture in Dry Regions of the Tropics.* N. Ft. Myers, FL: ECHO (17391 Durrance Rd., N. Ft. Myers, FL 33917), n.d. 16 pp.

National Academy of Sciences. *Tropical Legumes: Resources for the Future.* Washington, DC: National Academy of Sciences, 1979. 331 pp.

National Research Council. *Leucaena: Promising Forage and Tree Crop for the Tropics,* 2nd ed. Washington, DC: National Academy Press, 1984.

*Organic Matter Management and Tillage in Humid and Subhumid Africa.* IBSRAM Proceedings No. 10. Bangkok, Thailand: International Board for Soil Research and Management, 1990. 459 pp.

Rosemeyer, Martha. "Challenges to Sustainable Agriculture in Central America." *Dimensions of Sustainability Proceedings.* Amsterdam: Baden-Baden, 1996: 340–349.

*Sanchez, Pedro A. *Properties and Management of Soil in the Tropics.* New York: John Wiley & Sons, 1987. 618 pp.

Schwartz, H., and Marcial A. Pastor-Corrales, eds. *Bean Production Problems in the Tropics,* 2nd ed. Cali, Columbia: Centro Internacional de Agricultura Tropical (Apartado Aeréo 6713, Cali, Colombia), 1989. 725 pp.

Shiva, Vandana. *Staying Alive: Women, Ecology and Development in India.* New Delhi: Kali for Women, 1988. 224 pp.

*Soil Management, Compost Production and Use in Tropical and Subtropical Environments.* Rome: FAO of the United Nations (Via delle Terme di Caracalle, 00100 Rome, Italy), 1987. 177 pp.

*Soils of the Humid Tropics.* Washington, DC: National Academy of Sciences, 1972. 219 pp. Compiled by the Committee on Tropical Soils, Ag. Board, and National Research Committee.

Sommers, Paul. *Low-Cost Farming in the Humid Tropics: An Illustrated Handbook.* Metro Manila, Phillipines: Island Publishing House (STA Mesa P.O. Box 406, Metro Manila, Philippines), 1984. 38 pp.

Srivastava, Jitendre, et al. *Conserving Soil Moisture and Fertility in the Warm Seasonally Dry Tropics.* Washington, DC: The International Bank for Reconstruction and Development (1818 H St., NW, Washington, DC 20433), 1993. 75 pp.

Steiner, Kurt G. *Intercropping in Tropical Smallholders Agriculture with Special Reference to West Africa.* Eschborn, Germany: Deutsche Gesellschaft für Technische Zusammenarbeith (Postfach 5180, D-6236 Eschborn/Ts. 1, Germany), 1984. 304 pp.

Stoll, Gabriele. *Natural Crop Protection in the Tropics.* Weikersheim, Germany: Margraf Verlag (P.O. Box 1205, 97985 Weikersheim, Germany), 2000. 376 pp.

Thurston, H. David. Slash/Mulch Systems: Sustainable Methods for Tropical Agriculture. Boulder, CO: Westview Press, 1997. 196 pp.

UNICEF. *The UNICEF Home Gardens Handbook.* New York: UNICEF, 1982.

USDA, ARS Tropical Agriculture Research Station. 2200 Pedro Albizu Campos Ave., Ste. 201 Mayaguez, Puerto Rico 006800-5470 (formerly, Mayaquez Institute of Tropical Agriculture, SEA, Box 70, Mayaquez, Puerto Rico 00681).

Wicherley, W. *The Whole Art of Rubber Growing.* Philadelphia: J. B. Lippincott, 1911. 151 pp.

## Urban Agriculture

Wade, Isabel. *City Food: Crop Selection in Third World Cities.* San Francisco: Urban Resource Systems, 1986. 54 pp.

## Vegetables

Aaron, Chester. *The Great Garlic Book: A Guide with Recipes.* Berkeley, CA: Ten Speed Press, 1997. 146 pp.

Allan, Ken. *Sweet Potatoes for the Home Garden.* Kingston, Canada: Green Spade Books, 1998. 204 pp.

Allen, C. L. *Cabbage, Cauliflower and Allied Vegetables.* New York: Orange Judd, 1918. 125 pp.

Bailey, L. H. *Principles of Vegetable Gardening.* New York: Macmillan, 1901. 450 pp.

Barnes, James, and William Robinson. *Asparagus Culture: The Best Methods Employed.* New York: George Routledge & Sons, n.d. 84 pp.

Basse, H., et al. *Variétés de Laitues.* Wageningen, Holland: Instituut Voor De Veredeling Van Tuinbourwgewassen, 1960. 228 pp.

Blasdale, Walter C. *Some Chinese Vegetable Food Materials and Their Nutritive and Economic Value.* Bulletin No. 68. Washington, DC: USDA Office of Experiment Stations, July 15, 1899, 48 pp.

Blazey, Clive. *The Australian Vegetable Garden: What's New Is Old.* Sydney: New Holland Publishers, 1999. 126 pp.

Brewster, J. L. *Onions and Other Vegetable Alliums.* Wallingford, Oxon, UK: CAB International, 1994. 236 pp.

Brickell, Christopher, ed. *Vegetables.* New York: Simon & Schuster, 1980. 96 pp.

Bubel, Nancy. "Broccoli." *Country Journal,* September/October 1992: 14–15.

Burrage, Albert C. *Burrage on Vegetables.* Boston: Houghton Mifflin,

1975. 224 pp. Good notes on scheduling for continuous harvest.

Burton, W. G. *The Potato,* 3rd ed. New York: Halsted Press, 1989. 724 pp.

Butterfield, H. M. *The Home Vegetable Garden in Berkeley.* Reprint. Berkeley, CA: Ecology Center. 1944. 22 pp.

Chandler, Andrea Ray. "Preventing Tomato Diseases." *Organic Gardening,* May/June 2003: 28–30.

Decoteau, Dennis R. *Vegetable Crops.* Upper Saddle River, NJ: Prentice Hall, 2000. 464 pp.

DeWitt, Dave, and Paul W. Bosland. *The Pepper Garden.* Berkeley, CA: Ten Speed Press, 1993. 240 pp.

———. *Peppers of the World: An Identification Guide.* Berkeley, CA: Ten Speed Press, 1996. 219 pp.

Engeland, Ron L. *Growing Great Garlic.* Okanogan, WA: Filaree Productions (Rte. 2, P.O. Box 162, Okanogan, WA 98840), 1991. 213 pp.

Galloway, Willi Evans. "Parsnips." *Organic Gardening* February/ March 2006: 30–31.

Garnham, Peter. "Cut-and-Come-Again Lettuce Sampler." *Kitchen Gardener,* February/March 1999: 10–14.

Goldman, Amy. *The Compleat Squash: A Passionate Grower's Guide to Pumpkins, Squashes, and Gourds.* NY: Artisan, 2004. 214 pp.

Gregory, James J. H. *Cabbages: How to Grow Them.* Salem, MA: Observer Steam Printing Rooms, 1870. 73 pp.

———. *Onion Raising: What Kinds to Raise and the Way to Raise Them.* Marblehead, MA: Messenger Steam Printing House, 1878. 42 pp.

Greiner, T. *Celery for Profit.* Philadelphia, PA: W. Atlee Burpee, 1893. 85 pp.

Hand, F. E., and K. L. Cockerham. *The Sweet Potato.* New York: Macmillan, 1921. 261 pp.

Harrison, S. G., et al. *The Oxford Book of Food Plants.* New York: Oxford University Press, 1969. 207 pp.

Herklots, G. A. C. *Vegetable Cultivation in Hong Kong.* Hong Kong: The South China Morning Post, 1947. 208 pp.

Ivins, J. D., and F. L. Milthorpe, eds. *The Growth of the Potato: Proceedings of the Tenth Easter School in Agricultural Science, University of Nottingham, 1963.* London: Butterworths, 1963. 328 pp.

The Jefferson Institute. "Dry Edible Beans: A High Value Alternative Legume." Alternative Crop Guide. Columbia, MO: The Jefferson Institute, 2002.

Kains, Maurice G. *Chicory Growing as an Addition to the Resources of the American Farmer.* Washington, DC: Government Printing Office, 1898. 52 pp.

Langsner, Louise. "The Many Faces of Asian Greens." *Kitchen Garden,* June/July 1998: 20–25.

Larkcom, Joy. *Creative Vegetable Gardening.* New York: Abbeville Press, 1997. 208 pp.

Macself, A. J. *The Vegetable Grower's Treasury.* London: W. H. & L. Collingridge, n.d. 320 pp.

Maynard, Donald N., and George J. Hochmuth. *Knott's Handbook for Vegetable Growers,* 4th ed. New York: John Wiley & Sons, 1997. 582 pp.

Nordell, Eric. "Trashed Our Onions: Cultivating Pea Vines into Onions." *Small Farmer's Journal,* Vol. 18, No. 3: 24–29.

Ogden, Ellen Ecker. "Spicing Up Salad." *Organic Gardening,* February/March 2006: 38–43.

Ohio Agricultural Experiment Station. *The Relation of Weather to the Date of Planting Potatoes in Northern Ohio.* Wooster, Ohio: Ohio Agricultural Experiment Station, 1926. 43 pp.

Omohundro, John T. "One Potato, Two Potato." *Natural History Magazine,* June 1985: 22–27.

Peet, Mary. *Sustainable Practices for Vegetable Production in the South.* Newburyport, MA: Focus Publishing, 1996. 174 pp.

Pleasant, Barbara. "Pick the Perfect Onions." *Mother Earth News,* February/March 2006: 40–45.

Reed, Brenda H. "Grow Oriental Vegetables." *BackHome Magazine,* March/April 2005: 33–35.

Robinson, R. W., and D. S. Decker-Walters. *Cucurbits.* New York: CAB International, 1996. 226 pp.

Rodale Institute. *Legumes for Lasting Benefits.* Information Sheet #2. Kutztown, PA: International Ag-Sieve (Rodale Institute, 611 Siegfriedale Rd., Kutztown PA 19530), n.d. 4 pp.

*Rubatzky, Vincent, and Mas Yamaguchi. *World Vegetables,* 2nd ed. New York: Chapman & Hall, 1997. 842 pp. Very good.

Sanders, T. W. *Vegetables and Their Cultivation.* London: Q. H. & L. Collingridge, 1928. 508 pp.

Sherf, Arden F., and Alan A. MacNab. *Vegetable Diseases and Their Control.* New York: John Wiley & Sons, 1986. 728 pp.

Solomon, Steve. *Water-Wise Vegetables.* Seattle: Sasquatch Books, 1993. 93 pp.

Staub, Jack. "Faux Spinaches Can Stand the Heat." *Kitchen Gardener,* August/September 1999: 12–15.

Stiles, Shelly. "Hot Potatoes." *National Gardening,* July/August 1994: 29–34.

*Vilmorin-Andrieux, M. M. *The Vegetable Garden.* London: John Murray, 1905. 782 pp. Softcover edition: Berkeley, CA: Ten Speed Press, 1981. 620 pp. Hardcover edition: Willits, CA: The Jeavons-Leler Press (5798 Ridgewood Rd., Willits, CA 95490). 620 pp. Reprint of the excellent 1885 English edition by John Murray. This classic is still one of the most useful works on cultural directions in existence today.

Weaver, William Woys. *Heirloom Vegetable Gardening.* New York: Henry Holt, 1997. 439 pp.

Wickson, Edward J. *The California Vegetables in Garden and Field.* San Francisco: Pacific Rural Press, 1917. 319 pp.

Wilkinson, Albert E. *Muck Crops.* New York: Orange Judd Company, 1916. 257 pp.

Zuckerman, Larry. *The Potato: How the Humble Spud Rescued the Western World.* New York: North Point Press, 1998. 320 pp.

### *Water*

Agarwal, Anil, et al., eds. *Making Water Everybody's Business.* New Delhi: Center for Science and Environment, 2001. 456 pp.

Agarwal, Anil, and Sunita Narain, eds. *Dying Wisdom: Rise, Fall and Potential of India's Traditional Water Harvesting Systems.* New Delhi: Center for Science and Environment, 1997. 404 pp.

Brooks, Kenneth N., et al. *Hydrology and the Management of Watersheds.* Ames, IA: Iowa State Press, 2003. 574 pp.

Center for Science and Environment. *A Water Harvesting Manual: Case Studies from India.* New Delhi: Center for Science and Environment, 2001. 35 pp.

———. *Water Links-2: Water Harvesters Directory.* New Delhi: Center for Science and Environment, 2000. 362 pp.

Cocannouer, Joseph A. *Water and the Cycle of Life.* Old Greenwich, CT: Devin-Adair, 1962. 142 pp. All his books are fascinating and easy to read.

Costello, Laurence R., et al. *Estimating Water Requirements of Landscape Plantings: The Landscape Coefficient Method.* Oakland, CA: University of California, 1991. 9 pp.

Cummings, Ronald, et al. *Waterworks: Improving Irrigation Management in Mexican Agriculture.* Washington, DC: World Resources Institute (1709 New York Ave., NW, Washington, DC 20006), 1989. 51 pp.

Davies, Rodney. *Dowsing.* London: The Aquarian Press (77-85 Fulham Palace Rd., Hammersmith, London W6 8JB, England), 1991. 112 pp.

Department of Water Resources. *Water Conservation in California.* Sacramento, CA: California Resources Agency, 1976. 95 pp.

DripWorks. 190 Sanhedrin Circle, Willits, CA 95490. (800) 616-8322. Complete line of drip irrigation.

East Bay Municipal Utility District. *Water-Conserving Plants & Landscapes for the Bay Area.* Oakland, CA: EBMUD, 1986. 107 pp.

Emoto, Masaru. *The Hidden Messages in Water.* Hillsboro, OR: Beyond Words Publishing, 2004. 157 pp.

Gleick, Peter H., et al. *California Water 2020: A Sustainable Vision.* Oakland, CA: Pacific Inst. for Studies in Development, Environment, and Security, 1995. 113 pp.

Ingram, Colin. *The Drinking Water Book.* Berkeley, CA: Ten Speed Press, 1995. 198 pp.

James, I. C., et al. *How Much Water in a 12-Ounce Can?* Washington, DC: U.S. Geological Survey, 1976. 18 pp.

———. *Principles of Irrigation Practice.* New York: Macmillan, 1920. 496 pp.

King, F. H. *Irrigation and Drainage: Principles and Practice of Their Cultural Phases.* New York: Macmillan, 1906. 502 pp.

Kourik, Robert. *Drip Irrigation for Every Landscape and All Climates.* Metamorphic Press: Santa Rosa, CA, 1992. 103 pp.

———. *Graywater Use in the Landscape: How to Make Your Landscape Prosperous with Recycled Water.* Santa Rosa, CA: Metamorphic Press, 1988. 28 pp.

Lester, Stephen U., and Brian Lipsett. *Drinking Water Filters: What You Need to Know.* Arlington, VA: Citizen's Clearinghouse for Hazardous Wastes, 1988. 44 pp.

Ludwig, Art. *Greywater Information: How to Manage Greywater and Rainwater in the Landscape.* Santa Barbara, CA: Developer of Oasis Biocompatible Laundry Detergent, 1991. 17 pp.

Matson, Tim. *Earth Ponds Sourcebook: The Pond Owner's Manual and Resource Guide.* Woodstock, VT: The Countryman Press, 1997. 171 pp.

Mellin, Bob. *Waterhole: A Guide to Digging Your Own Well.* San Anselmo, CA: Balboa Publishing (11 Library Place, San Anselmo, CA 94960), 1991. 71 pp.

National Academy of Sciences. *Eutrophication: Causes, Consequences, Correctives.* Washington, DC: NAS, 1969. 661 pp. Proceedings of a symposium in 1965.

Pimentel, David, et al., "Water Resources: Agriculture, the Environment, and Society." *BioScience,* Vol. 47, No. 2 (February 1997): 97–106.

Postel, Sandra. *Last Oasis Facing Water Scarcity.* New York: W.W. Norton & Co., 1992. 239 pp.

———. *Pillar of Sand: Can the Irrigation Miracle Last?* New York: W. W. Norton, 1999. 313 pp.

Richardson, Gail, and Peter Mueller-Beilschmidt. *Winning with Water: Soil-Moisture Monitoring for Efficient Irrigation.* New York: Inform, 1988. 173 pp.

Riotte, Louise. *Catfish, Ponds and Lilypads.* Pownal, VT: Storey, 1997. 186 pp.

Robinson, Peter. *The American Horticultural Society Complete Guide to Water Gardening.* New York: DK Publishing, 1997. 216 pp.

Romanelli, Vince. "How to Drive a Well." *Countryside and Small Stock Journal,* July/August 1994: 34–35.

Stadelmann, Peter. *Water Gardens.* Haupauge, NY: Barron's Educational Series (250 Wireless Blvd., Haupauge, NY 11788), 1994. 143 pp.

State of California. *Water Conservation in California.* Sacramento, CA: Department of Water Resources, 1976. 95 pp.

Swindells, Philip. *Container Water Gardens.* Pownal, VT: Storey, 1998. 128 pp.

The Urban Farmer Store. 2833 Vicente St., San Francisco, CA 94116. Drip irrigation products.

USDA. *Building a Pond.* Washington, D.C.: Soil Conservation Service, 1973. 14 pp.

Van den Heuvel, Kick. *Wood and Bamboo for Rural Water Supply.* Delft, The Netherlands: Delft University Press, 1983. 76 pp.

Vogt, Evon, and Ray Hyman. *Water Witching USA.* Chicago: The University of Chicago Press, 1918. 248 pp.

Walters, Gregg L., ed. *Hach Water Analysis Handbook.* Loveland, CO: Hach, 1989. 691 pp.

Yarger, Larry, and Dawn Berkelaar. "Gray Water and Crop Irrigation." *ECHO Development Notes,* July 2005: 1–4.

Yeomans, Ken B. *Water for Every Farm.* Australia: Griffin Press, 1993. 261 pp.

### Weeds

Cocannouer, Joseph A. *Weeds: Guardians of the Soil.* New York: Devin-Adair, 1948. 179 pp. How weeds help your garden. **BL**

Cramer, Craig and staff of the New Farm, eds. *Controlling Weeds with Fewer Chemicals.* Emmaus, PA: Rodale Institute, 1991. 138 pp.

Darr, Sheila. "Installing Lawns without Herbicides." *Common Sense Pest Control Quarterly,* Spring 1989: 6–7.

———. "Safe Ways to Outwit Poison Ivy and Poison Oak." *Common Sense Pest Control Quarterly,* Fall 1991: 7–14.

Gilman, Steve. *Organic Weed Management.* White River Junction, VT: Chelsea Green, 2002. 62 pp.

Harris, Ben Charles. *Eat the Weeds.* Barre, MA: Barre Publishing, 1968. 223 pp.

Hatfield, Audry W. *How to Enjoy Your Weeds.* New York: Sterling, 1971. 192 pp. Delightful. Includes an herbal lawn, flower salads, and other charming ideas.

Kummer, Anna P. *Weed Seedlings.* Chicago: The University of Chicago Press, 1951. 435 pp.

Martin, Alexander C. *Weeds.* New York: Golden Press, 1972. 160 pp. Inexpensive identification guide.

Muenscher, Walter C., and Peter A. Hyypio. *Weeds.* Ithaca, NY: Cornell University Press, 1980. 586 pp.

Nordell, Anne and Eric. "A Strategy for Weed-Free Onions." *Organic Farms, Folks and Food,* Harvest 1996: 57.

Olkowski, Helga and William. "Using Animals for Weed Management." *Common Sense Pest Control Quarterly,* Spring 1992: 5–13.

Pleasant, Barbara. *The Gardener's Weed Book: Earth-Safe Controls.* Pownal, VT: Storey, 1996. 201 pp.

Quarles, William. "Non-Toxic Weed Control in the Lawn and Garden." *Common Sense Pest Control Quarterly,* Summer 1999: 4–14.

———. "Non-Toxic Weed Control, Specific Situations." *Common Sense Pest Control Quarterly,* Summer 1999: 15–17.

Robbins, W. W., et al. *Weeds of California.* Sacramento, CA: Department of Agriculture, 1951. 547 pp.

Walters, Charles, Jr. *Weeds: Control Without Poison.* Austin, TX: Acres U.S.A. (P.O. Box 91299, Austin, TX 78709), 1991. 320 pp.

*Weeds of the North Central States.* North Central Regional Publication No. 36, Circular 718. Urbana, IL: Univ. of Illinois Ag. Experiment Station, 1954. 239 pp.

Whitson, Tom D., et al. *Weeds of the West.* Jackson, WY: Pioneer of Jackson Hole, 1991. 630 pp.

# THE EFFICACY OF THE GROW BIOINTENSIVE METHOD IN INCREASING SUSTAINABLE YIELDS AND BUILDING SOILS

APPENDIX

A s the charts below show, at some point during the years 2014 to 2021, there probably will not be enough land to produce all the nutrition needed for most of the world's population using current standard agricultural practices. These practices currently require about 7,000 to 63,000 square feet of farmable land per person, and most people will have access to only 9,000 square feet of arable soil as early as 2014. Further, most of the current practices are growing only *food* in the areas indicated, yielding insignificant net amounts of organic matter to produce the soil-nurturing humus needed to ensure the development of healthy soil. With many of these practices, an additional equal area will be needed to produce the amount of organic matter necessary to sustain soil fertility for both the food-growing farm area and the organic matter–growing farm area.

## APPROXIMATE AREA REQUIRED TO GROW 1 PERSON'S DIET USING CONVENTIONAL MECHANIZED *CHEMICAL* OR *ORGANIC* TECHNIQUES

| | |
|---|---|
| High animal product diet (fossil fuels available) currently | 31,000–63,000 sq ft |
| Average U.S. diets[1] (fossil fuels available) currently | 15,000–30,000 sq ft |
| Average U.S. vegan (fossil fuels available) currently | 7,000 sq ft |
| Average U.S. vegan diet (no animal products) (post–fossil fuel era) | 21,000–28,000 sq ft |
| Average of actual areas needed for diets eaten in developing nations, using actual agricultural practices (fossil fuels available) | 1977: 30,000 sq ft |
| | 1988: 22,000 sq ft |
| | 2000: 16,000 sq ft |

1. Assuming average amounts of vegetables, fruits, grains, beans, eggs, milk, cheese, and meat are eaten.

## ESTIMATED ARABLE LAND AVAILABLE TO GROW 1 PERSON'S DIET WITH DIFFERENT LEVELS OF WATER AVAILABILITY

| | |
|---|---|
| Year 2000, developing nations (where 80% of the world's population will be living) with water available | 16,000 sq ft |
| Year 2014–2021, developing nations (where 90% of the world's population will be living) with water available | 9,000 sq ft |
| Year 2000, in water-scarce areas around the world | 4,000 sq ft |

## AREA REQUIRED TO GROW 1 PERSON'S DIET WITH THE GROW BIOINTENSIVE METHOD, INCLUDING CROPS THAT PRODUCE A HIGH LEVEL OF CALORIES PER UNIT OF AREA (SEE PAGES 24–25)

| | |
|---|---|
| GROW BIOINTENSIVE intermediate yields with soil fertility sustained | 4,000 sq ft |

By the years 2014–2021, with an average of 9,000 square feet available (see above), sufficient land and resources may be available in many developing-nation areas with GROW BIOINTENSIVE, leaving up to 5,000 square feet of surplus land for the preservation of plant and animal genetic diversity in situations with adequate water.

## WILL THERE BE ENOUGH LAND TO GROW A COMPLETE DIET FOR 1 PERSON USING CONVENTIONAL MECHANIZED CHEMICAL OR ORGANIC TECHNIQUES OR USING THE GROW BIOINTENSIVE METHOD?

| Land Available with Different Levels of Water | *Diet* *Agricultural Technique* | High Animal Product — Conventional or Organic | Avg. U.S. — Conventional or Organic | Vegan — Conventional or Organic | Vegan — Conventional or Organic (post fossil fuel) | Vegan with Special Root Crops — GROW BIOINTENSIVE (intermediate yields/sustainable) |
|---|---|---|---|---|---|---|
| 16,000 sq ft (year 2000, water available) | | Insufficient | Insufficient | Sufficient land and 9,000 sq ft surplus[2] | Insufficient | Sufficient land and 12,000 sq ft[2] surplus |
| 9,000 sq ft (year 2014–2021, water available) | | Insufficient | Insufficient | Sufficient land and 2,000 sq ft surplus[2] | Insufficient | Sufficient land and 5,000 sq ft[2] surplus |
| 4,000 sq ft (year 2000, water scarce) | | Insufficient | Insufficient | Insufficient | Insufficient | Sufficient land and no surplus |

2. Number of square feet represents the area that is in surplus, not needed for food production, that could be left in a natural state to preserve plant and animal genetic diversity and ecosystems.

## GROW BIOINTENSIVE Applications

The GROW BIOINTENSIVE method, with its high yields, low water and fertilizer consumption, and soil-building techniques, is eminently practical for serious small-scale food production. Some possible applications are:

- One mini-farmer may be able to net $20,000 to $40,000+ a year on a ⅛-acre mini-farm. He or she might work a 40-hour week and take a 4-month vacation each year. (For more details, see Ecology Action's *Backyard Homestead, Mini-Farm and Garden Log Book* and *Cucumber Bonanza,* Self-Teaching Mini-Series Booklet 1.)

- A backyard gardener in the United States could grow a year's supply of vegetables and soft fruits (322 pounds) on 200 square feet in a 6-month growing season, assuming GROW BIOINTENSIVE intermediate yields. This food would be worth more than $600 and could eventually be grown in about 30 minutes (for 2 beds) a day, making the gardener's time worth $20 to $40+ per hour.

- An entire balanced diet could be grown at intermediate yields on as little as 1,000 square feet per person in an 8-month growing season with another 1,000 square feet needed to make it sustainable (for a total of 2,000 square feet). (See David Duhon and Cindy Gebhard's *One Circle,* published by Ecology Action, and Ecology Action's *Designing a GROW BIOINTENSIVE® Sustainable Mini-Farm* for more information. More usually it will take about 4,000 square feet to sustainably grow a complete diet for 1 person.) Using commercial agricultural techniques, it takes approximately 22,000 square feet per person in India, 7,000 square feet in the United States, and 3,400 square feet in Japan to grow similar diets unsustainably.

- Eventually we hope to produce as much food per hour by hand as commercial agriculture produces with machines.

Perhaps it is unfair to compare the yields we obtained in our hard clay subsoil in Palo Alto with commercial agricultural yields. The stunted broccoli plant on the *left* was grown using *normal backyard techniques,* loosening the soil and adding chemical fertilizer. The broccoli shown in the *middle* was obtained by loosening the soil *12 inches deep* and incorporating a 3-inch layer of aged manure with some compost. The broccoli on the *right* demonstrates the superiority of the GROW BIOINTENSIVE method, with soil loosened 24 inches deep and compost incorporated.

- Key points such as the low start-up cost, low water usage, and diversity of crops make the GROW BIOINTENSIVE approach especially viable for small farmers in the developing world.
- This decentralized, self-sufficient approach is consistent with the current emphasis on enabling countries and communities to provide their own food.

## Sustainability

The most important element in assessing agricultural systems is whether or not the yields are sustainable in an environmentally balanced way. For thousands of years the Chinese practiced a manual, organic form of intensive farming using only

POTENTIAL OF SMALL-SCALE GROW BIOINTENSIVE FOOD RAISING
AS INDICATED BY ECOLOGY ACTION'S RESEARCH TO DATE

**Potential production ranges as compared to local averages, per unit area**

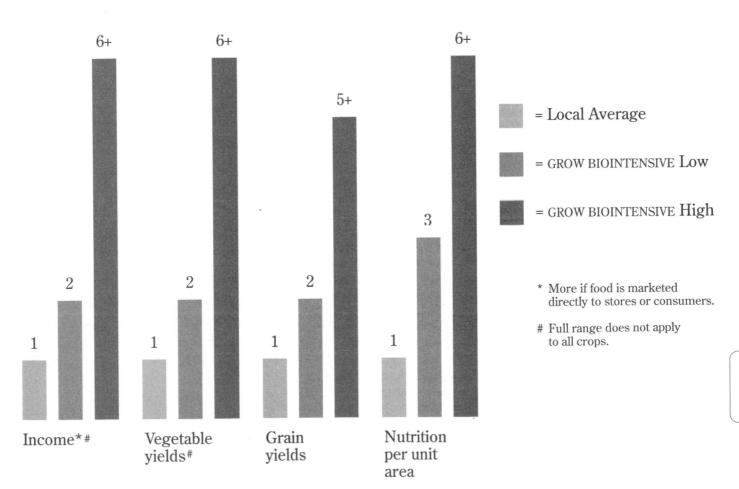

= Local Average

= GROW BIOINTENSIVE Low

= GROW BIOINTENSIVE High

\* More if food is marketed directly to stores or consumers.

\# Full range does not apply to all crops.

APPENDIX

## Pounds of food produced per hour

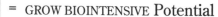
= U.S. Commercial
Agriculture Average

= GROW BIOINTENSIVE Potential

Potentially can reach the same yield per hour as with machines as soil and practitioner's skills improve and yields increase, and through the use of new, simple, labor-saving hand devices—when all labor inputs for both approaches are evaluated.

## Potential resource use ranges as compared with local averages, per pound of food produced

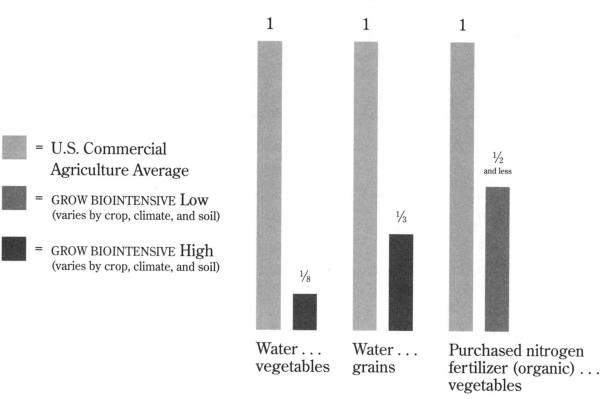

= U.S. Commercial
Agriculture Average

= GROW BIOINTENSIVE Low
(varies by crop, climate, and soil)

= GROW BIOINTENSIVE High
(varies by crop, climate, and soil)

1

1

1

½
and less

⅓

⅛

Water . . .
vegetables

Water . . .
grains

Purchased nitrogen
fertilizer (organic) . . .
vegetables

fertilizers grown or produced on the farmstead. They were able to feed 1.5 to 2 times more people per acre than the United States presently does with mechanized chemical or mechanized organic techniques (assuming similar nonmeat diets). In addition, chemical techniques deplete the soil's capacity to produce. Wilson Clark, in the January 1975 issue of *Smithsonian,* noted: "Even though more corn was produced per acre in 1968 than in the 1940s, the efficiency with which crops used available [nitrogen] fertilizer actually declined fivefold."

Chemical agriculture requires ever-increasing amounts of fertilizer at an increasing cost as petroleum supplies dwindle. The use of chemical fertilizers depletes beneficial microbial life, breaks down soil structure, and adds to soil salinity. Impoverished soil makes crops more vulnerable to disease and insect attack and requires increasing amounts of pesticides to sustain production. "A modern agriculture, racing one step ahead of the apocalypse, is not ecologically sane, no matter how productive, efficient, or economically sound it may seem" (John Todd, in *The New Alchemy Institute Bulletin,* No. 2). Biointensive agriculture can sustain yields because it puts back into the soil those elements needed to sustain fertility. A small-scale personal agriculture recycles the nutrients and humus so important to the microbial life-forms that fix atmospheric nitrogen and produce disease-preventing antibiotics.

## SOIL BUILD-UP RATE WITH GROW BIOINTENSIVE PRACTICES AT PALO ALTO SITE COMPARED WITH NORMAL BUILDUP RATE

**A.** ■ ■ ■ ■ ■ ■ ■ ■
Observed increase (buildup) in carbon soil (which was subsoil to begin with) at the Ecology Action Research Site (tentative figures). The program began in June 1972.

*Question:* What would the fate of the carbon curve (or nitrogen curve) be if the bed were now left fallow after the normal "intense" organic matter input?

**1.** ☐ ☐ ☐ ☐ ☐ ☐ ☐ ☐
Remains at "natural" steady-state level?

*—Unlikely.*

**2.** ● ● ● ● ● ● ● ● ● ●
Substantial drop, but leveling off, then rising again under "natural development"?

*—Most likely.* Accelerated gain of hundreds of years of soil development (in as little as 6 months or as much as 8 years time with Ecology Action–type cultivation).

**3.** ○ ○ ○ ○ ○ ○ ○ ○ ○
Drastic drop back down to zero?

*—Unlikely.*

**B.** ▬▬▬▬▬
Normal buildup of soil by natural processes.

*Curve shows what happens in good soil if organic matter is artificially added in excess. If left alone the carbon content of the soil will return to the "steady state" level.*

*% C Times ~1.7 ≅ % Organic Matter

APPENDIX

THE EFFICACY OF THE GROW BIOINTENSIVE METHOD   253

Biointensive techniques are being used to improve people's diets in over 110 countries around the world. Here a raised bed garden is planted in India.

Preliminary studies by soil scientists at the University of California, Berkeley, indicate that in as little as a 6-month period (and in as many as 8 years), the soil involved in our tests (which was only a "C-horizon" subsoil material at the beginning) was built up to a humified carbon level equal to hundreds of years of natural soil development! If maintained, this improvement may make possible not only the maintenance of sustainable soil fertility, but also the reclamation of deteriorated and marginal lands (see the preceding graph). The GROW BIOINTENSIVE method also nurtures the soil life and structure, utilizes renewable resources, can be productive economically on a small manual scale, and provides higher yields.

---

For more information about Ecology Action's history, current programs, workshops, and classes, or to become a member and support our work, go to www.growbiointensive.org or write to Ecology Action, 5798 Ridgewood Road, Willits, CA 95490-9730. To order Ecology Action's other publications, see page 261.

## Ecology Action Publications

Beeby, John. *Future Fertility: Transforming Human Waste into Human Wealth.* Willits, CA: Ecology Action, 1995. 168 pp.

Duhon, David, and Cindy Gebhard. *One Circle: How to Grow a Complete Diet in Less Than 1,000 Square Feet.* Willits, CA: Ecology Action, 1984. 200 pp. This book helps you to explore your nutritional needs and to design and produce a smallest-scale complete diet.

Gridley, Karen, ed. *Man of the Trees: Selected Writings of Richard St. Barbe Baker.* Willits, CA: Ecology Action, 1989. 120 pp. This collection of excerpts from Richard St. Barbe Baker's most important writings provides a fascinating glimpse of one of this century's most farsighted individuals. Beyond mere human interest, however, the book carries an urgent message about the vital role of trees in planetary survival. (Also in Spanish.)

Jeavons, John. *How to Grow More Vegetables, Fruits, Nuts, Berries, and Other Crops Than You Ever Thought Possible on Less Land Than You Can Imagine.* 7th Edition. Berkeley, CA: Ten Speed Press, 2006. 288 pp. Ecology Action's popular primer gives the most complete instructions and information for the GROW BIOINTENSIVE method.

————. *Cultivo Biointensivo de Alimentos: Más Alimentos en Menos Espacio.* Willits, CA: Ecology Action, 2002. Spanish translation of the 6th edition of *How to Grow More Vegetables.*

————. *Comment Faire Pousser.* Berkeley, CA: Ten Speed Press, 1982. 192 pp. French translation of the 2nd edition of *How to Grow More Vegetables.*

————. *Mehr Gemuse im Eigenen Garten.* Willits, CA: Ecology Action, 1981. 82 pp. German translation of the 1st edition of *How to Grow More Vegetables.*

————. *Kak Vyraschivat' Bol'she Ovoschei.* Moscow: BVL Publishers, 1997. 220 pp. Russian translation of the 5th edition of *How to Grow More Vegetables.*

————. Arabic translation of the 5th edition of *How to Grow More Vegetables.* Willits, CA: Ecology Action, 1997. 300 pp.

————. Braille version of the 3rd edition of *How to Grow More Vegetables.* Willits, CA: Ecology Action, 1981. For details on how to obtain a copy, write Monterey County Braille Transcribers, P.O. Box DF, Pacific Grove, CA 93950.

————. Hindi translation of the 1st edition of *How to Grow More Vegetables.* Willits, CA: Ecology Action, 1987. 70 pp.

————. *1972 Preliminary Research Report.* Palo Alto, CA: Ecology Action of the Midpeninsula, 1973. 22 pp. Ecology Action's first data report on the Biointensive method and implications for small farmers.

————. *1972–1975 Research Report Summary.* Palo Alto, CA: Ecology Action, 1976. 19 pp. Summary of data and projections of Ecology Action's first 4 years of research with Biointensive techniques.

————. "Quantitative Research on the Biodynamic/French Intensive Method." In *Small Scale Intensive Food Production—Improving the Nutrition of the Most Economically Disadvantaged Families,* pp. 32–38. Washington, DC: League for International Food Education, 1977. Workshop proceedings prepared on behalf of the Office of Nutrition, Bureau for Technical Assistance, U.S. Agency of International Development.

Jeavons, John, and Carol Cox. *The Sustainable Vegetable Garden.* Berkeley, CA: Ten Speed Press, 1999. 118 pp. The basic GROW BIOINTENSIVE book for those just starting. Also gives specific recommendations on the best crops to grow and how much to grow for an entire family.

Jeavons, John, J. Mogador Griffin, and Robin Leler. *Backyard Homestead, Mini-Farm and Garden Log Book.* Willits, CA: Ecology Action, 1983. 224 pp. A handbook for everyday use in developing greater self-sufficiency in a backyard homestead or in actually earning an income from a small farm. There is material covering tools and crop testing, as well as calendars, graphs, charts, and plenty of space for record keeping. It also includes information on creating your own self-fertilizing herbal lawns.

Roberts, Hugh, ed. *Intensive Food Production on a Human Scale: Proceedings of the Third International Conference on Small Scale and Intensive Food Production.* Willits, CA: Ecology Action, 1982. 224 pp. The result of a gathering of 100 people representing projects in 16 countries.

————. *Proceedings of the Soil, Food, and People Conference.* Willits, CA: Ecology Action, 2001, 180 pp. The result of a gathering of 276 people from 26 countries focusing on the role of Biointensive food raising in the new century.

Shepard, Michael, and John Jeavons. *Appropriate Agriculture.* Menlo Park, CA: Intermediate Technology, 1977. 14 pp. Paper given by Peter N. Gillingham at the "Small Is Beautiful" conference, featuring Dr. E. F. Schumacher, at the University of California at Davis.

## Self-Teaching Mini-Series and Other Booklets

*Annual Report.* 1993. 30 pp.

*Another Way to Wealth.* Booklet P1. 1991. 16 pp.

*Backyard Garden Research.* Booklet 17. 1988. 32 pp. Improving your garden's performance through observation. (Also in Spanish.)

*Biointensive Mini-Farming: A Rational Use of Natural Resources.* Booklet 0. 1985. 15 pp. Explains what Ecology Action is doing and why. (Also in Spanish, French, German, Russian, Portuguese, and Chinese.)

*Biointensive Micro-Farming: A Seventeen-Year Perspective.* Booklet 19. 1989. 20 pp. (Also in Spanish.)

*The Complete 21-Bed Biointensive Mini-Farm: Fertility, Nutrition, and Income.* Booklet 14. 1986. 39 pp. Explores

Mini-greenhouses fit right over the growing beds. Plans for this one are available in Ecology Action's *Backyard Homestead, Mini-Farm and Garden Log Book.*

sustainably growing all your own food and composting crops and making a small income, in as little as 2,100 square feet. (Also in Spanish and Russian.)

*Cucumber Bonanza.* Booklet 1. 1979. 24 pp. Takes cucumbers as an example of a crop history and goes through 7 years of work, bringing the 1973 yield of 140 pounds of marketable cucumbers per 100 square feet to over 400 pounds in 1979. An excellent introduction to mini-farming and the variables that can be examined in obtaining improved yields. (Also in Spanish.)

*Cultivating Our Garden.* A detailed article on GROW BIOINTENSIVE methods. 4 pp. (Also in Spanish, Russian, Arabic, and Japanese.)

*Designing a GROW BIOINTENSIVE® Sustainable Mini-Farm— A Working Paper.* Booklet 31. 2003. 45 pp.

*Dried, Cut, and Edible Flowers for Pleasure, Food, and Income.* Booklet 18. 1990. 61 pp. (Also in Spanish.)

*An Ecology Action Reading Guide.* Booklet 20. 1989. 36 pp. Design your own curriculum.

*Ecology Action's Comprehensive Definition of Sustainability.* Booklet 24. 2005. 4 pp. (Also in Spanish.)

*Examining the Tropics: A Small-Scale Approach to Sustainable Agriculture.* Booklet 11. 1982. 31 pp. (Also in Spanish.)

*Foliar Feeding.* Booklet 16. 1987. 9 pp. (Also in Spanish.)

*Grain Culture.* Booklet 33. 2006. How to grow grain and seed crops.

*GROW BIOINTENSIVE® Apprentice Possibilities.* 2005. 28 pp.

*GROW BIOINTENSIVE® Composting and Growing Compost Materials.* Booklet 32. 2004. 35 pp.

*GROW BIOINTENSIVE® Sustainable Mini-Farming Teacher Training and Certification Program—Revised.* Booklet 30. 2005. 43 pp.

*Grow Your Manure for Free.* Booklet 22. 1989. 32 pp. Summary of compost crops to grow for improving your soil's fertility. (Also in Spanish.)

*Growing and Gathering Your Own Fertilizers.* Booklet 12. 1984. 125 pp. (Also in Russian.)

*Growing Medicinal Herbs in as Little as Fifty Square Feet—Uses and Recipes.* Booklet 27. 1995. 40 pp.

*Growing to Seed.* Revised. Booklet 13. 1999. 45 pp. How to grow your own seed in the smallest possible area while preserving genetic diversity. (Also in Spanish.)

*Learning to Grow All Your Own Food: One-Bed Model for Compost, Diet, and Income Crops.* Booklet 26. 1991. 25 pp.

*Micro-Farmers as a Key to the Revitalization of the World's Agriculture and Environment.* Booklet 21. 1989. 13 pp.

*One Basic Kenyan Diet: With Diet, Income, and Compost Designs in a Three-Growing-Bed Learning Model.* Booklet 25. 1991. 28 pp.

Using a U-bar digging tool cuts digging time and helps make GROW BIOINTENSIVE mini-farming competitive with mechanized techniques.

*One Basic Mexican Diet.* Booklet 15. 1987. 32 pp. Explores complete nutritional self-sufficiency in a small area with 1 Mexican diet as a focal point. (Also in Spanish.)

*One Crop Test Booklet: Soybeans.* Booklet 2. 1980. 24 pp., plus data sheet and log form. Contains step-by-step instructions for conducting comparative tests for spacing and yield (with optional water monitoring) for soybeans—an important protein crop throughout the world. This booklet lets you participate in Ecology Action's research or simply grow better soybeans for yourself.

*A Perspective.* Booklet 9. 1981. 17 pp. Speech given by John Jeavons at the Second International Conference on Small-Scale Intensive Food Production, October 1981.

*The Smallest Possible Area to Grow Food and Feed.* Booklet 28. 1997. 45 pp.

*Solar Water Heater.* 2000. 12 pp.

*Test Your Soil with Plants.* Booklet 29. 1997. 86 pp.


## Information Packets

Topical treatments on the latest information from our garden research, and our work around the world. Topics range from "Data for Common Compost Crops" (in the *Sustainable Soil Fertility* packet) to "Double-Digging vs. the U-Bar" (in the *Gardening Techniques* packet) to "About Amaranth and Quinoa" (in the *Crops* packet). The information is presented as short complete articles on a given subject area, and the information tends to be interrelated.

*Children's Gardening Resources.* 3 pp.

*Cooking with Sunshine.* 2 pp.

*Crops.* 9 topics, 15 pp. Information on specific crops and things to look for in certain useful crops.

*Data Report for One Crop.* 2 pp., free. The form to use to send data from your garden to Ecology Action.

*Gardening Techniques.* 12 topics, 31 pp. Some greening-edge techniques and observations on the art of gardening.

*GROW BIOINTENSIVE Projects.* 5 topics, 14 pp. Profiles of some of the major Biointensive projects around the world.

*Insect and Animal Life.* 5 topics, 10 pp. Useful hints and tips for dealing with our wilder neighbors.

*Inspiration.* 6 topics, 13 pp. The bigger picture. Articles that are Ecology Action's key position papers and put our work in perspective.

*Limited Water Growing.* 4 topics, 6 pp. Water-saving techniques.

*Small Cabin/Land Trust Information.* 2 pp.

*Sustainable Soil Fertility.* 16 topics, 41 pp. The heart of our work—finding out how to have a really sustainable garden or mini-farm.

*Yields.* 4pp. Outlines the factors master yield figures are based upon.

## Reprints

*Composting for the Tropics.* 28 pp.
*Living Quarters for Plant Roots.* 6 pp.
*Plant Species Index for the Pacific Northwest and General
    Reference.* 20 pp.

## Related Publications by Other Organizations

*Intensive Small Farms and the Urban Fringe.* Sausalito, CA:
    Landal Institute for Small Farm Research, 1976. 93 pp.
    Based in part on Ecology Action's research.
Jeavons, John. "Biointensive Sustainable Mini-Farming: I.
    The Challenge; II. Perspective, Principles, Techniques,
    and History; III. System Performance—Initial Trials; IV.
    System Performance—Continuing Trials in a More Diffi-
    cult Environment and Soil; V. Future Potential, Some
    Representative World Applications, Future Challenges,
    and Research Opportunities." *Journal of Sustainable
    Agriculture,* pp. 49–105. Birmingham, NY: Haworth
    Press, 2001.
Martinez, Juan Manuel. *Huertos Familiares.* ECOPOL: (c.o.
    Edif. H10-1-2. Col. Lomas de Plateros, Mexico, D.F. CP
    01480, Mexico), 1992. Booklet used by the nationwide
    program in Mexico to teach Biointensive mini-farming at
    the introductory level.
———. *Rotofolio Huertos Familiares.* ECOPOL: (c.o. Edif.
    H10-1-2. Col. Lomas de Plateros, Mexico, D.F. CP 01480,
    Mexico), 1992. Flipchart used for teaching Biointensive
    mini-farming in villages in Mexico.
*A Preliminary Assessment of the Applicability of French
    Intensive/Biodynamic Gardening Techniques in Tropical
    Settings.* Santa Barbara, CA: Direct International Develop-
    ment/Direct Relief Foundation, 1978. 47 pp. Report from
    on-site visits to 4 intensive demonstration gardens in
    Central America.
Seshadri, C. V., et al. *Biodynamic Gardening.* Vol. 4. Tharamani,
    Tamil Nadu: Shri AMM Murugappa Chettiar Research
    Centre (Tharamani, Tamil Nadu, 600 113, India), 1980. 38 pp.
———. *Biodynamic Horticulture—Improvements & Extension.*
    Vol. 15. Tharamani, Tamil Nadu: Shri AMM Murugappa
    Chettiar Research Centre (Tharamani, Tamil Nadu, 600
    113, India), 1983. 43 pp.
Yang, Y. K. "Home Gardens as a Nutrition Intervention," in
    *Small Scale Intensive Food Production: Improving the Nutri-
    tion of the Most Economically Disadvantaged Families,* pp.
    60–80, Washington, D.C.: League for International Food
    Education, 1977.

## Accredited Classes in Biointensive Mini-Farming

Dr. Ed Glenn and Dr. Mary Olsen of the Environmental Research Laboratory (at the University of Arizona) give a Biointensive course for arid areas each semester based on their 10 years' experience. Contact them at 2601 E. Airport Drive, Tucson International Airport, Tucson, AZ 85706-6985, or fax (602) 573-0852.

## Videotapes of Our Work

(Available from Bountiful Gardens)

Two award-winning PBS specials documenting our work have been televised nationally.

*Circle of Plenty* (1987) is about our Willits garden and the Menos y Mejores project in northern Mexico. *Circle of Plenty* addresses some serious problems in world agriculture and shows that the Biointensive method is a viable solution even under Third World conditions with poor soil.

*Gardensong* (1983) is a beautiful film about Alan Chadwick's work, our own work, and that of others.

*El Huerto Ecologico* (1992). This video is used to introduce biointensive practices in Mexico.

*A Journey in Kenya—Biointensive Farmers* (1993). Sandra Mardigian and Doug Burck revisit graduates from Manor House Agricultural Centre whom they sponsored, and document the amazing, positive changes that have resulted from Biointensive gardens—both for individuals and for whole villages! Wonderful, hope-filled scenes of African gardens and gardeners. About 20 minutes.

*A Perspective: The Living Land* (1999). This PBS TV special is available from the Foundation for Global Community, 222 High Street, Palo Alto, CA, 94301, phone (800) 707-7932. The program focuses on the bases of our lives: the soil, farming, and food. Beautifully done. Interviews with John Jeavons of Ecology Action, Wes Jackson of the Land Institute, Alice Waters of Chez Panisse, and Mas Masumoto, author of *Epitaph for a Peach* and *Harvest Son* are woven into a beautiful fabric.

## Ecology Action / GROW BIOINTENSIVE

Ecology Action teaches people worldwide to better feed themselves while feeding the soil and conserving resources. Ecology Action is a 501(c)(3) nonprofit organization with its headquarters and Common Ground Mini-Farm located at 5798 Ridgewood Road, Willits, CA 95490. Also visit www.growbiointensive.org; for a synopsis of initiatives in and results from this work since 1972, see "The Story So Far…" on this website. Become a member to support this growing-edge work.

## Bountiful Gardens

International gardening and mini-farming mail order service. An Ecology Action nonprofit project. For a free catalog of gardening publications, fertilizers, tools, and seeds, write to Bountiful Gardens, 18001 Shafer Ranch Road, Willits, California 95490-9626, or call (707) 459-6410, or fax (707) 459-1925. Visit Bountiful Gardens at www.bountifulgardens.org. Also, visit www.growbiointensive.org.

## Common Ground Garden Supply and Education Center

Organic gardening store and education center with library, classes, over 500 open-pollinated seed varieties and nursery starts—vegetables, herbs, flowers, grains, and much more. An Ecology Action nonprofit project. Common Ground is located at 559 College Avenue, Palo Alto, California 94306, or call (650) 493-6072. Visit Common Ground at www.commonground-inpaloalto.org.

## Latin America

Ecology Action's international partner for the Spanish speaking world is ECOPOL. Contact: Juan Manuel Martinez Valdez, Director, ECOPOL, Apartado Postal Numero 2, Aculco, Estado de Mexico, Mexico; ecopolac@aol.com and onaledar@yahoos.com; tel 011-52 (55) 565-111-43 or 011-52 (55) 130-860-40.

## Africa

Ecology Action's international partner for Africa is Manor House Agricultural Centre. Contact: Emmanuel Omondi, Director, Manor House Agriculture Centre, Private Bag, Kitale, Kenya.

## Help in Kenya

You can help support a Kenyan villager's training at a basic Biointensive Skills Workshop. To make this happen, send a tax-deductible donation to the Kilili Self Help Project, 260 Marion Avenue, Mill Valley, California 94141: $50 will train 10 farmers and $100 will train 20. Help the world grow!

## Help in Russia

To assist Biointensive work in Russia, contact: Biointensive for Russia, 831 Marshall Drive, Palo Alto, California 94303-3614, fax (650) 424-8767, e-mail cvesecky@igc.org, or visit www.igc.org/biointensiveforrussia.

# PLEASE JOIN US.

*Membership donations provide a reliable financial base that secures continued education and research programs for sustainable* GROW BIOINTENSIVE *food-raising worldwide. Our thanks to all of our friends who are investing in the future by making this work possible.*

**I would like to be part of Ecology Action's work. Enclosed is my membership donation for one year, which includes Ecology Action's newsletter.**

- ❏ $20 Newsletter     ❏ $40 Supporting     ❏ $60 Family
- ❏ $100 Sustaining
- ❏ $250 Outreach Supporter
- ❏ $400 Research Supporter
- ❏ $1,000 Lifetime Membership
- ❏ Gift membership at $_____     ❏ Other _____

**Please also send:**

- ❏ *How to Grow More Vegetables*, 2006 edition, by John Jeavons, $19.95 (U.S. funds). California residents add $1.45 tax. For shipping and handling please add $4 for U.S., $6 for Canada, $9 for Mexico, and $14 for all other countries.
- ❏ *The Sustainable Vegetable Garden*, 1999 edition, by John Jeavons and Carol Cox, $12.95 (U.S. funds). California residents add $0.94 tax. For shipping and handling please add $3 in U.S., $4 for Canada, $5 for Mexico, and $8.50 for all other countries.
- ❏ *Proceedings of the Soil, Food, and People Conference: A Biointensive Model for the New Century,* $30 (U.S. funds). California residents add $2.18 tax. For shipping and handling please add $6 for U.S., $7.50 for Canada, $11 for Mexico, and $17 for all other countries.
- ❏ Sample Newsletter, $1.50 postpaid.
- ❏ Rare Seeds Catalog, $2.50 postpaid.
- ❏ Membership brochures, free.

Name _____

Address _____

_____

*Send to:* ECOLOGY ACTION, 5798 Ridgewood Road, Willits, CA 95490-9730

MEMBERSHIP

# INDEX

## G

Gaillardia, 128
Gardening, rewards of, ix–x
Garden plans
  making, 131–32
  sample, 134–51
Gardens for Humanity, 29
Garden year, 133
Garlic
  as area- and weight-efficient
      crop, 25
  companions and antagonists, 166,
      168
  Master Charts, 90–93
  temperature range for, 79
Gazania, 128
Geraniums, 129
Glenn, Ed, 23, 28
Good King Henry, 129
Gopher plant, 110–13, 164
Gophers, 164, 173, 174
Gourds, 67, 110–13
Grains
  crop rotation and, 156–58
  as high-carbon-producing
      crops, 24
  Master Charts, 98–105
  protecting from birds, 75
  yields of, 83–84
Granite, crushed, 51
Grapefruit, 118–21
Grapes, 24, 118–21
Grasses, 106–9
Grass family, 158
Greece, xvi, 57
Greenhouses, 63, 75, 256
Green manures, 43
GROW BIOINTENSIVE techniques
  applications of, 250–51
  Biointensive vs., vi
  features of, xvii–xviii
  history of, xv–xvii
  philosophy of, xiv
  worldwide use of, 28–29, 47
Guatemala, 57
Guava, 118–21
Guayule, 110–13
Gypsum, 50, 52

## H

Hand-picking, 175
Hazelnuts. *See* Filberts
Henbit, 168
Herbs. *See also individual herbs*
  companion planting for, 167–69
  spacing chart, 129

Hickory, 118–21
Hollyhock, 128
Honey locust, 118–21
Horehound, 129
Horseradish, 79, 90–93, 168
Human Diet Experiment, 28
Humic acid, 19
Hummingbirds, 165
Humus
  amount of, 20
  definition of, 34
  initially adding, 19–20
  loss of, 19
  role of, 34–35
Hyssop, 129, 168

## I

Iceland poppy, 128
Income crops, viii, 24
India, 28, 47, 254
Insects
  controlling, 163–64, 170–78
  importance of, 170–71, 173
Irrigation. *See* Watering

## J

Jacob's ladder, 128
Japanese beetle, 177
Jenny, Hans, 82–83
Jerusalem artichokes, 25, 86–89
Jojoba, 110–13
June bug, 177

## K

Kafka, Stephen, v, vi
Kale, 79, 90–93, 163, 166
Kenaf, 110–13
Kenya, 28, 261
Koch, Frank, v
Kohlrabi, 79, 90–93, 166
Kudzu, 106–9

## L

Ladybugs, 173
Lamb's quarters, 168
LaMotte soil test kit, 48
Land
  crop area percentages for, 23,
      24–27
  lack of, xiii, 248, 249
  square footage requirements, xiii,
      27, 248–49
Lavender, 129
Leeks, 25, 79, 90–93, 166

Legumes. *See also individual*
      *legumes*
  crop rotation and, 156–58
  nitrogen fixing and, 43, 156, 159
Leler, Rachael, ix
Lemon balm, 129, 154, 168
Lemons, 118–21
Lemon verbena, 129
Lentils, 98–101
Lettuce
  companions, 162, 166
  leaf vs. head, 132
  Master Charts, 90–93
  root system of, 14
  soil temperature for germination
      of, 80
  temperature range for, 79
Lily family, 158
Lime (soil amendment), 52
Limes (fruit), 118–21
Living mulch, 59, 160
Lovage, 129, 168

## M

Magnesium, 52
Malo family, 158
Mangels, 25, 90–93
Mangos, 118–21
Manor House Agricultural Centre,
      28, 261
Manure, 32, 42, 44, 52–53, 55
Marguerite, 128
Marigold, 128, 163, 164, 168
Marjoram, 129, 154, 168
Master Charts
  calorie, grain, protein source, and
      vegetable oil crops, 98–105
  compost, carbon, organic matter,
      fodder, and cover crops,
      106–9
  energy, fiber, paper, and other
      crops, 110–13
  tree and cane crops, 114–25
  using, 81–85
  vegetables and garden
      crops, 86–97
Maturity. *See* Master Charts
Melons
  Master Charts, 90–93
  soil temperature for germination
      of, 80
  temperature range for, 79
  turning stems back, 67
  watering, 71–72
Mesquite, 118–21
Mexican marigold, 163, 164
Mexico, 28

INDEX